HTML

Complete Concepts and Techniques

THIRD EDITION

Gary B. Shelly
Thomas J. Cashman
Denise M. Woods

THOMSON
COURSE TECHNOLOGY™

COURSE TECHNOLOGY
25 THOMSON PLACE
BOSTON MA 02210

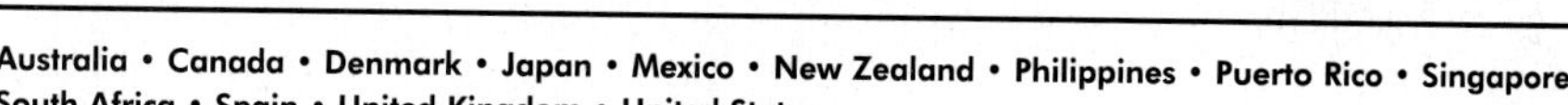
Australia • Canada • Denmark • Japan • Mexico • New Zealand • Philippines • Puerto Rico • Singapore
South Africa • Spain • United Kingdom • United States

THOMSON
COURSE TECHNOLOGY

HTML Complete Concepts and Techniques, Third Edition

Gary B. Shelly
Thomas J. Cashman
Denise M. Woods

Executive Director:
Cheryl Costantini

Senior Acquisitions Editor:
Dana Merk

Senior Editor:
Alexandra Arnold

Editorial Assistant:
Selena Coppock

Series Consulting Editor:
Jim Quasney

Print Buyer:
Laura Burns

Production Editor:
Jennifer Goguen

Development Editor:
Lisa Strite

Copy Editor:
Nancy Lamm

Proofreader:
Lori Silfen

Cover Image:
John Still

Compositor:
GEX Publishing Services

Indexer:
Cristina Haley

Printer:
Banta Menasha

Printed in the United States of America

1 2 3 4 5 6 7 8 9 10 BM 09 08 07 06 05

For more information, contact
Course Technology
25 Thomson Place
Boston, Massachusetts 02210

Or find us on the World Wide Web at:
www.course.com

ISBN 0-619-25502-1

Complete Concepts and Techniques
THIRD EDITION

Contents

Preface vi

Project One

Introduction to HTML

Objectives **HTM 4**
Introduction **HTM 4**
What Is the Internet? **HTM 4**
What Is the World Wide Web? **HTM 6**
Web Servers HTM 6
Web Site Types and Purposes HTM 7
Web Browsers HTM 9
What Is Hypertext Markup Language? **HTM 9**
HTML History HTM 11
HTML Elements HTM 12
HTML Coding Practices HTM 12
HTML Versions HTM 12
Dynamic HTML (DHTML) HTM 13
Extensible Hypertext Markup Language (XHTML) HTM 13
Tools for Creating HTML Documents **HTM 14**
Web Development Life Cycle **HTM 15**
Web Site Planning HTM 15
Web Site Analysis HTM 16
Web Site Design and Development HTM 17
Web Site Testing HTM 20
Web Site Implementation and Maintenance HTM 21
Project Summary **HTM 22**
What You Should Know **HTM 22**
Learn It Online **HTM 23**
Apply Your Knowledge **HTM 24**
In the Lab **HTM 25**
Cases and Places **HTM 28**

Project Two

Creating and Editing a Web Page

Objectives **HTM 30**
Introduction **HTM 30**
Project Two — The Campus Tutoring Service **HTM 30**
Elements of a Web Page **HTM 32**
Window Elements HTM 32
Text Elements HTM 32
Image Elements HTM 33
Hyperlink Elements HTM 33
Starting Notepad **HTM 33**
The Notepad Window **HTM 35**
Title Bar HTM 35
Menu Bar HTM 35
Text Area HTM 35
Scroll Bar HTM 35
Enabling Word Wrap in Notepad **HTM 35**
Entering HTML Tags and Text **HTM 36**
Entering HTML Tags to Define the Web Page Structure HTM 36
Entering Headings HTM 39
Entering a Paragraph of Text HTM 40
Creating a List HTM 41
Saving an HTML File **HTM 44**
Using a Browser to View a Web Page **HTM 47**
Starting a Browser HTM 47
Viewing a Web Page in a Browser HTM 48
Activating Notepad **HTM 50**
Web Page Images **HTM 51**
Image Types HTM 51
Image Attributes HTM 51
Improving the Appearance of Your Web Page **HTM 52**
Adding an Image HTM 53
Adding Background Color HTM 54
Centering the Heading HTM 56
Adding a Horizontal Rule HTM 56
Refreshing the View in a Browser HTM 58
Viewing HTML Source Code for a Web Page **HTM 58**
Printing a Web Page and an HTML File **HTM 60**
Quitting Notepad and a Browser **HTM 62**
Project Summary **HTM 62**
What You Should Know **HTM 62**
Learn It Online **HTM 63**
Apply Your Knowledge **HTM 64**
In the Lab **HTM 65**
Cases and Places **HTM 68**

Project Three

Creating Web Pages with Links, Images, and Formatted Text

Objectives **HTM 70**
Introduction **HTM 70**
Project Three — Plant World Web Site **HTM 71**
Starting Notepad HTM 72
Using Links on a Web Page **HTM 72**
Linking to Another Web Page within the Same Web Site HTM 75
Linking to a Web Page in Another Web Site HTM 76
Linking within a Web Page HTM 77
Linking to an E-Mail Address HTM 77
Creating a Home Page **HTM 78**
Entering HTML Tags to Define the Web Page Structure HTM 78
Adding an Image HTM 79
Adding a Left-Aligned Heading with a Font Color HTM 80
Entering a Paragraph of Text HTM 82
Creating Unordered (Bulleted) Lists HTM 83
Adding a Background Image HTM 85

Adding a Text Link **HTM 85**
Adding a Text Link to Another Web Page within the Same Web Site HTM 86
Adding an E-Mail Link **HTM 88**
Saving and Printing the HTML File HTM 89
Viewing, Testing Links, and Printing a Web Page **HTM 90**
Editing the Second Web Page **HTM 94**
Formatting Text HTM 96
Formatting Text in Bold HTM 96
Formatting Text in Italics HTM 98
Format Text with a Font Color HTM 99
Adding an Image with Wrapped Text **HTM 100**
Adding an Image with Wrapped Text HTM 103
Clearing the Text Wrapping HTM 104
Using Horizontal and Vertical Spacing HTM 106
Using Thumbnail Images HTM 106
Obtaining Images HTM 107
Adding a Text Link to Another Web Site **HTM 108**
Adding a Text Link to a Web Page in Another Web Site HTM 108
Adding Links within a Web Page **HTM 109**
Setting Link Targets HTM 110
Adding Links to Link Targets within a Web Page HTM 112
Adding Links to a Link Target at the Top of the Page HTM 114
Adding an Image Link to a Web Page HTM 115
Saving and Printing the HTML File and Web Page HTM 117
Project Summary **HTM 120**
What You Should Know **HTM 120**
Learn It Online **HTM 121**
Apply Your Knowledge **HTM 122**
In the Lab **HTM 124**
Cases and Places **HTM 129**

Project Four

Creating Tables in a Web Site

Objectives **HTM 132**
Introduction **HTM 132**
Project Four — Bell Video **HTM 132**
Creating Web Pages with Tables **HTM 134**
Table Elements HTM 136
Table Borders, Headers, Captions, and Rules HTM 137
Planning, Designing, and Coding a Table **HTM 138**
Determining if a Table Is Needed HTM 139
Planning the Table HTM 139
Coding the Table HTM 141
Table Tag Attributes HTM 142
Creating a Home Page **HTM 143**
Starting Notepad HTM 143
Entering HTML Tags to Define the Web Page Structure HTM 143
Using Borderless Tables to Position Images **HTM 145**
Creating a Borderless Table to Position Images HTM 146
Inserting Images in a Table HTM 147
Creating a Vertical Menu Bar with Text Links HTM 148
Adding Text to a Table Cell HTM 151
Viewing and Printing the Web Page Using the Browser HTM 154
Creating a Secondary Web Page **HTM 155**
Changing the Title HTM 157
Deleting an Image HTM 158
Creating a Horizontal Menu Bar with Text Links HTM 158
Creating a Table with Borders **HTM 160**
Creating a Table with Borders and Inserting Text into Cells HTM 162
Adding Cellspacing, Cellpadding, and a Caption **HTM 169**
Adding Cellspacing and Cellpadding to a Table HTM 170
Adding a Table Caption HTM 172
Spanning Rows and Columns **HTM 174**
Spanning the Main Heading across All Columns HTM 177
Creating Additional Headings that Span Rows and Columns HTM 178
Project Summary **HTM 183**
What You Should Know **HTM 184**
Learn It Online **HTM 185**
Apply Your Knowledge **HTM 186**
In the Lab **HTM 187**
Cases and Places **HTM 192**

Project Five

Creating an Image Map

Objectives **HTM 194**
Introduction **HTM 194**
Project Five — Ibrahim Real Estate **HTM 195**
Introduction to Image Maps **HTM 196**
Using Image Maps with Text Links HTM 197
Image Map Uses HTM 197
Server-Side versus Client-Side Image Maps HTM 201
Creating an Image Map **HTM 201**
Selecting Images HTM 201
Sketching the Borders of Hotspots HTM 203
Mapping Image Coordinates HTM 204
Coding the Map HTM 206
Using Paint to Locate X- and Y-Coordinates **HTM 207**
The Paint Window HTM 207
Opening an Image File in Paint HTM 208
Locating X- and Y-Coordinates of an Image HTM 209
Creating the Home Page **HTM 213**
Starting Notepad and Entering Initial HTML Tags HTM 213
Creating a Table HTM 214
Inserting an Image in a Table HTM 215
Adding Text to a Table Cell **HTM 216**
Adding an Image to Use as an Image Map HTM 217
Creating a Horizontal Menu Bar with Text Links HTM 219
Coding the Image Map Using HTML Tags and Attributes **HTM 220**
Creating an Image Map HTM 221
Changing Link Colors HTM 223
Viewing and Printing the Web Page Using a Browser HTM 225
Creating a Second Web Page **HTM 226**
Changing the Title HTM 228
Adding a Heading and Paragraphs of Text HTM 229
Adding an Image HTM 231
Creating a Horizontal Menu Bar HTM 232
Viewing and Printing the Web Page HTM 234
Testing the Links HTM 236
Project Summary **HTM 237**
What You Should Know **HTM 237**
Learn It Online **HTM 238**
Apply Your Knowledge **HTM 239**
In the Lab **HTM 241**
Cases and Places **HTM 245**

Project Six

Using Frames in a Web Site

Objectives HTM 248
Introduction HTM 248
Project Six — Bill Thomas Illustrations HTM 249
Creating Frames HTM 250
Creating a Frame Definition File HTM 250
Defining Columns and Rows in a Frameset HTM 252
Defining Frame Attributes HTM 254
Planning and Laying Out Frames HTM 258
Creating a Frame Definition File HTM 260
Starting Notepad and Entering Initial HTML Tags HTM 260
Defining the Frameset Columns and Rows HTM 262
Identifying Attributes of the Header and Menu Frames HTM 265
Identifying Attributes of the Main Frame HTM 266
Saving the HTML File HTM 267
Creating the Header Page HTM 268
Creating the Menu Page HTM 270
Adding Links with Targets to the Menu Page HTM 272
Creating the Home Page HTM 273
Viewing, Testing, and Printing Web Pages and HTML Code HTM 275
Viewing and Printing the Frame Definition File Using a Browser HTM 275
Testing the Links HTM 277
Printing the HTML Files HTM 277
Project Summary HTM 279
What You Should Know HTM 279
Learn It Online HTM 280
Apply Your Knowledge HTM 281
In the Lab HTM 282
Cases and Places HTM 287

Project Seven

Creating a Form on a Web Page

Objectives HTM 290
Introduction HTM 290
Project Seven — Creating Forms on a Web Page HTM 291
Creating Web Page Forms HTM 292
Input Controls HTM 292
HTML Tags Used to Create Forms HTM 296
Attributes of HTML Tags Used to Create Forms HTM 296
Creating a Form On a Web Page HTM 298
Creating a Form and Identifying the Form Process HTM 299
Changing the Text Message HTM 300
Adding Text Boxes HTM 301
Adding Check Boxes HTM 303
Adding a Selection Menu HTM 304
Adding More Advanced Selection Menus HTM 306
Adding Additional Text Boxes HTM 307
Adding Radio Buttons and a Textarea HTM 309
Adding Radio Buttons HTM 309
Adding a Textarea HTM 310
Submit and Reset Buttons HTM 312
Adding Submit and Reset Buttons HTM 312
Organizing a Form Using Form Groupings HTM 313
Using Fieldset Controls to Create Form Groupings HTM 314
Saving the HTML File HTM 316
Viewing, Testing, and Printing the Web Page and HTML Code HTM 317
Project Summary HTM 321
What You Should Know HTM 321
Learn It Online HTM 322
Apply Your Knowledge HTM 323
In the Lab HTM 324
Cases and Places HTM 328

Project Eight

Creating Style Sheets

Objectives HTM 330
Introduction HTM 330
Project Eight — Using Style Sheets in the Stained Glass Club Web Site HTM 331
Creating Style Sheets HTM 334
Style Sheet Precedence HTM 334
Style Statement Format HTM 334
Inline Style Sheets HTM 336
Embedded Style Sheets HTM 336
External Style Sheets HTM 337
Working with Classes in Style Sheets HTM 338
Adding Style Sheets to the Stained Glass Club Web Site HTM 340
Adding an Embedded Style Sheet HTM 341
Setting the Paragraph Style HTM 343
Setting a Style for All Links HTM 344
Setting the Link Hover Style HTM 345
Saving, Viewing, and Printing the HTML File HTM 345
Adding an External Style Sheet HTM 348
Setting a Body Style HTM 349
Setting Link and Paragraph Styles HTM 350
Setting Table and Caption Styles HTM 350
Creating an External Style Sheet HTM 350
Linking to an External Style Sheet HTM 352
Linking the Remaining HTML Files to an External Style Sheet HTM 353
Adding an Inline Style Sheet HTM 355
Viewing and Printing Framed Web Pages HTM 357
Viewing and Printing HTML Files HTM 359
Quitting Notepad and a Browser HTM 361
Project Summary HTM 361
What You Should Know HTM 361
Learn It Online HTM 362
Apply Your Knowledge HTM 363
In the Lab HTM 364
Cases and Places HTM 368

Appendix A

HTML Quick Reference

HTML Tags and Attributes APP 1

Appendix B

Browser-Safe Color Palette

Browser-Safe Colors APP 11

Appendix C

Style Sheet Browser Compatibility Tables

Style Sheet Properties and Values APP 13

Index IND 1

Preface

The Shelly Cashman Series® offers the finest textbooks in computer education. We are proud of the fact that our previous HTML books have been so well received. With each new edition of our HTML books, we have made significant improvements based on the comments made by instructors and students. The *HTML, Third Edition* books continue with the innovation, quality, and reliability you have come to expect from the Shelly Cashman Series.

In this HTML book, you will find an educationally sound, highly visual, and easy-to-follow pedagogy that combines a vastly improved step-by-step approach with corresponding screens. All projects and exercises in this book are designed to take advantage of enhancements to the HTML and XHTML standards. The popular More About feature offers in-depth knowledge of HTML. The new Q&A feature offers students a way to solidify important HTML concepts. The Learn It Online page presents a wealth of additional exercises to ensure your students have all the reinforcement they need. The project material is developed to ensure that students will see the importance of learning HTML for future coursework.

Objectives of This Textbook

HTML: Complete Concepts and Techniques, Third Edition is intended for use in combination with other books in an introductory course on creating Web pages. This book also is suitable for use as a stand alone in a two-credit hour course or a continuing education course. No experience with Web page development or computer programming is required. Specific objectives of this book are as follows:

- To teach the fundamentals of developing Web pages using HTML
- To acquaint students with the XHTML guidelines
- To show students how to create Web pages suitable for course work, professional purposes, and personal use
- To expose students to common Web page formats and functions
- To promote curiosity and independent exploration of World Wide Web resources
- To develop an exercise-oriented approach that allows students to learn by example
- To encourage independent study and help those who are learning how to create Web pages in a distance education environment

The Shelly Cashman Approach

Features of the Shelly Cashman Series *HTML, Third Edition* books include:

- **Project Orientation:** Each project in the book presents a practical problem and complete solution using an easy-to-understand methodology.
- **Step-by-Step, Screen-by-Screen Instructions:** Each of the tasks required to complete a project is identified throughout the project. Full-color screens accompany the steps.
- **Thoroughly Tested Projects:** Unparalleled quality is ensured because every screen in the book is produced by the author only after performing a step, and then each project must pass Course Technology's award-winning Quality Assurance program.
- **More About and Q&A Features:** These marginal annotations provide background information, tips, and answers to common questions that complement the topics covered, adding depth and perspective to the learning process.
- **Integration of the World Wide Web:** The World Wide Web is integrated into the HTML learning experience by (1) More About annotations that send students to Web sites for up-to-date information and alternative approaches to tasks; (2) an HTML Quick Reference Summary Web page that summarizes HTML tags and attibutes; and (3) the Learn It Online page at the end of each project, which has project reinforcement exercises, learning games, and other types of student activities.

Organization of This Textbook

HTML: Complete Concepts and Techniques, Third Edition is comprised of eight projects and three appendices. Each project ends with a large number of exercises to reinforce what students learn in the project. The projects and appendices are organized as follows:

Project 1 - Introduction to HTML This introductory project provides students with an overview of the Internet, World Wide Web, Web pages, HTML, and Web development. Topics include the types and purposes of Web sites; Web browsers; HTML standards; Dynamic Hypertext Markup Language (DHTML) and Extensible Hypertext Markup Language (XHTML) and their relationship to HTML. Additionally, Web editors; the five phases of the Web development life cycle, and the importance of usability testing are defined.

Project 2 - Creating and Editing a Web Page In Project 2, students are introduced to basic HTML tags and the various parts of a Web page. Topics include starting and quitting Notepad and a browser; entering headings and text into an HTML file; creating a bulleted list with HTML; adding background color, a horizontal rule, and an image; saving the HTML file and viewing it in the browser; printing the HTML file and the Web page; and Web page design.

Project 3 - Creating Web Pages with Links, Images, and Formatted Text In Project 3, students are introduced to linking terms and definitions. Topics include adding an e-mail link; linking to another page on the same Web site; linking to another Web site; setting link targets within a page; linking to targets; types of image files; alternative text for images; defining image size; wrapping text around an image; and inserting images onto Web pages.

Project 4 - Creating Tables in a Web Site In Project 4, students learn how to create tables using HTML tags. First, students assess table needs and then plan the table. Topics include table definitions and terms; table uses; creating borderless tables; inserting images into tables; vertical and horizontal alignment within a table; adding color to a cell; adding links to another page; adding an e-mail link; using the rowspan and colspan attributes; adding captions; and spacing within and between cells.

Project 5 - Creating an Image Map In Project 5, students learn how to use an image map to create more advanced Web pages. Topics include image mapping purpose and considerations; selecting images for mapping; dividing an image into hotspots; creating links with hotspots; and using text to describe links. Students also use graphics software to determine the coordinates needed for image mapping.

Project 6 - Using Frames in a Web Site In Project 6, students are introduced to using frames for Web page creation. Topics include purpose and considerations when using frames; resizing frames; frame headers; scroll bars; frame navigation; linking frames; and two-frame and three-frame Web pages. Additional topics include using the noresize attribute and creating four-frame Web pages.

Project 7 - Creating a Form on a Web Page In Project 7, students create a form that will allow readers to complete a survey online and send the entered information via e-mail. Topics include form purposes and basics; selecting check boxes on a form; choosing menu items on a form; form text boxes for free-form text; and creating an e-mail link to transfer the form information back to the Web page developer. Students also are introduced to using advanced selection menus and fieldset tags to segregate groups of information.

Project 8 – Creating Style Sheets In Project 8, students are introduced to the three different types of cascading style sheets -- embedded style sheet, an external style sheet, and an inline style sheet. Topics include adding an embedded style sheet to change the link styles, adding an external style sheet to format a Web page, and adding an inline style sheet to change a text style.

Appendix A - HTML Quick Reference Appendix A includes an HTML quick reference that contains the most frequently used tags and their associated attributes.

Appendix B – Browser-Safe Color Palette Appendix B summarizes the 216 browser-safe colors that display equally well on different monitors, operating systems, and browsers – including both the Windows and Mac OS operating systems and Internet Explorer and Netscape browsers.

Appendix C – Style Sheet Browser Compatibility Tables Appendix C provides a listing of the CSS (cascading style sheet) properties and values supported by versions 4.x, 5.x, and 6.x of Internet Explorer and versions 4.x, 6.x, and 7.x of Netscape Navigator.

End-of-Project Student Activities

A notable strength of the Shelly Cashman Series *HTML* books is the extensive student activities at the end of each project. Well-structured student activities can make the difference between students merely participating in a class and students retaining the information they learn. The activities in the Shelly Cashman Series *HTML* books include the following.

- **What You Should Know** A listing of the tasks completed within a project together with the pages on which the step-by-step, screen-by-screen explanations appear.
- **Learn It Online** Every project features a Learn It Online page that contains 12 exercises. These exercises include True/False, Multiple Choice, Short Answer, Flash Cards, Practice Test, Learning Games, Tips and Tricks, Newsgroup usage, Expanding Your Horizons, Search Sleuth, and Online Help.
- **Apply Your Knowledge** This exercise usually requires students to open and manipulate a file on the Data Disk that parallels the activities learned in the project. To obtain a copy of the Data Disk, follow the instructions on the inside back cover of this textbook.
- **In the Lab** Three in-depth assignments per project require students to utilize the project concepts and techniques to solve problems on a computer.
- **Cases and Places** Five unique real-world case-study situations, including one small-group activity.

Instructor Resources CD-ROM

The Shelly Cashman Series is dedicated to providing you with all of the tools you need to make your class a success. Information on all supplementary materials is available through your Course Technology representative or by calling one of the following telephone numbers: Colleges and Universities, 1-800-648-7450; High Schools, 1-800-824-5179; Private Career Colleges, 1-800-347-7707; Canada, 1-800-268-2222; Corporations with IT Training Centers, 1-800-648-7450; and Government Agencies, Health-Care Organizations, and Correctional Facilities, 1-800-477-3692.

The Instructor Resources for this textbook include both teaching and testing aids. The contents of each item on the Instructor Resources CD-ROM (ISBN 0-619-25520-X) are described below.

INSTRUCTOR'S MANUAL The Instructor's Manual is made up of Microsoft Word files, which include detailed lesson plans with page number references, lecture notes, teaching tips, classroom activities, discussion topics, projects to assign, and transparency references. The transparencies are available through the Figure Files described below.

LECTURE SUCCESS SYSTEM The Lecture Success System consists of intermediate files that correspond to certain figures in the book, allowing you to step through the creation of an application in a project during a lecture without entering large amounts of data.

SYLLABUS Sample syllabi, which can be customized easily to a course, are included. The syllabi cover policies, class and lab assignments and exams, and procedural information.

FIGURE FILES Illustrations for every figure in the textbook are available in electronic form. Use this ancillary to present a slide show in lecture or to print transparencies for use in lecture with an overhead projector. If you have a personal computer and LCD device, this ancillary can be an effective tool for presenting lectures.

POWERPOINT PRESENTATIONS PowerPoint Presentations is a multimedia lecture presentation system that provides slides for each project. Presentations are based on project objectives. Use this presentation system to present well-organized lectures that are both interesting and knowledge based. PowerPoint Presentations provides consistent coverage at schools that use multiple lecturers.

SOLUTIONS TO EXERCISES Solutions are included for the end-of-project exercises, as well as the Project Reinforcement exercises.

TEST BANK & TEST ENGINE The ExamView test bank includes 110 questions for every project (25 multiple choice, 50 true/false, and 35 short answer) with page number references and, when appropriate, figure references. A version of the test bank you can print also is included. The test bank comes with a copy of the test engine, ExamView, the ultimate tool for your objective-based testing needs. ExamView is a state-of-the-art test builder that is easy to use. ExamView enables you to create paper-, LAN-, or Web-based tests from test banks designed specifically for your Course Technology textbook. Utilize the ultra-efficient QuickTest Wizard to create tests in less than five minutes by taking advantage of Course Technology's question banks, or customize your own exams from scratch.

DATA FILES FOR STUDENTS All the files that are required by students to complete the exercises are included. You can distribute the files on the Instructor Resources CD-ROM to your students over a network, or you can have them follow the instructions on the inside back cover of this book to obtain a copy of the Data Disk.

ADDITIONAL ACTIVITIES FOR STUDENTS These additional activities consist of Project Reinforcement Exercises, which are true/false, multiple choice, and short answer questions that help students gain confidence in the material learned.

Online Content

Course Technology offers textbook-based content for Blackboard, WebCT, and MyCourse 2.1.

BLACKBOARD AND WEBCT As the leading provider of IT content for the Blackboard and WebCT platforms, Course Technology delivers rich content that enhances your textbook to give your students a unique learning experience.

MYCOURSE 2.1 MyCourse 2.1 is Course Technology's powerful online course management and content delivery system. MyCourse 2.1 allows nontechnical users to create, customize, and deliver Web-based courses; post content and assignments; manage student enrollment; administer exams; track results in the online grade book; and more.

HTML

HTML

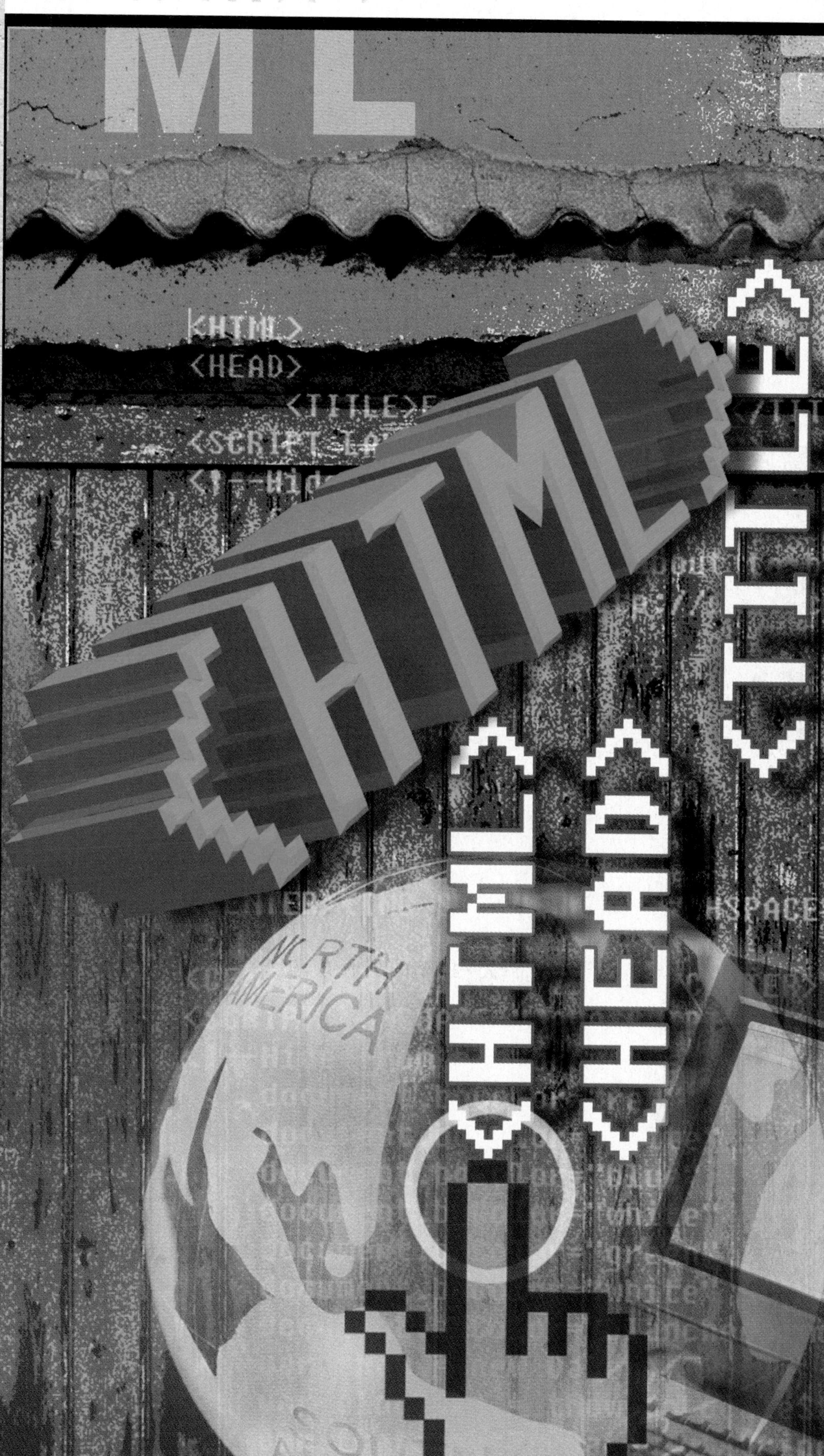

ML
<HTML>
<HEAD>
<TITLE>
<SCRIPT LA
HTML
<HTML>
<HEAD>
<TITLE>
HSPACE=
NORTH AMERICA

HTML

Introduction to HTML

PROJECT 1

CASE PERSPECTIVE

Shomir Kini has been selected as the project leader for the company's Web development effort. This project includes the development of a corporate Internet site that displays information about the company to prospective customers and a corporate intranet that displays information about the company to employees. In order for this to be a successful project, Shomir formed a development team that included people from several functional areas of the company, including the Human Resources, Marketing, Finance, and Engineering departments. You represented the Information Technology (IT) department at the kick-off meeting. Shomir was very concerned about the lack of Internet knowledge from the employees who represented their functional areas. The majority of questions appeared to be the result of employees not understanding the main concepts behind Internet and Hypertext Markup Language (HTML) technology. You suggested that Shomir work with you to develop a seminar on Internet and HTML basics that he can present to the development team. In this seminar, you want to describe the Internet, the World Wide Web, and intranets. You want to discuss Web browsers, definitions of HTML and the associated key terms, the five phases of the Web development life cycle, and what role each team member will play in the Web development effort.

Introduction to HTML

PROJECT

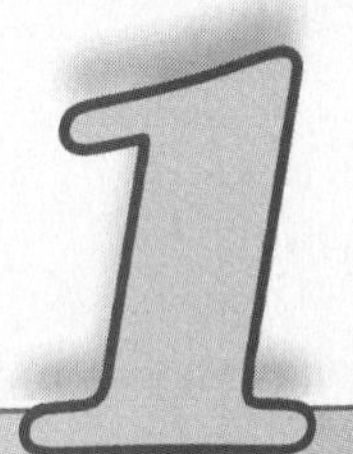

Objectives

You will have mastered the material in this project when you can:

- Describe the Internet and its associated key terms
- Describe the World Wide Web and its associated key terms
- Identify the types and purposes of Web sites
- Discuss Web browsers and identify their purpose
- Define Hypertext Markup Language (HTML) and the standards used for Web development
- Define Dynamic Hypertext Markup Language (DHTML) and describe its relationship to HTML
- Define Extensible Hypertext Markup Language (XHTML) and describe its relationship to HTML
- Describe tools used to create HTML documents
- Discuss the five phases of the Web development life cycle
- Describe Web site structures and the purpose of each structure
- Describe the importance of testing throughout the Web development life cycle

Introduction

Each day, you make decisions in all areas of your life. Having quick access to information to help you make good, informed decisions is vitally important. Today, computers and networks allow people to gather, analyze, and use information to make decisions and to communicate with others around the world. The world's largest network is the Internet — a worldwide network of computers that houses information on a multitude of subjects.

What Is the Internet?

The **Internet** is a worldwide collection of computer networks that links together millions of computers used by businesses, the government, educational institutions, organizations, and individuals using modems, telephone lines, television cables, and other communications devices and media (Figure 1-1). A **network** is a group of two or more computers that are connected together to share resources and information. Today, high-, medium-, and low-speed data lines connect networks. These data lines allow data to move from one computer to another. The **Internet backbone** is a collection of high-speed data lines that connect major computer systems located around the world. An

FIGURE 1-1 The Internet is a worldwide collection of computer networks.

Internet service provider (**ISP**) is a company that has a permanent connection to the Internet backbone. ISPs utilize high- or medium-speed data lines to allow individuals and companies to connect to the backbone for access to the Internet. A consumer's Internet connection at home generally is a low-speed data line that connects to the ISP.

More than 650 million people in 240 countries connect to the Internet using computers in their homes, offices, schools, and public locations such as libraries. Users with computers connected to the Internet can access a variety of services, including e-mail, newsgroups, and the World Wide Web (Figure 1-2).

FIGURE 1-2 The Internet makes available a variety of services such as e-mail, newsgroups, and the World Wide Web.

More About

Internet and WWW History

Many Web sites are dedicated to telling the story of the creation of the Internet and the World Wide Web. The World Wide Web Consortium (W3C), the de facto organization to govern HTML, provides a rich history of the Internet and the World Wide Web. To view their history, visit the HTML More About Web page (scsite.com/html3e/more) and then click History.

What Is the World Wide Web?

The **World Wide Web**, also called the **Web**, is the part of the Internet that supports multimedia and consists of a collection of linked documents. To support multimedia, the Web relies on the **Hypertext Transfer Protocol** (**HTTP**), which is a set of rules for exchanging text, graphic, sound, video, and other multimedia files. The linked documents, or pages of information, on the Web are known as **Web pages**. Because the Web supports multimedia, text, graphics, sound, and video, a Web page can include any of these elements.

A **Web site** is a related collection of Web pages that is created and maintained by an individual, company, educational institution, or other organization. For example, as shown in Figure 1-3, many colleges and universities, such as Arizona State University, publish and maintain Web sites. Each Web site contains a **home page**, which is the first document users see when they access the Web site. The home page often serves as an index or table of contents to other documents and files stored on the site.

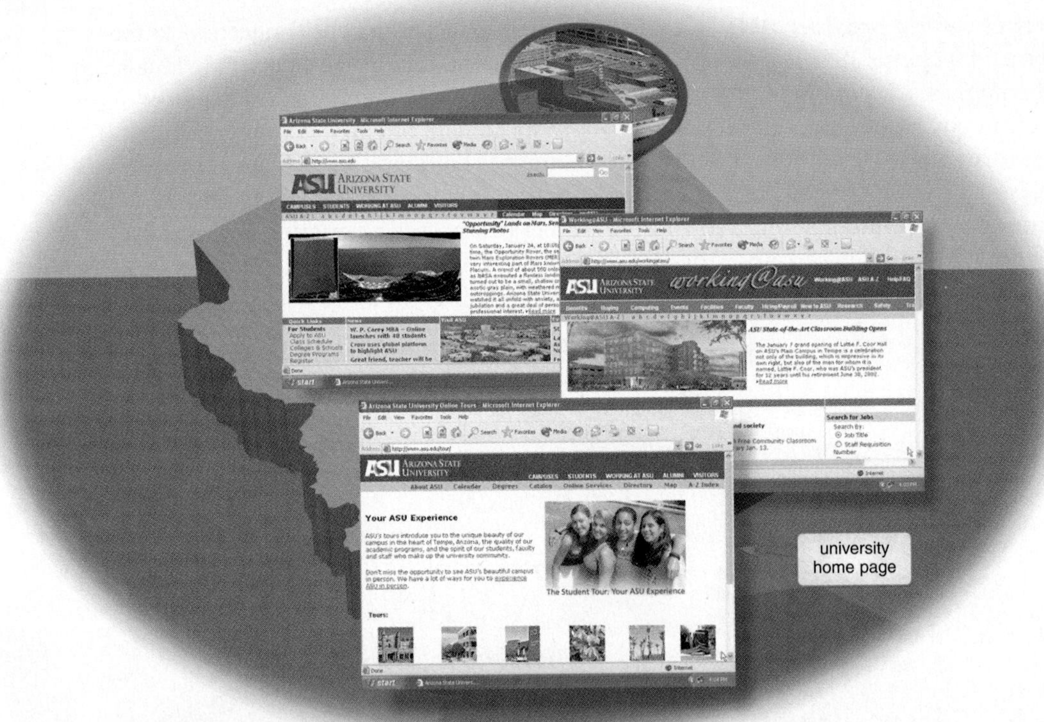

FIGURE 1-3 A Web site is a related collection of Web pages that is created and maintained by an individual, company, educational institution, or other organization.

Web Servers

Web pages are stored on a **Web server**, or **host**, which is a computer that stores and sends (serves) requested Web pages and other files. Any computer that has Web server software installed and is connected to the Internet can act as a Web server. Every Web site is stored on, and runs from, one or more Web servers. A very large Web site may be spread over a number of servers in different geographic locations.

Publishing is copying Web pages and other files to a Web server. Once a Web page is published, anyone who has access to the Internet can view it, regardless of where the Web server is located. For example, although the Arizona State University Web site is stored on a Web server in Tempe, Arizona, it is available for viewing by anyone in the world.

Web Site Types and Purposes

The three general types of Web sites are Internet, intranet, and extranet. Table 1-1 lists characteristics of each of these three types of Web sites.

Table 1-1 Types of Web Sites

TYPE	USERS	ACCESS	APPLICATIONS
Internet	Anyone	Public	Share information (personal information, product catalogs, classroom information, etc.) with the public
Intranet	Employees or members of organization	Private	Share information (forms, manuals, schedules, etc.) with employees or members
Extranet	Select business partners or customers	Private	Share information (inventory updates, product specifications, financial information, etc.) with partners and customers

An **Internet site**, also known as a Web site, is a site generally available to the public. Individuals, groups, companies, and educational institutions use Internet sites, or Web sites, for a variety of purposes. An individual, for example, might create a personal Web site that includes his or her résumé to make it easily accessible to any interested employers. Another personal Web site might present information about a person's hobbies or interests. Families also can share photographs of special events, schedules, or other information with each other via Web sites (Figure 1-4).

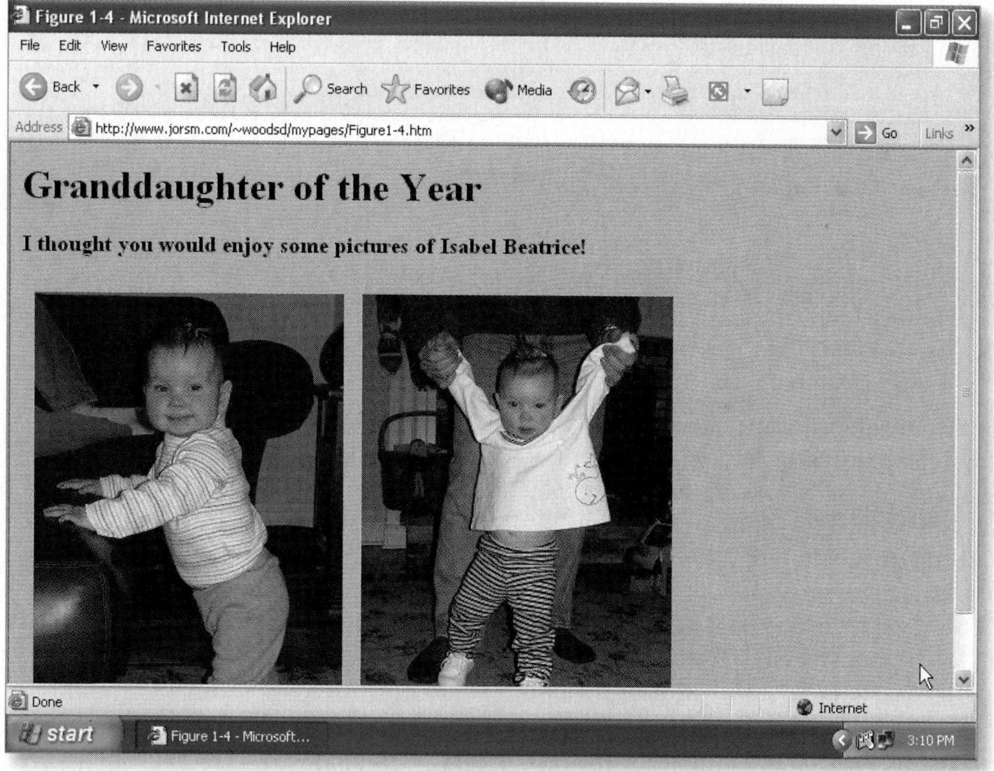

FIGURE 1-4 Web page on a personal Web site.

> *More About*
>
> **E-Commerce**
>
> Today, e-commerce is a standard part of doing business. E-commerce technologies, however, continue to change, offering new applications and potential uses. Several online magazines are dedicated to providing an in depth look at e-commerce. To learn more about e-commerce, visit the HTML More About Web page (scsite.com/html3e/more) and then click E-commerce.

Companies use Web sites to advertise or sell their products and services worldwide, as well as to provide technical and product support for their customers. Many company Web sites also support **electronic commerce** (**e-commerce**), which is the buying and selling of goods and services on the Internet. Using e-commerce technologies, these Web sites allow customers to browse product catalogs, comparison shop, and order products online. Many company Web sites also provide job postings and announcements, a frequently asked questions (FAQs) section, customer feedback links to solicit comments from their customers, and searchable technical support databases.

Colleges, universities, and other schools use Web sites to distribute information about areas of study, provide course information, or register students for classes online. Instructors use their Web sites to issue announcements, post questions on the reading material, list contact information, and provide easy access to their lecture notes and slides, as shown in Figure 1-5.

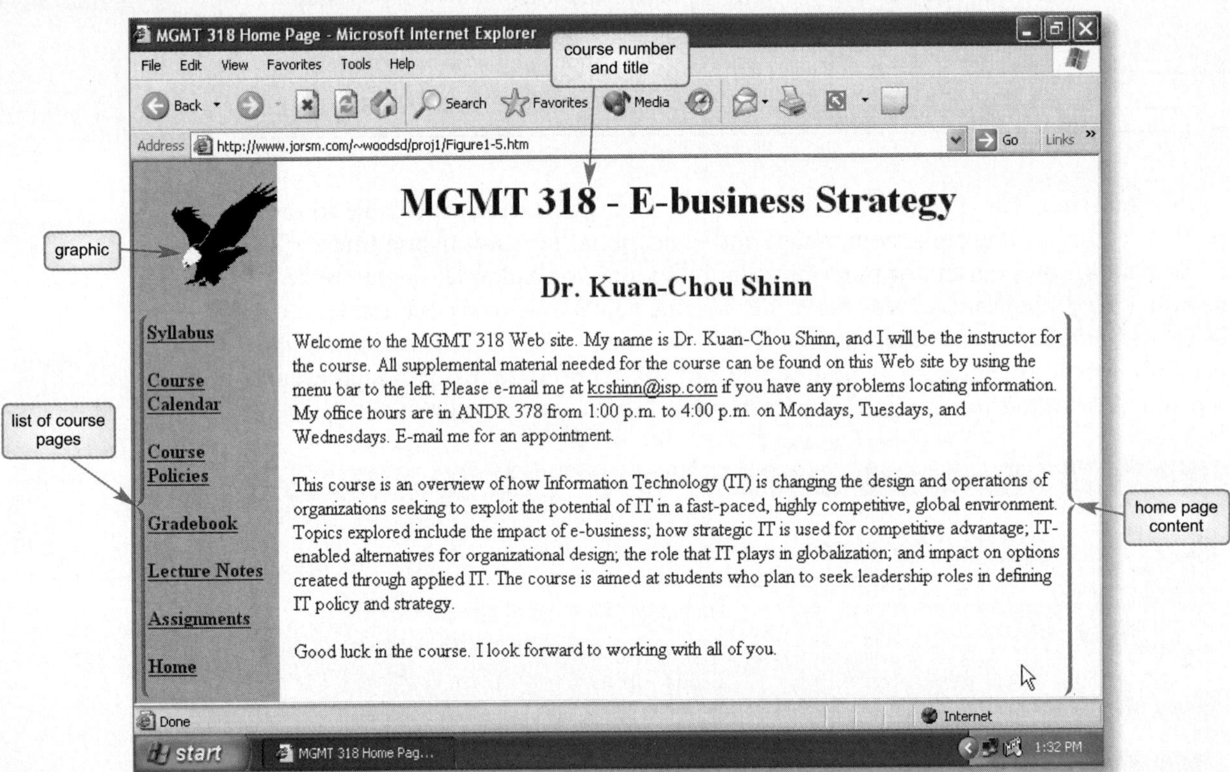

FIGURE 1-5 Web page from a university's Web site.

> *More About*
>
> **Intranets and Extranets**
>
> The CIO Intranet/Extranet Research Center provides valuable information on building and maintaining an intranet or extranet, along with additional resources. To view their Web site, visit the HTML More About Web page (scsite.com/html3e/more) and then click Intranets/Extranets.

An **intranet** is a private network that uses standard Internet technologies to share company information among employees. An intranet is contained within a company or organization's network; some intranets also are password-protected to provide additional security. Policy and procedure manuals usually are found on an intranet, in addition to a variety of forms. Other documents, such as employee directories, company newsletters, product catalogs, and training manuals, often are distributed via an intranet. An intranet also can be used to facilitate working in groups and collecting feedback from employees.

An **extranet** is a private network that uses Internet technologies to share business information with select corporate partners or key customers. Most extranets are password-protected to restrict access to specific suppliers, vendors, partners, or customers. Companies and organizations can use an extranet to share product manuals, training modules, inventory status, and order information. An extranet also might support e-commerce to allow retailers to purchase inventory directly or to pay bills online, which is more efficient than calling partners to check on inventory levels or account status.

Web Browsers

In order to view a Web page on any type of Web site, a computer needs to have a Web browser installed. A **Web browser**, also called a **browser**, is a program that interprets and displays Web pages and enables you to view and interact with a Web page. The two more popular browsers in use today are Microsoft Internet Explorer and Netscape Navigator. Browsers provide a variety of features, including the capability to locate Web pages, to move forward and backward between Web pages, to bookmark favorite Web pages, and to choose security settings.

To locate a Web page using a browser, you type its Uniform Resource Locator (URL) in the browser's Address, or Location, bar. A **Uniform Resource Locator** (**URL**) is the address of a document or other file accessible on the Internet. An example of a URL on the Web is:

http://www.scsite.com/html3e/index.htm

The URL indicates to the browser to use the Hypertext Transfer Protocol (http) to locate a Web page named index.htm in the html3e folder on a Web server named scsite.com. Web page URLs can be found in a wide range of places, including school catalogs, business cards, product packaging, and advertisements.

Hyperlinks are used to link one Web page to other Web pages. A **hyperlink**, also called a **link**, is an element used to connect one Web page to another Web page on the same, or a different, Web server located anywhere in the world. Clicking a hyperlink allows you to move quickly from one Web page to another. You also can click hyperlinks to move to a different section of the same Web page.

Hyperlinks are an essential part of the World Wide Web. With hyperlinks, a Web site user does not have to view information linearly. Instead, he or she can choose to click the available hyperlinks in order to view the information in a variety of ways. Many different Web page elements, including text, graphics, and animations, can serve as hyperlinks. Figure 1-6 on the next page shows examples of several different Web page elements used as hyperlinks.

> **Q&A**
>
> **Q:** What are browser-safe colors and why should they be used?
>
> **A:** The browser limits the colors that a user can see on a Web page to 216 colors. Because a browser can display these colors correctly, they are called browser-safe colors. To ensure that the majority of your users can see Web page colors as intended, Web developers should use only browser-safe colors when designing Web pages. Appendix B provides a list of the 216 browser-safe colors that can be used without worry.

What Is Hypertext Markup Language?

Web pages are created using **Hypertext Markup Language** (**HTML**), which is the authoring language used to create documents on the World Wide Web. HTML uses a set of special instructions called **tags** or **markup** to define the structure and layout of a Web document and specify how the page is displayed in a browser.

A Web page is a file that contains both text and HTML tags. HTML tags *mark* the text to define how it displays when viewed as a page on the Web. HTML includes hundreds of tags used to format Web pages and create hyperlinks to other documents or Web pages. For instance, the HTML tags <strong> and </strong> are used to indicate bold text, <p> and </p> are used to indicate a new paragraph, and <hr /> is used to display a horizontal rule across the page. Figure 1-7a on the next page shows the HTML tags needed to create the Web page shown in Figure 1-7b.

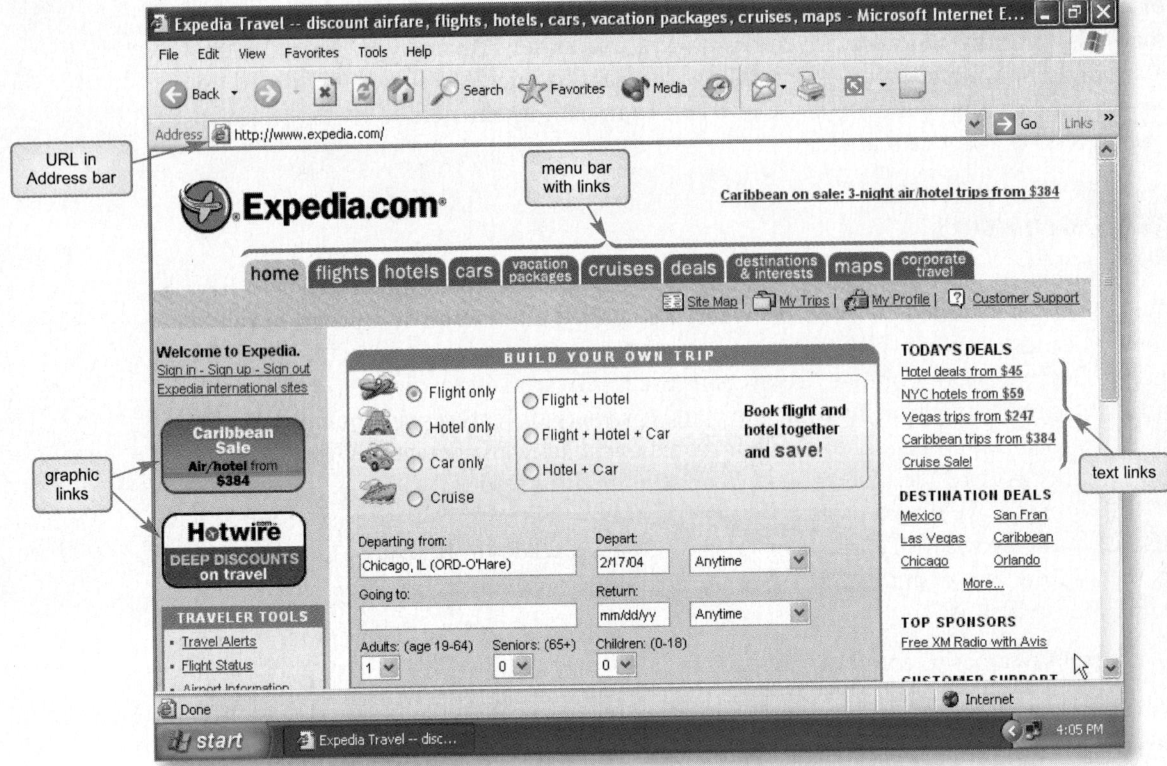

FIGURE 1-6 A Web page can use several different Web page elements as hyperlinks.

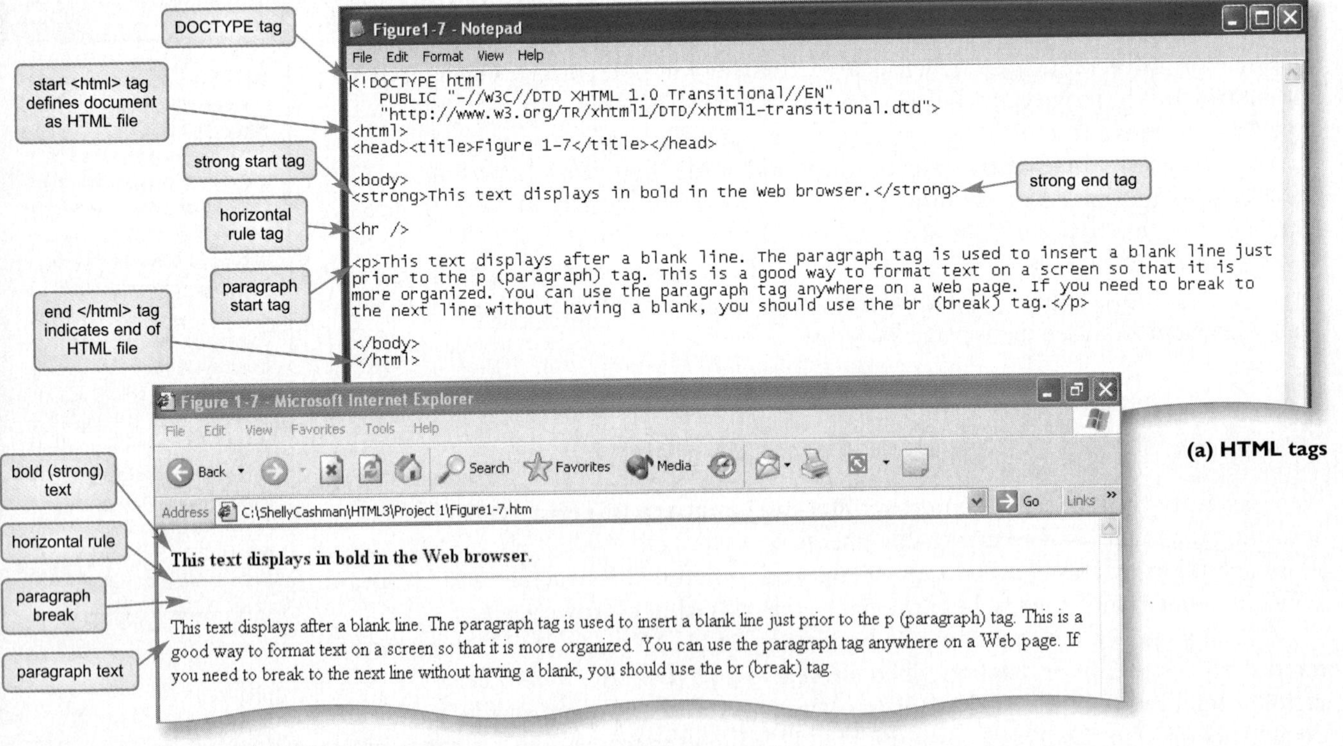

FIGURE 1-7 A Web page is a file that contains both text and HTML tags.

HTML is **platform independent**, meaning you can create, or *code*, an HTML file on one type of computer and then use a browser on another type of computer to view that file as a Web page.

HTML History

In 1989, Tim Berners-Lee and Robert Calliau set out to improve their process for handling hundreds of research documents. Over the next two years, Berners-Lee developed a collection of tags that described how a document should look when viewed in a browser. For example, the tags defined text displayed as a header, in a paragraph, or as regular text. In addition, these tags made it possible to create hyperlinks to connect documents together. Berners-Lee's system of tags became known as HTML and created the use of hyperlinks that now define the World Wide Web.

In 1994, Tim Berners-Lee founded the World Wide Web Consortium in an effort to encourage the universality and interoperability of HTML and to promote an open forum for discussion among Web developers. The **World Wide Web Consortium** (**W3C**) is an industry consortium that seeks to promote standards for the evolution of the Web and Web technologies. Although no one organization dictates the rules or standards for HTML, the W3C is regarded as the de facto organization to govern HTML.

In addition to information about HTML standards, the W3C Web site (w3.org) also includes information about accessibility, privacy, internationalization, and new Web development languages and techniques (Figure 1-8). Membership in the W3C is open to all types of organizations, including educational, government, and commercial entities. Members generally include technology vendors, content providers, corporations, research laboratories, standards bodies, and governments, all of which help to ensure the strength and direction of the consortium.

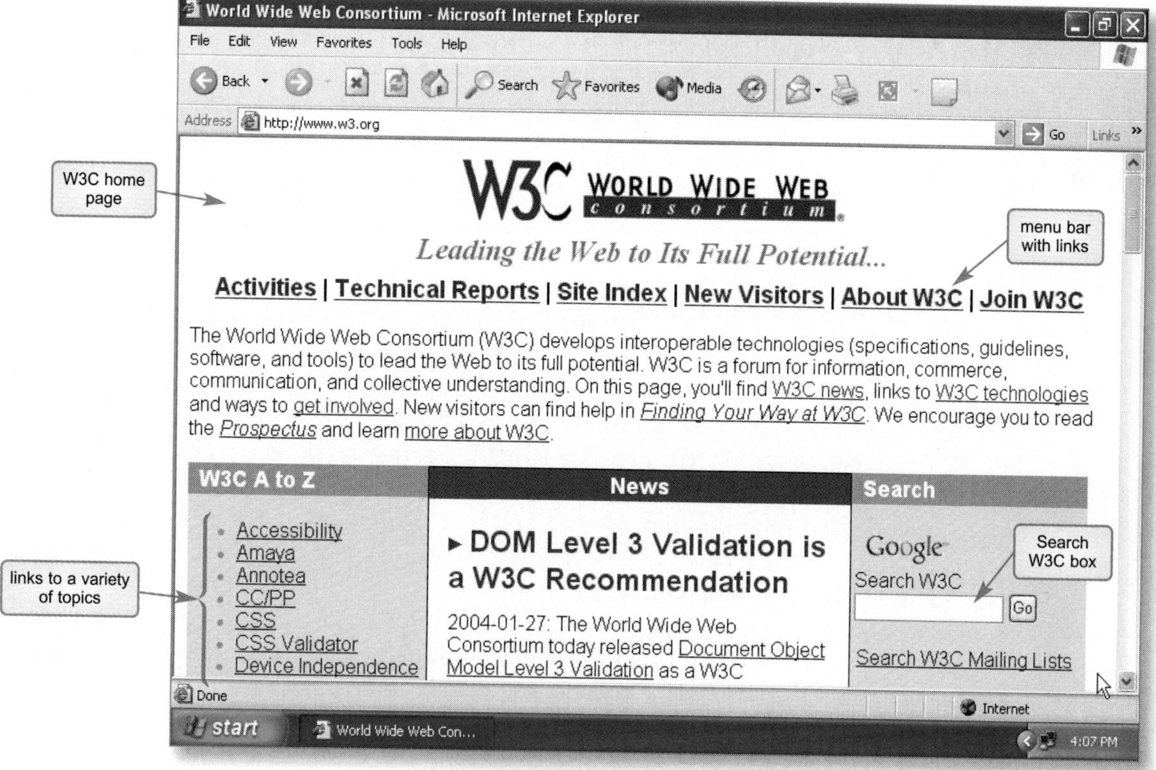

FIGURE 1-8 W3C Web site home page.

HTML Elements

HTML is a subset of Standard Generalized Markup Language (SGML), which is a standard for how to organize and tag elements of a document. SGML itself does not specify any particular formatting; rather, it specifies the rules for tagging elements. Government agencies and publishers use SGML to create books and reference documentation.

HTML combines the descriptive tags of SGML with special tags that denote formatting styles for how a document should display in a Web browser. HTML elements include headings, paragraphs, hyperlinks, lists, images, and more. Most HTML elements consist of three parts: a start tag, content, and an end tag. For example, to specify that text should display in bold on a Web page, you would enter the following HTML code:

```
<strong>sample text</strong>
```

where <strong> is the start tag, sample text is the content that will display in bold, and </strong> is the end tag. Table 1-2 shows examples of some HTML elements.

More About

HTML Elements

Numerous sources of information about HTML elements are available. The W3C provides the most comprehensive list of tags and attributes together with examples of their use. To view this comprehensive list, visit the HTML More About Web page (scsite.com/html3e/more) and then click HTML Elements.

Table 1-2 HTML Elements

HTML ELEMENT	HTML TAGS	PURPOSE
Title	<title>...</title>	Indicates title to display on the title bar on the Web page
Body	<body>...</body>	Specifies what displays on the Web page; all Web page content is inserted within the start <body> tag and end </body> tag
Paragraph	<p>...</p>	Inserts a blank line before paragraph text
Line Break	 	Inserts a line break before next element (no blank line)

HTML Coding Practices

Similar to all programming languages, HTML has a set of coding practices designed to simplify the process of creating and editing HTML files and to ensure the Web pages display correctly in different browsers.

When creating an HTML file, you should separate sections of the HTML code with spaces. Adding spaces between sections gives you an immediate view of the sections of code that relate to one another and helps you view the HTML elements in your document more clearly. HTML browsers ignore spaces that exist between the tags in your HTML document, so the spaces inserted within the code will not display on the Web page. Figure 1-9 shows an example of an HTML file, with code sections separated by space lines. Another developer looking at this code can see immediately where the table (lines 9 through 18) and bulleted list (lines 20 through 23) are located in the code.

HTML Versions

HTML has gone through several versions, each of which expands the capabilities of HTML. The most recent version of HTML is HTML 4.01, although most browsers still support the previous HTML versions 3.2 and 2.0. To ensure that browsers can interpret each new version of HTML, the W3C maintains HTML standards, or specifications, which it makes publicly available on its Web site.

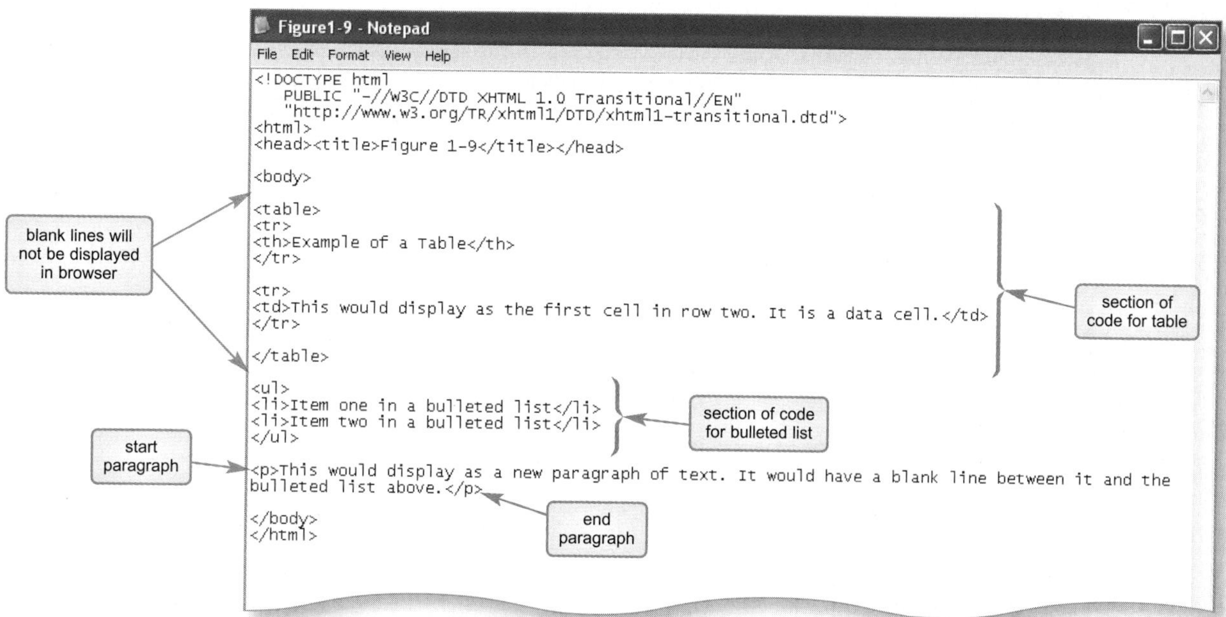

FIGURE 1-9 Adding spaces to HTML code separates sections to make reading easier.

Dynamic HTML (DHTML)

HTML can be used with other Web technologies to provide additional Web page functionality. For example, **Dynamic HTML** (**DHTML**) is a term that describes a combination of HTML tags, cascading style sheets (CSS), and a scripting language such as JavaScript. DHTML allows users to create interactive, animated Web pages. CSS, JavaScript, and DHTML are covered in later projects in this book.

Extensible Hypertext Markup Language (XHTML)

Extensible Markup Language (**XML**) is a markup language that uses tags to describe the structure and content of a document, not the format. **Extensible Hypertext Markup Language** (**XHTML**) is a reformulation of HTML so it conforms to Extensible Markup Language (XML) rules. As you have learned, HTML uses tags to describe how a document should be displayed in a Web browser. By incorporating HTML and XML, XHTML combines the benefits of the display features of HTML and the stricter coding standards required by XML.

If you create a Web page in HTML and do not follow HTML coding standards exactly (for example, by not using an end </p> tag), the Web browser on your computer still can interpret and display the Web page correctly. Newer types of browsers, such as those for mobile phones or handheld computers, are not able to interpret HTML code that does not meet the HTML standards. Because XHTML has such strict coding standards, it helps ensure that Web pages created in XHTML will be readable by many different types of applications.

Table 1-3 on the next page lists some of the XHTML coding rules that Web developers should follow to ensure that their HTML code conforms to XHTML standards. All of the projects in this book follow XHTML standards and adhere to the rules outlined in Table 1-3. The specifics of each rule will be explained in detail as it is used in a project.

Table 1-3 XHTML Coding Practices

PRACTICE	INVALID EXAMPLE	VALID EXAMPLE
HTML file must include a DOCTYPE statement	<html> <head><title>sample Web page</title>	<!DOCTYPE html PUBLIC "-//W3C//DTD XHTML 1.0 Transitional//EN" "http://www.w3.org/TR/xhtml1/DTD/xhtml1-transitional.dtd"> <html> <head><title>sample Web page</title>
All tags and attributes must be written in lowercase	<TABLE WIDTH="100%">	<table width="100%">
All attribute values must be enclosed by single or double quotes	<table width=100%>	<table width="100%">
All tags must be closed, including tags such as img, hr, br, which do not have end tags	<p>This is a paragraph <hr> <p>This is another paragraph	<p>This is a paragraph</p> <hr /> <p>This is another paragraph</p>
All elements must be nested properly	<p><strong>This is a bold paragraph</p></strong>	<p><strong>This is a bold paragraph</strong></p>

Tools for Creating HTML Documents

You can create Web pages using HTML with a simple text editor, such as Notepad, WordPad, or SimpleText. A **text editor** is a program that allows a user to enter, change, save, and print text, such as HTML. Text editors do not have many advanced features, but they do allow you to develop HTML documents easily. For instance, if you want to mark text to be displayed in italics on a Web page, type the text in the text editor and then surround the text with the start (<em>) and end (</em>) tags as shown in Figure 1-10.

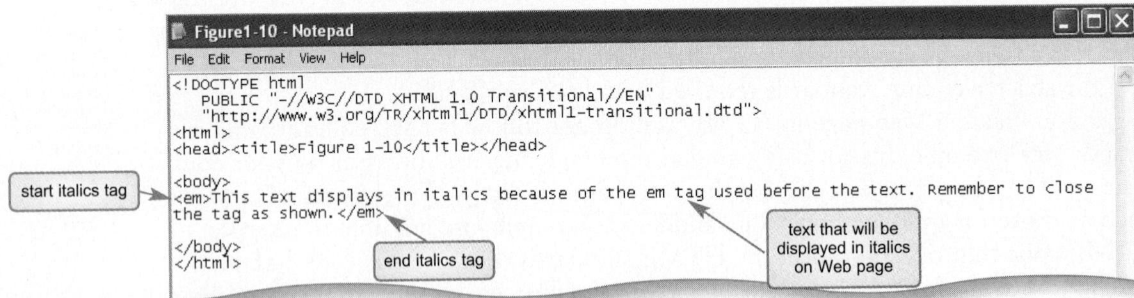

FIGURE 1-10 With a text editor, such as Notepad, you type HTML tags directly in the document.

You also can create Web pages using an HTML editor, such as Macromedia HomeSite or BBEdit. An **HTML editor** is a program that provides basic text-editing functions, as well as more advanced features such as color-coding for various HTML tags, menus to insert HTML tags, and spell checkers.

Many popular software applications also provide features that enable you to develop Web pages easily. Microsoft Word, for example, has a Save as Web Page feature that converts a Word document into an HTML file by automatically adding the HTML tags into the document. Microsoft Excel and Microsoft PowerPoint also have Save as Web Page features. Using Microsoft Access, you can create a Web page that allows you to add, edit, or view data in a database. Each of these applications also provides the capability of inserting hyperlinks, drop-down boxes, option buttons, or scrolling text to the Web page.

These advanced Web features make it simple to save any document, spreadsheet, database, or presentation to display as a Web page. Corporate policy and procedures manuals and PowerPoint presentations, for example, easily can be saved as Web pages and published to the company's intranet site. Extranet users can be given access to Web pages that allow them to view or update information stored in a database.

You also can create Web pages using a WYSIWYG editor, such as Microsoft FrontPage, Macromedia Dreamweaver, or Sausage Software HotDog. A **WYSIWYG editor** is a program that provides a graphical user interface that allows a developer to preview the Web page during its development. WYSIWYG (pronounced *wizzywig*) is an acronym for What You See Is What You Get. A WYSIWYG editor creates the HTML code for you as you add elements to the Web page, which means that you do not have to enter HTML tags directly.

Regardless of which type of program you use to create Web pages, it is important to understand the specifics of HTML so you can make changes outside of the editor. It also is important to understand the Web development life cycle, so the Web pages in your Web site are consistent and complete.

More About

Microsoft FrontPage

Microsoft's FrontPage is a popular WYSIWYG editor used by many novice Web developers to create well-designed, interactive Web sites. To get a 30-day trial of the latest version of FrontPage, visit the HTML More About Web page (www.scsite.com/html/more.htm) and click FrontPage.

Web Development Life Cycle

In any software development project, a systematic methodology, or process, should be followed through the life cycle of the project to ensure consistency and completeness. The Web development life cycle outlined in this section is one that can be utilized for any size of Web development project. The life cycle includes the following phases: planning, analysis, design and development, testing, and implementation and maintenance. Table 1-4 on the next page lists several questions that should be asked during each phase in the Web development life cycle.

Web Site Planning

Web site planning, which is the first phase of the Web development life cycle, involves identifying the goals or purpose of the Web site. The first step in the Web site planning phase is to answer the question, What is the purpose of this Web site? As you have learned, individuals and groups design and publish Web sites for a variety of purposes. Individuals develop Web sites to share their hobbies, to post résumés, or just to share ideas on personal interests. Organizations create Web sites to keep members informed of upcoming events or to recruit new members. Businesses create Web sites to advertise and sell products or to give their customers 24-hour online support. Instructors publish Web sites to inform students of course policies and requirements. Until you adequately can identify the intended purpose of the Web site, you should not proceed with the Web development project.

In addition to understanding the Web site's purpose, you also should understand who will use the Web site and the computing environments of most of the users. Knowing the makeup of your target audience — including age, gender, general demographic background, and level of computer literacy — will help you design a Web site appropriate for all users. Understanding their computing environments will determine what types of Web technologies to use. For example, if most users had low-speed Internet connections, you would not want to create pages with large graphics or multimedia elements.

Table 1-4 Web Development Phases and Questions

WEB DEVELOPMENT PHASE	QUESTIONS TO ASK
Planning	• What is the purpose of this Web site? • Who will use this Web site? • What are the users' computing environments? • Who owns and authors the information on the Web site? • Who decides if/where the information goes on the Web site?
Analysis	• What tasks do the users need to perform? • What information is useful to the users? • What process considerations must be made?
Design and Development	• How will the Web pages be organized? • What type of Web site structure is appropriate for the content? • What forms of multimedia contribute positively to the Web site? • How can accessibility issues be addressed so as not to limit usability? • Do we need to design for an international audience?
Testing	• Is the Web site content correct? • Does the Web site functionality work correctly? • Are users able to find the information they need and to complete desired tasks? • Is the navigation easy to use?
Implementation and Maintenance	• How is the Web site published? • How is the Web site updated? • Who is responsible for content updates? • Who is responsible for structure updates? • How do we notify users about updates to the Web site? • Will the Web site be monitored?

More About

Accessibility Standards

Creating a Web site that is accessible to all users allows your Web site to reach the widest audience. Further, under Section 508 law, any Web site or technology used by a Federal agency must be usable by people with disabilities. To learn more about Section 508 guidelines and how they impact Web page development, visit the HTML More About Web page (scsite.com/html3e/more) and then click Accessibility Standards.

A final aspect to the Web site planning phase is to identify the content owners and authors. To determine this, you need to ask the questions:

- Who owns and authors the information on the Web site?
- Who decides if/where the information goes on the Web site?

Once you have identified who will provide and authorize the Web site content, you can include those individuals in all aspects of the Web development project.

Web Site Analysis

During the analysis phase, you make decisions about the Web site content and functionality. To help define the appropriate Web site content and functionality, you first should identify the tasks that users need to perform. Answering that question allows you to define necessary content to facilitate those tasks and determine useful information for the users. Extraneous content should be eliminated from the Web site, as it does not serve any purpose.

In the analysis phase, it also is important to consider the processes required to support Web site features. For example, if you determine that users should be able to order products via the Web site, then you also need to define the processes or actions to be taken each time an order is submitted. For instance, after an order is submitted, how will that order be processed throughout the back-office business applications, such as inventory control and accounts payable? Will users receive e-mail confirmations with details about their orders?

The analysis phase is one of the more important phases in the Web development life cycle. Clearly, understanding and defining the desired content and functionality of the Web site will direct the type of Web site that you design and reduce changes during Web site development.

Web Site Design and Development

After determining the purpose of the Web site and defining the content and functionality, you need to consider the Web site's design. Some key considerations in Web site design are defining how to organize Web page content, selecting the appropriate Web site structure, determining how to use multimedia, addressing accessibility issues, and designing pages for an international audience.

Many ways to organize a Web page exist, just as many ways to organize a report or paper exist. Table 1-5 lists some organizational standards for creating a Web page that is easy to read and navigate.

Table 1-5 Web Page Organizational Standards

ELEMENT	ORGANIZATIONAL STANDARD	REASON
Titles	Use simple titles that clearly explain the purpose of the page	Titles help users understand the purpose of the page; a good title explains the page in the search engine results lists
Headings	Use headings to separate main topics	Headings make a Web page easier to read; simple headlines clearly explain the purpose of the page
Horizontal rules	Insert horizontal rules to separate main topics	Horizontal rules provide graphical elements to break up Web page content
Paragraphs	Use paragraphs to help divide large amounts of text	Paragraphs provide shorter, more-readable sections of text
Lists	Utilize bulleted or numbered lists when appropriate	Lists provide organized, easy-to-read text that readers can scan easily
Page length	Maintain suitable Web page lengths	Web users do not always scroll to view information on longer pages; appropriate page lengths increase likelihood that users view key information
Information	Emphasize the most important information by placing it at the top of a Web page	Web users are quick to peruse a page; placing critical information at the top of the page increases the likelihood that users will view key information
Other	Incorporate a contact e-mail address; include the date of the last modification	E-mail addresses and dates give users a way to contact a Web developer with questions; the date last modified helps users determine the timeliness of site information

Web sites can use any of several different types of structures, including linear, hierarchical, and webbed. Each structure links, or connects, the Web pages in a different way to define how users navigate through the site and view the Web pages. You should select a structure for the Web site based on how users will navigate through the site to complete tasks and view the Web site content.

A **linear** Web site structure connects Web pages in a straight line, as shown in Figure 1-11. A linear Web site structure is appropriate if the information on the Web pages should be read in a specific order. For example, if the information on the first Web page was necessary for understanding information on the second Web page, you

FIGURE 1-11 Linear Web site structure.

More About

User Interface Design

The user interface design is a very important aspect of a Web site. If a site is designed poorly, users may be unable to find the desired information or complete a task, which makes the Web site ineffective. To learn more about good Web design principles, visit the HTML More About Web page (scsite.com/html3e/more) and then click Design.

should use a linear structure. Each page would have links from one Web page to the next, as well as a link back to the home page.

A **hierarchical** Web site structure connects Web pages in a tree-like structure, as shown in Figure 1-12. A hierarchical Web site structure works well on a site with a main index or table of contents page that links to all other Web pages. With this structure, the main index page would display general information and secondary pages would include more detailed information.

A **webbed** Web site structure has no set organization, as shown in Figure 1-13. A webbed Web site structure works best on Web sites with information that does not need to be read in a specific order and with many navigation options users can select. The World Wide Web itself uses a webbed structure, so users can navigate among Web pages in any order they choose.

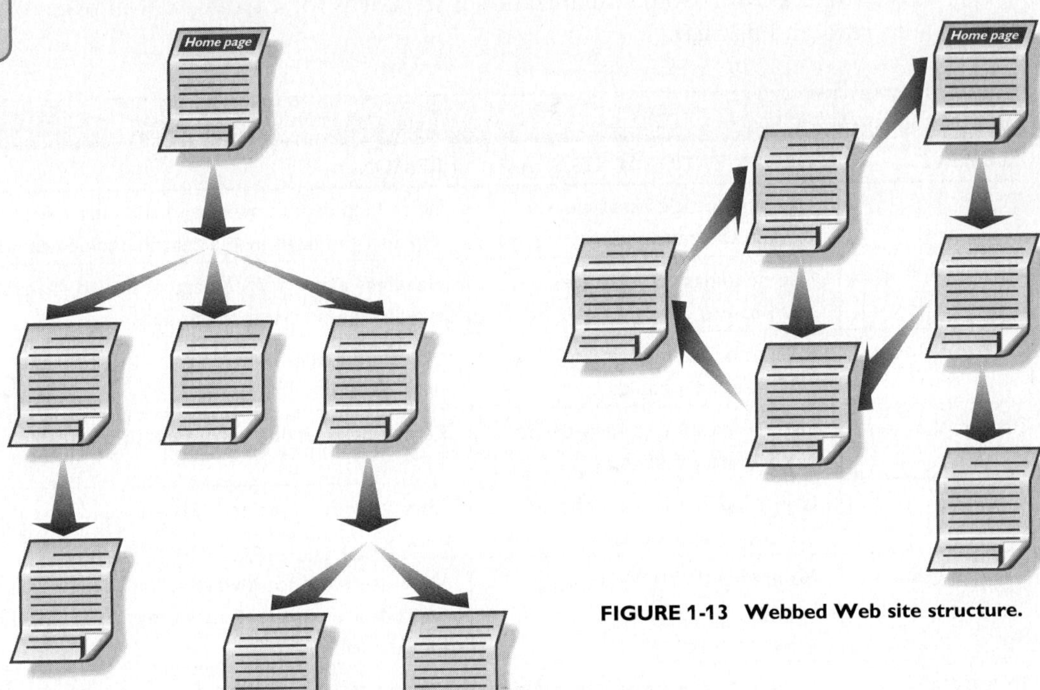

FIGURE 1-12 Hierarchical Web site structure.

FIGURE 1-13 Webbed Web site structure.

Most Web sites are a combination of the linear, hierarchical, and webbed structures. Some information on the Web site might be organized hierarchically from an index page; other information might be accessible from all areas of the site; while other information might be organized linearly to be read in a specific order. Using a combination of the three structures is appropriate, if it helps users navigate through the site easily.

Regardless of the structure or structures that you use, you should balance the narrowness and depth of the Web site. A **broad Web site** is one in which the home page is the main index page, and all other Web pages are linked individually to the home page (Figure 1-14). By making the other Web pages accessible only through the home page, a broad Web site forces the user to return to the home page in order to move from one Web page to another. The structure makes navigation time-consuming and limiting for users. A better structure would present a user with navigation alternatives that allow for direct movement between the Web pages.

FIGURE 1-14 Broad Web site.

A **deep Web site** is one that has many levels of pages, requiring the user to click many times to reach a particular Web page (Figure 1-15). By requiring a visitor to move through several Web pages before reaching the desired Web page, a deep Web site forces a user to spend time viewing interim pages with little or no content.

As a Web developer, you must select an appropriate structure for the Web site and work to balance breadth and depth. Users go to a Web site looking for information to complete a task. Good design provides ease of navigation to allow users to find content quickly and easily.

During the design and development phase, you also should consider what, if any, types of multimedia could contribute positively to the Web site experience. For instance, adding a video message from the company CEO might be useful, but if the computing environment of your users cannot accommodate video playback, then the video serves no purpose. In general, do not use advanced multimedia technologies in a Web site, unless they make a positive contribution to the Web site experience.

Finally, consider accessibility issues and internationalization. A Web developer should always design for viewing by a diverse audience, including physically impaired and global users. A key consideration is that the software used by physically impaired individuals does not work with some Web features. For instance, if you use graphics on the Web site, always include alternate text for each graphic. To support an international audience, use generic icons that can be understood globally, avoid slang expressions in the content, and build simple pages that load quickly over lower-speed connections.

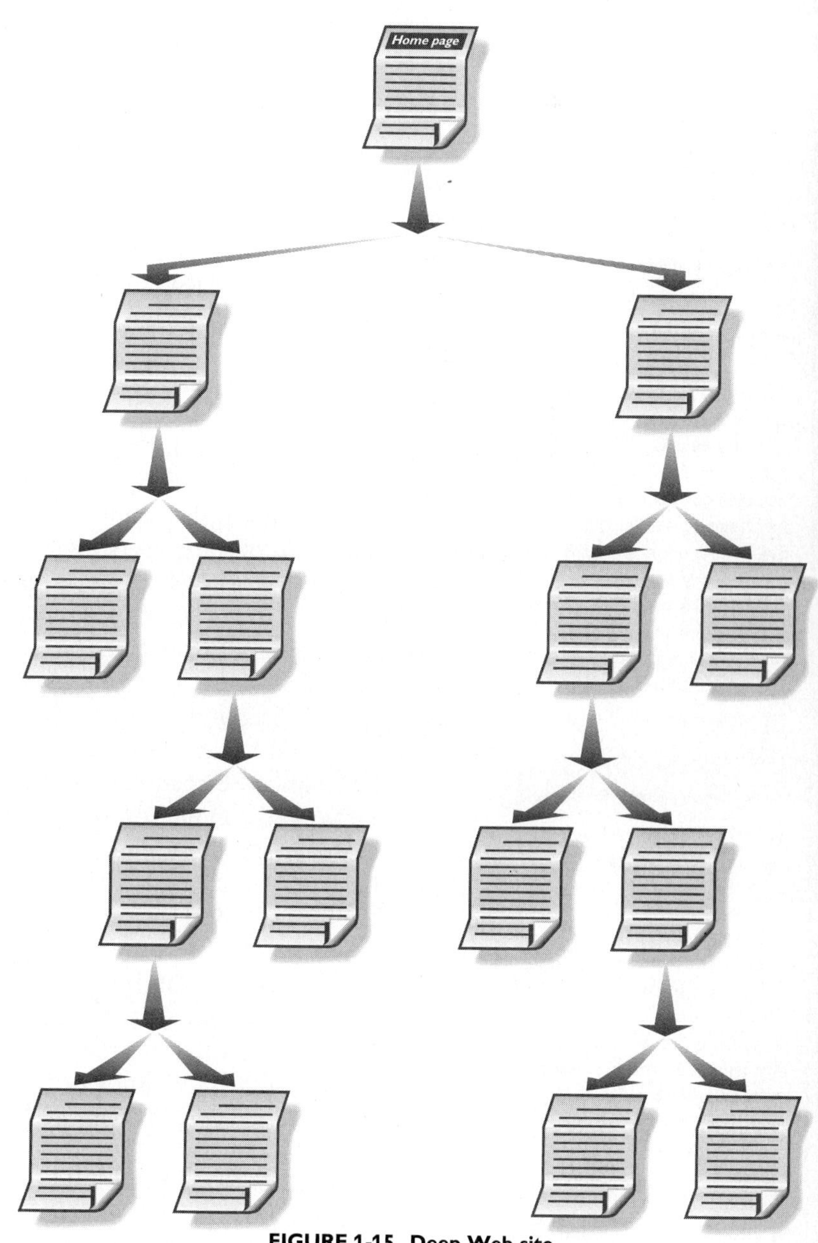

FIGURE 1-15 Deep Web site.

The design issues just discussed above are only a few of the basic Web page design issues that you need to consider. Throughout this book, design issues will be addressed as they relate to each project. Many excellent Web page design resources also are available on the Internet.

Web Site Testing

A Web site should be tested at various stages of the Web design and development processes. The testing process should be comprehensive and include a review of Web page content, functionality, and usability. Some basic steps to test content and functionality include:

- Proofreading content and page titles to review for accurate spelling and grammar
- Checking links to ensure they are not broken and are linked correctly
- Checking graphics to confirm they display properly and are linked correctly
- Ensuring that accessibility and internationalization issues are addressed
- Testing forms and other interactive page elements
- Testing pages to make sure they load quickly over lower-speed connections
- Printing each page to check how pages print
- Reviewing the HTML to ensure it meets W3C standards

Q: What other types of testing should be considered, in addition to usability testing?

A: For a newly implemented or maintained Web site, several types of tests should be conducted. Functionality testing involves determining if the Web site functions as it is designed to do. Compatibility testing is done to verify that the Web site works with a variety of browser versions. Stress testing determines what happens on your Web site when greater numbers of users access the site.

You also should test each Web page in several different browser types and versions. Different browsers display some aspects of Web pages differently, so it is important to test Web pages in several different browsers to verify they display correctly in each browser. If you have used technologies that are not supported by older browsers or that require plug-ins, consider changing the content or providing alternate Web pages for viewing in older browsers.

Usability is the measure of how well a product, such as a Web site, allows a user to accomplish his or her goals. **Usability testing** is a method by which users of a Web site or other product are asked to perform certain tasks in an effort to measure the product's ease-of-use and the user's perception of the experience. Usability testing for a Web site should focus on three key aspects: content, navigation, and presentation.

Usability testing can be conducted in several ways. One good way to test a Web site's usability is to observe users interfacing with (or using) the Web site. As you observe users, you can track the links they click and record their actions and comments. You even can ask the users to explain what tasks they were trying to accomplish while navigating through the site. The information gained by observing users can be invaluable in helping to identify potential problem areas in the Web site. For example, if you observe that users have difficulty finding the Web page that lists store locations and hours of operation, you may want to clarify the link descriptions or make the links more prominent on the Web page.

Q: What browsers should I use to test Web pages?

A: Use the browsers your audience is most likely to use. If your audience uses both PC and Macintosh computers, consider testing the Web pages using browsers on both platforms. You also may want to test the Web pages in several versions of the same browser (usually the two most recent versions), in the event users have not yet upgraded.

Another way to conduct usability testing is to give users a specific task to complete (such as finding the product price list) and then observe how they navigate through the site to complete the task. If possible, ask them to explain why they selected certain links. Both of these observation methods are extremely valuable, but require access to users in order to conduct this type of testing.

Usability testing also can be completed using a questionnaire or survey. When writing a questionnaire or survey, be sure to write open-ended questions that can give you valuable information. For instance, asking the yes/no question, "Is the Web site visually appealing?," will not gather useful information. If you change that question to use a scaled response, such as, "Rate the visual appeal of this Web site, using a scale of 1 for low and 5 for high," you can get more valuable input from the users.

A usability testing questionnaire always should include space for users to write additional explanatory comments. For example, if a user rates the Web site's visual appeal as low and then adds a comment, you might learn that the user viewed the

Web site on a smaller monitor that cut off the right side of the page, or you might find that the user disliked the site's background color.

Figure 1-16 shows some examples of types of questions and organization that you might include in a Web site usability testing questionnaire.

do not require name unless necessary

ask for user's relationship to organization

sample question structure

another sample question structure

area for additional comments

range of choices for answers

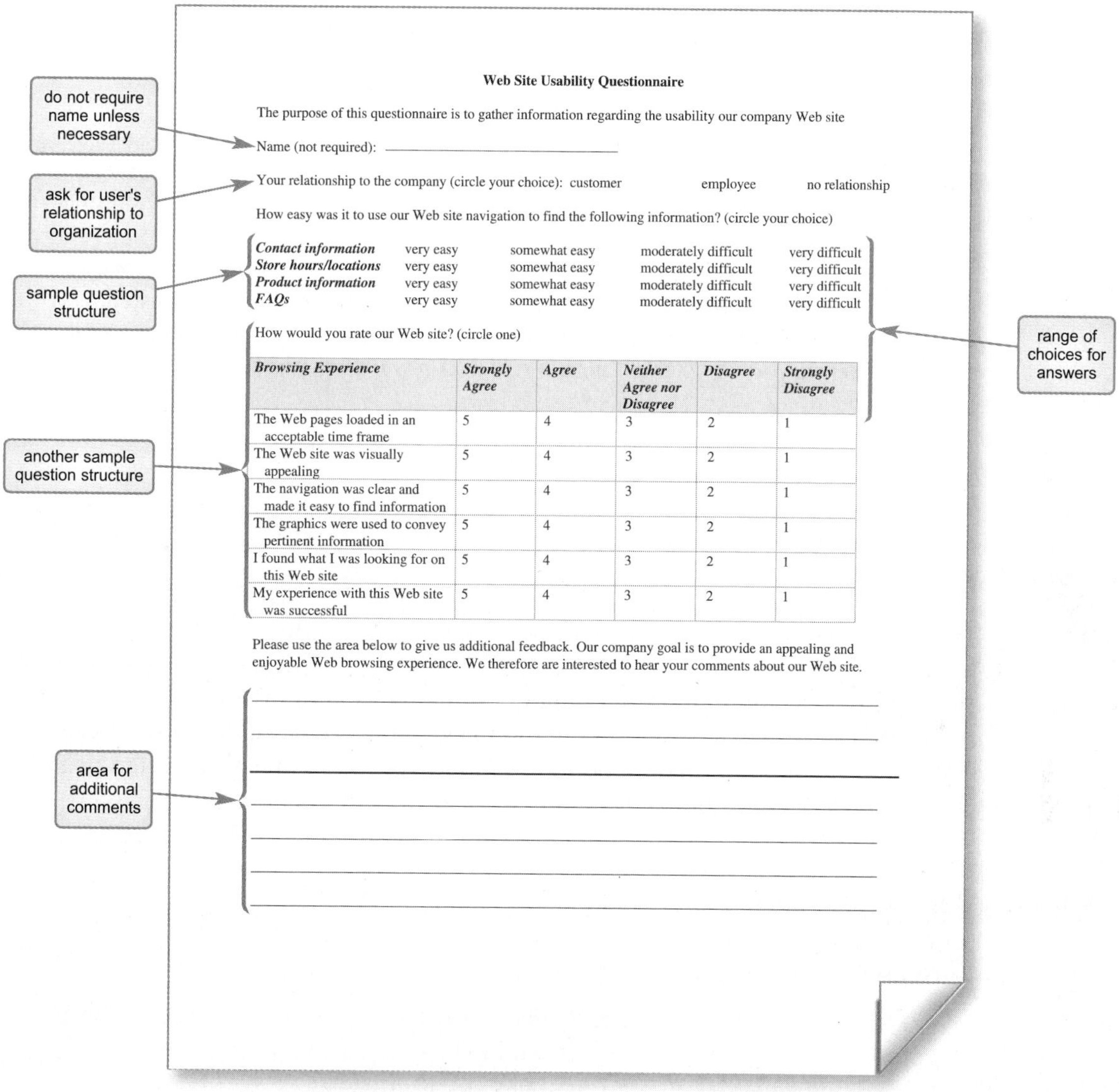

Web Site Usability Questionnaire

The purpose of this questionnaire is to gather information regarding the usability our company Web site

Name (not required): ____________________

Your relationship to the company (circle your choice): customer employee no relationship

How easy was it to use our Web site navigation to find the following information? (circle your choice)

Contact information	very easy	somewhat easy	moderately difficult	very difficult
Store hours/locations	very easy	somewhat easy	moderately difficult	very difficult
Product information	very easy	somewhat easy	moderately difficult	very difficult
FAQs	very easy	somewhat easy	moderately difficult	very difficult

How would you rate our Web site? (circle one)

Browsing Experience	*Strongly Agree*	*Agree*	*Neither Agree nor Disagree*	*Disagree*	*Strongly Disagree*
The Web pages loaded in an acceptable time frame	5	4	3	2	1
The Web site was visually appealing	5	4	3	2	1
The navigation was clear and made it easy to find information	5	4	3	2	1
The graphics were used to convey pertinent information	5	4	3	2	1
I found what I was looking for on this Web site	5	4	3	2	1
My experience with this Web site was successful	5	4	3	2	1

Please use the area below to give us additional feedback. Our company goal is to provide an appealing and enjoyable Web browsing experience. We therefore are interested to hear your comments about our Web site.

FIGURE 1-16 Web site usability testing questionnaire.

Web Site Implementation and Maintenance

Once Web site testing is complete and any required changes have been made, the Web site can be implemented. Implementation of a Web site involves the actual publishing of the Web pages to a Web server. Many HTML editors and WYSIWYG editors provide publishing capabilities. You also can use FTP software, such as WS_FTP, to publish your Web pages to a Web server. After you publish a Web site, you should test the Web pages again to confirm no obvious errors exist, such as broken links or missing graphics.

Once a site is implemented, develop a process to maintain the Web site. The one constant about Web development is that users will request changes and content will require updates. You need to ensure, however, that updates to the Web site do not compromise the site's integrity and consistency. For example, if you have a number of different people updating various Web pages on a large Web site, you might find it difficult to maintain a consistent look on pages across the Web site.

Q: How often should I update my Web site?

A: Plan to update your Web site on a regular basis to keep content up-to-date after your Web site is up and running. Do not allow your content to become stale, outdated, or include links to Web pages that no longer exist.

To help manage the task of Web site maintenance, first determine who is responsible for updates to content, structure, functionality, and so on. Then, limit the capability to update the Web site to specific users. Be sure the implementation is controlled by one or more Web developers who can verify that pages are tested thoroughly before the pages are published.

As updates and changes are made to a Web site, consider notifying users with a graphic banner or a "What's New" announcement, explaining any new features and how the features will benefit them. This technique not only keeps users informed, but also encourages them to come back to the Web site to see what is new.

Finally, Web site monitoring is another key aspect of maintaining a Web site. Usually, the Web servers that host Web sites keep logs of information about Web site usage. A **log** is the file that lists all of the Web pages that have been requested from the Web site. Web site logs are an invaluable source of information for a Web developer. Obtaining and analyzing the logs allows you to determine such things as: the number of visitors, browser types and versions, connection speeds, pages most commonly requested, and usage patterns. With this information, you can design a Web site that is effective for your targeted audience, providing them with a rich and rewarding experience.

More About

Log Files

Usage statistics can provide a wealth of information about who is visiting your Web site and how they navigate through the Web site. To learn more about how log files work and how to analyze the information in those logs, visit the HTML More About Web page (scsite.com/html3e/more) and then click Log Files.

Project Summary

Project 1 provided an overview of the Internet and the World Wide Web and the key terms associated with those technologies. You then were introduced to the features and purposes of three different types of Web sites (the Internet, intranets, and extranets) and Web browsers used to view these sites. You also were presented with information about HTML, its history, elements, and coding standards, and its relationship to DHTML and XHTML. After reviewing various tools used to create HTML documents, you were provided an overview of the five phases of the Web development life cycle, along with pertinent questions to be addressed at each phase. It is important that a Web development project follow the life cycle methodology so the finished Web site is effective and efficient for the users. As you read the projects that follow in this book, you will gain an understanding of the power of HTML, as you learn how to develop many interesting and useful Web pages.

What You Should Know

Having completed this project, you should be able to perform the tasks below.

1. Describe the Internet (HTM 4)
2. Describe the World Wide Web (HTM 6)
3. Define Web servers (HTM 6)
4. Describe the Internet, intranets, and extranets (HTM 7)
5. Discuss Web browsers (HTM 9)
6. Define Hypertext Markup Language (HTM 9)
7. Outline the history of HTML (HTM 11)
8. Describe HTML elements (HTM 12)
9. List HTML coding practices (HTM 12)
10. Explain HTML versions (HTM 12)
11. Define Dynamic Hypertext Markup Language (HTM 13)
12. Define Extensible Hypertext Markup Language (HTM 13)
13. Describe tools for creating HTML documents (HTM 14)
14. Discuss the Web development life cycle (HTM 15)
15. Describe steps in the Web development planning phase (HTM 15)
16. Explain the Web development analysis phase (HTM 16)
17. Discuss Web design and development (HTM 17)
18. Describe various Web site structures (HTM 17)
19. Discuss the importance of Web site testing, including usability testing (HTM 20)
20. Discuss Web site implementation and maintenance (HTM 21)

Learn It Online

Instructions: To complete the Learn It Online exercises, start your browser, click the Address bar, and then enter the Web address `scsite.com/html3e/learn`. When the HTML Learn It Online page is displayed, follow the instructions in the exercises below. Each exercise has instructions for printing your results, either for your own records or for submission to your instructor.

1 Project Reinforcement TF, MC, and SA

Below HTML Project 1, click the Project Reinforcement link. Print the quiz by clicking Print on the File menu for each page. Answer each question.

2 Flash Cards

Below HTML Project 1, click the Flash Cards link and read the instructions. Type `20` (or a number specified by your instructor) in the Number of playing cards text box, type your name in the Enter your Name text box, and then click the Flip Card button. When the flash card is displayed, read the question and then click the ANSWER box arrow to select an answer. Flip through Flash Cards. If your score is 15 (75%) correct or greater, click Print on the File menu to print your results. If your score is less than 15 (75%) correct, then redo this exercise by clicking the Replay button.

3 Practice Test

Below HTML Project 1, click the Practice Test link. Answer each question, enter your first and last name at the bottom of the page, and then click the Grade Test button. When the graded practice test is displayed on your screen, click Print on the File menu to print a hard copy. Continue to take practice tests until you score 80% or better.

4 Who Wants To Be a Computer Genius?

Below HTML Project 1, click the Computer Genius link. Read the instructions, enter your first and last name at the bottom of the page, and then click the PLAY button. When your score is displayed, click the PRINT RESULTS link to print a hard copy.

5 Wheel of Terms

Below HTML Project 1, click the Wheel of Terms link. Read the instructions, and then enter your first and last name and your school name. Click the PLAY button. When your score is displayed, right-click the score and then click Print on the shortcut menu to print a hard copy.

6 Crossword Puzzle Challenge

Below HTML Project 1, click the Crossword Puzzle Challenge link. Read the instructions, and then enter your first and last name. Click the SUBMIT button. Work the crossword puzzle. When you are finished, click the Submit button. When the crossword puzzle is redisplayed, click the Print Puzzle button to print a hard copy.

7 Tips and Tricks

Below HTML Project 1, click the Tips and Tricks link. Click a topic that pertains to Project 1. Right-click the information and then click Print on the shortcut menu. Construct a brief example of what the information relates to in HTML to confirm you understand how to use the tip or trick.

8 Newsgroups

Below HTML Project 1, click the Newsgroups link. Click a topic that pertains to Project 1. Print three comments.

9 Expanding Your Horizons

Below HTML Project 1, click the Expanding Your Horizons link. Click a topic that pertains to Project 1. Print the information. Construct a brief example of what the information relates to in HTML to confirm you understand the contents of the article.

10 Search Sleuth

Below HTML Project 1, click the Search Sleuth link. To search for a term that pertains to this project, select a term below the Project 1 title and then use the Google search engine at google.com (or any major search engine) to display and print two Web pages that present information on the term.

11 Online Help I

Below HTML Project 1, click the Online Help I link. Follow the instructions on the page to access Web pages that provide additional help on project topics. Hand in any printed information to your instructor.

12 Online Help II

Below HTML Project 1, click the Online Help II link. Follow the instructions on the page to access Web pages that provide additional help on project topics. Hand in any printed information to your instructor.

Apply Your Knowledge

1 Web Page Organizational Standards

Instructions: Start your word processing program. Open the file, apply1-1.doc, from the Project01\AYK folder on the HTML Data Disk. See the inside back cover of this book for instructions for downloading the Data Disk or see your instructor for information on accessing the files required for this book. As shown in Table 1-6, the apply1-1.doc file lists Web page organizational standards and the related reasons, but contains blanks in the Element column.

Table 1-6 Web Page Organizational Standards

ELEMENT	ORGANIZATIONAL STANDARD	REASON
	Use to explain purpose of page clearly	Helps user understand purpose of the page; identifies the page in search engine results
	Use to separate main topics	Makes a Web page easier to read; clearly explains what the page is about
	Use as a graphical element to separate main topics	Provides a graphic to break up Web page content
	Use to help divide large amounts of text	Provides shorter, more-readable sections of text
	Utilize these elements to organize text, when appropriate	Provides organized, easy-to-read text that readers can scan easily
	Use suitable amounts of information on each Web page	Increases likelihood that users view key information on a page, without needing to scroll

Perform the following tasks:

1. Without referring to Table 1-5 (on page HTM 17), determine the correct element that is described in the Organizational Standard and Reason columns.
2. Add the correct elements in the Element column.
3. Save the document using the file name, apply1-1solution.doc.
4. Print the document. Write your name on the printout and hand it in to your instructor.

1 Web Site Redesign

Problem: Figure 1-17 shows the popular online bookstore, Amazon.com. As you learned in this project, three common Web site structures include linear, hierarchical, and webbed. Based on that information, determine the structure used in the Amazon.com Web site. Review other similar Web sites and determine which Web site design features are beneficial to a user. Incorporate those ideas into a new Web site design for Amazon.com. Use paper to sketch out the new Web site design for the Amazon.com Web site.

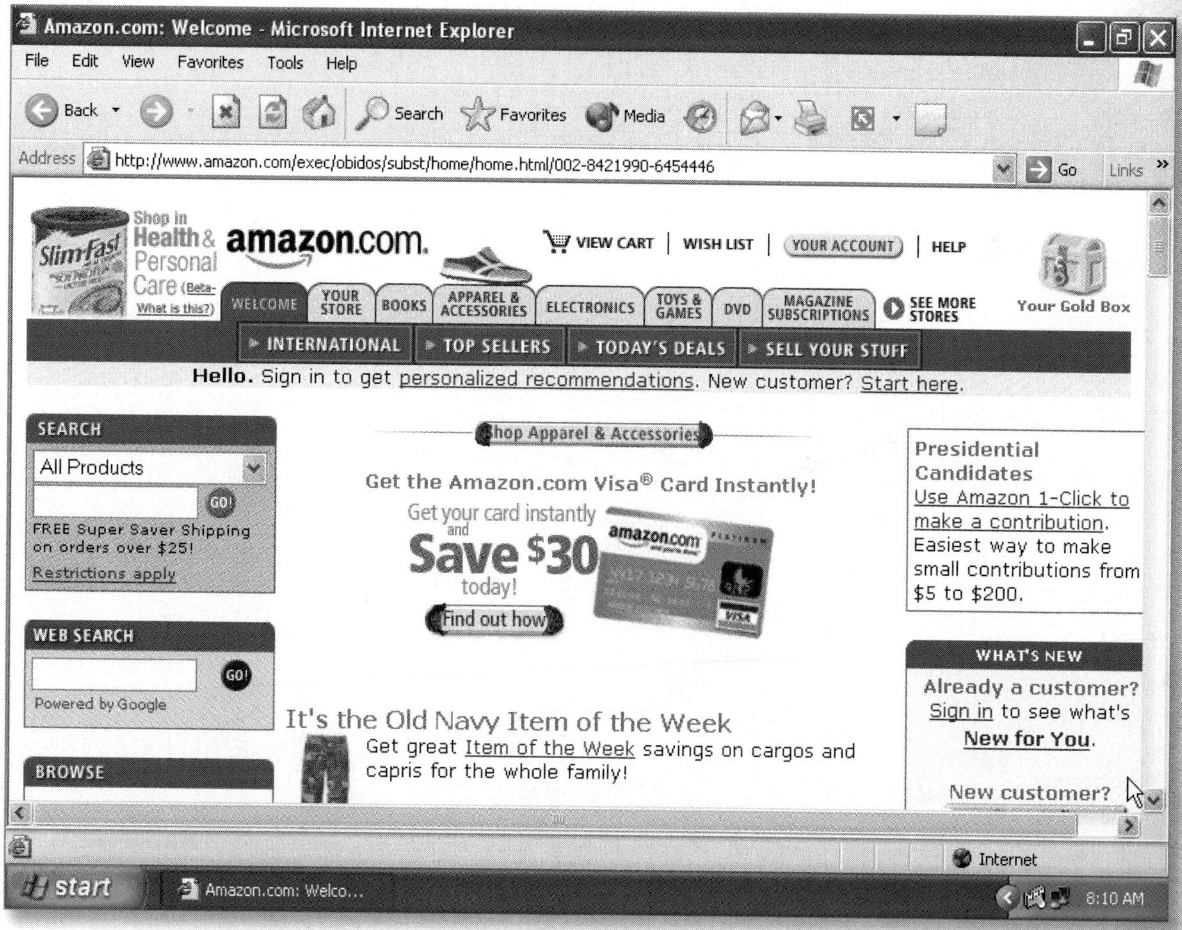

FIGURE 1-17

Instructions: Perform the following steps using your browser and paper.

1. Start your browser. Open the Amazon.com Web site in your browser. Print the home page by clicking Print on the File menu.
2. Navigate through the Amazon.com Web site and determine the structure that the Web site utilizes (linear, hierarchical, or webbed) and write that on the printout.
3. Find two other online bookstore Web sites. Print the home pages for each of those sites by clicking Print on the File menu. Navigate through these Web sites to identify any Web site design features that are beneficial to a user.
4. Using ideas from the online bookstore Web sites that you found in Step 3, sketch a new Web site structure and design for the Amazon.com site on paper.
5. Write your name on the printouts and the sketch and hand them in to your instructor.

2 Student Club Web Site Design

Problem: You have decided to design a Web site that you can share with your student club members. In order to do this, you must complete the planning and analysis phases by answering such questions as:

- What tasks will the student club members want to complete on the Web site?
- What types of information should be included?
- Who will provide information on the Web site content?

Interview several members of the student club and determine the answers to these questions. Based on that information, you will draw a sketch of a design for the home page of the student club Web site, such as the design shown in Figure 1-18.

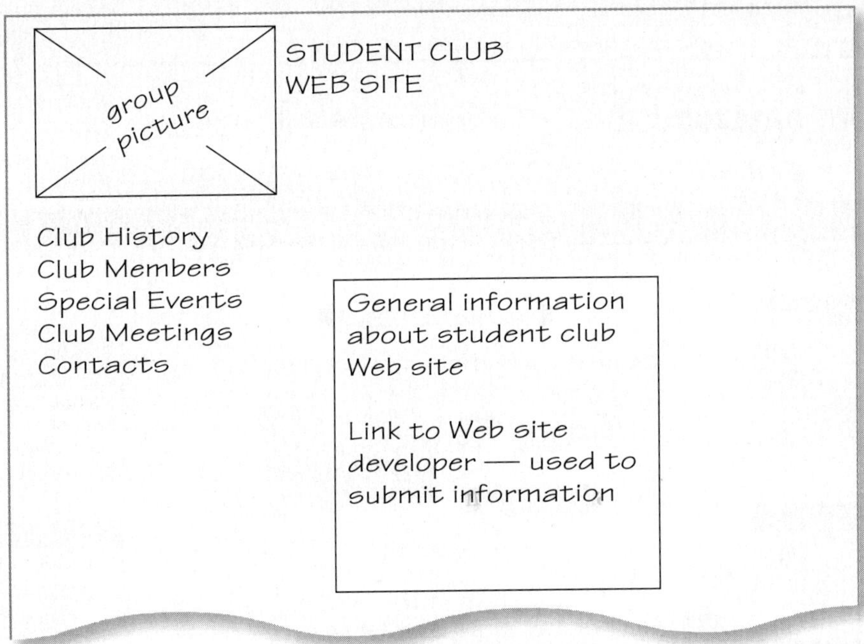

FIGURE 1-18

Instructions: Perform the following tasks using your word processing program and paper.

1. Review the questions in the planning and analysis phases of the Web development life cycle, as shown in Table 1-4 (on page HTM 16).
2. Assess the value of those questions listed in the table. Add other questions that you think are relevant to the planning and analysis of a student club Web site.
3. Start your word processing program. If necessary, open a new document. Enter the questions you will use for planning and analysis. Save the document using the file name, lab1-2solution.doc. Print the document.
4. Using the questions that you developed, interview student club members to determine what information should be included in the Web site, who will provide the information, and so on.
5. After gathering the required information, sketch a design for the home page of the Web site on paper.
6. Share your design sketch with members of the student club and get their opinions on your design.
7. Redraw the design on paper, making any changes based on the input from the club members.
8. Write Original Design on the first design sketch.
9. Write Second Design on the second design sketch.
10. Write your name on the printout and sketches and hand them in to your instructor.

3 Internet, Intranet, and Extranet Design

Problem: Three different types of Web sites were discussed in this project — Internet, intranet, and extranet. Each type of Web site type is designed for a different target audience. Think of a business (e.g., music, university, or bookstore) you frequently visit and how that business might use an Internet, intranet, and extranet site. Using the Planning phase questions found in Table 1-4 on page HTM 16, determine the answers to the questions listed in Table 1-7. Enter your ideas in the table. If there are questions that are difficult/impossible to answer directly (e.g., What are their computing environments?), list ways that you can use to find the answers to those questions.

Table 1-7 Planning Phase Questions

TYPE OF BUSINESS			
PLANNING QUESTION	INTERNET	INTRANET	EXTRANET
What is the purpose of this Web site?			
Who will use this Web site?			
What are users' computing environments?			
Who owns and authors the information on the Web site?			
Who decides if/where the information goes on the Web site?			

Instructions: Perform the following tasks using your word processing program.

1. Start your word processing program and then open the file, lab1-3.doc, from the Project01\IntheLab folder on the HTML Data Disk.
2. Enter the type of business in the first row. Determine the answers to the first question for all three types of Web sites and then enter the answers in the appropriate table cells.
3. Continue answering the other four questions.
4. Save the file using the file name, lab1-3solution.doc. Print the document.
5. Write your name on the printout and hand it in to your instructor.

Cases and Places

The difficulty of these case studies varies:
■ are the least difficult and ■■ are the most difficult. The last exercise is a group exercise.

1 ■ A local job placement office wants to offer several of your company's online courses to their employees. A requirement of the job placement contract, however, is that the online courses must be accessible to users with disabilities and be Bobby Approved. Your manager has asked you to learn more about accessibility guidelines to determine what changes are needed to get the current online courses Bobby Approved. Visit the Bobby Web site at the URL, http://bobby.watchfire.com/bobby/html/en/index.jsp. Read the Web page to learn more about the Bobby tool. What types of disabilities do you have to consider when developing Web pages? What recommendations does Bobby make for accessibility? What does this mean for the Web page developer? View the information about getting your Web site Bobby Approved and read about the issues that are discussed there.

2 ■ As a Web developer at D2 Design, you often are asked to restructure a client's existing Web sites to make them more user-friendly and easier to navigate. Find a Web site that utilizes more than one Web site structure (linear, hierarchical, and/or webbed). Is the information conveyed on the Web site displayed in the appropriate structure? Does the structure effectively support the information communicated? Print the home page of the Web site that you found. On a blank sheet of paper, sketch a design that you think might be more appropriate for the message. Use a word processing program to create a document that explains why your new design is more effective.

3 ■■ Johnson Smythe Interiors sells high-end furniture and carpets, along with its interior design services. The owner has hired you to give its Web site a new design that better captures the company's brand. Before starting on the design, you decide to create a list of Web design principles to which the Web site will adhere. Search the Web for more information about Web site design. Find three Web sites that give information about Web design principles. In a word processing document, take the ideas presented in this project together with the ideas presented in the other Web sites and make a comprehensive list of Web design principles. Where appropriate, identify any conflicting design principles discussed in the Web sites.

4 ■■ As the CarFoundry Webmaster, you are hoping to update your Web site to XHTML, but first want to learn more about how XHTML differs from HTML. Visit the W3Schools Web site (w3schools.com) to learn more about HTML and XHTML. In a word processing document, briefly describe HTML and XHTML, how they are related, and how they differ.

5 ■■ **Working Together:** Your manager at Travel Tours has asked your team to develop a usability survey or questionnaire that you can give to a group of users to evaluate the new online travel booking Web site. What types of information do you hope to gain by distributing this survey or questionnaire? How can you convey information on the survey or questionnaire so it clearly identifies what you are asking? Create a usability survey using your word processing program. Give the survey or questionnaire to at least five people. Allow them to complete the survey or questionnaire and then look at the results. If possible, ask the users what they thought the various questions conveyed. Is that what you wanted to convey? If not, think of other ways to gather the information that you need in a format that is self-explanatory.

HTML

Creating and Editing a Web Page

PROJECT 2

CASE PERSPECTIVE

Dr. Isabel Myers, the Dean of Student Services, is very concerned about the academic success of all students, especially freshman students. Recent statistics, however, show that many students do not pass several freshman-level classes their first time taken. Dr. Myers has an idea to use student workers, who previously have passed these courses with a grade of A, as tutors for struggling students. She thinks students who recently completed the courses successfully will have an easier time relating to the questions asked by the students who need some help. Dr. Myers knows something about the World Wide Web (also called the Web) and wonders if the Campus Tutoring Service should develop its own Web site to advertise the new service. She came to you, an MIS major, to ask for your help.

After working with Dr. Myers to plan the Web site and analyze required Web site content and functionality, you start to design and develop a Web page that promotes the Campus Tutoring Service's key services (Figure 2-1a on page HTM 31). To develop this Web page, you will use Hypertext Markup Language (HTML), as shown in Figure 2-1b. You begin the project with a simple text Web page. You then will visually enhance the Web pages by using various text sizes and formats, adding color, and including an image and a horizontal rule. You also will add a bulleted list to organize the information on the Web page. Once finished with the development, you will review the Web page with Dr. Myers for modifications, enhancements, or additional Web page developments.

As you read through this project, you will learn how to use Notepad to create a Web page using HTML, enhance the look of a Web page, and save and print an HTML file.

PROJECT

Creating and Editing a Web Page

Objectives

You will have mastered the material in this project when you can:

- Identify elements of a Web page
- Start Notepad and describe the Notepad window
- Enable word wrap in Notepad
- Enter the HTML tags
- Enter headings and a paragraph of text
- Create an unordered, ordered, or definition list
- Save an HTML file
- Use a browser to view a Web page
- Activate Notepad
- Identify Web page image types and attributes
- Add an image, change the background color of a Web page, center a heading, and add a horizontal rule
- View the HTML source code in a browser
- Print a Web page and an HTML file
- Quit Notepad and a browser

Introduction

With an understanding of the Web development life cycle, you should have a good idea about the importance of proper Web site planning, analysis, and design. After completing these phases, the next phase is the actual development of a Web page using HTML. As discussed in Project 1, Web pages are created using HTML, which uses a set of special tags to define the structure, layout, and appearance of a Web page. In this project, you will learn to create a Web page by entering HTML into the Notepad window and then saving the file as an HTML file. After entering basic HTML tags and adding text to the file, you will learn the tags used to organize the text by adding headings and creating a bulleted list. You then will learn how to enhance the Web page's appearance by inserting an image, changing the background color of the Web page, centering a heading, and adding a horizontal rule. Finally, you will learn to view the Web page and HTML code in your browser and then print the Web page from your browser.

Project Two — The Campus Tutoring Service

Project 2 illustrates how to use HTML to create a Web page for the Campus Tutoring Service, as shown in Figure 2-1a. Before building the first Web page, you must plan the purpose of the Web page and then analyze what content to include. The Campus Tutoring Service Web page will include general information about the new tutoring service, along with contact information and the list of courses for which tutors are available. To make the Web page interesting, you will use various HTML tags to format the paragraphs and add a bulleted list. You also will insert a colorful image, add a horizontal rule, and change the background color to make the Web page more appealing.

To edit text and HTML tags used to create the Web page, you use a program called Notepad, as shown in Figure 2-1b. **Notepad** is a basic text editor you can use for simple documents or for creating Web pages using HTML. You also will use the Microsoft Internet Explorer browser to view your Web page as you create it. By default, Notepad and Internet Explorer are installed with Windows, so these two programs should be available on most computers running Windows. If you do not have Notepad or Internet Explorer available on your computer, other text editor or browser programs will work.

> *Q&A*
>
> **Q:** I plan to use a WYSIWYG editor to create Web pages. Why should I learn HTML?
>
> **A:** Understanding HTML is an important aspect of being a well-rounded Web developer. Although popular WYSIWYG editors, such as Microsoft FrontPage and Macromedia Dreamweaver, automatically create HTML code as you add elements to the Web page, you still should understand the resulting HTML code. Understanding HTML will allow you to edit the HTML code directly to make modifications not supported by the WYSIWYG editor.

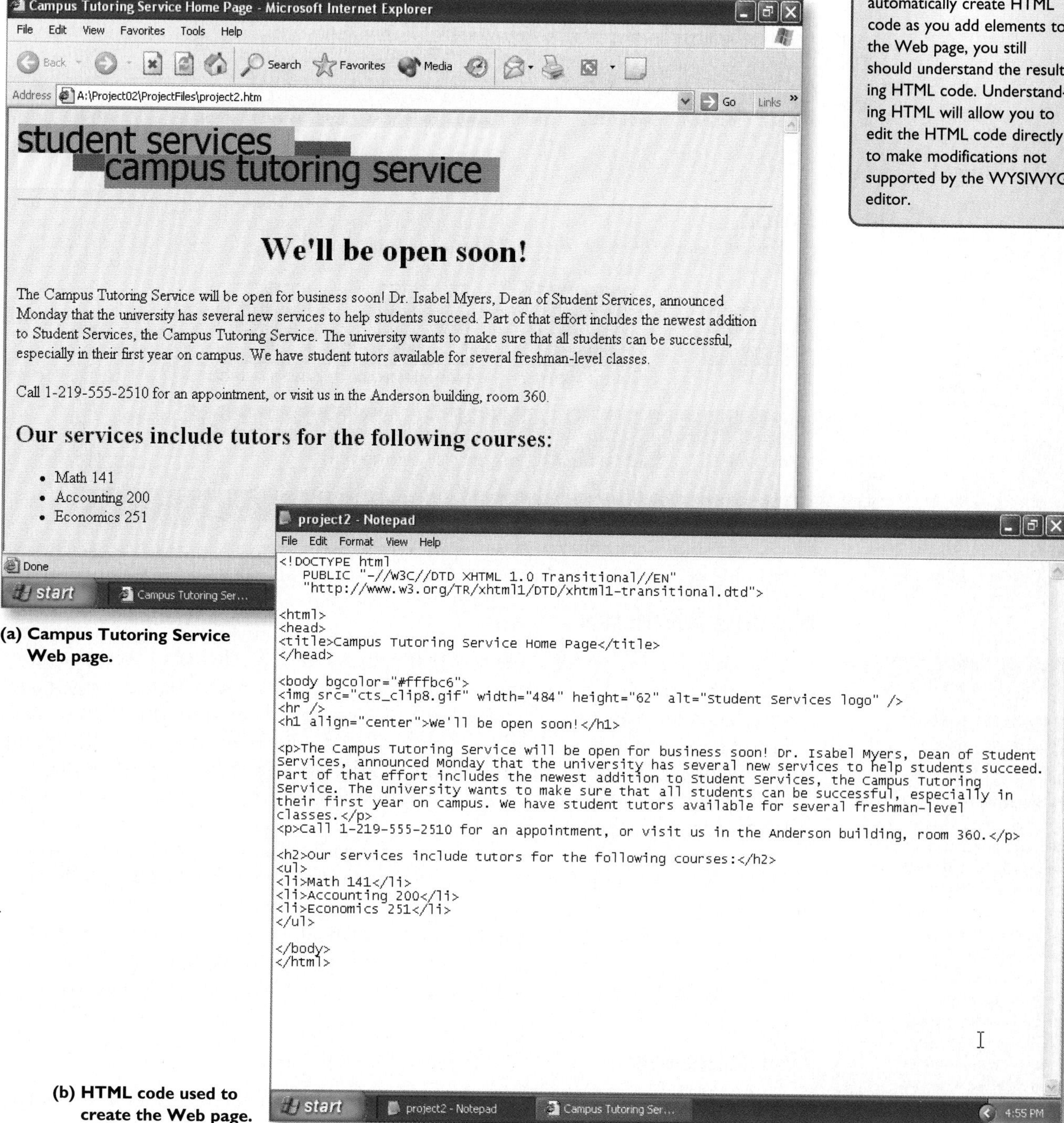

(a) Campus Tutoring Service Web page.

(b) HTML code used to create the Web page.

FIGURE 2-1

Elements of a Web Page

Today, many people — individuals, students, teachers, business executives, Web developers, and others — are developing Web pages for personal or professional reasons. Each person has his or her own style and the resulting Web pages are as diverse as the people who create them. Most Web pages, however, include several basic features, or elements, as shown in Figure 2-2.

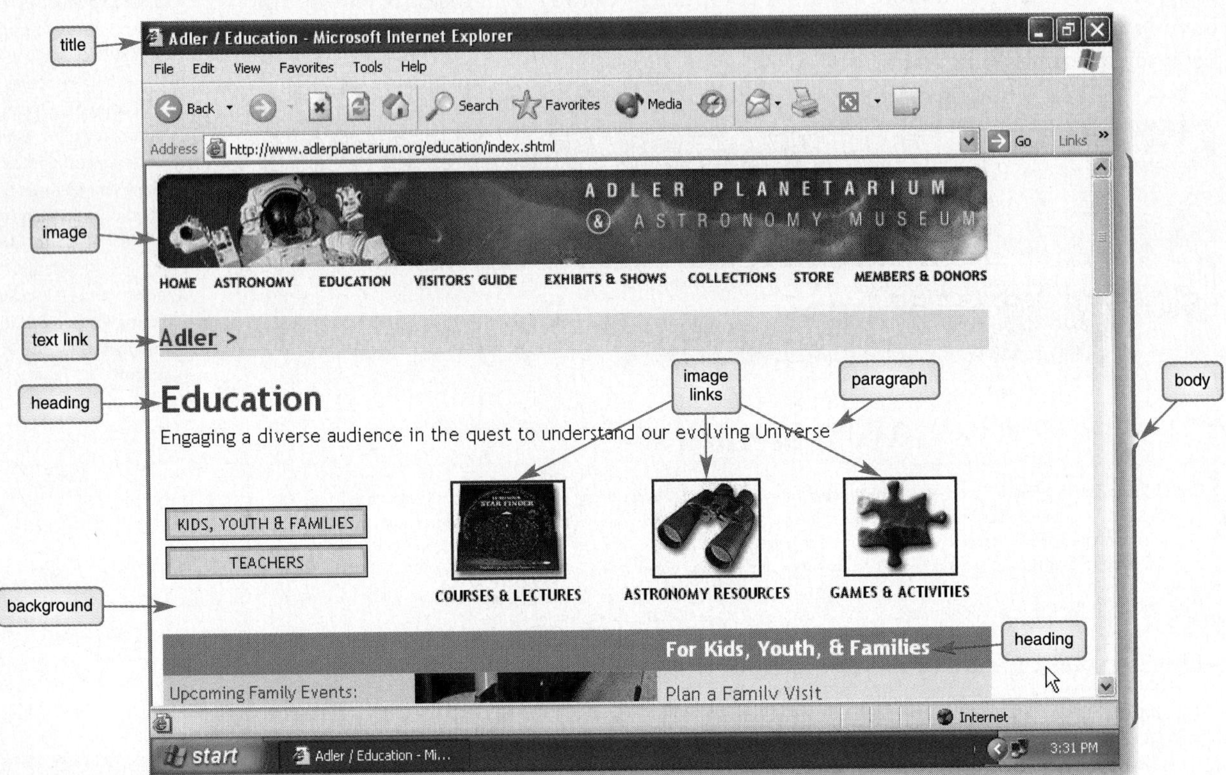

FIGURE 2-2 Elements of a Web page.

Window Elements

The **title** of a Web page is the text that appears on the title bar of the browser window when the Web page appears. The title also is the name assigned to the page if a user adds the page to the browser's list of **favorites**, or **bookmarks**. Because of its importance, you always should include a title on your Web page. The title, which usually is the first element you see, should identify the subject or purpose of the page. The title should be concise yet descriptive and briefly explain the page's content or purpose to the visitor.

The **body** of the Web page contains the information that is displayed in the browser window. The body can include text, graphics, and other elements. The **background** of a Web page is a solid color or a picture or graphic against which the other elements on the Web page appear. When choosing your background, be sure it does not overpower the information on the Web page. If you use an image for the background, the image is tiled, or repeats across and down the page, similar to the Wallpaper in Windows.

More About

Favorites and Bookmarks

Internet Explorer and Netscape Navigator both have a feature that allows you to add Web pages to a list, so you quickly can access them in the future. Internet Explorer refers to these as Favorites, while Navigator calls them Bookmarks. To learn more about adding Web pages to your list of Favorites or Bookmarks, visit the HTML More About Web page (scsite.com/html3e/more) and then click Favorites or Bookmarks.

Text Elements

Normal text is the default text format used for the main content of a Web page. Normal text can be used in a standard paragraph or formatted to appear as bold (<strong>), italic (<em>), or underlined text (<u>); in different colors; and so on.

Normal text also can be used in a series of text items called a **list**. Typically, lists are bulleted or numbered.

Headings, such as those in Figure 2-2, are used to set off different paragraphs of text or different sections of a page. Headings are a larger font size than normal text and often are bold or italic or a different color than normal text. HTML has six different sizes, or levels, of headings numbered 1 through 6, with 1 being the largest. When using headings to organize content and emphasize key points on a Web page, be sure to use headings consistently. That is, if you use a Heading 2 (<h2>) style for a specific level of text, you always should use a Heading 2 style to break up information at that level. Also, do not skip levels of headings in your document. For example, do not start with a Heading 1 (<h1>) style and then use a Heading 3 (<h3>) style.

Image Elements

Web pages typically use several different types of graphics, or images, such as an icon, bullet, line, photo, illustration, or other picture. An image used in a Web page also is called an **inline image**, which means the image or graphic file is not part of the HTML file. Instead, the Web browser merges the separate graphic file into the Web page as it is displayed in the browser window. The HTML file contains <img> tags that tell the browser which graphic file to request from the server, where to insert it on the page, and how to display it.

Web pages typically use several different types of inline images. An **image map** is a special type of inline image in which you define one or more areas as hotspots. A **hotspot** is an area of an image that activates a function when selected. For example, each hotspot in an image map can link to a different Web page. Some inline images are **animated**, meaning they include motion and can change in appearance.

Horizontal rules are lines that are displayed across a Web page to separate different sections of the page. Although the appearance of a horizontal rule can vary, many Web pages use an inline image as a horizontal rule. Alternatively, you can use the horizontal rule tag (<hr />) to add a simple horizontal rule, such as the one used in this project.

When including images on a Web page, be cautious about overuse. Using too many images may give your Web page a cluttered look or distract the visitor from the purpose of the Web page. An image should have a purpose, such as to convey content, visually organize a page, provide a hyperlink, or serve another function.

More About

HTML

The Web has many wonderful sources of information on HTML and Web page development. One of the better sources is the HTML Goodies Web site, which has primers and tutorials on a variety of topics as well as free downloads and discussion areas. To learn more about this Web site, visit the HTML More About Web page (scsite.com/html3e/more) and then click HTML Goodies.

Hyperlink Elements

One of the more important elements of a Web page is a hyperlink, or link. A **link** is text, an image, or another Web page element that you click to instruct the browser to go to a location in a file or to request a file from a server. On the Web, links are the primary way to navigate between Web pages and among Web sites. Links point not only to Web pages, but also to graphics, sound, video, program files, e-mail addresses, and parts of the same Web page. Text links, also called hypertext links, are the most commonly used hyperlinks. When text identifies a hyperlink, it usually appears as underlined text, in a color different from the rest of the Web page text.

Starting Notepad

With the planning, analysis, and design of the Web page complete, you can begin developing the Web page by entering HTML in the Notepad window. The steps on the next page show how to start Notepad.

To Start Notepad

1

- **Click the Start button on the Windows taskbar.**
- **Click All Programs on the Start menu.**
- **Point to Accessories on the All Programs submenu and then point to Notepad on the Accessories submenu (Figure 2-3).**

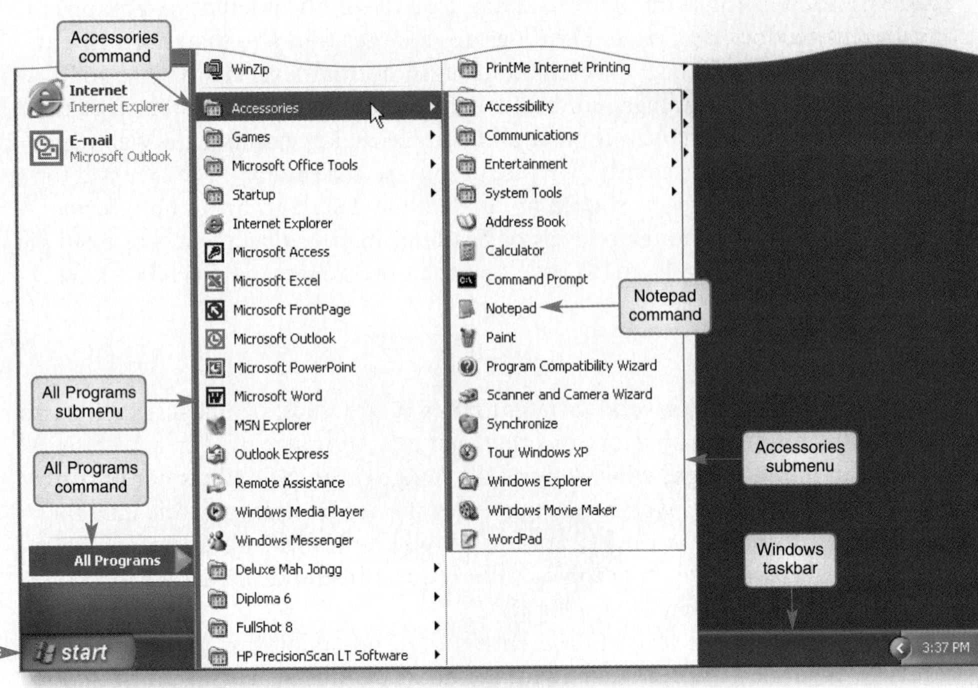

FIGURE 2-3

2

- **Click Notepad.**

The Notepad window is displayed (Figure 2-4).

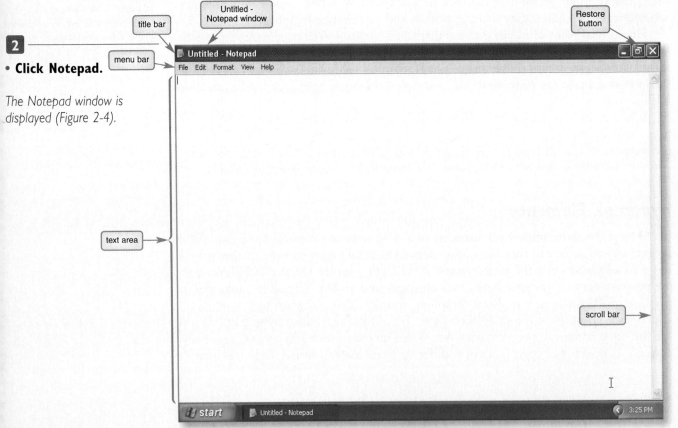

FIGURE 2-4

If the Notepad window is not maximized, click the Maximize button on the Notepad title bar to maximize it.

The Notepad Window

The Notepad window contains several elements similar to document windows in other applications. The main elements of the Notepad window are the title bar, the menu bar, the text area, and the scroll bars (Figure 2-4).

Title Bar

The **title bar** appears at the top of the Notepad window. The name of the document open in the Notepad window is displayed. When you first start Notepad, the default document is named Untitled.

More About

WordPad

WordPad is another text editor that you can use to create HTML files. To start WordPad, click the Start button on the taskbar, point to All Programs on the Start menu, point to Accessories on the All Programs submenu, and then click WordPad on the Accessories submenu. WordPad help provides tips on how to use the product.

Menu Bar

The **menu bar** appears at the top of the window just below the title bar (Figure 2-4). The menu bar shows Notepad menu names. Each **menu name** represents a menu. A **menu** provides a list of commands you can use to open, save, and print the text in the file and perform other tasks.

Text Area

The **text area** is the main part of the Notepad window (Figure 2-4). As you type, text is displayed in the text area.

Scroll Bar

On the right side of the Notepad window is a vertical **scroll bar**, which is used to view different portions of the text area (Figure 2-4). The **scroll box** on the scroll bar indicates your current location in the file. If all of the text in the file appears in the Notepad window, as shown in Figure 2-4, the scroll bar is dimmed and the scroll box does not display.

Enabling Word Wrap in Notepad

In Notepad, the text entered in the text area scrolls continuously to the right unless the Word Wrap feature is enabled, or turned on. **Word wrap** causes text lines to break at the right edge of the window and appear on a new line, so all entered text is visible in the Notepad window. Word wrap does not affect the way text prints. When word wrap is enabled, a check mark precedes the Word Wrap command on the Format menu. The steps on the next page show how to enable word wrap in Notepad.

To Enable Word Wrap in Notepad

1

• **Click Format on the menu bar (Figure 2-5).**

2

• **If the Word Wrap command does not have a check mark next to it, click Word Wrap.**

Notepad enables word wrap so the text will not scroll off the screen as you type.

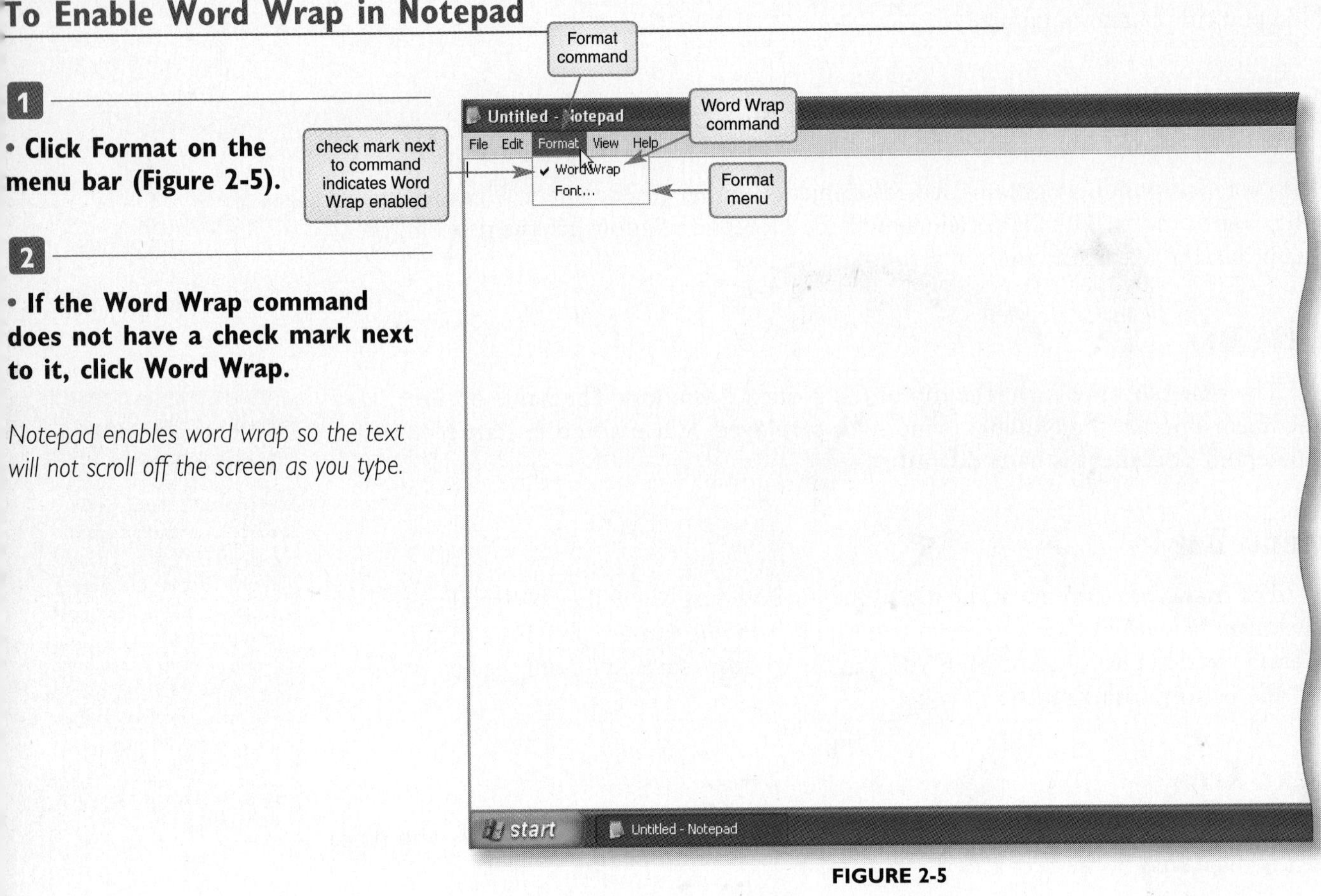

FIGURE 2-5

Entering HTML Tags and Text

To create an HTML document, you begin by inserting a <!DOCTYPE> tag and four sets of tags (<html>, <head>, <title>, and <body>). These tags define the overall structure of a standard Web page and divide the HTML file into its basic sections, such as the header information and the body of the page that contains text and graphics.

> **Q&A**
>
> **Q:** What is the purpose of using the Word Wrap feature in Notepad?
>
> **A:** Using the Word Wrap feature wraps the text in the Notepad window so you can see all of the text in the Notepad window as you work. Enabling Word Wrap does not affect the way text appears when it is printed.

Entering HTML Tags to Define the Web Page Structure

The **<!DOCTYPE>** tag is used to tell the browser which HTML or XHTML version and type the document uses. The W3C supports three document types for HTML or XHTML: *strict*, *transitional*, and *frameset*. The **strict** document type is specified when you want to prohibit the use of deprecated tags. **Deprecated tags** are tags that the W3C has earmarked for eventual removal from their specifications, because they have replaced those tags with newer, more functional tags. The **transitional** document type allows the use of deprecated tags. The **frameset** document type, which is used to support frames on a Web page, also allows the use of deprecated tags. The <!DOCTYPE> tag includes a URL that references a Document Type Definition found on the W3C Web site. A **Document Type Definition** (**DTD**) is a file containing definitions of tags and how they should be used in a Web page. Projects 2 through 5 use a transitional document type. Projects 6 and 7 use a frameset document type, because those projects utilize frames.

The second set of tags, **<html>** and **</html>**, indicates the start and end of an HTML document. Software tools, such as browsers, use these tags to determine where the HTML code in a file begins and ends. The third set of tags, **<head>** and **</head>**, contains the Web page title and other document header information. The fourth set of tags, **<title>** and **</title>**, indicates the title of the Web page. As previously noted, the title appears on the browser title bar when the Web page is displayed in the browser window. The title also is the name that appears in the favorite or bookmark when a user adds the page to the favorite or bookmark list. The final set of tags, **<body>** and **</body>**, indicates the boundaries of the Web page. All text, images, links, and other content is contained within this final set of tags.

To make your HTML files compliant with XHTML standards, always enter tags in lowercase (with the exception of the <!DOCTYPE> tag, which is always uppercase). Throughout this book, the project directions follow these standards to help you learn good HTML and XHTML coding standards.

Most HTML start tags, such as <html>, <head>, <title>, and <body>, also have corresponding end tags, </html>, </head>, </title>, and </body>. Table 2-1 lists the functions of those tags as well as other tags that you use in this project. Note that, for tags that do not have end tags, such as <hr /> and <br />, the tag is closed using a space and a forward slash.

Table 2-1 HTML Tags and Their Functions

HTML TAG	FUNCTION
<!DOCTYPE>	Indicates the version and type of HTML used; includes a URL reference to a DTD
<html> </html>	Indicates the start and end of an HTML document
<head> </head>	Indicates the start and end of a section of the document used for the title and other document header information
<title> </title>	Indicates the start and end of the title. The title does not appear in the body of the Web page, but appears on the title bar of the browser.
<body> </body>	Indicates the start and end of the Web page body
<hn> </hn>	Indicates the start and end of the text section called a heading; sizes range from <h1> through <h6>. See Figure 2-8a on page HTM 39 for heading size samples.
<p> </p>	Indicates the start of a new paragraph; inserts a blank line above the new paragraph
<ul> </ul>	Indicates the start and end of an unordered (bulleted) list
<li> </li>	Indicates that the item that follows the tag is an item within a list
<hr />	Inserts a horizontal rule
 	Inserts a line break at the point where the tag appears

The steps on the next page illustrate how to enter the initial tags that define the structure of the Web page.

More About

HTML and XHTML Tags

The Web has excellent sources that list HTML and XHTML tags. For more information about HTML and XHTML, visit the HTML More About Web page (scsite.com/html3e/more.htm) and then click HTML and XHTML.

More About

The DOCTYPE Tag

The W3Schools Web site provides additional information about the DOCTYPE tags used for the strict, transitional, and frameset document types. To learn more about the DOCTYPE tag, visit the HTML More About Web page (scsite.com/html3e/more.htm) and then click DOCTYPE tags.

To Enter HTML Tags to Define the Web Page Structure

1

- **Type** `<!DOCTYPE html` **and then press the ENTER key.**
- **Press the SPACEBAR three times, type** `PUBLIC "-//W3C//DTD XHTML 1.0 Transitional//EN"` **as the entry, and then press the ENTER key.**
- **Press the SPACEBAR three times, type** `"http://www.w3.org/TR/xhtml1/DTD/xhtml1-transitional.dtd">` **as the entry, and then press the ENTER key twice.**
- **Type** `<html>` **and then press the ENTER key.**
- **Type** `<head>` **and then press the ENTER key.**
- **Type** `<title>Campus Tutoring Service Home Page</title>` **and then press the ENTER key.**
- **Type** `</head>` **and then press the ENTER key.**

The HTML tags are displayed in the Notepad window (Figure 2-6). The text between the title tags is displayed when you view the Web page using a browser. The </title> tag indicates the title is complete and the </head> tag indicates the headings are complete.

Untitled - Notepad

File Edit Format View Help

```
<!DOCTYPE html
   PUBLIC "-//W3C//DTD XHTML 1.0 Transitional//EN"
   "http://www.w3.org/TR/xhtml1/DTD/xhtml1-transitional.dtd">

<html>
<head>
<title>Campus Tutoring Service Home Page</title>
</head>
```

DOCTYPE statement

URL references XHTML 1.0 Transitional DTD

start <html> tag

indicates the start and end of header section

defines Web page title

insertion point

start | Untitled - Notepad

FIGURE 2-6

2

- **Type** `<body>` **and then press the ENTER key twice.**
- **Type** `</body>` **and then press the ENTER key.**
- **Type** `</html>` **as the end tag.**

The <body> tag starts the body section of the Web page and the </body> tag ends the body section. The </html> tag (Figure 2-7) ends the HTML file itself. The remainder of the HTML tags will be entered between the <body> and </body> tags.

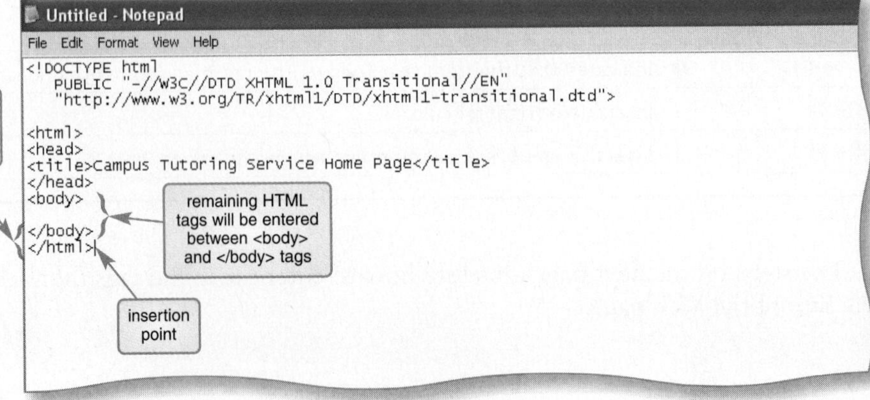

FIGURE 2-7

If you notice an error in the text, use the BACKSPACE key to delete all the characters back to and including the incorrect characters and then continue typing.

Entering Headings

Headings serve to separate text and introduce new topics on Web pages. The headings used for this purpose vary in size. The tags used to specify the heading style or sizes range from <h1> through <h6>, with <h1> being the largest. Figure 2-8a shows a Web page using various sizes of headings. One method of maintaining a consistent look on a Web page is to use the same heading size for headings at the same topic level (Figure 2-8b).

The step on the next page explains how to enter the first heading for the Web page.

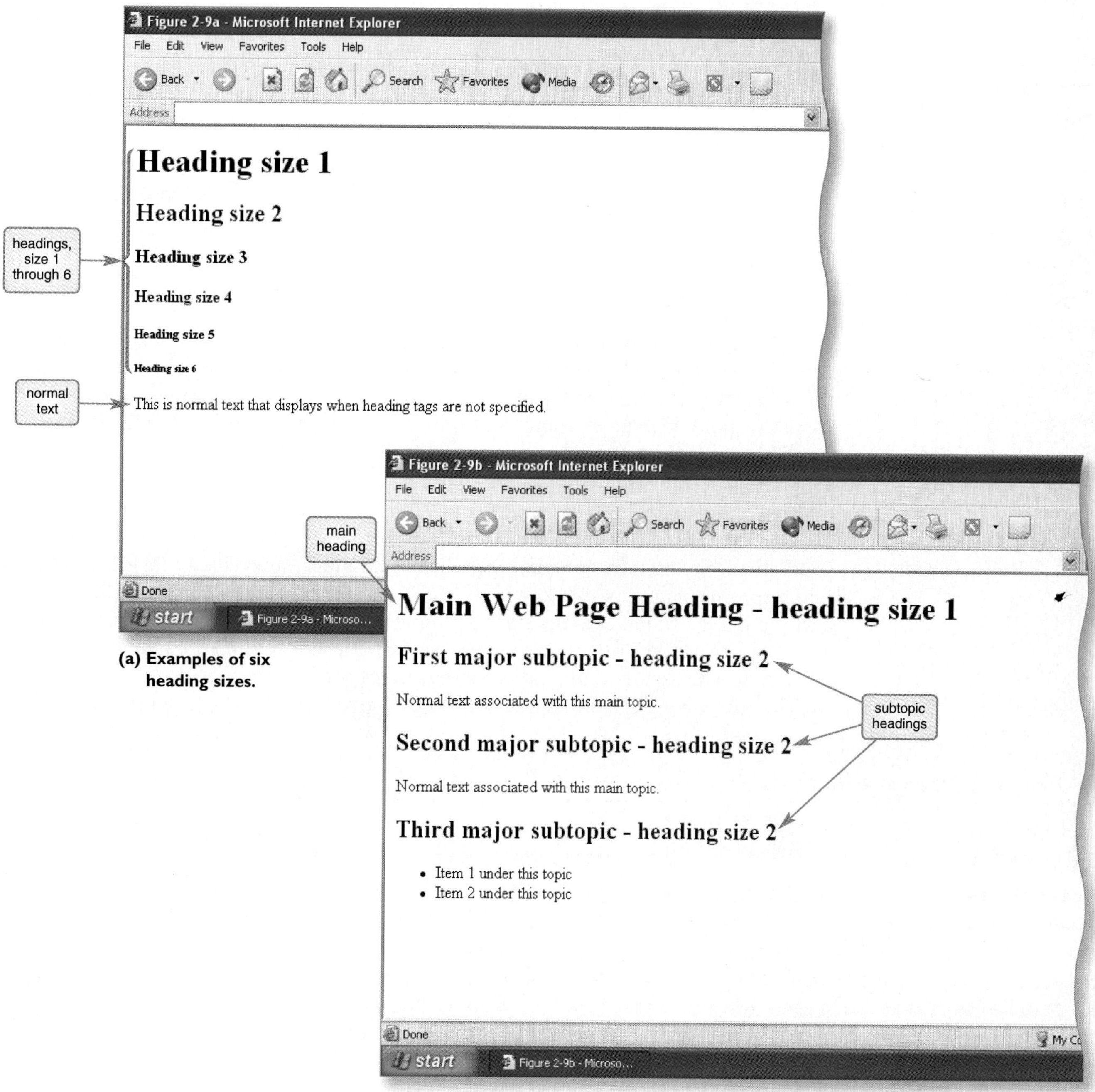

(a) Examples of six heading sizes.

(b) A consistent use of headings can help organize Web page content.

FIGURE 2-8

To Enter a Heading

1

- **Click the blank line below the <body> tag, type** `<h1>We'll be open soon!</h1>` **in the text area, and then press the ENTER key twice.**

The HTML code is displayed (Figure 2-9). The main heading is formatted using the Heading 1 (<h1>) style. An additional space line was inserted for readability.

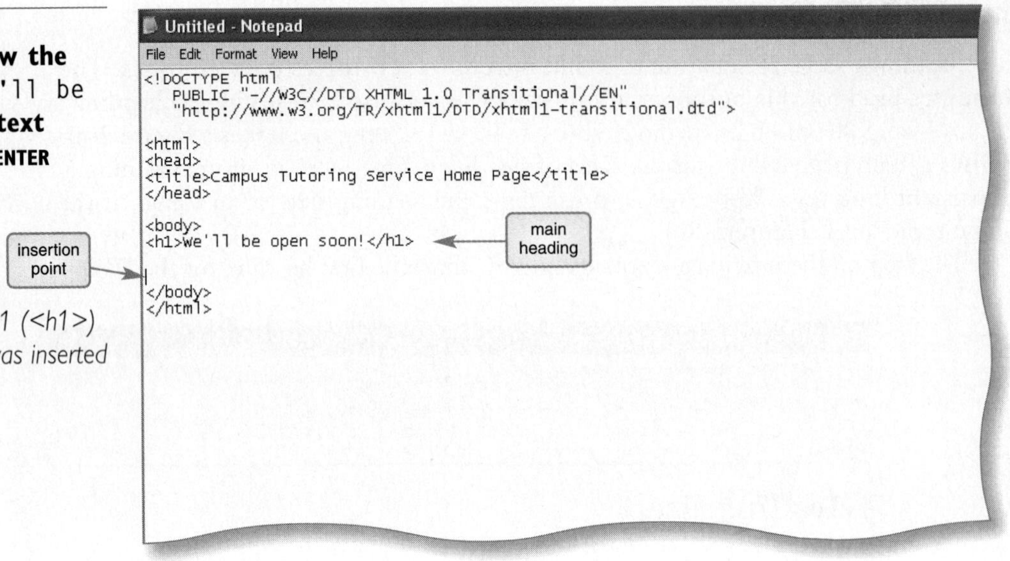

Untitled - Notepad

File Edit Format View Help

```
<!DOCTYPE html
   PUBLIC "-//W3C//DTD XHTML 1.0 Transitional//EN"
   "http://www.w3.org/TR/xhtml1/DTD/xhtml1-transitional.dtd">

<html>
<head>
<title>Campus Tutoring Service Home Page</title>
</head>

<body>
<h1>We'll be open soon!</h1>

</body>
</html>
```

insertion point

main heading

FIGURE 2-9

The <h1> tag is used to apply a Heading 1 style to the main heading on a Web page because it is the largest heading size. The main heading often presents the most important message on a Web page or contains the name of the business, school, or organization. A Web page usually has only one main heading; the HTML file for that Web page thus usually has only one set of <h1> </h1> tags.

Entering a Paragraph of Text

Web pages generally contain a significant amount of text. Breaking the text into paragraphs helps to separate key ideas and make the text easier to read. The <p> start tag is used to indicate the start of a new paragraph. When the browser finds a <p> tag in an HTML file, it starts a new line and inserts a blank line above the new paragraph. The </p> end tag indicates the end of the paragraph.

The following steps illustrate how to enter a paragraph of text in an HTML file.

To Enter a Paragraph of Text

1

- **With the insertion point on line 12, press the ENTER key and then type** `<p>The Campus Tutoring Service will be open for business soon! Dr. Isabel Myers, Dean of Student Services, announced Monday that the university has several new services to help students succeed. Part of that effort includes the newest addition to Student Services, the Campus Tutoring Service. The university wants to make sure that all students can be successful, especially in their first year on campus. We have student tutors available for several freshman-level classes.</p>` **and then press the ENTER key.**

2

- **With the insertion point on line 19, type** `<p>Call 1-219-555-2510 for an appointment, or visit us in the Anderson building, room 360.</p>` **and then press the ENTER key twice (Figure 2-10).**

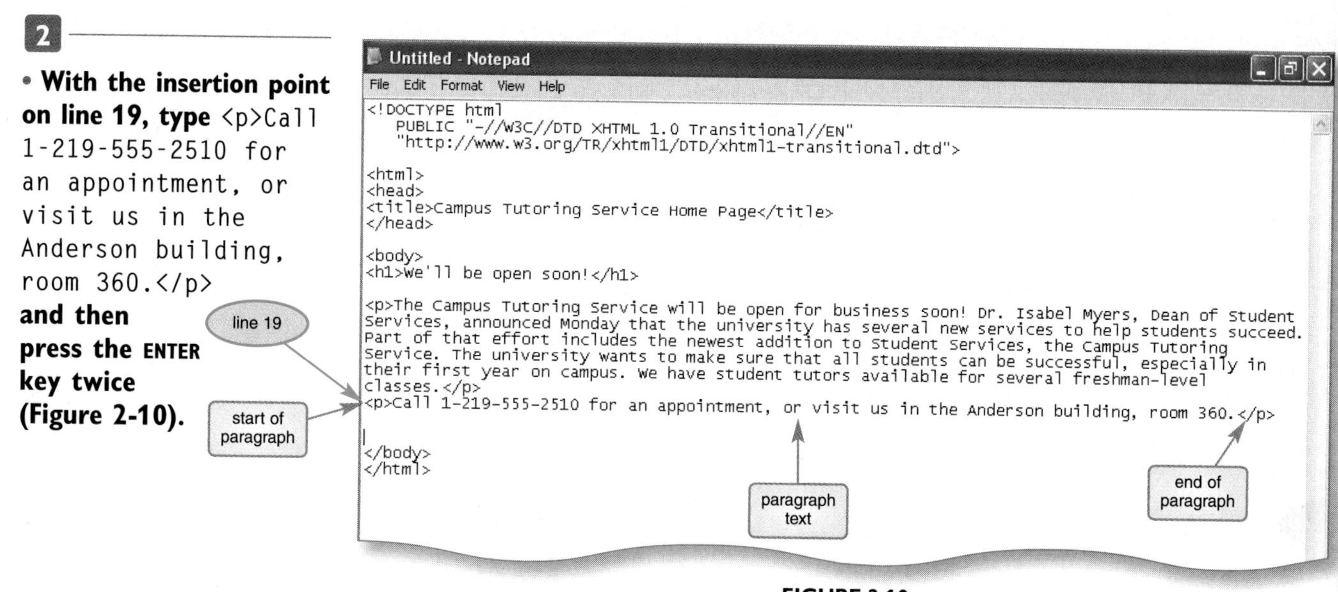

FIGURE 2-10

The <br /> tag also is used to break a line of text. As soon as the browser encounters a <br /> tag, it starts a new line with the text that follows the tag. Unlike the <p> tag, using the <br /> tag does not insert a blank line above the new line of text. The <br /> tag is used later in this book.

Creating a List

Text on a Web page sometimes is easier for users to read and understand when it is formatted as a list, instead of as a paragraph format. Lists structure text into an itemized format. Typically, lists are bulleted (unordered) or numbered (ordered).

An **unordered list**, which also is called a **bulleted list**, formats information using small images called bullets. Figure 2-11 on the next page shows Web page text formatted as unordered, or bulleted, lists and the HTML code used to create the lists.

An **ordered list**, which also is called a **numbered list**, formats information in a series using numbers or letters. An ordered list works well to organize items where order must be emphasized, such as a series of steps. Figure 2-12 on the next page shows Web page text formatted as ordered, or numbered, lists and the HTML tags used to create the lists.

The **<ul>** and **</ul>** tags must be at the start and end of an unordered or bulleted list. The **<ol>** and **</ol>** tags are used at the start and end of an ordered or numbered list. Unordered and ordered lists have optional bullet and number types. As shown in Figure 2-11, an unordered list can use one of three different bullet options: disc, square, or circle. If no type is identified, the default, disc, is used. An ordered list can use numbers, letters, or Roman numerals, as shown in Figure 2-12. The default option is to use Arabic numbers, such as 1, 2, and 3.

The format of the start tag for a list without a bullet and number type specified is <ul> or <ol>. To change the default bullet or number type, the **type** attribute is entered within the <ol> or <ul> tags. The tags <ul type=" "> or <ol type=" "> create lists that use a specific bullet and number type, where the specified type is found within the quotation marks.

After the <ul> or <ol> tag is entered to define the type of list, the **<li>** and **</li>** tags are used to define a list item in an ordered or unordered list. As shown in Figures 2-11 and 2-12, each item in a list must have the <li> tag at the start and the </li> tag at the end.

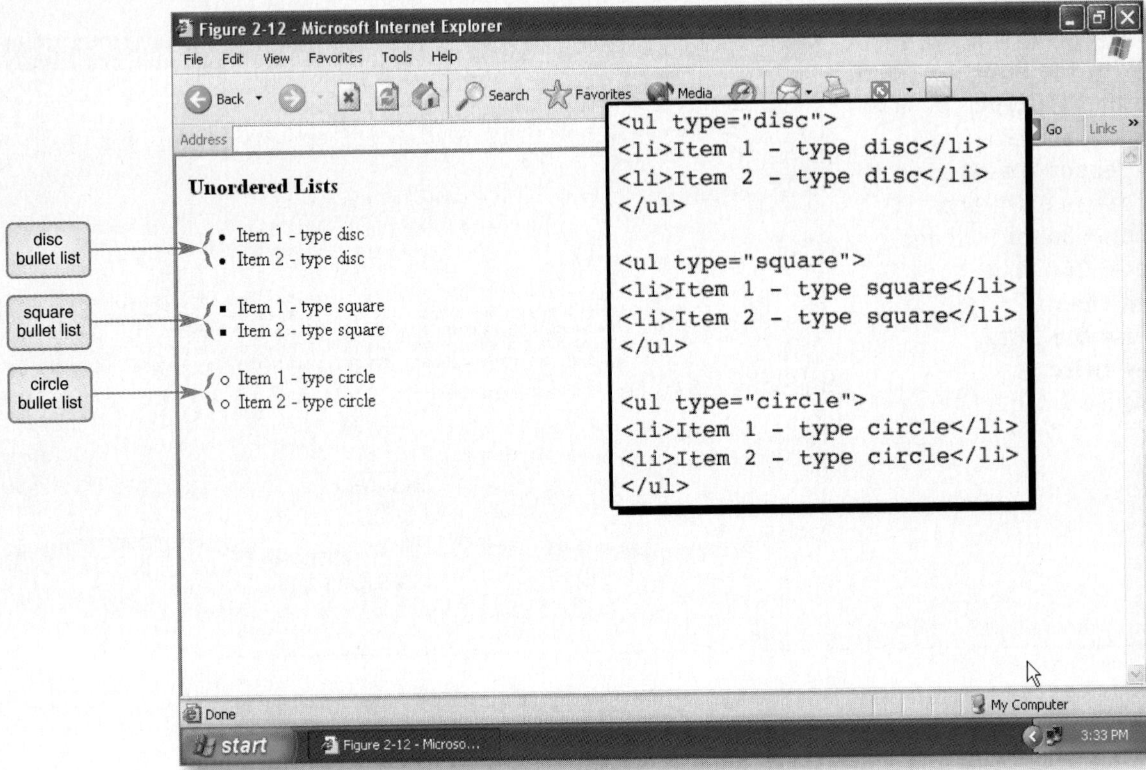

FIGURE 2-11 **Examples of unordered (bulleted) lists.**

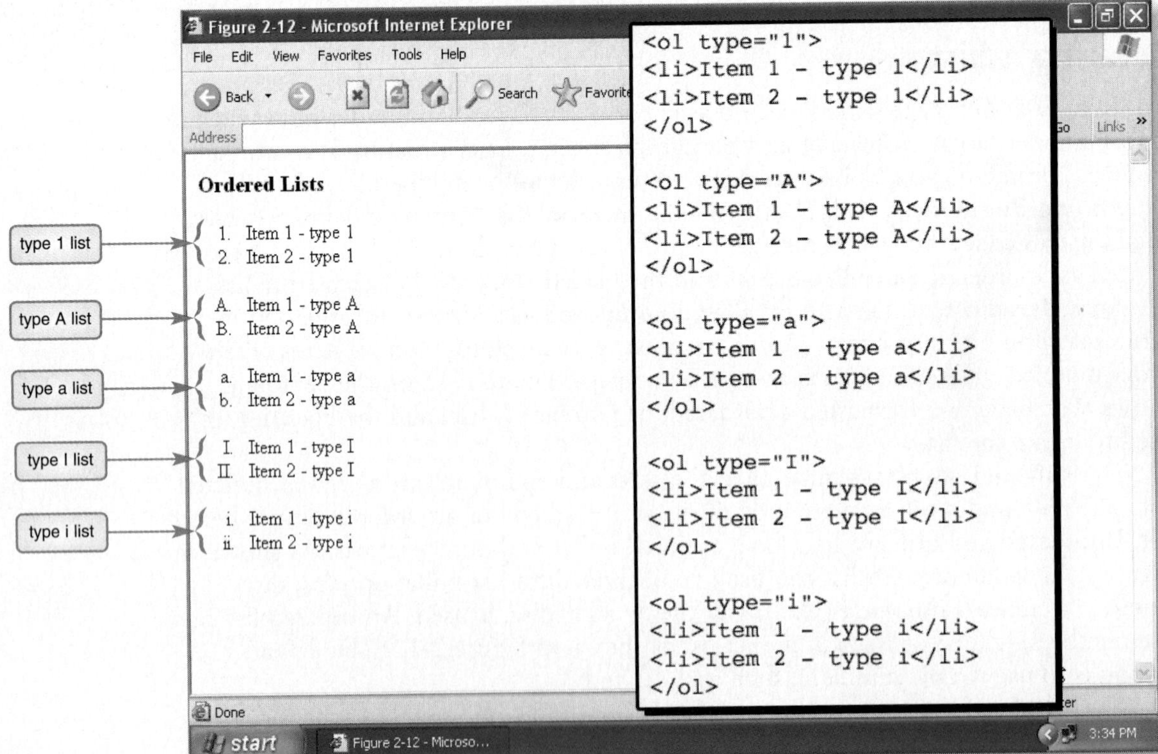

FIGURE 2-12 **Examples of ordered (numbered) lists.**

The following steps illustrate how to create an unordered, or bulleted, list using the default bullet style.

To Create an Unordered List

1

- **With the insertion point on line 20, press the ENTER key, type** `<h2>Our services include tutors for the following courses:</h2>` **as the entry, and then press the ENTER key.**

2

- **Type** `<ul>` **as the start tag and then press the ENTER key.**
- **Type** `<li>Math 141</li>` **and then press the ENTER key.**
- **Type** `<li>Accounting 200</li>` **and then press the ENTER key.**
- **Type** `<li>Economics 251</li>` **and then press the ENTER key.**
- **Type** `</ul>` **as the end tag and then press the ENTER key.**

The HTML code creates a bulleted list with three items (Figure 2-13). Because the code does not specify a type attribute, the list uses the default disc bullet.

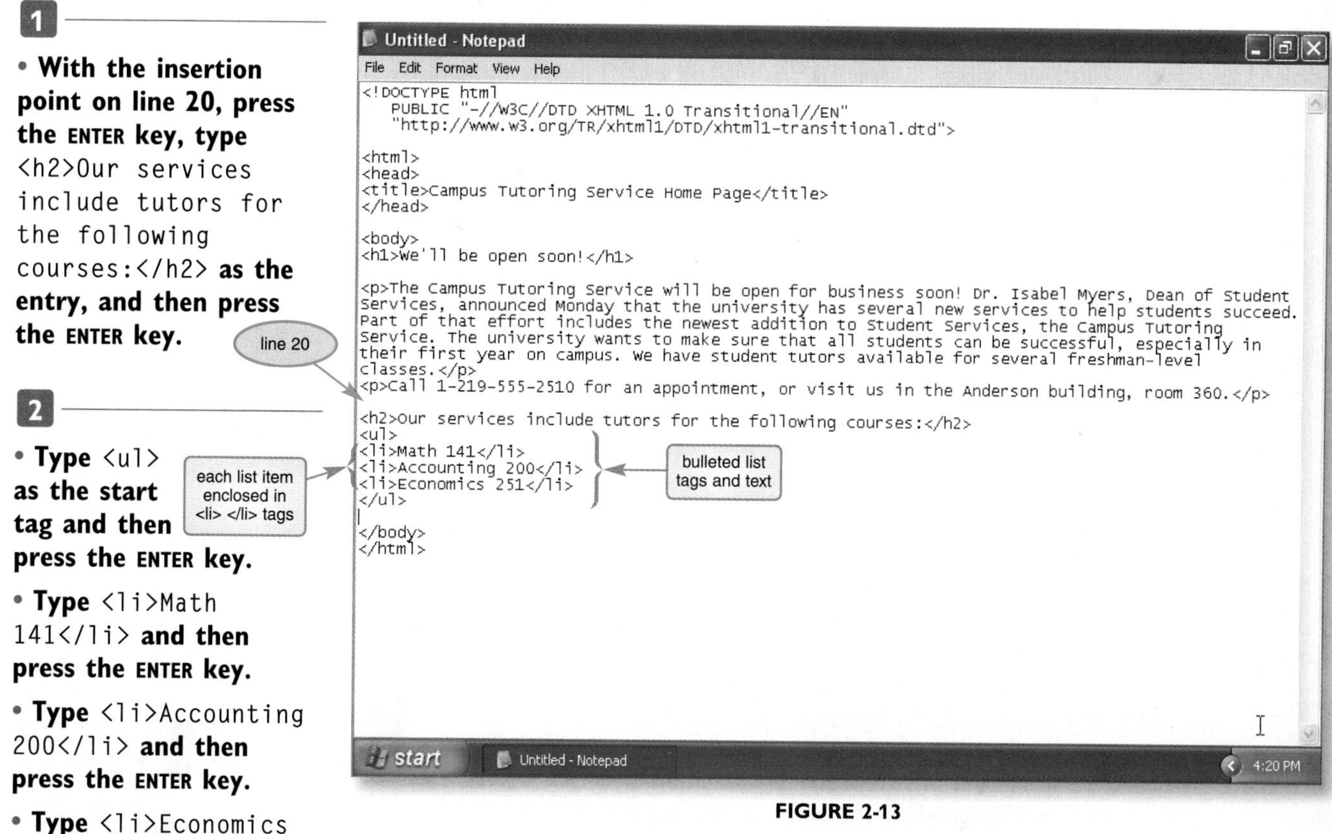

FIGURE 2-13

A third type of list, called a **definition list**, offsets information in a dictionary-like style. While used less often than unordered or ordered lists, definition lists are useful to create a glossary-like list of terms and definitions, as shown in Figure 2-14a on the next page. Figure 2-14b shows the HTML code used to create the definition list.

The syntax for definition lists is not as straightforward as the <ul>, <ol>, or <li> structure that is used in the unordered and ordered list styles. With definition lists, you use the **<dl>** and **</dl>** tags to start and end the list. A **<dt>** tag indicates a term and a **<dd>** tag identifies the definition of that term by offsetting the definition from the term. Table 2-2 on the next page lists the elements of a definition list and their purposes.

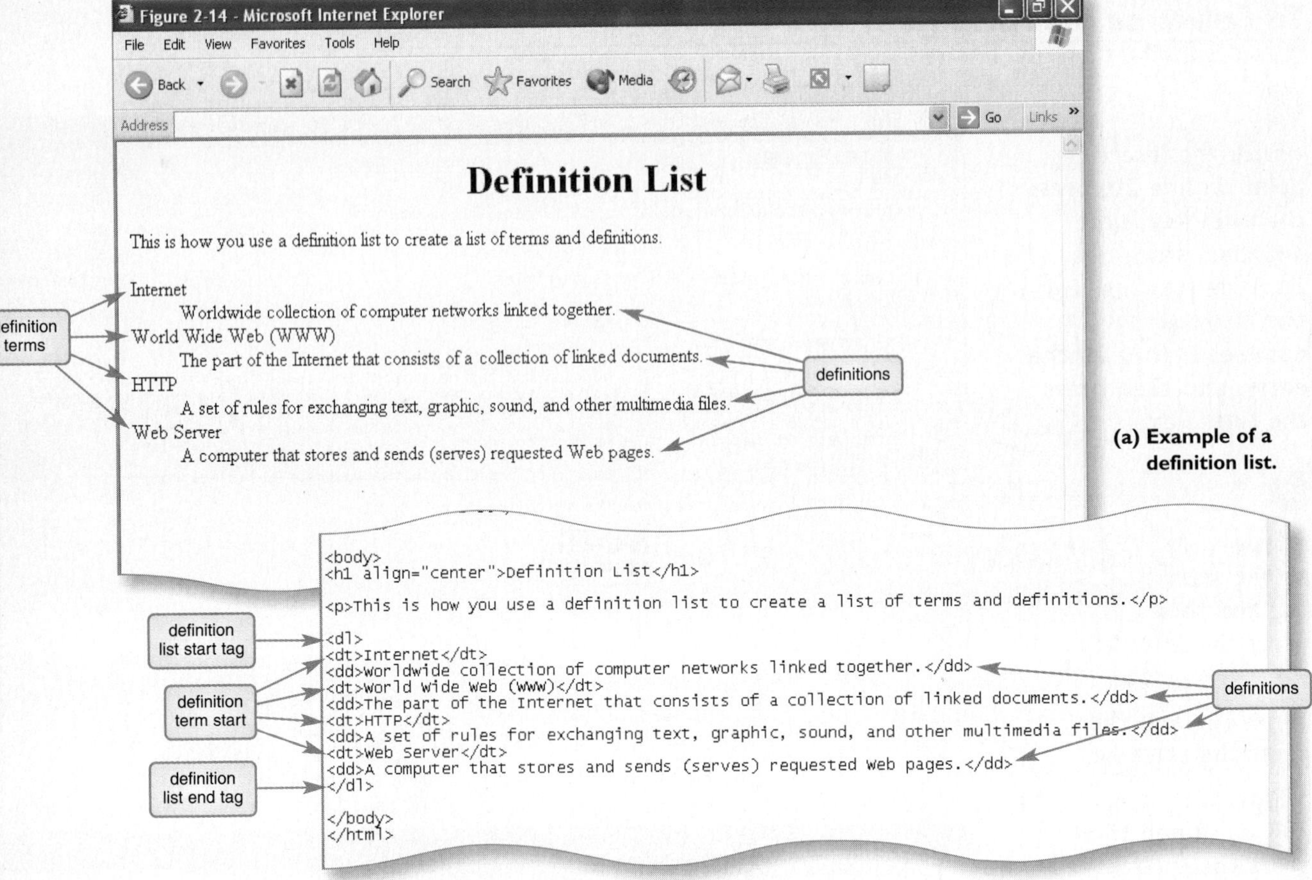

(a) Example of a definition list.

(b) HTML code used to create a definition list.

FIGURE 2-14

Table 2-2 Definition List Elements and Purposes

DEFINITION LIST ELEMENT	PURPOSE
<dl> </dl>	Used to start and end a definition list
<dt>	Used to identify a term
<dd>	Used to identify the definition of the term directly above

The start <dl> tag indicates the start of a definition list. After the <dl> tag, the <dt> tag is used to identify a term, followed by the <dd> tag to provide the definition of that term. The end </dl> tag identifies the end of a definition list. As shown in Figures 2-14a and 2-14b, by default, the definition term is left-aligned on the line and the definition for each term is indented so it easily is distinguishable as the definition for the term above.

Saving an HTML File

After entering code in the HTML file, you should view the Web page in a browser to see what the Web page looks like up to this point. In general, viewing the Web page periodically during development is good coding practice, as it allows you to see the effect of various HTML tags on the text. To view the Web page in a browser, the HTML file first must be saved.

HTML files must end with an extension of **.htm** or **.html**. HTML files with an extension of .html can be viewed on Web servers running an operating system that allows long file names. Web servers with Windows Server 2003, Windows XP, Windows 2000, Windows NT, or Macintosh operating systems all allow long file names. For Web servers that run an operating system that does not accept long file names, you need the .htm extension. In this book, all files are saved using the .htm extension. The following steps show how to save an HTML file.

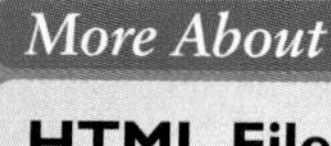

More About

HTML File Names

HTML files have an extension of .html or .htm. Generally, the home page of a Web site is called index.html or index.htm. Many service providers default to this name as the first page of a Web site to display.

To Save an HTML File

1

- **With a floppy disk in drive A, click File on the menu bar (Figure 2-15).**

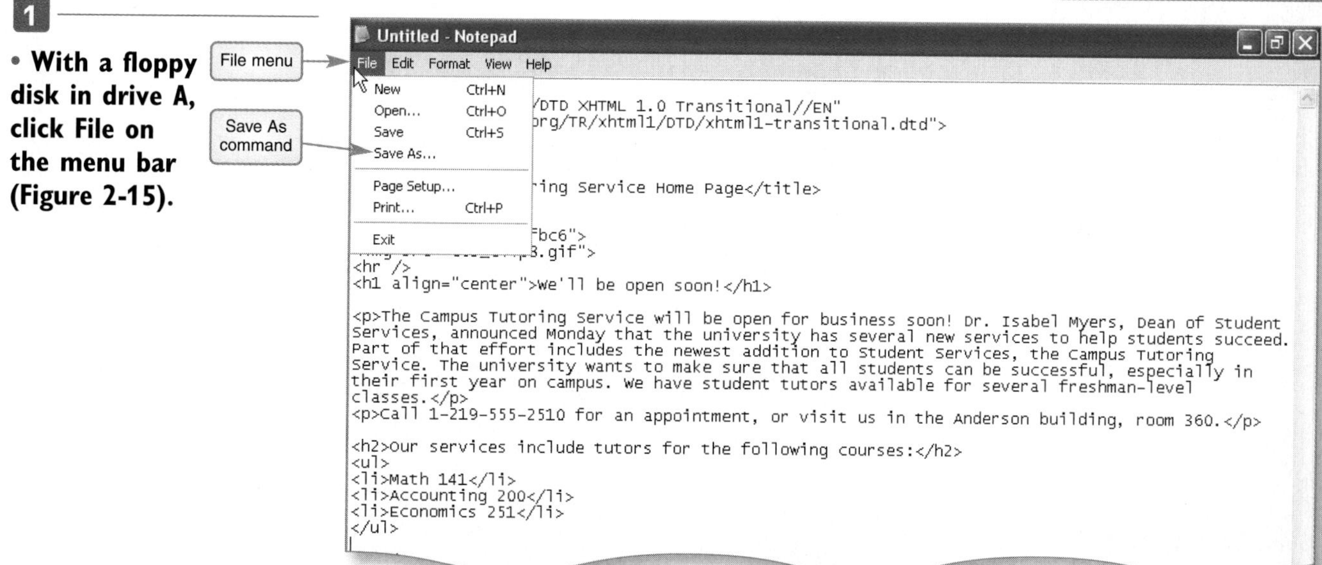

FIGURE 2-15

2

- **Click Save As on the File menu.**

The Save As dialog box is displayed (Figure 2-16).

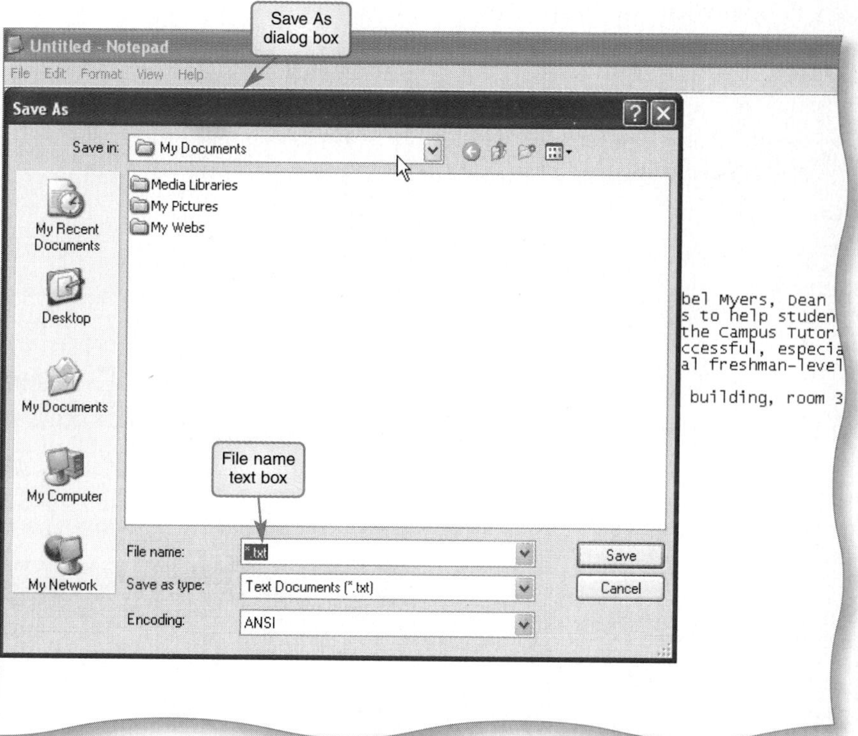

FIGURE 2-16

3

- **Type** `project2.htm` **in the File name text box.**
- **Click the Save in box arrow.**

The file name, project2.htm, appears in the File name text box (Figure 2-17). Notepad displays a list of available drives and folders.

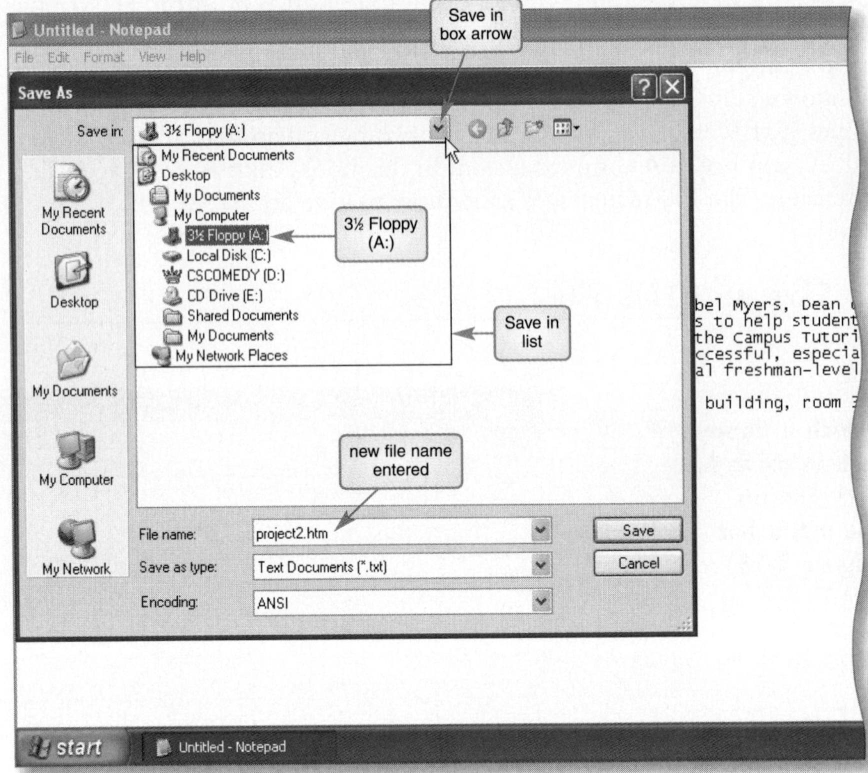

FIGURE 2-17

4

- **Click 3½ Floppy (A:) in the Save in list.**
- **Click the Project02 folder and then double-click the ProjectFiles folder in the list of available folders.**

The Project02\ProjectFiles folder on Drive A becomes the selected drive (Figure 2-18).

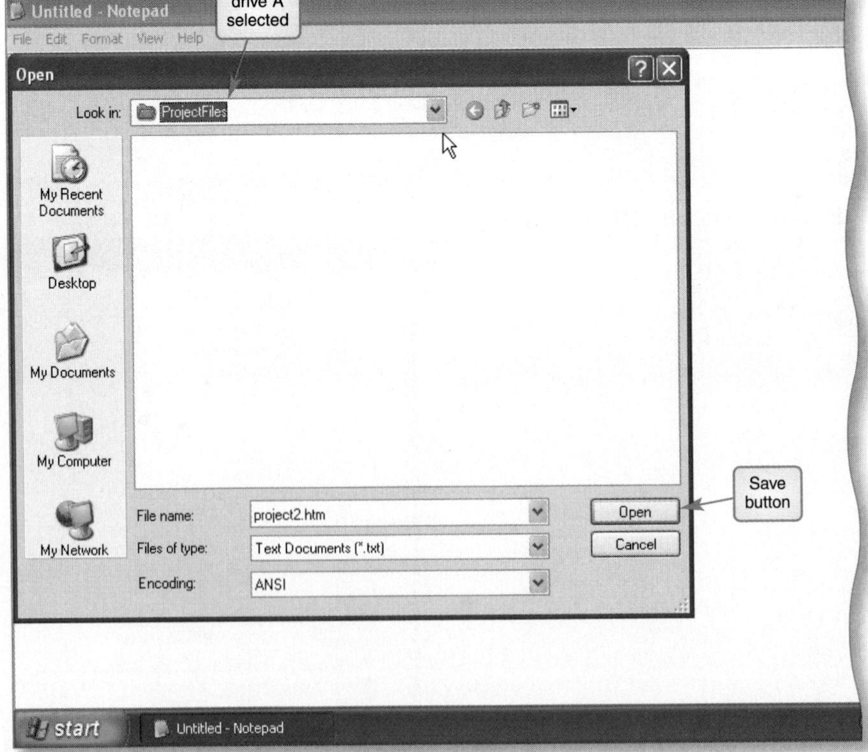

FIGURE 2-18

5

• **Click the Save button in the Save As dialog box.**

Notepad saves the HTML file in the Project02\ProjectFiles folder on the floppy disk in drive A using the file name, project2.htm. Although the HTML file is saved on a floppy disk, it also remains in memory and is displayed on the screen (Figure 2-19). Notepad displays the new file name on the title bar.

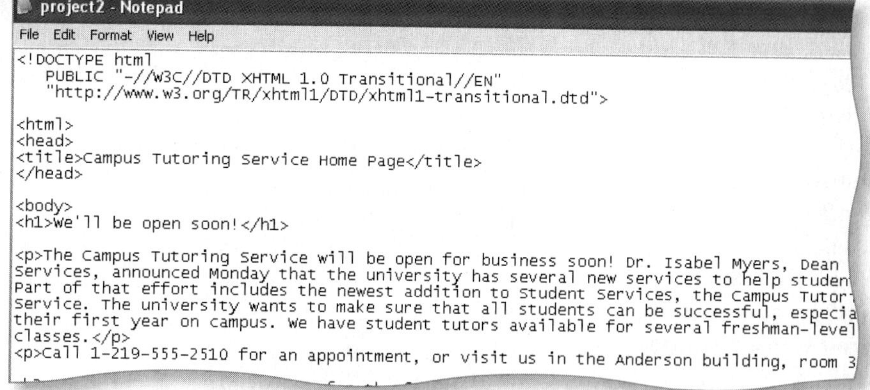

FIGURE 2-19

c:\Documents and Settings\chipo 1\My Documents\ProjectFiles\project

Using a Browser to View a Web Page

After saving an HTML file, you can use a browser to view your Web page. The HTML file is displayed in the browser as if the file were available on the Web.

Starting a Browser

An important feature of Windows is its **multitasking** capability — that is, its capability to have more than one program or process running at the same time. With the HTML file saved on a floppy disk in drive A, the next step is to view the Web page using a browser. The following steps illustrate how to start a browser to view a Web page.

To Start a Browser

1

• **Click the Start button on the Windows taskbar and then point to All Programs on the Start menu (Figure 2-20).**

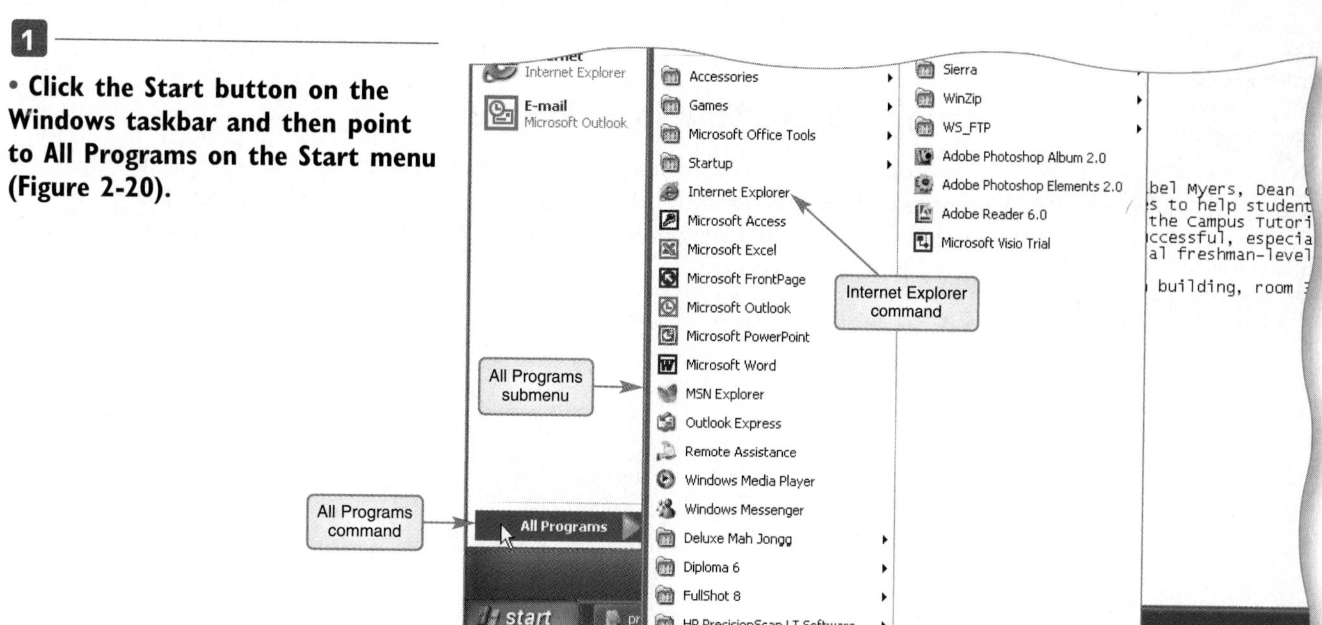

FIGURE 2-20

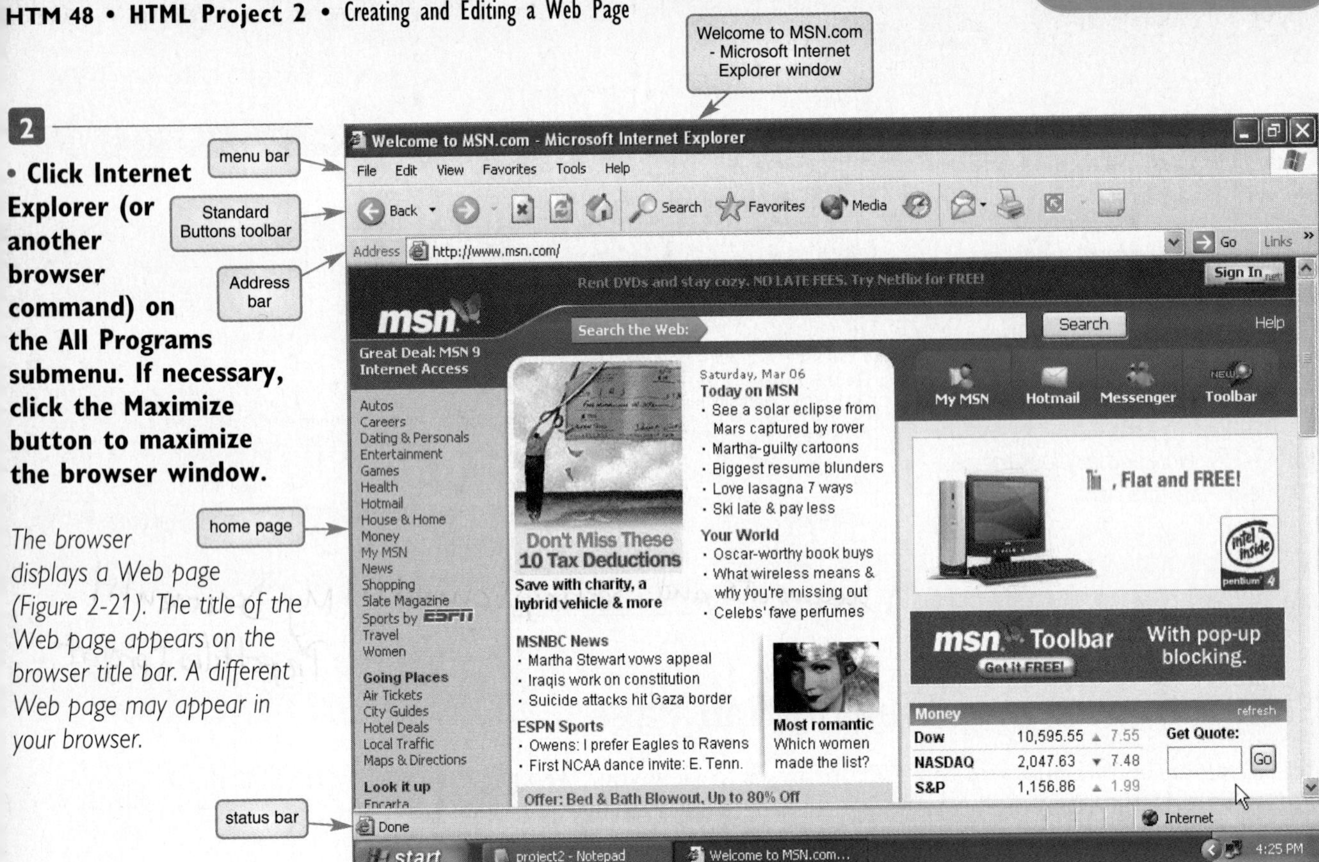

2

- **Click Internet Explorer (or another browser command) on the All Programs submenu. If necessary, click the Maximize button to maximize the browser window.**

The browser displays a Web page (Figure 2-21). The title of the Web page appears on the browser title bar. A different Web page may appear in your browser.

FIGURE 2-21

> *More About*
>
> **User Interface Design**
>
> The user interface design is a very important aspect of a Web site. If a site is designed poorly, users may be unable to find the desired information or complete a task, which makes the Web site ineffective. To learn more about good Web design principles, visit the HTML More About Web page (scsite.com/html3e/more) and then click Web Design.

If your computer is connected to the Internet when the browser window opens, it displays a **home page**, or **start page**, which is a Web page that appears each time Internet Explorer starts. Because it is possible to customize browser settings to change the Web page that appears as the home page, the home page displayed by your browser may be different. Schools and organizations often set a main page on their Web sites as the home page for browsers installed on lab or office computers.

Viewing a Web Page in a Browser

A browser allows you to open a file located on your computer and have full browsing capabilities, as if the Web page were stored on a Web server and made available on the Web. The following steps use this technique to view the HTML file, project2.htm, in a browser.

To View a Web Page in a Browser

1

• **When the browser window appears, click the Address bar.**

• **Type** `a:\Project02\ProjectFiles\project2.htm` **in the Address box.**

The URL is displayed in the Address box (Figure 2-22). If you type an incorrect letter or symbol in the Address box and notice the error before moving to the next step, use the BACKSPACE key to erase all the characters back to and including the one that is incorrect and then continue typing.

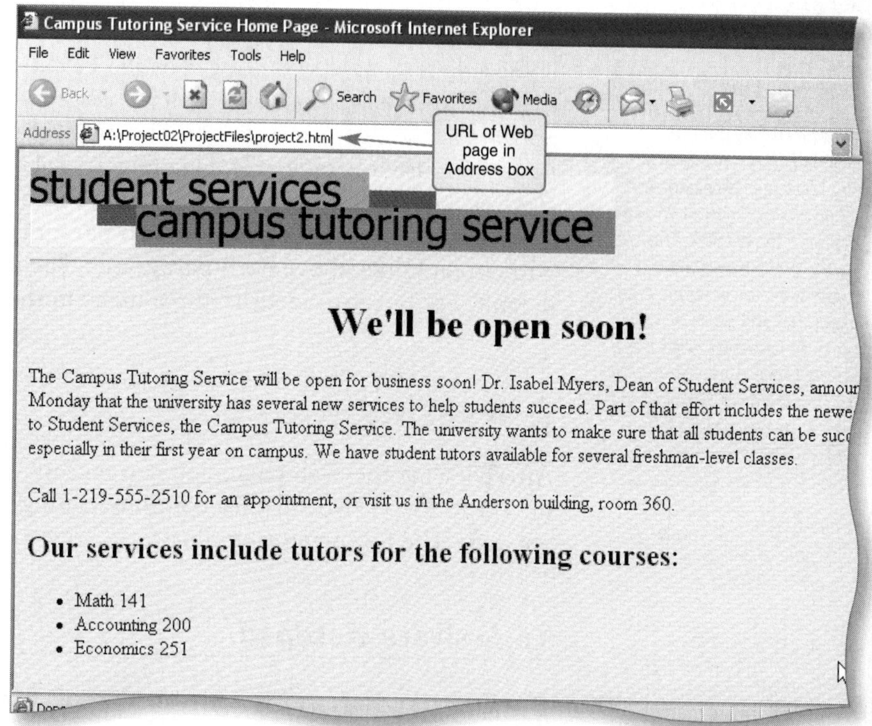

FIGURE 2-22

2

• **Press the ENTER key.**

The browser displays the Web page, project2.htm (Figure 2-23). The Address box appears with A:\Project02\ProjectFiles\project2.htm, which indicates the HTML file is saved on the floppy disk in drive A.

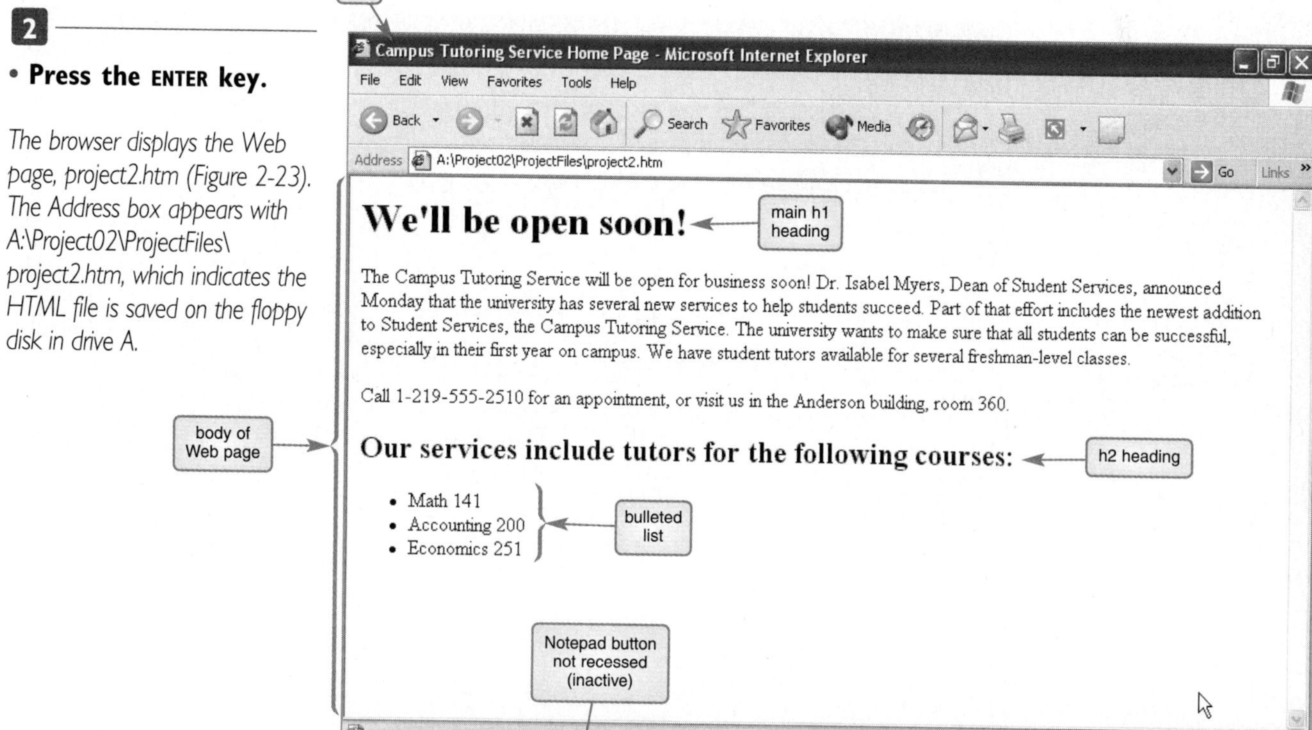

FIGURE 2-23

More About

Developing Web Pages for Multiple Browsers

When developing Web pages, you must consider the types of browsers visitors will use, including Internet Explorer and Netscape Navigator for Windows or Safari or Internet Explorer for MacOS. The Apple Web site provides suggestions for creating Web pages that will work in a wide range of browsers. Visit the HTML More About Web page (scsite.com/html3e/more) and then click Developing for Multiple Browsers.

The browser displays the Web page as if it were available on the Web. Viewing Web pages periodically during development ensures that the Web pages appear in the manner you intend. To understand the HTML code used to create the Web page, compare the Web page displayed in the browser with the HTML file in Notepad. The title bar, for example, displays the Campus Tutoring Service Home Page, which is the title text entered on line 7 of the HTML file. All the information contained in the body of the Web page — that is, between the <body> and </body> tags — now appears in the browser window. The main heading, We'll be open soon!, appears larger because it is tagged as Heading 1 (<h1>) style, whereas the heading, Our services include tutors for the following courses:, appears smaller because it is tagged as a Heading 2 (<h2>) style. The two paragraphs of text appear using normal font, with a blank line above each paragraph. The unordered (bulleted) list uses the default disc bullet to identify three items in the list.

Activating Notepad

After viewing the Web page, you can modify the Web page by adding additional tags or text to the HTML file. To continue editing, you first must return to the Notepad window. The following step illustrates how to activate Notepad.

To Activate Notepad

1 **Click the Notepad button on the taskbar.**

The maximized Notepad window becomes the active window (Figure 2-24).

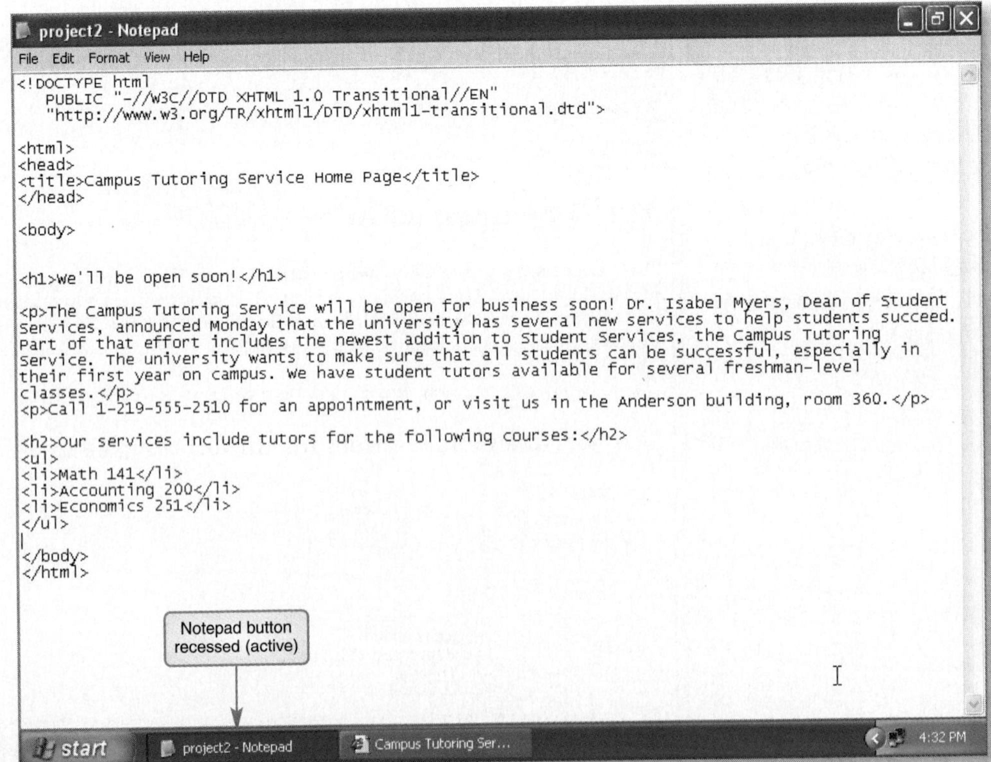

FIGURE 2-24

Web Page Images

Images are used in many ways to enhance the look of a Web page and make it more interesting and colorful. Images can be used to add background color, to help organize a Web page, to help clarify a point being made in the text, or to serve as links to other Web pages. Images also often are used to break up Web page sections (such as a horizontal rule) or as directional elements that allow a visitor to navigate through a Web site.

Image Types

Web pages use three types of files as images: GIF, JPEG, and PNG. **Graphics Interchange Format** (**GIF**) files have an extension of .gif. A graphic image saved as a GIF (pronounced *jiff* or *giff*) also is saved using compression techniques to make it smaller for download on the Web. The technique used to compress GIF files (called LZW compression) is patented, however, which means companies making products that use the GIF format must obtain a license. This does not apply to typical Web users or businesses that include GIFs in their Web pages. Standard (or non-interlaced) GIF images are displayed one line at a time when loading. Interlaced GIF images load all at once, starting with a blurry look and becoming sharper as they load. Using interlaced GIFs for large images is a good technique, because a Web page visitor can see a blurred outline of the image as it loads. Users with faster Internet connections most likely will see little difference between an interlaced GIF and a non-interlaced GIF.

Joint Photographic Experts Group (**JPEG**) files have an extension of .jpg, .jpe, or .jpeg. A JPEG (pronounced *JAY-peg*) is a graphic image saved using compression techniques to make it smaller for download on the Web. When creating a JPEG image, you can specify the image quality to reach a balance between image quality and file size. JPEG files often are used for more complex images, such as photographs, because the JPEG file format supports more colors and resolutions than the other file types.

A third type of image file is **Portable Network Graphics** (**PNG**), which has a .png or .ping extension. The PNG (pronounced *ping*) format also is a compressed file format that supports multiple colors and resolutions. The World Wide Web Consortium developed the PNG format as a graphics standard and patent-free alternative to the GIF format. Most newer browsers support PNG images.

If an image is not in one of these formats, you can use a paint or graphics-editing program to convert an image to a .gif, .jpg, or .png format. Some paint programs even allow you to save a GIF image as interlaced. A number of paint and graphics-editing programs, such Adobe Photoshop, Corel Painter, and Jasc Paint Shop Pro, are available in the marketplace today.

> *More About*
>
> **Images**
>
> Images on Web pages are viewed in a variety of environments, including slow connections to the Internet and slower computers. Optimizing your images is important to increase the speed of download for all of your Web page visitors. Visit the HTML More About Web page (scsite.com/html3e/more) and then click Optimization.

Image Attributes

Table 2-3 on the next page lists the attributes that can be used with the <img> tag. In this project, the src and alt attributes are used in the <img> tag. The **src** attribute is used to define the URL of the image to load. The **alt** attribute is used to provide alternative text, in the event the image is not displayed. The alt text is especially useful to vision-impaired users who use a screen reader, which translates information on a computer screen into audio output. The text should be a brief representation of the purpose of the image, not a description of the image, with the goal of helping those who cannot see the image use the site most effectively. Although the text can be any length, you generally should stick to 50 characters or less to avoid the browser wrapping the text. <img> tag attributes will be explained in detail as they are used in later projects. The width and height attributes will define the image size. It is important to include the height and width attributes so the browser knows the size of the image without having to calculate it.

Table 2-3 Image Attributes

ATTRIBUTE	FUNCTION
align	• Controls alignment • Can select from bottom, middle, top, left, or right
alt	• Alternative text to display when an image is being loaded
border	• Defines the border width
height	• Defines the height of the image • Improves loading time
hspace	• Defines the horizontal space that separates the image from the text
src	• Defines the URL of the image to be loaded
vspace	• Defines the vertical space that separates the image from the text
width	• Defines the width of the image • Improves loading time

Improving the Appearance of Your Web Page

One goal in Web page development is to create a Web page that is visually appealing and maintains the interest of the visitors. The Web page developed thus far in the project is functional, but lacks in visual appeal. The following steps illustrate how to improve the appearance of the Web page from the one shown in Figure 2-25a to the one shown in Figure 2-25b by adding an image, adding a background color, centering a heading, and adding a horizontal rule.

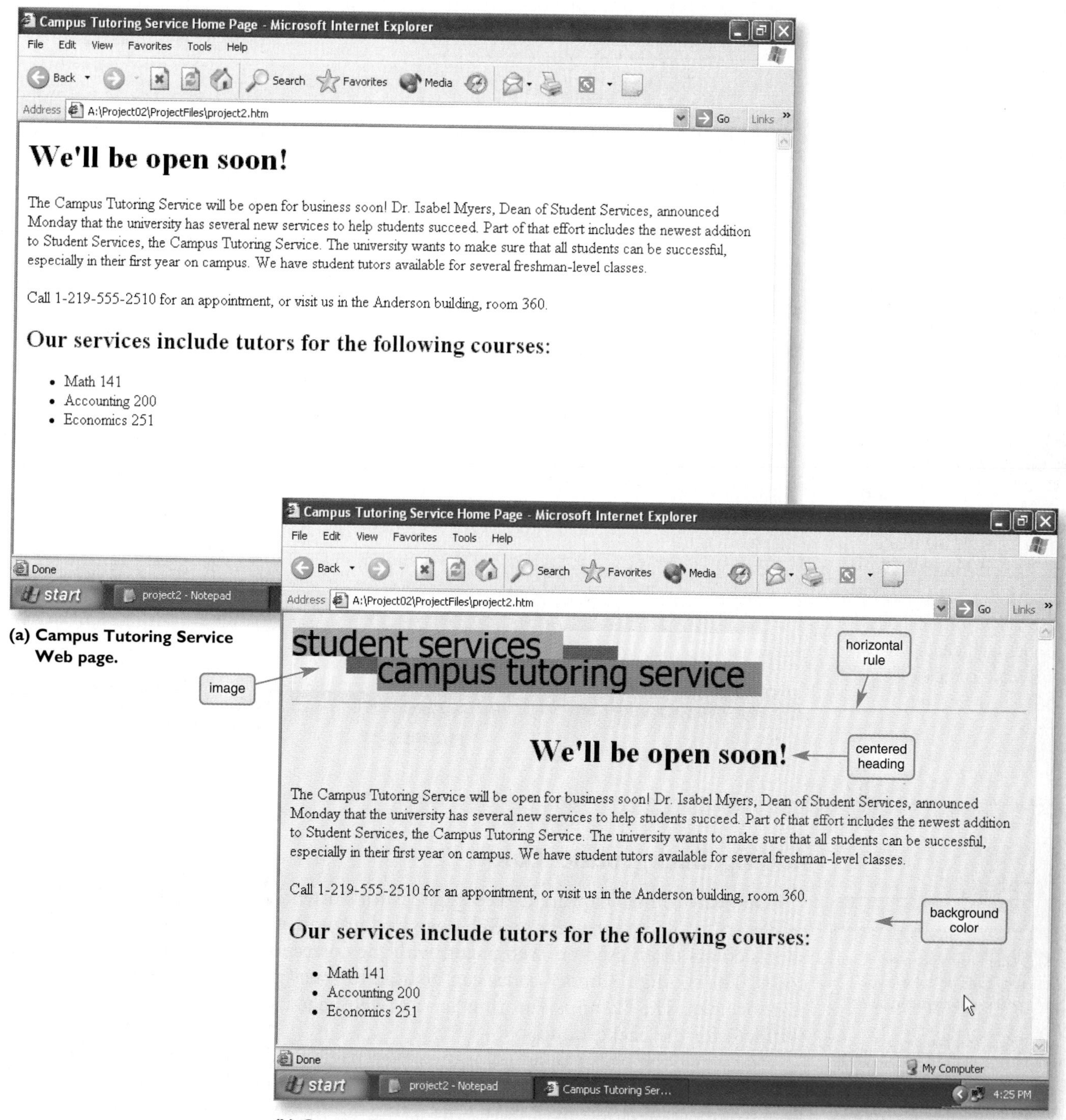

(a) Campus Tutoring Service Web page.

(b) Campus Tutoring Service Web page formatted to improve appearance.

FIGURE 2-25

Adding an Image

Early in the use of the Web, when the Web was used mostly by researchers needing to share information with each other, having purely functional, text-only Web pages was the norm. Today, however, the Web also serves as a communications and advertising medium, competing with television, radio, and print. Web page visitors are used to a more graphically oriented world. Because of this, Web page visitors have come to expect Web pages to use images that provide visual interest. The steps on the next page illustrate how to add an image to a Web page by entering an <img> tag in the HTML file.

To Add an Image

1

- **Click after the > symbol on line 10 and then press the ENTER key.**

2

- **Type** `<img src="cts_clip8.gif" width="484" height="62" alt="Student Services logo" />` **as the tag.**

The HTML code inserts an image with the file name cts_clip8.gif (Figure 2-26). Because the image only uses a few colors, a GIF image provides high enough quality. For a more complex image, a JPEG would be used.

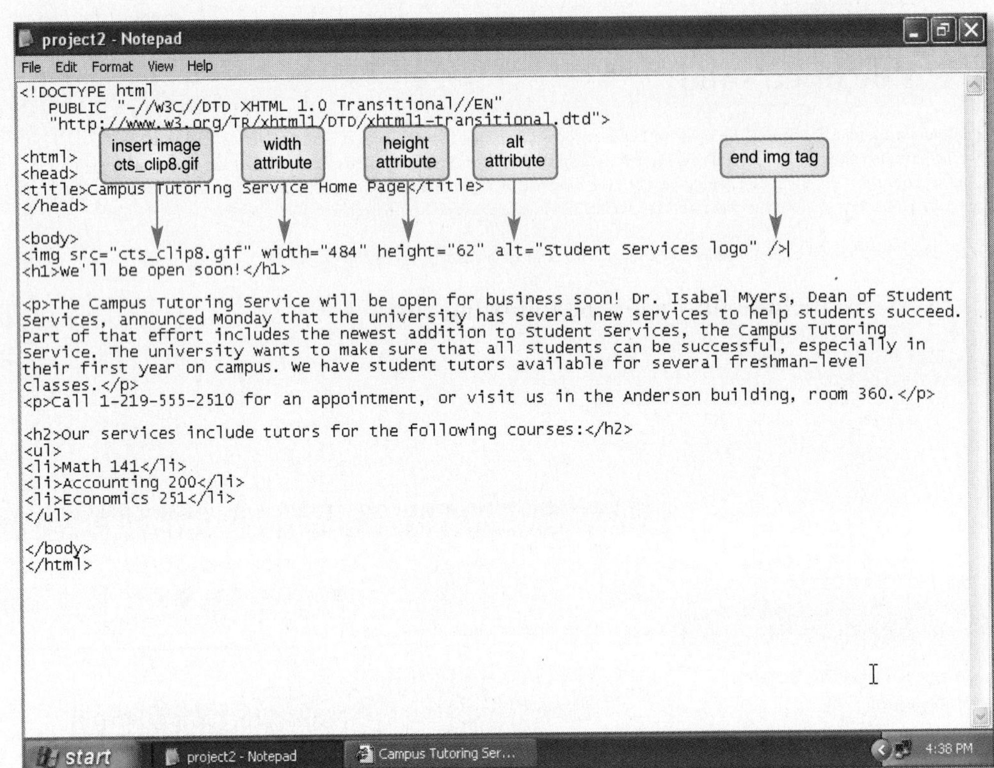


```
<!DOCTYPE html
   PUBLIC "-//W3C//DTD XHTML 1.0 Transitional//EN"
   "http://www.w3.org/TR/xhtml1/DTD/xhtml1-transitional.dtd">

<html>
<head>
<title>Campus Tutoring Service Home Page</title>
</head>

<body>
<img src="cts_clip8.gif" width="484" height="62" alt="Student Services logo" />
<h1>We'll be open soon!</h1>

<p>The Campus Tutoring Service will be open for business soon! Dr. Isabel Myers, Dean of Student
Services, announced Monday that the university has several new services to help students succeed.
Part of that effort includes the newest addition to Student Services, the Campus Tutoring
Service. The university wants to make sure that all students can be successful, especially in
their first year on campus. We have student tutors available for several freshman-level
classes.</p>
<p>Call 1-219-555-2510 for an appointment, or visit us in the Anderson building, room 360.</p>

<h2>Our services include tutors for the following courses:</h2>
<ul>
<li>Math 141</li>
<li>Accounting 200</li>
<li>Economics 251</li>
</ul>

</body>
</html>
```

FIGURE 2-26

Adding Background Color

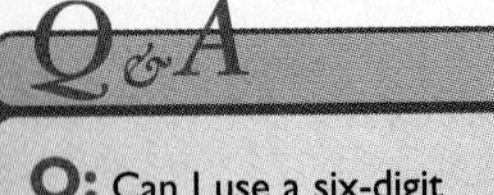

Q: Can I use a six-digit number code or color name to specify a background color?

A: Yes. You can use a six-digit number code or a color name as a background color choice. Figure 2-27 lists several predefined color names that can be used for background or font colors. The HTML attribute, background="navy", uses one of the predefined color choices.

One way to help capture a Web page visitor's attention is to use color. Many colors are available for use as a Web page background, text, or link. Figure 2-27 shows colors often used on Web pages, with the corresponding six-digit number codes. The six-digit number codes can be used to specify a color for a background, text, or links. The Campus Tutoring Service Web page uses a pale yellow color (#fffbc6) for the background.

To change the background color on a Web page, the bgcolor attribute must be added in the <body> tag of the HTML file. The **bgcolor** attribute lets you change the background color of the Web page. The following steps show how to add a background color using the bgcolor attribute.

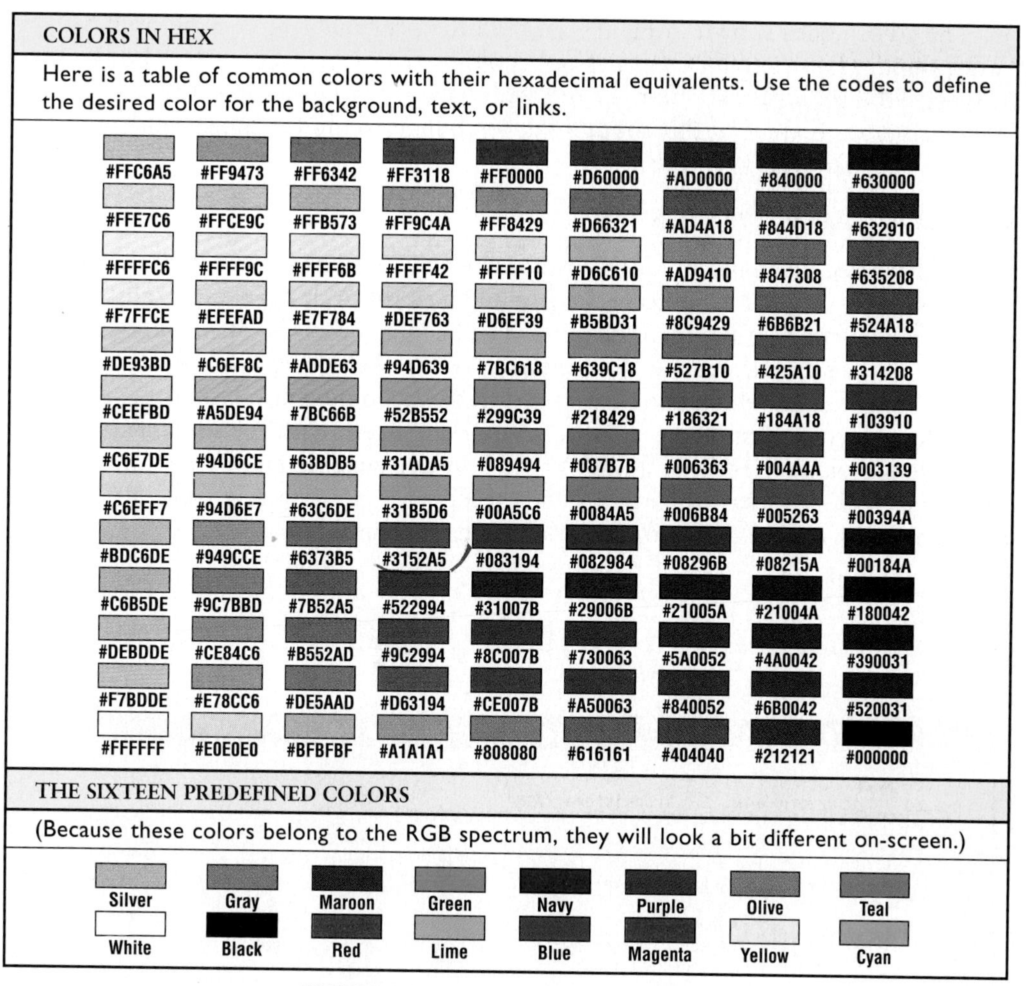

COLORS IN HEX

Here is a table of common colors with their hexadecimal equivalents. Use the codes to define the desired color for the background, text, or links.

#FFC6A5	#FF9473	#FF6342	#FF3118	#FF0000	#D60000	#AD0000	#840000	#630000
#FFE7C6	#FFCE9C	#FFB573	#FF9C4A	#FF8429	#D66321	#AD4A18	#844D18	#632910
#FFFFC6	#FFFF9C	#FFFF6B	#FFFF42	#FFFF10	#D6C610	#AD9410	#847308	#635208
#F7FFCE	#EFEFAD	#E7F784	#DEF763	#D6EF39	#B5BD31	#8C9429	#6B6B21	#524A18
#DE93BD	#C6EF8C	#ADDE63	#94D639	#7BC618	#639C18	#527B10	#425A10	#314208
#CEEFBD	#A5DE94	#7BC66B	#52B552	#299C39	#218429	#186321	#184A18	#103910
#C6E7DE	#94D6CE	#63BDB5	#31ADA5	#089494	#087B7B	#006363	#004A4A	#003139
#C6EFF7	#94D6E7	#63C6DE	#31B5D6	#00A5C6	#0084A5	#006B84	#005263	#00394A
#BDC6DE	#949CCE	#6373B5	#3152A5	#083194	#082984	#08296B	#08215A	#00184A
#C6B5DE	#9C7BBD	#7B52A5	#522994	#31007B	#29006B	#21005A	#21004A	#180042
#DEBDDE	#CE84C6	#B552AD	#9C2994	#8C007B	#730063	#5A0052	#4A0042	#390031
#F7BDDE	#E78CC6	#DE5AAD	#D63194	#CE007B	#A50063	#840052	#6B0042	#520031
#FFFFFF	#E0E0E0	#BFBFBF	#A1A1A1	#808080	#616161	#404040	#212121	#000000

THE SIXTEEN PREDEFINED COLORS

(Because these colors belong to the RGB spectrum, they will look a bit different on-screen.)

Silver	Gray	Maroon	Green	Navy	Purple	Olive	Teal
White	Black	Red	Lime	Blue	Magenta	Yellow	Cyan

FIGURE 2-27 Common Web page colors.

More About

Colors

Figure 2-27 does not list all possible Web colors. Many other colors are available that you can use for Web page backgrounds or text fonts. For more information about colors, see Appendix B or visit the HTML More About Web page (scsite.com/html3e/more.htm) and then click Colors.

To Add a Background Color

1

- **Click after the y in <body> on line 10 and then press the SPACEBAR.**

2

- **Type** `bgcolor="#fffbc6"` **as the color code.**

The HTML code is displayed (Figure 2-28). The bgcolor attribute uses a six-digit number code of fffbc6 to specify a pale yellow background.

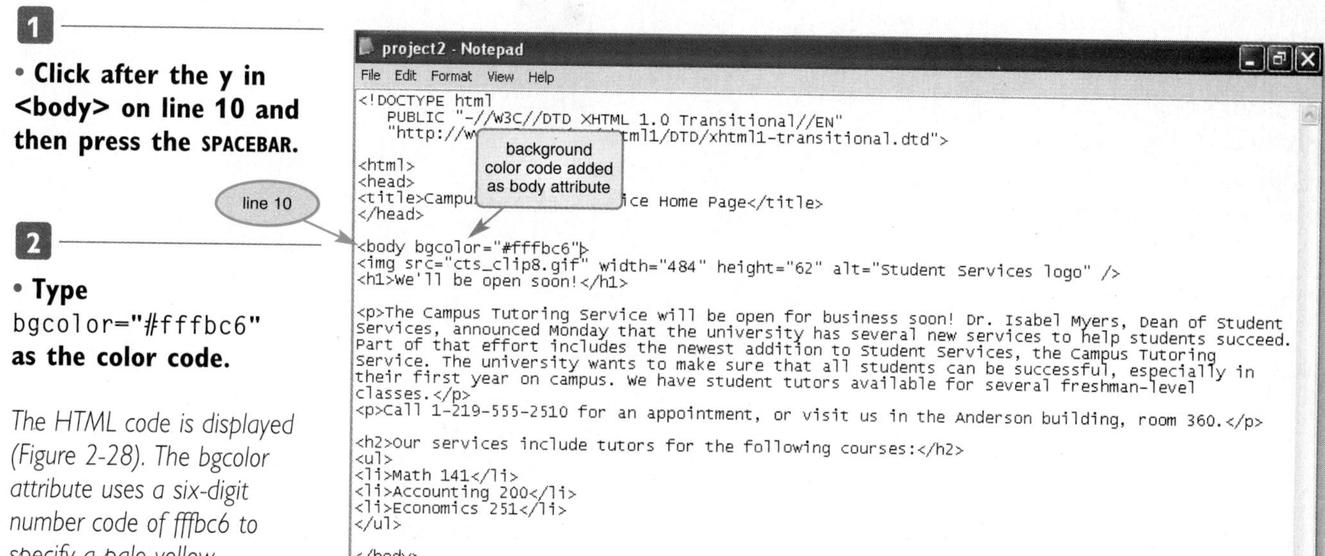

FIGURE 2-28

The color codes shown in Figure 2-27 on the previous page can be used for background, text, and link colors. The bgcolor attribute is used in the <body> tag to specify the background color for the Web page. In later projects, the text and link attributes are used in the <body> tag to change colors for those elements.

Centering the Heading

As discussed, headings are used to separate new sections of text from each other. A main heading is used to indicate the beginning of the Web page. Generally, you use the Heading 1 style for the main heading. The heading, We'll be open soon!, is the main heading and indicates the main message of the Web page. You can highlight the main heading further by aligning the text differently on the page. Using the **align** attribute, you can specify left-, right-, or center-alignment with the statements align="left", align="right", or align="center" in any heading tag. By default, headings are left-aligned; if an alignment is not specified, a heading is left-aligned. The following steps illustrate how to center-align the heading.

To Center a Heading

1

- **Click line 12 just after the 1 in the <h1> tag and then press the SPACEBAR.**

2

- **Type `align="center"` as the attribute.**

The insertion point is positioned before the > symbol (Figure 2-29). The code to center-align the heading is added as a heading attribute.

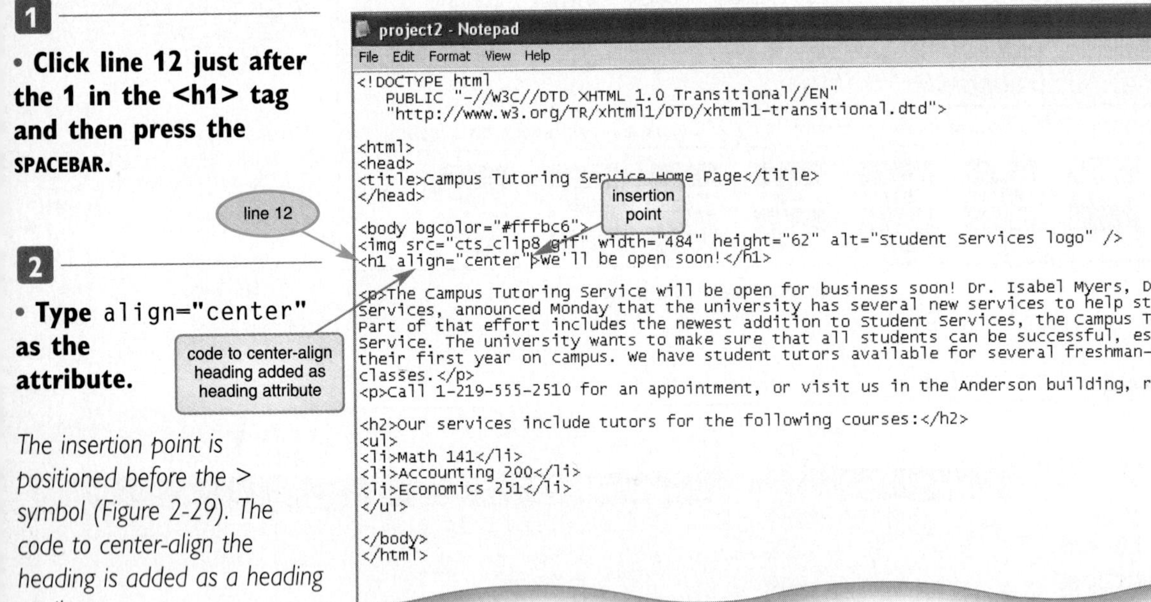

FIGURE 2-29

Adding a Horizontal Rule

As discussed earlier in the project, horizontal rules are lines that act as dividers in a Web page to provide a visual separation of sections on the page. You can use an inline image to add a horizontal rule or you can use the horizontal rule tag (<hr />) to add a simple horizontal rule, as shown in the steps below. Figure 2-30 shows examples of a variety of horizontal rules and the HTML code used to add them. The default horizontal rule is shown in the first line of the page. Dimension is added to a horizontal rule by increasing the number of pixels that are displayed. Another possibility is to turn the shading off using the noshade option, as shown in the last horizontal rule in Figure 2-30.

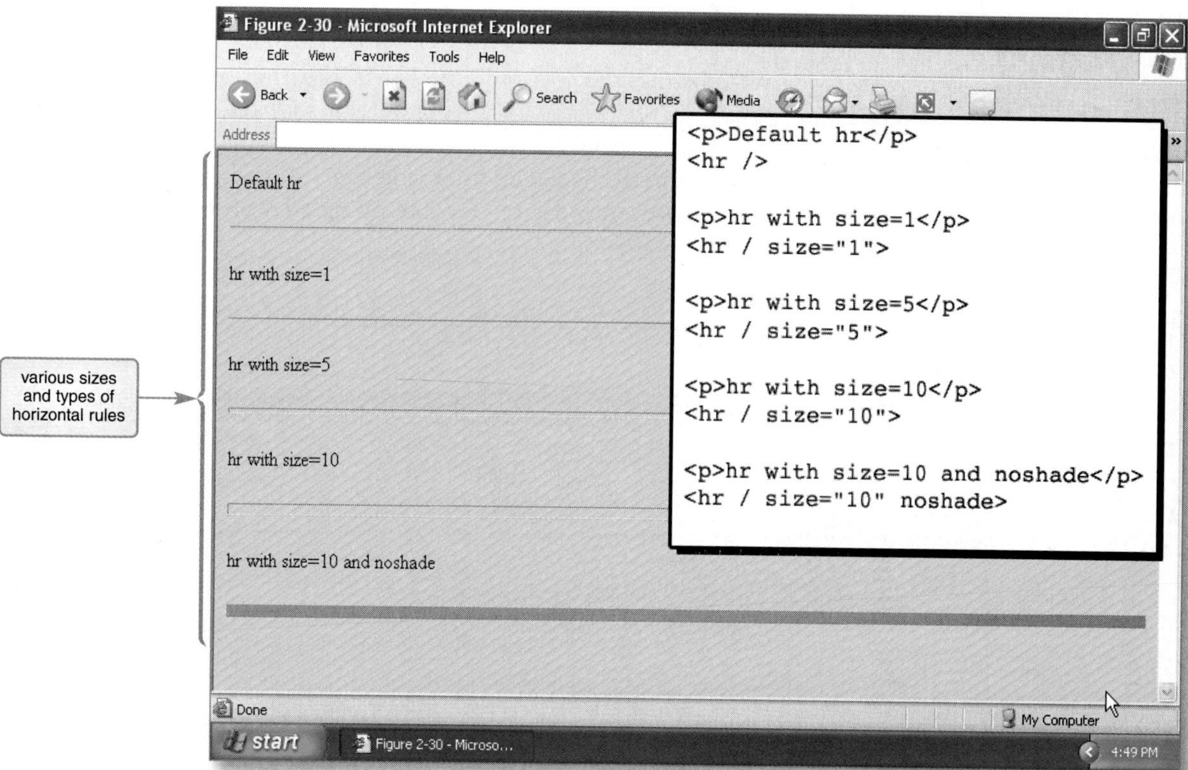

FIGURE 2-30 Examples of horizontal rules.

The following steps illustrate how to add a horizontal rule to a Web page.

To Add a Horizontal Rule

1 **Click line 11 just after the > symbol in the <img> tag and then press the ENTER key.**

2 **Type** `<hr />` **as the HTML tag.**

3 **Click File on the menu bar and then click Save.**

The project2 - Notepad window is displayed (Figure 2-31).

```
<!DOCTYPE html
   PUBLIC "-//W3C//DTD XHTML 1.0 Transitional//EN"
   "http://www.w3.org/TR/xhtml1/DTD/xhtml1-transitional.dtd">

<html>
<head>
<title>Campus Tutoring Service Home Page</title>
</head>

<body bgcolor="#fff
<img src="cts_clip8.       th="484" height="62" alt="Student Services logo" />
<hr />
<h1 align="center">We'll be open soon!</h1>

<p>The Campus Tutoring Service will be open for business soon! Dr. Isabel Myers, Dean of Student
Services, announced Monday that the university has several new services to help students succeed.
Part of that effort includes the newest addition to Student Services, the Campus Tutoring
Service. The university wants to make sure that all students can be successful, especially in
their first year on campus. We have student tutors available for several freshman-level
classes.</p>
<p>Call 1-219-555-2510 for an appointment, or visit us in the Anderson building, room 360.</p>

<h2>Our services include tutors for the following courses:</h2>
<ul>
<li>Math 141</li>
<li>Accounting 200</li>
<li>Economics 251</li>
</ul>

</body>
</html>
```


FIGURE 2-31

Refreshing the View in a Browser

After you have saved the modifications to the HTML file, the modified Web page can be viewed in a browser to review the background color, inserted image, centered heading, and horizontal rule. To view the latest version of the Web page in a browser, the page must be reloaded, or refreshed. The following steps show how to refresh the view of a Web page in a browser in order to view the modified Web page.

To Refresh the View in a Browser

1

- **Click the Campus Tutoring Service Home Page button on the taskbar.**

2

- **Click the Refresh button on the Standard toolbar.**

The latest version of project2.htm is displayed (Figure 2-32).

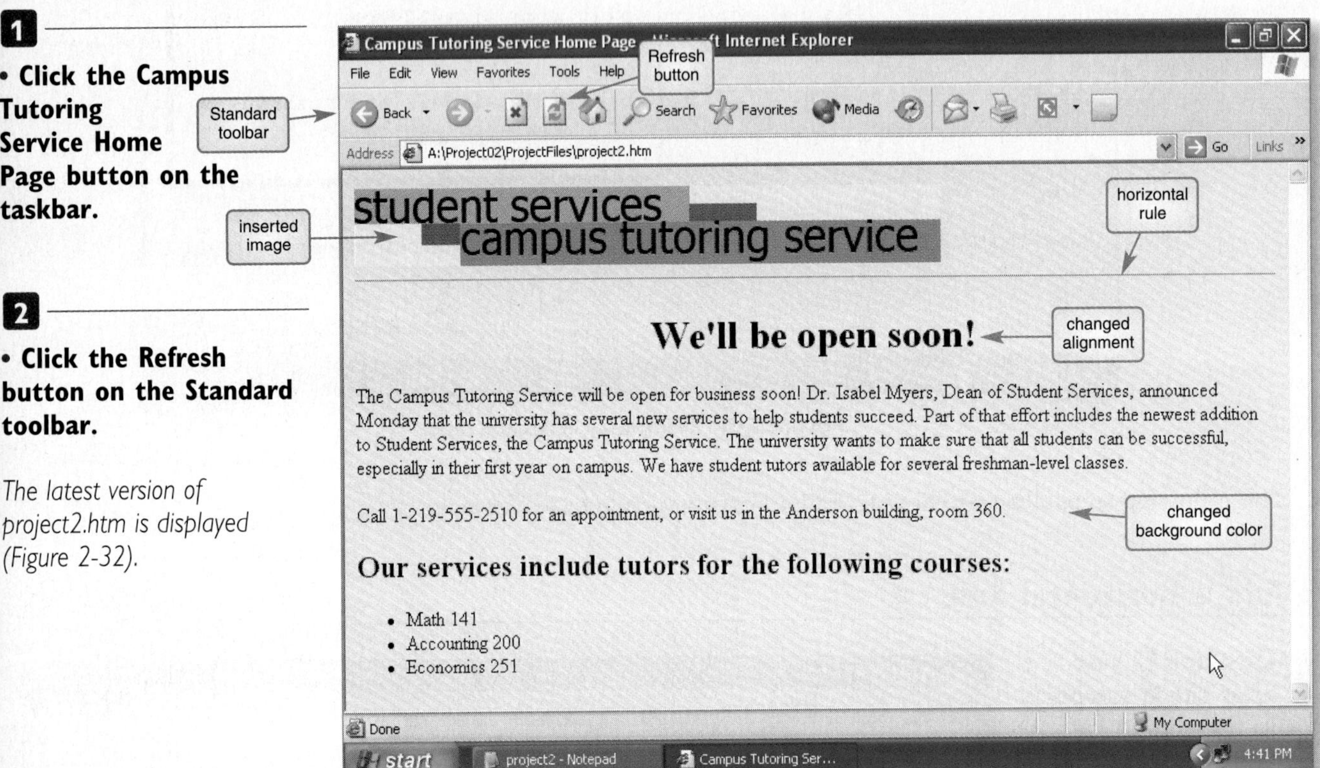

FIGURE 2-32

As discussed earlier in the project, Windows supports multitasking, so you can have Notepad and your browser open at the same time. You can continue developing the HTML file in Notepad and then view the modified file in your browser by clicking the appropriate button on the taskbar to switch between Notepad and the browser. Be sure to click the Refresh button when viewing the modified Web page in the browser, to ensure the latest version of the Web page is displayed.

Viewing HTML Source Code for a Web Page

Source code is the code or instructions used to create a Web page or program. For a Web page, the source code is the HTML code, which then is translated by a browser into a graphical Web page. You can view the HTML source code for any Web page from within your browser. This feature allows you to check your own HTML source code, as well as to see the HTML code other developers used to create their Web pages. If a feature on a Web page is appropriate or appealing for your Web page, you can view the source to understand the HTML required to add that feature and then copy sections of the HTML code to put in your own Web pages.

The following steps show how to view the HTML source code for a Web page using a browser.

To View HTML Source Code for a Web Page

1

- **Click View on the menu bar (Figure 2-33).**

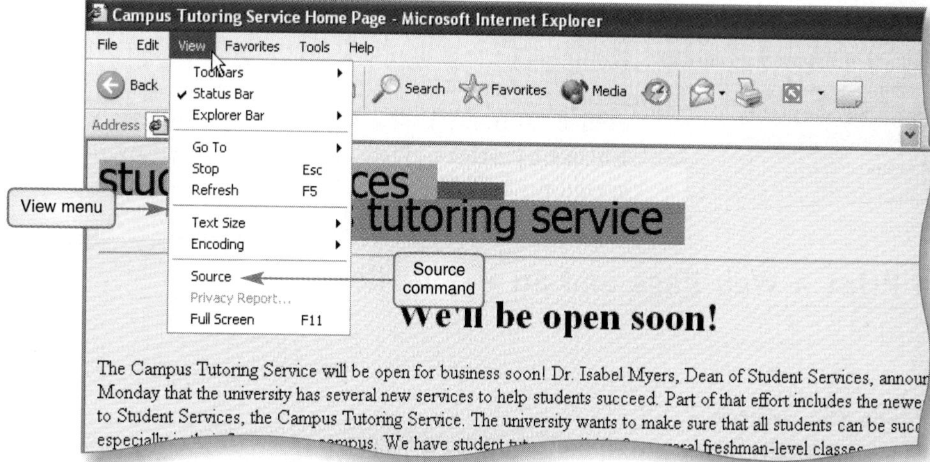

FIGURE 2-33

2

- **Click Source on the View menu.**

A Notepad window opens and displays the HTML source code for the Web page (Figure 2-34).

3

- **Click the Close button on the Notepad title bar.**

The Notepad window closes.

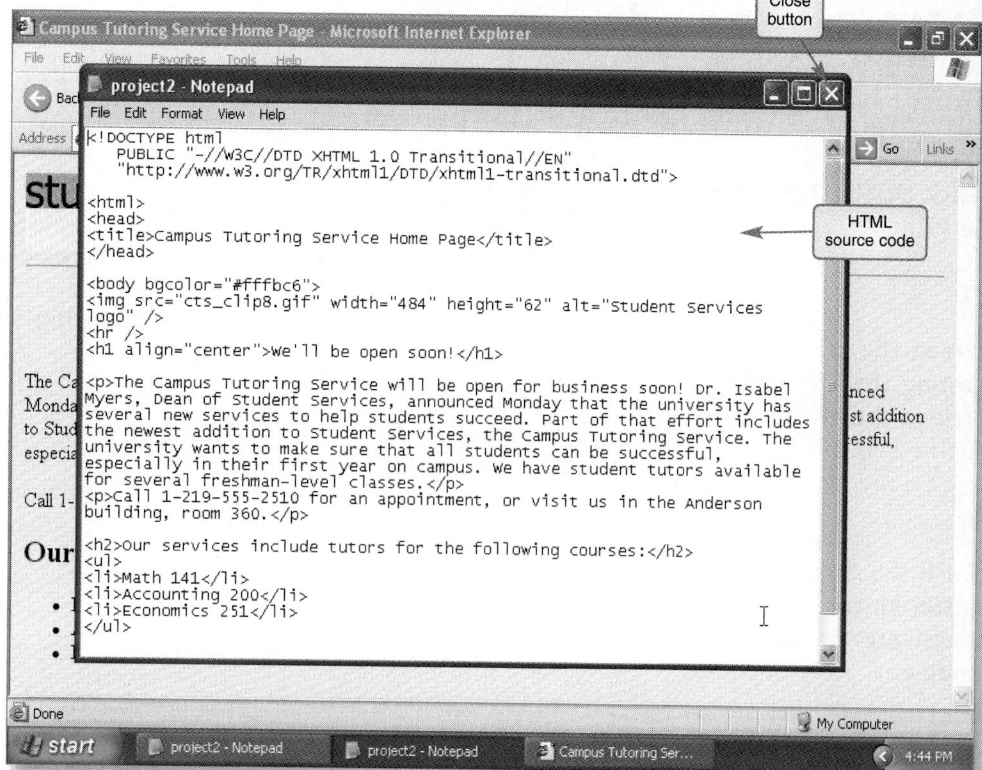

FIGURE 2-34

The HTML source code opens in the default text editor when you view the source. Although one Notepad window already was open, clicking View and then Source opened a second Notepad window.

More About

Printing HTML Files and Web Pages

Notepad and Internet Explorer both provide other ways to print a document or Web page. Pressing CTRL + P in Notepad or Internet Explorer opens the Print dialog box, where you can select print options. Alternatively, you can print a Web page in Internet Explorer by clicking the Print button on the Standard Buttons toolbar.

Printing a Web Page and an HTML File

After you have created the HTML file and saved it, you might want to print a copy of the HTML code and the resulting Web page. A printed version of a file, Web page, or other document is called a **hard copy** or **printout.**

Printouts are used for several reasons. Printouts allow you to present information to someone who does not have immediate access to a computer. A printout, for example, can be handed out in a meeting at which you are discussing sample Web pages. In addition, printed copies of HTML files and Web pages can be kept for reference. In many cases, HTML files and Web pages are printed and kept in binders for use by others. The following steps show how to print a Web page and its corresponding HTML file.

To Print a Web Page and an HTML File

1

- **Ready the printer according to the printer instructions.**
- **With the project2.htm Web page open in the browser window, click File on the menu bar and then click Print on the File menu.**
- **Click the OK button in the Print dialog box.**

2

- **When the printer stops printing the Web page, retrieve the printout (Figure 2-35).**

3

- **Click the Notepad button on the taskbar to activate the Notepad window.**

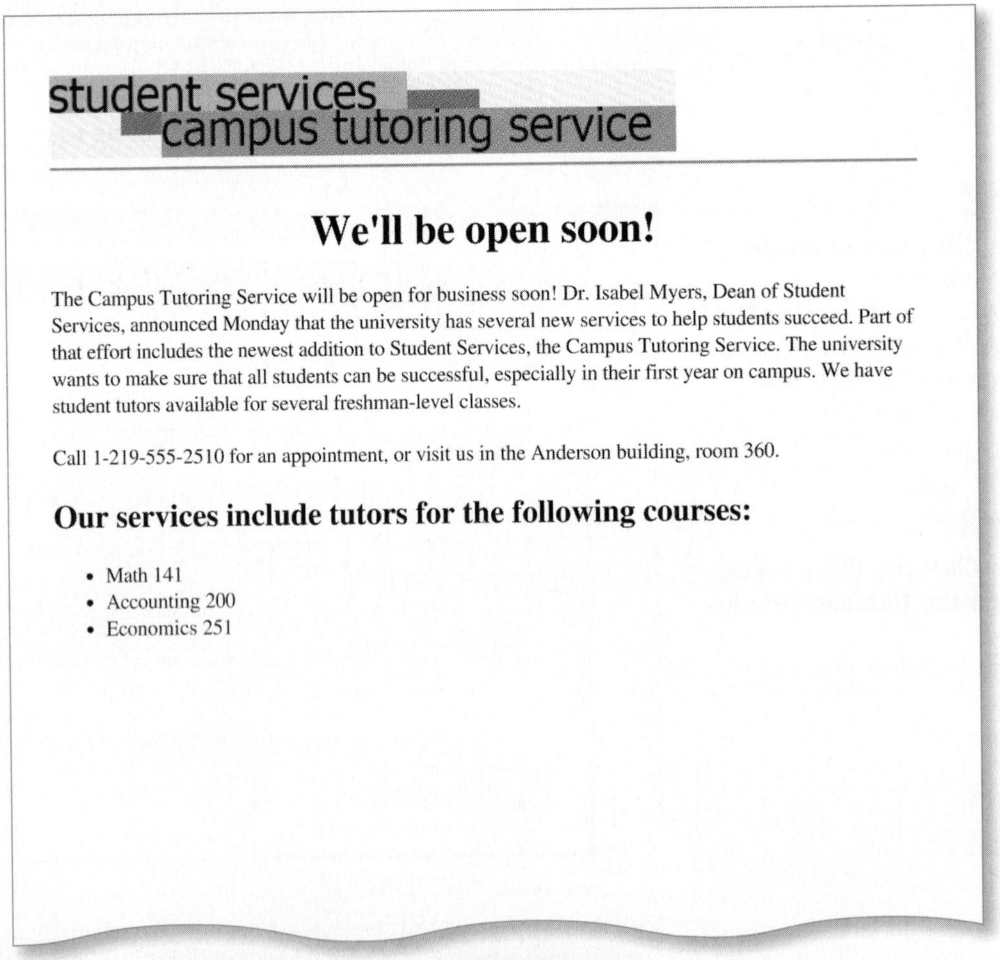

student services
campus tutoring service

We'll be open soon!

The Campus Tutoring Service will be open for business soon! Dr. Isabel Myers, Dean of Student Services, announced Monday that the university has several new services to help students succeed. Part of that effort includes the newest addition to Student Services, the Campus Tutoring Service. The university wants to make sure that all students can be successful, especially in their first year on campus. We have student tutors available for several freshman-level classes.

Call 1-219-555-2510 for an appointment, or visit us in the Anderson building, room 360.

Our services include tutors for the following courses:

- Math 141
- Accounting 200
- Economics 251

FIGURE 2-35

4

• Click File on the menu bar and then click Print on the File menu.

Notepad prints the HTML file (Figure 2-36).

```
<!DOCTYPE html
   PUBLIC "-//W3C//DTD XHTML 1.0 Transitional//EN"
   "http://www.w3.org/TR/xhtml1/DTD/xhtml1-transitional.dtd">

<html>
<head>
<title>Campus Tutoring Service Home Page</title>
</head>

<body bgcolor="#fffbc6">
<img src="cts_clip8.gif">
<hr />
<h1 align="center">We'll be open soon!</h1>

<p>The Campus Tutoring Service will be open for business soon! Dr. Isabel Myers,
Dean of Student

Services, announced Monday that the university has several new services to help
students succeed.

Part of that effort includes the newest addition to Student Services, the Campus
Tutoring

Service. The university wants to make sure that all students can be successful,
especially in

their first year on campus. We have student tutors available for several
freshman-level

classes.</p>
<p>Call 1-219-555-2510 for an appointment, or visit us in the Anderson building,
room 360.</p>

<h2>Our services include tutors for the following courses:</h2>
<ul>
<li>Math 141</li>
<li>Accounting 200</li>
<li>Economics 251</li>
</ul>

</body>
</html>
```

FIGURE 2-36

Having a printout of HTML code is an invaluable tool for beginning developers. A printed copy can help you immediately see the relationship between the HTML tags and the Web page that you view in the browser.

Quitting Notepad and a Browser

The following steps show how to quit Notepad and a browser.

To Quit Notepad and a Browser

1

- **Click the Close button on the Notepad title bar.**

The Notepad window closes and the Campus Tutoring Service Home Page window is displayed.

2

- **Click the Close button on the Campus Tutoring Service Home Page title bar.**

The browser closes and the Windows desktop is displayed.

Project Summary

Project 2 introduced the steps to start Notepad and create an HTML text file. You learned about the elements of a Web page and the HTML tags used to add those elements. You learned how to enter HTML tags and text using Notepad and then save the file. After learning how to view a Web page in a browser, you learned to modify the HTML file to improve the Web page appearance by using an image, adding a background color, centering a heading, and adding a horizontal rule. You then learned to refresh the view of the Web page in the browser to see the changes. Finally, you learned how to save the changes, print the Web page and HTML file, and quit Notepad and the browser.

What You Should Know

Having completed this project, you should be able to perform the tasks below. The tasks are listed in the same order they were presented in this project.

1. Start Notepad (HTM 34)
2. Enable Word Wrap in Notepad (HTM 36)
3. Enter HTML Tags to Define the Web Page Structure (HTM 38)
4. Enter a Heading (HTM 40)
5. Enter a Paragraph of Text (HTM 40)
6. Create an Unordered List (HTM 43)
7. Save an HTML File (HTM 45)
8. Start a Browser (HTM 47)
9. View a Web Page in a Browser (HTM 49)
10. Activate Notepad (HTM 50)
11. Add an Image (HTM 54)
12. Add a Background Color (HTM 55)
13. Center a Heading (HTM 56)
14. Add a Horizontal Rule (HTM 57)
15. Refresh the View in a Browser (HTM 58)
16. View HTML Source Code for a Web Page (HTM 59)
17. Print a Web Page and an HTML File (HTM 60)
18. Quit Notepad and a Browser (HTM 62)

Learn It Online

Instructions: To complete the Learn It Online exercises, start your browser, click the Address bar, and then enter the Web address `scsite.com/html3e/learn`. When the HTML Learn It Online page is displayed, follow the instructions in the exercises below. Each exercise has instructions for printing your results, either for your own records or for submission to your instructor.

1 Project Reinforcement TF, MC, and SA

Below HTML Project 2, click the Project Reinforcement link. Print the quiz by clicking Print on the File menu for each page. Answer each question.

2 Flash Cards

Below HTML Project 2, click the Flash Cards link and read the instructions. Type 20 (or a number specified by your instructor) in the Number of playing cards text box, type your name in the Enter your Name text box, and then click the Flip Card button. When the flash card is displayed, read the question and then click the ANSWER box arrow to select an answer. Flip through Flash Cards. If your score is 15 (75%) correct or greater, click Print on the File menu to print your results. If your score is less than 15 (75%) correct, then redo this exercise by clicking the Replay button.

3 Practice Test

Below HTML Project 2, click the Practice Test link. Answer each question, enter your first and last name at the bottom of the page, and then click the Grade Test button. When the graded practice test is displayed on your screen, click Print on the File menu to print a hard copy. Continue to take practice tests until you score 80% or better.

4 Who Wants To Be a Computer Genius?

Below HTML Project 2, click the Computer Genius link. Read the instructions, enter your first and last name at the bottom of the page, and then click the PLAY button. When your score is displayed, click the PRINT RESULTS link to print a hard copy.

5 Wheel of Terms

Below HTML Project 2, click the Wheel of Terms link. Read the instructions, and then enter your first and last name and your school name. Click the PLAY button. When your score is displayed, right-click the score and then click Print on the shortcut menu to print a hard copy.

6 Crossword Puzzle Challenge

Below HTML Project 2, click the Crossword Puzzle Challenge link. Read the instructions, and then enter your first and last name. Click the SUBMIT button. Work the crossword puzzle. When you are finished, click the Submit button. When the crossword puzzle is redisplayed, click the Print Puzzle button to print a hard copy.

7 Tips and Tricks

Below HTML Project 2, click the Tips and Tricks link. Click a topic that pertains to Project 2. Right-click the information and then click Print on the shortcut menu. Construct a brief example of what the information relates to in HTML to confirm you understand how to use the tip or trick.

8 Newsgroups

Below HTML Project 2, click the Newsgroups link. Click a topic that pertains to Project 2. Print three comments.

9 Expanding Your Horizons

Below HTML Project 2, click the Expanding Your Horizons link. Click a topic that pertains to Project 2. Print the information. Construct a brief example of what the information relates to in HTML to confirm you understand the contents of the article.

10 Search Sleuth

Below HTML Project 2, click the Search Sleuth link. To search for a term that pertains to this project, select a term below the Project 2 title and then use the Google search engine at google.com (or any major search engine) to display and print two Web pages that present information on the term.

11 Online Help I

Below HTML Project 2, click the Online Help I link. Follow the instructions on the page to access Web pages that provide additional help on project topics. Hand in any printed information to your instructor.

12 Online Help II

Below HTML Project 2, click the Online Help II link. Follow the instructions on the page to access Web pages that provide additional help on project topics. Hand in any printed information to your instructor.

Apply Your Knowledge

1 Editing the Apply Your Knowledge Web Page

Instructions: Start Notepad. Open the file, apply2-1.htm, from the Project02\AYK folder on the HTML Data Disk. If you did not download the HTML Data Disk, see the inside back cover for instructions or see your instructor. The apply2-1.htm file is a partially completed HTML file that contains some errors. Figure 2-37 shows the Apply Your Knowledge Web page as it should be displayed in a browser after the errors are corrected.

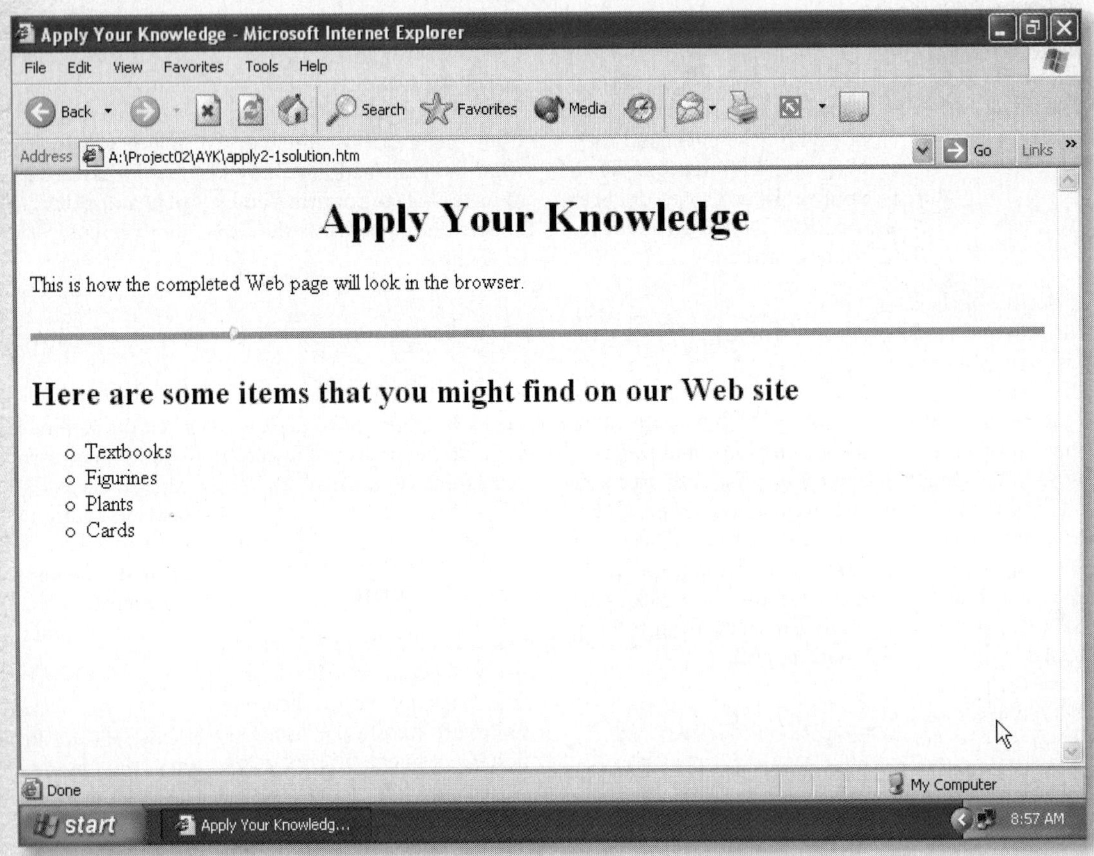

FIGURE 2-37

Perform the following steps using a computer:

1. Enter `a:\Project02\AYK\apply2-1.htm` as the URL to view the Web page in your browser.
2. Examine the HTML file and its appearance in the browser.
3. Use Notepad to open the file, `apply2-1.htm`, from the Project02\AYK folder on the HTML Data Disk. Correct the HTML errors, making the Web page look similar to the one shown in Figure 2-37.
4. Add any HTML code necessary for additional features shown in the Web page.
5. Save the revised HTML file in the Project02\AYK folder on the HTML Data Disk using the file name apply2-1solution.htm.
6. Print the revised HTML file.
7. Enter `a:\Project02\AYK\apply2-1solution.htm` as the URL to view the revised Web page in your browser.
8. Print the Web page.
9. Write your name on both printouts and hand them in to your instructor.

In the Lab

1 Creating a Personal Web Page

Problem: Your instructor would like to create a Web page that lists key Internet concepts and make the Web page available on the World Wide Web. You have been asked to create a Web page to display this information, similar to the one shown in Figure 2-38.

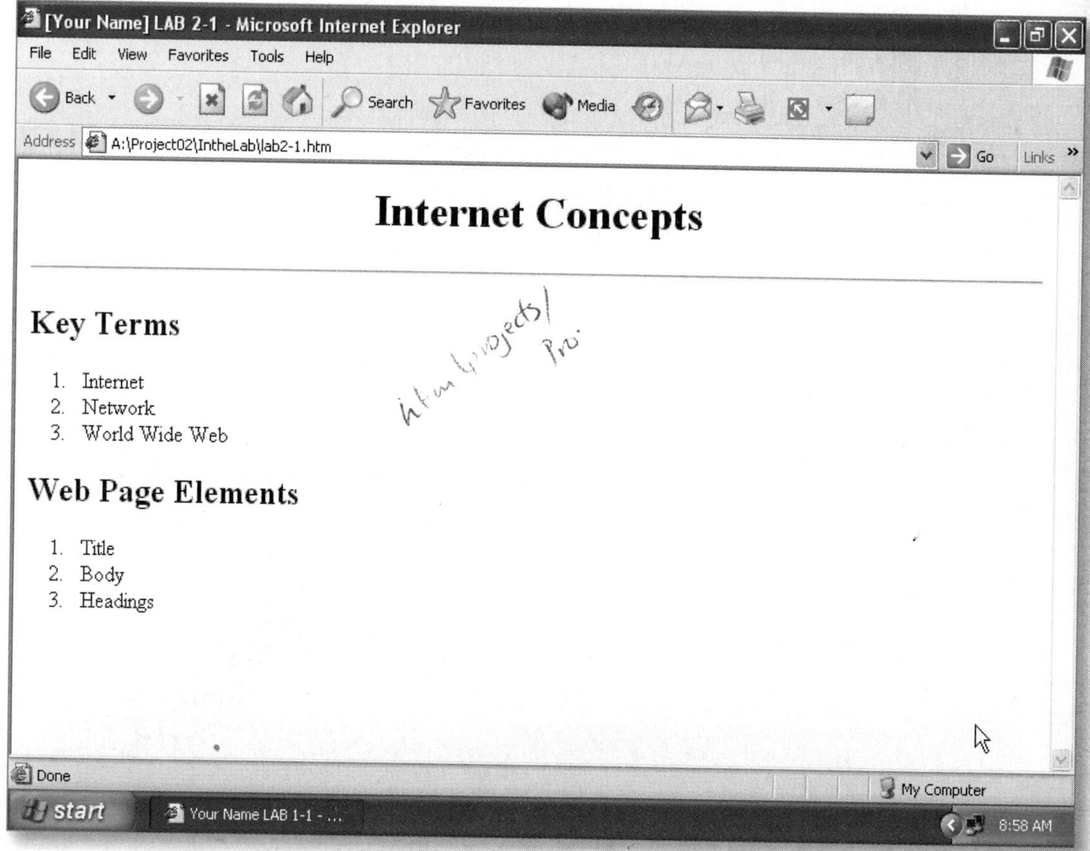

FIGURE 2-38

Instructions: Start Notepad. Perform the following steps using a computer:

1. Start a new HTML file with the title, [Your Name] LAB2-1, in the main heading section.
2. Begin the body section by adding the heading, Internet Concepts. Format the heading to use the Heading 1 style and be centered on the Web page.
3. Add a horizontal rule below the Internet Concepts heading.
4. Add two headings, Key Terms and Web Page Elements, using the Heading 2 style.
5. Add two ordered lists of topics as shown in Figure 2-38.
6. Save the HTML file in the Project02\IntheLab folder on the HTML Data Disk using the file name lab2-1.htm.
7. Print the lab2-1.htm file.
8. Enter `a:\Project02\IntheLab\lab2-1.htm` as the URL to view the Web page in your browser.
9. Print the Web page.
10. Write your name on the printouts and hand them in to your instructor.

2 Creating an Information Web Page

Problem: You are the president of the academic honor society, Phi Kappa Phi, and decide to prepare a Web page announcement, such as the one shown in Figure 2-39, to share the club's history and to invite new members to join the club.

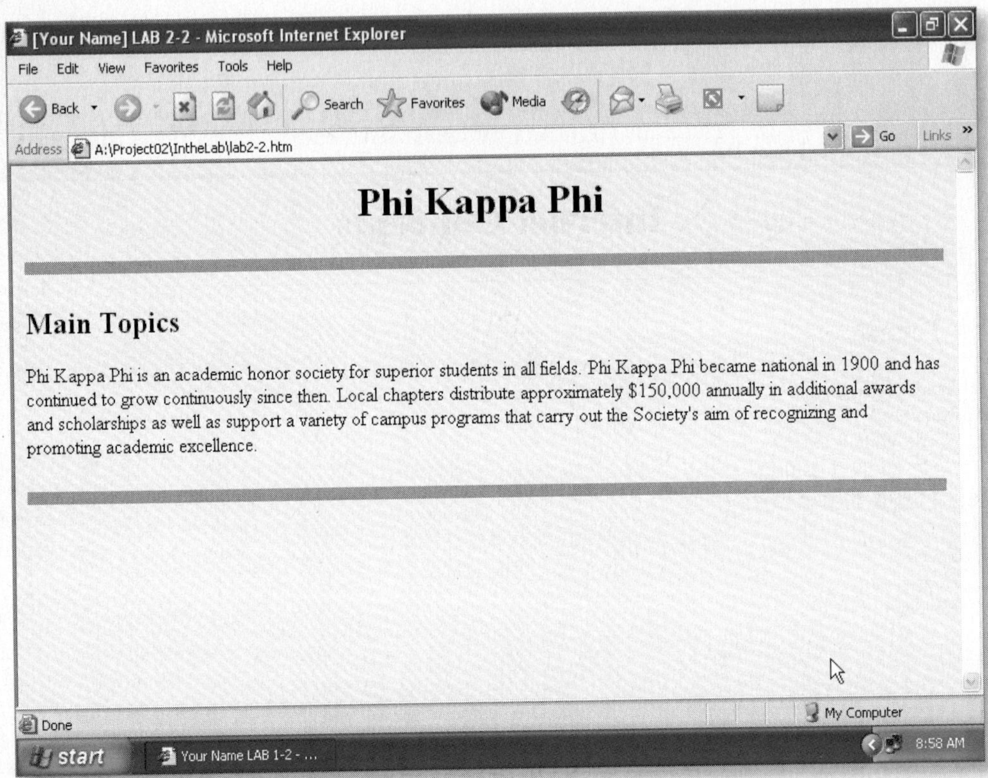

FIGURE 2-39

Instructions: Start Notepad. Perform the following steps using a computer:

1. Start a new HTML file with the title [Your Name] LAB2-2 in the main heading section.
2. Add a colored background to the Web page using the #ffffcc color code.
3. Begin the body section by adding the heading, Phi Kappa Phi. Format the heading to use the Heading 1 style and be center-aligned on the Web page.
4. Add a size 10 horizontal rule with noshade below the heading.
5. Add a heading, Main Topics, using a left-aligned Heading 2 style.
6. Add a paragraph of text, as shown in Figure 2-39.
7. Add a size 10 horizontal rule with noshade below the paragraph.
8. Save the HTML file in the Project02\IntheLab folder on the HTML Data Disk using the file name lab2-2.htm.
9. Print the lab2-2.htm file.
10. Enter `a:\Project02\IntheLab\lab2-2.htm` as the URL to view the Web page in your browser.
11. Print the Web page.
12. Write your name on the printouts and hand them in to your instructor.

3 Composing a Personal Web Page

Problem: Your manager at Student Services asked you to create a personal Web page to tell people about yourself, your experience tutoring students, and why you think using the Campus Tutoring Service can be beneficial for students. You plan to use paragraphs of text and a bulleted list, as shown in Figure 2-40.

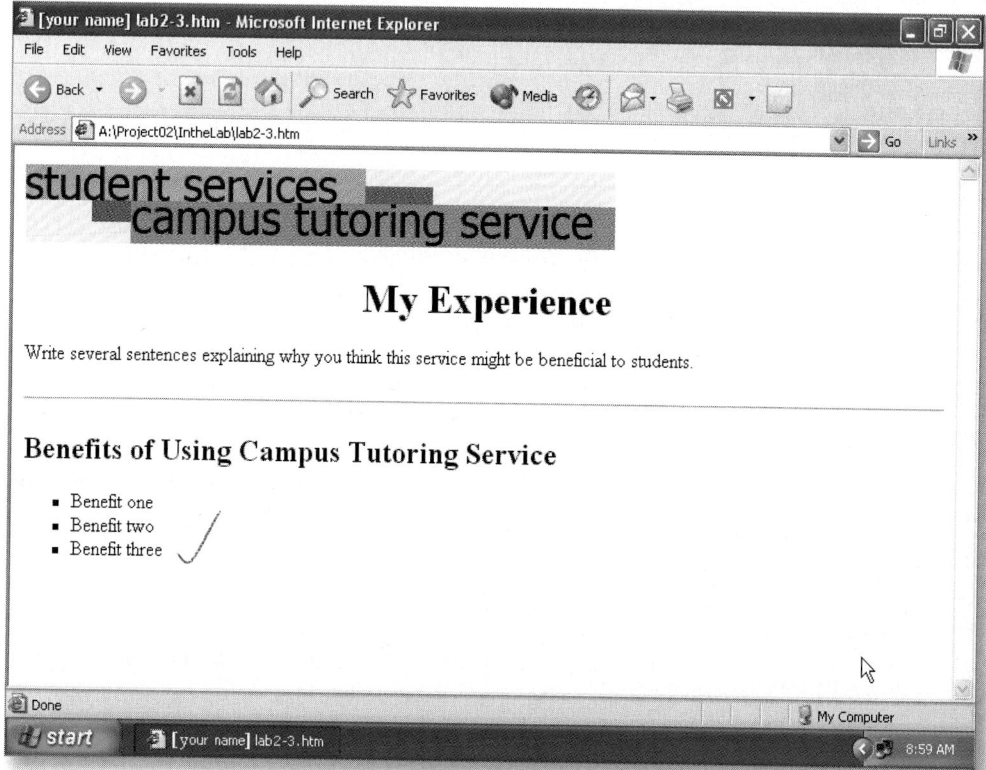

FIGURE 2-40

Instructions: Start Notepad. Perform the following steps using a computer:

1. Start a new HTML file with the title [your name] lab2-3 in the main heading section.
2. Include a short paragraph of information and a bulleted list, using a format similar to the one shown in Figure 2-40, to provide information about your tutoring experience.
3. Save the HTML file in the Project02\IntheLab folder on the HTML Data Disk using the file name lab2-3.htm.
4. Enter `a:\Project02\IntheLab\lab2-3.htm` as the URL to view the Web page in your browser.
5. Print the Web page from your browser.
6. Write your name on the printout and hand it in to your instructor.

Cases and Places

The difficulty of these case studies varies:
■ are the least difficult and ■■ are the most difficult. The last exercise is a group exercise.

1 ■ Dr. Meyers likes the Campus Tutoring Service Web page created in Project 2. Now that the Campus Tutoring Service is open, she would like you to update it with new information on available tutors and hours of availability. Before updating the page, search the Web to review the student services and tutoring services Web pages at other schools and universities for ideas on content to include or formatting to change. What do their Web sites look like? Are there changes you can make to the Project 2 Web page that reflect what other schools have done? Using the concepts presented in this project, include additional information or change the formatting to make the page more interesting and timely.

2 ■ Your class instructor wants to post all of the students' Web pages on the school server to show what her students have learned in class. Create a Web page of personal information, listing items such as your school major, jobs that you have had in the past, and your hobbies and interests. In order to make your personal Web page more visually interesting, search the Web for images that reflect your interests (be sure that the image is not copyrighted or you cannot use it on a personal Web page). Insert an image or two onto the Web page to help explain who you are.

3 ■■ As an instructor at NewCourses training, you often update your Web site with information to help students in your classes. For an upcoming HTML class, you have decided to create a Web page with a definition list of HTML tags and their usage. Using the concepts presented in this project, use Notepad to create a Web page with the information listed in Table 2-1 on page HTM 37. Add the heading, HTML Tags and Their Functions, at the top of the page. Use the HTML tag as the term (<dt>) and function as the definition of the term (<dd>).

4 ■■ You are creating a new Web site for a local KidDayz childcare center. The director of the center has asked that you use descriptive alt attributes for images on the Web page, as the parents of many of the children have very slow Internet connections and images often do not load quickly. Search the Web for information on adding useful, descriptive alt attributes for images. Create a document with a brief paragraph explaining the various purposes of alt attributes. Include three examples of good, descriptive alt attributes and three examples of less descriptive alt attributes.

5 ■■ **Working Together** You are part of a Web usability team for Axcelent, a local Web design firm. As part of a new project on the use of color on the Web, your team is doing research on which background colors are more appealing to users. Search the Web for information about browser-safe colors on the Web. Create three Web pages with the same information but vary the background color. Be sure to save each different page as a different file name. Show those pages to some friends or family members to have them evaluate which color of background they like and explain why they prefer one color to another. View these three Web pages on different computers used by members of the team. Do the colors look different? Why do you think they would? What factors contribute to the way in which a colored background would be displayed?

HTML

Creating Web Pages with Links, Images, and Formatted Text

PROJECT 3

CASE PERSPECTIVE

Plant World is a local nursery that specializes in landscape design and the sale of indoor and outdoor plants at its 38 New England store locations. You want to advance your current company position by using the knowledge you gained from recently finishing an HTML course. You can envision developing Web pages that advertise the company to current and prospective customers and help promote specific types of plants, by providing information on planting and seasonal care.

You know that, once you have some sample Web pages to show your boss, Jared Smith, you will be able to convince him that this idea will offer the company Internet exposure and a marketing presence on the Web. With this in mind, you develop two Web pages using HTML. The first Web page includes information about Plant World, a link to a second Web page, and an e-mail link to the company e-mail address. The second Web page includes information on several different types of plants, as well as a link to a Web page with additional information. Because it is long, you also used links within the second Web page to make it easier to navigate. After these Web pages are completed, you plan to take them to Jared to explain your idea.

In this project, you will learn how to use Notepad to create, save, and print an HTML file to create a Web page, as well as to open and edit an existing HTML file. You also will learn how to use different types of links, including an e-mail link, a text link and an image link to a second Web page, internal links to navigate within a single Web page, and an external link to a different Web site. Finally, you will learn to add a background image, wrap text around an image, and format text using bold, italic, and colored fonts.

HTML

Creating Web Pages with Links, Images, and Formatted Text

PROJECT 3

Objectives

You will have mastered the material in this project when you can:

- Describe linking terms and definitions
- Create a home page and enhance a Web page using images
- Align and add bold, italics, and color to text
- Change the bullet type used in an unordered list
- Add a background image
- Add a text link to a Web page in the same Web site
- Add an e-mail link
- View the HTML file and test the links
- Open an HTML file
- Add an image with wrapped text
- Add a text link to a Web page on another Web site
- Add links to targets within a Web page
- Copy and paste HTML code
- Add an image link to a Web page in the same Web site

Introduction

As you have learned, hyperlinks, or links, are an essential part of the World Wide Web, allowing developers to connect one Web page to another Web page on the same, or a different, Web server located anywhere in the world. Using hyperlinks, a Web site visitor can move from one page to another, to view information in any order. Many different Web page elements, including text, graphics, and animations, can serve as hyperlinks.

In this project, you will learn how to create Web pages using the following types of links:

- text and image links to another Web page in the same Web site
- text links to another Web page in a different Web site
- text links within a Web page
- e-mail links

You also will learn to add a background image and bulleted (unordered) lists to a Web page. After learning how to open an existing HTML file in Notepad, you will learn to write HTML code to insert and wrap text around an image and to format text using bold, italics, and colored fonts. Finally, you will learn to view the Web pages, test the links, and then print the HTML code and the Web page.

Project Three — Plant World Web Site

Project 3 illustrates how to use HTML to create a home page for the Plant World Web site (Figure 3-1a) and to edit the existing Desert Plants Web page (Figure 3-1b) to improve the appearance and function. The Plant World home page, which displays information about Plant World and its services, includes a logo image, headings, two unordered (bulleted) lists, an e-mail link, and a link to the Desert Plants Web page. The Desert Plants Web page contains images with text wrapped around them and internal links that allow visitors to move easily from section to section within the Web page. This page also includes a text link to a Web page on another Web site and an image link back to Plant World's home page. The basic HTML for the Desert Plants Web page is included on the HTML Data Disk.

image link back to home page

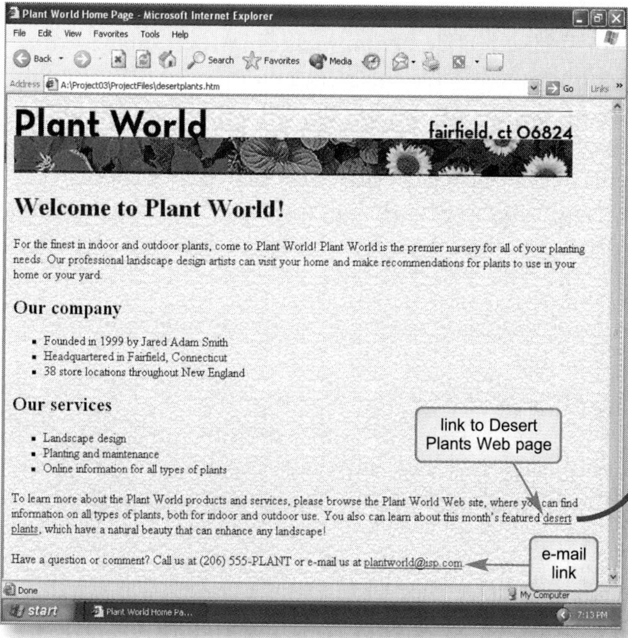

(a) Plant World home page.

(c) Linked Web page in external Web site.

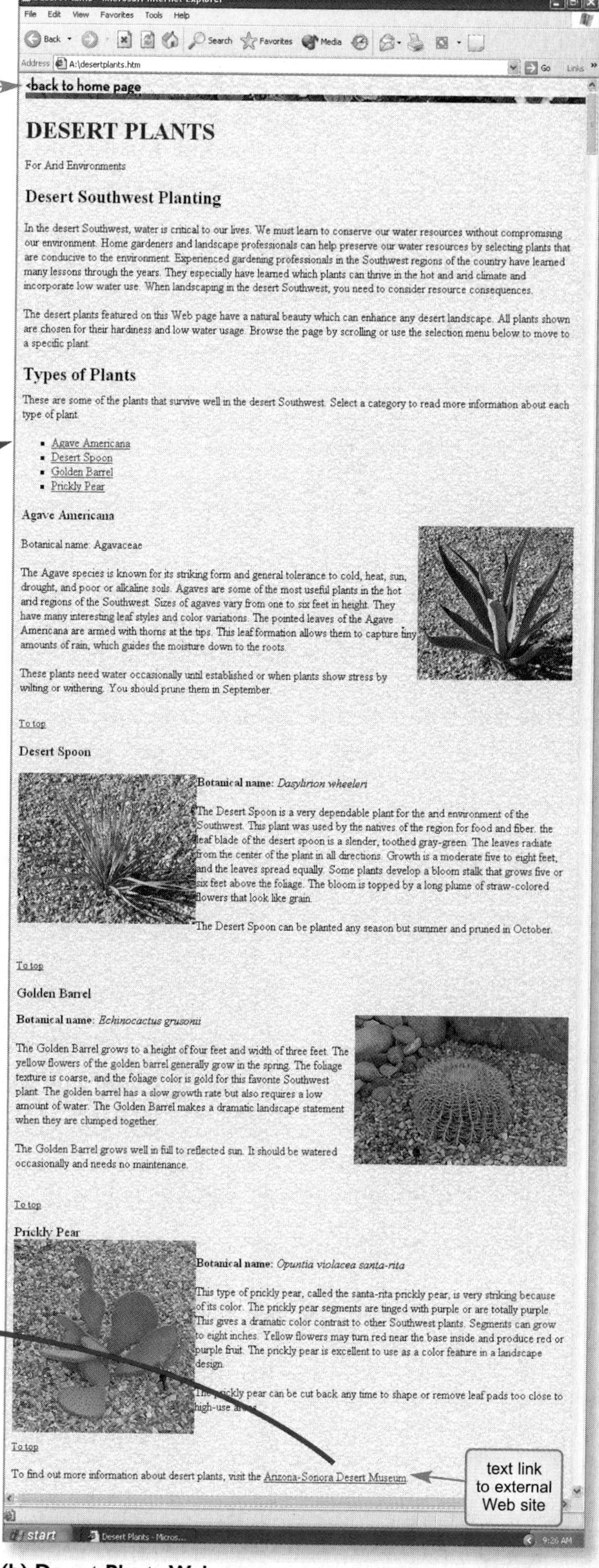

(b) Desert Plants Web page.

FIGURE 3-1

Starting Notepad

The first step in creating a home page for the Plant World Web site is to start Notepad. The following steps show how to start Notepad and maximize the window.

To Start Notepad

1. **Click the Start button on the taskbar and then point to All Programs on the Start menu.**
2. **Point to Accessories on the All Programs submenu and then point to Notepad on the Accessories submenu.**
3. **Click Notepad.**
4. **If the Notepad window is not maximized, click the Maximize button on the Notepad title bar to maximize it.**
5. **Click Format on the menu bar.**
6. **If Word Wrap is not checked, click Word Wrap.**

The Notepad window is displayed and Word Wrap is enabled.

> *More About*
>
> **Link Help**
>
> Many World Wide Web sites provide help for new HTML developers. For more information about links, visit the HTML More About Web page (scsite.com/html3e/more.htm) and then click Link Help.

Using Links on a Web Page

As you have learned, many different Web page elements, including text, images, and animations, can serve as links. Text and images are the elements most widely used as links. Figure 3-2 shows an example of a text link, and Figure 3-3 shows an example of an image link. Generally, moving the mouse pointer over a link causes the mouse pointer to change to a pointing hand. This change notifies the user that a link is available from that text or image. As shown in Figure 3-2, moving the mouse pointer over a link also displays the URL of the linked page, document, or other file on the status bar of the browser.

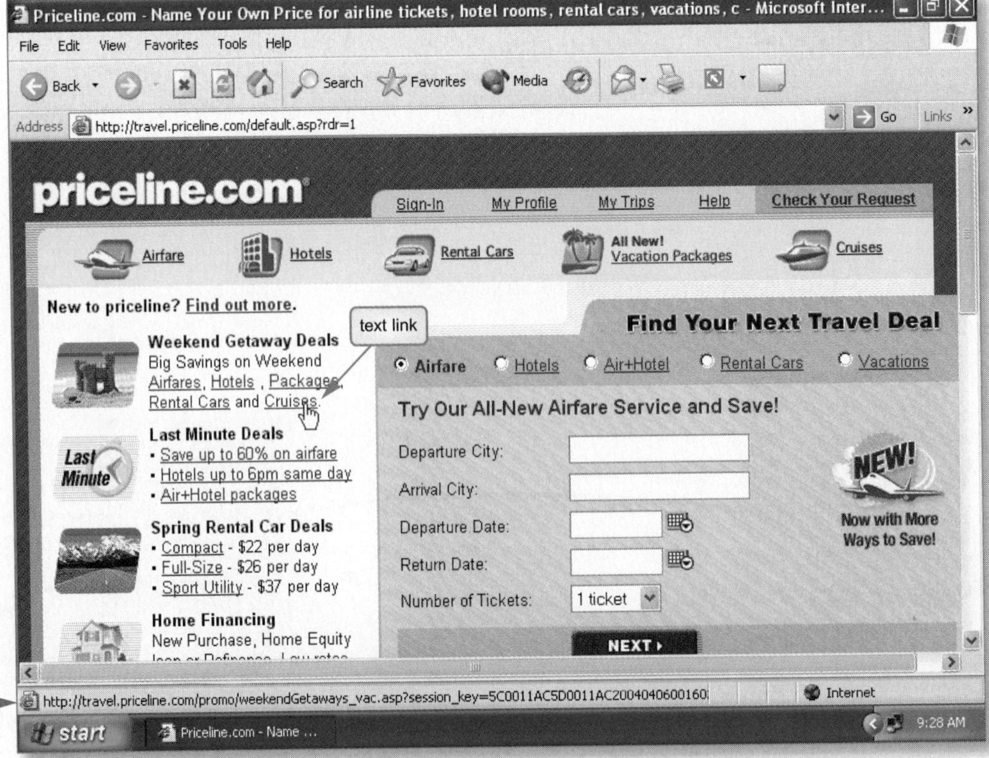

FIGURE 3-2 Text link on Web page.

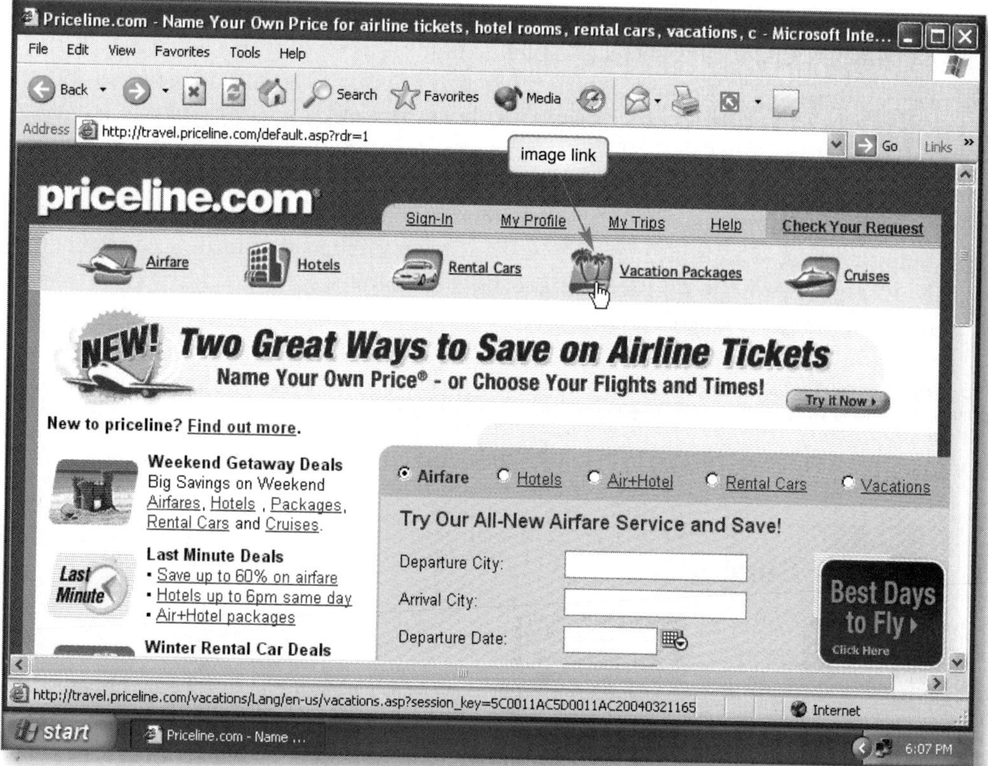

FIGURE 3-3 Image link on Web page.

When using text links on a Web page, use descriptive text as the clickable word or phrase. For example, the phrase, Click here, does not explain the purpose of the link to the visitor. By contrast, the phrase, Save up to 60% on airfare, indicates that the link connects to a Web page with discounted airline tickets. As shown in Figure 3-2, when text identifies a link, it often appears as underlined text, in a color different from the rest of the Web page text.

Unless otherwise coded in the <body> tag, the browser settings define the colors of text links throughout a Web page. For example, with Internet Explorer, the default color for a normal link that has not been clicked (or visited) is blue, a visited link is purple, and an active link (a link just clicked by a user) is green. Figure 3-4 shows examples of text links in all three states (normal, visited, and active).

More About

Linking Colors

You can change the link colors in popular browsers. In Microsoft Internet Explorer, you find color selection on the Tools menu using Internet Options. In Netscape Communicator, click Preferences on the Edit menu. In both products, you change colors by clicking the color bars.

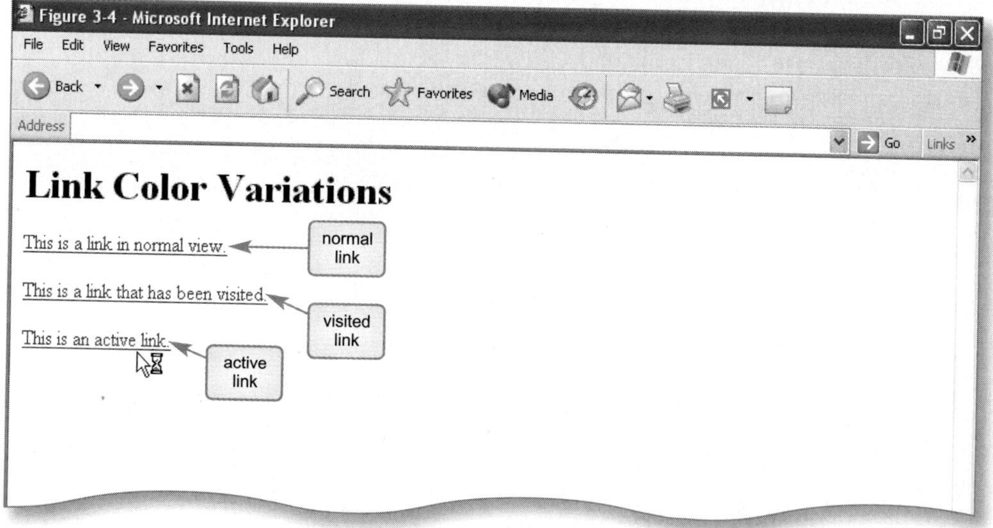

FIGURE 3-4 Examples of text link color variations.

The same color defaults apply to the border color around an image link. A border makes the image display as if it has a frame around it, as shown in Figure 3-5. If the image has no border, no color will display around the image. If the image has a border but is not used as a link, the border displays in black, as shown in the left image in Figure 3-5. If the image is used as a link, the default link colors display as the image border when the link is normal, active, or visited. The center image in Figure 3-5 shows an image with a border, which is used as a link. The link displays in the default color, which indicates it has not been clicked (visited). The image on the right in Figure 3-5 shows the changed border color after the link has been visited, giving the image an entirely different look.

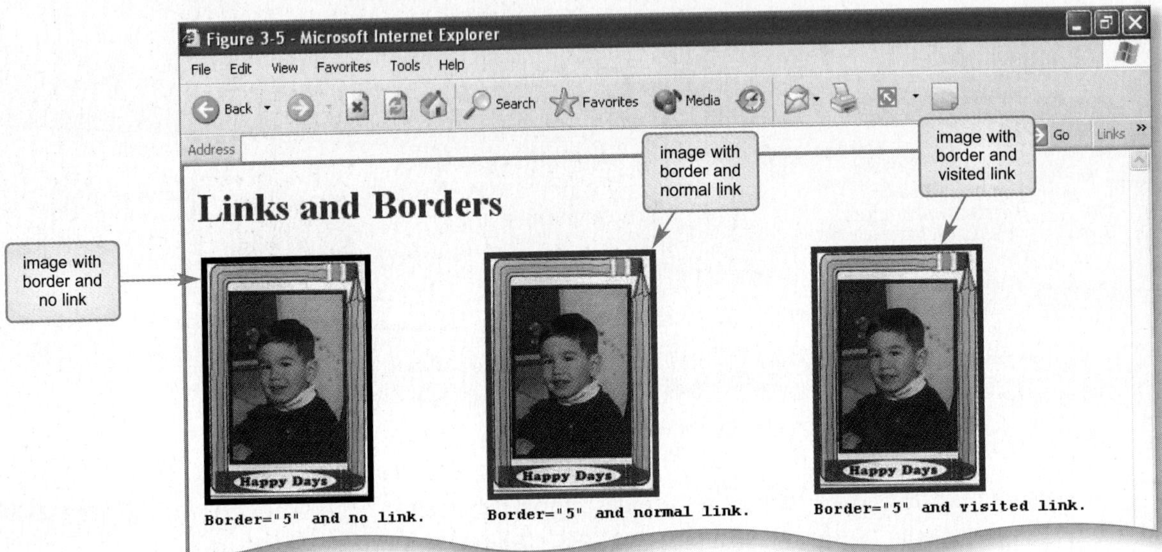

FIGURE 3-5 Examples of image border and link color variations.

If you want to change the colors of text links or image link borders to override the browser defaults, you must enter attributes and values in the <body> tag. The format of the tag used to change normal, visited, and active link colors from the default is

```
<body link="color" vlink="color" alink="color">
```

where color is a designated color code, such as #6633CC. Table 3-1 lists the link color attributes that can be specified in the <body> tag.

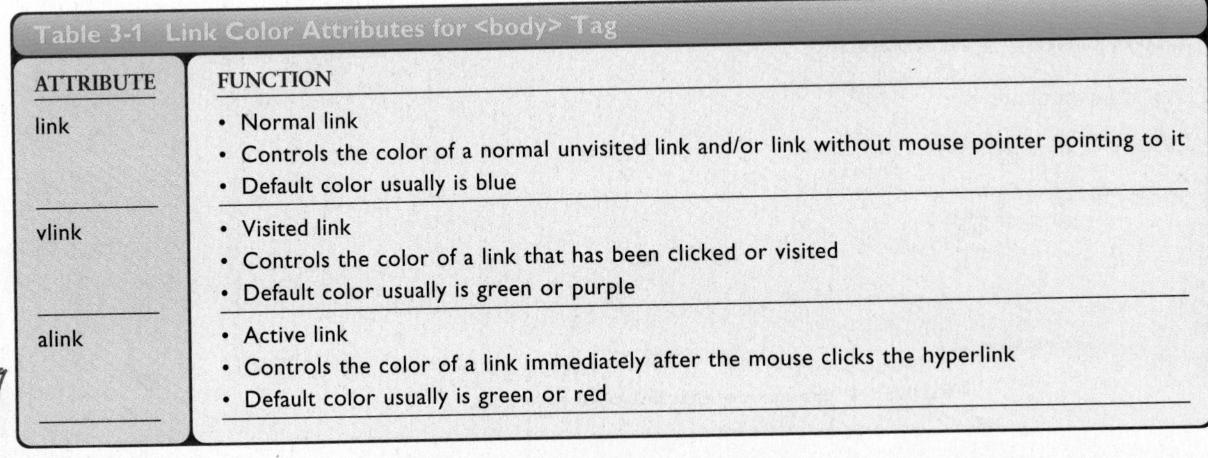

Table 3-1 Link Color Attributes for <body> Tag

ATTRIBUTE	FUNCTION
link	• Normal link • Controls the color of a normal unvisited link and/or link without mouse pointer pointing to it • Default color usually is blue
vlink	• Visited link • Controls the color of a link that has been clicked or visited • Default color usually is green or purple
alink	• Active link • Controls the color of a link immediately after the mouse clicks the hyperlink • Default color usually is green or red

Linking to Another Web Page within the Same Web Site

Web pages often include links to connect one Web page to another page within the same Web site. For example, a visitor can click a link on the home page of a Web site (Figure 3-6a) to connect and view another Web page on the same Web site (Figure 3-6b). Links between pages on a Web site allow visitors to move from one Web page to another, in a Web site with multiple pages. The Web pages created in this project include links to other pages in the same Web site: (1) the Plant World home page includes a text link to the Desert Plants Web page and (2) the Desert Plants Web page includes an image link to the Plant World home page.

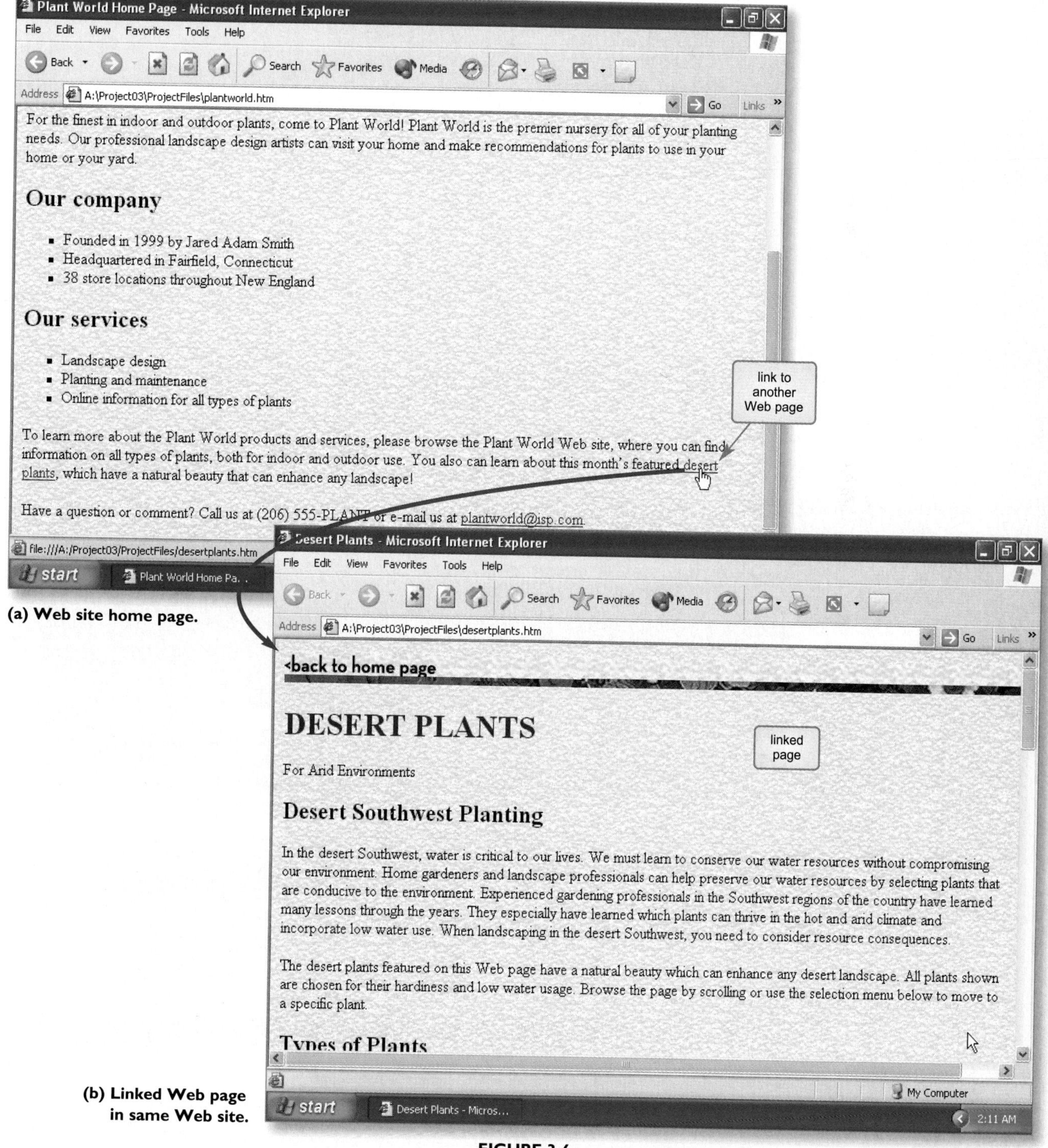

(a) Web site home page.

(b) Linked Web page in same Web site.

FIGURE 3-6

Linking to a Web Page in Another Web Site

A very important feature of the Web is the capability of linking a Web page on one Web site to a Web page on another external Web site. Web developers use these links to connect their Web pages to other Web pages with information on the same topic. In this project, the Desert Plants Web page (Figure 3-7a) includes a link to a page on another Web site, where the visitor can find additional desert plant information. (Figure 3-7b).

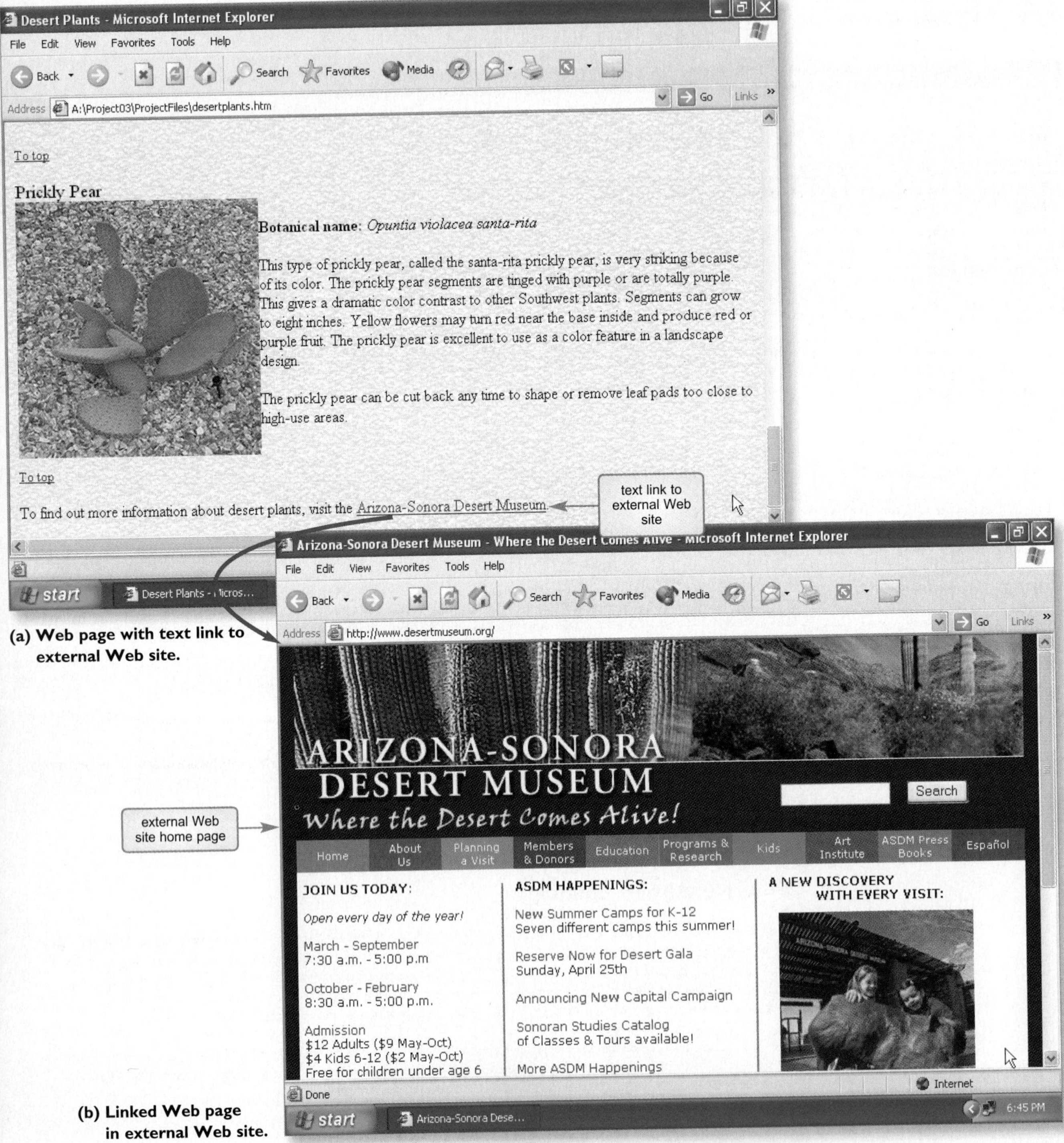

(a) Web page with text link to external Web site.

(b) Linked Web page in external Web site.

FIGURE 3-7

Linking within a Web Page

Links within a Web page allow visitors to move quickly from one section of the Web page to another. This is especially important in Web pages that are long and require a visitor to scroll down to see all of the content. By including links within a Web page, a visitor can click a link to move directly to a section of interest, rather than scrolling through the entire Web page. Many Web pages contain a list of links like a menu or table of contents at the top of the page, with links to sections within the Web page (Figure 3-8). In this project, the Desert Plants Web page includes links from the top section of the Web page to other sections within the page, as well as links back to the top of the Web page.

> *More About*
>
> **Links on a Web Page**
>
> An anchor tag also allows visitors to move within a single Web page. Use the name attribute to allow movement from one area to another on the same page. This linking technique is useful particularly on long pages. An index of links also can provide easy access to various areas within the Web page.

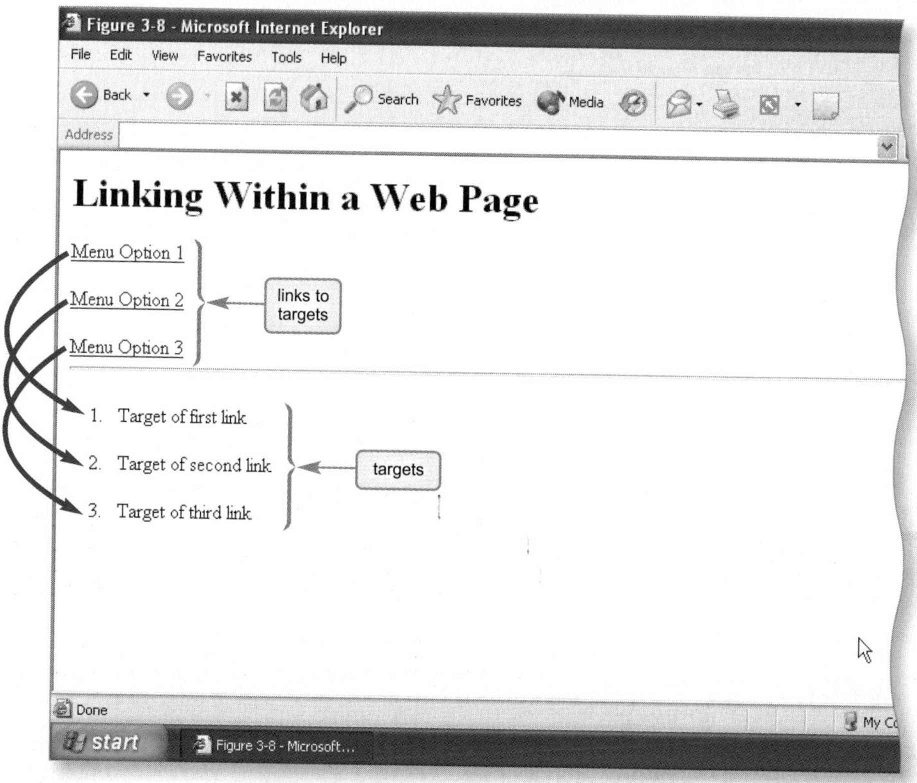

FIGURE 3-8 Web page with internal links.

Linking to an E-Mail Address

A well-designed Web page always provides a way for visitors to contact the person at the company responsible for maintaining the Web site or addressing customer questions and comments. An easy way to provide contact information is to include an e-mail link on the Web site's home page, as well as on other pages in the Web site. As shown in Figure 3-9 on the next page, when a visitor clicks the **e-mail link**, it automatically opens a new message in the default e-mail program and inserts the appropriate contact e-mail address in the To field. Visitors then can type and send an e-mail to request additional information, comment on the Web site, or notify the company of a problem with its Web site.

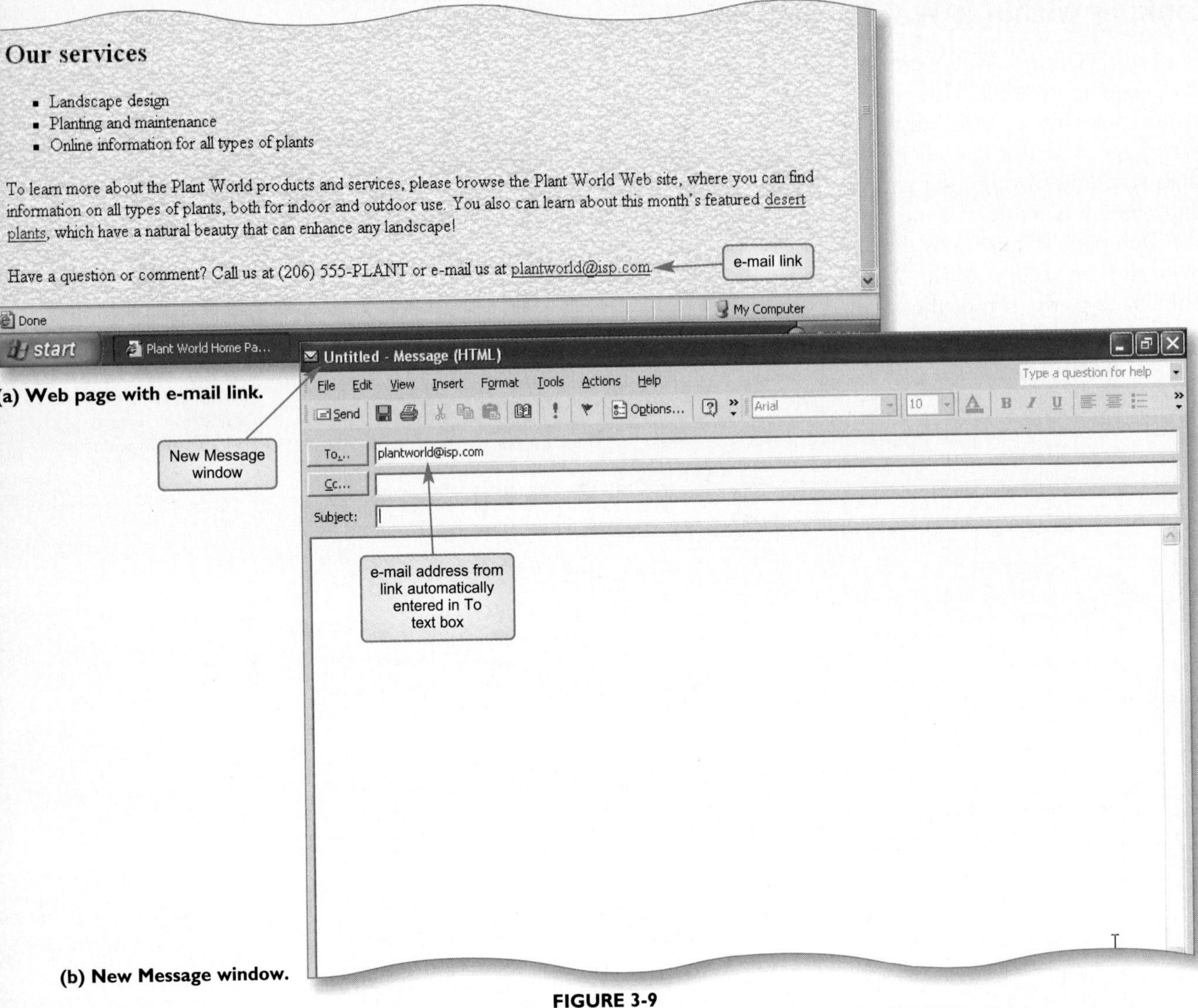

(a) Web page with e-mail link.

(b) New Message window.

FIGURE 3-9

Creating a Home Page

The first Web page developed in this project is the home page of the Plant World Web site. A home page is the main page of a Web site, which visitors to a Web site generally will view first. A Web site home page should identify the purpose of the Web site, by briefly stating what content, services, or features it provides. The home page also should indicate clearly what links the visitor should click to move from one Web page on the Web site to another. A Web developer should design the Web site in such a way that the links from one Web page to another are apparent and the navigation is clear. The Web site home page also should include an e-mail link, so visitors easily can find contact information for the individual or organization.

Entering HTML Tags to Define the Web Page Structure

As you have learned, every HTML file includes HTML tags that define the overall structure of a standard Web page and divide the HTML file into its basic sections. The following steps show how to enter the HTML tags that define the structure of the Plant World home page.

To Enter HTML Tags to Define the Web Page Structure

1. **Type** `<!DOCTYPE html` **and then press the ENTER key.**
2. **Press the SPACEBAR three times, type** `PUBLIC "-//W3C//DTD XHTML 1.0 Transitional//EN"` **as the entry, and then press the ENTER key.**
3. **Press the SPACEBAR three times, type** `"http://www.w3.org/TR/xhtml1/DTD/xhtml1-transitional.dtd">` **as the entry, and then press the ENTER key twice.**
4. **Type** `<html>` **and then press the ENTER key.**
5. **Type** `<head>` **and then press the ENTER key.**
6. **Type** `<title>Plant World Home Page</title>` **and then press the ENTER key.**
7. **Type** `</head>` **and then press the ENTER key.**
8. **Type** `<body>` **and then press the ENTER key twice.**
9. **Type** `</body>` **and then press the ENTER key.**
10. **Type** `</html>` **as the final tag.**
11. **Position the insertion on the blank line (line 10) between the <body> and </body> tags.**

The HTML code is displayed (Figure 3-10).

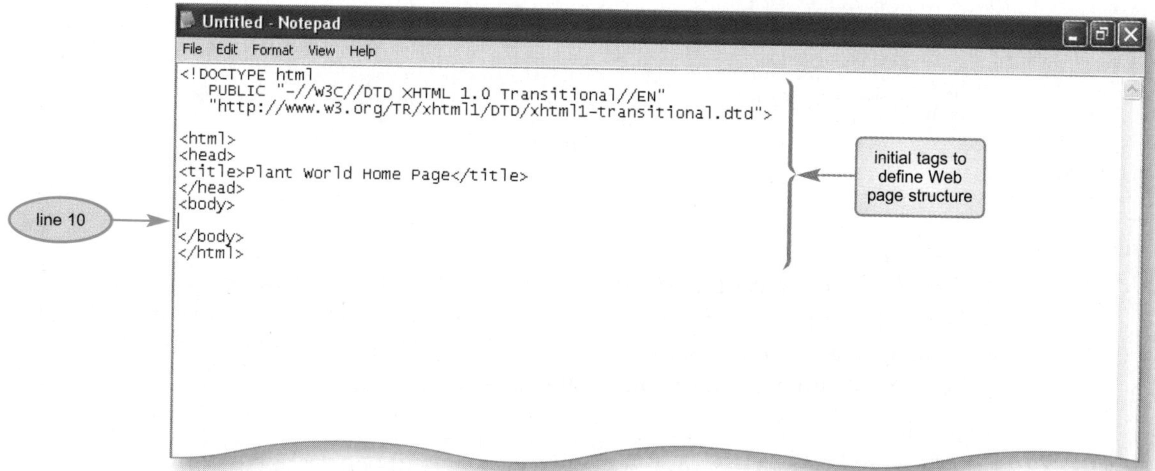

FIGURE 3-10

Adding an Image

Many Web developers utilize images to enhance the look of a Web page. In this project, the Plant World home page includes an image logo to provide visual appeal, catch the visitor's interest, and promote the company's brand. The logo image contains the name of the company and the city, state, and zip information. Often, a logo image on a company's Web site is the same image that is printed on company stationary, cards, and other promotional material distributed by the company. Using the same graphical image on all marketing materials, including the Web site, is a good way to provide a consistent visual and brand message to customers, so they connect your Web site with your product, signage, direct mail pieces, and so on.

As introduced in Project 2, the HTML tag used to include an image in a Web page also should include the width, height, and alt attributes. Identifying the width and height attributes can improve page loading time, because the browser does not have to determine the width and height of the image. The alt attribute displays as the Web page is loading and when a user moves the mouse over the image to provide additional information on the purpose of the image.

The following step illustrates how to add an image to a Web page by entering an <img> tag in the HTML file. The image file is stored on the HTML Data Disk. See the inside back cover for instructions for downloading the HTML Data Disk, or see your instructor.

To Add an Image

1

- **Type** `<img src="plantworldlg.jpg" width="720" height="84" alt="Plant World logo" />` **and then press the ENTER key.**

The HTML code inserts an image with the file name, plantworldlg.jpg (Figure 3-11).

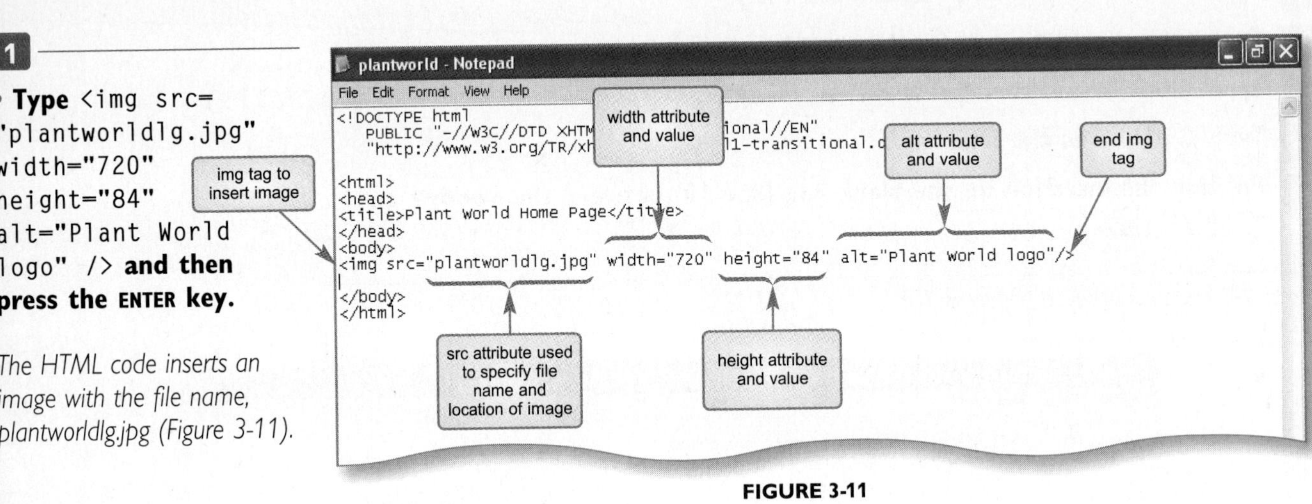

FIGURE 3-11

The attributes specified for the image indicate that the image is 720 pixels wide by 84 pixels high and will display the text, Plant World logo, when the mouse points to the image. Because the logo image uses photo elements, it is added as a JPEG image, which supports more colors and resolutions than GIF or PNG images.

Adding a Left-Aligned Heading with a Font Color

As discussed in Project 2, the <h1> tag assigns the largest possible size to a heading. Using the align attribute of the heading tag, you can specify left-, right-, or center-alignment with the statements align="left", align ="right", or align ="center". By default, headings are left-aligned, which means that, if an alignment is not specified, the heading will be left-aligned. The design of the Plant World home page makes it appropriate to left-align the heading on the Web page. Because the heading will be left-aligned, you do not have to specify an align attribute and value in the <h1> tag.

Text can be formatted using different colors and styles to make it stand out further on a Web page. Any text on a Web page, including headings, can be formatted with a different color or style by using attributes of the <font> tag. Table 3-2 lists the different font attributes that can be used to enhance standard text on a Web page.

Table 3-2 Font Attributes and Values

ATTRIBUTE AND VALUE	FUNCTION
color="#xxxxxx"	• Changes the font color • Value inside quotation marks is a six-digit color code or color name
face="fontname"	• Changes the font face or type • Value inside quotation marks is the name of a font, such as Verdana or Arial; text appears using the default font if the font face is not specified
size="x"	• Changes the font size • Value inside quotation marks is a number that represents size • Values can be an actual font size of 1 (smallest) to 7 (largest) or a relative font size, such as +2 or -1, which specifies a number of sizes larger or smaller than the preset font size

Q&A

Q: What if a Web page uses a font visitors do not have on their computers?

A: If a Web page uses a font that Web page visitors do not have on their computers, the Web page appears using a default font (usually Times New Roman). If you want a heading with a specific font, create the heading as a graphic using the desired font.

Figure 3-12 lists several of these attributes and how they affect the text.

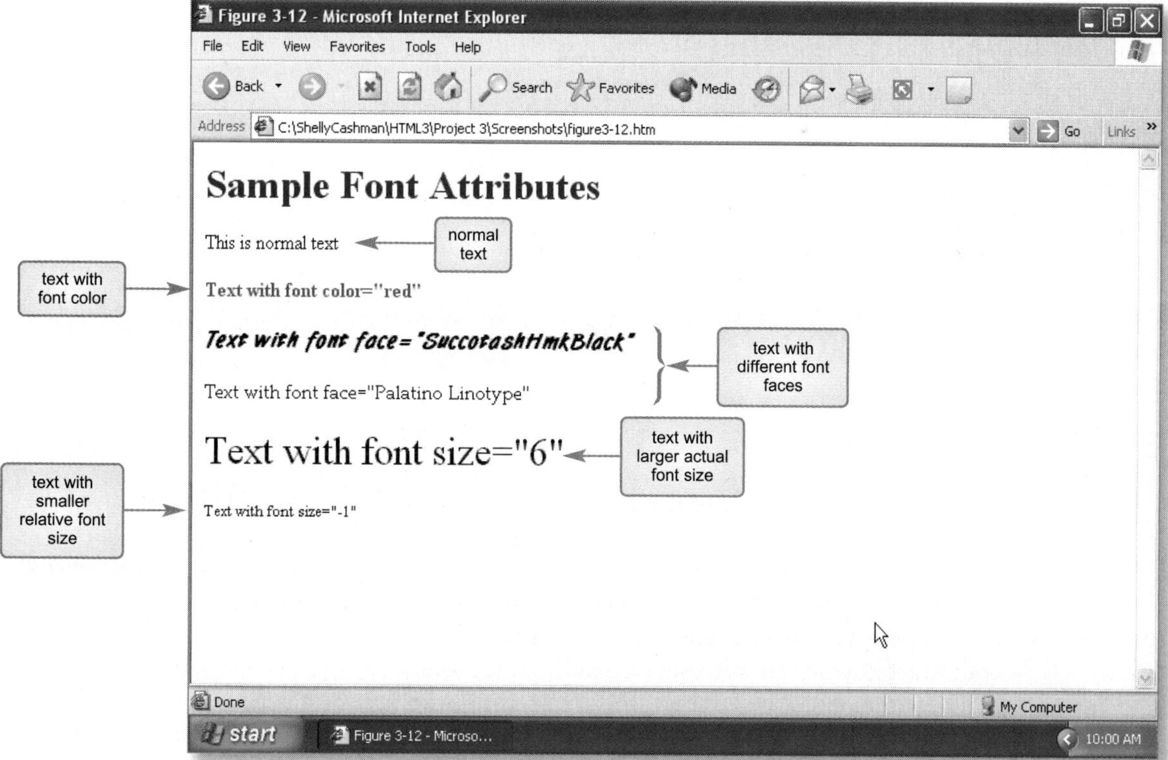

FIGURE 3-12 Examples of various font attributes.

The following step shows how to enter HTML code to add a left-aligned heading formatted in color to provide visual impact.

To Add a Left-Aligned Heading with a Font Color

1

• **With the insertion point on line 11, type `<h1><font color="#000066">Welcome to Plant World!</font></h1>` and then press the ENTER key.**

The HTML code for the heading is displayed (Figure 3-13). The color attribute uses a six-digit number code of #000066 to specify that the heading should appear in a navy blue color.

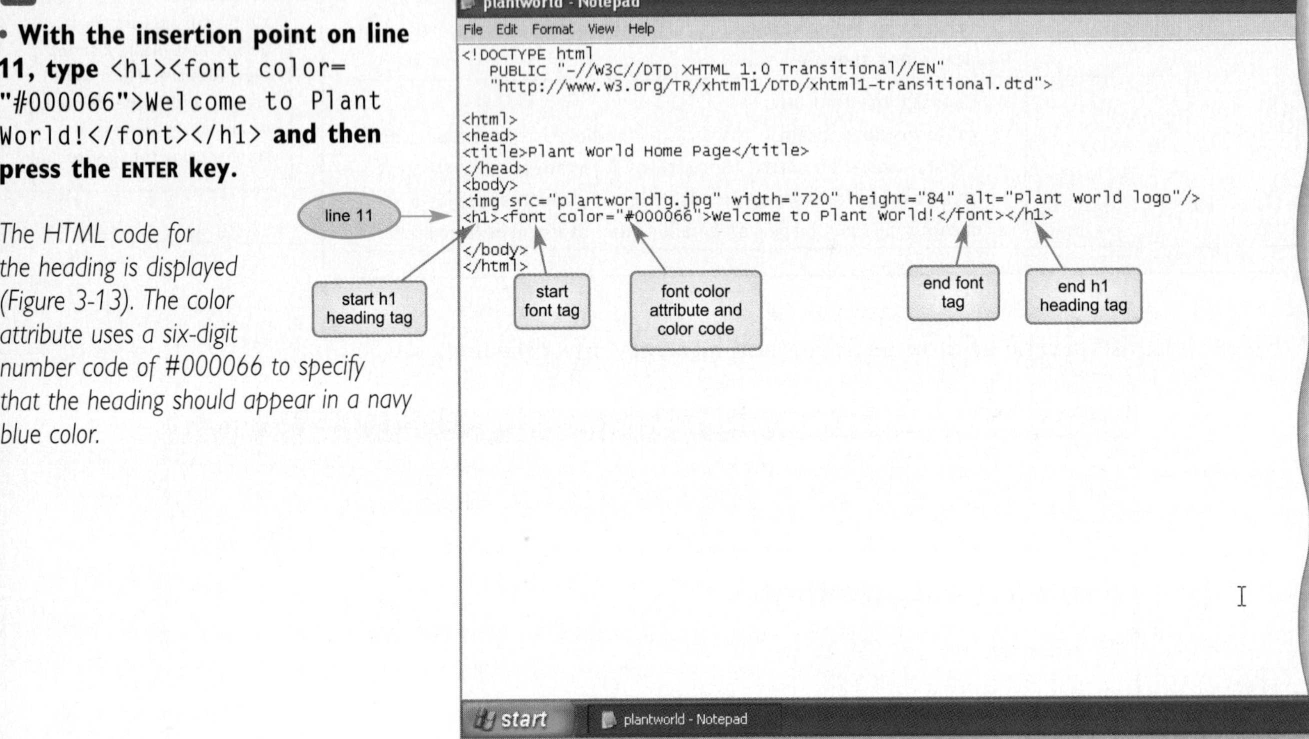

FIGURE 3-13

For additional color options, reference Figure 2-27 on page HTM 55 to see the list of possible color codes and names.

As discussed in Project 1, XHTML coding standards require that tags be nested properly. Nesting tags properly means that you always must enter end tags in an order opposite from the start tags. For example, as shown in Figure 3-13, the HTML code started with the start <h1> heading tag, followed by the start <font> tag. The end tags thus must be entered in the opposite order, with the end </font> tag first, followed by the end </h1> heading tag. This technique is similar to math equations.

More About

Font Sizes

The most frequently used font attribute is size. The values of font sizes range from 1 to 7, with 3 being the default. You also can specify the font size as a relative value using a + (plus) or – (minus) sign. These relative values range from –3 to +4.

Entering a Paragraph of Text

After the heading for the Plant World home page is entered, a paragraph of Web page text introducing Plant World can be entered. The following steps illustrate how to enter a paragraph of text in an HTML file.

To Enter a Paragraph of Text

1 **With the insertion point on line 12, type** `<p>For the finest in indoor and outdoor plants, come to Plant World! Plant World is the premier nursery for all of your planting needs. Our professional landscape design artists can visit your home and make recommendations for plants to use in your home or your yard.</p>` **as the first paragraph in the HTML file.**

2 **Press the ENTER key twice.**

The paragraph text is displayed in the HTML file (Figure 3-14).

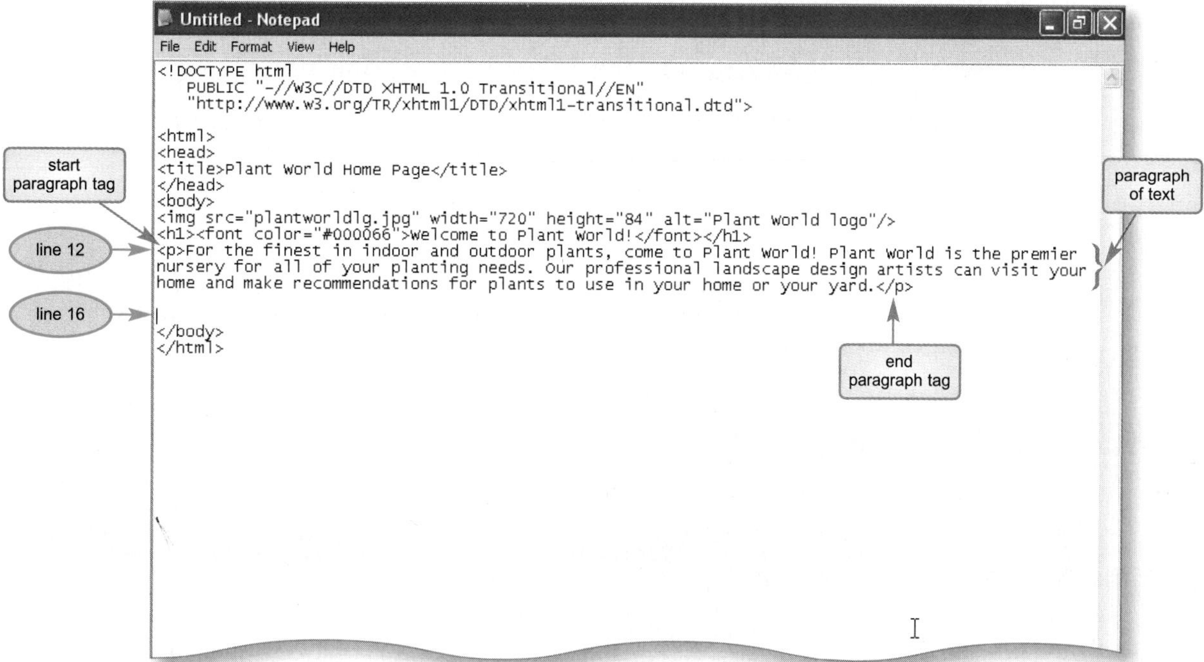
Untitled - Notepad
File Edit Format View Help
<!DOCTYPE html
PUBLIC "-//W3C//DTD XHTML 1.0 Transitional//EN"
"http://www.w3.org/TR/xhtml1/DTD/xhtml1-transitional.dtd">
<html>
<head>
<title>Plant World Home Page</title>
</head>
<body>
<img src="plantworldlg.jpg" width="720" height="84" alt="Plant World logo"/>
<h1><font color="#000066">Welcome to Plant World!</font></h1>
<p>For the finest in indoor and outdoor plants, come to Plant World! Plant World is the premier
nursery for all of your planting needs. Our professional landscape design artists can visit your
home and make recommendations for plants to use in your home or your yard.</p>
</body>
</html>
start paragraph tag
line 12
line 16
paragraph of text
end paragraph tag

FIGURE 3-14

Creating Unordered (Bulleted) Lists

In Project 2, you learned how to create an unordered (bulleted) list on a Web page. Because the HTML code for the list did not specify a bullet type, the list used the default disc bullet. The Plant World home page uses square bullets to identify items in the lists and to give the page a more distinctive look. To change the bullet type from the default (disc) to a square or circle, the <ul> tag is entered using the form

```
<ul type="bullettype">
```

where the bullettype value in quotation marks can be disc, square, or circle. If you want to use the default disc bullet, the type attribute does not need to be included.

Table 3-3 on the next page shows the HTML code used to create two unordered (bulleted) lists for the Plant World home page. An h2 heading above each unordered list visually separates the list from other elements on the Web page and indicates what the items in the list describe. The h2 heading tags are used so the list headings are slightly smaller than the main h1 heading.

Table 3-3 HTML Code for Creating Unordered (Bulleted) Lists

LINE	HTML TAG AND TEXT
16	<h2>Our company</h2>
17	<ul type="square">
18	<li>Founded in 1999 by Jared Adam Smith</li>
19	<li>Headquartered in Fairfield, Connecticut</li>
20	<li>38 store locations throughout New England</li>
21	</ul>
22	
23	<h2>Our services</h2>
24	<ul type="square">
25	<li>Landscape design</li>
26	<li>Planting and maintenance</li>
27	<li>Online information for all types of plants</li>
28	</ul>

The steps below show how to create the two unordered (bulleted) lists that appear on the Plant World home page.

To Create Unordered (Bulleted) Lists

1

- **If necessary, click line 16.**

2

- **Enter the HTML code shown in Table 3-3.**

3

- **Press the ENTER key twice to insert a blank line on line 29, after the second </ul> in the HTML code.**

The HTML code creates two unordered, or bulleted, lists, with three items each (Figure 3-15). Because the code specifies a type attribute and value of square, the lists will appear in the Web page using a square bullet.

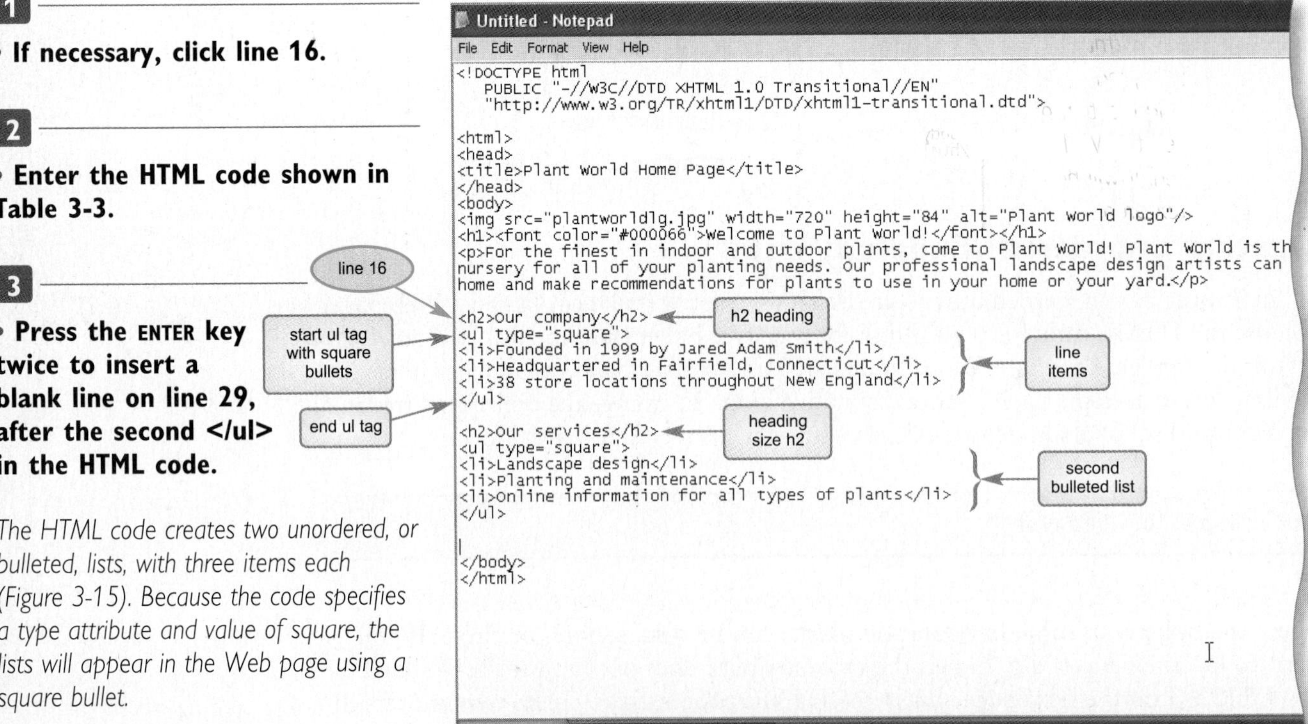
Untitled - Notepad
File Edit Format View Help
<!DOCTYPE html
PUBLIC "-//W3C//DTD XHTML 1.0 Transitional//EN"
"http://www.w3.org/TR/xhtml1/DTD/xhtml1-transitional.dtd">
<html>
<head>
<title>Plant World Home Page</title>
</head>
<body>
<img src="plantworldlg.jpg" width="720" height="84" alt="Plant World logo"/>
<h1><font color="#000066">Welcome to Plant World!</font></h1>
<p>For the finest in indoor and outdoor plants, come to Plant World! Plant World is th
nursery for all of your planting needs. Our professional landscape design artists can
home and make recommendations for plants to use in your home or your yard.</p>
<h2>Our company</h2>
<ul type="square">
<li>Founded in 1999 by Jared Adam Smith</li>
<li>Headquartered in Fairfield, Connecticut</li>
<li>38 store locations throughout New England</li>
</ul>
<h2>Our services</h2>
<ul type="square">
<li>Landscape design</li>
<li>Planting and maintenance</li>
<li>Online information for all types of plants</li>
</ul>
</body>
</html>
line 16
start ul tag with square bullets
end ul tag
h2 heading
line items
heading size h2
second bulleted list
start
Untitled - Notepad

FIGURE 3-15

Adding a Background Image

The Web page created in Project 2 used the bgcolor attribute in the <body> tag to add a background color. The Plant World home page created in this project will use the background attribute of the <body> tag to add the image, greyback.jpg, as the Web page background. Using this image will give the background a grey, lightly textured look.

The following steps show how to add a background image to the Plant World home page. The image file, greyback.jpg, is saved on the HTML Data Disk. See the inside back cover for instructions for downloading the HTML Data Disk, or see your instructor.

To Add a Background Image

1

- **Click immediately to the right of the y in the <body> tag on line 9 and then press the SPACEBAR.**

2

- **Type** `background="greyback.jpg"` **as the attribute.**

The HTML code is displayed (Figure 3-16). The attribute value, greyback.jpg, indicates the file name and location of the image. When the Web page is displayed, it will have a grey, lightly textured background.

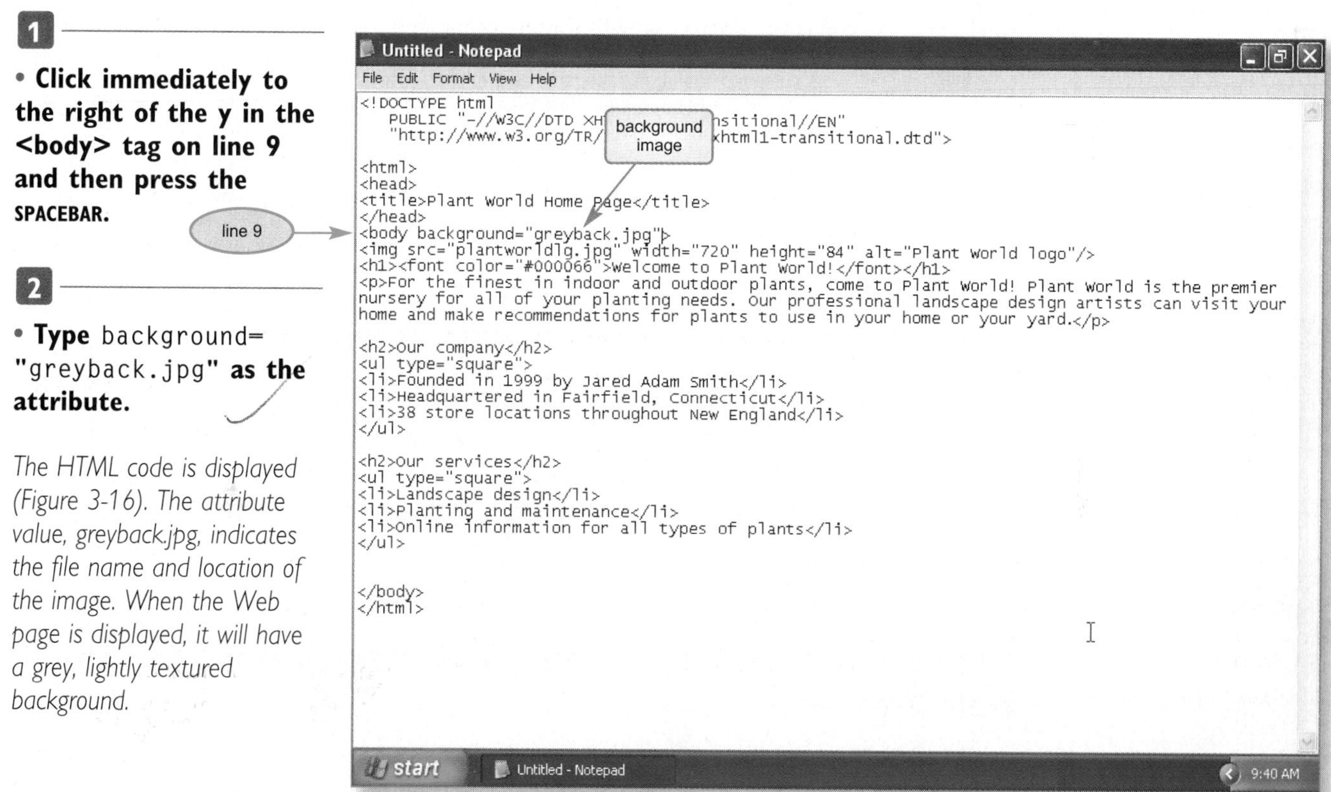
line 9
background image
Untitled - Notepad
File Edit Format View Help
<!DOCTYPE html
<html>
<head>
<title>Plant World Home Page</title>
</head>
<body background="greyback.jpg">
<img src="plantworldlg.jpg" width="720" height="84" alt="Plant World logo"/>
<h1><font color="#000066">Welcome to Plant World!</font></h1>
<p>For the finest in indoor and outdoor plants, come to Plant World! Plant World is the premier nursery for all of your planting needs. Our professional landscape design artists can visit your home and make recommendations for plants to use in your home or your yard.</p>
<h2>Our company</h2>
<ul type="square">
<li>Founded in 1999 by Jared Adam Smith</li>
<li>Headquartered in Fairfield, Connecticut</li>
<li>38 store locations throughout New England</li>
</ul>
<h2>Our services</h2>
<ul type="square">
<li>Landscape design</li>
<li>Planting and maintenance</li>
<li>Online information for all types of plants</li>
</ul>
</body>
</html>
start
Untitled - Notepad
9:40 AM

FIGURE 3-16

Adding a Text Link

As you have learned, a Web site is a collection of Web pages created and maintained by a group or individual. Web pages often include links to connect one Web page to another page within the same Web site, so users can move easily from page to page. In this project, the Plant World home page includes a text link to the Desert Plants Web page, which is part of the same Web site.

The <a> and </a> tags are used to create links in a Web page. The <a> tag also is called the anchor tag because it is used to create anchors for links to another page in the same Web site, to a Web page in an external Web site, within the same Web page, and for e-mail links. The basic form of the tag used to create a link is:

```
<a href="URL">linktext</a>
```

where linktext is the clickable word or phrase that appears on the Web page and the value for href (hypertext reference) is the name or URL of the linked page or file. Table 3-4 shows some of the <a> tag attributes and their functions.

Table 3-4 <a> Tag Attributes and Functions

ATTRIBUTE	FUNCTION
href	Specifies the URL of the linked page or file.
name	Defines a name for the current anchor so it may be the target or destination of another link. Each anchor in a Web page must use a unique name.
rel	Indicates a forward relationship from the current document to the linked document. The value of the rel attribute is a link type, such as prev, next, index, or copyright. For example, the chapter5.htm Web page might include the tag, <a rel="next" href="chapter6.htm"> to indicate a link to the Web page for the next chapter, chapter6.htm.
rev	Indicates a reverse (backward) relationship from the current document to the linked document. The value of the rev attribute is a link type, such as prev, next, index, or copyright. For example, the chapter5.htm Web page might include the tag, <a rel="prev" href="chapter4.htm"> to indicate a link to the Web page for the previous chapter, chapter4.htm.
type	Specifies the content type (also known as media types or MIME types) of the linked page or file to help a browser determine if it can handle the resource type. Examples of content types include text/html, image/jpeg, video/quicktime, application/java, text/css, and text/javascript.

Adding a Text Link to Another Web Page within the Same Web Site

As discussed, the Plant World home page includes a text link to the Desert Plants Web page, which is part of the same Web site. When a visitor clicks the link on the home page, the browser will display the Desert Plants Web page.

Before creating the link, be sure you know the URL or name of the file to be linked and the text that will serve as the clickable word or phrase. The words should be descriptive and tell the Web page visitor the purpose of the link. For the Plant World home page, the text link is a phrase in a paragraph at the bottom of the Web page.

The following steps illustrate how to add a text link to another Web page within the same Web site.

To Add a Text Link to Another Web Page within the Same Web Site

1

- **Click immediately to the right of the </ul> tag on line 28 and then press the DOWN ARROW key twice.**

2

- **With the insertion point on line 30, type** `<p>To learn more about the Plant World products and services, please browse the Plant World Web site, where you can find information on all types of plants, both for indoor and outdoor use. You also can learn about this month's featured desert plants, which have a natural beauty that can enhance any landscape!</p>` **and then press the ENTER key (Figure 3-17).**

Untitled - Notepad
File Edit Format View Help
<!DOCTYPE html
PUBLIC "-//W3C//DTD XHTML 1.0 Transitional//EN"
"http://www.w3.org/TR/xhtml1/DTD/xhtml1-transitional.dtd">
<html>
<head>
<title>Plant World Home Page</title>
</head>
<body background="greyback.jpg">
<img src="plantworldlg.jpg" width="720" height="84" alt="Plant World logo"/>
<h1><font color="#000066">Welcome to Plant World!</font></h1>
<p>For the finest in indoor and outdoor plants, come to Plant World! Plant World is the premier
nursery for all of your planting needs. Our professional landscape design artists can visit your
home and make recommendations for plants to use in your home or your yard.
<h2>Our company</h2>
<ul type="square">
<li>Founded in 1999 by Jared Adam Smith</li>
<li>Headquartered in Fairfield, Connecticut</li>
<li>38 store locations throughout New England</li>
</ul>
<h2>Our services</h2>
<ul type="square">
<li>Landscape design</li>
<li>Planting and maintenance</li>
<li>Online information for all types of plants</li>
</ul>
<p>To learn more about the Plant World products and services, please browse the Plant World Web
site, where you can find information on all types of plants, both for indoor and
outdoor use. You also can learn about this month's featured desert plants, which have a natural
beauty that can enhance any landscape!</p>
</body>
</html>
line 30
second paragraph of text
start
Untitled - Notepad
9:47 AM

FIGURE 3-17

3

- **Click immediately to the left of the d in desert on line 32.**
- **Type** `<a href="desertplants.htm">` **to start the link.**
- **Click immediately to the right of the s in plants on line 33. Type** `</a>` **to end the link and then press the ENTER key.**

The HTML code is displayed (Figure 3-18).

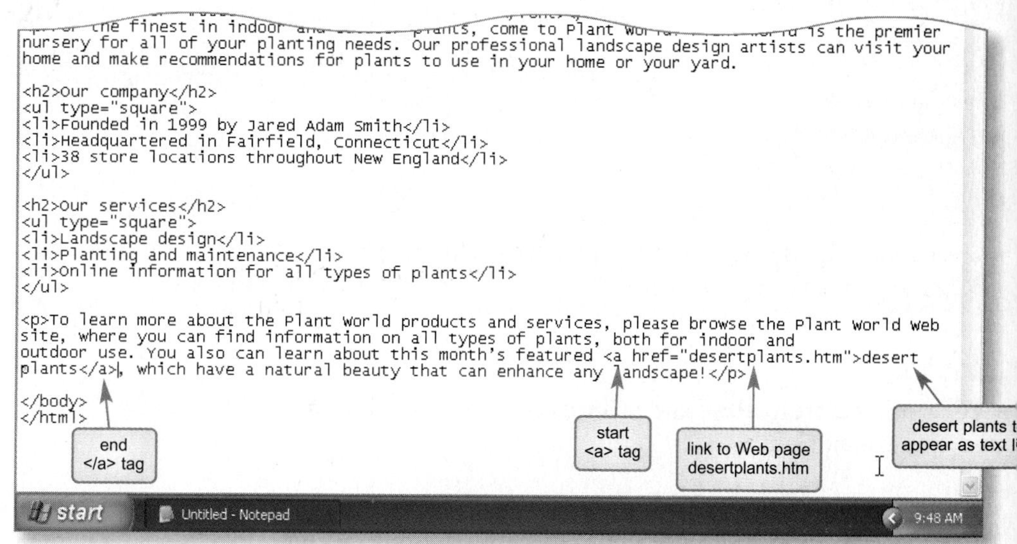
nursery for all of your planting needs. Our professional landscape design artists can visit your
home and make recommendations for plants to use in your home or your yard.
<h2>Our company</h2>
<ul type="square">
<li>Founded in 1999 by Jared Adam Smith</li>
<li>Headquartered in Fairfield, Connecticut</li>
<li>38 store locations throughout New England</li>
</ul>
<h2>Our services</h2>
<ul type="square">
<li>Landscape design</li>
<li>Planting and maintenance</li>
<li>Online information for all types of plants</li>
</ul>
<p>To learn more about the Plant World products and services, please browse the Plant World Web
site, where you can find information on all types of plants, both for indoor and
outdoor use. You also can learn about this month's featured <a href="desertplants.htm">desert
plants</a>, which have a natural beauty that can enhance any landscape!</p>
</body>
</html>
end </a> tag
start <a> tag
link to Web page desertplants.htm
start
Untitled - Notepad
9:48 AM

FIGURE 3-18

As shown in Figure 3-17, the <a> and </a> tags enclose the text, desert plants, which will appear on the Plant World home page as a clickable text link. The href attribute value sets the Web page, desertplants.htm, as the linked Web page.

Adding an E-Mail Link

The Plant World home page also includes an e-mail link so customers can contact Plant World for additional information or to comment on the Web page. The <a> and </a> tags used to create a text link to a Web page also are used to create an e-mail link. Instead of using a URL as the href attribute value, the href attribute value for an e-mail link uses the form,

```
<a href="mailto:address@email.com">linktext</a>
```

where the href attribute value uses the word, mailto, to indicate it is an email link, followed by a colon and the e-mail address to which to send the e-mail message. When the browser recognizes a **mailto** URL in a clicked link, it automatically opens a new message in the default e-mail program and inserts the appropriate contact e-mail address in the To field. The clickable text used for an e-mail link typically is the e-mail address used in the e-mail link. The Web page also should provide some information before the link, so visitors know the purpose of the e-mail link.

The following steps show how to add an e-mail link to a Web page.

To Add an E-Mail Link

1

• **With the insertion point on line 34, type** `<p>Have a question or comment? Call us at (206) 555-PLANT or e-mail us at plantworld@isp.com.</p>` **as a new paragraph of text.**

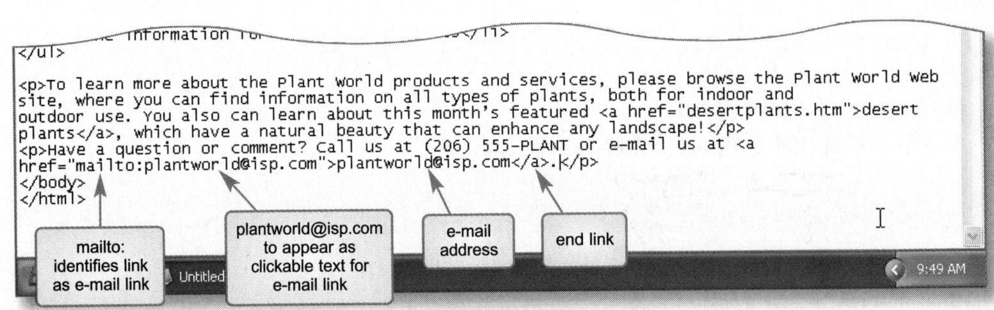

FIGURE 3-19

2

• **Click immediately before the p in plantworld on line 34. Type** `<a href="mailto: plantworld@isp.com">` **to start the e-mail link.**

3

• **Click immediately after the m in com in the e-mail address text. Type** `</a>` **to end the e-mail link.**

The HTML code for the e-mail link is displayed (Figure 3-19). The HTML code for the Plant World home page is complete.

As shown in Figure 3-19, the <a> and </a> tags enclose the text, plantworld@isp.com, which will appear on the Plant World home page as a clickable e-mail link. The href attribute value, mailto:plantworld@isp.com, indicates that clicking the e-mail link will start a new message addressed to plantworld@isp.com.

Saving and Printing the HTML File

With the HTML code for the Plant World home page complete, the file should be saved and a copy should be printed as a reference.

To Save and Print an HTML File

1. **With a floppy disk in drive A, click File on the menu bar and then click Save As. Type** `plantworld.htm` **in the File name text box.**
2. **If necessary, click 3½ Floppy (A:) in the Save in list. Click the Project03 folder and then click the ProjectFiles folder in the list of available folders. Click the Save button in the Save As dialog box.**
3. **Click File on the menu bar and then click Print on the File menu.**

Notepad saves the HTML file in the Project03\ProjectFiles folder on the floppy disk in drive A using the file name, plantworld.htm. Notepad prints the HTML file (Figure 3-20).

```
<!DOCTYPE html
   PUBLIC "-//W3C//DTD XHTML 1.0 Transitional//EN"
   "http://www.w3.org/TR/xhtml1/DTD/xhtml1-transitional.dtd">

<html>
<head>
<title>Plant World Home Page</title>
</head>
<body background="greyback.jpg">
<img src="plantworldlg.jpg" width="720" height="84" alt="Plant World logo"/>
<h1><font color="#000066">Welcome to Plant World!</font></h1>
<p>For the finest in indoor and outdoor plants, come to Plant World! Plant World is
the premier nursery for all of your planting needs. Our professional landscape
design artists can visit your home and make recommendations for plants to use in
your home or your yard.

<h2>Our company</h2>
<ul type="square">
<li>Founded in 1999 by Jared Adam Smith</li>
<li>Headquartered in Fairfield, Connecticut</li>
<li>38 store locations throughout New England</li>
</ul>

<h2>Our services</h2>
<ul type="square">
<li>Landscape design</li>
<li>Planting and maintenance</li>
<li>Online information for all types of plants</li>
</ul>

<p>To learn more about the Plant World products and services, please browse the
Plant World Web site, where you can find information on all types of plants, both
for indoor and
outdoor use. You also can learn about this month's featured <a
href="desertplants.htm">desert plants</a>, which have a natural beauty that can
enhance any landscape!</p>
<p>Have a question or comment? Call us at (206) 555-PLANT or e-mail us at <a
href="mailto:plantworld@isp.com">plantworld@isp.com</a>.</p>

</body>
</html>
```

FIGURE 3-20

Viewing, Testing Links, and Printing a Web Page

After the HTML file for the Plant World home page is saved, it should be viewed in a browser to confirm the Web page appears as desired. It also is important to test the two links in the Plant World home page to verify they function as expected. With the home page displayed in the browser, click the e-mail hyperlink and the desert plants link to verify they work correctly. The second Web page, desertplants.htm, will display, although it is not completed. In the remainder of this project, the HTML code in the desertplants.htm file will be edited to create the Web page shown in Figure 3-1b on page HTM 71.

More About

Web Page Testing

An important part of Web page development is testing Web page links. For more information about link testing, visit the HTML More About Web page (scsite.com/html3e/more.htm) and then click Web Page Testing.

To View a Web Page

1. **Click the Start button on the Windows taskbar and then point to All Programs on the Start menu. Click Internet Explorer (or another browser command) on the All Programs submenu.**
2. **If necessary, click the Maximize button to maximize the browser window.**
3. **When the browser window appears, click the Address bar.**
4. **Type** `a:\Project03\ProjectFiles\plantworld.htm` **in the Address text box.**
5. **Press the ENTER key.**

Your browser displays the Web page, plantworld.htm (Figure 3-21).

The Plant World home page appears, with the grey textured image as a background and the Plant World logo. The home page uses two different sizes of headings to separate visually the paragraph text and the two unordered lists, which use a square bullet type. Finally, the home page includes a text link to another Web page in the same Web site and an e-mail link.

After confirming that the Web page appears as desired, the two links in the Plant World home page should be tested to verify they function as expected. The following steps show how to test the links in the Plant World home page.

Plant World Home Page - Microsoft Internet Explorer
Print button
Standard toolbar
Plant World logo image
h1 heading
paragraph of text
h2 heading
bulleted list with square bullet type
h2 heading
bulleted list with square bullet type
text link to Web page in same Web site
e-mail link
Plant World
fairfield, ct 06824
Welcome to Plant World!
For the finest in indoor and outdoor plants, come to Plant World! Plant World is the premier nursery for all of your planting needs. Our professional landscape design artists can visit your home and make recommendations for plants to use in your home or your yard.
Our company
Founded in 1999 by Jared Adam Smith
Headquartered in Fairfield, Connecticut
38 store locations throughout New England
Our services
Landscape design
Planting and maintenance
Online information for all types of plants
To learn more about the Plant World products and services, please browse the Plant World web site, where you can find information on all types of plants, both for indoor and outdoor use. You also can learn about this month's featured desert plants, which have a natural beauty that can enhance any landscape!
Have a question or comment? Call us at (206) 555-PLANT or e-mail us at plantworld@isp.com.

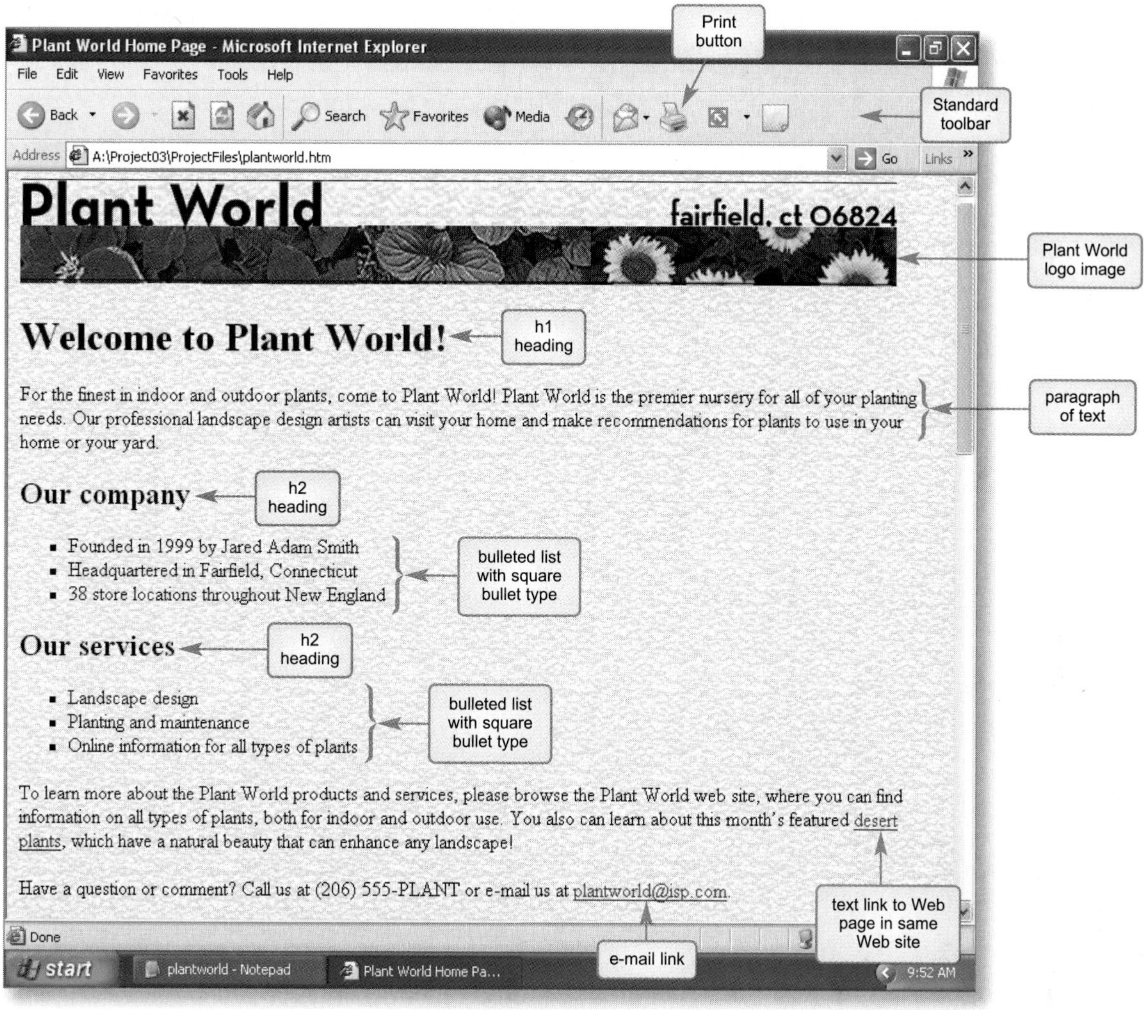

FIGURE 3-21

To Test Links in a Web Page

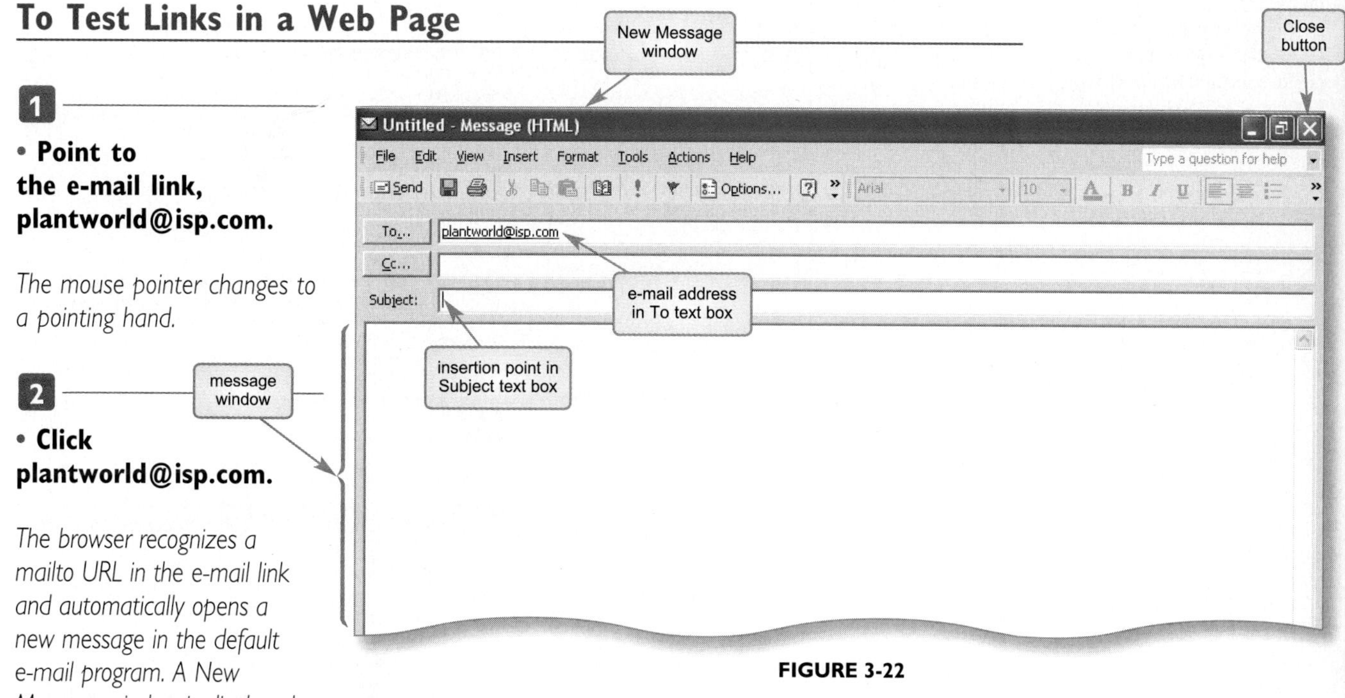
New Message window
Close button
Untitled - Message (HTML)
plantworld@isp.com
e-mail address in To text box
insertion point in Subject text box
message window

FIGURE 3-22

1

- **Point to the e-mail link, plantworld@isp.com.**

The mouse pointer changes to a pointing hand.

2

- **Click plantworld@isp.com.**

The browser recognizes a mailto URL in the e-mail link and automatically opens a new message in the default e-mail program. A New Message window is displayed (Figure 3-22). The address, plantworld@isp.com, is displayed in the To text box.

3

• **Click the Close button in the New Message window.**

4

• **With the HTML Data Disk in drive A, point to the link, desert plants.**

The mouse pointer changes to a pointing hand.

5

• **Click desert plants.**

The desertplants.htm page is displayed (Figure 3-23). This Web page is an HTML document stored in the Project03\ProjectFiles folder on the HTML Data Disk.

> *More About*
>
> **Web Page Improvement**
>
> Web page development is an ongoing process. In Web page development, you create a Web page, view it in a browser, and then look for ways to improve the appearance of the page. For more information about Web page improvement, visit the HTML More About Web page (scsite.com/html3e/more.htm) and then click Web Page Improvement.

Desert Plants Web page prior to editing

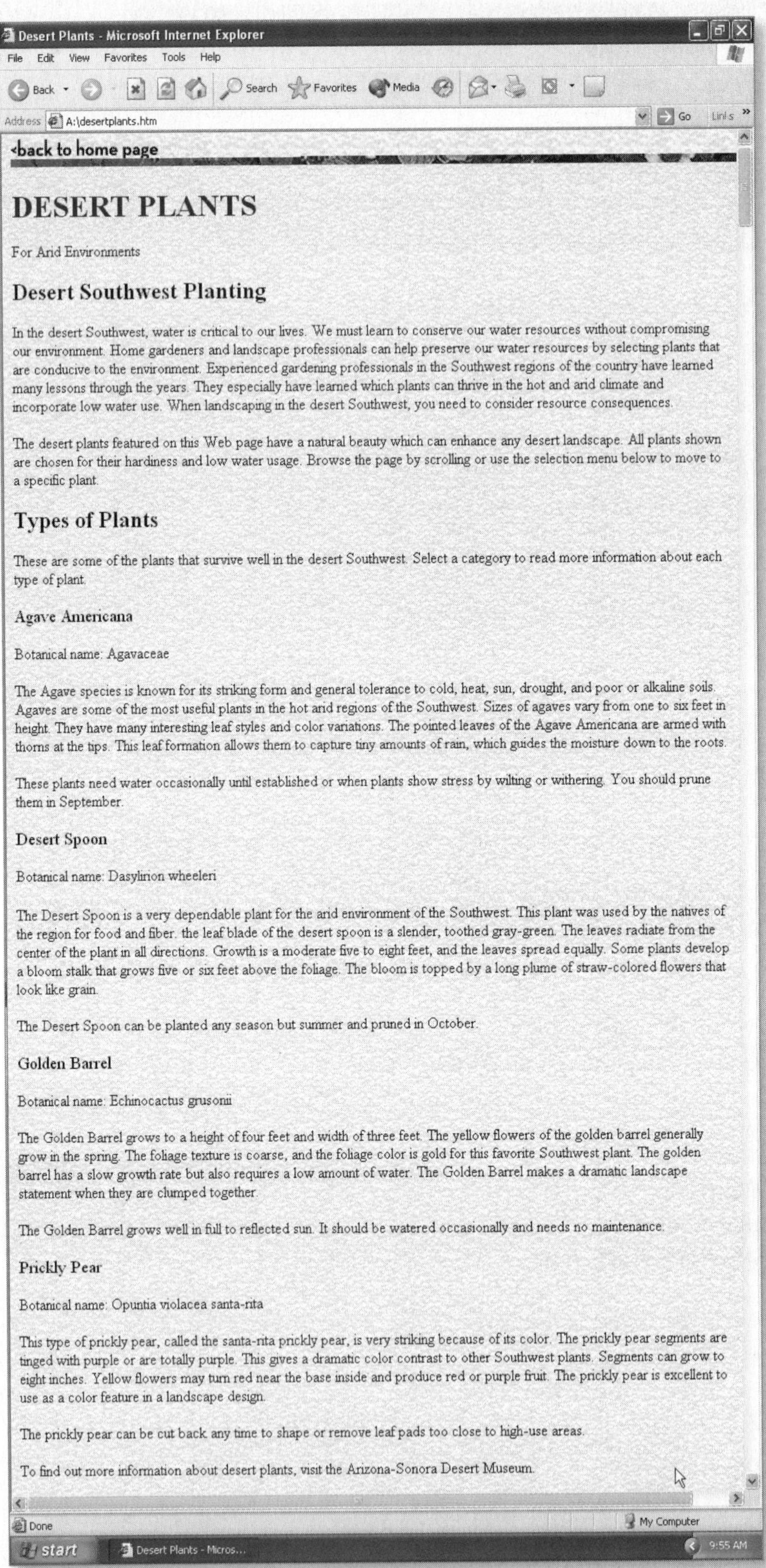

FIGURE 3-23

After verifying that the two links work, scroll through the Web page, desertplants.htm, to view its appearance. The following step shows how to print the Web page for future reference.

To Print a Web Page

1 **Click the Back button on the Standard toolbar to return to the Plant World home page.**

2 **Click the Print button on the Standard toolbar.**

The displayed Web page is printed (Figure 3-24).

<back to home page

DESERT PLANTS

For Arid Environments

Desert Southwest Planting

In the desert Southwest, water is critical to our lives. We must learn to conserve our water resources without compromising our environment. Home gardeners and landscape professionals can help preserve our water resources by selecting plants that are conducive to the environment. Experienced gardening professionals in the Southwest regions of the country have learned many lessons through the years. They especially have learned which plants can thrive in the hot and arid climate and incorporate low water use. When landscaping in the desert Southwest, you need to consider resource consequences.

The desert plants featured on this Web page have a natural beauty which can enhance any desert landscape. All plants shown are chosen for their hardiness and low water usage. Browse the page by scrolling or use the selection menu below to move to a specific plant.

Types of Plants

These are some of the plants that survive well in the desert Southwest. Select a category to read more information about each type of plant.

- Agave
- Desertspoon
- Golden Barrel
- Prickly Pear

Agave Americana

Botanical name: *Agavaceae*

The Agave species is known for its striking form and general tolerance to cold, heat, sun, drought, and poor or alkaline soils. Agaves are some of the most useful plants in the hot arid regions of the Southwest. Sizes of agaves vary from one to six feet in height. They have many interesting leaf styles and color variations. The pointed leaves of the Agave Americana are armed with thorns at the tips. This leaf formation allows them to capture tiny amounts of rain, which guides the moisture down to the roots.

These plants need water occasionally until established or when plants show stress by wilting or withering. You should prune them in September.

To top

Desert Spoon

Botanical name: *Dasylirion wheeleri*

The Desert Spoon is a very dependable plant for the arid environment of the Southwest. This plant was used by the natives of the region for food and fiber. the leaf blade of the desert spoon is a slender, toothed gray-green. The leaves radiate from the center of the plant in all directions. Growth is a moderate five to eight feet, and the leaves spread equally. Some plants develop a bloom stalk that grows five or six feet above the foliage. The bloom is topped by a long plume of straw-colored flowers that look like grain.

The Desert Spoon can be planted any season but summer and pruned in October.

To top

Golden Barrel

Botanical name: *Echinocactus grusonii*

The Golden Barrel grows to a height of four feet and width of three feet. The yellow flowers of the golden barrel generally grow in the spring. The foliage texture is coarse, and the foliage color is gold for this favorite Southwest plant. The golden barrel has a slow growth rate but also requires a low amount of water. The Golden Barrel makes a dramatic landscape statement when they are clumped together.

The Golden Barrel grows well in full to reflected sun. It should be watered occasionally and needs no maintenance.

To top

Prickly Pear

Botanical name: *Opuntia violacea santa-rita*

This type of prickly pear, called the santa-rita prickly pear, is very striking because of its color. The prickly pear segments are tinged with purple or are totally purple. This gives a dramatic color contrast to other Southwest plants. Segments can grow to eight inches. Yellow flowers may turn red near the base inside and produce red or purple fruit. The prickly pear is excellent to use as a color feature in a landscape design.

The prickly pear can be cut back any time to shape or remove leaf pads too close to high-use areas.

To top

To find out more information about desert plants, visit the Arizona-Sonora Desert Museum.

FIGURE 3-24

In the following sections, the HTML code in the desertplants.htm file is edited to add images with wrapped text, links within the Desert Plants Web page, a link to another Web site, and an image link back to the home page.

Editing the Second Web Page

The current version of the desertplants.htm Web page is stored on the HTML Data Disk. As shown in Figure 3-23 on page HTM 92, the Desert Plants Web page includes many Web page elements, such as headings, paragraph text, and images.

In this section, you will learn to open the existing Web page file and edit the HTML code so the Desert Plants Web page appears as shown in Figure 3-25. You will learn to enhance the text by adding bold, italics, and color. You also will learn how to add an image and set text to wrap around the image. You also will learn to add three additional types of links: (1) links within the same Web page, (2) a text link to a Web page in another Web site, and (3) and an image link to a Web page in the same Web site.

As you have learned, the <a> tag used to create a link must specify the page, file, or location to which it links. In the case of a link within a Web page, the <a> tag specifies a **target**, or named location, in the same file. Before adding the links and targets in the Desert Plants Web page, an unordered (bulleted) list that contains four items — Agave Americana, Desert Spoon, Golden Barrel, and Prickly Pear — must be added to the page. The list items will serve as the links that are directed to the heading at the top of each major section of the Desert Plants Web page. When clicked, these links will move the Web page visitor to the targets, which are the headings named Agave Americana, Desert Spoon, Golden Barrel, and Prickly Pear, respectively.

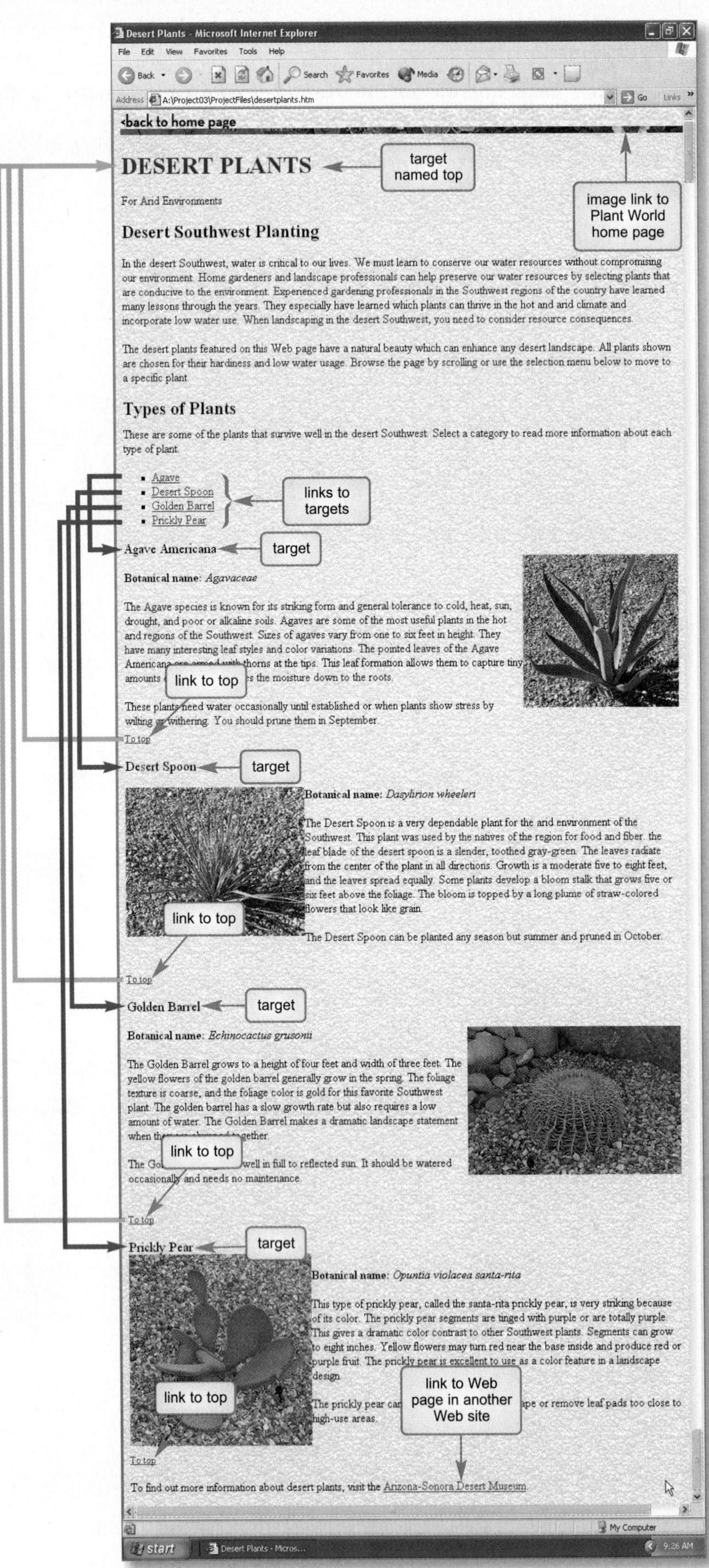

FIGURE 3-25 Completed Desert Plants Web page.

Because the Web page is so long, it is a good design practice to provide users with a quick way to move back to the top of the Web page, without scrolling back. For this purpose, the Web page includes four text links named, To top. These links are located just above the Desert Spoon, Golden Barrel, and Prickly Pear headings, and at the bottom of the page above the link to the Arizona-Sonora Desert Museum. When clicked, the To top link takes the Web page visitor back to the top of the page.

To complete the Desert Plants Web page, an image link will be created, so users can click the back to home page link to return to the Plant World home page. A text link also will be created from the Desert Plants Web page to an external Web site, the Arizona-Sonora Desert Museum.

The following steps illustrate how to open the desertplants.htm file in Notepad.

To Open an HTML File

1. **Click the Notepad button on the taskbar.**
2. **With the HTML Data Disk in drive A, click File on the menu bar and then click Open on the File menu.**
3. **If necessary, click the Look in box arrow and then click 3½ Floppy (A:). Click the Project03 folder and then click the Project Files folder in the list of available folders.**
4. **If necessary, click the Files of type box arrow and then click All Files. Click desertplants.htm in the list of files.**
5. **Click the Open button in the Open dialog box.**

The first 39 lines of the HTML code for desertplants.htm are displayed (Figure 3-26).

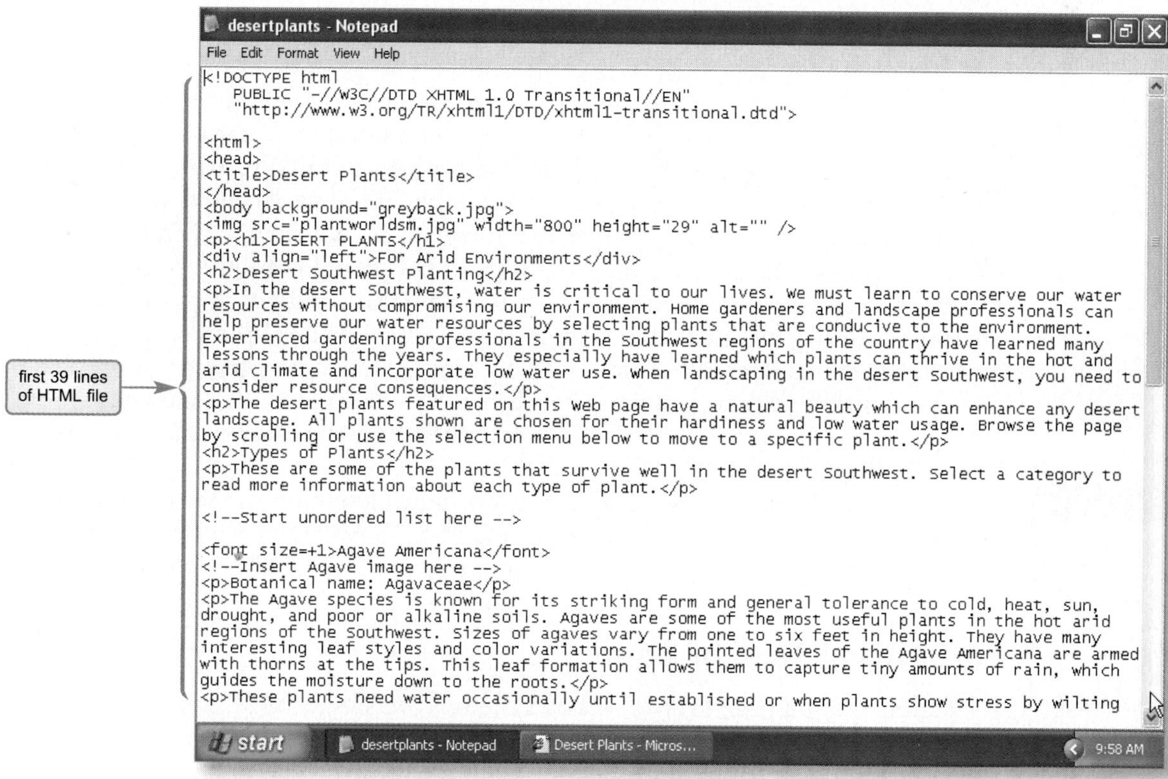

FIGURE 3-26

Formatting Text

Earlier in the project, the color attribute of the <font> tag was used to change the color of text on the Web page. HTML provides a number of other tags to format text, several of which are listed in Table 3-5.

Table 3-5 Text Formatting Tags

HTML TAG	FUNCTION
<b> </b>	Physical style tag that displays text as bold
<big> </big>	Increases the font size in comparison to the surrounding text
<blockquote> </blockquote >	Designates a long quotation; indents margins on sections of text
<em> </em>	Logical style tag that displays text with emphasis (usually appears as italicized)
<i> </i>	Physical style tag that displays text as italicized
<pre> </pre>	Sets enclosed text as preformatted material, meaning it preserves spaces and line breaks; often used for text in column format in another document pasted into HTML code
<small> </small>	Decreases the font size in comparison to the surrounding text
<strong> </strong>	Logical style tag that displays text with strong emphasis (usually appears as bold)
	Displays text as subscript (below normal text)
	Displays text as superscript (above normal text)
<tt> </tt>	Displays text as teletype or monospace text
<u> </u>	Displays text as underlined

Figure 3-27 shows a sample Web page with some of the text format tags. These tags fall into two categories: logical style tags and physical style tags. Logical styles allow a browser to interpret the tag based on browser settings, relative to other text in a Web page. The <h2> heading tag, for example, is a logical style that indicates that the heading text should be larger than regular text but smaller than text formatted using an <h1> heading tag. The <strong> </strong> tag is another logical style, which indicates that text should have a strong emphasis, and which most browsers interpret as displaying the text in bold font. Physical style tags specify a particular font change that is interpreted strictly by all browsers. For example, to ensure that text appears as bold font, you would enclose it between a start <b> and end </b> tag. In practice, the <strong> and <b> tags usually have the same result when the Web page displays.

Changing the characteristics of text can help call attention to that portion of text. You should use these elements with discretion, however. A Web page with too much bold, italicized, or other types of formatted text can be difficult to read.

More About

Text Formatting

You can indent entire blocks of text by using the <blockquote> </blockquote> tags. Both Internet Explorer and Netscape Communicator indent the text on either side by 40 pixels. You can use <p> and <br /> tags within the blockquote tags to control line breaking within the text.

Formatting Text in Bold

Figure 3-25 on page HTM 94 shows the final version of the Desert Plants Web page. As shown in the figure, bold text is used for the phrase, Botanical Name:, which appears once for each of the four plant types listed. The following steps illustrate how to format text in bold.

Figure 3-27 - Microsoft Internet Explorer
File Edit View Favorites Tools Help
Back Search Favorites Media
Address
Go Links
Sample Formatting Tags
This is normal text with no formatting.
normal unformatted text
strong (bold) text
This is bold text.
This is big text.
big text
blockquote
This text is put between the start and end blockquote tags. By using the blockquote tags, you block the text in from the right and left margins.
This is italicized text using the em tag.
emphasized (italicized) text
subscript and superscript text
This is text that uses the subscript and superscript tags.
This is teletype or monospace text.
teletype or monospace text
underlined text
This is underlined text.
Done
My Computer
start
Figure 3-27 - Microso...
10:00 AM

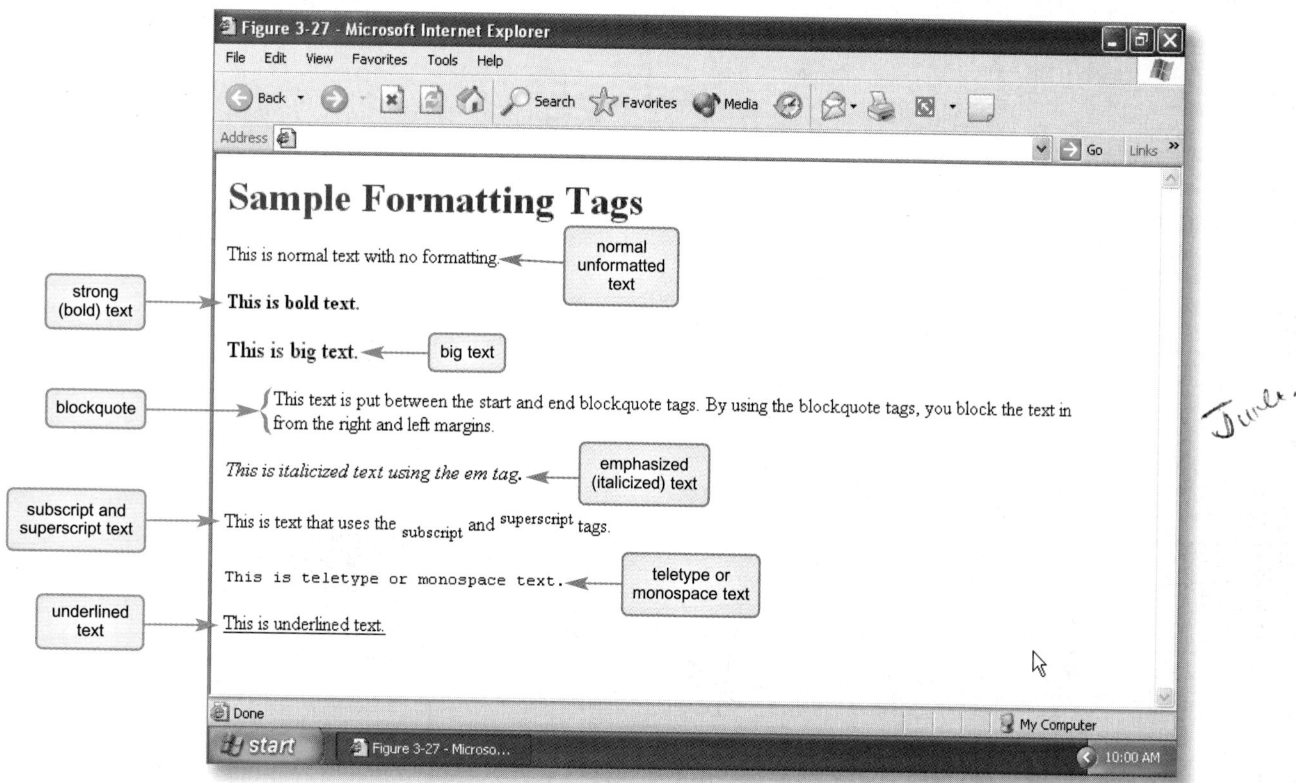

FIGURE 3-27 Examples of various text formatting tags.

To Format Text in Bold

1

- **Click immediately to the left of the B in Botanical on line 32. Type <b> as the start tag (Figure 3-28).**

2

- **Click immediately to the right of the colon (:) in Botanical name: on line 32 and then type </b> as the end tag.**

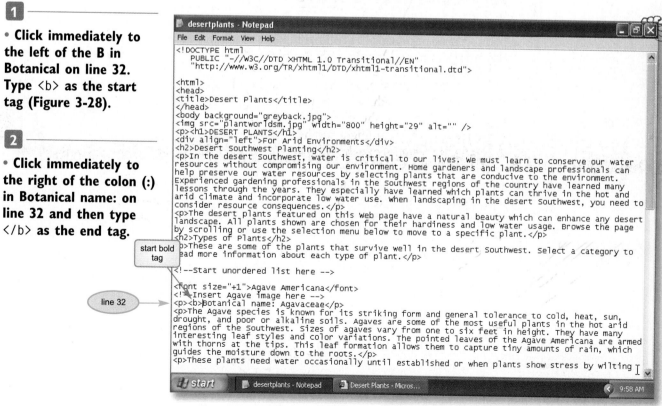

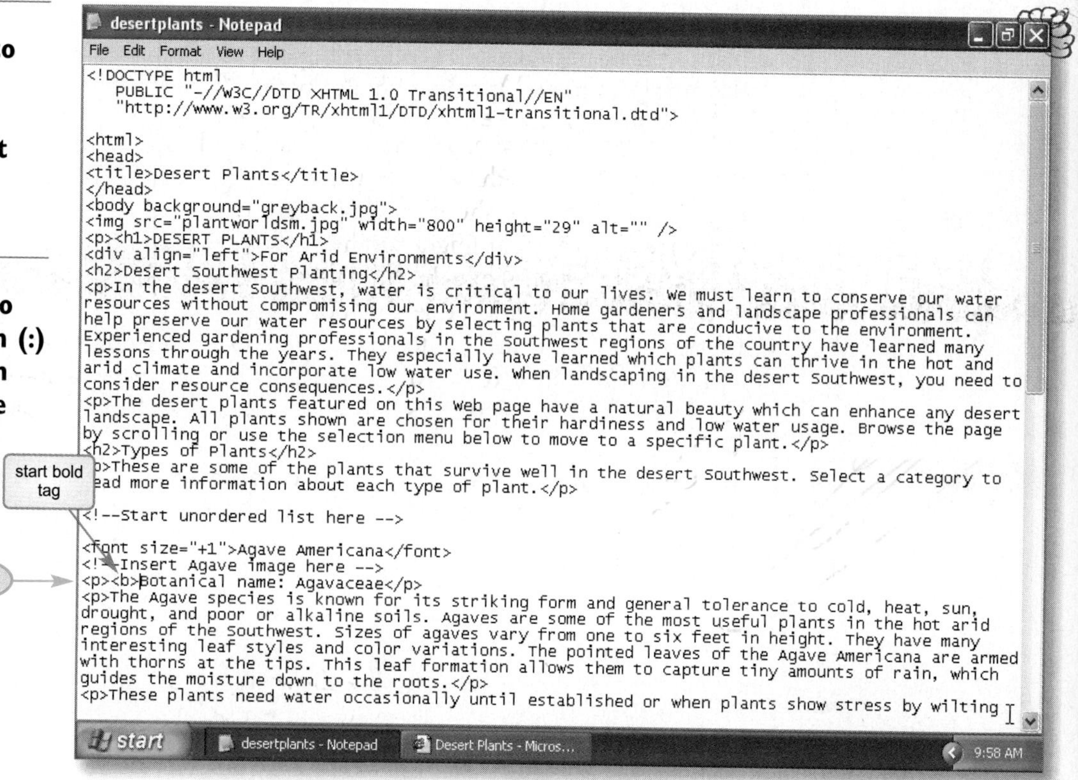

desertplants - Notepad
File Edit Format View Help
<!DOCTYPE html
PUBLIC "-//W3C//DTD XHTML 1.0 Transitional//EN"
"http://www.w3.org/TR/xhtml1/DTD/xhtml1-transitional.dtd">
<html>
<head>
<title>Desert Plants</title>
</head>
<body background="greyback.jpg">
<img src="plantworldsm.jpg" width="800" height="29" alt="" />
<p><h1>DESERT PLANTS</h1>
<div align="left">For Arid Environments</div>
<h2>Desert Southwest Planting</h2>
<p>In the desert Southwest, water is critical to our lives. We must learn to conserve our water resources without compromising our environment. Home gardeners and landscape professionals can help preserve our water resources by selecting plants that are conducive to the environment. Experienced gardening professionals in the Southwest regions of the country have learned many lessons through the years. They especially have learned which plants can thrive in the hot and arid climate and incorporate low water use. When landscaping in the desert Southwest, you need to consider resource consequences.</p>
<p>The desert plants featured on this Web page have a natural beauty which can enhance any desert landscape. All plants shown are chosen for their hardiness and low water usage. Browse the page by scrolling or use the selection menu below to move to a specific plant.</p>
<h2>Types of Plants</h2>
<p>These are some of the plants that survive well in the desert Southwest. Select a category to read more information about each type of plant.</p>
<!--Start unordered list here -->
<font size="+1">Agave Americana</font>
<!--Insert Agave image here -->
<p><b>Botanical name: Agavaceae</p>
<p>The Agave species is known for its striking form and general tolerance to cold, heat, sun, drought, and poor or alkaline soils. Agaves are some of the most useful plants in the hot arid regions of the Southwest. Sizes of agaves vary from one to six feet in height. They have many interesting leaf styles and color variations. The pointed leaves of the Agave Americana are armed with thorns at the tips. This leaf formation allows them to capture tiny amounts of rain, which guides the moisture down to the roots.</p>
<p>These plants need water occasionally until established or when plants show stress by wilting
start bold tag
line 32
start
desertplants - Notepad
Desert Plants - Micros...
9:58 AM

FIGURE 3-28

3

- **Repeat Steps 1 and 2 to bold the other three occurrences of the phrase, Botanical name:, on lines 45, 57, and 69.**

The bold tags surround the words, Botanical name:, on line 32, 45, 57, and 69 (Figure 3-29).

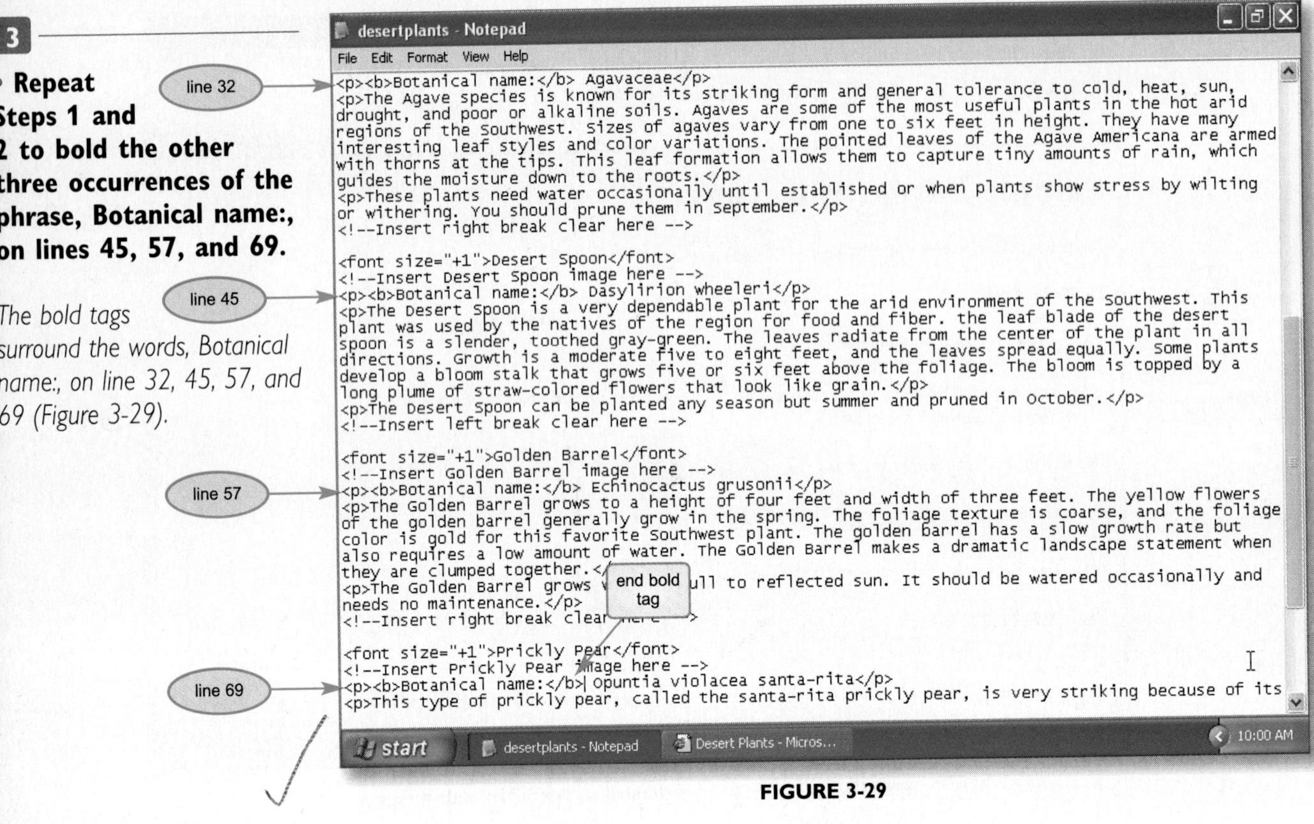

FIGURE 3-29

Formatting Text in Italics

As shown in Figure 3-25 on page HTM 94, the botanical names for each type of plant appear in italics. The following steps show how to use the <em> tag to italicize the botanical names for each type of plant.

To Format Text in Italics

1

- **Click immediately to the right of the </b> on line 32. Type <em> as the start tag.**

2

- **Click immediately to the right of the e at the end of Agavaceae on line 32. Type </em> as the end tag.**

3

- **Repeat Steps 1 and 2 to italicize the other botanical names on lines 45, 57, and 69.**

The tags, <em> and </em>, surround the botanical names Agavaceae, Dasylirion wheeleri, Echinocactus grusonii, and Opuntia violacea santa-rita on lines 32, 45, 57, and 69 (Figure 3-30).

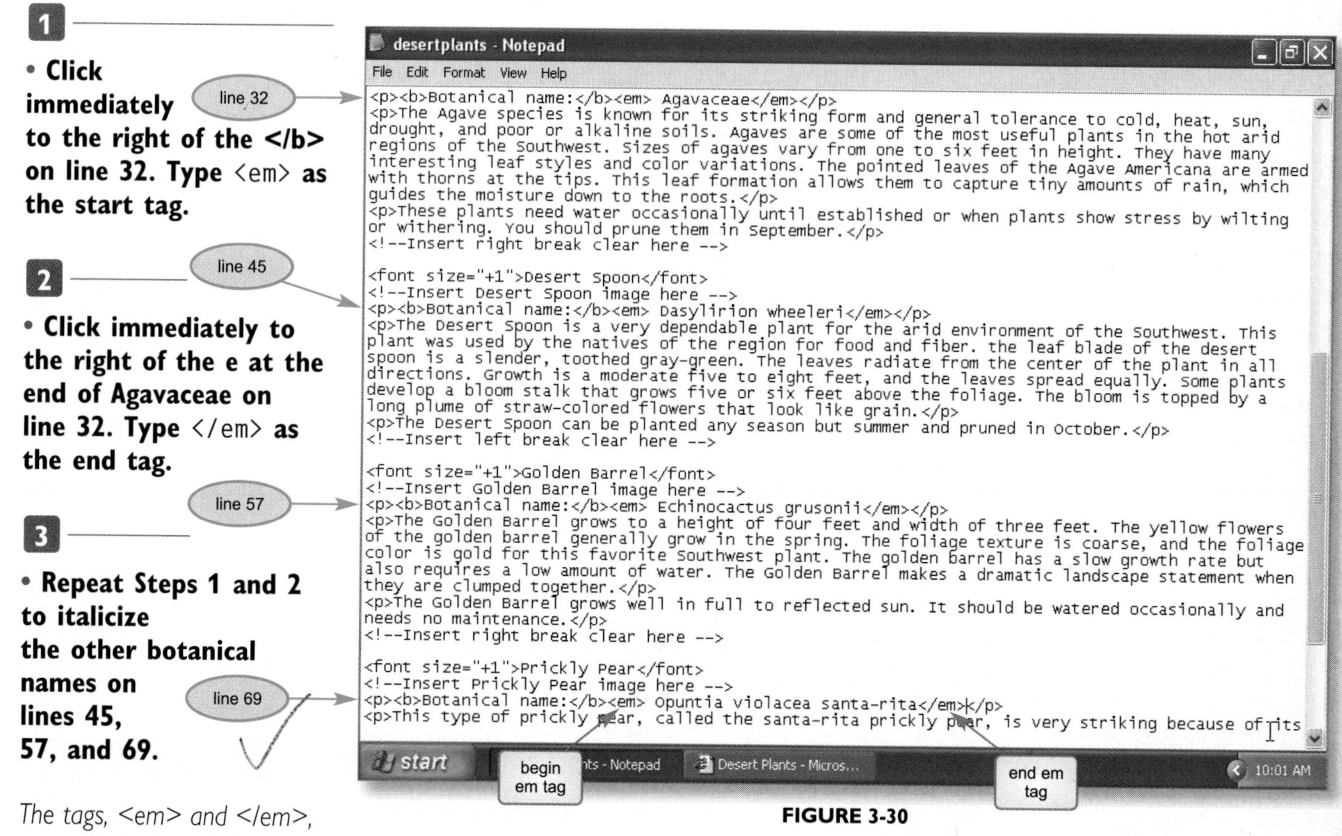

FIGURE 3-30

Format Text with a Font Color

Changing the color of the text also can enhance its look. As shown in Figure 3-25 on page HTM 94, the main heading, DESERT PLANTS, displays in dark blue. The following steps show how to use the color attribute of the <font> tag to format a heading in color.

> ***More About***
>
> **HTML Colors**
>
> Color is an important aspect of Web development. Visually appealing Web sites attract visitors. For more information about HTML color, visit the HTML More About Web page (scsite.com/html3e/more.htm) and then click Coloring Web Graphics.

To Format Text with a Font Color

1

- **Click immediately to the left of the word, DESERT, on line 11. Type `<font color="#000099">` as the start tag.**

2

- **Click immediately to the right of the word, PLANTS, on line 11. Type `</font>` as the end tag.**

The HTML code used to format the heading is displayed (Figure 3-31). The color attribute uses a six-digit number code of #000099 to specify that the heading should appear in a dark blue color.

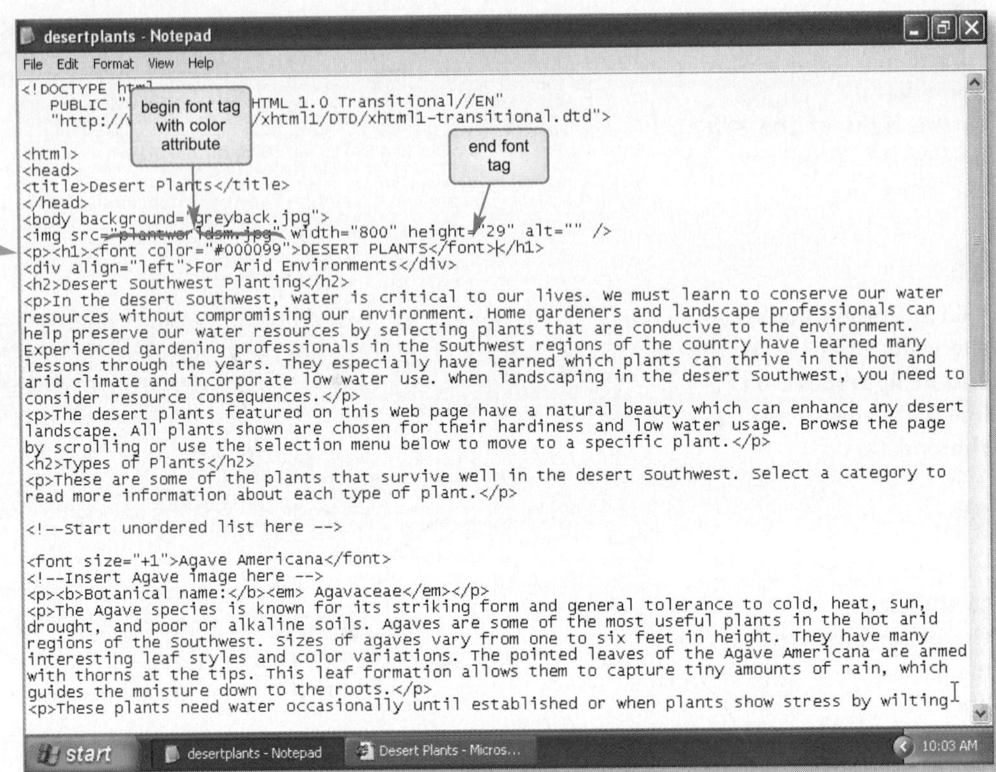

FIGURE 3-31

Adding an Image with Wrapped Text

As shown in Table 2-3 on page HTM 52, the <img> tag has many attributes, including attributes to specify height, width, alignment, alternate text, and so on. In Project 2, the HTML code used the height and width attributes to identify the size of the image to the browser and the alt attribute to define the text that displays when the user moves the mouse over the image.

Alignment also is a key consideration when inserting an image. Alignment can give an image and the surrounding text completely different looks. Figure 3-32 shows an image that is right-aligned, which wraps any text to the left of the image. The format of the HTML code to add the right-aligned image is

```
<img src="agave.jpg" align="right" alt= "Agave" width="212"
height="203" />.
```

where the src attribute indicates the file name of the image file, align="right" aligns the image to the right of the text, the height and width are in number of pixels, and the alt attribute displays the alternate text as the image is loading. The text used in the alt attribute helps to keep the visitor informed of what is going to display when the image has loaded completely.

The completed Desert Plants Web page, as shown in Figure 3-25 on page HTM 94, uses both right-aligned and left-aligned images. After specifying an image alignment and defining how text wraps, you also must enter a break (<br />) tag to stop the text wrapping. To end right-aligned text wrap, enter the <br clear="right" /> tag where the text should stop wrapping to the right. Figure 3-33 shows a left-aligned image, with text wrapped to its left. In the left-aligned example, the <br clear="left" /> tag is used to end the text wrap. The <br clear="all" /> tag clears both left and right alignments.

In addition to aligning text to the right and left of an image, the align attribute also supports values to align text with the top, middle, or bottom of the image, vertically. Figure 3-34a on the next page shows an example of one line of text with align="top" used in the <img> tag. This aligns the tagged text with the top of the image, with the remainder of the text displaying below the image. Figure 3-34b shows the same text with the align="middle" attribute, and Figure 3-34c on the following page shows the same text with the align="bottom" attribute.

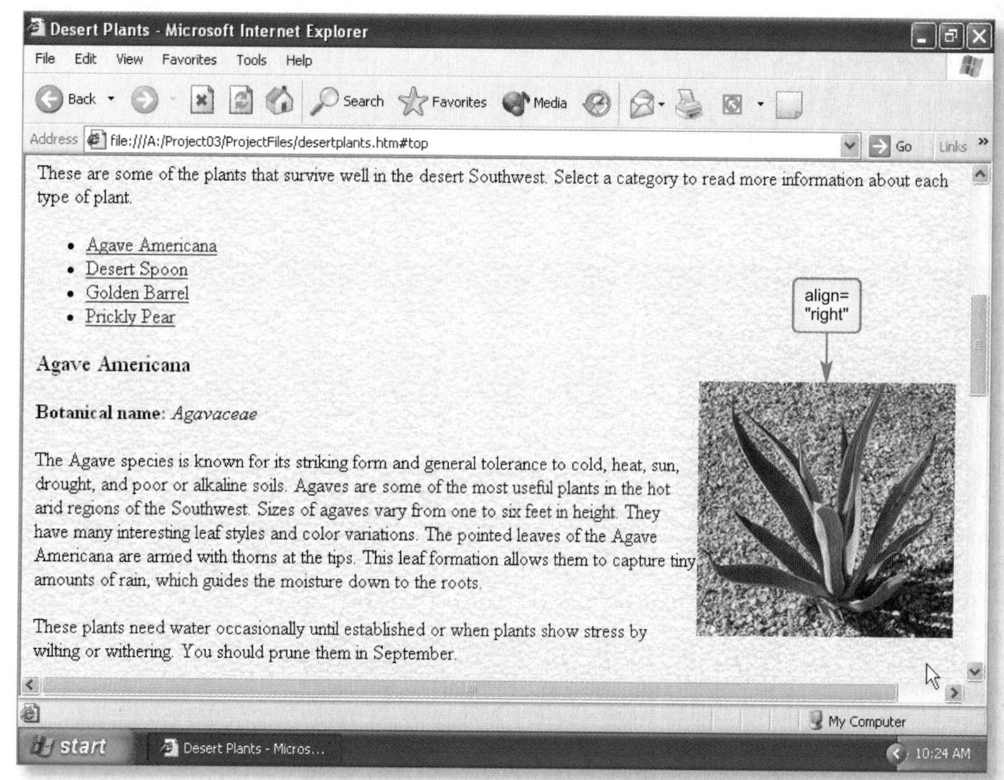

FIGURE 3-32 Right-aligned image.

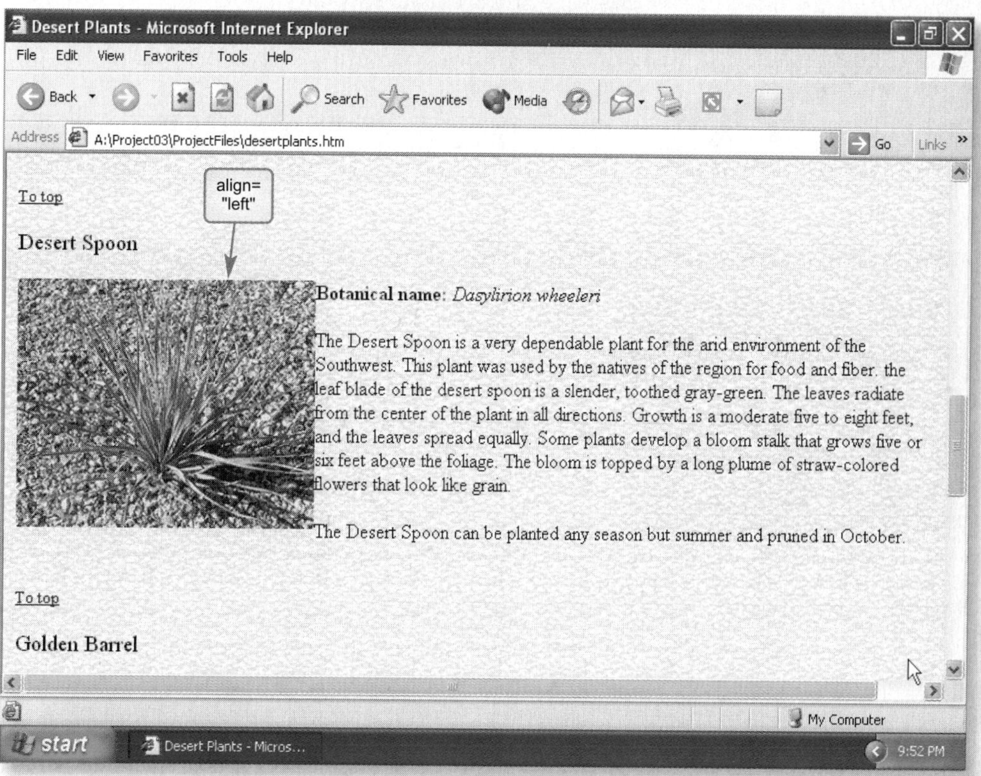

FIGURE 3-33 Left-aligned image.

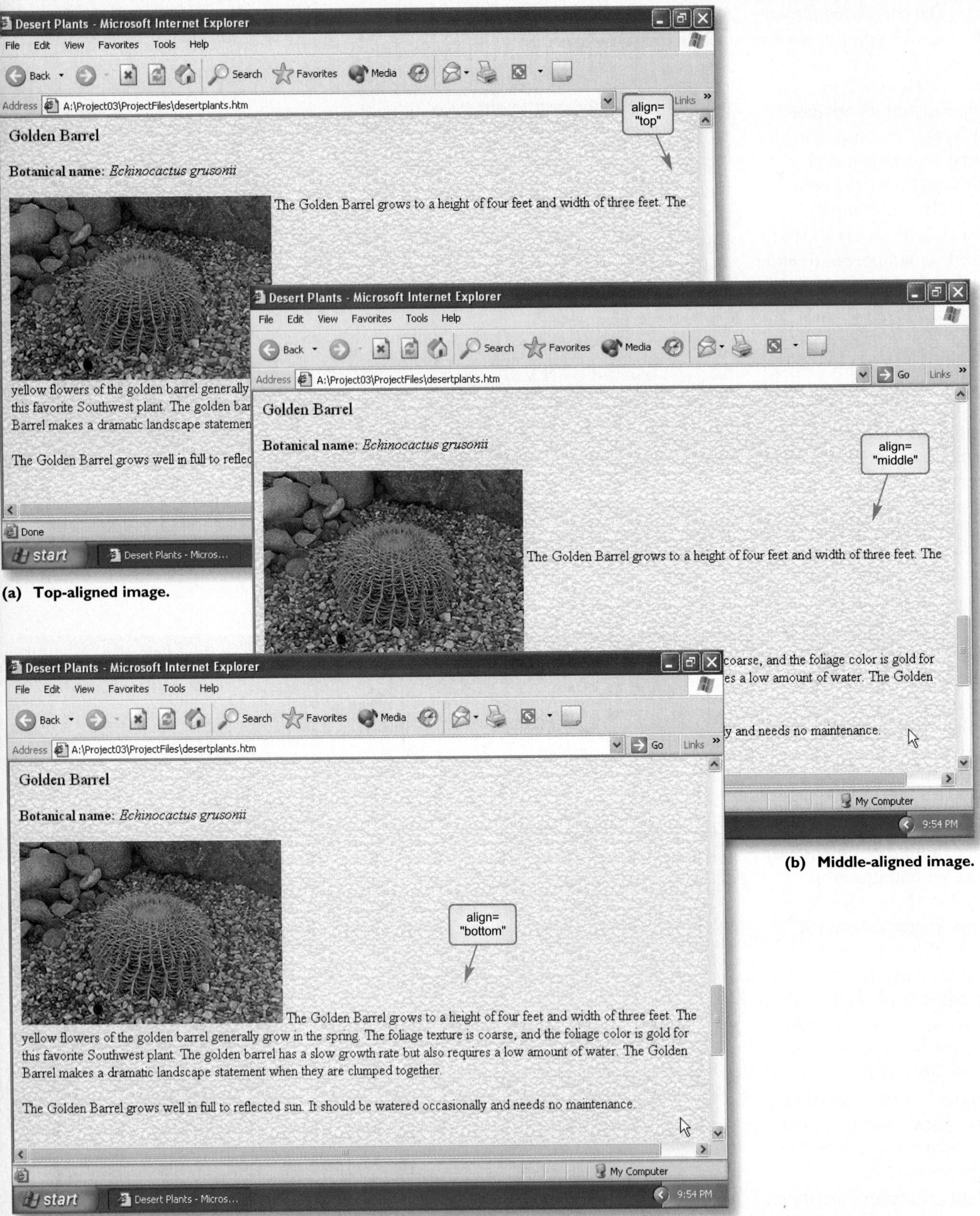

(a) Top-aligned image.

(b) Middle-aligned image.

(c) Bottom-aligned image.

FIGURE 3-34

Adding an Image with Wrapped Text

The following steps show how to insert right-aligned images with wrapped text, as shown in Figure 3-32 on page HTM 101. The images are saved on the HTML Data Disk in the Project03\ProjectFiles folder. See the inside back cover for instructions for downloading the HTML Data Disk, or see your instructor.

To Add an Image with Wrapped Text

1

• **Highlight the words <!--Insert Agave image here --> on line 31.**

2

• **Type** `<img src="agave.jpg" align="right" alt= "Agave" width="212" height="203" />` **and do not press the ENTER key.**

The HTML code inserts an image with the file name, agave.jpg (Figure 3-35). The image will be right-aligned on the Web page, with text wrapped to its left.

line 31

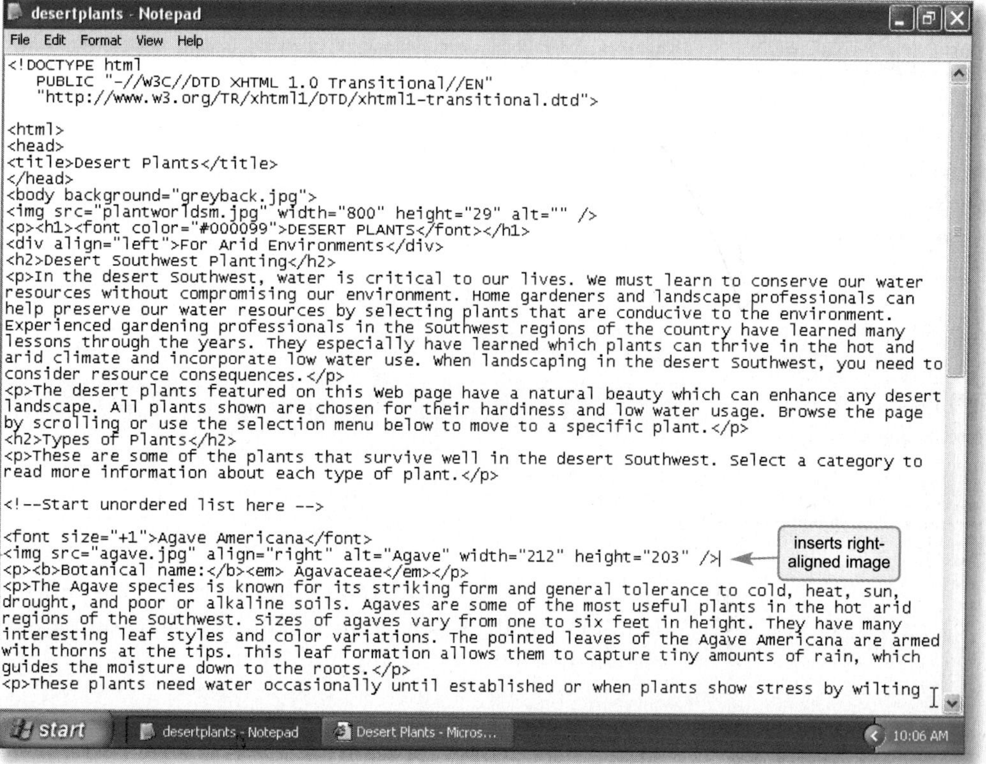


```
<!DOCTYPE html
   PUBLIC "-//W3C//DTD XHTML 1.0 Transitional//EN"
   "http://www.w3.org/TR/xhtml1/DTD/xhtml1-transitional.dtd">

<html>
<head>
<title>Desert Plants</title>
</head>
<body background="greyback.jpg">
<img src="plantworldsm.jpg" width="800" height="29" alt="" />
<p><h1><font color="#000099">DESERT PLANTS</font></h1>
<div align="left">For Arid Environments</div>
<h2>Desert Southwest Planting</h2>
<p>In the desert Southwest, water is critical to our lives. We must learn to conserve our water
resources without compromising our environment. Home gardeners and landscape professionals can
help preserve our water resources by selecting plants that are conducive to the environment.
Experienced gardening professionals in the Southwest regions of the country have learned many
lessons through the years. They especially have learned which plants can thrive in the hot and
arid climate and incorporate low water use. When landscaping in the desert Southwest, you need to
consider resource consequences.</p>
<p>The desert plants featured on this Web page have a natural beauty which can enhance any desert
landscape. All plants shown are chosen for their hardiness and low water usage. Browse the page
by scrolling or use the selection menu below to move to a specific plant.</p>
<h2>Types of Plants</h2>
<p>These are some of the plants that survive well in the desert Southwest. Select a category to
read more information about each type of plant.</p>

<!--Start unordered list here -->

<font size="+1">Agave Americana</font>
<img src="agave.jpg" align="right" alt="Agave" width="212" height="203" />
<p><b>Botanical name:</b><em> Agavaceae</em></p>
<p>The Agave species is known for its striking form and general tolerance to cold, heat, sun,
drought, and poor or alkaline soils. Agaves are some of the most useful plants in the hot arid
regions of the Southwest. Sizes of agaves vary from one to six feet in height. They have many
interesting leaf styles and color variations. The pointed leaves of the Agave Americana are armed
with thorns at the tips. This leaf formation allows them to capture tiny amounts of rain, which
guides the moisture down to the roots.</p>
<p>These plants need water occasionally until established or when plants show stress by wilting
```

FIGURE 3-35

3

• **Highlight the words <!--Insert Desert Spoon image here --> on line 44.**

4

• **Type** `<img src="desertspoon.jpg" align="left" alt= "Desert Spoon" width="245" height="198" />` **to insert a left-aligned image with wrapped text.**

5

• **Highlight the words <!--Insert Golden Barrel image here --> on line 56.**

6

• **Type** `<img src="goldenbarrel.jpg" align="right" alt= "Golden Barrel" width="292" height="197" />` **to insert a right-aligned image with wrapped text.**

More About

Background Images

When choosing a background image, do not select an image that either overpowers the Web page or makes the text difficult to read. The Internet has a variety of Web sites with background images. Many require you name the Web site as a source for the image. For more information about background images, visit the HTML More About Web page (scsite.com/html3e/more.htm) and then click Background Images.

7

- **Highlight the words <!--Insert Prickly Pear image here --> on line 68.**

8

- **Type** `<img src="pricklypear.jpg" align="left" alt= "Prickly Pear" width="250" height="255" />` **to insert a left-aligned image with wrapped text.**

The HTML code for all four images appears, as shown in Figure 3-36.

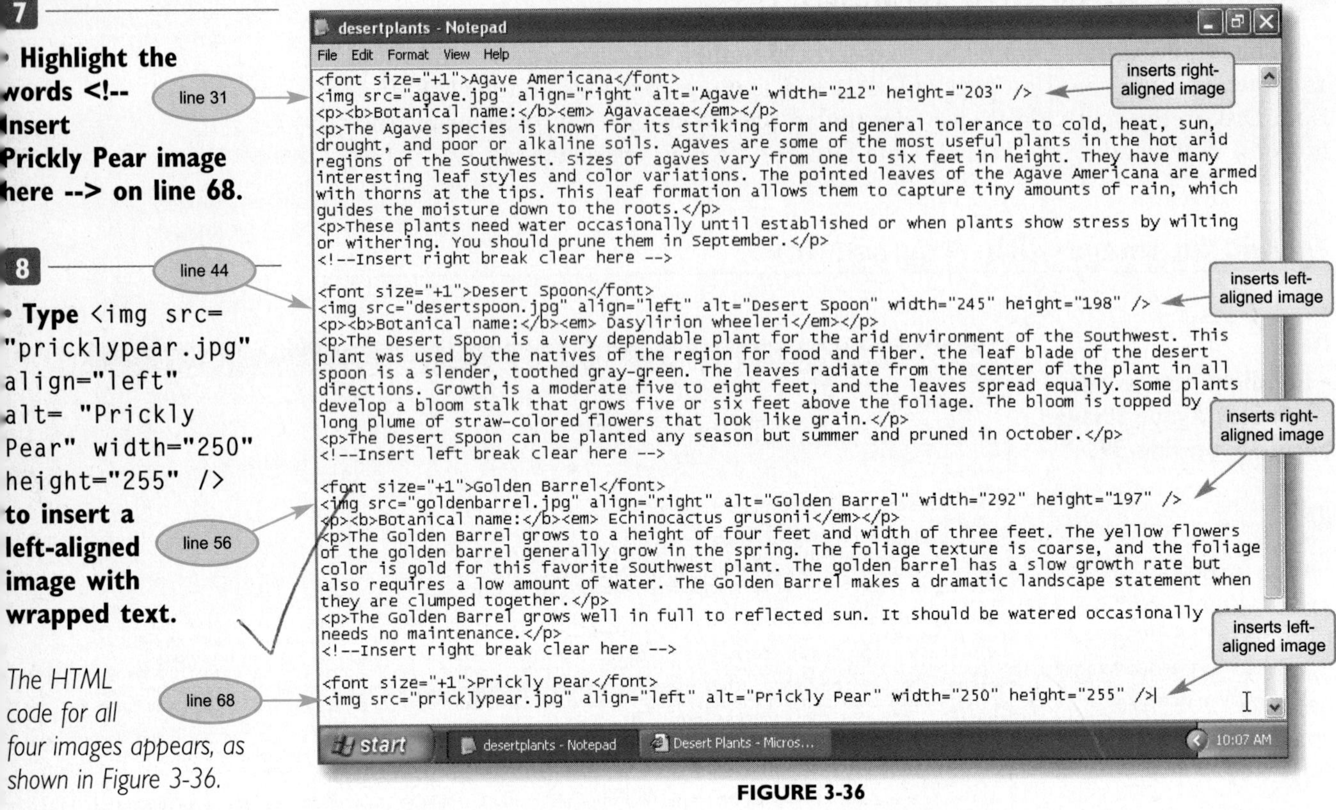

FIGURE 3-36

The HTML code entered in the previous steps sets the images to alternate alignment (first right, then left, then right, then left) down the Desert Plants Web page to provide a visually appealing and balanced Web page.

Clearing the Text Wrapping

The steps above illustrate how to insert an image and wrap the text to the right or the left. Next, the break tags to clear the text wrapping must be entered, using the <br clear=" " /> tag, with right, left, or all as the clear attribute value in the quotation marks. The following steps show to enter code to clear the text wrapping.

To Clear the Text Wrapping

1

- **Highlight the words <!--Insert right break clear here --> on line 41 and then type** `<br clear="right" />` **as the tag.**

2

- **Highlight the words <!--Insert right break clear here --> on line 65 and then type `<br clear="right" />` as the tag.**

The HTML code to clear the text wrapping for both right-aligned images is displayed (Figure 3-37).

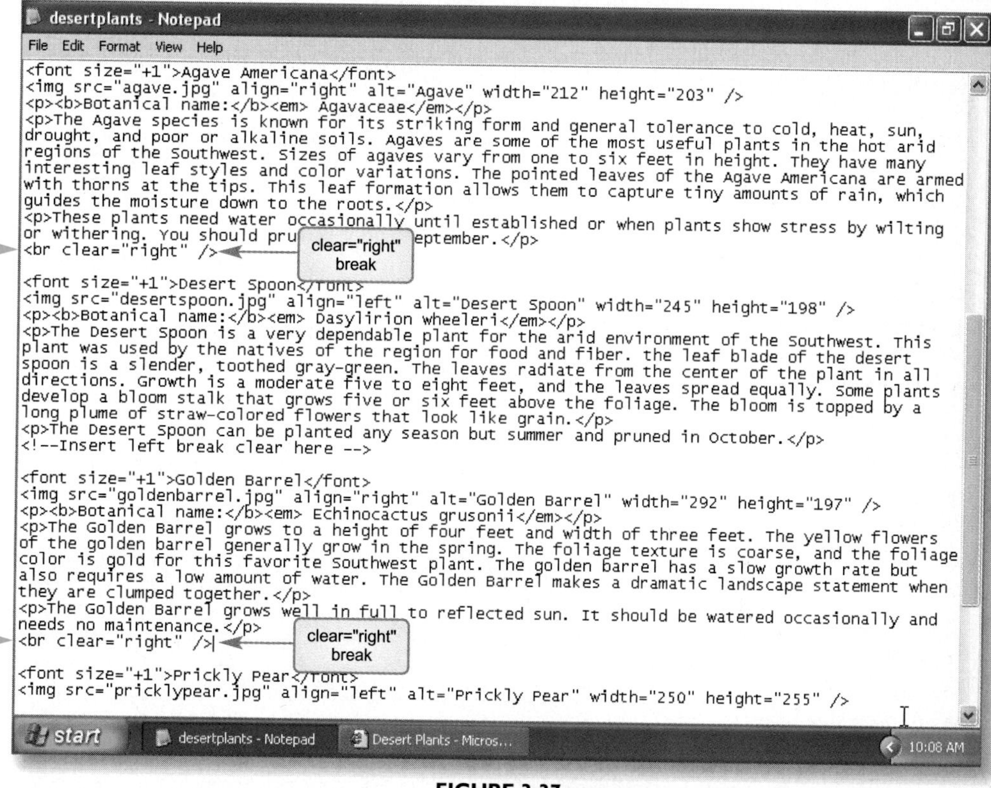

```
desertplants - Notepad
File Edit Format View Help
<font size="+1">Agave Americana</font>
<img src="agave.jpg" align="right" alt="Agave" width="212" height="203" />
<p><b>Botanical name:</b><em> Agavaceae</em></p>
<p>The Agave species is known for its striking form and general tolerance to cold, heat, sun,
drought, and poor or alkaline soils. Agaves are some of the most useful plants in the hot arid
regions of the Southwest. Sizes of agaves vary from one to six feet in height. They have many
interesting leaf styles and color variations. The pointed leaves of the Agave Americana are armed
with thorns at the tips. This leaf formation allows them to capture tiny amounts of rain, which
guides the moisture down to the roots.</p>
<p>These plants need water occasionally until established or when plants show stress by wilting
or withering. You should pru                eptember.</p>
<br clear="right" />

<font size="+1">Desert Spoon</font>
<img src="desertspoon.jpg" align="left" alt="Desert Spoon" width="245" height="198" />
<p><b>Botanical name:</b><em> Dasylirion wheeleri</em></p>
<p>The Desert Spoon is a very dependable plant for the arid environment of the Southwest. This
plant was used by the natives of the region for food and fiber. the leaf blade of the desert
spoon is a slender, toothed gray-green. The leaves radiate from the center of the plant in all
directions. Growth is a moderate five to eight feet, and the leaves spread equally. Some plants
develop a bloom stalk that grows five or six feet above the foliage. The bloom is topped by a
long plume of straw-colored flowers that look like grain.</p>
<p>The Desert Spoon can be planted any season but summer and pruned in October.</p>
<!--Insert left break clear here -->

<font size="+1">Golden Barrel</font>
<img src="goldenbarrel.jpg" align="right" alt="Golden Barrel" width="292" height="197" />
<p><b>Botanical name:</b><em> Echinocactus grusonii</em></p>
<p>The Golden Barrel grows to a height of four feet and width of three feet. The yellow flowers
of the golden barrel generally grow in the spring. The foliage texture is coarse, and the foliage
color is gold for this favorite Southwest plant. The golden barrel has a slow growth rate but
also requires a low amount of water. The Golden Barrel makes a dramatic landscape statement when
they are clumped together.</p>
<p>The Golden Barrel grows well in full to reflected sun. It should be watered occasionally and
needs no maintenance.</p>
<br clear="right" />

<font size="+1">Prickly Pear</font>
<img src="pricklypear.jpg" align="left" alt="Prickly Pear" width="250" height="255" />
start   desertplants - Notepad   Desert Plants - Micros...   10:08 AM
```


FIGURE 3-37

3

- **Highlight the words <!--Insert left break clear here --> on line 53 and then type `<br clear="left" />` as the tag.**

4

- **Highlight the words <!--Insert left break clear here --> on line 77 and then type `<br clear="left" />` as the tag.**

The HTML code to clear the text wrapping for both left-aligned images is displayed (Figure 3-38). The text wrapping breaks all are in place on lines 41, 53, 65, and 77.

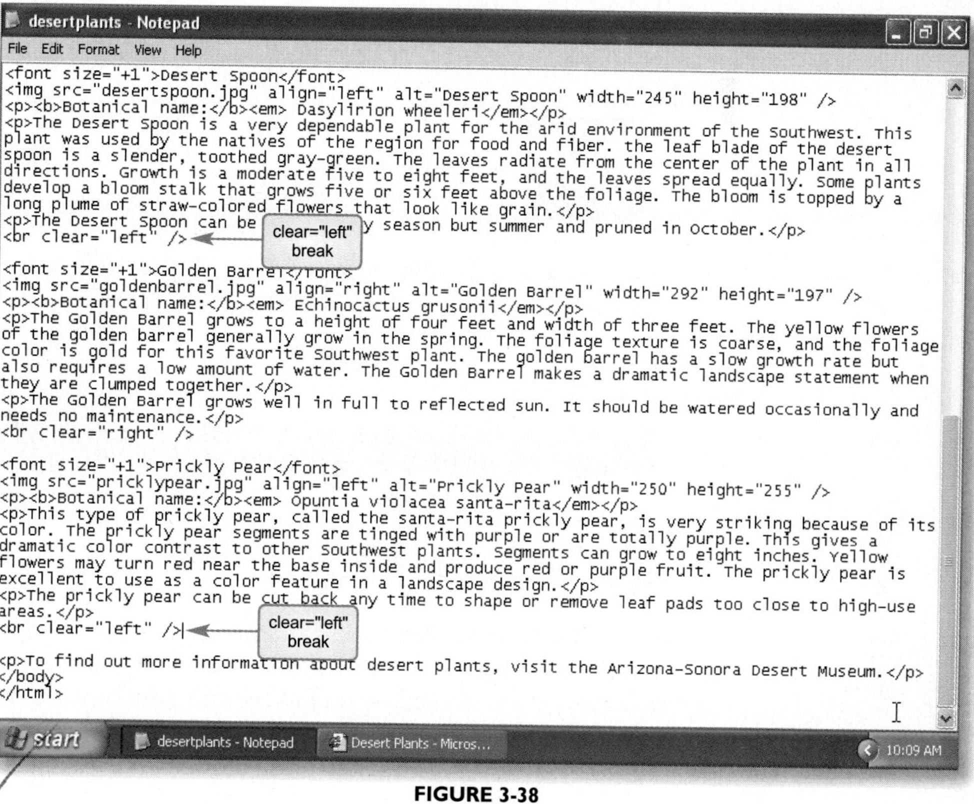

```
desertplants - Notepad
File Edit Format View Help
<font size="+1">Desert Spoon</font>
<img src="desertspoon.jpg" align="left" alt="Desert Spoon" width="245" height="198" />
<p><b>Botanical name:</b><em> Dasylirion wheeleri</em></p>
<p>The Desert Spoon is a very dependable plant for the arid environment of the Southwest. This
plant was used by the natives of the region for food and fiber. the leaf blade of the desert
spoon is a slender, toothed gray-green. The leaves radiate from the center of the plant in all
directions. Growth is a moderate five to eight feet, and the leaves spread equally. Some plants
develop a bloom stalk that grows five or six feet above the foliage. The bloom is topped by a
long plume of straw-colored flowers that look like grain.</p>
<p>The Desert Spoon can be              y season but summer and pruned in October.</p>
<br clear="left" />

<font size="+1">Golden Barr
<img src="goldenbarrel.jpg" align="right" alt="Golden Barrel" width="292" height="197" />
<p><b>Botanical name:</b><em> Echinocactus grusonii</em></p>
<p>The Golden Barrel grows to a height of four feet and width of three feet. The yellow flowers
of the golden barrel generally grow in the spring. The foliage texture is coarse, and the foliage
color is gold for this favorite Southwest plant. The golden barrel has a slow growth rate but
also requires a low amount of water. The Golden Barrel makes a dramatic landscape statement when
they are clumped together.</p>
<p>The Golden Barrel grows well in full to reflected sun. It should be watered occasionally and
needs no maintenance.</p>
<br clear="right" />

<font size="+1">Prickly Pear</font>
<img src="pricklypear.jpg" align="left" alt="Prickly Pear" width="250" height="255" />
<p><b>Botanical name:</b><em> Opuntia violacea santa-rita</em></p>
<p>This type of prickly pear, called the santa-rita prickly pear, is very striking because of its
color. The prickly pear segments are tinged with purple or are totally purple. This gives a
dramatic color contrast to other Southwest plants. Segments can grow to eight inches. Yellow
flowers may turn red near the base inside and produce red or purple fruit. The prickly pear is
excellent to use as a color feature in a landscape design.</p>
<p>The prickly pear can be cut back any time to shape or remove leaf pads too close to high-use
areas.</p>
<br clear="left" />

<p>To find out more informa               desert plants, visit the Arizona-Sonora Desert Museum.</p>
</body>
</html>
start   desertplants - Notepad   Desert Plants - Micros...   10:09 AM
```


FIGURE 3-38

The previous steps used several image attributes when adding images, including the alignment, the height and width, and the alternate text. The <img> tag also supports additional attributes to control the spacing around images and text.

More About

Web Page Size

The size of a Web page is the total file size of all elements, including the HTML file and any images. The more images a Web page contains, the longer it takes to download. When adding images, test the download time; if it takes more than 10 seconds, most users will not wait to view the page.

Using Horizontal and Vertical Spacing

Using spacing between and around images and text can help create an easy-to-read Web page, as shown in Figure 3-39. The hspace and vspace attributes of the <img> tag control the amount of horizontal and vertical space around an image. If text is wrapped around an image, as it is on the Desert Plants Web page, adding space around the image helps ensure that the text does not appear to run into the image. Figure 3-39 shows images added to a Web page using hspace and vspace attributes. Additional vertical space displays above and below the image where the <img> tag uses the attribute and value, vspace="20". Additional horizontal space displays to the right and the left of the image where the <img> tag uses the attribute and value, hspace="20".

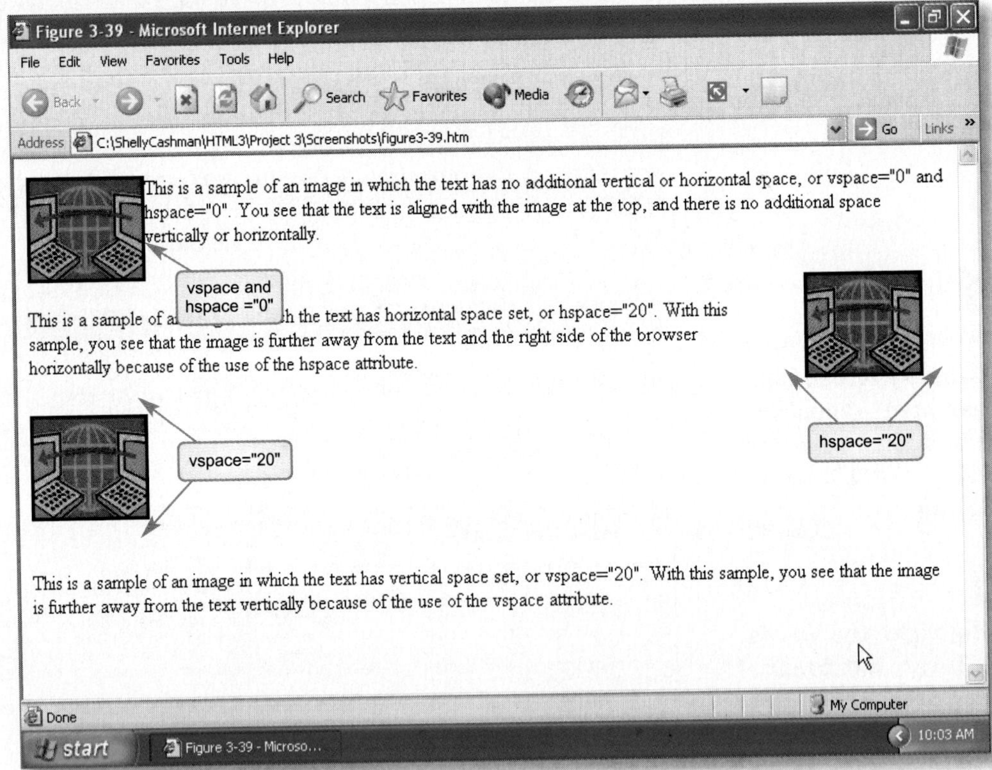

FIGURE 3-39 Examples of horizontal and vertical spacing.

Using Thumbnail Images

Many Web developers use thumbnail images to improve page loading time. A **thumbnail image** is a smaller version of the image itself. The thumbnail is used as a link that, when clicked, will load the full-sized image. Figure 3-40a shows an example of a thumbnail image. When the image is clicked, the browser loads the full-sized image (Figure 3-40b). Loading images can take a long time, depending on the size and the complexity of the image. Using a thumbnail image gives a visitor the opportunity to decide whether to view the full-sized image.

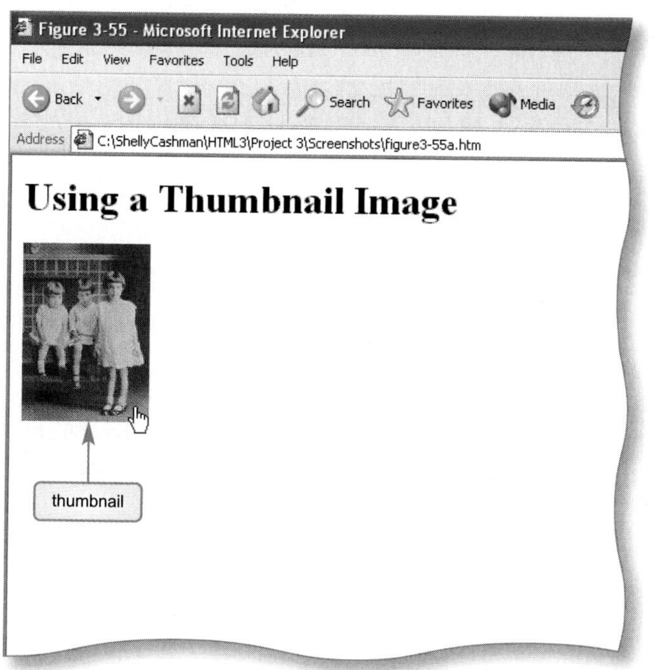

(a) Thumbnail image.

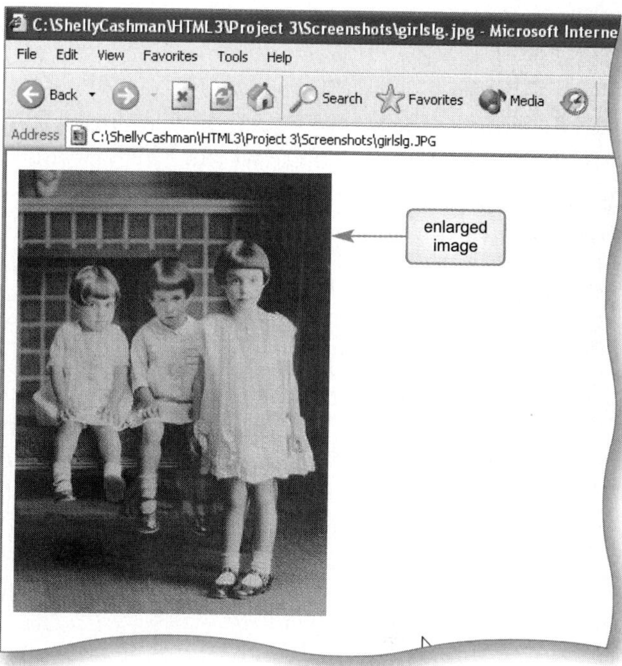

(b) Full-sized

FIGURE 3-40

To create a thumbnail version of an image, the image can be resized to a smaller size in a paint or image-editing project and then saved with a different file name. The thumbnail image then is added to a Web page as an image link to the larger version of the image. The HTML code to add a thumbnail image that links to a larger image takes the form

```
<a href="largeimage.gif"><img src="thumbnail.gif" /></a>
```

where largeimage.gif is the name of the full-sized image and thumbnail.gif is the name of the smaller version of the image. If a visitor clicks the thumbnail image to view the larger image, he or she can use the Back button on the browser's Standard toolbar to return to the original Web page displaying the thumbnail image.

Obtaining Images

You can obtain images from a number of different sources. The Web contains many Web sites with thousands of image files on countless subjects that can be downloaded free and used for noncommercial purposes. Using a search engine, enter a search for the phrases, free GIFs or free Web images, to find collections of images for use on a Web site. If you find a graphic you want to use, right-click the image, click Save Picture As on the shortcut menu, and then save the image to your computer.

Many applications come with clip art that can be used on Web pages. Other types of digital images, such as images scanned by a scanner or pictures taken with a digital camera, also can be included on a Web page. You also can create images using a paint or image-editing program. Regardless of where you get the images, always be aware of copyright rules and regulations.

More About

E-mail Links

Although it is not common, you can assign more than one e-mail address to a mailto: tag. Use the form "mailto:first@isp.com, second@isp.com" in the <a href=> tag. Some older browsers may not support this tag.

Adding a Text Link to Another Web Site

As you have learned, one of the more important features of the Web is the capability of linking a Web page in one Web site to a Web page in another Web site anywhere in the world. The <a> and </a> tags used to create a text link to a Web page within the same Web site also are used to create a link to a Web page in another Web site.

Adding a Text Link to a Web Page in Another Web Site

In this project, the Desert Plants Web page includes a link to a Web page on another Web site, where the visitor can find additional desert plant information. The <a> and </a> tags are used to create a link to a Web page in another Web site. The basic form of the tag used to create a link is the same as the previous links. To link to a Web page on an external Web site, the href (hypertext reference) attribute value includes the entire URL to the Web page (for example, http://www.desertmuseum.org). The phrase, Arizona-Sonora Desert Museum, is used as the clickable text link.

The following steps illustrate how to add a text link on the Desert Plants Web page to the home page of the Arizona-Sonora Desert Museum Web site.

To Add a Text Link to a Web Page in Another Web Site

1

- **Click immediately to the left of Arizona on line 80 and type `<a href="http://www.desertmuseum.org">` to add the text link.**

2

- **Click immediately to the right of Museum on line 81 and type `</a>` to end the tag.**

The HTML code is displayed (Figure 3-41).

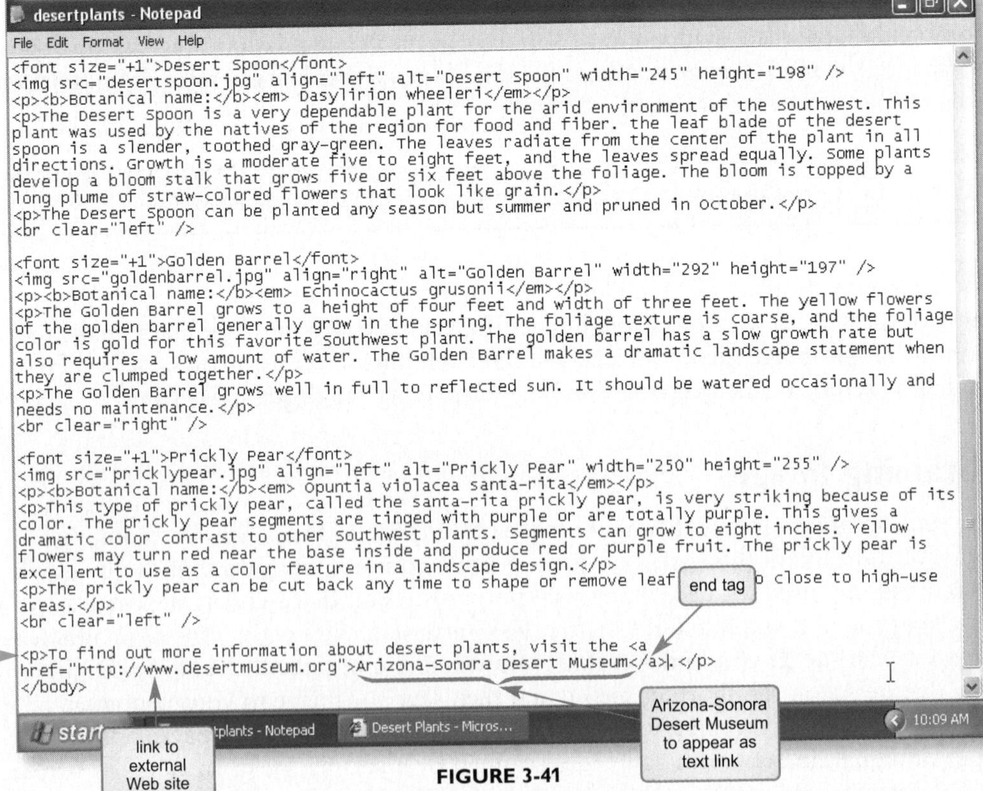

FIGURE 3-41

After adding this link, the Web page displays as shown in Figure 3-42. The text link displays in a blue, underlined font to indicate it is a link. The mouse pointer also changes to the pointing hand when moved over the link text.

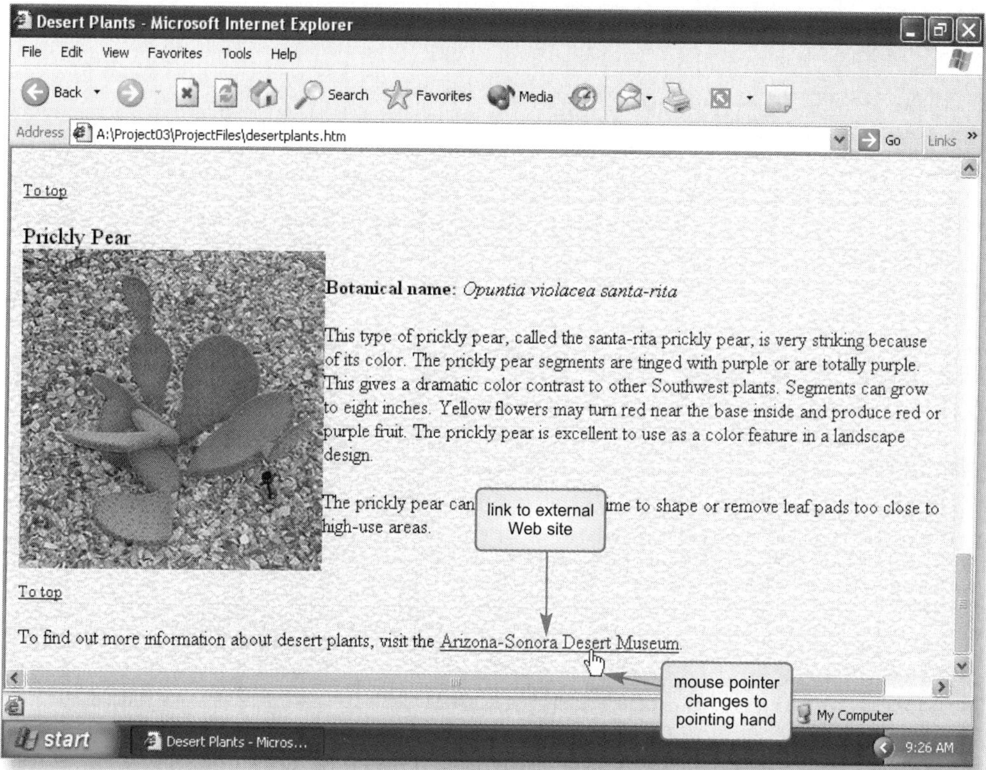

FIGURE 3-42 Web page with external link.

Adding Links within a Web Page

The final links to be added in this project are links within the Desert Plants Web page. Because the Desert Plants is a long page, it would be easier for the visitors to have a menu or list at the top of the Web page that facilitates immediate movement to another section. The Web page in Figure 3-25 on page HTM 94 shows how these links will appear when completed.

Figure 3-43a on the next page shows how clicking the text link, Agave Americana, at the top of the page, links to the Agave Americana section in another part of the Web page (Figure 3-43b). When the mouse pointer is moved over the word, Agave Americana, and clicked, the browser repositions, or links, the page to the target named Agave Americana.

To create links within the same Web page, the targets for the links first must be created. A **target** is a named location or anchor within a Web page to which a link can be created. In the Desert Plants Web page, the internal links are intended to make it easier for Web page visitors to go quickly from the top of the Desert Plants Web page to the Agave Americana, Desert Spoon, Golden Barrel, and Prickly Pear sections of the Web page. Targets thus must be set at the beginning of these four sections, so links then can be created to these targets. To do this, you create a list of words to use as links. The unordered (bulleted) list shown in Figure 3-25 is used as the series of links to the targets.

> *More About*
>
> **Other Links**
>
> You also can create a link to other Web pages (i.e., non-http), an FTP site, and newsgroups. To link to an FTP site, type `ftp://URL` rather than `http://URL` used in this project. For a newsgroup, type `news:newsgroup name` and for any particular article within the newsgroup, type `news:article name` as the entry.

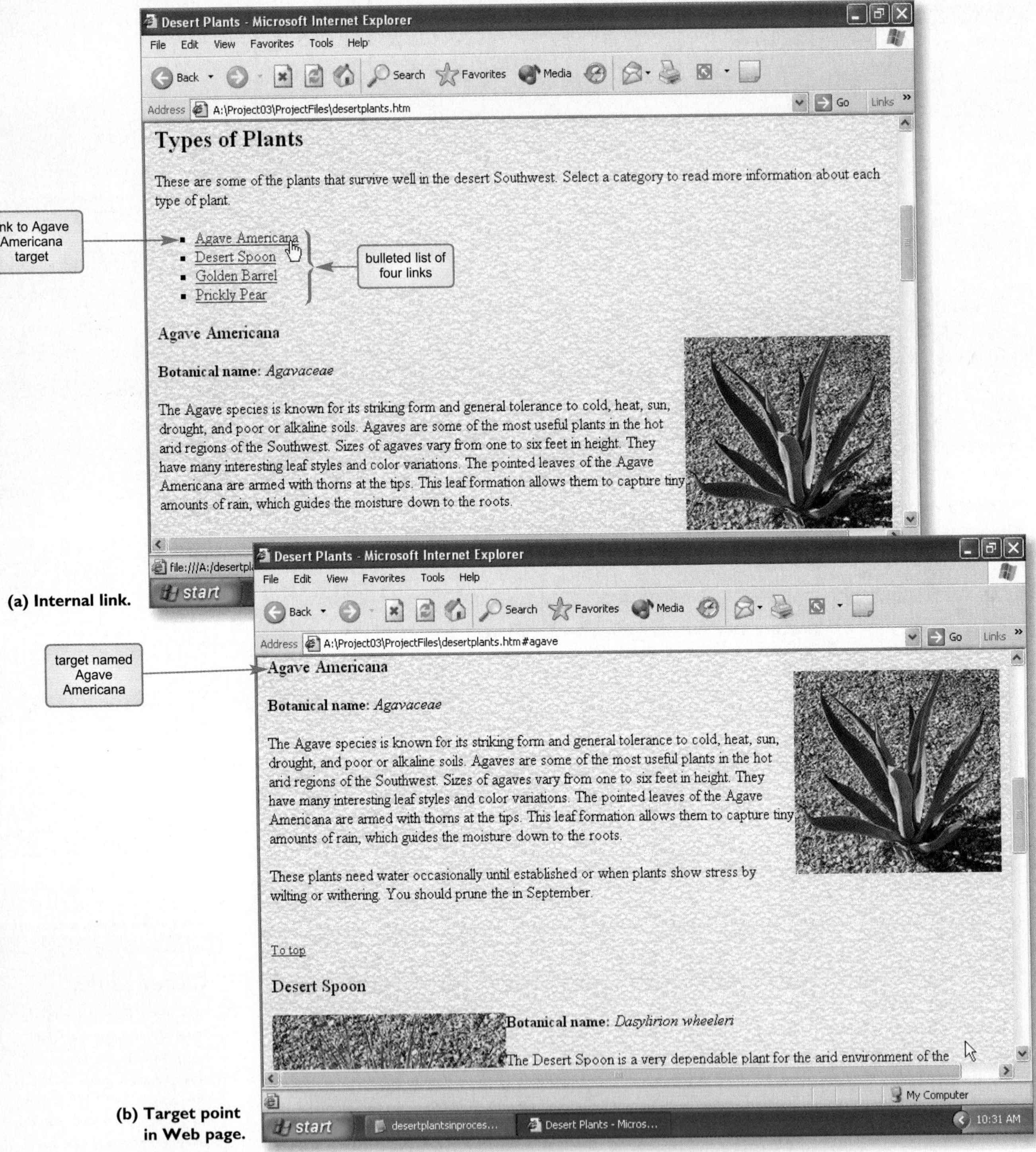

(a) Internal link.

(b) Target point in Web page.

FIGURE 3-43

Setting Link Targets

Link targets are created using the <a> tag with the name attribute, using the form

```
<a name= "targetname"></a>
```

where targetname is a unique name for a link target within that Web page. Notice that the tag uses the name attribute, rather than the href attribute, and that no text is included between the start <a> and end </a> tag, because the target is not intended to display on the Web page as a clickable link. Instead, the link target is intended to mark a specific area of the Web page, to which a link can be directed. The following steps show how to set the four link targets in the Desert Plants Web page.

To Set Link Targets

1

- **Click immediately to the left of the <font> tag on line 30.**
- **Type** `<a name="agaveamericana"></a>` **to create a link target named agaveamericana.**

2

- **Click immediately to the left of the <font> tag on line 43.**
- **Type** `<a name="desertspoon"></a>` **to create a link target named desertspoon.**

The HTML code is displayed (Figure 3-44). Two link targets, agaveamericana and desertspoon, are created in the Web page.

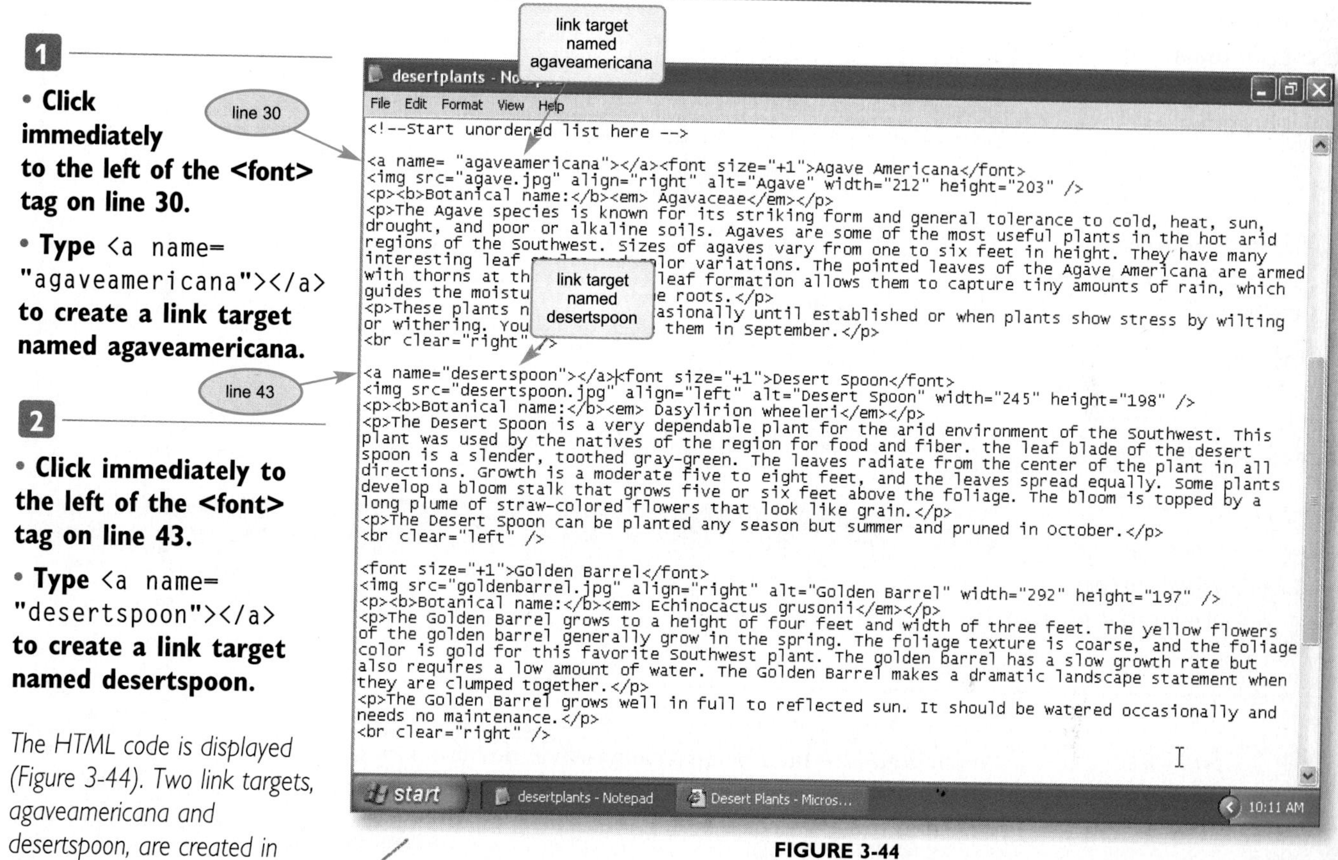

FIGURE 3-44

3

- **Click immediately to the left of the <font> tag on line 55.**
- **Type** `<a name="goldenbarrel"></a>` **to create a link target named goldenbarrel.**

4

- **Click immediately to the left of the <font> tag on line 67.**
- **Type** `<a name="pricklypear"></a>` **to create a link target named pricklypear.**

The HTML code is displayed (Figure 3-45). Two additional link targets, goldenbarrel and pricklypear, are created in the Web page.

desertplants - Notepad

File Edit Format View Help

```
<img src="desertspoon.jpg" align="left" alt="Desert Spoon" width="245" height="198" />
<p><b>Botanical name:</b><em> Dasylirion wheeleri</em></p>
<p>The Desert Spoon is a very dependable plant for the arid environment of the Southwest. This
plant was used by the natives of the region for food and fiber. the leaf blade of the desert
spoon is a slender, toothed gray-green. The leaves radiate from the center of the plant in all
directions. Growth is                  ive to eight feet, and the leaves spread equally. Some plants
develop a bloom stalk                  ive or six feet above the foliage. The bloom is topped by a
long plume of straw-co                 s that look like grain.</p>
<p>The Desert Spoon ca                  any season but summer and pruned in October.</p>
<br clear="left" />

<a name="goldenbarrel"></a><font size="+1">Golden Barrel</font>
<img src="goldenbarrel.jpg" align="right" alt="Golden Barrel" width="292" height="197" />
<p><b>Botanical name:</b><em> Echinocactus grusonii</em></p>
<p>The Golden Barrel grows to a height of four feet and width of three feet. The yellow flowers
of the golden barrel generally grow in the spring. The foliage texture is coarse, and the foliage
color is gold for this favorite Southwest plant. The golden barrel has a slow growth rate but
also requires a low amoun              The Golden Barrel makes a dramatic landscape statement when
they are clumped together
<p>The Golden Barrel grow              ll to reflected sun. It should be watered occasionally and
needs no maintenance.</p>
<br clear="right" />

<a name="pricklypear"></a><font size="+1">Prickly Pear</font>
<img src="pricklypear.jpg" align="left" alt="Prickly Pear" width="250" height="255" />
<p><b>Botanical name:</b><em> Opuntia violacea santa-rita</em></p>
<p>This type of prickly pear, called the santa-rita prickly pear, is very striking because of its
color. The prickly pear segments are tinged with purple or are totally purple. This gives a
dramatic color contrast to other Southwest plants. Segments can grow to eight inches. Yellow
flowers may turn red near the base inside and produce red or purple fruit. The prickly pear is
excellent to use as a color feature in a landscape design.</p>
<p>The prickly pear can be cut back any time to shape or remove leaf pads too close to high-use
areas.</p>
<br clear="left" />

<p>To find out more information about desert plants, visit the <a
href="http://www.desertmuseum.org">Arizona-Sonora Desert Museum</a>.</p>
</body>
</html>
```

line 55

link target named goldenbarrel

line 67

link target named pricklypear

start | desertplants - Notepad | Desert Plants - Micros... | 10:12 AM

FIGURE 3-45

The four link targets (agaveamericana, desertspoon, goldenbarrel, and pricklypear) now are added to the Desert Plants Web page. With the link targets added, links directed at those tags can be created.

Adding Links to Link Targets within a Web Page

Links to link targets are created using the <a> tag with the name attribute, using the form

```
<a href="#targetname">
```

where targetname is the name of a link target in that Web page. Notice that the tag uses the href attribute, followed by the pound sign (#) and the target name enclosed in quotation marks. The steps on the next page illustrate how to create an unordered (bulleted) list and then to use the list items as links to link targets within the Web page.

To Add Links to Link Targets within a Web Page

1

- **Highlight the words <!--Start unordered list here --> on line 28.**

2

- **Type** `<ul type="square">` **and then press the ENTER key.**

3

- **Type** `<li><a href="#agaveamericana"> Agave Americana </a></li>` **and then press the ENTER key.**

The HTML code is displayed (Figure 3-46). The first list item, which displays as a text link, links to the target named agaveamericana.

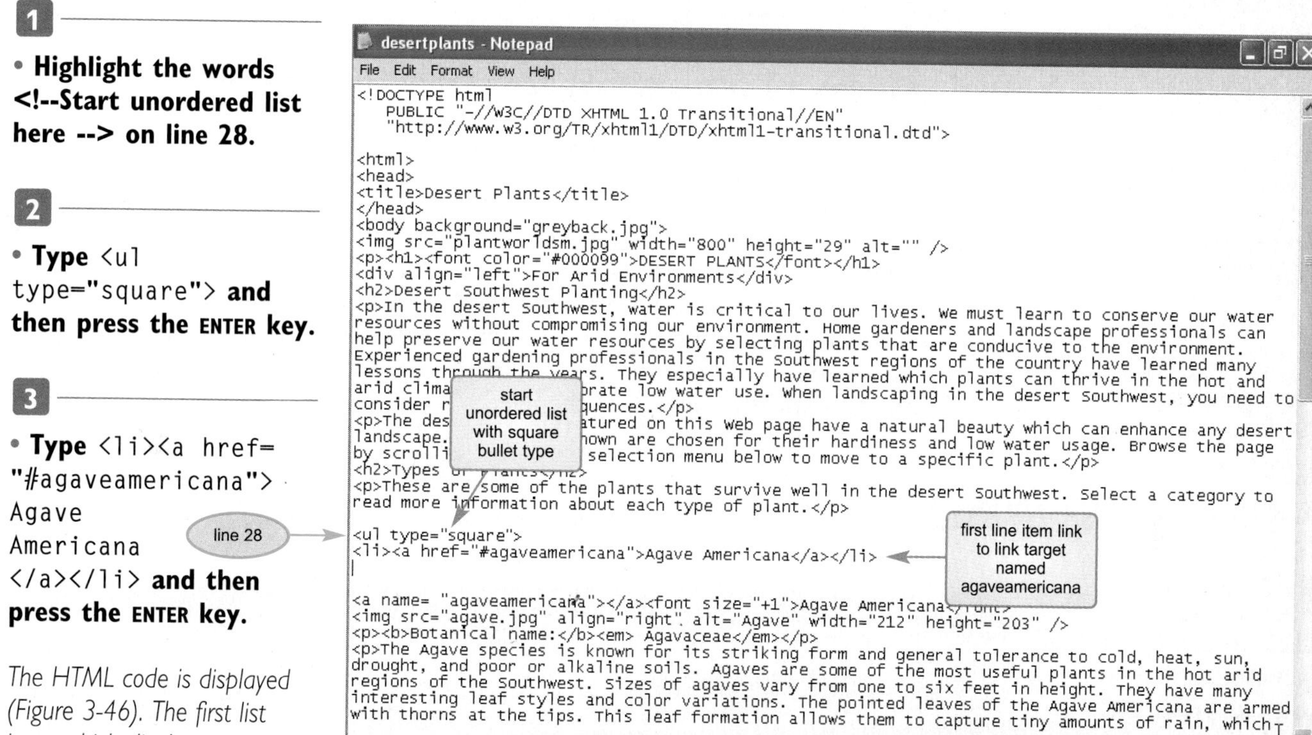

FIGURE 3-46

4

- **Type** `<li><a href="#desertspoon"> Desert Spoon</a></li>` **and then press the ENTER key.**

5

- **Type** `<li><a href= "#goldenbarrel"> Golden Barrel</a> </li>` **and then press the ENTER key.**

6

- **Type** `<li><a href="#pricklypear"> Prickly Pear</a> </li>` **and then press the ENTER key.**
- **Type** `</ul>` **and then press the ENTER key.**

The HTML code is displayed (Figure 3-47).

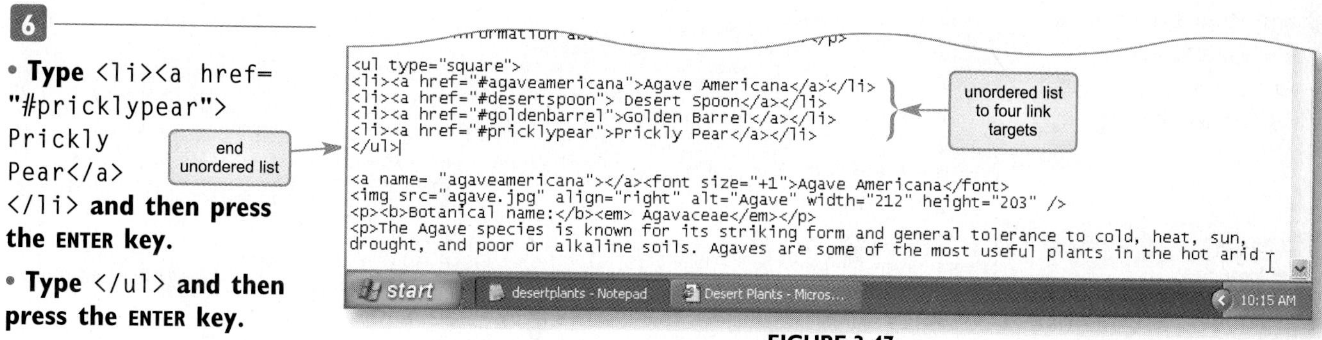

FIGURE 3-47

> **More About**
>
> **Specifying Alternative Fonts**
>
> If a Web page font is not available on users' computers, you can create a list of fonts and the browser will determine the font to use. For example, if the Web page uses a Geneva font, but would display well in Arial or Helvetica, you create a comma-separated list of acceptable fonts, using <font face="geneva,arial,helvetica">your text</font> as the code.

The HTML code added to the Desert Plants Web page creates a list with four items. Each item in the list is a text link to a specific, named link target in the Desert Plants Web page.

Adding Links to a Link Target at the Top of the Page

As discussed, it is good design practice to provide users with a quick way to move back to the top of a long Web page. The Desert Plants Web page thus includes four text links named To top, as shown in Figure 3-25 on page HTM 94. Clicking a To top link quickly moves the visitor back to the top of the page. To create these links, first you need to set the target at the top of the page. Then you create four links to that target after the Agave Americana, Desert Spoon, Golden Barrel, and Prickly Pear sections. The links will use a font size smaller than normal text (<font size="-1">), so they do not clutter the Web page. The following steps illustrate how to add links to a target at the top of the page.

To Add Links to a Target at the Top of the Page

1

- **Click to the left of the < symbol on line 10 and then press the ENTER key.**

2

- **Position the insertion point on line 10 and type `<a name="top"></a>` as the tag.**

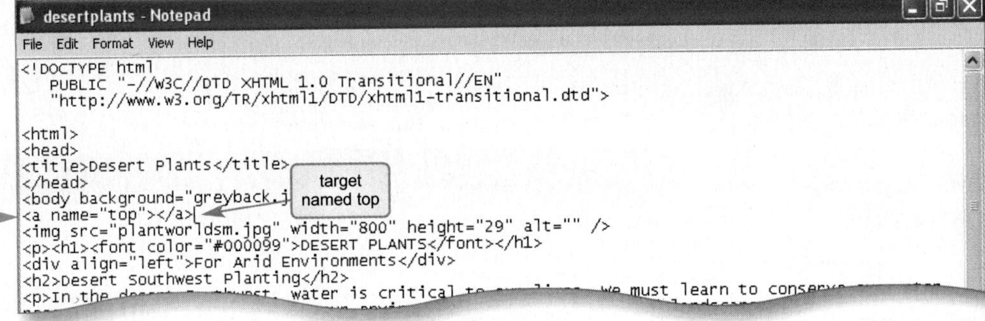

FIGURE 3-48

The target is set at the top of the Web page (Figure 3-48).

3

- **Position the insertion point on the blank line 48 and then type `<p><a href="#top"><font size=-1>To top</font></a></p>` as the tag.**

4

- **Press the ENTER key.**

```
desertplants - Notepad
File Edit Format View Help
<li><a href="#pricklypear">Prickly Pear</a></li>
</ul>

<a name= "agaveamericana"></a><font size="+1">Agave Americana</font>
<img src="agave.jpg" align="right" alt="Agave" width="212" height="203" />
<p><b>Botanical name:</b><em> Agavaceae</em></p>
<p>The Agave species is known for its striking form and general tolerance to cold, heat, sun,
drought, and poor or alkaline soils. Agaves are some of the most useful plants in the hot arid
regions of the Southwest. Sizes of agaves vary from one to six feet in height. They have many
interesting leaf styles and color variations. The pointed leaves of the Agave Americana are armed
with thorns at the tips. This leaf formation allows them to capture tiny amounts of rain, which
guides the moisture down to the roots.</p>
<p>These plants need water occasionally until established or when plants show stress by wilting
or withering. You should prune them in September.</p>
<br clear="right" />
<p><a href="#top"><font size="-1">To top</font></a></p>

<a name="desertspoon"></a><font size="+1">Desert Spoon</font>
<img src="desertspoon.jpg" align="left" alt="Desert Spoon" width="245" height="198" />
```

line 48

link to target named top

FIGURE 3-49

A text link to the top link target is added (Figure 3-49). The font size is set to -1, so the text link appears smaller than normal text.

After the code for one of the To top links is added, that code can be copied and pasted into other areas of the HTML code. Copying and pasting the code typically is much faster than retyping the code and is less prone to typing errors. The following steps show how to copy and paste the link code to three other lines in the HTML code.

To Copy and Paste HTML Code

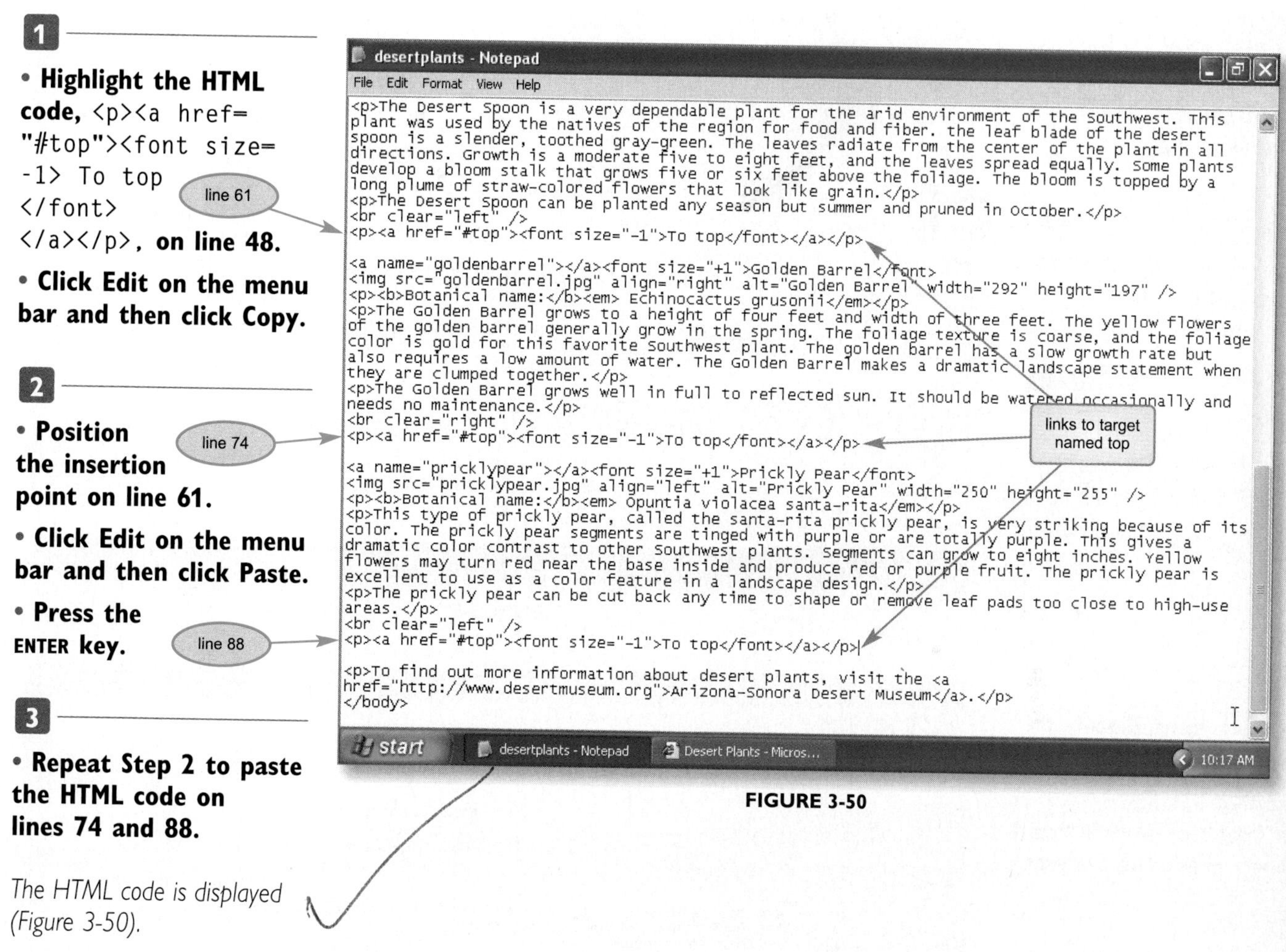

FIGURE 3-50

1

- **Highlight the HTML code, <p><a href="#top"><font size=-1> To top </font> </a></p>, on line 48.**
- **Click Edit on the menu bar and then click Copy.**

2

- **Position the insertion point on line 61.**
- **Click Edit on the menu bar and then click Paste.**
- **Press the ENTER key.**

3

- **Repeat Step 2 to paste the HTML code on lines 74 and 88.**

The HTML code is displayed (Figure 3-50).

The HTML code added to lines 48, 61, 74, and 88 creates four text links that are directed to the link target named, top, at the top of the Desert Plants Web page. For each text link, the HTML code creates a new paragraph using the <p> and </p> tags, sets the font to a small size using the <font size="-1"> and the </font> tags, and sets the link to the top target <a href="#top"></a> using the anchor tag.

Adding an Image Link to a Web Page

The last step in editing the Desert Plants Web page is to add an image link from the Desert Plants Web page back to the Plant World home page. The steps on the next page show how to create an image link at the top of the Desert Plants Web page that a visitor can click to return to the Plant World home page.

To Add an Image Link to a Web Page

1

- **Click immediately to the left of <img on line 11.**
- **Type** `<a href="plantworld.htm">` **as the tag and then press the ENTER key.**

2

- **Click immediately to the right of alt=" " /> on line 12.**
- **Type** `</a>` **as the tag.**

The HTML file is displayed (Figure 3-51). The image, plantworldsm.jpg is set as an image link to plantworld.htm.

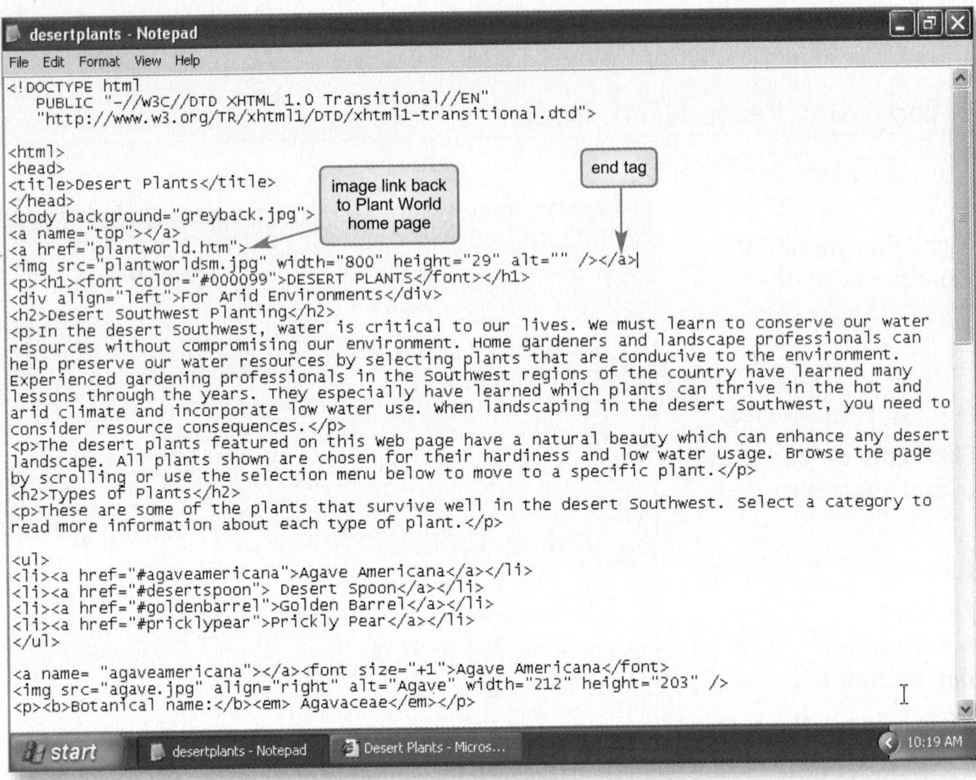

```
<!DOCTYPE html
   PUBLIC "-//W3C//DTD XHTML 1.0 Transitional//EN"
   "http://www.w3.org/TR/xhtml1/DTD/xhtml1-transitional.dtd">

<html>
<head>
<title>Desert Plants</title>
</head>
<body background="greyback.jpg">
<a name="top"></a>
<a href="plantworld.htm">
<img src="plantworldsm.jpg" width="800" height="29" alt="" /></a>
<p><h1><font color="#000099">DESERT PLANTS</font></h1>
<div align="left">For Arid Environments</div>
<h2>Desert Southwest Planting</h2>
<p>In the desert Southwest, water is critical to our lives. We must learn to conserve our water
resources without compromising our environment. Home gardeners and landscape professionals can
help preserve our water resources by selecting plants that are conducive to the environment.
Experienced gardening professionals in the Southwest regions of the country have learned many
lessons through the years. They especially have learned which plants can thrive in the hot and
arid climate and incorporate low water use. When landscaping in the desert Southwest, you need to
consider resource consequences.</p>
<p>The desert plants featured on this web page have a natural beauty which can enhance any desert
landscape. All plants shown are chosen for their hardiness and low water usage. Browse the page
by scrolling or use the selection menu below to move to a specific plant.</p>
<h2>Types of Plants</h2>
<p>These are some of the plants that survive well in the desert Southwest. Select a category to
read more information about each type of plant.</p>

<ul>
<li><a href="#agaveamericana">Agave Americana</a></li>
<li><a href="#desertspoon"> Desert Spoon</a></li>
<li><a href="#goldenbarrel">Golden Barrel</a></li>
<li><a href="#pricklypear">Prickly Pear</a></li>
</ul>

<a name= "agaveamericana"></a><font size="+1">Agave Americana</font>
<img src="agave.jpg" align="right" alt="Agave" width="212" height="203" />
<p><b>Botanical name:</b><em> Agavaceae</em></p>
```


FIGURE 3-51

3

- **Click immediately to the left of alt=" " /> on line 12.**
- **Type** `border="0"` **and then press the SPACEBAR.**

The HTML file is displayed (Figure 3-52).

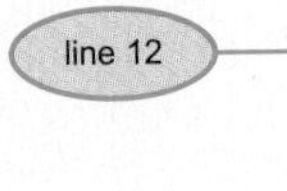

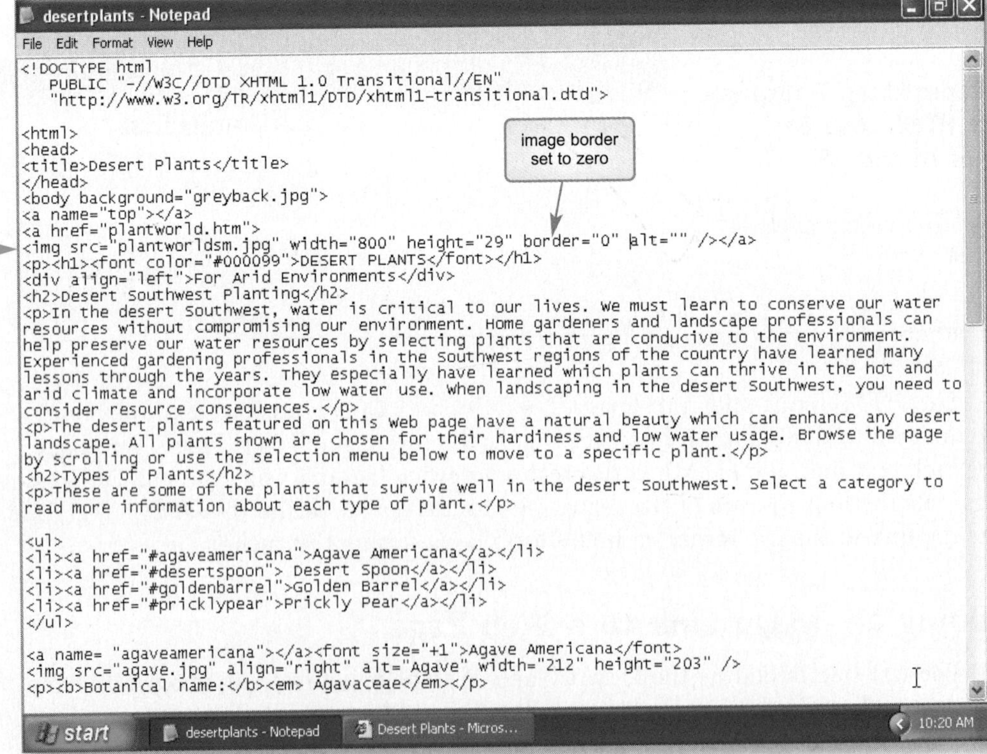

```
<!DOCTYPE html
   PUBLIC "-//W3C//DTD XHTML 1.0 Transitional//EN"
   "http://www.w3.org/TR/xhtml1/DTD/xhtml1-transitional.dtd">

<html>
<head>
<title>Desert Plants</title>
</head>
<body background="greyback.jpg">
<a name="top"></a>
<a href="plantworld.htm">
<img src="plantworldsm.jpg" width="800" height="29" border="0" alt="" /></a>
<p><h1><font color="#000099">DESERT PLANTS</font></h1>
<div align="left">For Arid Environments</div>
<h2>Desert Southwest Planting</h2>
<p>In the desert Southwest, water is critical to our lives. We must learn to conserve our water
resources without compromising our environment. Home gardeners and landscape professionals can
help preserve our water resources by selecting plants that are conducive to the environment.
Experienced gardening professionals in the Southwest regions of the country have learned many
lessons through the years. They especially have learned which plants can thrive in the hot and
arid climate and incorporate low water use. When landscaping in the desert Southwest, you need to
consider resource consequences.</p>
<p>The desert plants featured on this web page have a natural beauty which can enhance any desert
landscape. All plants shown are chosen for their hardiness and low water usage. Browse the page
by scrolling or use the selection menu below to move to a specific plant.</p>
<h2>Types of Plants</h2>
<p>These are some of the plants that survive well in the desert Southwest. Select a category to
read more information about each type of plant.</p>

<ul>
<li><a href="#agaveamericana">Agave Americana</a></li>
<li><a href="#desertspoon"> Desert Spoon</a></li>
<li><a href="#goldenbarrel">Golden Barrel</a></li>
<li><a href="#pricklypear">Prickly Pear</a></li>
</ul>

<a name= "agaveamericana"></a><font size="+1">Agave Americana</font>
<img src="agave.jpg" align="right" alt="Agave" width="212" height="203" />
<p><b>Botanical name:</b><em> Agavaceae</em></p>
```


FIGURE 3-52

The image, plantworldsm.jpg, is added to the top of the Desert Plants Web page. The <a> </a> tags are used to set the image as the clickable element for the link, which connects to the home page, plantworld.htm. Setting the image border attribute value to zero ensures that no border displays around the image. As previously discussed, if the image did have a border, the border would display using the default link colors to indicate that the link is normal, active, or visited. Because it does not have a border, no link colors display.

Saving and Printing the HTML File and Web Page

With the HTML code for the Desert Plants Web page complete, the HTML file should be saved and a copy should be printed as a reference.

To Save and Print the HTML File

1. **Save the HTML file by clicking File on the menu bar and then clicking Save on the File menu.**
2. **Click File on the menu bar and then click Print on the File menu.**

Notepad prints the HTML file (Figure 3-53). Notepad saves the HTML file in the Project03\ProjectFiles folder on the floppy disk in drive A using the file name, desertplants.htm.

```
<!DOCTYPE html
     PUBLIC "-//W3C//DTD XHTML 1.0 Transitional//EN"
      "http://www.w3.org/TR/xhtml1/DTD/xhtml1-transitional.dtd">

<html>
<head>
<title>Desert Plants</title>
</head>
<body background="greyback.jpg">
<a name="top"></a>
<a href="plantworld.htm">
<img src="plantworldsm.jpg" width="800" height="29" border="0" alt="" /></a>
<p><h1><font color="#000099">DESERT PLANTS</font></h1>
<div align="left">For Arid Environments</div>
<h2>Desert Southwest Planting</h2>
<p>In the desert Southwest, water is critical to our lives. We must learn to conserve our
water resources without compromising our environment. Home gardeners and landscape
professionals can help preserve our water resources by selecting plants that are conducive to
the environment. Experienced gardening professionals in the Southwest regions of the country
have learned many lessons through the years. They especially have learned which plants can
thrive in the hot and arid climate and incorporate low water use. When landscaping in the
desert Southwest, you need to consider resource consequences.</p>
<p>The desert plants featured on this Web page have a natural beauty which can enhance any
desert landscape. All plants shown are chosen for their hardiness and low water usage. Browse
the page by scrolling or use the selection menu below to move to a specific plant.</p>
<h2>Types of Plants</h2>
<p>These are some of the plants that survive well in the desert Southwest. Select a category
to read more information about each type of plant.</p>

<ul type="square">
<li><a href="#agaveamericana">Agave</a></li>
<li><a href="#desertspoon">Desertspoon</a></li>
<li><a href="#goldenbarrel">Golden Barrel</a></li>
<li><a href="#pricklypear">Prickly Pear</a></li>
</ul>

<a name="agaveamericana"></a><font size=+1>Agave Americana</font>
<img src="agave.jpg" align="right" alt= "Agave" width="212" height="203" />
<p><b>Botanical name:</b> <em>Agavaceae</em></p>
<p>The Agave species is known for its striking form and general tolerance to cold, heat, sun,
drought, and poor or alkaline soils. Agaves are some of the most useful plants in the hot arid
regions of the Southwest. Sizes of agaves vary from one to six feet in height. They have many
interesting leaf styles and color variations. The pointed leaves of the Agave Americana are
armed with thorns at the tips. This leaf formation allows them to capture tiny amounts of
rain, which guides the moisture down to the roots.</p>
<p>These plants need water occasionally until established or when plants show stress by
wilting or withering. You should prune them in September.</p>
<br clear="right" />
<p><a href="#top"><font size=-1>To top</font></a></p>

<a name="desertspoon"></a><font size=+1>Desert Spoon</font>
<img src="desertspoon.jpg" align="left" alt= "Desert Spoon" width="245" height="198" />
<p><b>Botanical name:</b> <em>Dasylirion wheeleri</em></p>
<p>The Desert Spoon is a very dependable plant for the arid environment of the Southwest. This
plant was used by the natives of the region for food and fiber. the leaf blade of the desert
spoon is a slender, toothed gray-green. The leaves radiate from the center of the plant in all
directions. Growth is a moderate five to eight feet, and the leaves spread equally. Some
plants develop a bloom stalk that grows five or six feet above the foliage. The bloom is
topped by a long plume of straw-colored flowers that look like grain.</p>
<p>The Desert Spoon can be planted any season but summer and pruned in October.</p>
<br clear="left" />
<p><a href="#top"><font size=-1>To top</font></a></p>

<a name="goldenbarrel"></a><font size=+1>Golden Barrel</font>
<img src="goldenbarrel.jpg" align="right" alt= "Golden Barrel" width="292" height="197" />

-1-
```

FIGURE 3-53

```
<p><b>Botanical name:</b> <em>Echinocactus grusonii</em></p>
<p>The Golden Barrel grows to a height of four feet and width of three feet. The yellow
flowers of the golden barrel generally grow in the spring. The foliage texture is coarse, and
the foliage color is gold for this favorite Southwest plant. The golden barrel has a slow
growth rate but also requires a low amount of water. The Golden Barrel makes a dramatic
landscape statement when they are clumped together.</p>
<p>The Golden Barrel grows well in full to reflected sun. It should be watered occasionally
and needs no maintenance.</p>
<br clear="right" />
<p><a href="#top"><font size=-1>To top</font></a></p>

<a name="pricklypear"></a><font size=+1>Prickly Pear</font>
<img src="pricklypear.jpg" align="left" alt= "Prickly Pear" width="250" height="255" />
<p><b>Botanical name:</b> <em>Opuntia violacea santa-rita</em></p>
<p>This type of prickly pear, called the santa-rita prickly pear, is very striking because of
its color. The prickly pear segments are tinged with purple or are totally purple. This gives
a dramatic color contrast to other Southwest plants. Segments can grow to eight inches. Yellow
flowers may turn red near the base inside and produce red or purple fruit. The prickly pear is
excellent to use as a color feature in a landscape design.</p>
<p>The prickly pear can be cut back any time to shape or remove leaf pads too close to
high-use areas.</p>
<br clear="left" />
<p><a href="#top"><font size=-1>To top</font></a></p>

<p>To find out more information about desert plants, visit the <a
href="http://www.desertmuseum.org">Arizona-Sonora Desert Museum</a>.</p>
</body>
</html>
```

-2-

FIGURE 3-53 (continued)

After the HTML file for the Desert Plants Web page is saved, it should be viewed in a browser to confirm that the Web page appears as desired. It also is important to test the links in the Desert Plants Web page to verify they function as expected. Finally, a copy of the Web page should be printed as a reference.

To View and Test a Web Page

1. **Click the Desert Plants button on the taskbar.**
2. **Click the Refresh button on the Standard toolbar.**

The edited Desert Plants Web page is displayed, as shown in Figure 3-25 on page HTM 94.

With the home page displayed in the browser, click each of the links in the page to verify each link connects to the appropriate Web page or link target. If possible, view the Web page in more than one browser type or version (for example, Microsoft Internet Explorer and Netscape Navigator) to ensure that the Web pages display correctly in different browsers. After testing the links, the Web page can be printed for future reference.

More About

Logical vs. Physical Styles

For more information about the differences between logical and physical styles, visit the HTML More About Web page (scsite.com/html3e/more.htm) and then click Logical vs. Physical Styles.

To Print a Web Page

1 **Click the Print button on the Standard toolbar.**

The Web page prints (Figure 3-54).

Both Web pages in the Plant World Web site are complete. The following steps show how to quit Notepad and a browser.

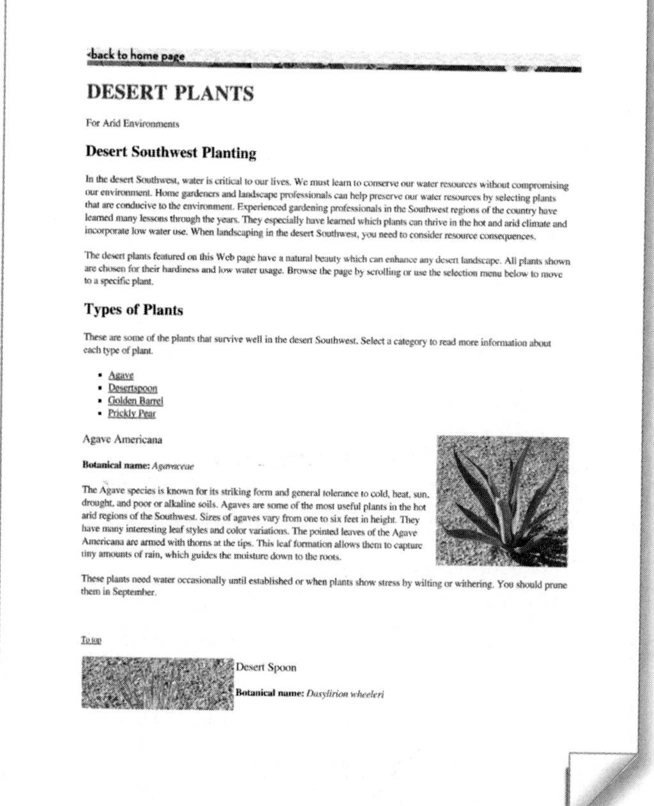

<back to home page

DESERT PLANTS

For Arid Environments

Desert Southwest Planting

In the desert Southwest, water is critical to our lives. We must learn to conserve our water resources without compromising our environment. Home gardeners and landscape professionals can help preserve our water resources by selecting plants that are conducive to the environment. Experienced gardening professionals in the Southwest regions of the country have learned many lessons through the years. They especially have learned which plants can thrive in the hot and arid climate and incorporate low water use. When landscaping in the desert Southwest, you need to consider resource consequences.

The desert plants featured on this Web page have a natural beauty which can enhance any desert landscape. All plants shown are chosen for their hardiness and low water usage. Browse the page by scrolling or use the selection menu below to move to a specific plant.

Types of Plants

These are some of the plants that survive well in the desert Southwest. Select a category to read more information about each type of plant.

- Agave
- Desertspoon
- Golden Barrel
- Prickly Pear

Agave Americana

Botanical name: *Agavaceae*

The Agave species is known for its striking form and general tolerance to cold, heat, sun, drought, and poor or alkaline soils. Agaves are some of the most useful plants in the hot arid regions of the Southwest. Sizes of agaves vary from one to six feet in height. They have many interesting leaf styles and color variations. The pointed leaves of the Agave Americana are armed with thorns at the tips. This leaf formation allows them to capture tiny amounts of rain, which guides the moisture down to the roots.

These plants need water occasionally until established or when plants show stress by wilting or withering. You should prune them in September.

To top

Desert Spoon

Botanical name: *Dasylirion wheeleri*

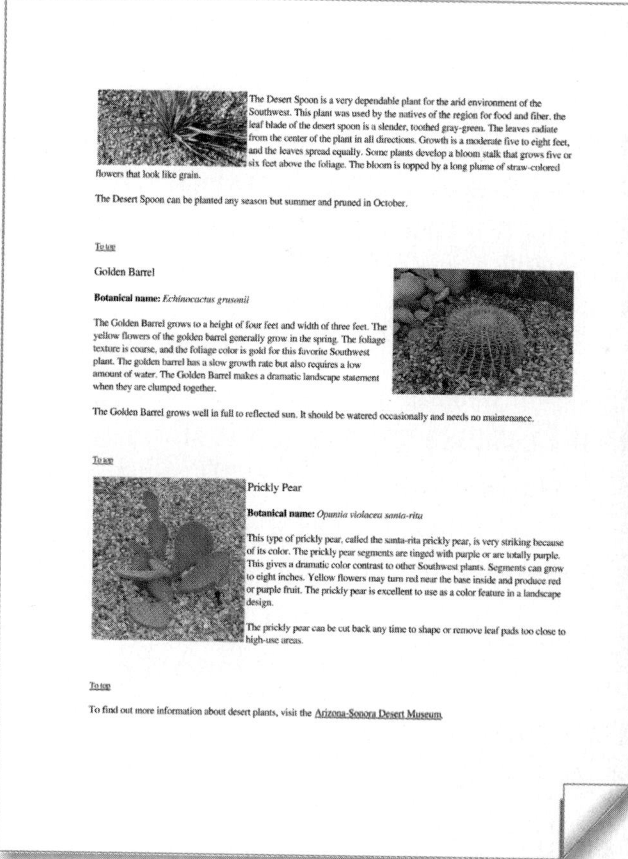

The Desert Spoon is a very dependable plant for the arid environment of the Southwest. This plant was used by the natives of the region for food and fiber. the leaf blade of the desert spoon is a slender, toothed gray-green. The leaves radiate from the center of the plant in all directions. Growth is a moderate five to eight feet, and the leaves spread equally. Some plants develop a bloom stalk that grows five or six feet above the foliage. The bloom is topped by a long plume of straw-colored flowers that look like grain.

The Desert Spoon can be planted any season but summer and pruned in October.

To top

Golden Barrel

Botanical name: *Echinocactus grusonii*

The Golden Barrel grows to a height of four feet and width of three feet. The yellow flowers of the golden barrel generally grow in the spring. The foliage texture is course, and the foliage color is gold for this favorite Southwest plant. The golden barrel has a slow growth rate but also requires a low amount of water. The Golden Barrel makes a dramatic landscape statement when they are clumped together.

The Golden Barrel grows well in full to reflected sun. It should be watered occasionally and needs no maintenance.

To top

Prickly Pear

Botanical name: *Opuntia violacea santa-rita*

This type of prickly pear, called the santa-rita prickly pear, is very striking because of its color. The prickly pear segments are tinged with purple or are totally purple. This gives a dramatic color contrast to other Southwest plants. Segments can grow to eight inches. Yellow flowers may turn red near the base inside and produce red or purple fruit. The prickly pear is excellent to use as a color feature in a landscape design.

The prickly pear can be cut back any time to shape or remove leaf pads too close to high-use areas.

To top

To find out more information about desert plants, visit the Arizona-Sonora Desert Museum.

FIGURE 3-54

To Quit Notepad and a Browser

1 **Click the Close button on the browser title bar.**

2 **Click the Close button on the Notepad window title bar.**

Both the browser and Notepad windows close, and the Windows desktop is displayed.

Project Summary

In this project, you learned how to develop a two-page Web site by creating a home page for Plant World and editing the Desert Plants Web page. You learned the terms and definitions related to linking, as well as how to create a text or link image to a Web page in the same Web site, how to create a text link to a Web page in another Web site, how to create links within the same Web page, and how to create an e-mail link. You also learned to format fonts using bold, italics, and colors. Finally, the project presented more about Web page images, including how to add a background image and how to add an image with wrapped text using various alignments.

What You Should Know

Having completed this project, you should be able to perform the tasks listed below. The tasks are listed in the same order they were presented in this project.

1. Start Notepad (HTM 72)
2. Enter HTML Tags to Define the Web Page Structure (HTM 79)
3. Add an Image (HTM 80)
4. Add a Left-Aligned Heading with a Font Color (HTM 82)
5. Enter a Paragraph of Text (HTM 83)
6. Create Unordered (Bulleted) Lists (HTM 84)
7. Add a Background Image (HTM 85)
8. Add a Text Link to Another Web Page within the Same Web Site (HTM 86)
9. Add an E-Mail Link (HTM 88)
10. Save and Print an HTML File (HTM 89)
11. View a Web Page (HTM 90)
12. Test Links in a Web Page (HTM 91)
13. Print a Web Page (HTM 93)
14. Open an HTML File (HTM 95)
15. Format Text in Bold (HTM 97)
16. Format Text in Italics (HTM 98)
17. Format Text with a Font Color (HTM 99)
18. Add an Image with Wrapped Text (HTM 103)
19. Clear the Text Wrapping (HTM 104)
20. Add a Text Link to a Web Page in Another Web Site (HTM 108)
21. Set Link Targets (HTM 111)
22. Add Links to Link Targets within a Web Page (HTM 113)
23. Add Links to a Target at the Top of the Page (HTM 114)
24. Copy and Paste HTML Code (HTM 115)
25. Add an Image Link to a Web Page (HTM 116)
26. Save and Print the HTML File (HTM 117)
27. View and Test a Web Page (HTM 118)
28. Print a Web Page (HTM 119)
29. Quit Notepad and a Browser (HTM 119)

Learn It Online

Instructions: To complete the Learn It Online exercises, start your browser, click the Address bar, and then enter the Web address `scsite.com/html3e/learn`. When the HTML Learn It Online page is displayed, follow the instructions in the exercises below. Each exercise has instructions for printing your results, either for your own records or for submission to your instructor.

1 Project Reinforcement TF, MC, and SA

Below HTML Project 3, click the Project Reinforcement link. Print the quiz by clicking Print on the File menu for each page. Answer each question.

2 Flash Cards

Below HTML Project 3, click the Flash Cards link and read the instructions. Type 20 (or a number specified by your instructor) in the Number of playing cards text box, type your name in the Enter your Name text box, and then click the Flip Card button. When the flash card is displayed, read the question and then click the ANSWER box arrow to select an answer. Flip through Flash Cards. If your score is 15 (75%) correct or greater, click Print on the File menu to print your results. If your score is less than 15 (75%) correct, then redo this exercise by clicking the Replay button.

3 Practice Test

Below HTML Project 3, click the Practice Test link. Answer each question, enter your first and last name at the bottom of the page, and then click the Grade Test button. When the graded practice test is displayed on your screen, click Print on the File menu to print a hard copy. Continue to take practice tests until you score 80% or better.

4 Who Wants To Be a Computer Genius?

Below HTML Project 3, click the Computer Genius link. Read the instructions, enter your first and last name at the bottom of the page, and then click the PLAY button. When your score is displayed, click the PRINT RESULTS link to print a hard copy.

5 Wheel of Terms

Below HTML Project 3, click the Wheel of Terms link. Read the instructions, and then enter your first and last name and your school name. Click the PLAY button. When your score is displayed, right-click the score and then click Print on the shortcut menu to print a hard copy.

6 Crossword Puzzle Challenge

Below HTML Project 3, click the Crossword Puzzle Challenge link. Read the instructions, and then enter your first and last name. Click the SUBMIT button. Work the crossword puzzle. When you are finished, click the Submit button. When the crossword puzzle is redisplayed, click the Print Puzzle button to print a hard copy.

7 Tips and Tricks

Below HTML Project 3, click the Tips and Tricks link. Click a topic that pertains to Project 3. Right-click the information and then click Print on the shortcut menu. Construct a brief example of what the information relates to in HTML to confirm you understand how to use the tip or trick.

8 Newsgroups

Below HTML Project 3, click the Newsgroups link. Click a topic that pertains to Project 3. Print three comments.

9 Expanding Your Horizons

Below HTML Project 3, click the Expanding Your Horizons link. Click a topic that pertains to Project 3. Print the information. Construct a brief example of what the information relates to in HTML to confirm you understand the contents of the article.

10 Search Sleuth

Below HTML Project 3, click the Search Sleuth link. To search for a term that pertains to this project, select a term below the Project 3 title and then use the Google search engine at google.com (or any major search engine) to display and print two Web pages that present information on the term.

11 Online Help I

Below HTML Project 3, click the Online Help I link. Follow the instructions on the page to access Web pages that provide additional help on project topics. Hand in any printed information to your instructor.

12 Online Help II

Below HTML Project 3, click the Online Help II link. Follow the instructions on the page to access Web pages that provide additional help on project topics. Hand in any printed information to your instructor.

1 Editing the Apply Your Knowledge Web Page

Instructions: Start Notepad. Open the file, apply3-1.htm, from the Project03\AYK folder on the HTML Data Disk. If you do not have the HTML Data Disk, see the inside back cover for instructions or see your instructor. The apply3-1.htm file is a partially completed HTML file that contains some errors. Figure 3-55 shows the Apply Your Knowledge Web page as it should display in your browser after the errors are corrected. Perform the following steps using a computer:

1. Enter the URL, `a:\Project03\AYK\apply3-1.htm`, to view the Web page in your browser.
2. Examine the HTML file in Notepad and its appearance as a Web page in the browser.
3. Correct the HTML errors, making the Web page look similar to the one shown in Figure 3-55, with all links working correctly. (*Hint*: review the hspace attribute of the <img> tag.)

Apply Your Knowledge - 3 - Microsoft Internet Explorer

File Edit View Favorites Tools Help

Back Search Favorites Media

Address A:\Project03\AYK\apply3-1solution.htm Go Links

Zhang Family Addition

We decided that we would buy a dog this summer. We bought a chocolate labrador retriever that we named Khunde, after a village in Nepal that we loved. Here are two pictures of Khunde when he was small and when he got bigger.

- Small
- Big

Summer 2003

You can see that Khunde was a puppy then. We put him next to the old boot to show his size. He was the runt of the litter but was very friendly when we first saw him. We liked that he came right up to us when we went into the pen to see all of the puppies.

He weighed 13 pounds when we brought him home. He did real well from the first time that he stepped into the house. We bought a dog bed for him to sleep in, but he liked sleeping right at the end of our bed on an old blanket. It was fun buying the dog toys for him.

To top

Summer 2004

This is just one year later and look how big he has gotten. Khunde now weighs 75 pounds and stands three feet tall at the shoulder. We hired a trainer who came to the house to train him. Khunde did real well with that and knows all of his commands, such as sit, stay, and lie down.

We also had a invisible fence installed around the front yard. This is so helpful, especially since we live on a relatively busy street. It makes us feel more comfortable that he is safe, and the small children who live nearby do not have to worry about a large dog approaching them.

To top

Done My Computer

start Apply Your Knowledg... 5:43 PM

FIGURE 3-55

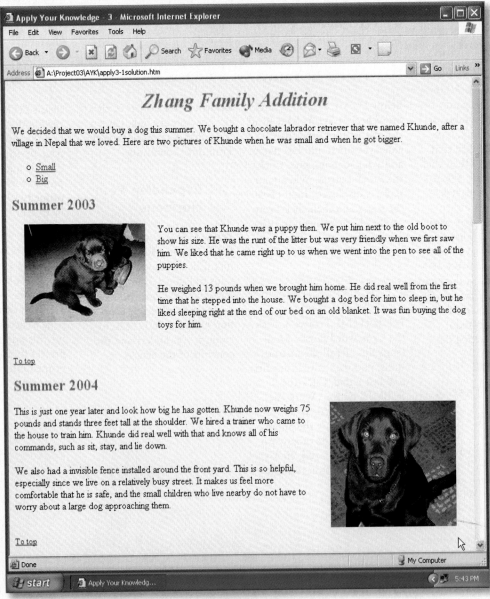

Apply Your Knowledge

4. Add any HTML code necessary for additional features shown in the Web page.
5. Save the revised file in the Project03\AYK folder using the file name, apply3-1solution.htm.
6. Print the revised HTML file.
7. Enter the URL, `a:\Project03\AYK\apply3-1solution.htm`, to view the Web page in your browser.
8. Print the Web page.
9. Write your name on both printouts and hand them in to your instructor.

1 Creating a Web Page with Target Links

Problem: Your instructor wants you to create a Web page demonstrating your knowledge of link targets. You have been asked to create a Web page to demonstrate this technique, similar to the one shown in Figure 3-56.

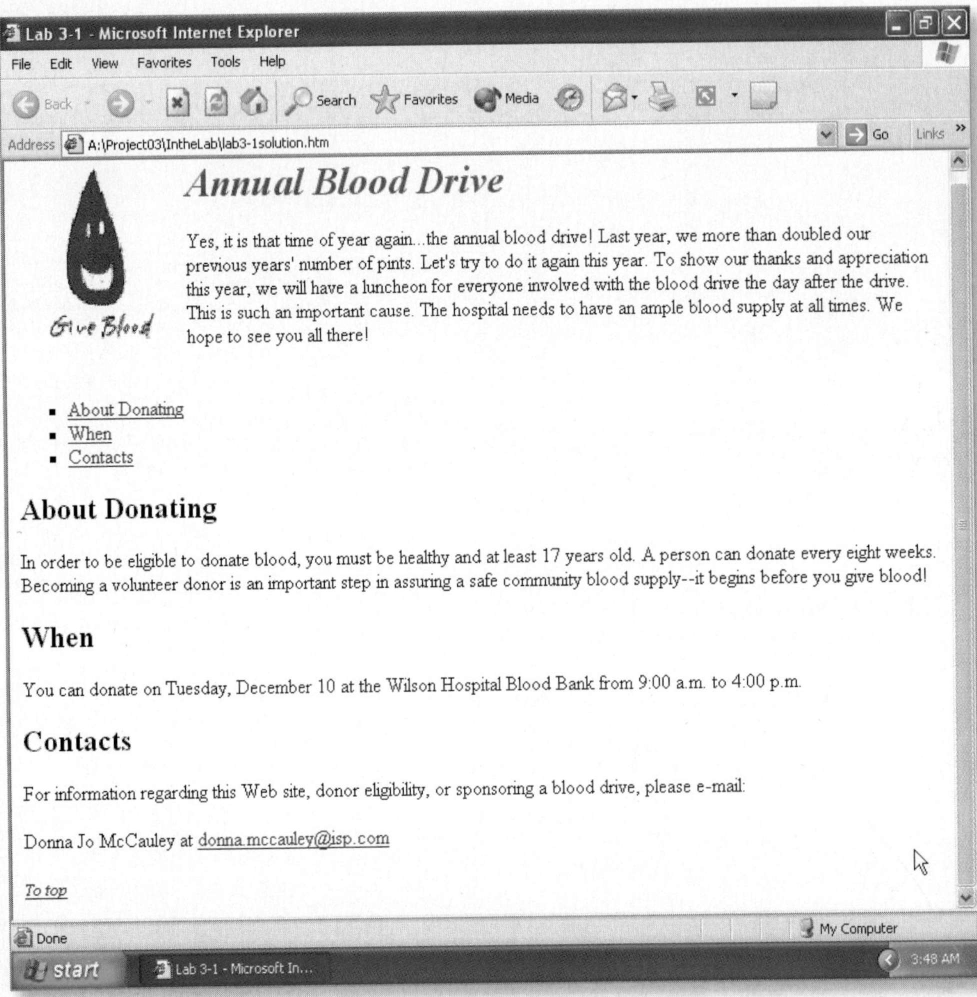

FIGURE 3-56

Instructions: Start Notepad. Perform the following steps using a computer:

1. Start a new HTML file with the title, Lab 3-1 [your name], in the main heading section.
2. Begin the body section by adding the image, blooddrop.gif, and aligning it to the left.
3. Begin the body section by adding the heading, Annual Blood Drive. Format the heading to use the Heading 1 style, be left-aligned, and use the font color red.
4. Add an unordered list with the three list items, as shown in Figure 3-56. Use a square bullet type for the bullet.
5. Add a Heading 2 style heading, About Donating, and type the paragraph of text shown in Figure 3-56.
6. Add a Heading 2 style heading, When, and the paragraph as shown in Figure 3-56.
7. Add a Heading 2 style heading, Contacts, and the paragraph as shown in Figure 3-56.
8. Create a target at the top of the page named, totop.
9. Create a To top link at the bottom of the page, as shown in Figure 3-56. Set the link to direct to the totop target at the top of the page.
10. Save the HTML file in the Project03\IntheLab folder using the file name, lab3-1solution.htm.
11. Print the lab3-1solution.htm file.
12. Enter the URL, `a:\Project03\IntheLab\lab3-1solution.htm`, to view the Web page in your browser.
13. Print the Web page.
14. Write your name on both printouts and hand them in to your instructor.

2 Creating a Web Page with Wrapped Text

Problem: You are the head of an after school volunteer program and decide to prepare a Web page announcement inviting people to join the group (Figure 3-57 on the next page). You decide to create a Web page with text wrapped around a left-aligned image to provide visual appeal.

(continued)

Creating a Web Page with Wrapped Text *(continued)*

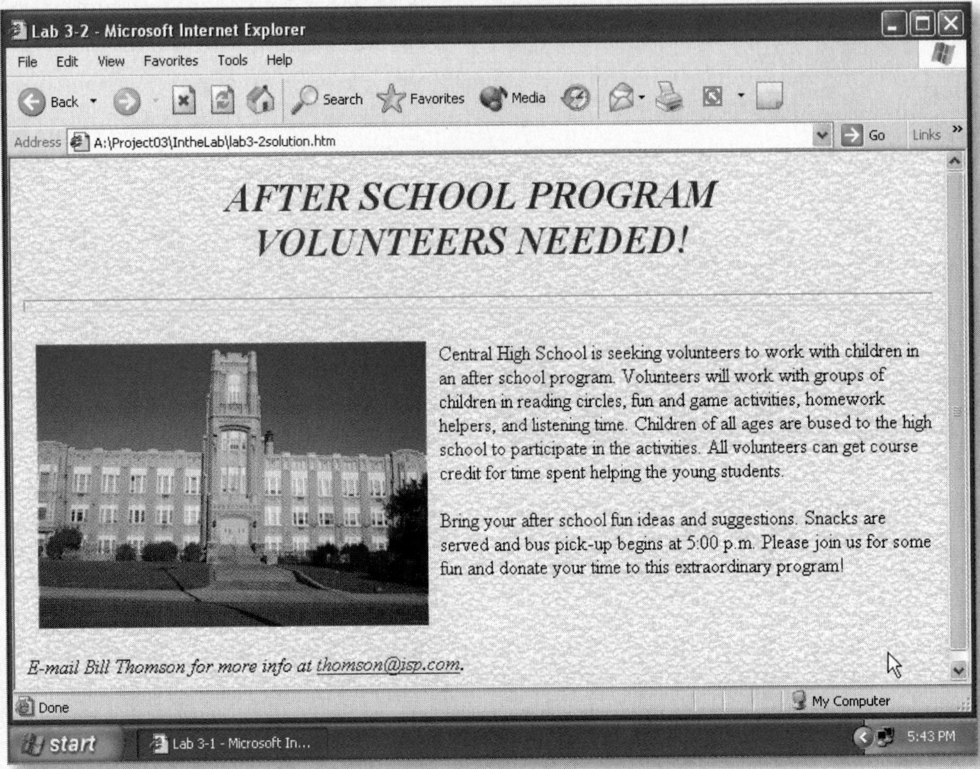

FIGURE 3-57

Instructions: Start Notepad. Perform the following tasks using a computer:

1. Start a new HTML file with the title, Lab 3-2 [your name], in the main heading section.
2. Add a background image to the Web page using the greyback.jpg image.
3. Begin the body section by adding the Heading 1 style heading, AFTER SCHOOL PROGRAM, using a centered, italicized, blue font. Insert a break <br /> tag and add the heading, VOLUNTEERS NEEDED!, using the same formatting as the previous heading. (*Hint*: use the word blue for the color code.)
4. Add a size 10 horizontal rule below the heading.
5. Add the image, school.jpg, using attributes so it is left-aligned with horizontal space of 10, height of 226, and width of 324. Left-alignment will wrap text to the right of the image.
6. Add the paragraphs of information as shown in Figure 3-57.
7. Add an italicized e-mail sentence at the bottom of the paragraph and create the e-mail link as shown in Figure 3-57.

In the Lab

8. Save the HTML file in the Project03\IntheLab folder using the file name, lab3-2solution.htm.
9. Print the lab3-2solution.htm file.
10. Enter the URL, `a:\Project03\IntheLab\lab3-2solution.htm`, to view the Web page in your browser.
11. Print the Web page.
12. Write your name on the printouts and hand them in to your instructor.

3 Composing Two Linked Web Pages

Problem: Your English Composition instructor has asked each student in the class to create a two-page Web site to help other students in the class get to know them. She suggested using the basic template shown in Figures 3-58a and 3-58b on the next page as a starting point. The first Web page (Figure 3-58a) is a home page that includes basic personal information and a link to the second Web page. The second Web page (Figure 3-58b) includes a paragraph of text and a numbered list with links.

Instructions: Start Notepad. Perform the following steps using a computer:

1. Start a new HTML file with the title, Lab 3-3 [your name], in the main heading section.
2. In the first Web page, include a Heading style 1 heading, similar to the one shown in Figure 3-58a, and a short paragraph of text.
3. Create a text link to the second Web page, lab3-3favorites.htm.
4. Save the HTML file in the Project03\IntheLab folder using the file name, lab3-3solution.htm. Print the lab3-3solution.htm file.
5. Start a new HTML file with the title, Lab 3-3 Favorites [your name], in the main heading section.
6. In the second Web page, include a Heading style 1 heading, similar to the one shown in Figure 3-58b, a short paragraph of text, and two Heading style 2 headings. Create two ordered (numbered) lists with at least two items that serve as links to Web pages on another Web site.
7. Save the HTML file in the Project03\IntheLab folder using the file name, lab3-3favorites.htm. Print the lab3-3favorites.htm file.
8. Enter the URL, `a:\Project03\IntheLab\lab3-3solution.htm`, to view the Web page in your browser. Click the text link to the second Web page. Click the links in the lists to test them.
9. Print the Web pages.
10. Write your name on the printouts and hand them in to your instructor.

(continued)

Composing Two Linked Web Pages *(continued)*

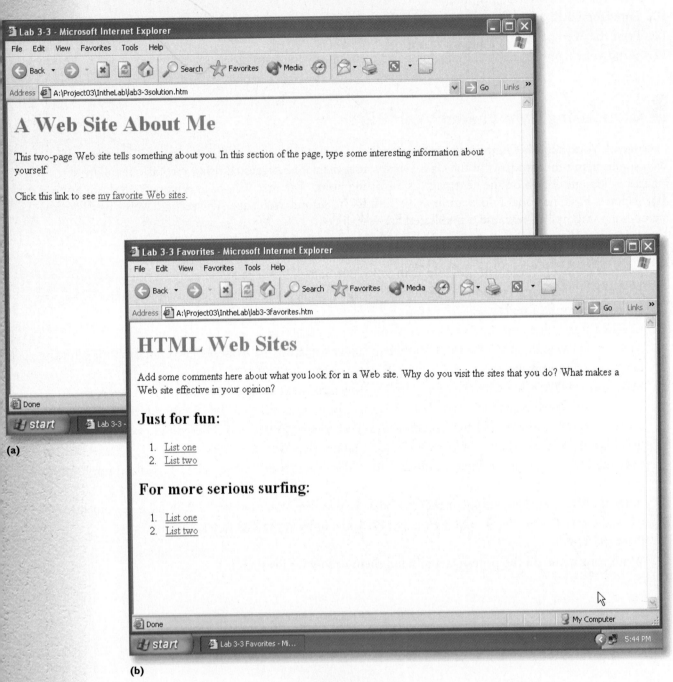

Lab 3-3 - Microsoft Internet Explorer

Address A:\Project03\IntheLab\lab3-3solution.htm

A Web Site About Me

This two-page Web site tells something about you. In this section of the page, type some interesting information about yourself.

Click this link to see my favorite Web sites.

(a)

Lab 3-3 Favorites - Microsoft Internet Explorer

Address A:\Project03\IntheLab\lab3-3favorites.htm

HTML Web Sites

Add some comments here about what you look for in a Web site. Why do you visit the sites that you do? What makes a Web site effective in your opinion?

Just for fun:

1. List one
2. List two

For more serious surfing:

1. List one
2. List two

(b)

FIGURE 3-58

Cases and Places

The difficulty of these case studies varies:
■ are the least difficult and ■■ are the most difficult. The last exercise is a group exercise.

1 ■ Jared Smith is very impressed with the Plant World Web pages and now would like to add a Web page listing online gardening resources. Search the Web to find at least four Web sites that contain information about plants and gardening. Create a Web page that includes a Heading 1 style heading, a brief paragraph of descriptive text, and list links to those Web sites. Use the greyback.jpg background image in the new Web page, so all of the pages in the Web site look consistent. Modify the Plant World home page to include a link to the new Web page.

2 ■ Your manager at LightSpace Photography has asked you to update the home page to make it more visually appealing. As a first step, you plan to create a Web page with sample text formats, such as the ones shown in Figure 3-27 on page HTM 97, to share with your manager and get his input on which types of formatting he prefers. Create such a Web page and include text formatted as bold, italic, underlined, superscript, and subscript; use different colors and sizes for each type of text. Be sure to include one sample using the <bold> tag and one using the <strong> tag to see how they compare when displayed together.

3 ■■ To update the Plant World Web site further, you want to add image links so the plant images on the Desert Plants Web page also are links to Web pages in an external Web site. Search the Web for information specific to each of the four desert plants used in the project. Modify the Desert Plants Web page so each plant image is used as a link to a Web page in an external Web site. After adding the links, you decide the text paragraphs on the page are too close to the pictures. Modify the Desert Plants Web page to use the <img> tag attributes hspace and vspace to add space around each image.

4 ■■ The Marketing Director at Steel Solutions is unhappy the links on the company Web pages appear in blue when unvisited and purple when visited, because those are the logo colors of Steel Solutions' closest competitor. She has asked you to update the Web pages to use navy for unvisited links, olive for visited links, and red for active links. Create a Web page similar to Figure 3-4 on page HTM 73, with three text links to a Web page in an external Web site. Add the appropriate link attributes in the body tag to define the link colors as requested by the Marketing Director.

5 ■■ **Working Together** Your manager at Axcelent has asked your team to create a simple five-page prototype of the Web pages in the new Entertainment section for the online magazine, CityStuff. The home page should include headings and brief paragraphs of text for Arts, Music, Movies, and Dining. Within each paragraph of text is a link to one of the four detailed Web pages for each section (for example, the Arts link should connect to the Arts Web page). The home page also includes an e-mail link at the bottom of the page. Add a To top link that connects to a target at the top of the page. The four detailed Web pages should include links to external Web sites of interest and a link back to the home page. If possible, also find appropriate images to use as a background or in the Web page and set text to wrap around the images.

Creating Tables in a Web Site

PROJECT 4

CASE PERSPECTIVE

The city's newest video rental store, Bell Video, is having trouble attracting new customers. As advertising director for Bell Video, you are trying to think of new ways to promote three key differentiating features of Bell Video: excellent customer service, low rental prices, and a wide selection of videos. In researching the subject, you find many articles and case studies in which companies learned that having a solid Web site made it easier for customers to find them, provided a way to communicate the company's brand, and allowed the company to provide additional services. As you begin to understand the importance of the Web to businesses like your own, your recommendation is to create a Web site for Bell Video to help increase the store's exposure to current and new customers.

One of the services you want to provide on the Bell Video Web site is a way for customers to browse through the store's database of videos. In designing the various ways customers will be able to browse the database, you consider the questions that customers ask about videos when they visit the store. Sometimes, customers want to know about new releases. Other times, they do not know the name of the movie, but do know one or more actors in the movie. Finally, customers sometimes want to select a certain type of movie, such as comedy or action, rather than a specific movie. Given that, you design three Web pages to allow customers to browse by new releases, by actor, or by type. You decide to develop the necessary Web pages with this information to show at the next staff meeting, so you can gather feedback from the team.

As you read through this project, you will learn how to plan, design, and code a table to create a user-friendly Web site. You also will learn to format tables and to combine table features to make the pages more readable. In addition, you will learn to create a menu bar with text links.

HTML

Creating Tables in a Web Site

PROJECT

Objectives

You will have mastered the material in this project when you can:

- Define table elements
- Describe the steps used to plan, design, and code a table
- Create a borderless table to organize images
- Create a vertical menu bar with text links
- Create a borderless table to organize text
- Create a horizontal menu bar with text links
- Create a table with borders
- Change the horizontal alignment of text
- Add background color to rows and cells
- Alter the spacing between and within cells using the cellspacing and cellpadding attributes
- Insert a caption below a table
- Use the rowspan and colspan attributes

Introduction

In the first three projects, you learned the fundamentals of Web page development, as well as how to create an HTML file and use paragraphs and lists of text items to present information on a Web page. This project adds to your HTML knowledge by teaching you how to present information on a Web page using tables with rows and columns. In this project, you will learn about the elements used in a table and how to plan, design, and code a table. You also will learn how to create tables to organize text and images and to use a table column to create a menu bar with text links. The project also discusses how to enhance tables by using a variety of attributes and formats, such as borders, colors, spacing, and blank cells, and by adding a caption to the table.

Project Four — Bell Video

When a Web page is developed, tables often are used to organize and position text and images to help make the Web pages look more organized and professional. Project 4 illustrates how to create two pages for the Bell Video Web site, including a home page and the New Releases Web page, and how to edit two existing pages, including the Actor and Type Web pages.

As shown in Figure 4-1a, the Bell Video home page includes a borderless table to position two images at the top of the page, as well as a second borderless table that organizes text and a vertical menu bar of text links that link to the other three Web pages.

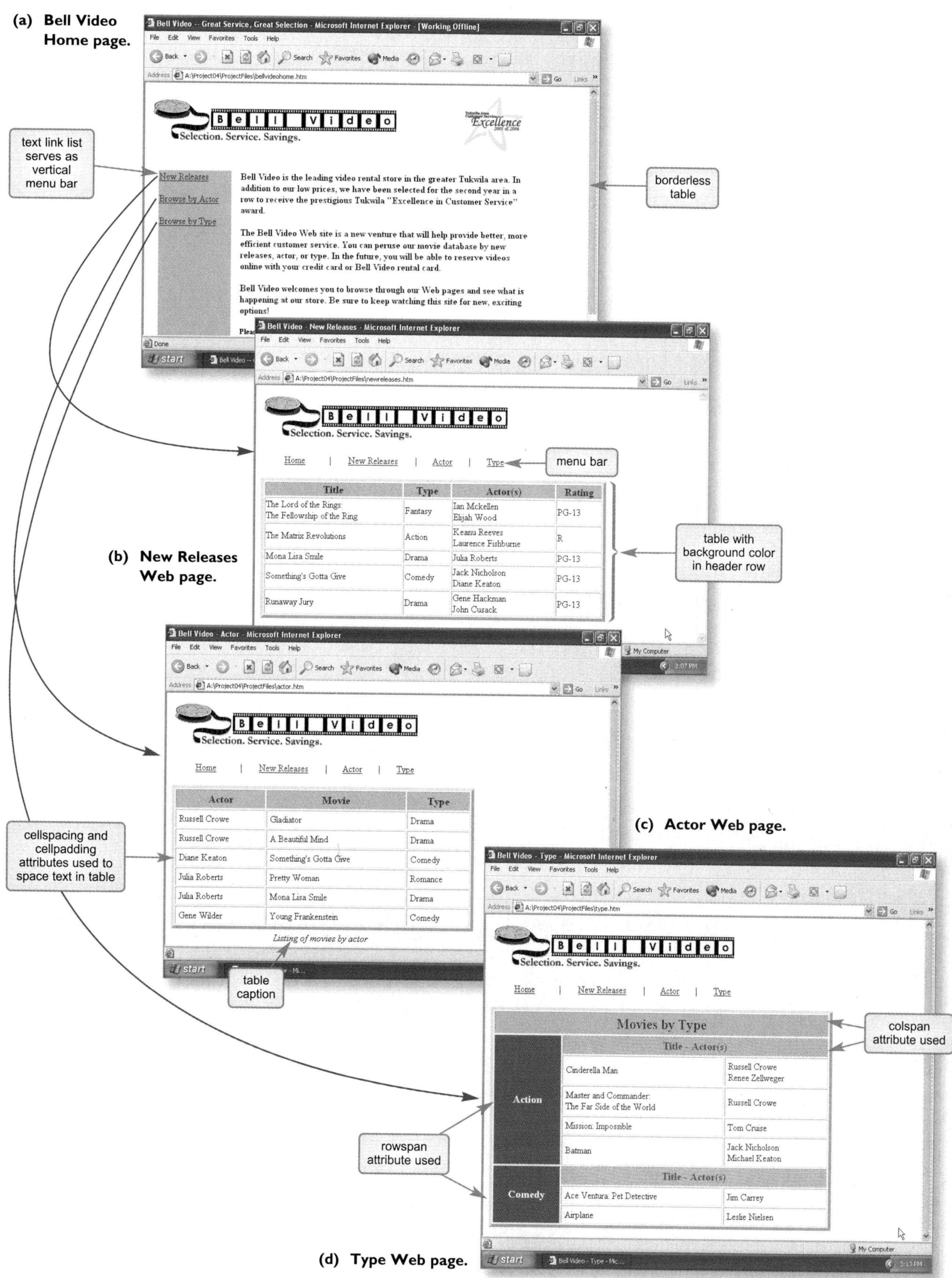
(a) Bell Video Home page.
text link list serves as vertical menu bar
borderless table
(b) New Releases Web page.
menu bar
table with background color in header row
(c) Actor Web page.
cellspacing and cellpadding attributes used to space text in table
table caption
colspan attribute used
rowspan attribute used
(d) Type Web page.

FIGURE 4-1

The New Releases, Actor, and Type Web pages all include two borderless tables: one to position the logo image and the other to create a horizontal menu bar of text links. The New Releases Web page (Figure 4-1b on the previous page) also includes a table with a background color to highlight the table headings. The basic HTML for the Actor and Type Web pages is included on the HTML Data Disk. The Actor Web page (Figure 4-1c) is edited to use cellspacing and cellpadding attributes and a caption to give the table a different appearance. The Type Web page (Figure 4-1d) is edited to use the colspan and rowspan attributes to create headings that span several columns and rows. As shown in Figure 4-1, all three of these Web pages use vertical alignment and color in specific cells to enhance the appearance of the table.

Creating Web Pages with Tables

Tables allow you to organize information on a Web page using HTML tags. Tables are useful when you want to arrange text and images into rows and columns in order to make the information straightforward and clear to the Web page visitor. You can use tables to create Web pages with two newspaper-type columns of text or structured lists of information. Tables can be complex, using the rowspan and colspan attributes to span rows and columns, background colors in cells, and borders to provide formatting (Figure 4-2a). Tables also can be simple, with a basic grid format and no color (Figure 4-2b). The purpose of the table helps to define what formatting is appropriate.

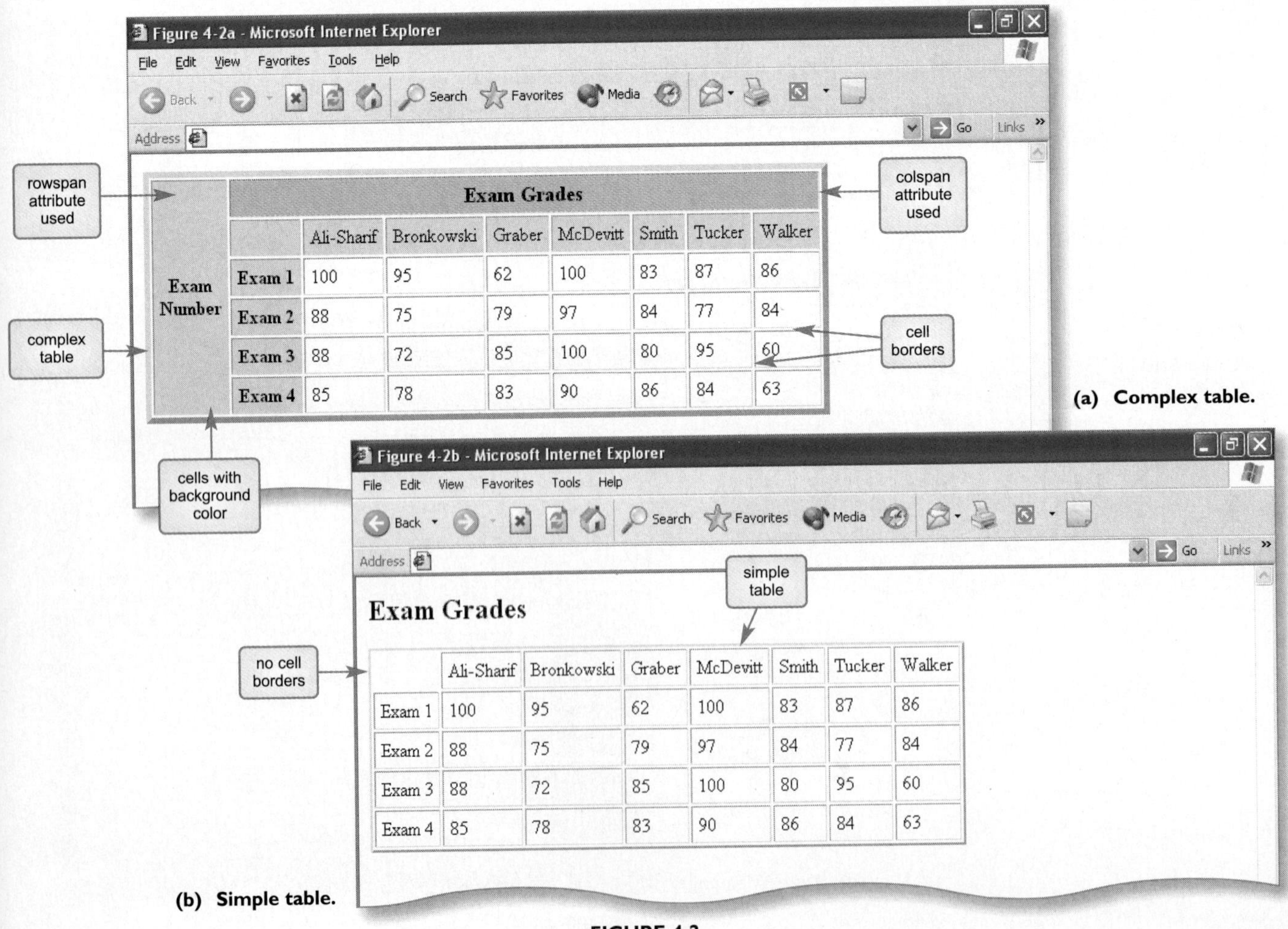

Exam Number	Exam Grades							
		Ali-Sharif	Bronkowski	Graber	McDevitt	Smith	Tucker	Walker
	Exam 1	100	95	62	100	83	87	86
	Exam 2	88	75	79	97	84	77	84
	Exam 3	88	72	85	100	80	95	60
	Exam 4	85	78	83	90	86	84	63

(a) Complex table.

Exam Grades

	Ali-Sharif	Bronkowski	Graber	McDevitt	Smith	Tucker	Walker
Exam 1	100	95	62	100	83	87	86
Exam 2	88	75	79	97	84	77	84
Exam 3	88	72	85	100	80	95	60
Exam 4	85	78	83	90	86	84	63

(b) Simple table.

FIGURE 4-2

Project 3 discussed wrapping text around an image. Tables also can be used to position text and images, such as the one shown in Figure 4-3, which uses a borderless table to position text to the left of the map images. An advantage to using a table to position text and images, instead of just wrapping the text around the image, is that you have more control over the placement of the text and image.

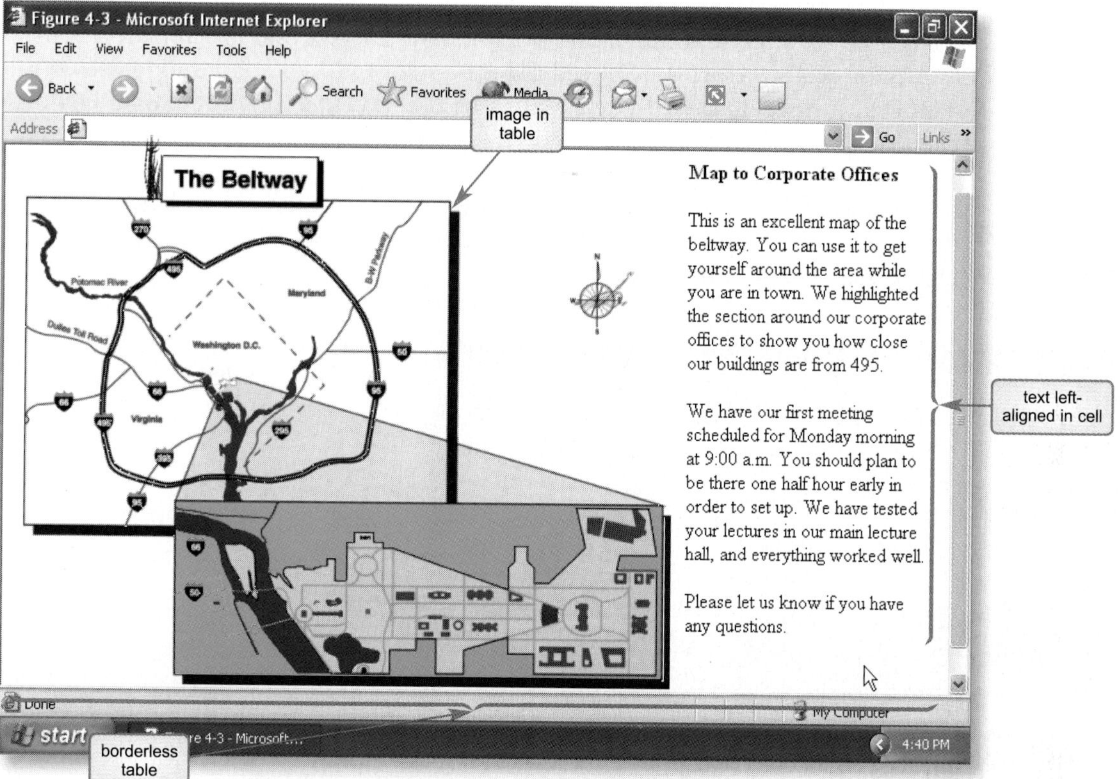

FIGURE 4-3 Image and text positioned in table.

Tables also can be used to create a border or frame around an image, as shown in Figure 4-4. The Web page shown in Figure 4-4 shows an image inserted into a table with one row and one cell. The border is set to a pixel width of 15 to create the appearance of a frame. Using a table to create a frame is a simple technique that gives an image a polished look and highlights the image.

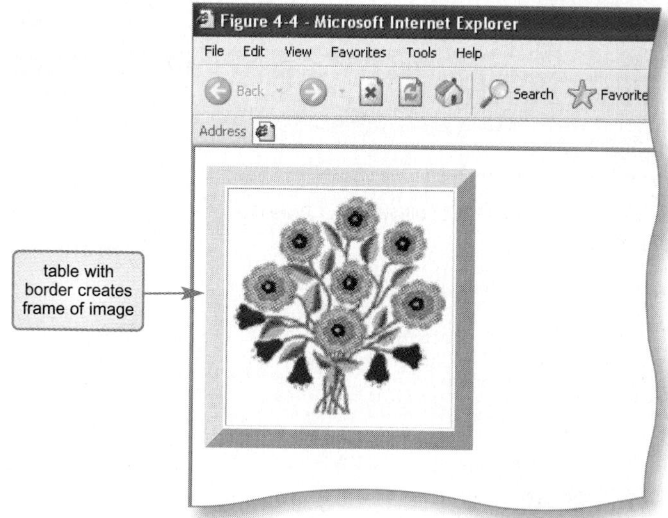

FIGURE 4-4 Table used as image frame.

Table Elements

Tables consist of rows, columns, and cells, much like spreadsheets. A **row** is a horizontal line of information. A **column** is a vertical line of information. A **cell** is the intersection of a row and a column. Figure 4-5 shows examples of these three elements. In Figure 4-5a, the fifth row in the table has a yellow background. In Figure 4-5b, the fourth column has a red background. In Figure 4-5c, the cell at the intersection of column 2 and row 2 has a lime green background.

As shown in Figure 4-5c, a cell can be one of two types: a heading cell or a data cell. A **heading cell** displays text as bold and center-aligned. A **data cell** displays normal text that is left-aligned.

Understanding the row, column, and cell elements is important, as you create a table using HTML. Attributes are set are relative to these table elements. For example, you can set attributes for an entire row of information, for a single cell, or for one or more cells within a row.

> *More About*
>
> **Tables**
>
> Tables are useful for a variety of purposes. They can store information in tabular form or create a layout on a Web page. Layouts created with tables give more flexibility to the Web developer. You have more control over the placement of information or images. Many popular Web sites use tables.

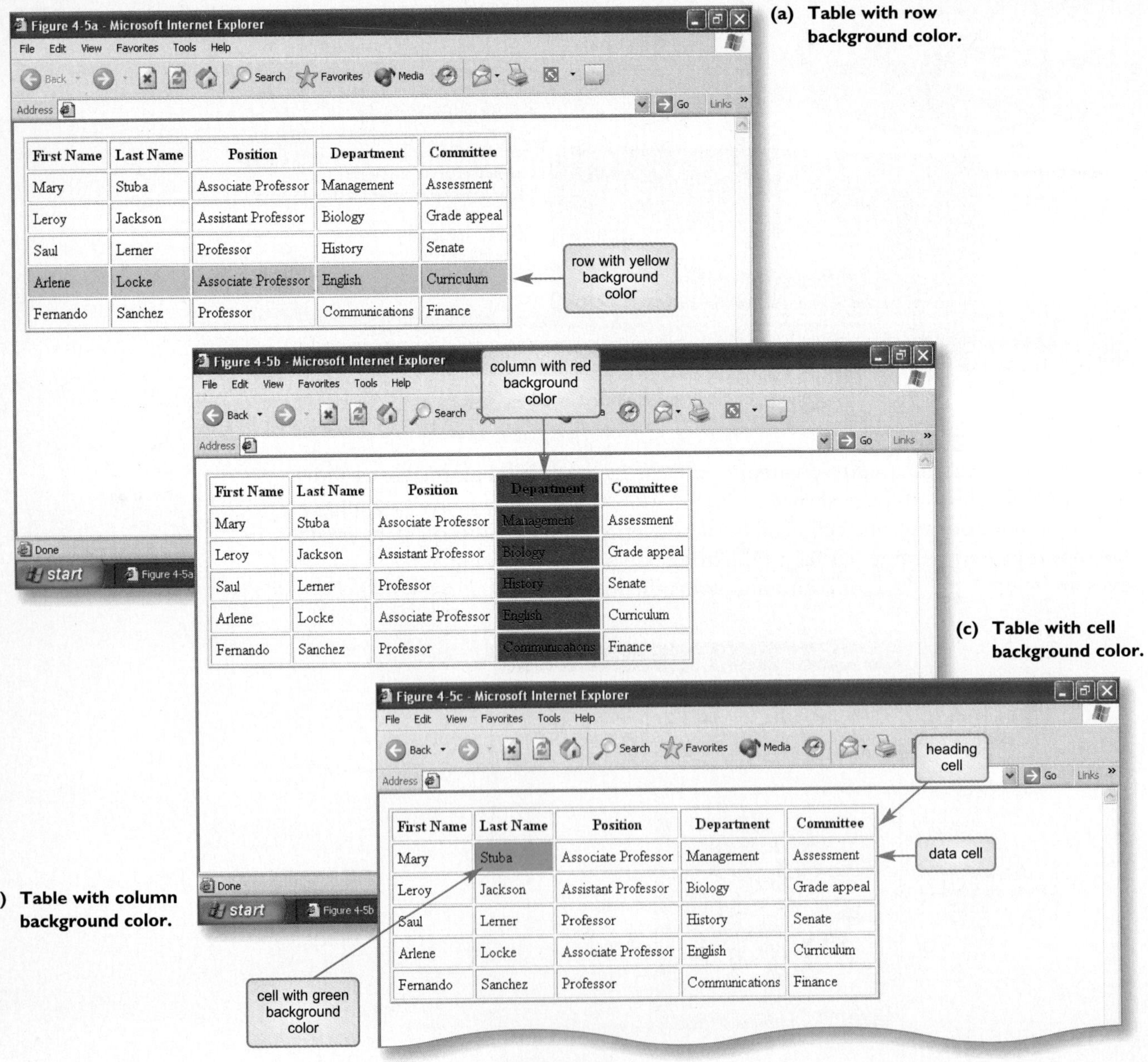

First Name	Last Name	Position	Department	Committee
Mary	Stuba	Associate Professor	Management	Assessment
Leroy	Jackson	Assistant Professor	Biology	Grade appeal
Saul	Lerner	Professor	History	Senate
Arlene	Locke	Associate Professor	English	Curriculum
Fernando	Sanchez	Professor	Communications	Finance

(a) Table with row background color.

(b) Table with column background color.

(c) Table with cell background color.

FIGURE 4-5

Table Borders, Headers, Captions, and Rules

Tables also include features such as table borders, table headers, table captions, and rules (Figure 4-6). A **table border** is the line that encloses the perimeter of the table. A **table header** is the same as a heading cell — that is, it is any cell with bold text that indicates the purpose of the row or column. A **table caption** is descriptive text located above or below the table that further describes the purpose of the table.

Tables can use each of these features or a combination of them. The purpose for the table dictates which of these features are used. For example, the table shown in Figure 4-6 lists columns of numbers. A header row is used to identify the meaning of the numbers in each column, and headings that span columns and rows are used to provide additional information. Finally, the table caption explains that each number is based on thousands (that is, the 10 listed in the table represents 10,000).

More About

Table Elements

Many Web sources discuss table parts, giving numerous examples and tips. For more information about HTML table parts, visit the HTML More About Web page (scsite.com/html3e/more.htm) and then click Table Elements.

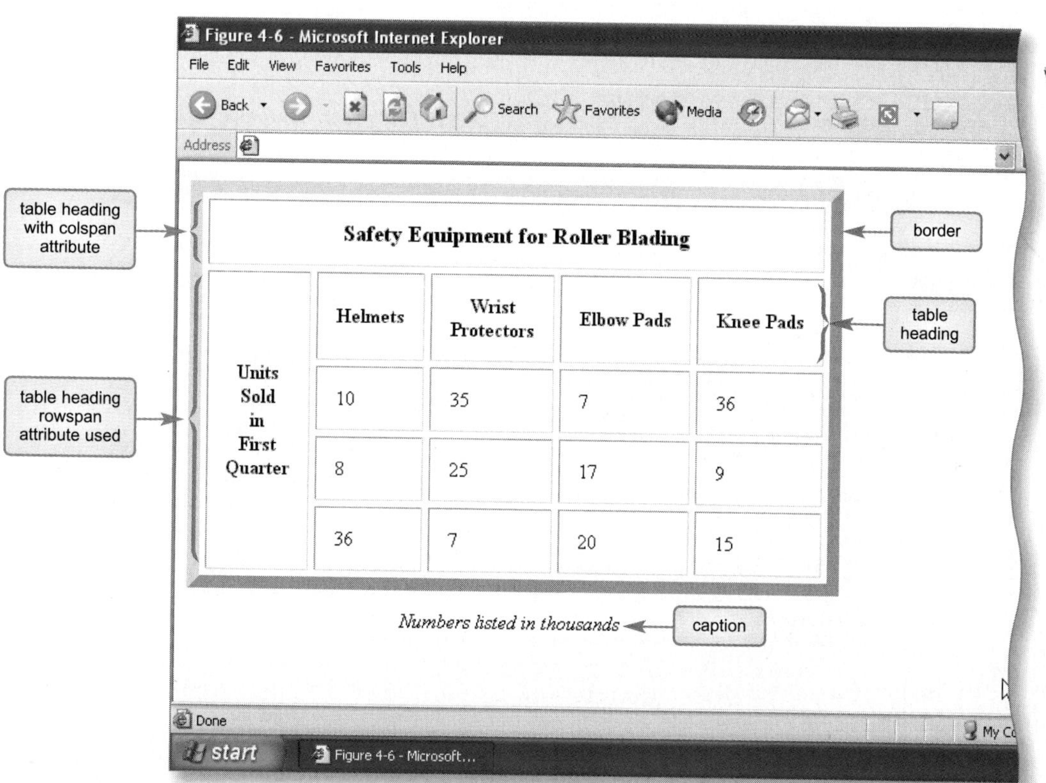

FIGURE 4-6 Table headers, border, and caption.

Another useful attribute of a table is the rules attribute. The **rules attribute** allows a Web developer to select which internal borders to show in a table. The rules attribute supports several values to provide different formatting options. For example, using the attribute and value rules="none" creates a table with no internal rules. Using the attribute and value rules="cols" creates a table with vertical rules between each column in the table (Figure 4-7a), while rules="rows" creates a table with horizontal rules between each row in the table (Figure 4-7b). Appendix A provides additional information on values supported by the rules attribute.

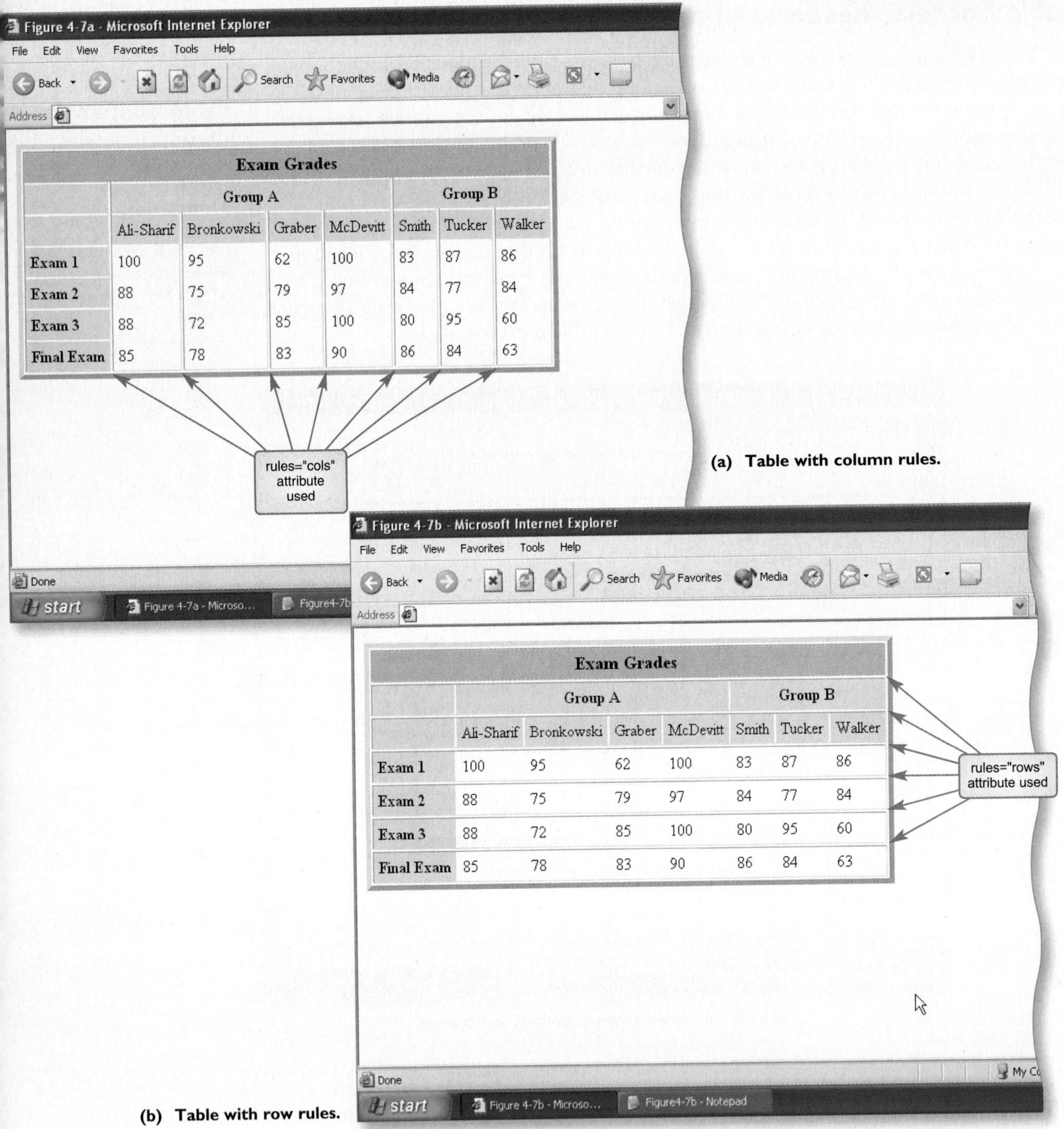

Exam Grades							
	Group A				Group B		
	Ali-Sharif	Bronkowski	Graber	McDevitt	Smith	Tucker	Walker
Exam 1	100	95	62	100	83	87	86
Exam 2	88	75	79	97	84	77	84
Exam 3	88	72	85	100	80	95	60
Final Exam	85	78	83	90	86	84	63

(a) Table with column rules.

(b) Table with row rules.

FIGURE 4-7

Planning, Designing, and Coding a Table

Creating tables for a Web page is a three-step process: (1) determining if a table is needed; (2) planning the table; and (3) coding the table. Each of these steps is discussed in detail in the following sections.

Determining if a Table Is Needed

First, you must determine whether or not a table is necessary. Not all Web pages require the use of tables. A general rule of thumb is that a table should be used when it will help organize information or Web page elements in such a way that it is easier for the Web page visitor to read. Tables generally are useful in a Web page if the Web page needs to display a structured, organized list of information or includes text and images that must be positioned in a very specific manner. Figure 4-8 shows an example of information displayed as text in both a table and a bulleted list. To present this information, a table might be the better choice. The bulleted list might give the Web page an acceptable look, but the table more clearly explains the topic.

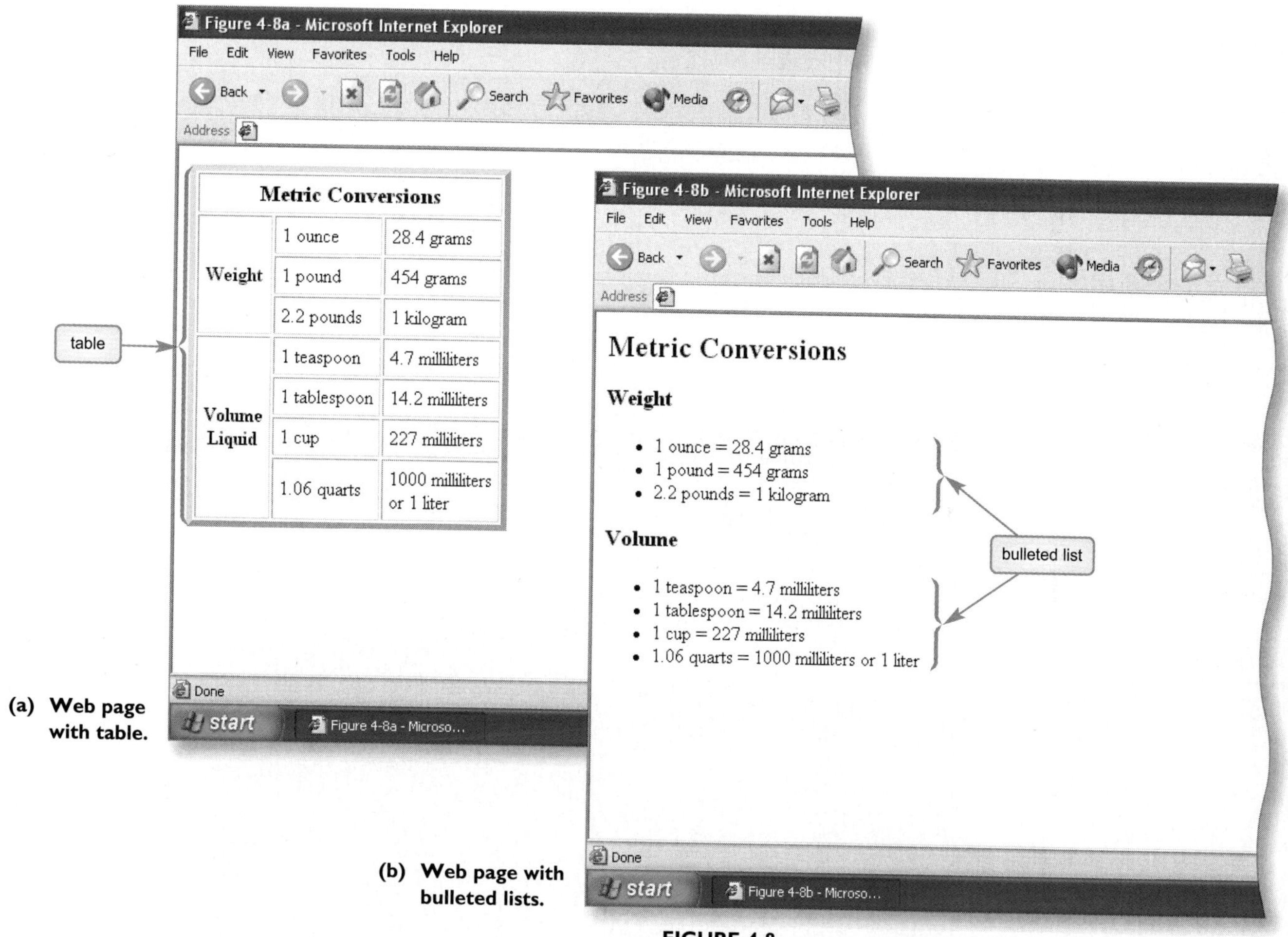

(a) Web page with table.

(b) Web page with bulleted lists.

FIGURE 4-8

Planning the Table

In order to create effective tables, you must begin by planning how the information will display in the table and create a good design. Before writing any HTML code, sketch the table out on paper. After the table is sketched on paper, it is easier to see how many rows and columns to create, if the table will include headings, and if any of the headings span rows or columns. Conceptualizing the table on paper first saves time trying to determine which HTML table tags to use to create the table.

For example, to create a simple table that lists the times run by various cross-country team members, you might sketch the table shown in Figure 4-9a on the next page. If runners participate in two different race lengths, such as 5K and 10K, that information can be included in a table designed as shown in Figure 4-9b. If the table needs to include

> ***More About***
>
> **Table Tutorial**
>
> Table tutorials are available via online sources. Tutorials take you step-by-step through a creation process. For more information about HTML tables, visit the HTML More About Web page (scsite.com/html3e/more.htm) and then click Table Tutorial.

different race dates for each race length, that information can be included in a table such as the one shown in Figure 4-9c. Finally, to make the table easier for the Web page visitor to understand, the table should include headings that span rows and columns and a caption, as shown in Figure 4-10. Design issues such as these should be considered while planning the table, before any HTML code is entered.

NAME1	NAME2	NAME3	NAME4
TIME	TIME	TIME	TIME

(a) Simple Table

5K		10K	
NAME1	NAME2	NAME3	NAME4
TIME	TIME	TIME	TIME

(b) Column Spanning Added

	5K		10K	
	NAME1	NAME2	NAME3	NAME4
MAY 5	TIME	TIME	TIME	TIME
MAY 12	TIME	TIME	TIME	TIME
MAY 19	TIME	TIME	TIME	TIME
MAY 26	TIME	TIME	TIME	TIME

(c) Row Spanning Added

FIGURE 4-9

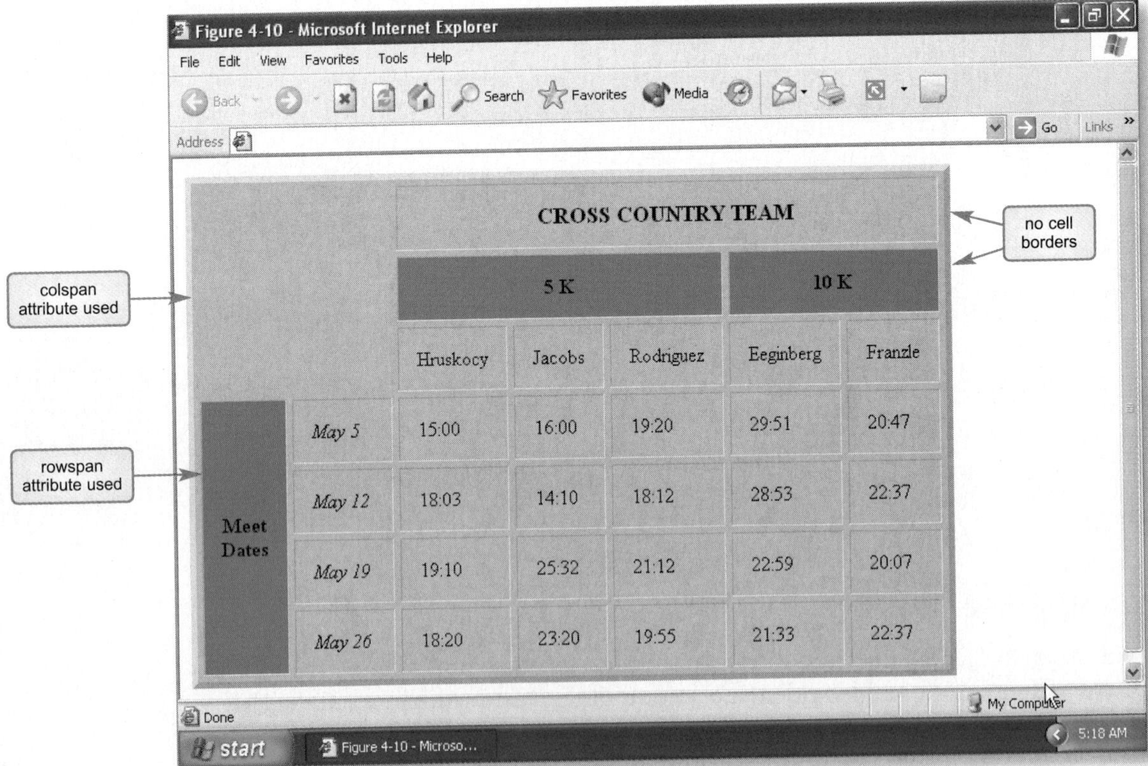

FIGURE 4-10 Table with row and column spanning.

Coding the Table

After the table design is complete, the table can be coded using HTML tags. Table 4-1 shows the four main HTML tags used to create a table. Each of these tags has a number of attributes, which are discussed later in this project.

Table 4-1 HTML Table Tags

TAG	FUNCTION
<table> </table>	• Indicates the start and end of a table • All other table tags are inserted within these tags
<tr> </tr>	• Indicates the start and end of a table row • Rows consist of heading or data cells
<th> </th>	• Indicates the start and end of a table heading (also called a heading cell) • Table headings default to bold text and center-alignment
<td> </td>	• Indicates the start and end of a data cell in a table • Data cells default to normal text and left-alignment

Figure 4-11a on the next page shows an example of these tags used in an HTML file and Figure 4-11b shows the resulting Web page. As shown in Figure 4-11b, the table has four rows (a table header and three rows of data cells) and two columns. The rows are indicated in the HTML file in Figure 4-11a by the start **<tr>** tags and the end **</tr>** tags. For this simple table, the number of columns in the table is determined based on the number of cells within each row. As shown in Figure 4-11b, each row has two cells, which results in a table with two columns. (Later in the project, you will learn how to indicate the number of columns within the <table> tag.)

As shown in the HTML in Figure 4-11a, the first row includes table heading cells, as indicated by the start **<th>** tag and end **</th>** tag. In the second, third, and fourth rows, the cells contain data, indicated by the start **<td>** tag and end **</td>** tag. In the resulting table, as shown in Figure 4-11b, the table header in row 1 displays bold and centered text. The text in the data cells in rows 2 through 4 is left-aligned and normal. The table in Figure 4-11b is borderless, because no border attribute was specified in the <table> tag. Cellspacing of 15 pixels was added to further highlight the differences between the cells.

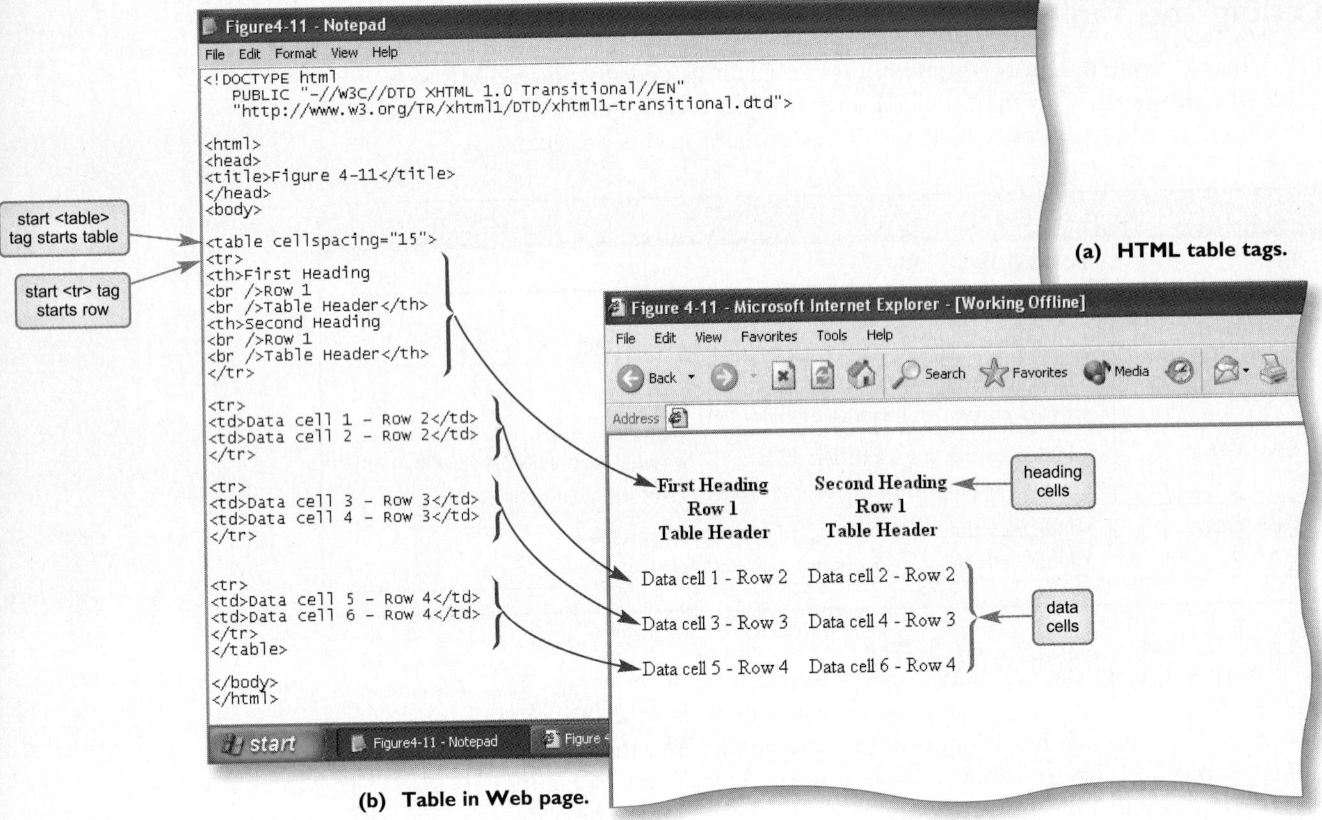

(a) HTML table tags.

(b) Table in Web page.

FIGURE 4-11

Table Tag Attributes

Each of the four main table tags listed in Table 4-1 has different attributes. Table 4-2 lists these tags and the main attributes associated with each tag. The <th> and <td> tags, which both are used to specify the contents of a cell, have the same attributes. Many of the table tags and attributes listed below are used in this project to create the Bell Video Web site.

Table 4-2 Table Tag Attributes and Functions

TAG	ATTRIBUTE	FUNCTION
<table> </table>	align bgcolor border cellspacing cellpadding cols width	• Controls table alignment (left, center, right) • Sets background color for table • Defines width of table border in pixels • Defines space between cells in pixels • Defines space within cells in pixels • Defines number of columns • Sets table width relative to window width
<tr> </tr>	align bgcolor valign	• Horizontally aligns row (left, center, right, justify) • Sets background color for row • Vertically aligns row (top, middle, bottom)
<th> </th> and <td> </td>	align bgcolor colspan rowspan valign	• Horizontally aligns cell (left, center, right, justify) • Sets background color for cell • Sets number of columns spanned by a cell • Sets number of rows spanned by a cell • Vertically aligns cell (top, middle, bottom)

Creating a Home Page

The first Web page developed in this project is the home page of the Bell Video Web site. As you have learned, the home page is the main page of a Web site, which Web site visitors generally view first. Visitors then click links to move from the home page to the other Web pages in the site. The Bell Video home page includes three links to other pages: the New Releases Web page, the Actor Web page, and the Type Web page. The home page also provides an e-mail link, so visitors easily can find contact information for Bell Video.

Starting Notepad

The first step in creating the Bell Video Web site is to start Notepad. The following steps show how to start Notepad and maximize the window.

To Start Notepad

1. **Click the Start button on the taskbar.**
2. **Point to All Programs on the Start menu, point to Accessories on the All Programs submenu, and then click Notepad on the Accessories submenu.**
3. **If the Notepad window is not maximized, click the Maximize button on the Notepad title bar to maximize it.**
4. **Click Format on the menu bar and, if necessary, click Word Wrap to turn Word Wrap on.**

The Notepad window is displayed and Word Wrap is enabled.

Entering HTML Tags to Define the Web Page Structure

As you have learned, every HTML file includes HTML tags that define the overall structure of a standard Web page and divide the HTML file into its basic sections. Table 4-3 shows the HTML tags entered to define the structure of the Bell Video home page. The following steps show how to enter the HTML tags that define the structure of the Bell Video home page.

More About

Table Borders

Table borders frame an image. You can insert a single image into a one-row, one-column table. Using a border gives the image a 3-D appearance, making the image appear to have a frame around it. A border of 1 pixel (border="1") is too small to use as a frame, but border="25" is too large.

Table 4-3 HTML Code to Define Web Page Structure

LINE	HTML TAG AND TEXT
1	`<!DOCTYPE html`
2	`PUBLIC "-//W3C//DTD XHTML 1.0 Transitional//EN"`
3	`"http://www.w4.org/TR/xhtml1/DTD/xhtml1-transitional.dtd">`
4	
5	`<html>`
6	`<head>`
7	`<title>Bell Video -- Great Service, Great Selection</title>`
8	`</head>`
9	`<body>`
10	
11	`</body>`
12	`</html>`

To Enter HTML Tags to Define the Web Page Structure

1 Enter the HTML code as shown in Table 4-3.

Notepad displays the HTML code (Figure 4-12).

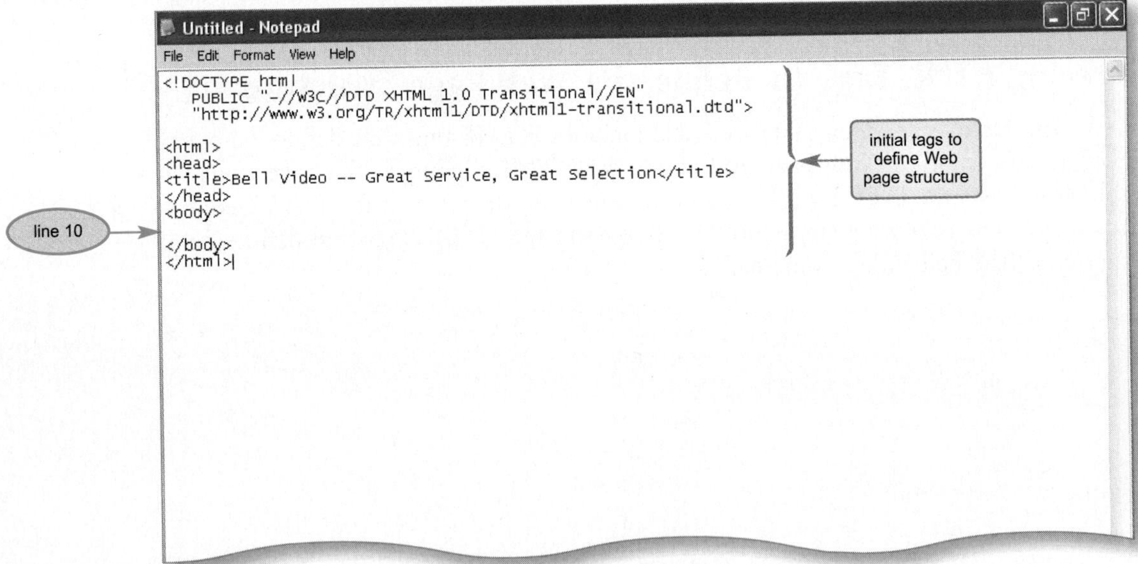

FIGURE 4-12

Using Borderless Tables to Position Images

Next, a borderless table is added to the Bell Video home page, in order to position the Bell Video logo image and the customer service excellence image at the top of the Web page (Figure 4-13).

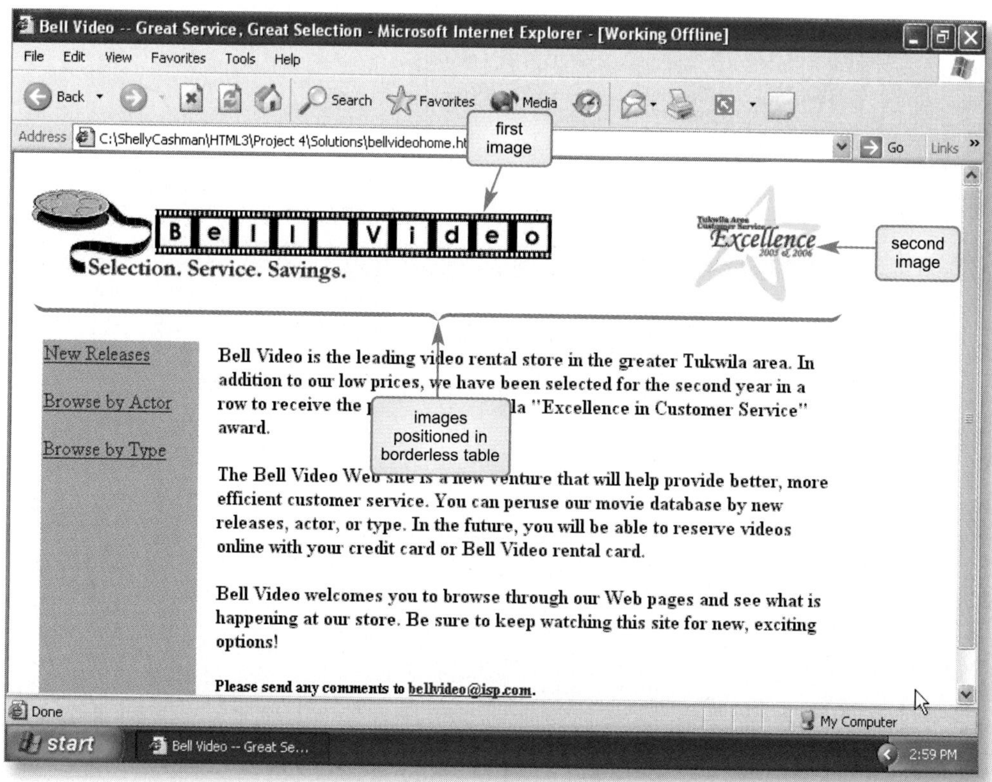

FIGURE 4-13 Bell Video Home page.

The HTML code to create a borderless table as shown in Figure 4-13 is as follows:

```
<table border="0" cols="2" width="90%">
```

where the border="0" attribute creates a borderless table, the cols="2" attribute indicates two columns are in the table, and the width="90%" indicates that the table should utilize 90% of the window's width. A benefit of using a percentage to set the table width is that it automatically changes the width of the table if the window is resized in the browser.

Figure 4-14a on the next page shows a sample of a table with the attributes border="2" and width="80%". The bordered table appears center-aligned on the Web page and utilizes 80% of the window's width. Figure 4-14b shows the same table with align="left", border="2", and width="100%" attributes. The bordered table appears left-aligned on the Web page and utilizes 100% of the window's width. Figure 4-14c shows the same table, with no attributes specified. The table uses the default left-alignment and appears with no borders. Because no width is specified, the table utilizes 100% of the window's width.

Q&A

Q: Is there another way to define table attributes?

A: You can define table attributes (e.g., colors, alignment) by using style sheets. This is the preferred technique to use when defining specific characteristics of a table. This project concentrates on table basics, which must be understood in order to utilize style sheets effectively for those characteristics.

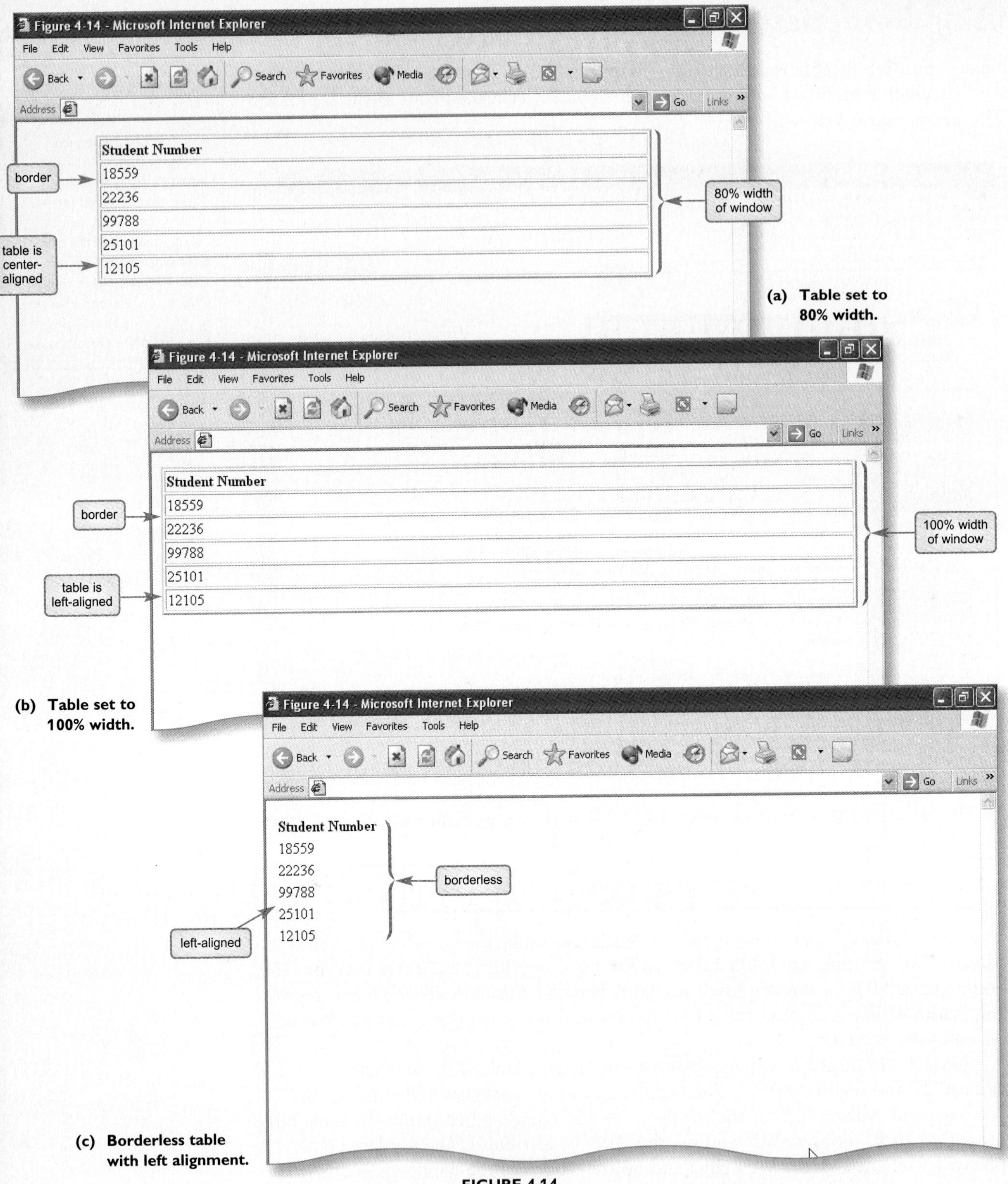

(a) Table set to 80% width.

(b) Table set to 100% width.

(c) Borderless table with left alignment.

FIGURE 4-14

Creating a Borderless Table to Position Images

Using these attributes, perform the steps on the next page to insert the heading table.

To Create a Borderless Table to Position Images

1

- **If necessary, click line 10.**

2

- **Type** `<table border="0" cols="2" width="90%">` **and then press the ENTER key.**

The <table> tag is displayed (Figure 4-15).

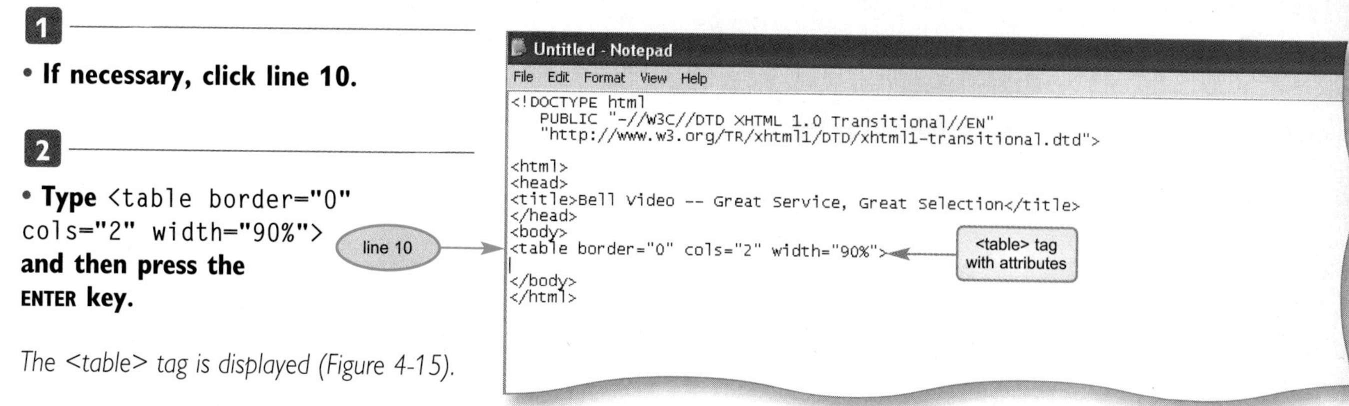

FIGURE 4-15

Inserting Images in a Table

The table shown in Figure 4-13 on page HTM 145 contains one row with two data cells in the row. The first data cell contains the image, bellvideologo.gif, and the second data cell contains the image, csexcellence.gif. To create data cells in a row, the HTML tags must include one or more sets of <td> </td> tags between the <tr> </tr> tags. Recall that the <tr> tag means table row, and the <td> tag means table data cell. Adding two sets of <td> </td> tags creates two data cells, one for each image. Data cell (<td> </td>) tags are used, rather than header cell (<th> </th>) tags, so that the image files can be left-aligned in the cell, instead of using the default center-alignment for heading cells. The following steps illustrate how to insert images in a table.

To Insert Images in a Table

1

- **If necessary, click line 11, type** `<tr>` **as the tag, and then press the ENTER key.**
- **Type** `<td><img src="bellvideologo.gif" width="430" height="74" alt="Bell Video Logo" /></td>` **and then press the ENTER key.**

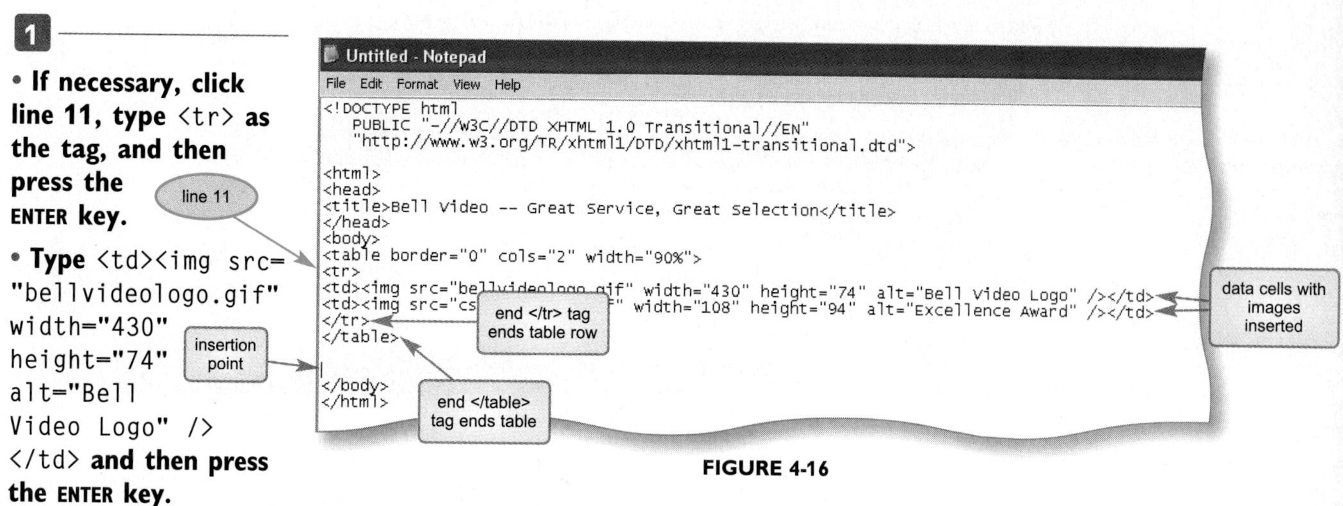

FIGURE 4-16

2

- **Type** `<td><img src="csexcellence.gif" width="108" height="94" alt="Excellence Award" /></td>` **and then press the ENTER key.**

3

• **Type** `</tr>` **and then press the ENTER key.**

4

• **Type** `</table>` **and then press the ENTER key twice.**

The HTML code is displayed (Figure 4-16).

The first table on the Bell Video home page is complete. The HTML code entered creates a borderless table that includes two images, bellvideologo.gif and csexcellence.gif, which are included on the HTML Data Disk. The attributes specified for the images indicate alt text and the height and width of these images in pixels. As you have learned, indicating the width and height of an image takes the burden off of the browser in calculating those dimensions and thus helps Web pages load faster. Later in the project, this HTML code is copied for use on the other three Web pages.

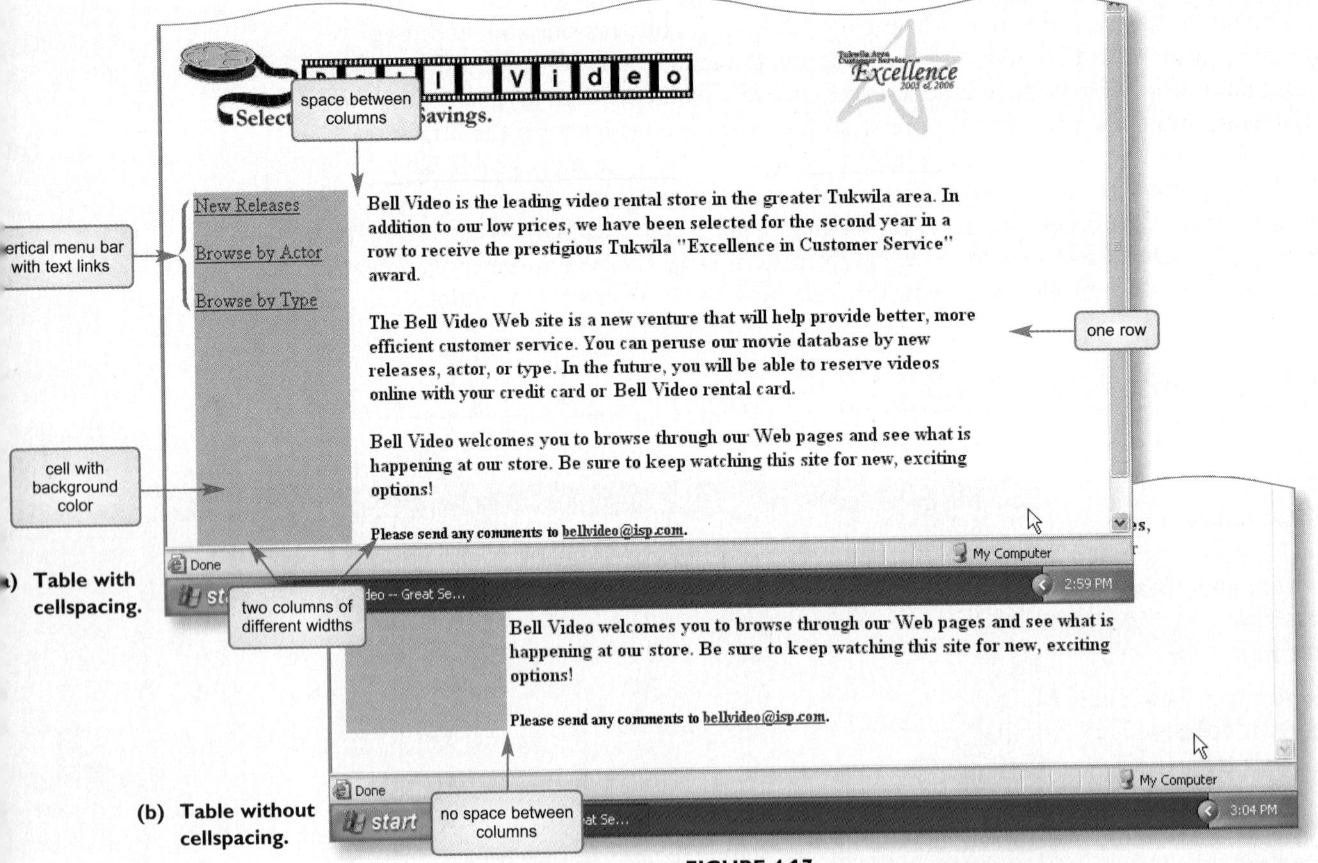

(a) Table with cellspacing.

(b) Table without cellspacing.

FIGURE 4-17

Creating a Vertical Menu Bar with Text Links

The Web site created in this project consists of four Web pages. Visitors should be able to move easily from one Web page to any of the other three Web pages. Providing a menu bar, either on the left side or top of the Web page, prevents the visitor from having to search the page for navigation links.

The following section shows how to create a one-row, two-column, borderless table, as shown in Figure 4-17a. The left column of the table is used to create a vertical menu bar of text links to the other three Web pages. The right column of the table is used to display text describing Bell Video.

To format the table as shown in Figure 4-17a, the cellspacing attribute in the <table> tag is used to insert some space between the left and right columns in the table. The **cellspacing** attribute sets the amount of space between cells. Figure 4-17a shows the home page with cellspacing used; Figure 4-17b shows the same page without cellspacing. As shown in these figures, the two columns are too close together when cellspacing is not used. Using cellspacing adds space between cells (or columns), which gives the table additional white space and creates a more polished look.

To create the table shown in Figure 4-17a, the <table> tag is used, along with four table attributes, as shown in Table 4-4.

More About

Navigation

Studies have been conducted to assess the best location on a Web page to place navigation bars and lists. The research results are varied, with indications that navigation options on the top, side, and bottom of a Web page show slight differences in visitor usability. The most important aspect of Web page navigation is to make the options easy enough to locate so visitors do not have to search for them.

Table 4-4 HTML Code to Create a Vertical Menu Bar of Text Links

LINE	HTML TAG AND TEXT
17	` <table border="0" cellspacing="15" cols="2" width="90%">`
18	`<tr>`
19	`<td valign="top" width="20%" bgcolor="lightsteelblue">`
20	`<a href="newreleases.htm">New Releases</a>`
21	
22	`<p><a href="actor.htm">Browse by Actor</a></p>`
23	
24	`<p><a href="type.htm">Browse by Type</a></p>`
25	`</td>`

Line 17 creates a table, where the border="0" attribute creates a borderless table, the cols="2" attribute indicates two columns are in the table, cellspacing="15" adds 15 pixels of space between table cells, width="90%" indicates that the table should display in 90% of the window's width, and align="center" centers the table on the Web page. The break tag <br /> at the beginning of the second table provides space between the two borderless tables. As in the first table, the width attribute sets the width of the entire table to a percentage of the window's width. This table also is set at 90%.

The columns of cells in the table are data cells, used to organize text and text links. The default vertical alignment for data cells is centered. As shown in Figure 4-17a, in this table, the text in the data cells should be aligned with the top of the cell. To change the alignment, the **valign="top"** attribute is used in the <tr> tag for the row (line 19). Using the valign="top" attribute aligns the information at the top of the cell. Vertical alignment also can be set in each individual cell of a row by using the **valign** attribute in the <td> tags in the row. If you want to set the vertical alignment for the entire row, using the valign attribute of the <tr> tag is more efficient.

Line 19 also shows the **bgcolor** attribute within the <td> tag of the first cell, which sets the background color for the first cell to light steel blue and provides a background for the menu bar. As with the valign attribute, the bgcolor attribute also can be used in the <tr> tag to set the background color for the entire row, instead of a specific cell.

Q&A

Q: How can I determine the height and width of an image?

A: You can determine the height and width of an image using a paint or image editing program. Once you know the height and width, you also can adjust the width and height by using the width and height attributes in the <img> tag. Be aware that, in doing so, you might cause the image to look distorted on the Web page.

Finally, the table in Figure 4-17a uses the **width** attribute within the <td> tag of each cell, to indicate the width of each column relative to the entire table. Columns of information in a table do not have to be equal widths, which allows the table to be formatted to organize text and images of different lengths and sizes. For example, in this table, the left column is set to 20% of the table width to contain short lines of text used as text links in a menu bar (lines 20 through 24). The right column will be set to 80% of the table width to contain paragraphs of text. The width attribute provides the flexibility to vary column widths in cases such as this. The width attribute of the <td> tag can be used to set the width to a specific number of pixels or as a percentage of the width of the table. Setting the width as a percentage is recommended, so that column widths are changed if the window is resized in the browser.

The following steps show how to create a borderless table and a vertical menu bar with text links.

To Create a Vertical Menu Bar with Text Links

1. **If necessary, click line 17 (Figure 4-18).**
2. **Enter the HTML code as shown in Table 4-4 on the previous page.**
3. **Press the ENTER key twice.**

The HTML code to create a borderless table with three text links is displayed (Figure 4-18).

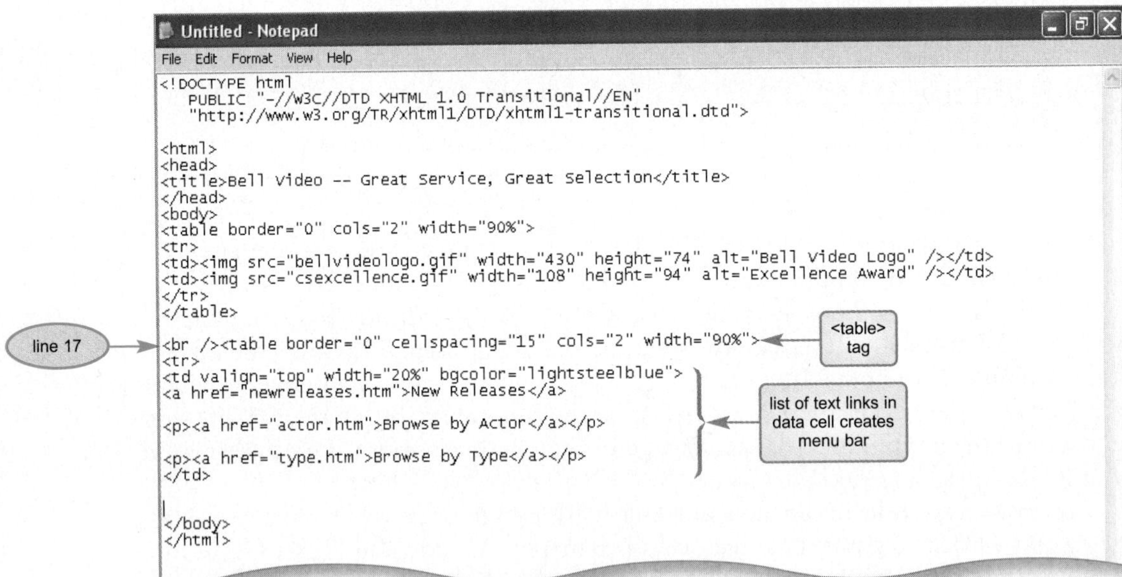


```
<!DOCTYPE html
   PUBLIC "-//W3C//DTD XHTML 1.0 Transitional//EN"
   "http://www.w3.org/TR/xhtml1/DTD/xhtml1-transitional.dtd">

<html>
<head>
<title>Bell Video -- Great Service, Great Selection</title>
</head>
<body>
<table border="0" cols="2" width="90%">
<tr>
<td><img src="bellvideologo.gif" width="430" height="74" alt="Bell Video Logo" /></td>
<td><img src="csexcellence.gif" width="108" height="94" alt="Excellence Award" /></td>
</tr>
</table>

<br /><table border="0" cellspacing="15" cols="2" width="90%">
<tr>
<td valign="top" width="20%" bgcolor="lightsteelblue">
<a href="newreleases.htm">New Releases</a>

<p><a href="actor.htm">Browse by Actor</a></p>

<p><a href="type.htm">Browse by Type</a></p>
</td>

</body>
</html>
```

FIGURE 4-18

The previous steps created a two-column, borderless table that is center-aligned and has cellspacing of 15 pixels between columns. The table was set to fill 90% of the window's width. The HTML code shown in Figure 4-18 also formatted the first data cell to be 20% of the table's width and use a light steel blue background color. Three links then were included in that data cell, to provide a vertical menu bar of links to the other three Web pages in the Web site. The vertical menu bar in the left column of this table allows the visitor to move from the home page to any other page quickly. Figure 4-19 shows the results of your work so far.

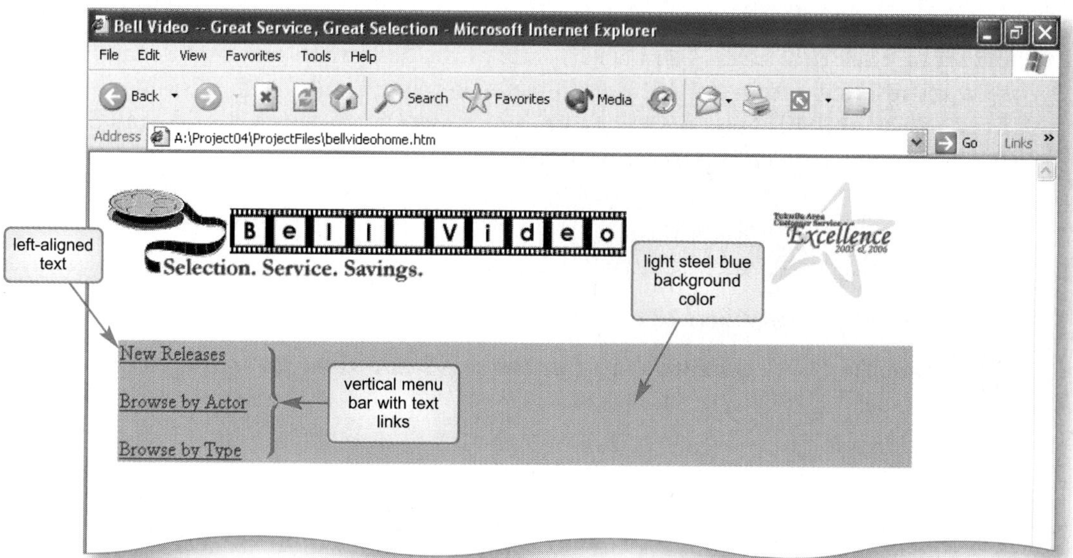

FIGURE 4-19 Web page with one-column table.

Adding Text to a Table Cell

Next, the paragraph of text must be added in the right column of the table, as shown in Figure 4-17a on page HTM 148. Table 4-5 shows the HTML code used to create a second column in the table, add text including an e-mail link, and then end the table.

Table 4-5 HTML Code to Add Text to a Table Cell

HTML TAG AND TEXT

```
<td valign=top width="80%"><b>Bell Video is the leading video rental store
in the greater Tukwila area. In addition to our low prices, we have been
selected for the second year in a row to receive the prestigious Tukwila
"Excellence in Customer Service" award.
<p>The Bell Video Web site is a new venture that will help provide better,
more efficient customer service. You can peruse our movie database by new
releases, actor, or type. In the future, you will be able to reserve videos online
with your credit card or Bell Video rental card.</p>
<p>Bell Video welcomes you to browse through our Web pages and see what is
happening at our store. Be sure to keep watching this site for new, exciting
options!</p>
<p><font size="-1">Please send any comments to <a
href="mailto:bellvideo@isp.com">bellvideo@isp.com</a>.</font></p></b>
</td>
</tr>
</table>
```

As shown in Table 4-5 on the previous page, the second column is created using the set of <td> </td> tags. The HTML code of the paragraph text and e-mail link then are inserted within the <td> </td> tags. To create blank lines, as shown in lines 31, 36, and 40, press the ENTER key twice after typing lines 30, 35, and 39.

The following steps illustrate how to add text to a table cell.

To Add Text to a Table Cell

1 **If necessary, click line 27.**

2 **Enter the HTML code as shown in Table 4-5 and then press the ENTER key.**

The HTML code is displayed (Figure 4-20).

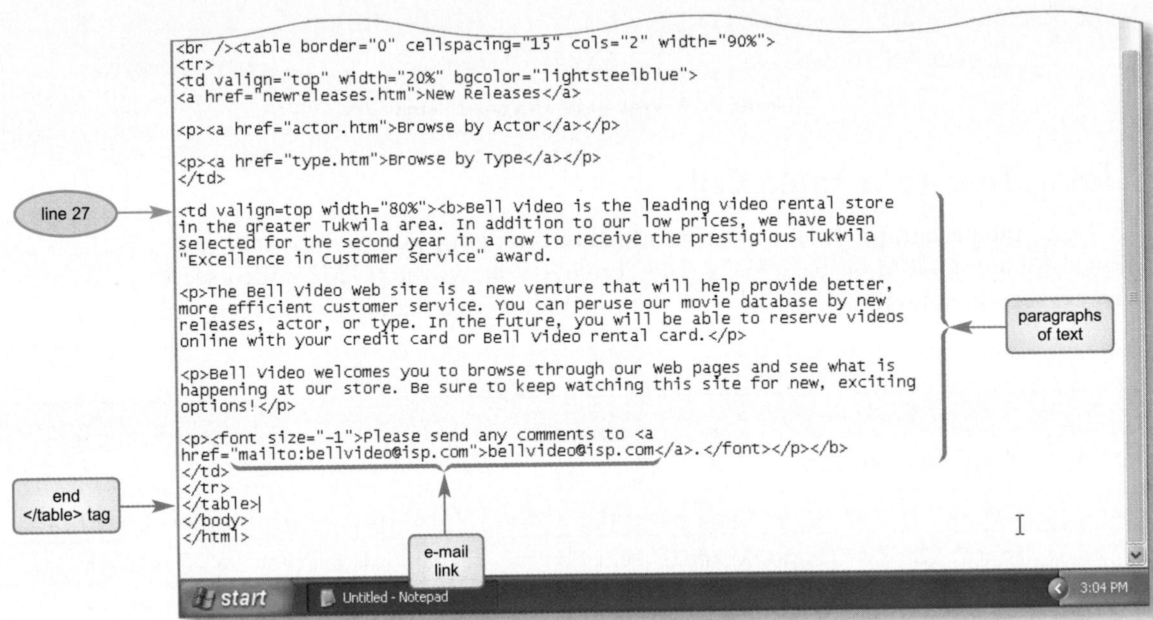

FIGURE 4-20

As shown in Figure 4-20, the <td> </td> tags create a new data cell set to 80% of the table's width. The <td> </td> tags enclose four paragraphs of text, including an e-mail link to bellvideo@isp.com. Finally, lines 43 through 45 end the current cell, the current row, and the table. The next step is to save and print the HTML file.

The HTML code for the Bell Video home page is complete. The Web page includes two tables used to organize images and text. The first table is a borderless, one-row, two-column table containing two images. The second is a borderless, one-row, two-column table containing text. The left column uses a background color to highlight a vertical menu bar of text links to the other Web pages in the Web site. The right column contains text describing Bell Video.

Two tables were used in the Bell Video home page, so that each table could be set to a different width. In the first table, the total width of the table is 80%. In the second table, the total width is 90%. The widths of the two columns in the second table are 20% of the table width and 70% of the table width, respectively.

With the HTML code for the Bell Video home page complete, the file should be saved and a copy should be printed as a reference.

To Save and Print the HTML File

1. **With a floppy disk in drive A, click File on the menu bar and then click Save As. Type** `bellvideohome.htm` **in the File name text box.**
2. **If necessary, click 3½ Floppy (A:) in the Save in list. Click the Project04 folder and then click the ProjectFiles folder in the list of available folders. Click the Save button in the Save As dialog box.**
3. **Click File on the menu bar and then click Print on the File menu.**

Notepad saves the HTML file in the Project04\ProjectFiles folder on the floppy disk in drive A using the file name, bellvideohome.htm. Notepad prints the HTML file (Figure 4-21).

```
<!DOCTYPE html
   PUBLIC "-//W3C//DTD XHTML 1.0 Transitional//EN"
   "http://www.w3.org/TR/xhtml1/DTD/xhtml1-transitional.dtd">

<html>
<head>
<title>Bell Video -- Great Service, Great Selection</title>
</head>
<body>
<table border="0" cols="2" width="90%">
<tr>
<td><img src="bellvideologo.gif" width="430" height="74" alt="Bell Video Logo" /></td>
<td><img src="csexcellence.gif" width="108" height="94" alt="Excellence Award" /></td>
</tr>
</table>

<br /><table border="0" cellspacing="15" cols="2" width="90%">
<tr>
<td valign="top" width="20%" bgcolor="lightsteelblue">
<a href="newreleases.htm">New Releases</a>

<p><a href="actor.htm">Browse by Actor</a></p>

<p><a href="type.htm">Browse by Type</a></p>
</td>

<td valign=top width="80%"><b>Bell Video is the leading video rental store
in the greater Tukwila area. In addition to our low prices, we have been
selected for the second year in a row to receive the prestigious Tukwila
"Excellence in Customer Service" award.

<p>The Bell Video Web site is a new venture that will help provide better,
more efficient customer service. You can peruse our movie database by new
releases, actor, or type. In the future, you will be able to reserve videos
online with your credit card or Bell Video rental card.</p>

<p>Bell Video welcomes you to browse through our Web pages and see what is
happening at our store. Be sure to keep watching this site for new, exciting
options!</p>

<p><font size="-1">Please send any comments to <a
href="mailto:bellvideo@isp.com">bellvideo@isp.com</a>.</font></p></b>
</td>
</tr>
</table>

</body>
</html>
```

FIGURE 4-21

Viewing and Printing the Web Page Using the Browser

After the HTML file for the Bell Video home page is saved, it should be viewed in a browser to confirm that the Web page appears as desired and that the links function as expected. To test the Bell Video home page, click the e-mail link to verify that it works correctly. Next, click each of the three vertical menu bar links. Clicking the New Releases link will display a blank page, as that Web page is developed later in the project. Clicking the Actor and Type links will display the Actor and Type Web pages, which are stored on the HTML Data Disk as they are developed thus far. Later in the project, edits will be made to both the Actor and Type Web pages.

The following steps show how to view and print the Web page.

To View and Print a Web Page

1

- **Click the Start button on the Windows taskbar and then point to All Programs on the Start menu.**
- **Click Internet Explorer (or another browser command) on the All Programs submenu.**
- **If necessary, click the Maximize button to maximize the browser window.**

2

- **Type** `a:\Project04\ProjectFiles\bellvideohome.htm` **in the Address text box and then press the ENTER key.**

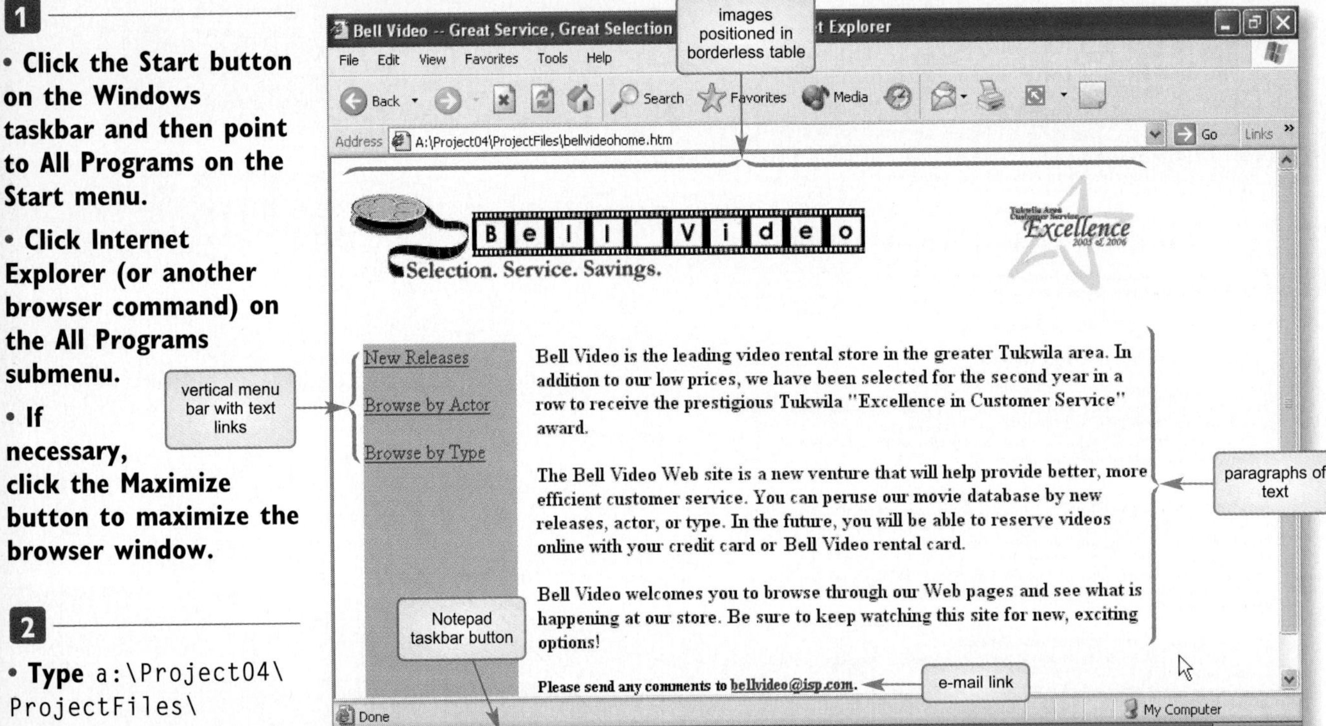

FIGURE 4-22

The Bell Video home page is displayed (Figure 4-22).

3

• **Click the Print button on the Standard Buttons toolbar.**

The home page prints (Figure 4-23).

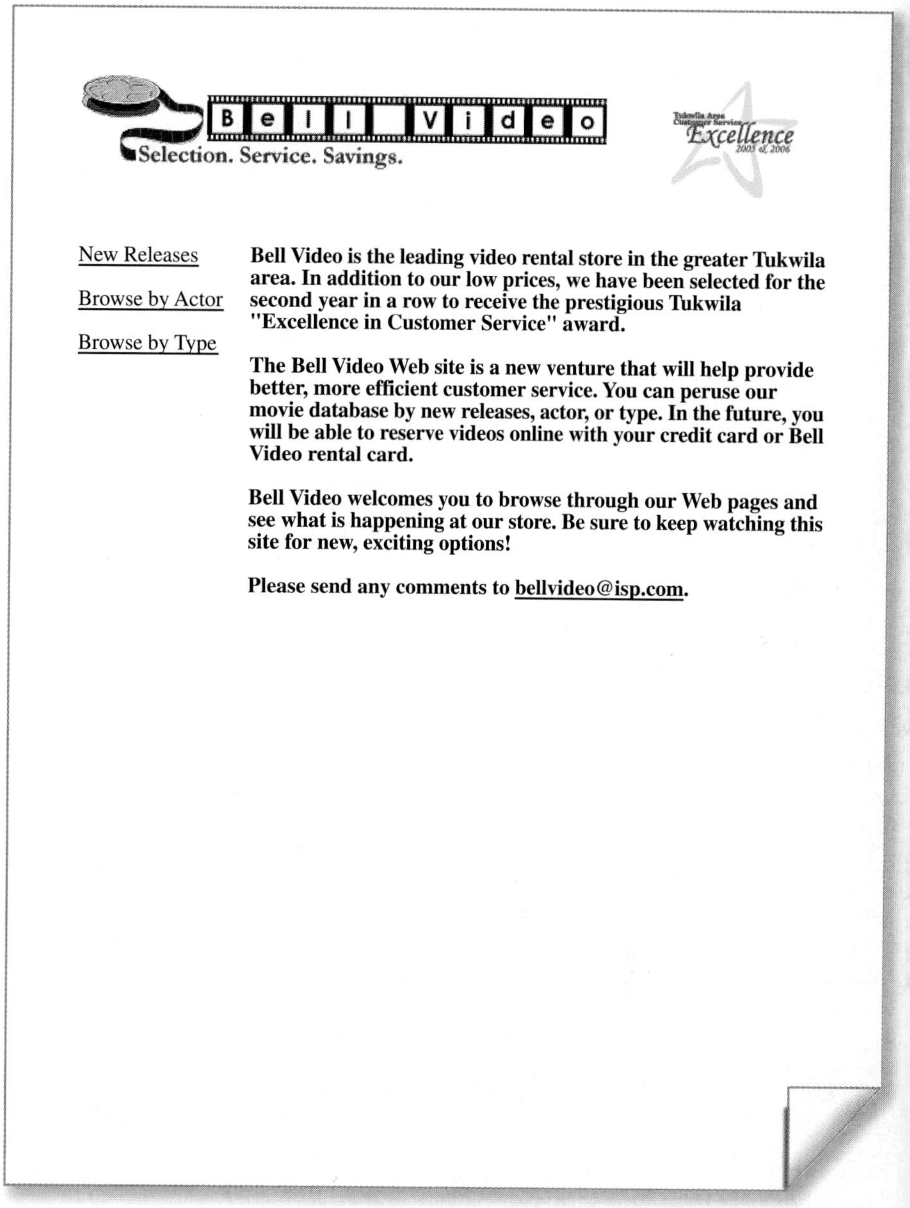

Tukwila Area Customer Service Excellence 2005 & 2006

New Releases

Browse by Actor

Browse by Type

Bell Video is the leading video rental store in the greater Tukwila area. In addition to our low prices, we have been selected for the second year in a row to receive the prestigious Tukwila "Excellence in Customer Service" award.

The Bell Video Web site is a new venture that will help provide better, more efficient customer service. You can peruse our movie database by new releases, actor, or type. In the future, you will be able to reserve videos online with your credit card or Bell Video rental card.

Bell Video welcomes you to browse through our Web pages and see what is happening at our store. Be sure to keep watching this site for new, exciting options!

Please send any comments to bellvideo@isp.com.

FIGURE 4-23

The home page is complete. The next step is to create the New Releases Web page with two tables: one to create a horizontal menu bar and another to organize a list of text.

Creating a Secondary Web Page

As previously discussed, it is important to give Web site visitors the option to move easily from one Web page to another without having to search for links. The Bell Video home page includes a vertical menu bar of text links to meet this need. The three remaining Web pages in the Bell Video Web site include a horizontal menu bar of text links, positioned toward the top of the Web page, just after the header table.

Figure 4-24 shows the New Releases Web page with a horizontal menu bar of text links. The menu bar lists the four Web pages — Home, New Releases, Actor, and Type — with a | (pipe) symbol between the four links.

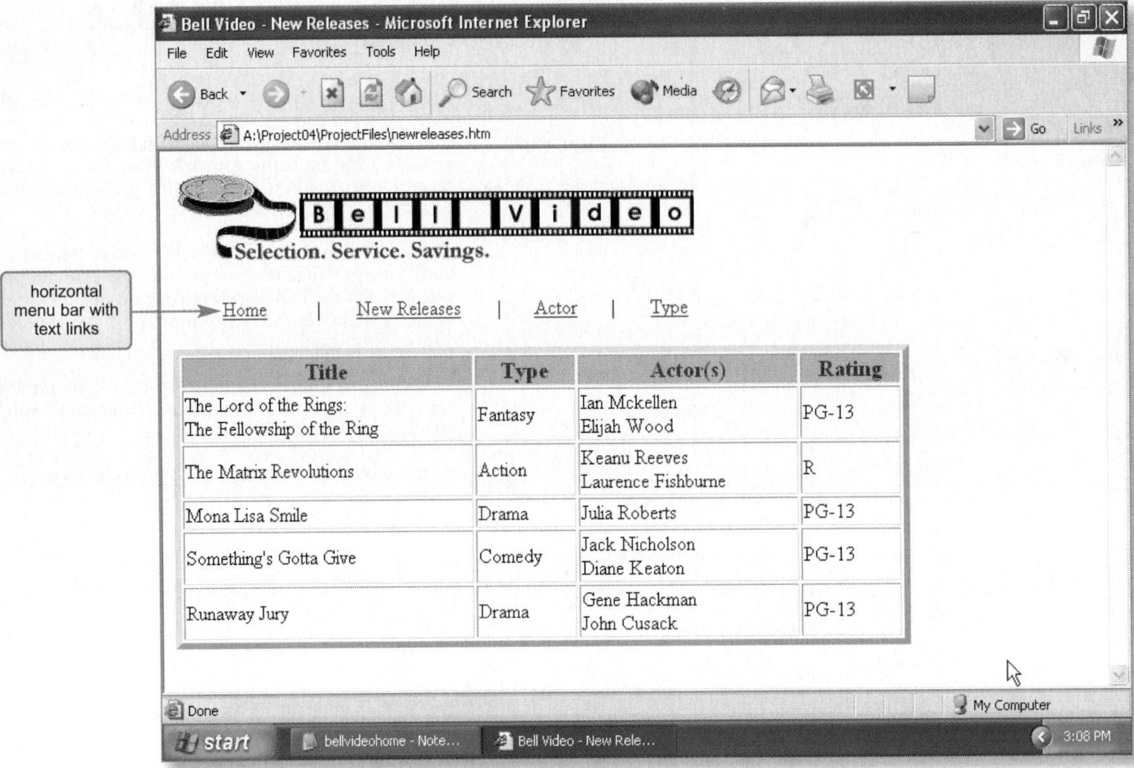

Bell Video - New Releases - Microsoft Internet Explorer
Address A:\Project04\ProjectFiles\newreleases.htm
Bell Video
Selection. Service. Savings.
horizontal menu bar with text links
Home | New Releases | Actor | Type
Title | Type | Actor(s) | Rating
The Lord of the Rings: The Fellowship of the Ring | Fantasy | Ian Mckellen Elijah Wood | PG-13
The Matrix Revolutions | Action | Keanu Reeves Laurence Fishburne | R
Mona Lisa Smile | Drama | Julia Roberts | PG-13
Something's Gotta Give | Comedy | Jack Nicholson Diane Keaton | PG-13
Runaway Jury | Drama | Gene Hackman John Cusack | PG-13
Done
My Computer
start
bellvideohome - Note...
Bell Video - New Rele...
3:08 PM

FIGURE 4-24 New Releases Web page.

To provide consistency throughout the Web site, as shown in Figure 4-1 on page HTM 133, the Bell Video logo should appear at the top of each Web page. The first steps in creating the New Releases Web page, as shown in Figure 4-24, thus is to add the HTML tags to define the Web page structure and create a borderless table with a Bell Video logo image. Recall that the Bell Video home page uses a borderless table with the Bell Video logo image and the customer service excellence image. Rather than entering this code again, the code from the Bell Video home page can be copied and pasted into the HTML file for the New Releases Web page and then edited to delete the image, csexcellence.gif. The following steps show how to copy the header table from the HTML file, bellvideohome.htm, to a new HTML file.

To Copy and Paste HTML Code to a New File

1. **Click the Notepad button on the taskbar.**
2. **Click immediately to the left of the < in the <!DOCTYPE html tag on line 1. Drag through the first </table> tag on line 15 to highlight lines 1 through 15.**
3. **Press CTRL+C to copy the selected lines to the Clipboard.**
4. **Click File on the menu bar and then click New.**
5. **Press CTRL+V to paste the contents from the Clipboard into a new file.**

The HTML code for the new file is displayed (Figure 4-25).

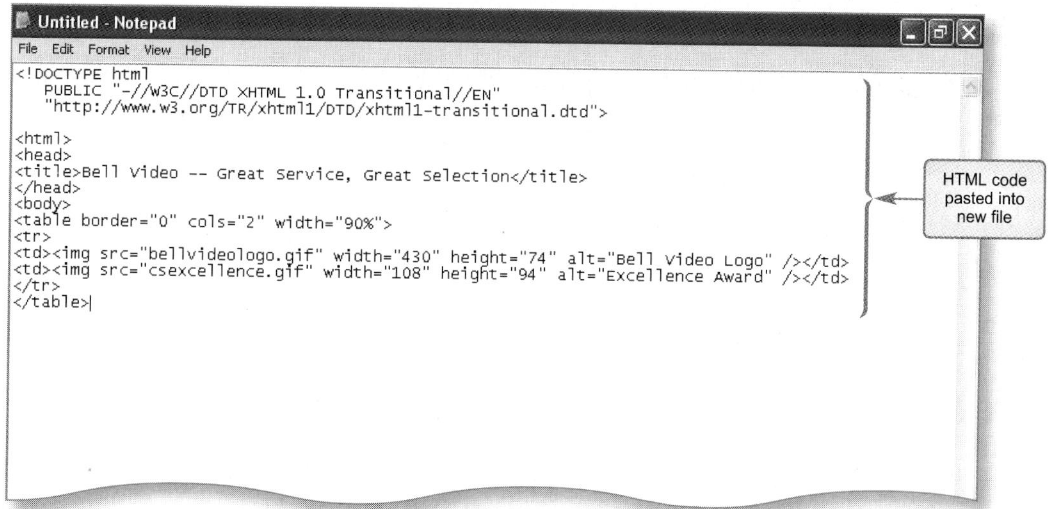

```
<!DOCTYPE html
   PUBLIC "-//W3C//DTD XHTML 1.0 Transitional//EN"
   "http://www.w3.org/TR/xhtml1/DTD/xhtml1-transitional.dtd">

<html>
<head>
<title>Bell Video -- Great Service, Great Selection</title>
</head>
<body>
<table border="0" cols="2" width="90%">
<tr>
<td><img src="bellvideologo.gif" width="430" height="74" alt="Bell Video Logo" /></td>
<td><img src="csexcellence.gif" width="108" height="94" alt="Excellence Award" /></td>
</tr>
</table>
```


FIGURE 4-25

Changing the Title

The next step is to edit the pasted code to change the title of the Web page and delete the image, csexcellence.gif. The title of the Web page should be changed to Bell Video - New Releases, so that the title of the current Web page is displayed on the title bar of the Web browser.

The following steps show how to change the title of the Web page.

To Change the Title

1. **Highlight the words, -- Great Service, Great Selection, between the <title> and </title> tags on line 7. Type** `- New Releases` **as the text.**
2. **Click immediately to the right of the </table> tag on line 15. Press the ENTER key three times.**
3. **Type** `</body>` **and then press the ENTER key.**
4. **Type** `</html>` **as the end tag.**

The HTML code is displayed (Figure 4-26).

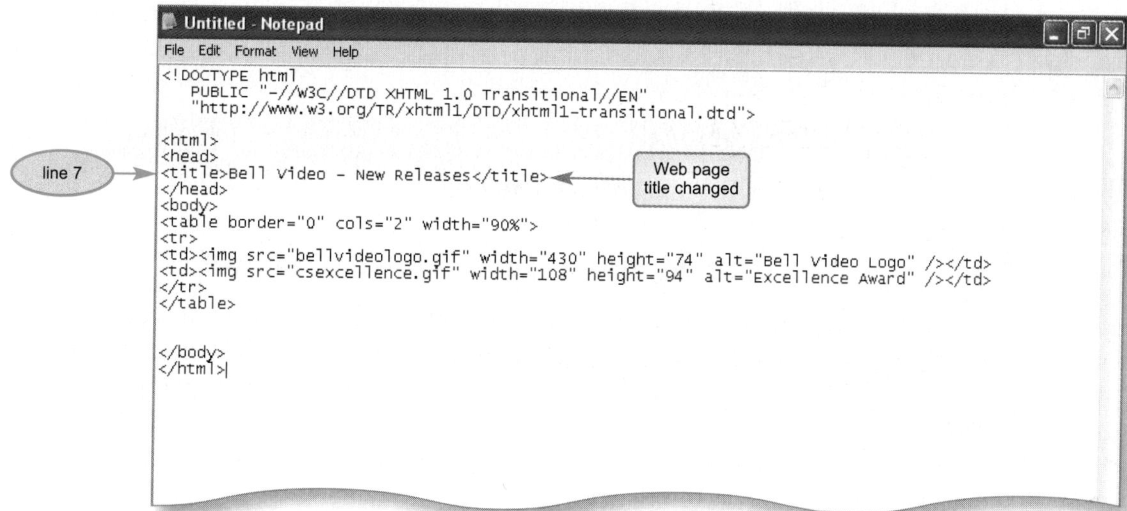

```
<!DOCTYPE html
   PUBLIC "-//W3C//DTD XHTML 1.0 Transitional//EN"
   "http://www.w3.org/TR/xhtml1/DTD/xhtml1-transitional.dtd">

<html>
<head>
<title>Bell Video - New Releases</title>
</head>
<body>
<table border="0" cols="2" width="90%">
<tr>
<td><img src="bellvideologo.gif" width="430" height="74" alt="Bell Video Logo" /></td>
<td><img src="csexcellence.gif" width="108" height="94" alt="Excellence Award" /></td>
</tr>
</table>


</body>
</html>
```


FIGURE 4-26

Deleting an Image

The customer service award image also should be deleted from the New Releases Web page, so that the Web page appears as shown in Figure 4-24 on page HTM 156. Because the New Releases Web page has a horizontal menu bar, including the customer service award image makes the Web page look very cluttered. Removing the customer service award image by deleting line 13 of the HTML code results in a more polished Web page.

The following steps show to delete the line of HTML code that inserts the customer service award image.

To Delete an Image

1. **Highlight line 13, which contains the code to insert the image, csexcellence.gif.**
2. **Press the DELETE key twice.**

The Web page with the completed changes is displayed (Figure 4-27).

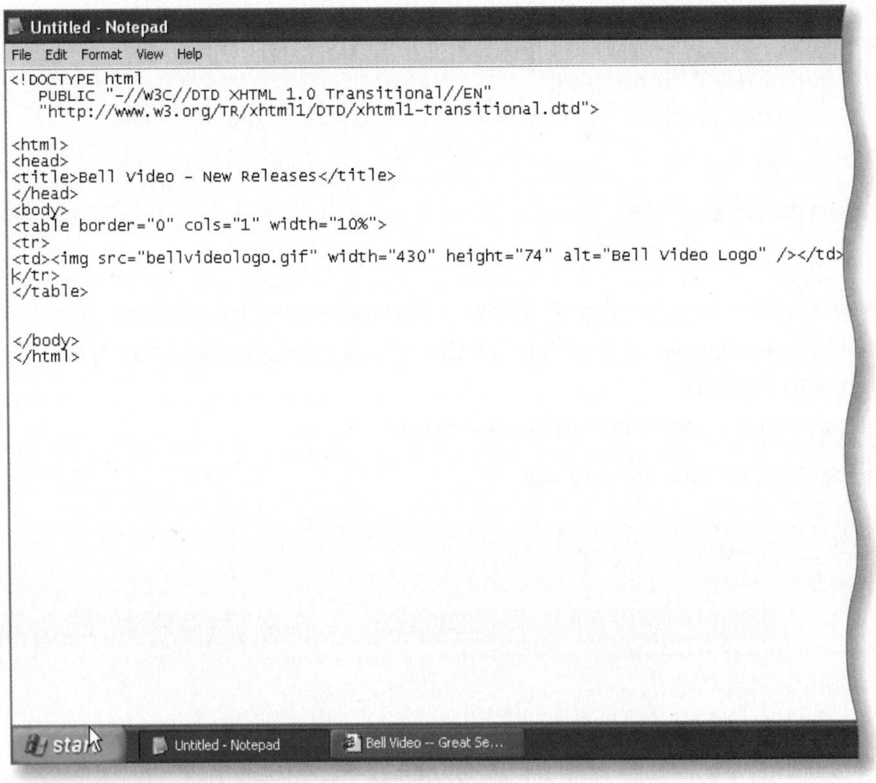

Untitled - Notepad

File Edit Format View Help

```
<!DOCTYPE html
   PUBLIC "-//W3C//DTD XHTML 1.0 Transitional//EN"
   "http://www.w3.org/TR/xhtml1/DTD/xhtml1-transitional.dtd">

<html>
<head>
<title>Bell Video - New Releases</title>
</head>
<body>
<table border="0" cols="1" width="10%">
<tr>
<td><img src="bellvideologo.gif" width="430" height="74" alt="Bell Video Logo" /></td>
</tr>
</table>


</body>
</html>
```

start | Untitled - Notepad | Bell Video -- Great Se...

FIGURE 4-27

Creating a Horizontal Menu Bar with Text Links

The next step in creating the New Releases Web page is to create a second borderless table that can be used as a horizontal menu bar, as shown in Figure 4-28 on page HTM 160. Table 4-6 lists the HTML tags and text are used to create the horizontal menu bar.

Table 4-6 HTML Code to Insert a Menu Bar

HTML TAG AND TEXT

```
<br /><table border="0" cols="7" width="60%">
<tr align="center">
<td width="20%"><a href="bellvideohome.htm">Home</a></td>
<td width="1%">|</td>
<td width="25%"><a href="newreleases.htm">New Releases</a></td>
<td width="1%">|</td>
<td width="15%"><a href="actor.htm">Actor</a></td>
<td width="1%">|</td>
<td width="15%"><a href="type.htm">Type</a></td>
</tr>
</table>
```

The table created by the HTML code in Table 4-6 is a borderless, one-row, seven-column table. To improve the appearance of the Web page, the table is set to 60% of the window's width, so that it is not as wide as the first table. The menu bar consists of four links — Home, New Releases, Actor, and Type — which link to the Web pages, bellvideohome.htm, newreleases.htm, actor.htm, and type.htm, respectively. Each link is inserted in a single column (cell). The | (pipe) symbol is included in a column between each of the four links to separate them visually.

As shown in Table 4-6, the width of each column in the table is specified using the width attribute of the <td> tag. For the four cells with text links, the column widths are set so that the text fits in the cell without wrapping. For example, the column used for New Releases is set a width of 25%, while the columns used for shorter words, Home, Actor, and Type, are set to 20%, 15%, and 15%, respectively. The column widths for the cells with the | (pipe) symbols are set to 1%, because the symbol does not require much space in the menu bar. If a width of 1% is not specified for the cells with the | symbols, all cells in the table are spaced evenly, which makes the cells for the | symbol unnecessarily large.

The steps on the next page show how to create a horizontal menu bar with text links for the New Releases Web page.

To Create a Horizontal Menu Bar with Text Links

1

- **If necessary, click line 16.**

2

- **Enter the HTML code as shown in Table 4-6 on the previous page.**

3

- **Press the ENTER key twice.**

The HTML code is displayed (Figure 4-28).

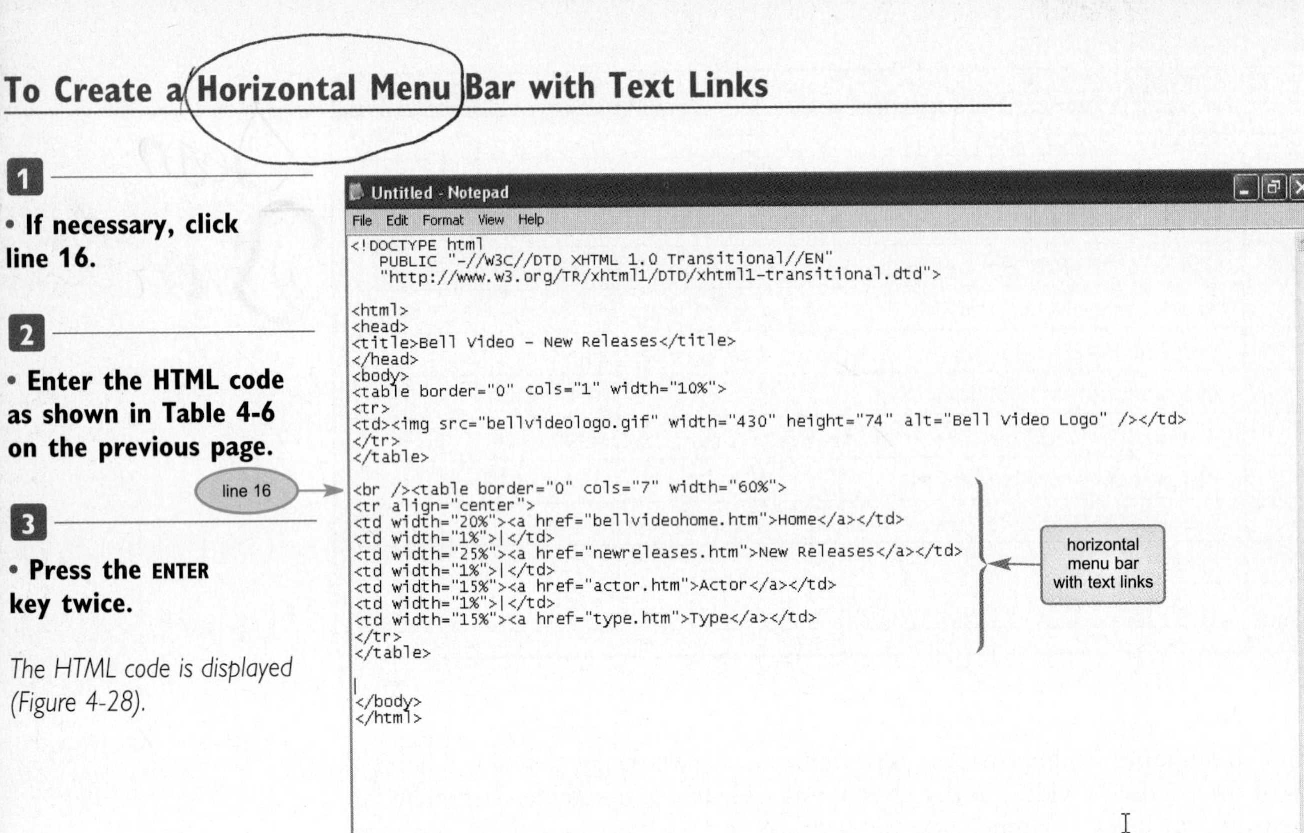

FIGURE 4-28

The HTML code for the horizontal menu bar is complete. As shown in Figure 4-28, line 16 created a new, borderless table with seven columns that fills 60% of the window's width. Line 18 added a data cell with a text link to the bellvideohome.htm Web page, while line 20 added a text link to the newreleases.htm Web page currently under development. Lines 22 and 24 created two other test links to the actor.htm (Actor) and type.htm (Type) Web pages. Lines 19, 21, and 23 add the | (pipe) symbols to separate all of these links.

Creating a Table with Borders

Up to this point, the tables created in the Bell Video home page and New Releases Web page have been borderless. Borderless tables often are appropriate when the tables are used to position text and image elements. In other instances, such as when a table is used to structure columns and rows of information, borders are appropriate. For example, the New Releases Web page lists four columns and six rows of information about newly released movies. Figure 4-29 shows this information in a table with borders, while Figure 4-30 shows the same table without borders. As shown in these figures, using a table with borders makes the information on the New Releases Web page easier to read and provides a frame that gives the table a three-dimensional appearance.

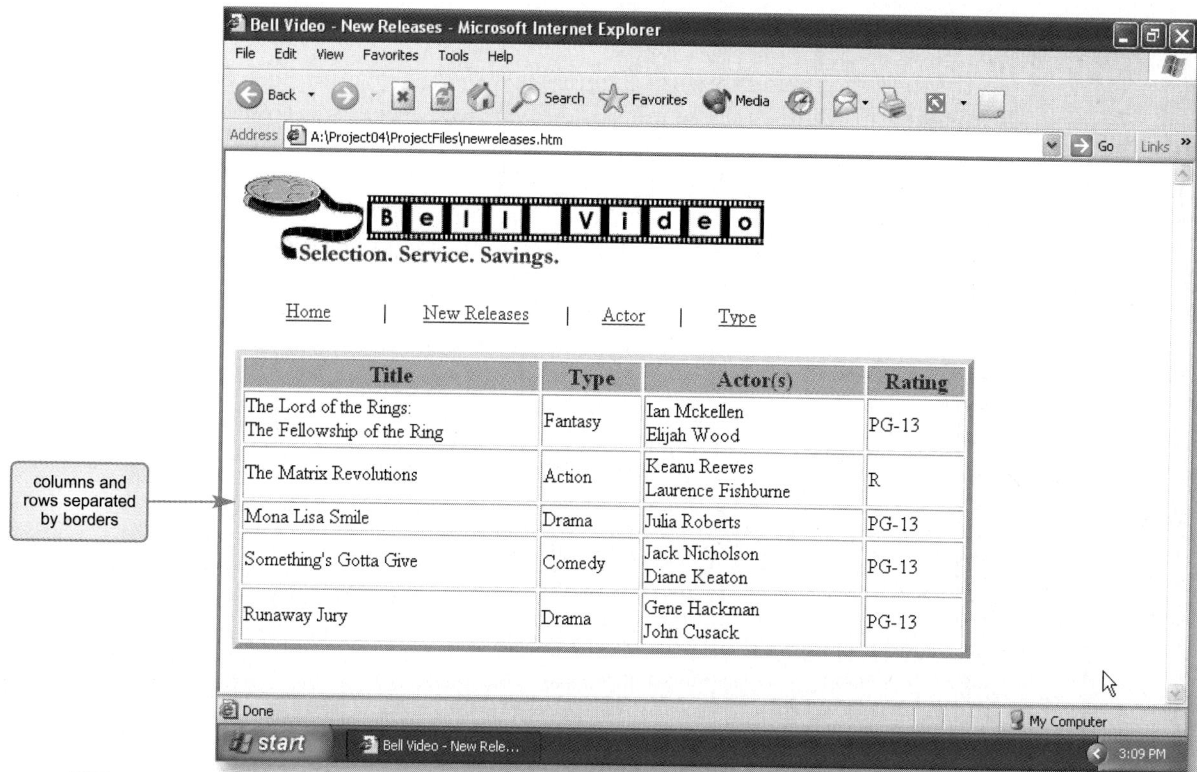

Title	Type	Actor(s)	Rating
The Lord of the Rings: The Fellowship of the Ring	Fantasy	Ian Mckellen Elijah Wood	PG-13
The Matrix Revolutions	Action	Keanu Reeves Laurence Fishburne	R
Mona Lisa Smile	Drama	Julia Roberts	PG-13
Something's Gotta Give	Comedy	Jack Nicholson Diane Keaton	PG-13
Runaway Jury	Drama	Gene Hackman John Cusack	PG-13

FIGURE 4-29 Table with border.

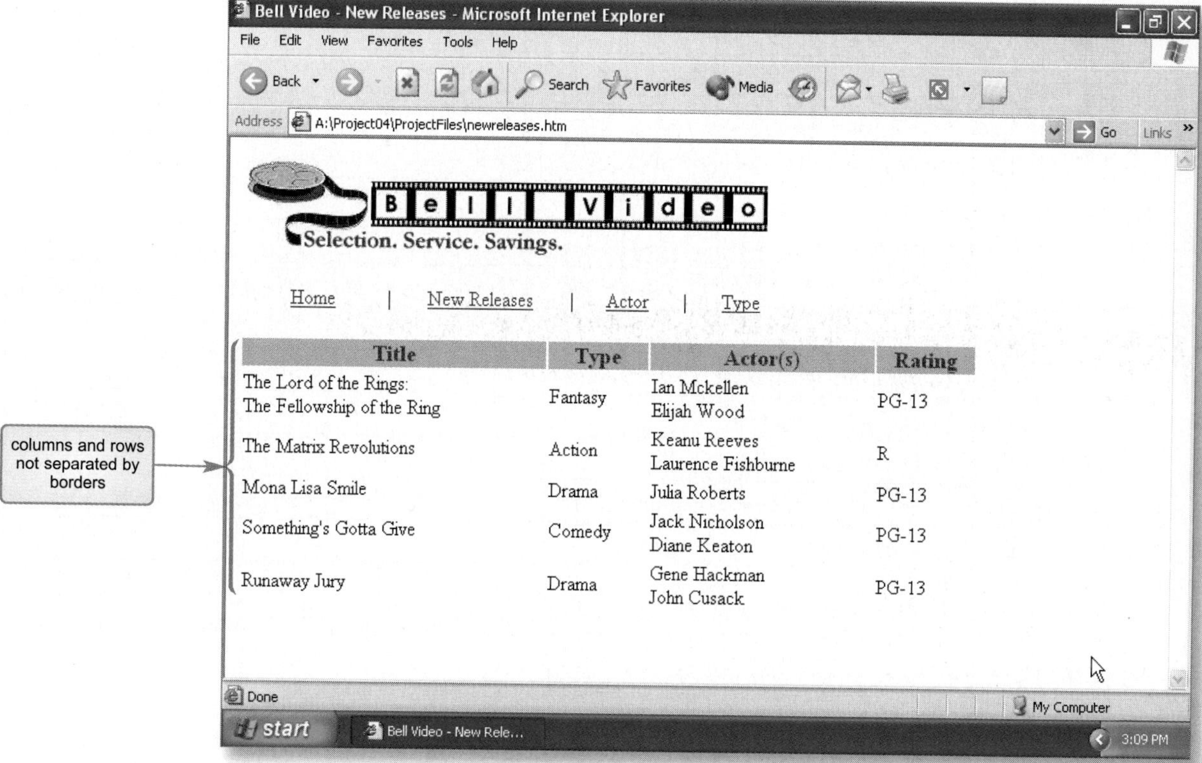

Title	Type	Actor(s)	Rating
The Lord of the Rings: The Fellowship of the Ring	Fantasy	Ian Mckellen Elijah Wood	PG-13
The Matrix Revolutions	Action	Keanu Reeves Laurence Fishburne	R
Mona Lisa Smile	Drama	Julia Roberts	PG-13
Something's Gotta Give	Comedy	Jack Nicholson Diane Keaton	PG-13
Runaway Jury	Drama	Gene Hackman John Cusack	PG-13

FIGURE 4-30 Borderless table.

Creating a Table with Borders and Inserting Text into Cells

Creating the table shown in Figure 4-29 on the previous page first involves creating a table with four columns and seven rows. The first row of the table is for column headings; the other rows are for data. As you have learned, heading cells differ from data cells in their appearance. Text in a heading cell appears as bold and centered, while text in a data cell appears as normal and left-aligned. Table 4-7 contains the HTML tags and text used to create the table of newly released movies on the New Releases Web page.

Table 4-7 HTML Code to Create a Table with Borders and Insert Text into Cells

HTML TAG AND TEXT

```
<br /><table cols="4" border="5" width="80%">
<tr bgcolor="lightsteelblue'>
<th><font color="#993366" size="+1">Title</font></th>
<th><font color="#993366" size="+1">Type</font></th>
<th><font color="#993366" size="+1">Actor(s)</font></th>
<th><font color="#993366" size="+1">Rating</font></th>
</tr>

<tr>
<td>The Lord of the Rings:
<br />The Fellowship of the Ring</td>
<td>Fantasy</td>
<td>Ian McKellen
<br />Elijah Wood</td>
<td>PG-13</td>
</tr>

<tr>
<td>The Matrix Revolutions</td>
<td>Action</td>
<td>Keanu Reeves
<br />Laurence Fishburne</td>
<td>R</td>
</tr>
```

The following steps illustrate how to create a table with borders and insert text into heading and data cells.

To Create a Table with Borders and Insert Text

1

- **If necessary, click line 28.**

2

- **Enter the HTML code as shown in Table 4-7.**

3

- **Press the ENTER key twice.**

The HTML code is displayed (Figure 4-31).

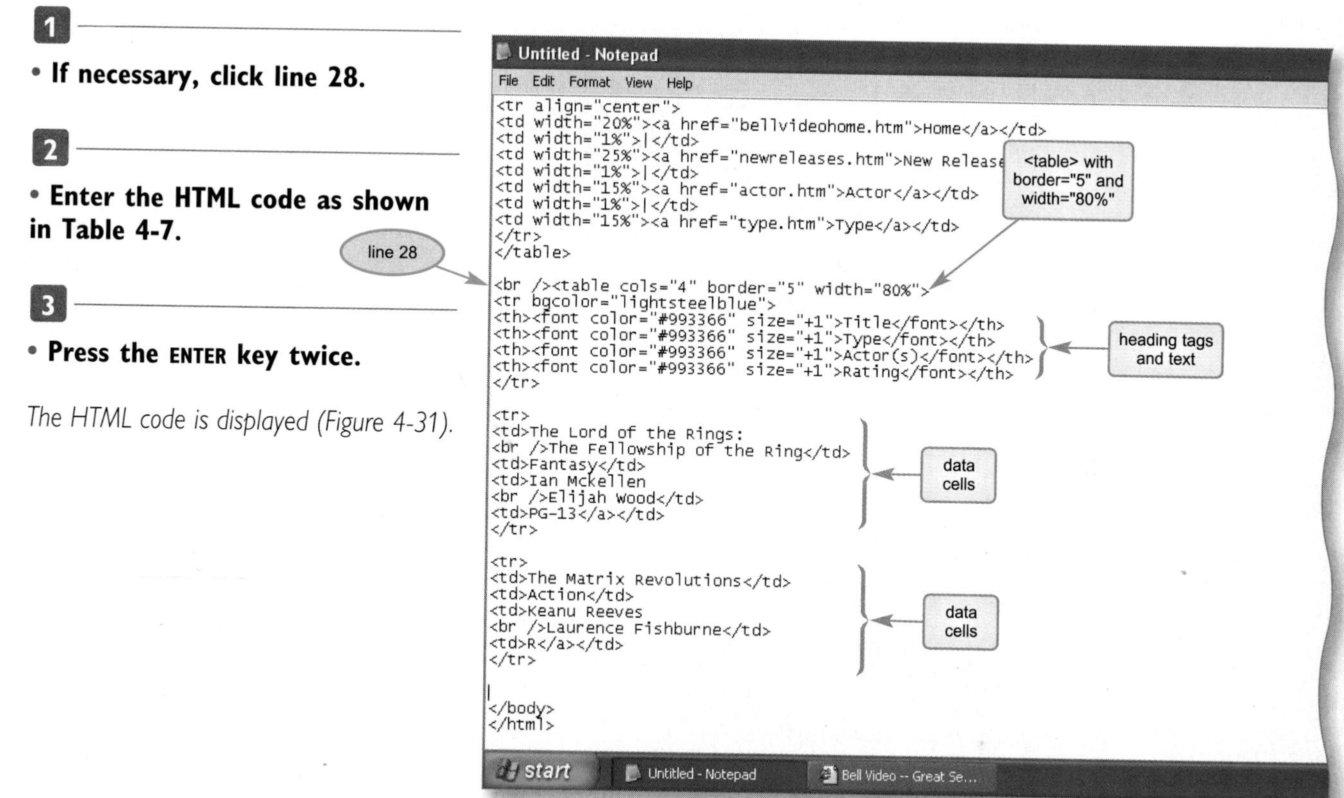

FIGURE 4-31

As shown in Figure 4-31, line 28 created a four-column table with a border that is five pixels wide. The table spans 80% of the window's width. Line 30 inserted a table header row with a light steel blue background and a large size (+1) font. Lines 31 through 33 added the three remaining headers. Lines 37 through 50 used the <td> </td> tags to create five rows with four data cells per row and then to insert text in the data cells.

Table 4-8 on the next page lists the HTML tags and text to create the remaining data cells and insert text.

> *More About*
>
> **Menu Bars**
>
> Many techniques are available to use when developing menu bars for navigation. Various Web sites contain some of the best ideas from current developers. For more information about menu bars, visit the HTML More About Web page (scsite.com/html3e/more.htm) and then click Menu Bars.

Table 4-8 HTML Code to Create Additional Cells and Insert Text

```
53 <tr>
54 <td>Mona Lisa Smile</td>
55 <td>Drama</td>
56 <td>Julia Roberts</td>
57 <td>PG-13</td>
58 </tr>
59
60 <tr>
61 <td>Something's Gotta Give</td>
62 <td>Comedy</td>
63 <td>Jack Nicholson
64 <br />Diane Keaton</td>
65 <td>PG-13</td>
66 </tr>
67
68 <tr>
69 <td>Runaway Jury</td>
70 <td>Drama</td>
71 <td>Gene Hackman
72 <br />John Cusack</td>
73 <td>PG-13</td>
74 </tr>
```

As shown in Table 4-8, each row of text is defined using the <tr> and </tr> tags. Each cell of text within that row is defined using the <td> and </td> tags. In this table, each row has four data cells, so four sets of <td> </td> tags are added per row. The following steps show how to create additional cells and insert text into those cells.

To Create Additional Cells and Insert Text

1. **If necessary, click line 53.**
2. **Enter the HTML code as shown in Table 4-8.**

The HTML code is displayed (Figure 4-32).

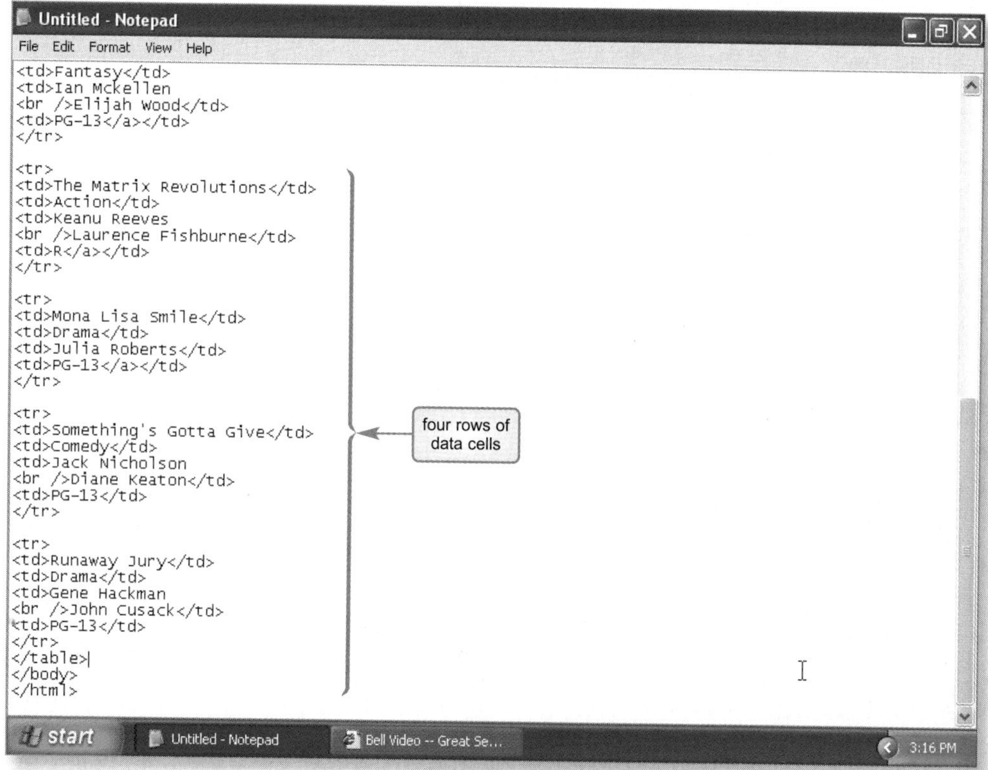

FIGURE 4-32

The HTML code for the table with borders is complete. Lines 53, 60, and 68 added three new rows of data cells using the <tr> (start table row) tag. Lines 58, 66, and 74 ended each row with a </tr> (end table row) tag. All of the text information was inserted into data cells between the <tr> and </tr> tags.

With the HTML code for the table with borders added, the New Releases Web page is complete. The HTML file thus should be saved and a copy should be printed as a reference.

To Save and Print an HTML File

1. **With a floppy disk in drive A, click File on the menu bar and then click Save As. Type** `newreleases.htm` **in the File name text box.**
2. **If necessary, click 3½ Floppy (A:) in the Save in list. Click the Project04 folder and then click the ProjectFiles folder in the list of available folders. Click the Save button in the Save As dialog box.**
3. **Click File on the menu bar and then click Print on the file menu.**

Notepad saves the HTML file in the Project04\ProjectFiles folder on the floppy disk in drive A using the file name, newreleases.htm. Notepad prints the HTML file (Figure 4-33 on the next page).

```
<!DOCTYPE html
  PUBLIC "-//W3C//DTD XHTML 1.0 Transitional//EN"
  "http://www.w3.org/TR/xhtml1/DTD/xhtml1-transitional.dtd">

<html>
<head>
<title>Bell Video - New Releases</title>
</head>
<body>
<table border="0" cols="1" width="10%">
<tr>
<td><img src="bellvideologo.gif" width="430" height="74" alt="Bell Video Logo" /></td>
</tr>
</table>

<br /><table border="0" cols="7" width="60%">
<tr align="center">
<td width="20%"><a href="bellvideohome.htm">Home</a></td>
<td width="1%">|</td>
<td width="25%"><a href="newreleases.htm">New Releases</a></td>
<td width="1%">|</td>
<td width="15%"><a href="actor.htm">Actor</a></td>
<td width="1%">|</td>
<td width="15%"><a href="type.htm">Type</a></td>
</tr>
</table>

<br /><table cols="4" border="5" width="80%">
<tr bgcolor="lightsteelblue">
<th><font color="#993366" size="+1">Title</font></th>
<th><font color="#993366" size="+1">Type</font></th>
<th><font color="#993366" size="+1">Actor(s)</font></th>
<th><font color="#993366" size="+1">Rating</font></th>
</tr>

<tr>
<td>The Lord of the Rings:
<br />The Fellowship of the Ring</td>
<td>Fantasy</td>
<td>Ian Mckellen
<br />Elijah Wood</td>
<td>PG-13</td>
</tr>

<tr>
<td>The Matrix Revolutions</td>
<td>Action</td>
<td>Keanu Reeves
<br />Laurence Fishburne</td>
<td>R</td>
</tr>

<tr>
<td>Mona Lisa Smile</td>
<td>Drama</td>
<td>Julia Roberts</td>
<td>PG-13</td>
</tr>

<tr>
<td>Somethingís Gotta Give</td>
<td>Comedy</td>
<td>Jack Nicholson
<br />Diane Keaton</td>
<td>PG-13</td>
</tr>

<tr>
<td>Runaway Jury</td>
<td>Drama</td>
<td>Gene Hackman
<br />John Cusack</td>
<td>PG-13</td>
</tr>
</table>

</body>
</html>
```

FIGURE 4-33

After saving and printing the HTML file, perform the following steps to view and print the Web page.

To View and Print the Web Page Using the Browser

1. **Click the Internet Explorer button on the taskbar.**
2. **Click the New Releases link in the vertical menu bar on the Bell Video home page.**
3. **Click the Print button on the Standard Buttons toolbar, when the New Releases Web page is displayed.**

The New Releases Web page is displayed (Figure 4-34).

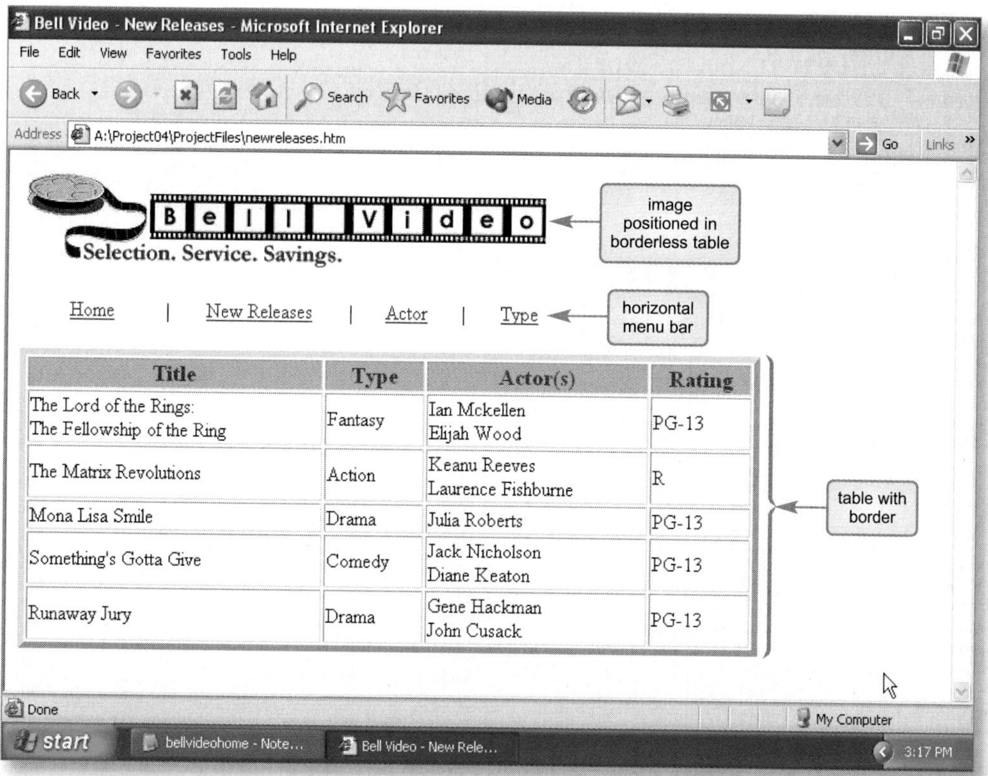

FIGURE 4-34

As shown in Figure 4-34, the New Releases Web page includes three tables: a two-row, one-column borderless table used to position the logo image; a one-row, seven-column table used to create a horizontal menu bar with links to all other Web pages; and a six-row, four-column table that contains the information about newly released movies available at Bell Video.

After confirming that the Web page appears as desired, the four links in the horizontal menu bar should be tested to verify that they function as expected. The steps on the next page show how to test the links in the New Releases Web page.

To Test Links in a Web Page

1. **Click the Home link in the horizontal menu bar on the New Releases Web page.**
2. **Click the New Releases link in the vertical menu bar on the home page to return to the New Releases Web page.**
3. **Click the Type link in the horizontal menu bar on the New Releases Web page.**
4. **Click the Actor link in the horizontal menu bar on the Type Web page.**

The Actor Web page is displayed (Figure 4-35).

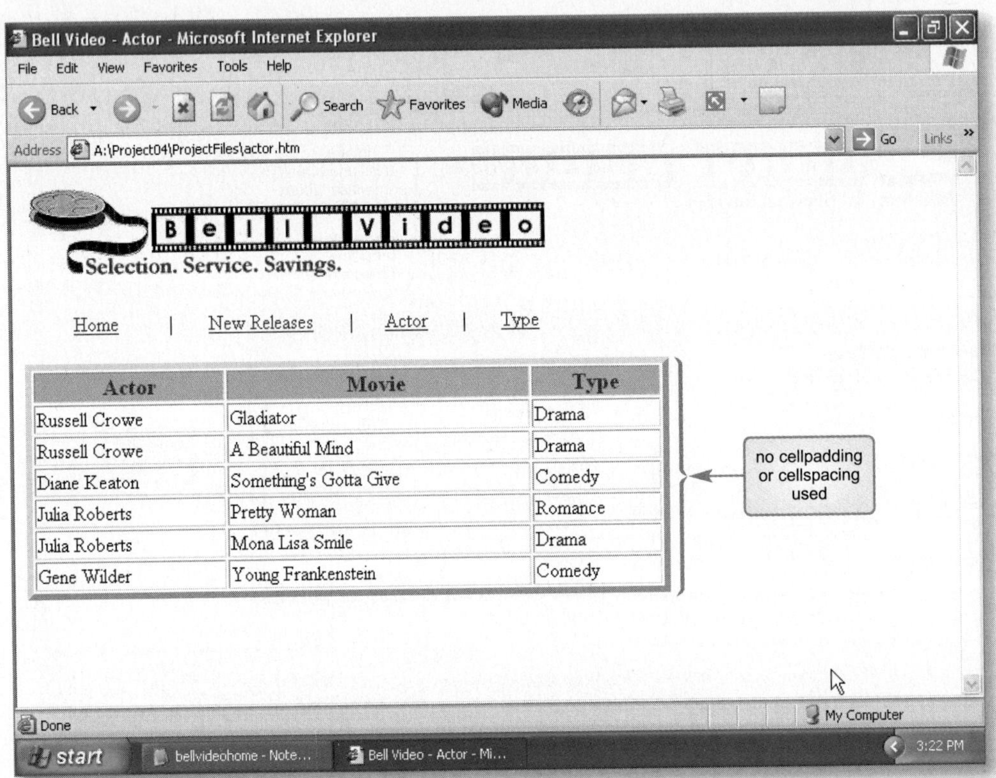

FIGURE 4-35

Thus far, the project has illustrated how to create the Bell Video home page and New Releases Web page. The HTML files for the other two Web pages (actor.htm and type.htm) are available in the Project04\ProjectFiles folder on the HTML Data Disk. Figure 4-35 shows the Actor Web page as saved on the HTML Data Disk. This Web page and the Type Web page both currently contain a borderless table with the logo image, a table used for a horizontal menu bar, and a table with borders used to organize text in data cells. The remaining sections in this project illustrate how to enhance the appearance of the actor.htm and type.htm Web pages using cellpadding, cellspacing, a caption, and headings that span rows and columns.

Adding Cellspacing, Cellpadding, and a Caption

The table of information on the New Releases Web page did not use the cellspacing or cellpadding attributes. The size of each data cell, therefore, automatically was set to the minimum size needed for the text inserted in the data cell.

The Actor Web page, however, should be modified to use cellspacing and cellpadding by adding the cellspacing and cellpadding attributes to the <table> tag. As shown in Table 4-2 on page HTM 142, **cellspacing** defines the number of pixels of space between cells in a table. **Cellpadding** defines the number of pixels of space within a cell. Figure 4-36 illustrates how using the <table> tag attributes cellspacing and cellpadding can affect a table's appearance.

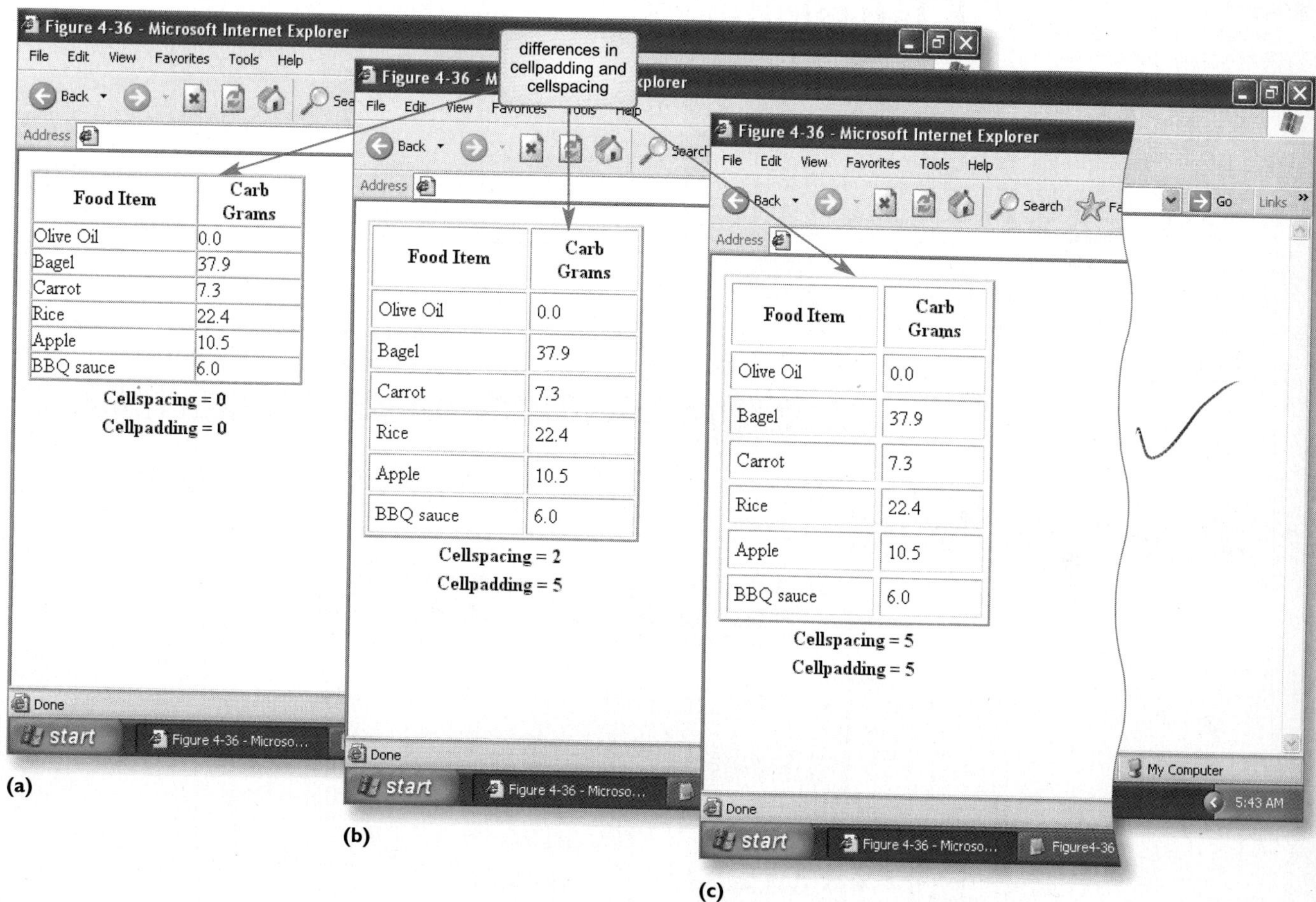

FIGURE 4-36 Tables with cellpadding and cellspacing.

Adding Cellspacing and Cellpadding to a Table

Figure 4-37a shows how the Actor Web page stored on the HTML Data Disk looks as currently designed. Figure 4-37b shows how the Actor Web page will appear after cellspacing, cellpadding, and a caption are added.

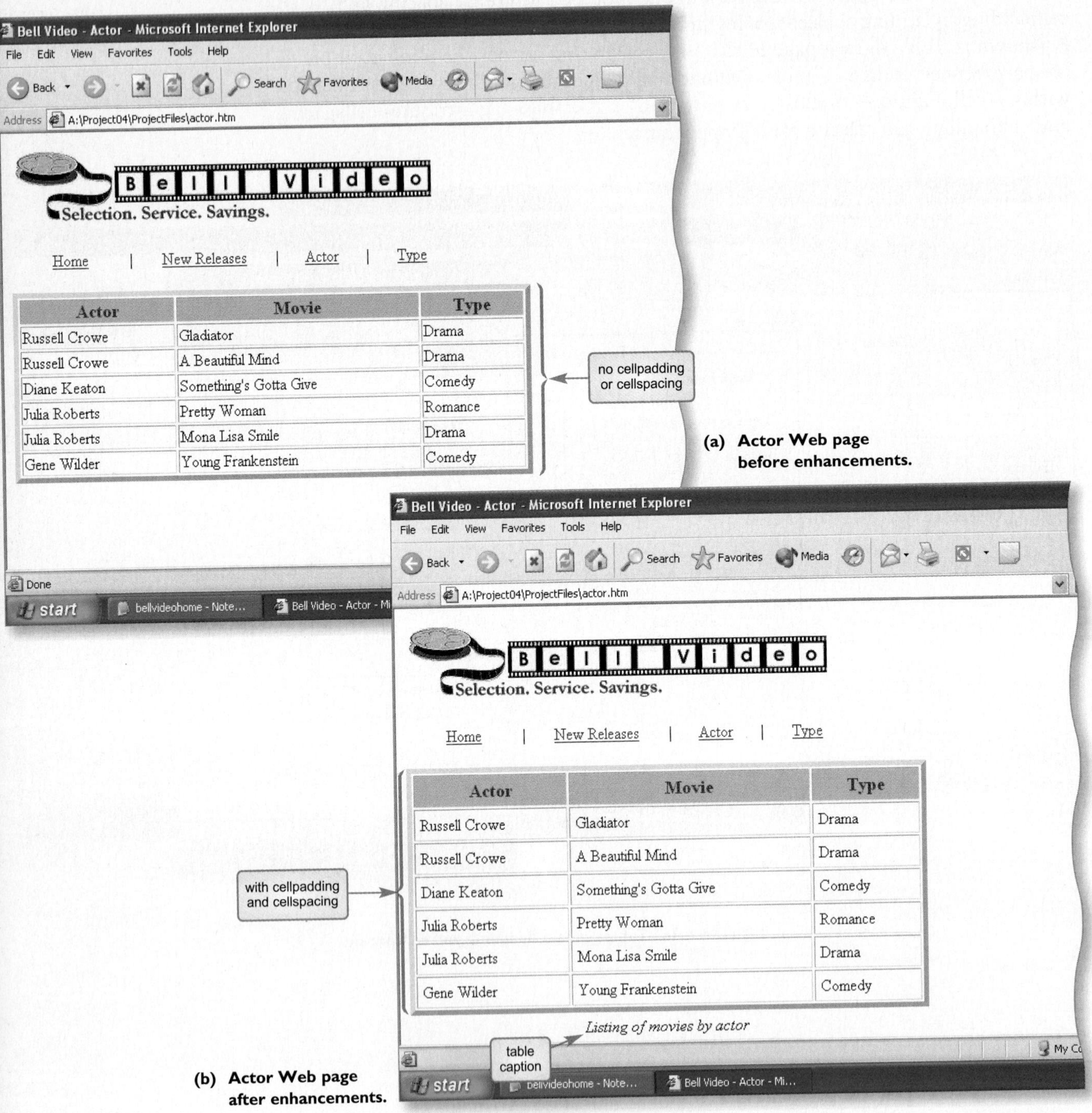

(a) **Actor Web page before enhancements.**

(b) **Actor Web page after enhancements.**

FIGURE 4-37

The following steps show to activate Notepad and open the Actor Web page file stored on the HTML Data Disk.

To Open an HTML File

1. **Click the Notepad button on the taskbar.**
2. **With the HTML Data Disk in drive A, click File on the menu bar and then click Open on the File menu.**
3. **If necessary, click the Look in box arrow and then click 3½ Floppy (A:). Click the Project04 folder and then click the ProjectFiles folder in the list of available folders.**
4. **If necessary, click the Files of type box arrow and then click All Files.**
5. **Click actor.htm in the list of files.**
6. **Click the Open button in the Open dialog box.**

Notepad opens the file, actor.htm (Figure 4-38). The first 40 lines of the HTML code for actor.htm are displayed.

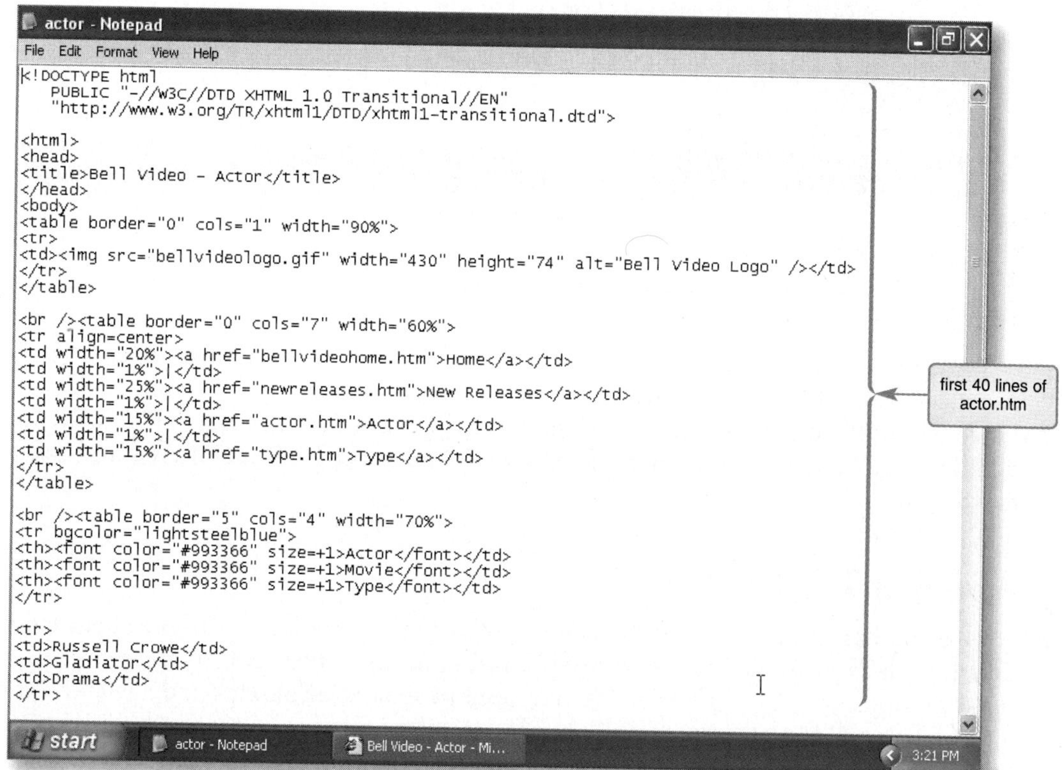

```
<!DOCTYPE html
   PUBLIC "-//W3C//DTD XHTML 1.0 Transitional//EN"
   "http://www.w3.org/TR/xhtml1/DTD/xhtml1-transitional.dtd">

<html>
<head>
<title>Bell Video - Actor</title>
</head>
<body>
<table border="0" cols="1" width="90%">
<tr>
<td><img src="bellvideologo.gif" width="430" height="74" alt="Bell Video Logo" /></td>
</tr>
</table>

<br /><table border="0" cols="7" width="60%">
<tr align=center>
<td width="20%"><a href="bellvideohome.htm">Home</a></td>
<td width="1%">|</td>
<td width="25%"><a href="newreleases.htm">New Releases</a></td>
<td width="1%">|</td>
<td width="15%"><a href="actor.htm">Actor</a></td>
<td width="1%">|</td>
<td width="15%"><a href="type.htm">Type</a></td>
</tr>
</table>

<br /><table border="5" cols="4" width="70%">
<tr bgcolor="lightsteelblue">
<th><font color="#993366" size=+1>Actor</font></td>
<th><font color="#993366" size=+1>Movie</font></td>
<th><font color="#993366" size=+1>Type</font></td>
</tr>

<tr>
<td>Russell Crowe</td>
<td>Gladiator</td>
<td>Drama</td>
</tr>
```


FIGURE 4-38

With the file actor.htm open, the HTML code to add cellspacing and cellpadding can be added. The steps on the next page show how to add cellspacing and cellpadding to a table.

To Add Cellspacing and Cellpadding to a Table

1

- **Click immediately to the right of the 5 in border="5" in line 28 and then press the SPACEBAR.**

2

- **Type** `cellspacing="2" cellpadding="5"` **as the attributes.**

The HTML code is displayed (Figure 4-39).

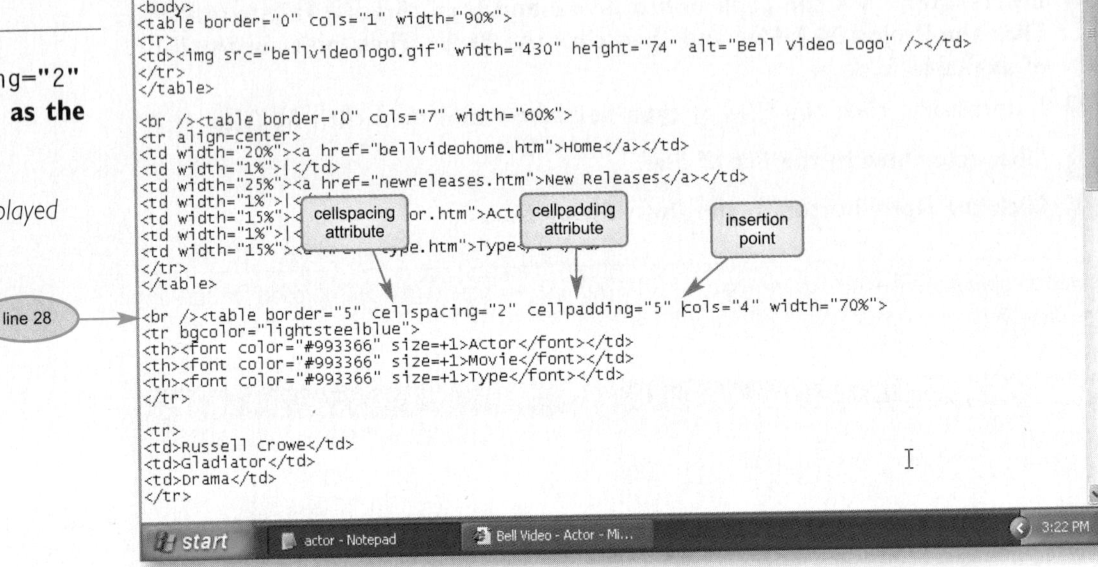

FIGURE 4-39

> ***More About***
>
> **Cellspacing**
>
> The cellspacing attribute adds pixels between cells. The purpose of cellspacing is to add additional space in the separation between the cells, whether or not a border exists. With a border, cellspacing increases the size of the border between the cells. Without a border, cellspacing increases the amount of white space between the cells.

Adding the <table> tag attributes, cellspacing="2" and cellpadding="5", enhances the table by adding two pixels of space between cells and five pixels of space within the cells in the table. As shown in Figure 4-37b on page HTM 170, adding space between and within cells makes the table appear less cluttered and easier to read.

Adding a Table Caption

As you have learned, a caption can help clarify the purpose of a table. For some tables, such as the table used to position images and the tables used to create menu bars, captions are not appropriate. Tables used to structure columns and rows of information, such as the Actor table, can benefit from having a caption to clarify the contents of the table. A table caption is added to a table using code such as:

```
<caption align="bottom"><em>Listing of movies by actor</em></caption>
```

where the <caption> </caption> tags enclose the caption text. This caption also uses the <em> </em> tags to italicize the caption text. The align attribute determines the placement of the caption. A caption can be placed above or below the table using the align="above" or align="bottom" attributes, respectively.

The following steps show how to add a caption below the Actor table.

To Add a Table Caption

1

- **Highlight the text <!--Insert caption here --> on line 69.**

2

- **Type** `<caption align="bottom"><em>Listing of movies by actor</em></caption>` **as the tag.**

The HTML code is displayed (Figure 4-40).

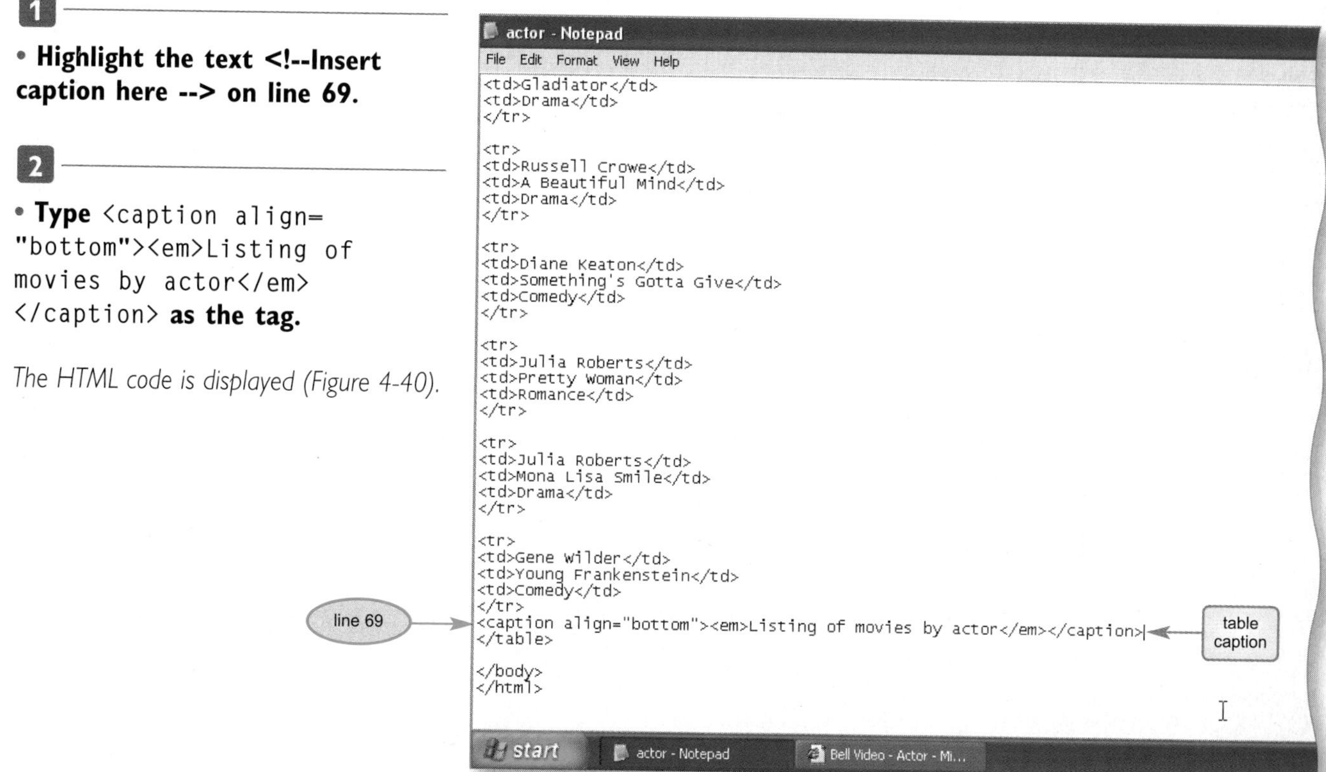

FIGURE 4-40

With the HTML code for the table caption added, the Actor Web page is complete. The HTML file thus should be saved and a copy should be printed as a reference. After saving and printing the HTML file, the Web page should be viewed and also printed as a reference.

To Save and Print the HTML File and View and Print the Web Page

1. **With the floppy disk in drive A, click File on the menu bar and then click Save.**
2. **Click File on the menu bar and then click Print.**
3. **Click the Internet Explorer button on the taskbar.**
4. **Click the Refresh button on the Standard Buttons toolbar.**
5. **Click the Print button on the Standard Buttons toolbar.**

Notepad saves the updated HTML file in the Project04\ProjectFiles folder on the floppy disk in drive A using the file name, actor.htm. The Actor Web page is displayed (Figure 4-41 on the next page). The HTML file and Web page are printed.

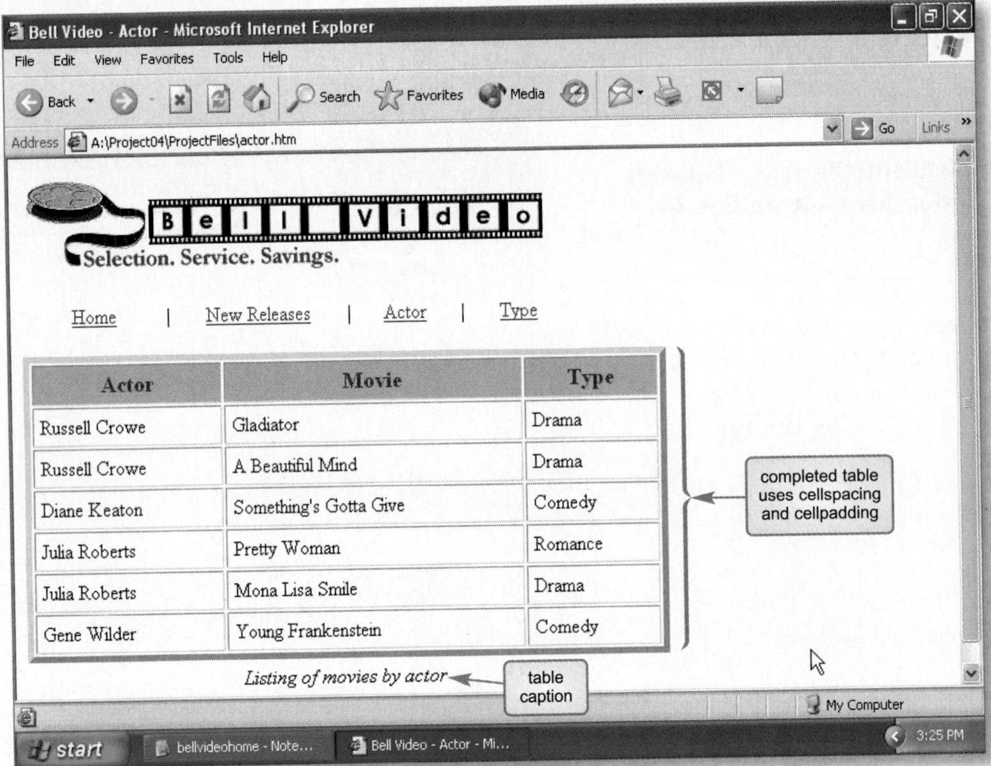

FIGURE 4-41

Spanning Rows and Columns

Spanning rows and columns is a technique used frequently to create a heading that goes across, or spans, rows or columns. As shown in Table 4-2 on page HTM 146, the **rowspan attribute** of the <th> or <td> tag sets the number of rows spanned by a cell, while the **colspan attribute** of the <th> or <td> tag sets the number of columns spanned by a cell. Figure 4-9 on page HTM 140 shows an example of a table that uses the rowspan and colspan attributes.

Figure 4-42 shows the Type Web page as saved on the HTML Data Disk. The table in this Web page is incomplete because the Web page visitor cannot tell what the table means without headings of any kind. Figure 4-43 shows how the Type Web page will appear after headings that span rows and columns are added.

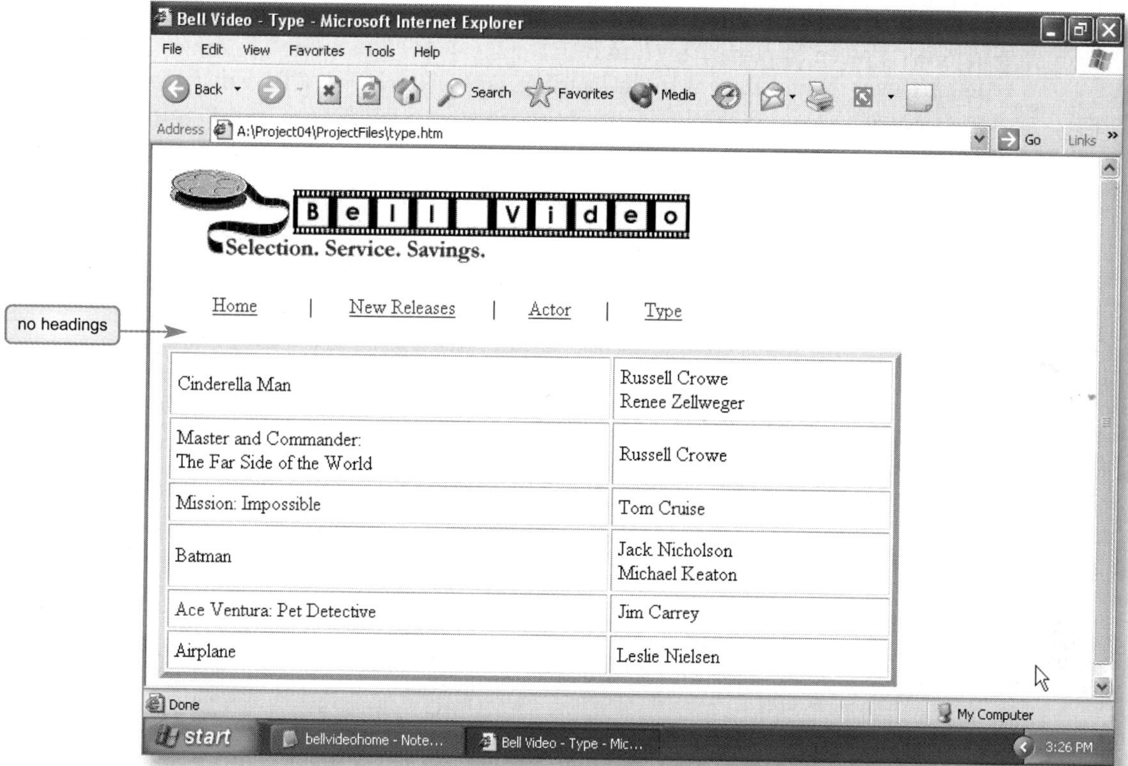

FIGURE 4-42 Type Web page before enhancements.

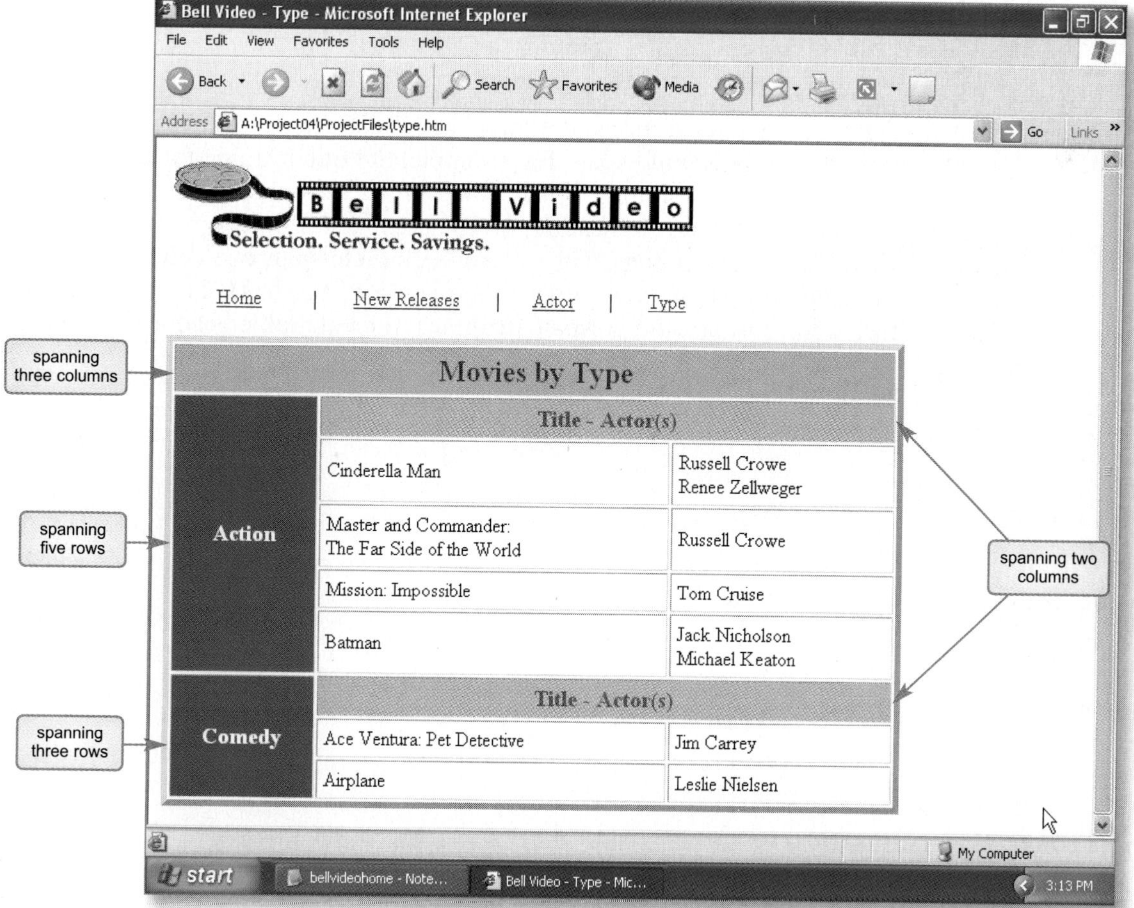

FIGURE 4-43 Type Web page after enhancements.

The first step when deciding to span rows or columns is to sketch the table design on a piece of paper, as shown in Figure 4-44. The table organizes movies by type and thus should have a main heading, Movies by Type. Two different types of movies are represented by the information in the rows: Action and Comedy. The columns in the table also require subheadings to indicate what information is included about each movie.

<table>
<tr><th colspan="3">Movies by Type</th></tr>
<tr><th rowspan="5">Action</th><th colspan="2">Title - Actor(s)</th></tr>
<tr><td>Cinderella Man</td><td>Russell Crowe
Renee Zellweger</td></tr>
<tr><td>Master and Commander:
The Far Side of the World</td><td>Russell Crowe</td></tr>
<tr><td>Mission: Impossible</td><td>Tom Cruise</td></tr>
<tr><td>Batman</td><td>Jack Nicholson
Michael Keaton</td></tr>
<tr><th rowspan="3">Comedy</th><th colspan="2">Title - Actor(s)</th></tr>
<tr><td>Ace Ventura: Pet Detective</td><td>Jim Carrey</td></tr>
<tr><td>Airplane</td><td>Leslie Nielsen</td></tr>
</table>

FIGURE 4-44

After defining the main sections of a table, you must determine how many rows or columns each heading should span. For example, the title heading for the table should span all three table columns. The heading for the first main section (Action) should span four rows, while the heading for the second section (Comedy) should span two rows. The row headings, Title - Actor(s), should span two columns.

The following steps show how to open the file, type.htm, from the HTML Data Disk and then add rowspan and colspan attributes to create table headings.

To Open an HTML File

1. Click the Notepad button on the taskbar.
2. With the HTML Data Disk in drive A, click File on the menu bar and then click Open on the File menu.
3. If necessary, click the Look in box arrow and then click 3½ Floppy (A:). Click the Project04 folder and then click the ProjectFiles folder in the list of available folders.
4. If necessary, click the Files of type box arrow, click All Files, and then double-click type.htm in the list of files.

Notepad displays the type.htm file.

Spanning the Main Heading across All Columns

As shown in Figure 4-43 on page HTM 175, the main heading for the table is in a new row, above the first row of text that currently is in the table. The main heading spans across both of the existing columns, as well as the new column that is created on the left. The main heading has one line — Movies by Type.

To Span the Main Heading across All Columns

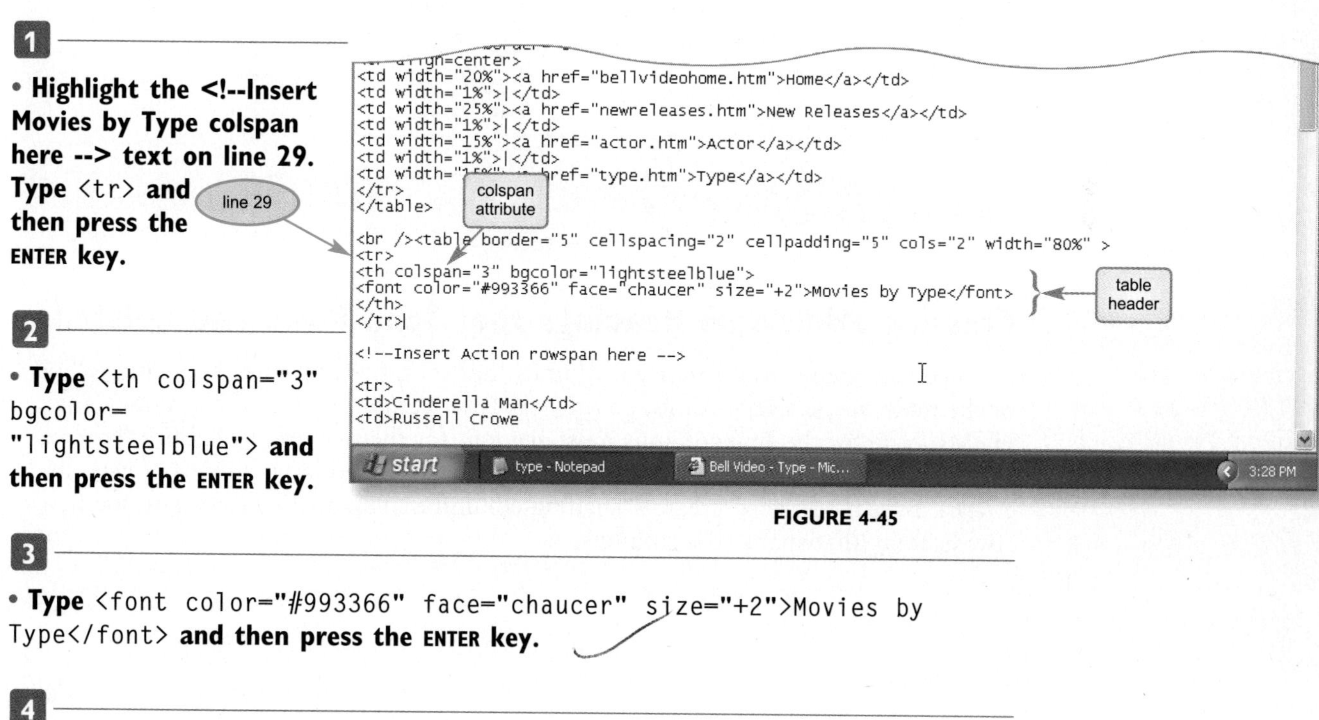

1

- **Highlight the <!--Insert Movies by Type colspan here --> text on line 29. Type `<tr>` and then press the ENTER key.**

2

- **Type `<th colspan="3" bgcolor="lightsteelblue">` and then press the ENTER key.**

FIGURE 4-45

3

- **Type `<font color="#993366" face="chaucer" size="+2">Movies by Type</font>` and then press the ENTER key.**

4

- **Type `</th>` and then press the ENTER key.**

5

- **Type `</tr>` as the end table row tag.**

The HTML code is displayed (Figure 4-45).

More About

Cellpadding

The cellpadding attribute adds pixels within a cell border. The purpose of cellpadding is to keep the content within each cell from looking too close to the content of another cell. Cellpadding will set a margin for the right, left, top, and bottom of the cell all at once with the specification of one tag.

Entering the <tr> tag in Step 1 created a new row. The <th> tag created a heading cell that spans three columns of the table and uses a light steel blue background color. The code entered in Step 3 changed the font to Chaucer using a larger (+2) size font. Finally, Steps 4 and 5 ended the heading cell and the row. If the HTML file was saved and viewed it in a browser at this point, the table would appear as shown in Figure 4-46.

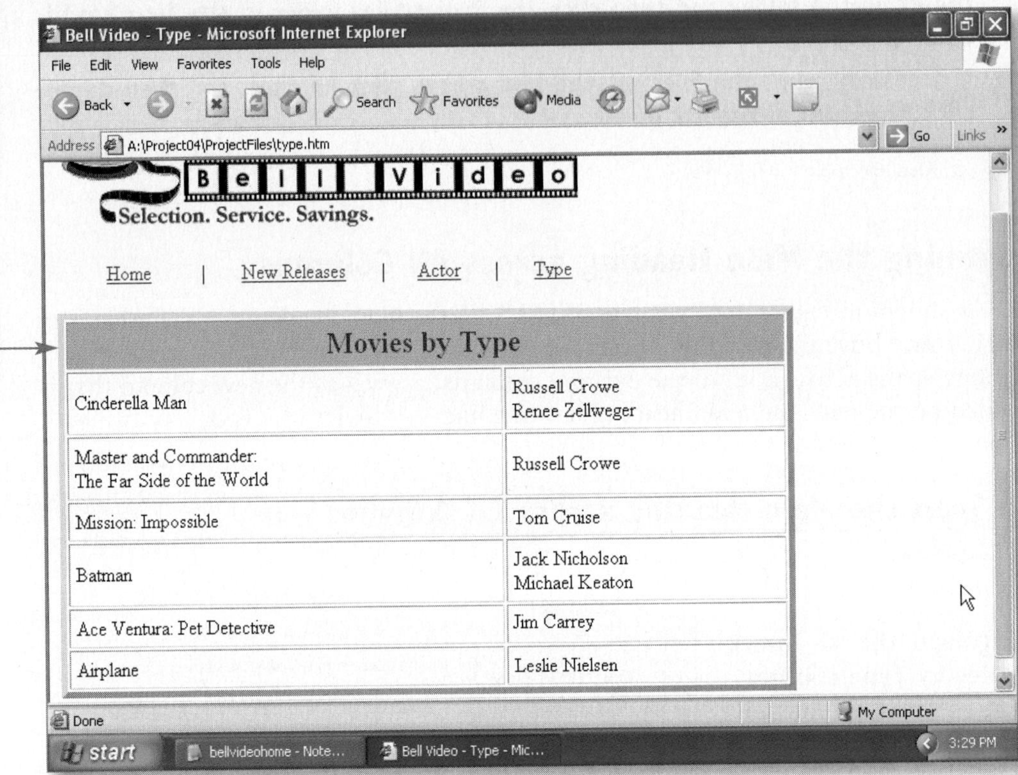

FIGURE 4-46

Creating Additional Headings that Span Rows and Columns

The next step is to create two columns that span five and three rows in the body of the table, respectively. Although only six rows contain cast member names, the HTML code for the two columns must account for the two additional header rows for another heading (Title - Actor(s)), which will be added later. Table 4-9 lists the HTML code required to create a heading column that spans five rows and the first row heading that spans two columns.

Table 4-9 HTML Code for Additional Headings

34	`<tr bgcolor="#ffffff">`
35	`<th rowspan="5" width="20%" bgcolor="#336699">`
36	`<font color="#ffffff" size=+1>Action</font>`
37	`</th>`
38	`<th colspan="2" bgcolor="thistle">`
39	`<font color="#336699" size="+1">Title - Actor(s)</font>`
40	`</th>`
41	`</tr>`

The following steps illustrate how to enter HTML code to create a heading column that spans five rows and the first row heading that spans two columns.

To Create Headings that Span Rows and Columns

1

• **Highlight <!--Insert Action rowspan here --> text on line 34.**

2

• **Enter the HTML code as shown in Table 4-9.**

The HTML code is displayed (Figure 4-47.)

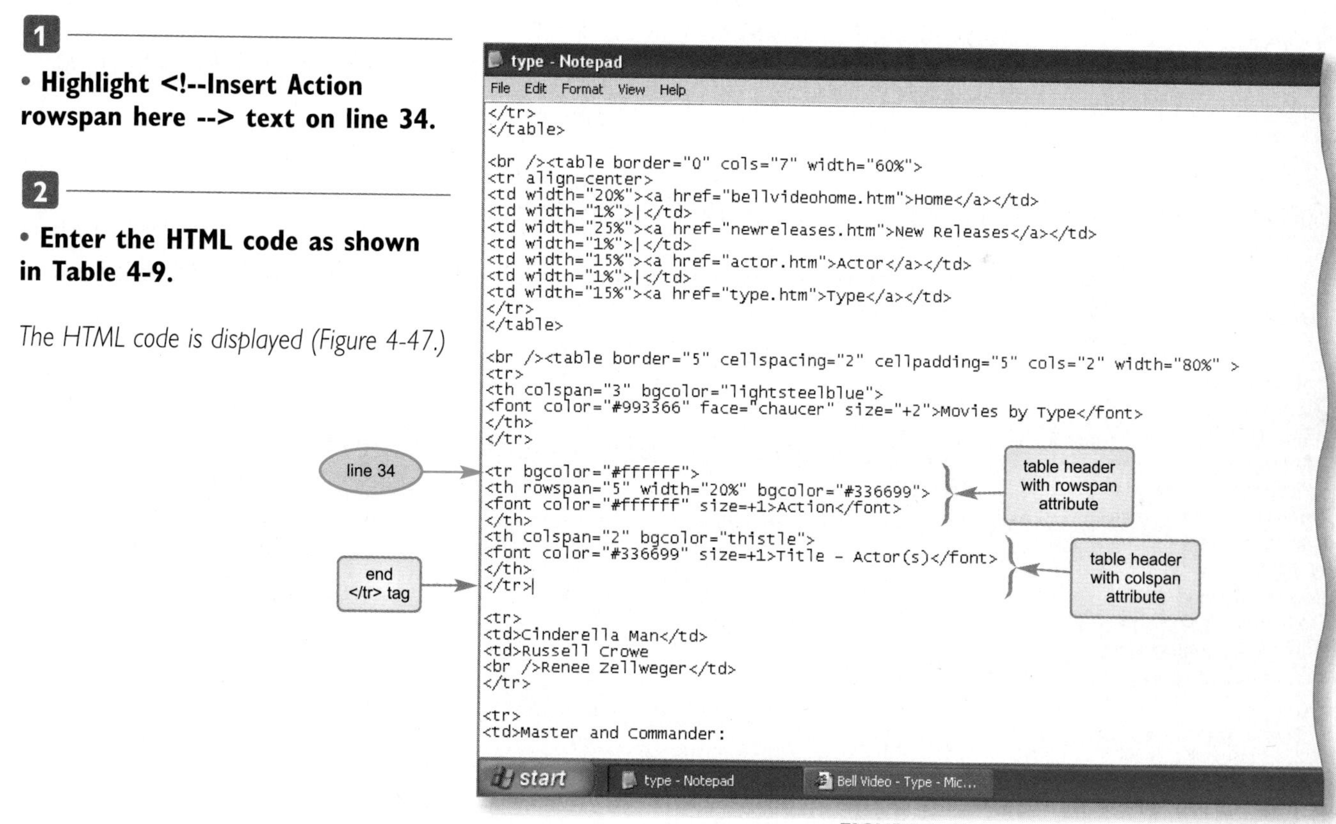

FIGURE 4-47

Line 34 created a new table row and line 35 added a table header that spans five rows of the table to identify Action movies listed in the table rows. Line 36 added the heading text, Action, in a white, larger (+1) size font. Line 38 created a new table header within the row and set it to span two table columns. Line 39 added the heading text, Title - Actor(s), in a light blue, larger (+1) size font. If the HTML file was saved and viewed in a browser at this point, the table would appear as shown in Figure 4-48 on the next page.

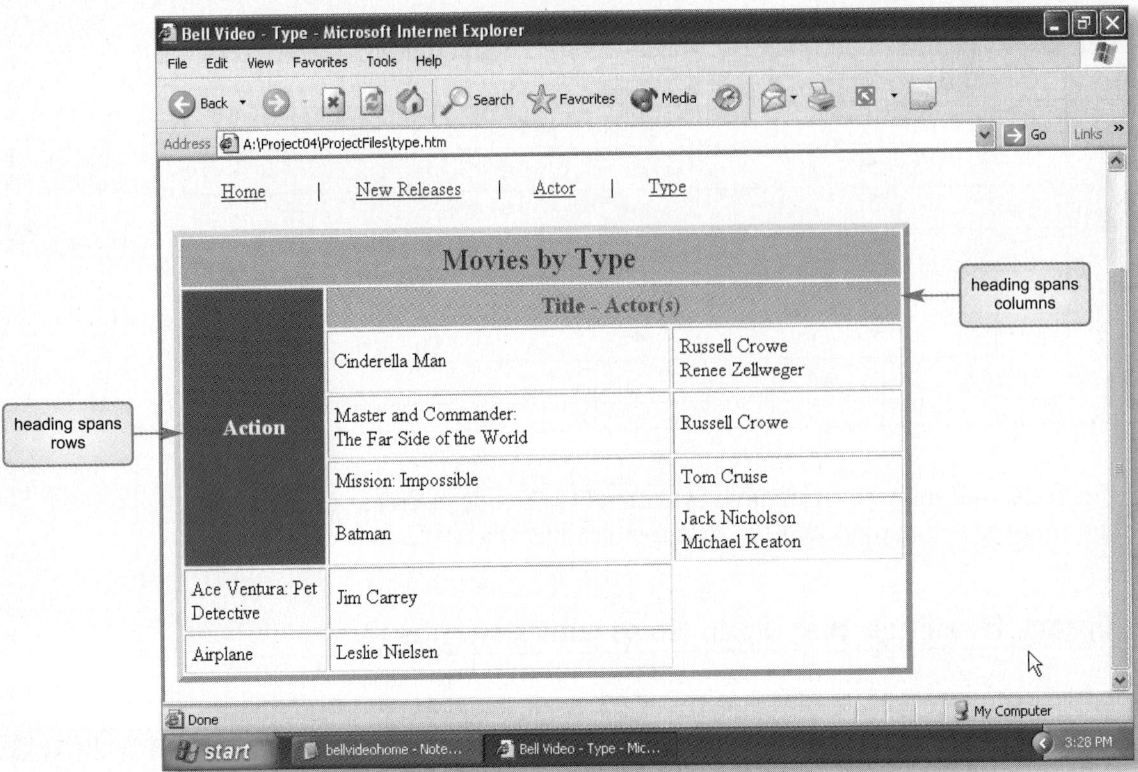

FIGURE 4-48

More About

Row and Column Spanning

Creating headings that span rows and columns defines tables more clearly. Many Web sties contain information about row and column spanning. For more information about row and column spanning, visit the HTML More About Web page (scsite.com/html3e/more.htm) and then click Row and Column Spanning.

To Create the Second Heading that Spans Rows

1. **Highlight the <!--Insert Comedy rowspan here --> text on line 66 and then press the DELETE key.**
2. **Type** `<tr>` **and then press the ENTER key.**
3. **Type** `<th rowspan="4" bgcolor="#336699">` **and then press the ENTER key.**
4. **Type** `<font color="#ffffff" size="+1">Comedy</font>` **and then press the ENTER key.**
5. **Type** `</th>` **as the tag.**

The HTML code is displayed (Figure 4-49).

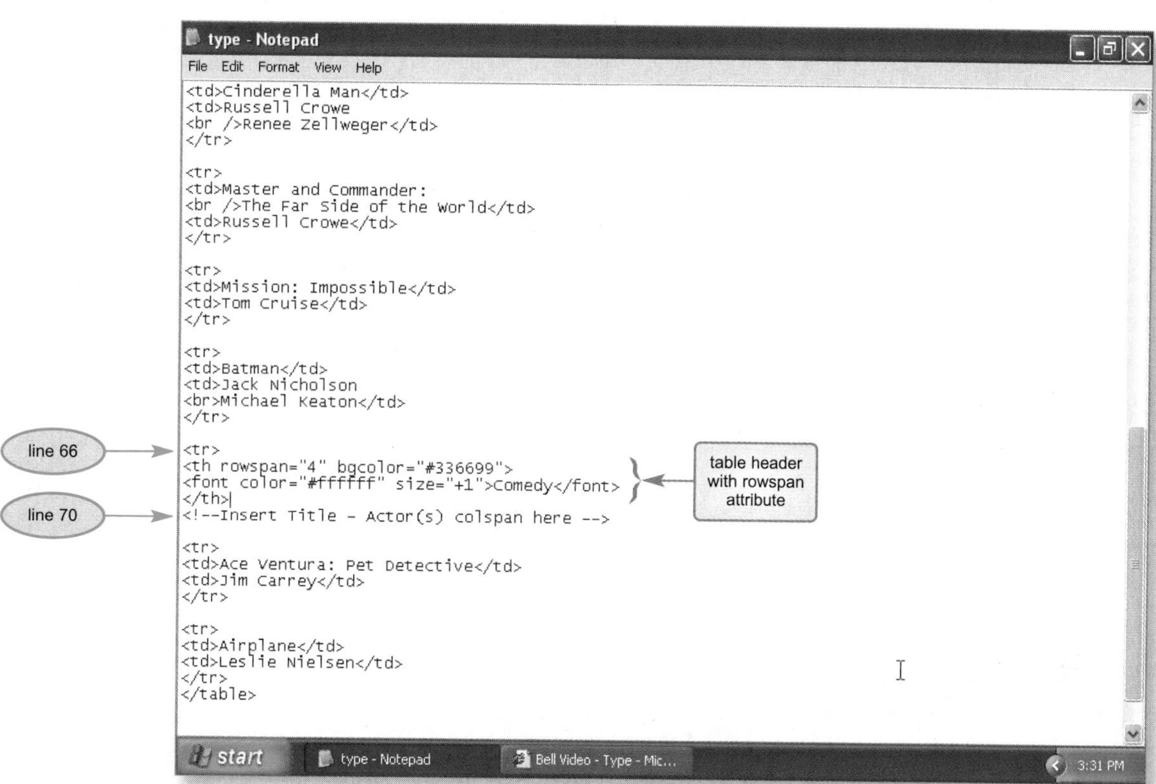

FIGURE 4-49

The previous steps added another table header that spans rows, to identify Comedy movies listed in the table rows. This second table header uses the same formatting as the Action table header added in previous steps.

The following steps illustrate how to enter HTML code to add the remaining heading that spans several columns.

To Create the Second Heading that Spans Columns

1. **Highlight the <!--Insert Title - Actor(s) colspan here --> text on line 70.**
2. **Type** `<th colspan="2" bgcolor="thistle">` **and then press the ENTER key.**
3. **Type** `<font color="#336699" size="+1">Title - Actor(s)</font>` **and then press the ENTER key.**
4. **Type** `</th>` **and then press the ENTER key.**
5. **Type** `</tr>` **and then press the ENTER key.**

The HTML code is displayed (Figure 4-50 on the next page).

In Steps 1 and 2, you added another heading, Title - Actor(s), that spans two columns. This table header uses the same formatting as the Title - Actor(s) header added in previous steps.

With the HTML code for the table headers added, the Type Web page is complete. The HTML file thus should be saved and a copy should be printed as a reference. After saving and printing the HTML file, the Web page should be viewed and also printed as a reference.

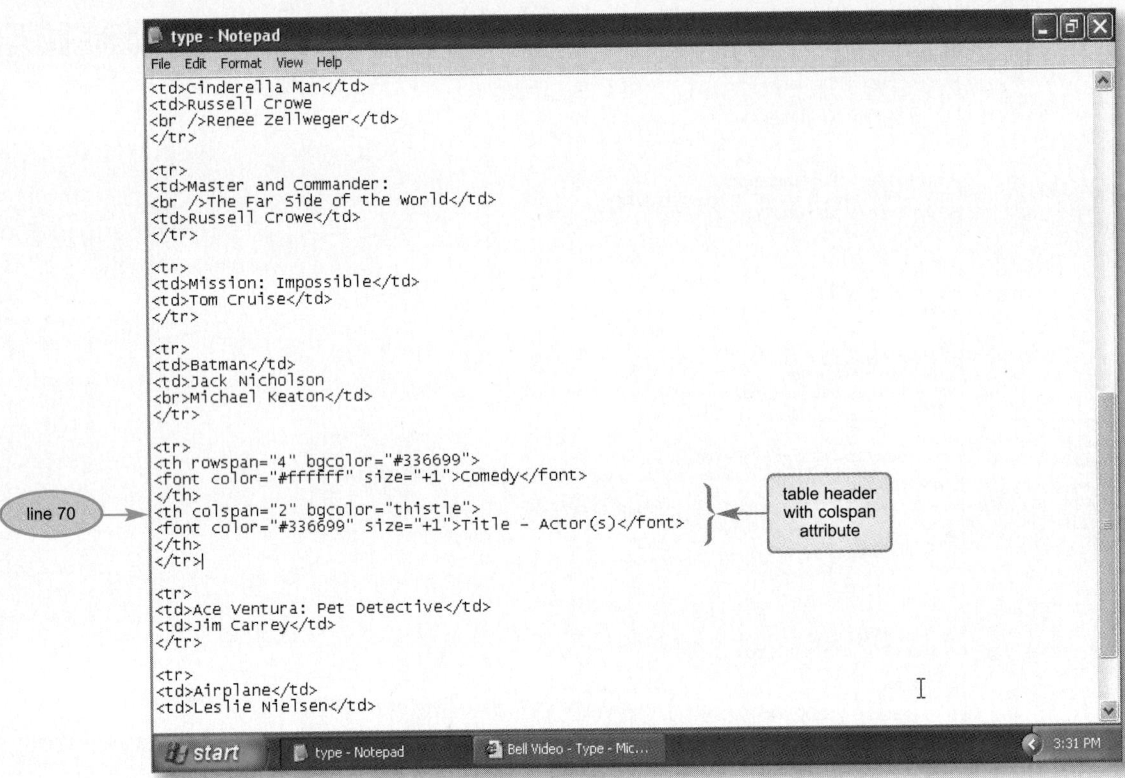
```
<td>Cinderella Man</td>
<td>Russell Crowe
<br />Renee Zellweger</td>
</tr>

<tr>
<td>Master and Commander:
<br />The Far Side of the World</td>
<td>Russell Crowe</td>
</tr>

<tr>
<td>Mission: Impossible</td>
<td>Tom Cruise</td>
</tr>

<tr>
<td>Batman</td>
<td>Jack Nicholson
<br>Michael Keaton</td>
</tr>

<tr>
<th rowspan="4" bgcolor="#336699">
<font color="#ffffff" size="+1">Comedy</font>
</th>
<th colspan="2" bgcolor="thistle">
<font color="#336699" size="+1">Title - Actor(s)</font>
</th>
</tr>

<tr>
<td>Ace Ventura: Pet Detective</td>
<td>Jim Carrey</td>
</tr>

<tr>
<td>Airplane</td>
<td>Leslie Nielsen</td>
```


FIGURE 4-50

To Save and Print the HTML File and View and Print the Web Page

1. **With the HTML Data Disk in drive A, click File on the menu bar and then click Save.**
2. **Click File on the menu bar and then click Print.**
3. **Click the Internet Explorer button on the taskbar.**
4. **Click the Refresh button on the Standard Buttons toolbar.**
5. **Click the Print button on the Standard Buttons toolbar.**

Notepad saves the updated HTML file in the Project04\ProjectFiles folder on the floppy disk in drive A using the file name, type.htm. The Type Web page is displayed (Figure 4-51). The HTML file and Web page are printed.

All four Web pages for the Bell Video Web site now are complete. In this project, two new Web pages (bellvideohome.htm and newreleases.htm) were created and two existing Web pages (actor.htm and type.htm) were enhanced by adding new formatting to existing tables.

With the Type page displayed in the browser, click each of the links in the page to verify that each link connects to the appropriate Web page or link target. If possible, view all of the Web pages in more than one browser type or version to ensure that the Web pages display correctly in different browsers.

After completing the project, quit Notepad and the browser. The following steps show how to quit Notepad and a browser.

> *More About*
>
> **Titles**
>
> A title is an important part of a Web page. Good titles are descriptive and indicate the content of the Web page. Visitors who bookmark or add a favorite Web page should be able to return to the page based on the title. The title is not part of the Web page text itself. It may not contain anchors, paragraph marks, or highlighting. Because of limited room to display the title, the title must consist of not more than 64 characters. Titles that are too long will be truncated.

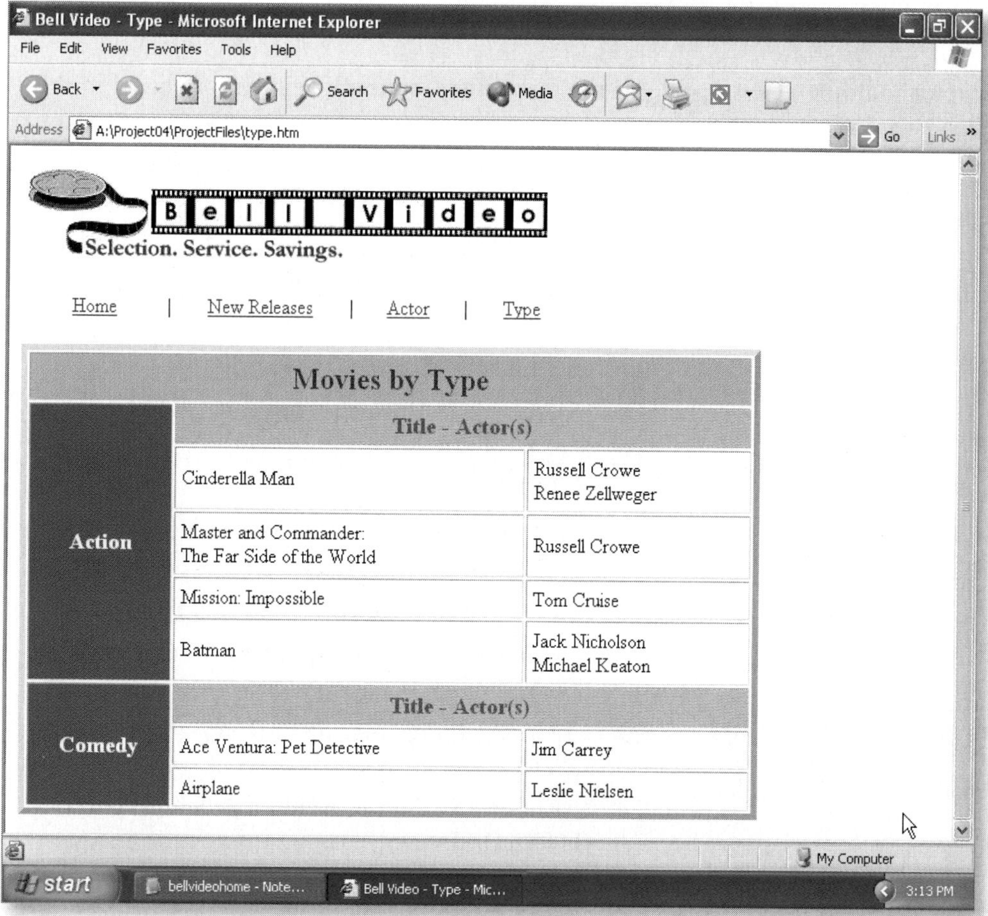

FIGURE 4-51

To Quit Notepad and a Browser

1. **Click the Close button on the browser title bar.**
2. **Click the Close button on the Notepad window title bar.**

Both the browser and Notepad windows close, and the Windows desktop is displayed.

Project Summary

In this project, you used Notepad to create and edit four HTML files and add links from each page to all three others. You learned to define table elements and the steps used to plan, design, and code a table. Using various table tags and attributes, you learned to create both bordered and borderless tables to organize images and text. You learned to use tables to create vertical and horizontal menu bars of text links, so users can navigate between all four pages in the Web site. Additionally, you learned to enhance a table format by adding background color to rows and cells, setting the spacing between and within cells using the cellspacing and cellpadding attributes, and adding a table caption. Finally, you learned how to create table headers that span rows and columns and help provide information about the data in a table.

What You Should Know

Having completed this project, you should be able to perform the tasks listed below. The tasks are listed in the same order they were presented in this project.

1. Start Notepad (HTM 143)
2. Enter HTML Tags to Define the Web Page Structure (HTM 144)
3. Create a Borderless Table to Position Images (HTM 147)
4. Insert Images in a Table (HTM 147)
5. Create a Vertical Menu Bar with Text Links (HTM 150)
6. Add Text to a Table Cell (HTM 152)
7. Save and Print the HTML File (HTM 153)
8. View and Print a Web Page (HTM 154)
9. Copy and Paste HTML Code to a New File (HTM 156)
10. Change the Title (HTM 157)
11. Delete an Image (HTM 158)
12. Create a Horizontal Menu Bar with Text Links (HTM 160)
13. Create a Table with Borders and Insert Text (HTM 163)
14. Create Additional Cells and Insert Text (HTM 164)
15. Save and Print an HTML File (HTM 165)
16. View and Print the Web Page Using the Browser (HTM 167)
17. Test Links in a Web Page (HTM 168)
18. Open an HTML File (HTM 171, HTM 177)
19. Add Cellspacing and Cellpadding to a Table (HTM 172)
20. Add a Table Caption (HTM 173)
21. Save and Print the HTML File and View and Print the Web Page (HTM 173, HTM 182)
22. Span the Main Heading across All Columns (HTM 177)
23. Create Headings that Span Rows and Columns (HTM 179)
24. Create the Second Heading that Spans Rows (HTM 180)
25. Create the Second Heading that Spans Columns (HTM 181)
26. Quit Notepad and a Browser (HTM 183)

Learn It Online

Instructions: To complete the Learn It Online exercises, start your browser, click the Address bar, and then enter the Web address `scsite.com/html3e/learn`. When the HTML Learn It Online page is displayed, follow the instructions in the exercises below. Each exercise has instructions for printing your results, either for your own records or for submission to your instructor.

1 Project Reinforcement TF, MC, and SA

Below HTML Project 4, click the Project Reinforcement link. Print the quiz by clicking Print on the File menu for each page. Answer each question.

2 Flash Cards

Below HTML Project 4, click the Flash Cards link and read the instructions. Type 20 (or a number specified by your instructor) in the Number of playing cards text box, type your name in the Enter your Name text box, and then click the Flip Card button. When the flash card is displayed, read the question and then click the ANSWER box arrow to select an answer. Flip through Flash Cards. If your score is 15 (75%) correct or greater, click Print on the File menu to print your results. If your score is less than 15 (75%) correct, then redo this exercise by clicking the Replay button.

3 Practice Test

Below HTML Project 4, click the Practice Test link. Answer each question, enter your first and last name at the bottom of the page, and then click the Grade Test button. When the graded practice test is displayed on your screen, click Print on the File menu to print a hard copy. Continue to take practice tests until you score 80% or better.

4 Who Wants To Be a Computer Genius?

Below HTML Project 4, click the Computer Genius link. Read the instructions, enter your first and last name at the bottom of the page, and then click the PLAY button. When your score is displayed, click the PRINT RESULTS link to print a hard copy.

5 Wheel of Terms

Below HTML Project 4, click the Wheel of Terms link. Read the instructions, and then enter your first and last name and your school name. Click the PLAY button. When your score is displayed, right-click the score and then click Print on the shortcut menu to print a hard copy.

6 Crossword Puzzle Challenge

Below HTML Project 4, click the Crossword Puzzle Challenge link. Read the instructions, and then enter your first and last name. Click the SUBMIT button. Work the crossword puzzle. When you are finished, click the Submit button. When the crossword puzzle is redisplayed, click the Print Puzzle button to print a hard copy.

7 Tips and Tricks

Below HTML Project 4, click the Tips and Tricks link. Click a topic that pertains to Project 4. Right-click the information and then click Print on the shortcut menu. Construct a brief example of what the information relates to in HTML to confirm you understand how to use the tip or trick.

8 Newsgroups

Below HTML Project 4, click the Newsgroups link. Click a topic that pertains to Project 4. Print three comments.

9 Expanding Your Horizons

Below HTML Project 4, click the Expanding Your Horizons link. Click a topic that pertains to Project 4. Print the information. Construct a brief example of what the information relates to in HTML to confirm you understand the contents of the article.

10 Search Sleuth

Below HTML Project 4, click the Search Sleuth link. To search for a term that pertains to this project, select a term below the Project 4 title and then use the Google search engine at google.com (or any major search engine) to display and print two Web pages that present information on the term.

11 Online Help I

Below HTML Project 4, click the Online Help I link. Follow the instructions on the page to access Web pages that provide additional help on project topics. Hand in any printed information to your instructor.

12 Online Help II

Below HTML Project 4, click the Online Help II link. Follow the instructions on the page to access Web pages that provide additional help on project topics. Hand in any printed information to your instructor.

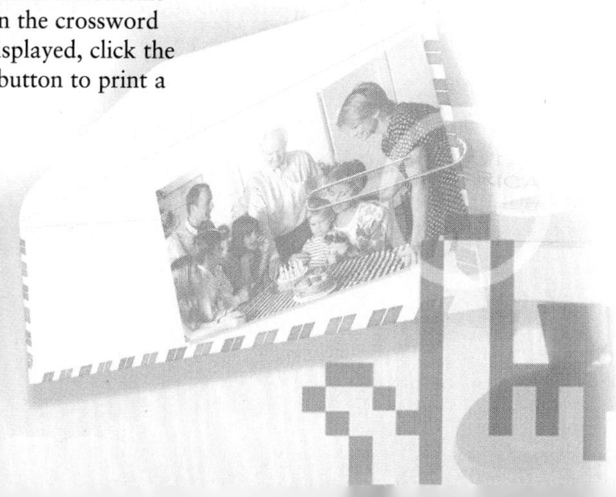

Apply Your Knowledge

1 Editing the Apply Your Knowledge Web Page

Instructions: Start Notepad. Open the file, apply4-1.htm, from the Project04\AYK folder on the HTML Data Disk. If you do not have the HTML Data Disk, see the inside back cover for instructions or see your instructor. The apply4-1.htm file is a partially completed HTML file that contains some errors. Figure 4-52 shows the Apply Your Knowledge Web page as it should display in the browser after the errors are corrected. Perform the following steps using a computer.

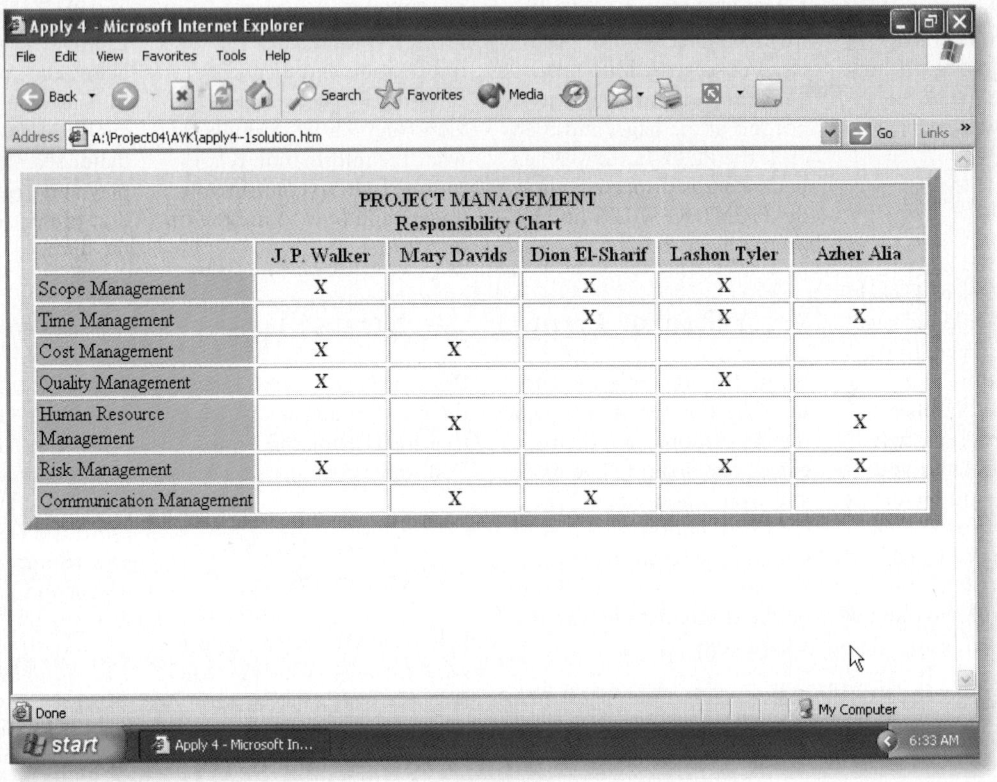

PROJECT MANAGEMENT Responsibility Chart					
	J. P. Walker	Mary Davids	Dion El-Sharif	Lashon Tyler	Azher Alia
Scope Management	X		X	X	
Time Management			X	X	X
Cost Management	X	X			
Quality Management	X			X	
Human Resource Management		X			X
Risk Management	X			X	X
Communication Management		X	X		

FIGURE 4-52

1. Enter the URL, `a:\Project04\AYK\apply4-1.htm`, to view the Web page in your browser.
2. Examine the HTML file and its appearance as a Web page in the browser.
3. Correct the HTML errors, making the Web page look similar to the Web page shown in Figure 4-52.
4. Add any HTML code necessary for additional features shown in the Web page in Figure 4-52.
5. Save the revised file in the Project04\AYK folder on the HTML Data Disk using the file name, apply4-1solution.htm.
6. Print the revised HTML file.
7. Enter the URL, `a:\Project04\AYK\apply4-1solution.htm`, to view the Web page in your browser.
8. Print the Web page.
9. Write your name on both printouts and hand them in to your instructor.

1 Creating a Table with Multiple Images

Problem: Bell Video wants to review other customer service award logos for potential use on the home page and compare them with the image currently being used, csexcellence.gif. You have been asked to create a Web page that shows the four logo samples, similar to the one shown in Figure 4-53.

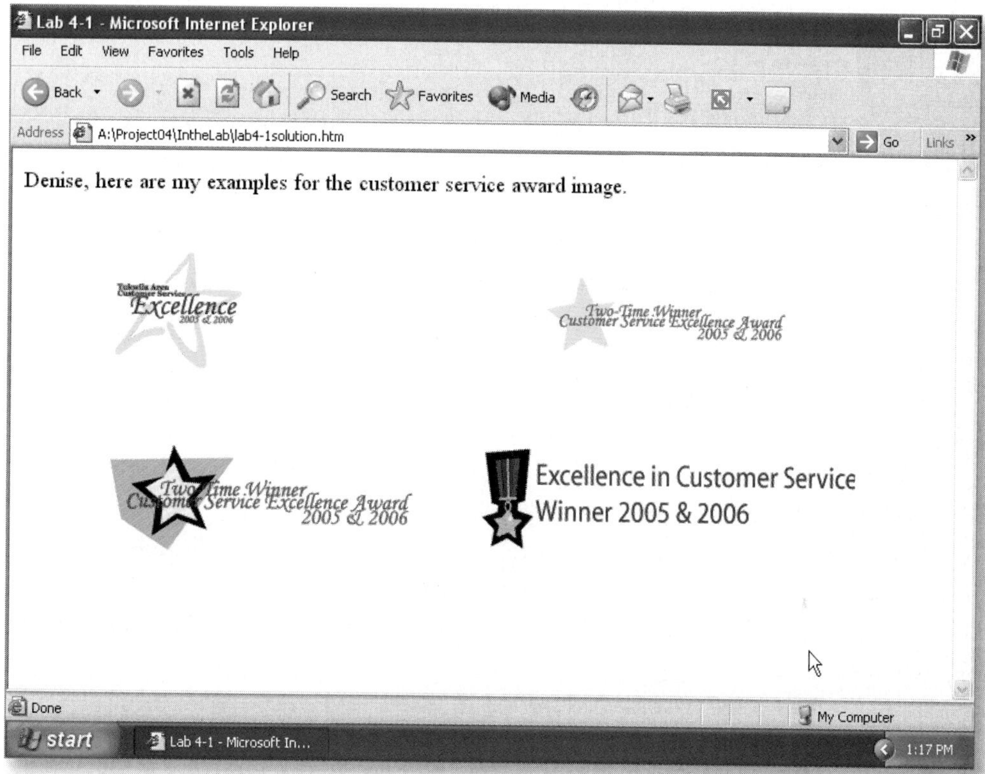

FIGURE 4-53

Instructions: Start Notepad. Perform the following steps using a computer.

1. Start a new HTML file with the title [your name] lab4-1 in the main heading section.
2. Insert the text shown in the top line of the Web page.
3. Add a centered borderless table with two columns and two rows and cellpadding of 25.
3. Insert the image, csexcellence.gif, in the first column of the first row.
4. Add the second image, csexcellence_v1.gif, to that same row in a second column.
5. Start a new row and add the images, csexcellence_v2.gif and csexcellence_v3.gif.
6. Save the HTML file in the Project04\IntheLab folder on the HTML Data Disk using the file name, lab4-1solution.htm.
8. Print the lab4-1solution.htm file.
9. Open the file, lab4-1solution.htm, in your browser to view it as a Web page.
10. Print the Web page.
11. Write your name on the printouts and hand them in to your instructor.

2 Creating Two Borderless Tables

Problem: Your manager at Mirimar Web Group, L.L.C. has asked you to create two Web pages, similar to the ones shown in Figures 4-54a and 4-54b. The first Web page is a home page that presents information about Mirimar Web Group, L.L.C., together with two links. The Samples link in the first page will be linked to the Bell Video home page created in Project 4. The second Web page lists the pricing structure Mirimar charges for various Web development phases.

Instructions: Start Notepad. Perform the following steps using a computer.

1. Start a new HTML file with the title [your name] lab4-2a in the main heading section.
2. Create a 50% wide, one-row, two-column borderless table with the image, computer.gif, in the left-hand data cell and the image, webgrouplogo.gif, in the right-hand data cell.
3. Create a second one-row, two-column borderless table. Make the first column 20% wide with a background color of yellow and then add two links to the column: Pricing (lab4-2bsolution.htm) and Samples (ProjectFiles\bellvideohome.htm). Make the second column 70% wide and include the text and an e-mail link as shown in Figure 4-54a.
4. Save the HTML file using the file name, lab4-2asolution.htm, in the Project04\IntheLab folder on the HTML Data Disk. Print the HTML file.
5. Start a new HTML file with the title [your name] lab4-2b in the main heading section.
6. Create a five-row, two-column table with a five-pixel border, cellpadding of 15, and cellspacing of 5. Use yellow for the background color of the top row and the color #e0e0e0 for all other rows.
7. Span the first heading across both columns, as shown in Figure 4-54b.
8. Enter the headings, Service and Hourly Rate, and additional information in the appropriate table cells, as shown in Figure 4-54b.
9. Save the HTML file in the Project04\IntheLab folder on the HTML Data Disk using the file name, lab4-2bsolution.htm. Print the HTML file.
10. Open the file, lab4-2asolution.htm, in your browser and test the Pricing link to verify it links to the lab4-2bsolution.htm Web page.
11. Print both Web pages.
12. Write your name on all printouts and hand them in to your instructor.

In the Lab

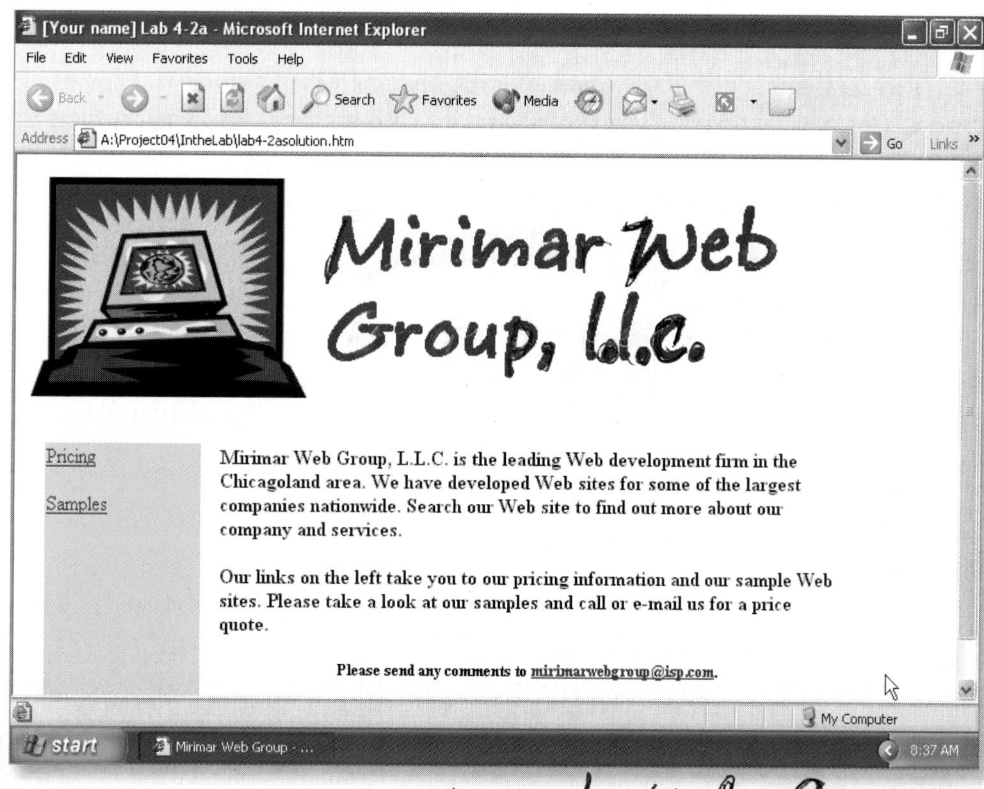

(a)

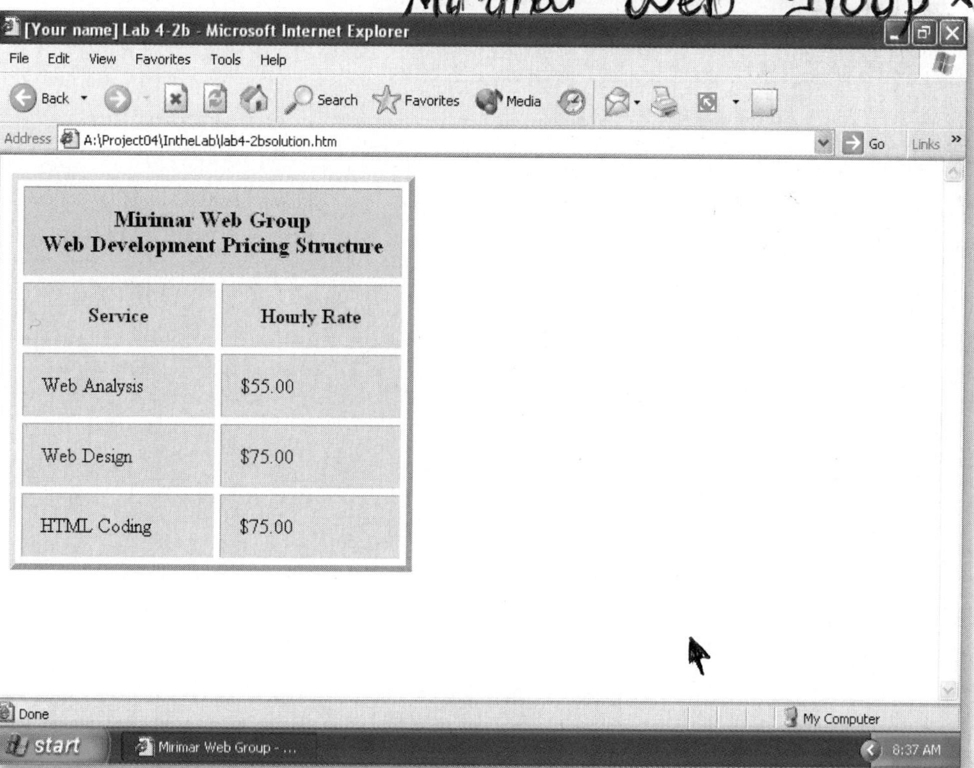

Service	Hourly Rate
Web Analysis	$55.00
Web Design	$75.00
HTML Coding	$75.00

(b)

FIGURE 4-54

3 Creating Linked Schedules

Problem: You want to create two Web pages similar to the ones shown in Figures 4-55a and 4-55b, which list your school and work schedule. The Web pages will use tables with headings that span several rows and columns to organize the information and will include links from one page to the other.

Instructions: Start Notepad. Perform the following steps using a computer.

1. Start two new HTML files with the titles [your name] lab4-3a and [your name] lab4-3b, respectively, in the main heading section.
2. In the lab4-3a file (School), create a borderless table with a menu bar (Figures 4-55a). In the lab 4-3b file (Work), create a one-pixel-bordered table with a menu bar (Figures 4-55b).
3. Include the headings and data cells as shown in both pages, with valid information in the data cells.
4. Add background colors for cells, as you see fit.
5. Save the HTML files in the Project04\IntheLab folder on the HTML Data Disk using the file names lab4-3asolution.htm and lab4-3bsolution.htm, respectively. Print the HTML files.
7. Open the file, lab4-3asolution.htm, in your browser and test the Work link to verify it links to the lab4-3bsolution.htm Web page. Test the School link to verify it links to the lab4-3asolution.htm Web page. Print both Web pages from your browser.
8. Write your name on all printouts and hand them in to your instructor.

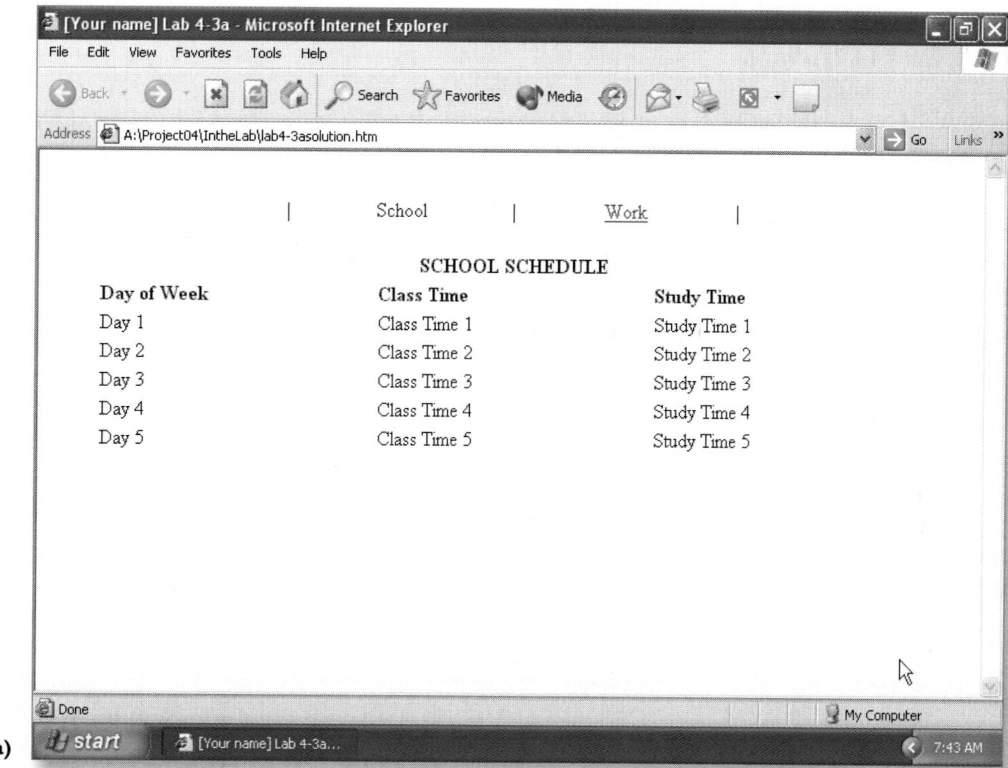

(a)

[Your name] Lab 4-3b - Microsoft Internet Explorer

File Edit View Favorites Tools Help

Address A:\Project04\IntheLab\lab4-3bsolution.htm

| School | Work |

WORK SCHEDULE		
	Day of Week	**Time**
Nursing Home Job	Day 1	Time 1
	Day 2	Time 2
	Day 3	Time 3
	Day 4	Time 4
Volunteer Programs	Day 5	Time 5
	Day 6	Time 6

Done — My Computer — start — [Your name] Lab 4-3b... — 7:44 AM

(b)

FIGURE 4-55

Cases and Places

The difficulty of these case studies varies:
■ are the least difficult and ■■ are the most difficult. The last exercise is a group exercise.

1 ■ In the Lab 1 you created a Web page that includes three new customer service award logos that could be used on the Bell Video home page. After seeing the new logos, the management staff at Bell Video has asked you to modify the Bell Video home page to test the new logos and determine if one of them is a better fit for the Web page. They also have asked you to insert a logo image on the three other Bell Video Web pages, so they can review how that would look. After modifying the Bell Video Web pages, have other students evaluate the new pages, comparing them with what was created in Project 4.

2 ■■ Browse the Web to find three Web pages that contain borderless tables and three Web pages that contain tables with borders. To verify, you can check the Web page source code from within the browser. Print all six pages and indicate if these are appropriate uses of each type of table and why. Next, find three Web pages that do not use tables currently but that should, in your opinion. Determine how these pages might display their content more effectively with the use of tables. Print those three pages and sketch Web page designs that incorporate tables.

3 ■■ Last week, you and the owner of Trailways Bus Lines sketched out a basic table format to use on the Updated Prices Web page of the Trailways Bus Lines Web site. As you begin to build the Web page, you start thinking about other table attributes that could make the Web pages look even better. Create a Web page with a basic five-row, two-column table with a one-pixel border. Review the additional table attributes listed in Appendix A, including the rules attribute. Find information on those attributes on other Web sites, including the W3C Web site (www.w3.org). Modify the basic table in the Updated Prices Web page to incorporate at least four of these attributes.

4 ■■ Several developers on your Web design team at Solid Graphics have asked if you can create a Web page with a table listing the six-digit number codes for browser-safe colors. Browse the Web to find Web pages with browser-safe color charts that are created using tables. To verify, you can check the Web page source code from within the browser. Using these Web pages and Figure 2-27 on page HTM 55 as a reference, create a Web page with a table that shows at least twelve browser-safe colors. For each cell, include the six-digit number code as the text and set the background color of that cell to the same six-digit number code.

5 ■■ **Working Together** Yakima Web Design recently has been hired to build a new Web site for a local coffee shop. Your team is working creating a basic four-page Web site to share with the owners for their input. On the home page, include a menu of items (Coffees, Teas, Bakery Items) and link those items to subsequent Web pages with more detailed information about each topic. On each linked Web page, use a table to organize lists of information related to each topic (Coffees, Teas, Bakery Items). Format each table slightly differently to demonstrate topics learned in this project, such as the use of the cellspacing and cellpadding attributes, the rowspan and colspan attributes, captions, background colors, and so on.

HTML

Creating an Image Map

PROJECT 5

CASE PERSPECTIVE

You recently started working part-time for Ibrahim Real Estate. Because the real estate market is highly competitive, you try to determine a creative and cost-effective way to publicize new home offerings for your company. While browsing the Web, you have used Web sites that utilize a technique called image mapping. With image mapping, a single image is divided into sections, each of which serves as a link. A Web page visitor can click a section of the image to link to another Web page. You realize that using an image map is a creative way to allow users to "tour" a home, by clicking on a floor plan to view Web pages with photos of different areas of the home.

You create a sample Home Tour Web site that consists of several Web pages to share with several of the real estate agents. On the home page, you use an image of a floor plan for a currently listed home. You divide the image into five rectangular areas, one for each different room of the house. Each rectangular area will be mapped to link to another Web page that contains a brief description and photo of the room.

As you read this project, you will learn how to create an image map with links to multiple Web pages. You also will learn the importance of using text links in conjunction with the image map.

Creating an Image Map

PROJECT 5

Objectives

You will have mastered the material in this project when you can:

- Define terms relating to image mapping
- List the differences between server-side and client-side image maps
- Name the two components of an image map and describe the steps to implement an image map
- Distinguish between appropriate and inappropriate images for mapping
- Sketch hotspots on an image
- Describe how the x- and y-coordinates relate to vertical and horizontal alignment
- Open an image in Paint and use Paint to map the coordinates of an image
- Create the home page and additional Web pages
- Create a table, insert an image into a table, and use the usemap attribute to define a map
- Add text to a table cell and create a horizontal menu bar with text links
- Use the <map> </map> tags to start and end a map
- Use the <area> tag to indicate the shape, coordinates, and URL for a mapped area
- Change link colors

Introduction

In Projects 2, 3, and 4, many of the Web pages used the <img> tag to add images. In Project 3, an image also was used as a link back to the home page, by using the <a> </a> tags to define the image as the clickable element for the link. When an image is used as a link, as in Project 3, the entire image becomes the clickable element, or hotspot. With an image map, the entire image does not have to be clickable. Instead, one or more specific areas serve as the hotspots.

As discussed in Project 2, an image map is a special type of inline image in which you define one or more areas as hotspots. For example, each hotspot in an image map can link to another part of the same Web page or to a different Web page. Using an image map in this way gives Web page developers significant flexibility, as well as creative ways to include navigation options on a Web site. Instead of using only text links, a Web page can include an image map that highlights key sections of a Web site and allows a user to navigate to that section by clicking the appropriate area of the image map.

In this project, you will learn how to create an image map with links to multiple Web pages. You will learn to use a program called Paint to create hotspots, by determining the screen pixel coordinates of each hotspot based on the horizontal and vertical axes of an image and then entering the coordinates for each hotspot in the image map within the <area> tag. You then will use HTML to create a link within each hotspot, so users can click the hotspot to link to another Web page. You will use your browser to view your Web pages as you develop them.

Project Five — Ibrahim Real Estate

Project 5 illustrates how to create an image map with links to other Web pages within the Ibrahim Real Estate Web site. The Ibrahim Real Estate Web site includes six Web pages, each of which is linked to the home page via an image map and text links, as shown in Figure 5-1. Project 5 describes how to create two Web pages in the Web

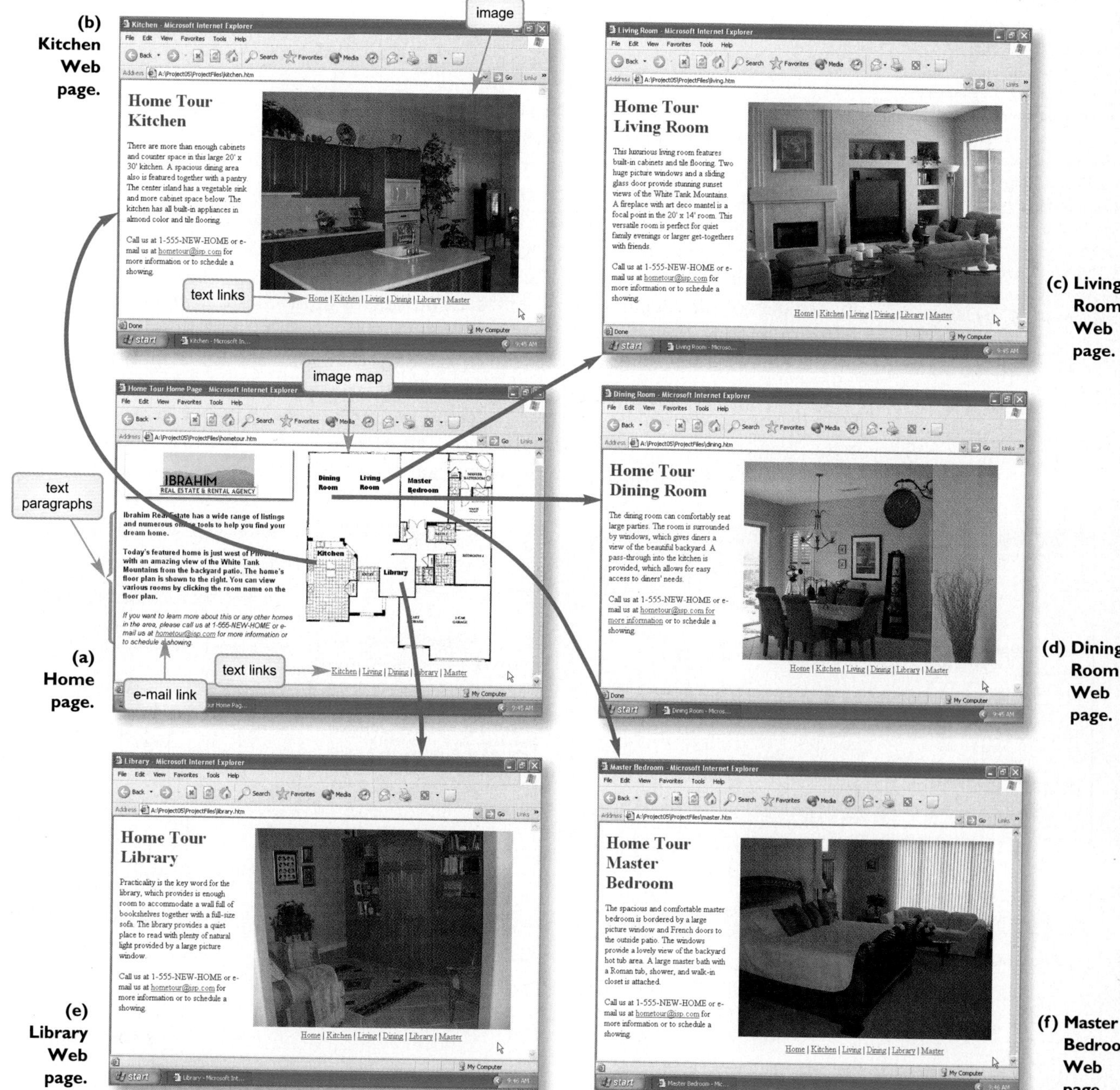

FIGURE 5-1

site: the home page (Figure 5-1a on the previous page) and the Kitchen Web page (Figure 5-1b). The Web pages shown in Figures 5-1c through 5-1f are included on the HTML Data Disk.

As shown in Figures 5-1a through 5-1f, the home page includes an image map, which is an image of the home's floor plan. The image map is divided into five hotspots, which link to five other Web pages: the Kitchen Web page (Figure 5-1b), the Living Room Web page (Figure 5-1c), the Dining Room Web page (Figure 5-1d), the Library Web page (Figure 5-1e), and the Master Bedroom Web page (Figure 5-1f). The home page also contains text information about the real estate company and text links that mirror the image map links.

Project 5 then describes how to create the Kitchen Web page (Figure 5-1b). The Kitchen Web page contains an image (kitchen.jpg) of the room, text describing the room, and text links to all other Web pages, including a link to the home page.

> *More About*
>
> **Image Maps**
>
> Image maps are used frequently for Web site navigation. Many online HTML sources address the purposes of image maps and give suggestions for their use. An online style guide produced by the World Wide Web Consortium is available for use by Web developers. For more information, visit the HTML More About Web page (scsite.com/html3e/more.htm) and then click Image Maps.

Introduction to Image Maps

In this project, you use an image map to create five clickable areas within a single image, each with a link to a different Web page, as shown in Figures 5-1a through 5-1f. Each clickable area is rectangular in shape and positioned over a room on the floor plan image. Figure 5-2a shows the borders of the five clickable areas, each of which encloses a specific room on the floor plan. These outlines, although visible in the figure, are not visible on the Web page. A Web page visitor clicking anywhere within one of the rectangular clickable areas will link to the associated Web page. Figure 5-2b shows areas that are not part of the clickable areas. Any area outside of those clickable areas is not linked to another Web page.

HTML tags are used to create the image map that supports the five clickable areas in the image. One of the key features of the Web is its support for graphics, so Web visitors expect to view many images on the Web pages that they visit. Images make Web pages more exciting and interesting to view and, in the case of image maps, provide a creative way to make navigational elements available to users.

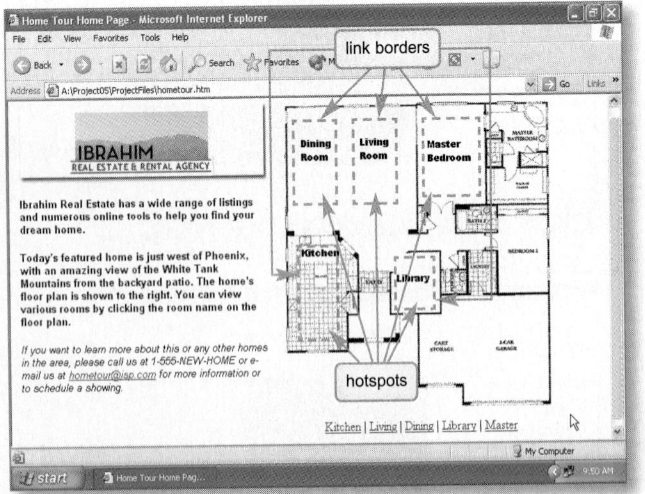

(a) Clickable areas.

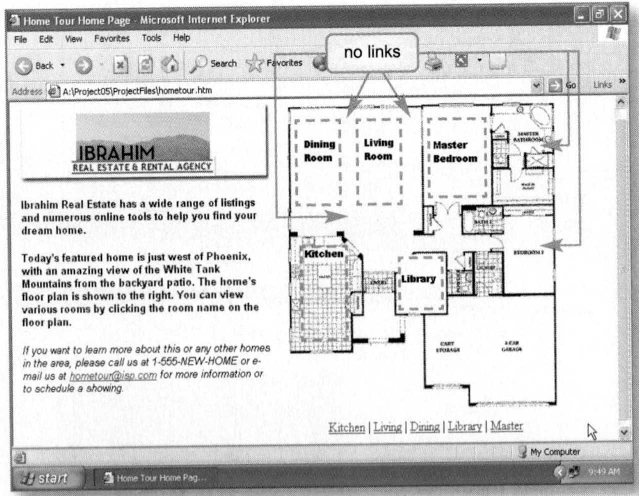

(b) Not clickable areas.

FIGURE 5-2

Using Image Maps with Text Links

One of the risks in using image maps to provide navigational elements is that if the image does not load, a user will not have the ability to navigate to other linked Web pages. Another potential issue is that using a large image for an image map may increase the amount of time required for pages to download over lower-speed connections. To avoid such performance issues, some people turn off the viewing of images when they browse Web pages, electing to display only text in their browsers. These users, and users of text-based browsers, also will not be able to navigate a Web page that relies on an image map to provide navigation. For these reasons, a Web page that uses an image map for navigation also should include text links to the URLs reflected in the image map, as shown in Figure 5-3a. Using text links in conjunction with the image map ensures that if the image does not download or a Web page visitor has images turned off, as shown in Figure 5-3b, a user still can navigate to other Web pages using the text links.

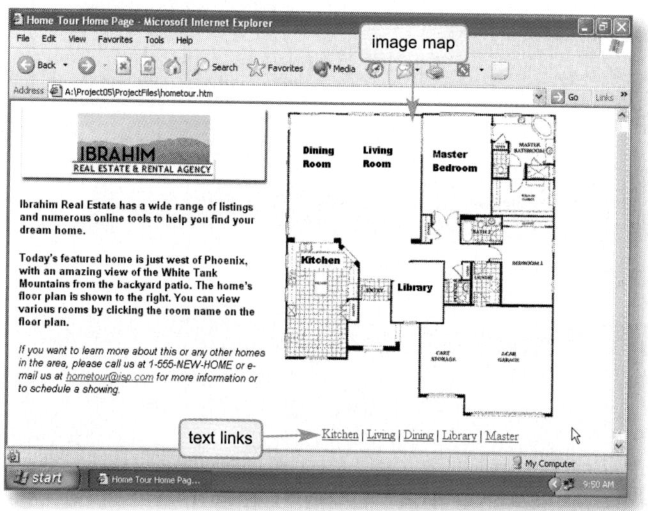

(a) Web page with images turned on.

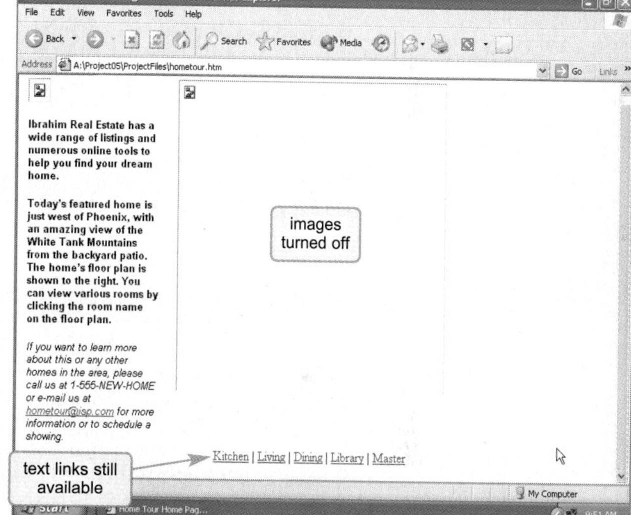

(b) Web page with images turned off.

FIGURE 5-3

Image Map Uses

Image maps can enhance the functionality and appeal of Web pages in many ways. For example, an image map can be used as an **image map button bar**, which is a menu bar that uses graphical images, as shown in Figure 5-4 on the next page. This makes the menu bar a more attractive feature of the Web page.

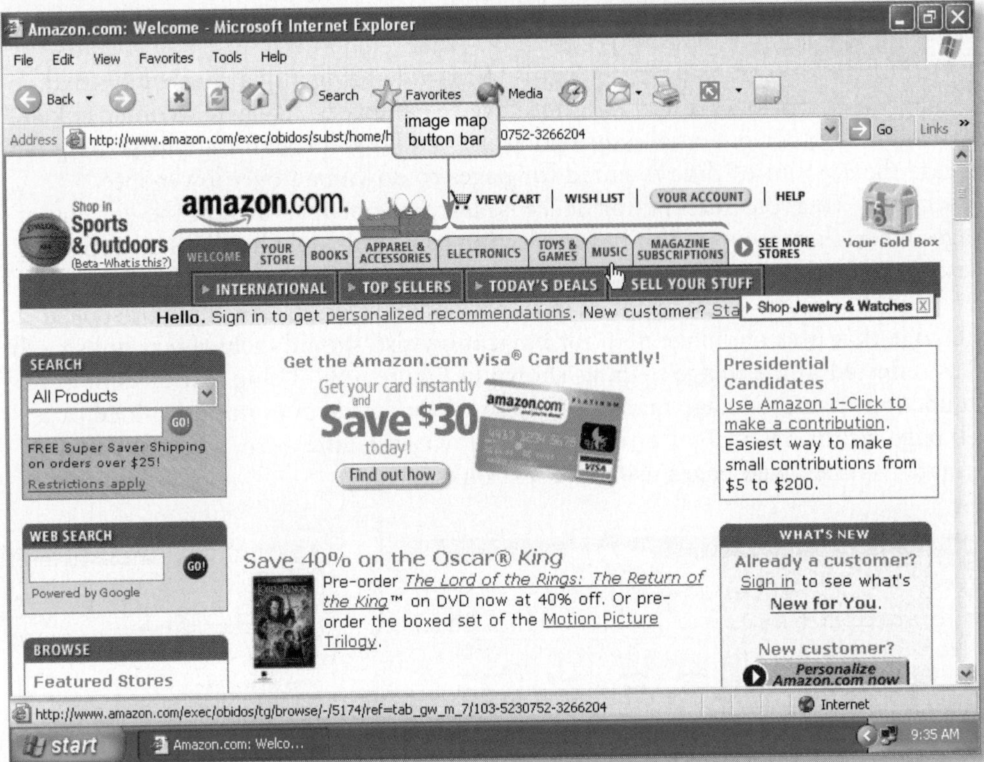

FIGURE 5-4 Image map on e-commerce site.

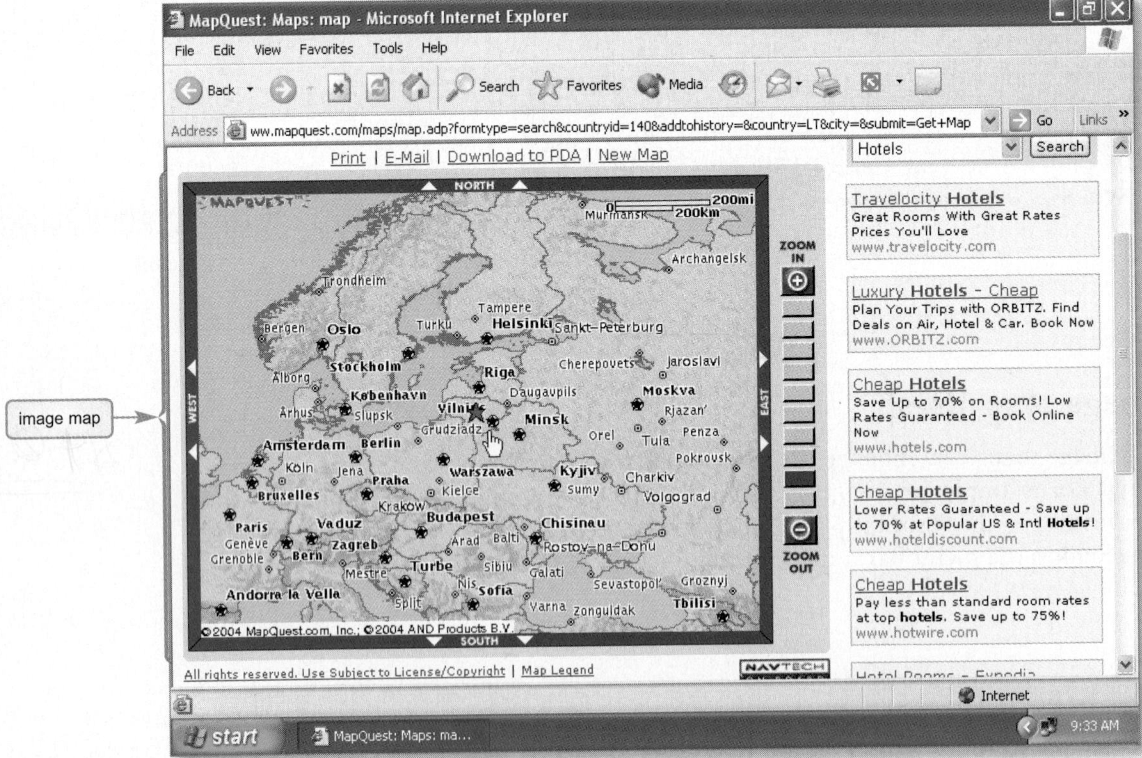

FIGURE 5-5 Image map on mapping Web page.

Image maps also are utilized to divide a geographical map into hotspots, as shown in Figure 5-5. A Web page visitor can click a geographical area on the map and be linked to additional information about that location.

As illustrated in this project, image maps also are used for commercial applications, such as real estate, in which a visitor can click a room within an image of a building (Figure 5-6a) and link to a Web page with specifics about that room (Figure 5-6b).

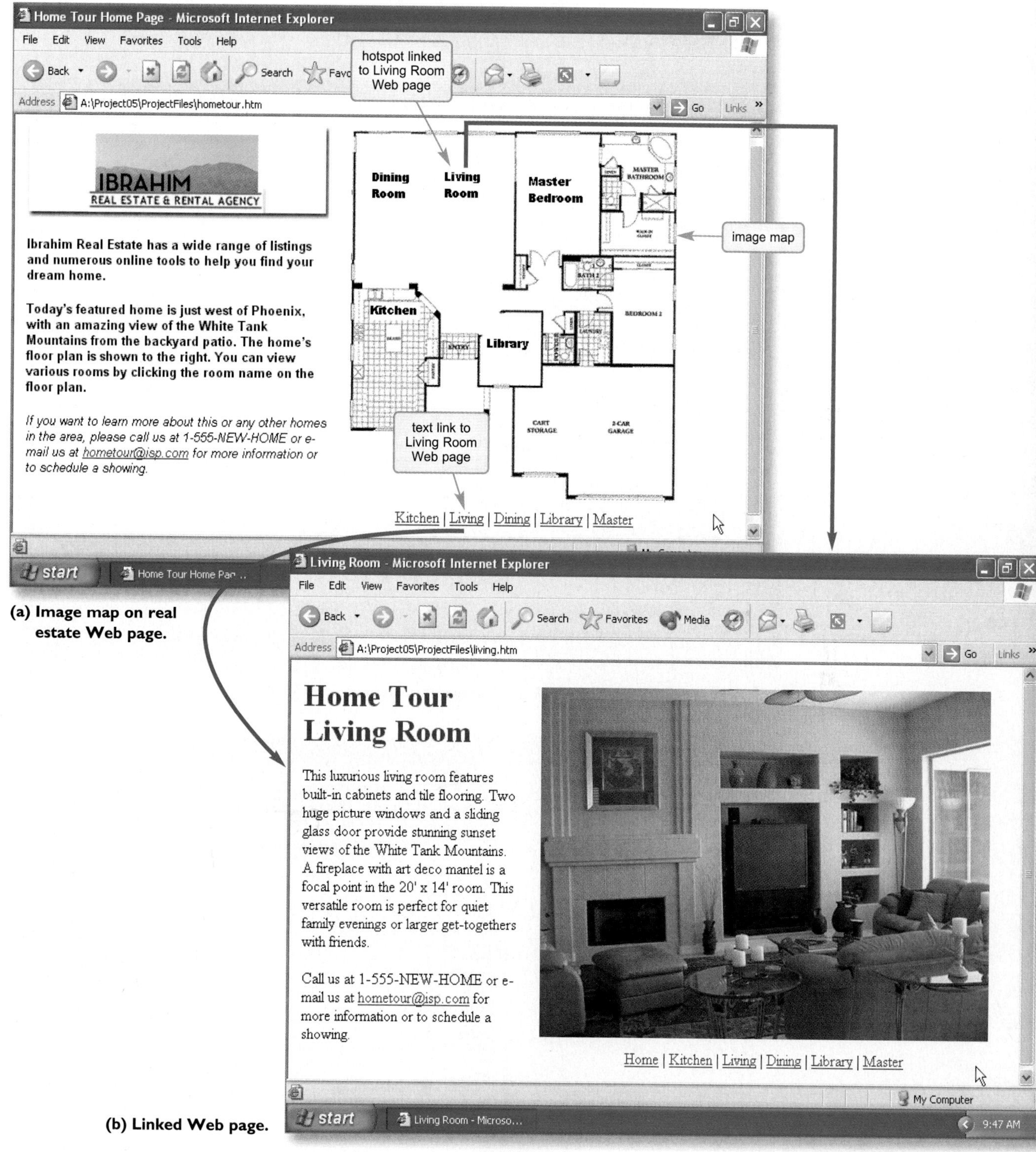

(a) Image map on real estate Web page.

(b) Linked Web page.

FIGURE 5-6

Companies also use image maps to create hotspots that link different functional areas of the company, as shown in Figure 5-7, to Web pages that contain more information about that specific area or department.

A company with a number of products or services can use an image map as a creative way to provide links to more specific information about those products or services (Figure 5-8).

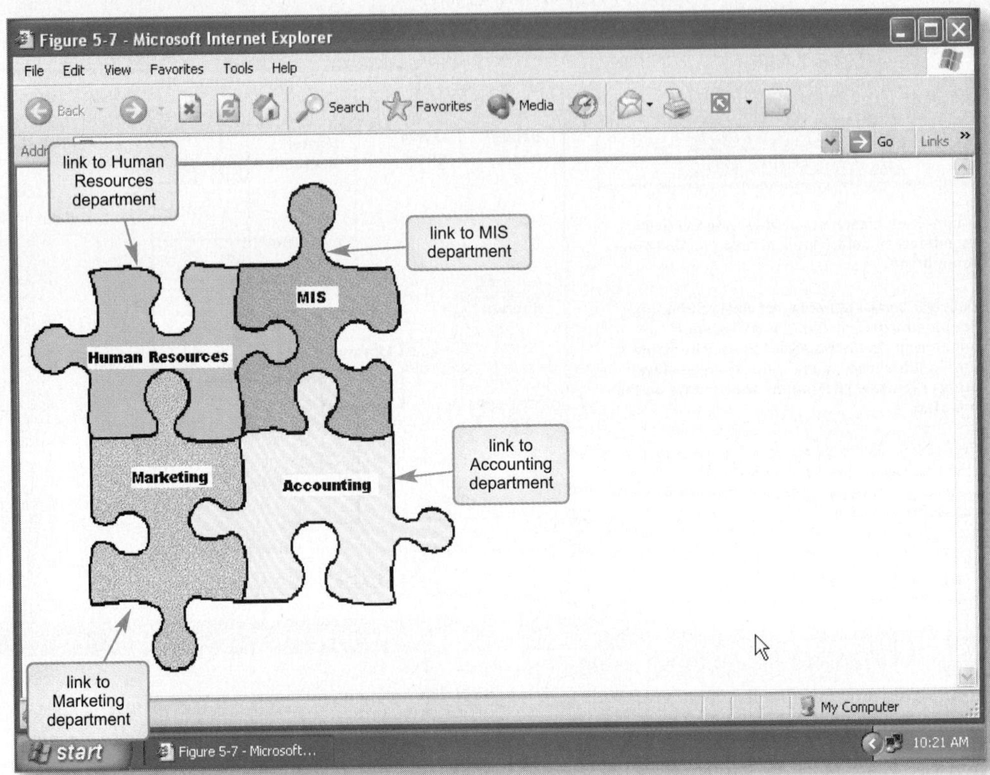

FIGURE 5-7 Image map on corporate Web page.

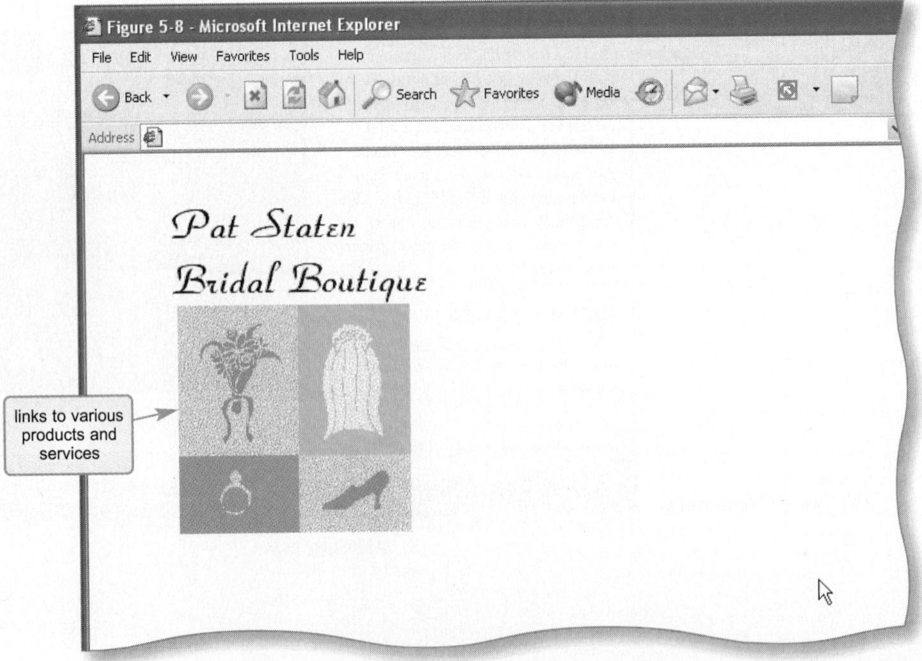

FIGURE 5-8 Image map on products and services Web page.

Server-Side versus Client-Side Image Maps

Two types of image maps exist: server-side and client-side. In a **server-side image map**, the image is displayed by the client (browser) and implemented by a program that runs on the Web server. When a Web page visitor clicks a link on a server-side image map, the browser sends the x- and y-coordinates of the mouse click to the Web server, which interprets them and then links the visitor to the correct Web page based on those coordinates. Thus, with a server-side image map, the Web server does all the work.

With a **client-side image map**, the browser does all the work. It does not have to send the x- and y-coordinates of the mouse click to the Web server to be interpreted. Instead, the coordinates are included in the HTML file along with the URL to which to link. When a visitor to a Web page clicks within a client-side image map, the browser processes the data without interaction with the Web server.

One advantage of server-side image mapping is that most, if not all, browsers support server-side image maps, while some older browsers do not support client-side image maps. Server-side image maps have disadvantages, however. They require that additional software run on the Web server. Also, an image map available on a particular Web site's server must be registered to the server before it can be used. Although this process is simple, it must be done. Further, all changes to that registered image map must be coordinated on the Web server, which does not allow for quick updates. Client-side image maps help to reduce the load on the Web server, generally download faster, and provide faster response when a user clicks a link. In this project, you will create a client-side image map with five links on the home page of the Ibrahim Real Estate Web site.

More About

Images

Not all images are appropriate for image mapping. It is helpful to hear from Web development experts about things to consider when selecting or creating images. For some great tips and suggestions, visit the HTML More About Web page (scsite.com/html3e/more.htm) and then click Images.

Creating an Image Map

An image map consists of two components: an image and a map definition that defines the hotspots and the URLs to which they link. Creating a client-side image map for a Web page is a four-step process:

1. select an image to use as an image map,
2. sketch in the hotspots on the image,
3. map the image coordinates for each hotspot, and
4. create the HTML code for the image map.

The following sections review each of these steps in greater detail.

Selecting Images

Not all images are appropriate candidates for image mapping. An appropriate image is one that has obvious visual sections, which makes a good choice as an image map. The globe image shown in Figure 5-9a on the next page, for example, has very distinct and easy to see sections, which serve as ideal hotspots. A user easily could select an individual area on the map to link to more information about each region.

FIGURE 5-9

An inappropriate image is an image that does not have obvious visual sections and therefore is not a good choice as an image map. Figure 5-9b shows a sample of a globe image not suitable for image mapping because it has no distinct sections.

Sketching the Borders of Hotspots

After an appropriate image is selected for use as the image map, the next step is to sketch the hotspots (clickable areas) within the image. Figure 5-10 shows an example of an image map with the borders of the hotspots sketched on the image. A map of the United States is used, with three states (Arizona, Nevada, and Wyoming) defined as hotspots. The image map thus will include a hotspot for three states, each of which can link to a different Web page.

> *More About*
>
> **Server-Side versus Client-Side Maps**
>
> Web sites exist that provide information about server-side versus client-side image maps. To see an example of how image maps can be used for Web pages and which type is more efficient, visit the HTML More About Web page (scsite.com/html3e/more.htm) and then click Maps.

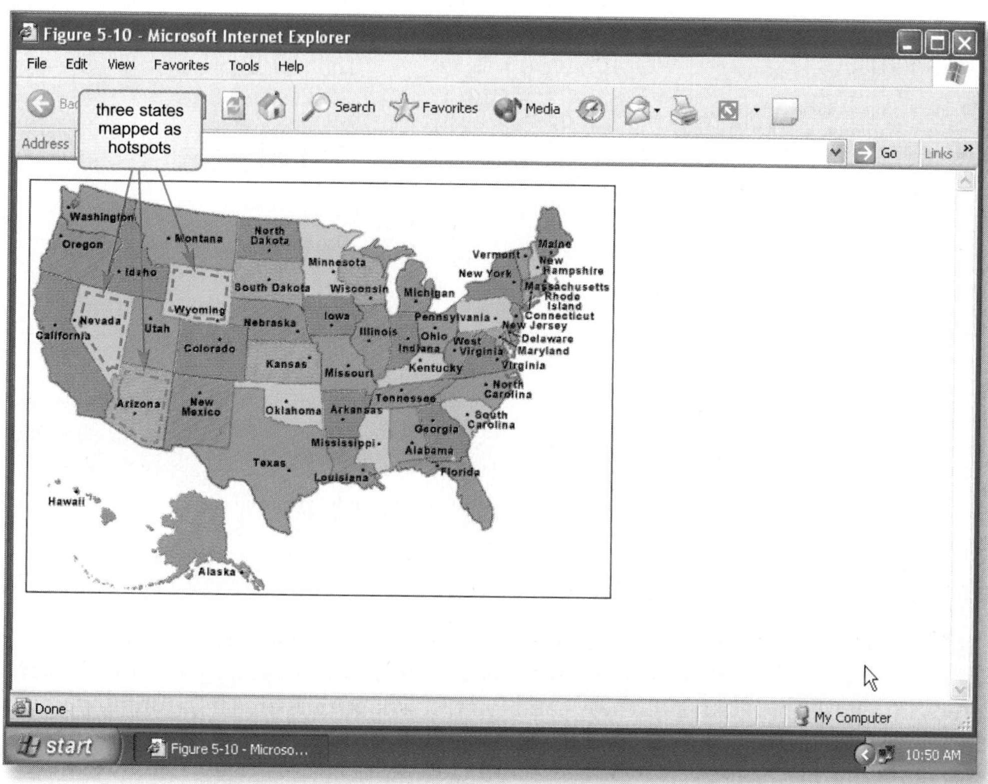

FIGURE 5-10 Sketched areas for United States image map.

Figure 5-11 on the next page shows the floor plan image used as an image map in this project, with the hotspots sketched in. This image, floorplan.gif, is included on the HTML Data Disk. Each room is defined as a hotspot, which will link to another Web page that contains information about the specific room. The process of mapping the image coordinates for each hotspot is based on this initial sketch.

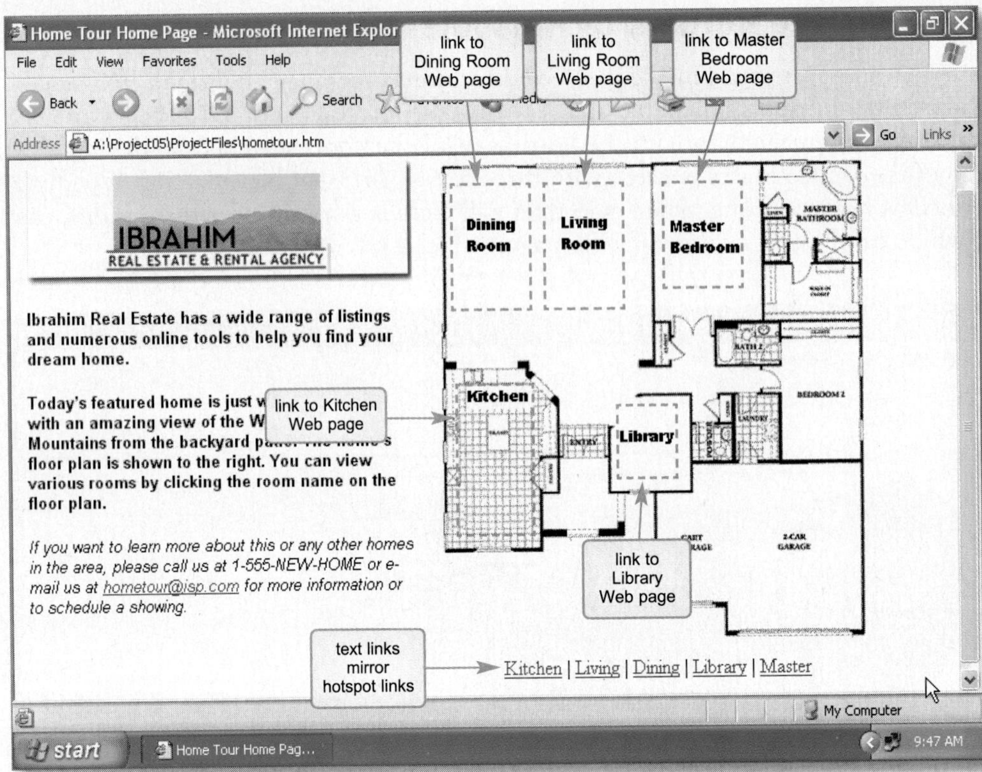

FIGURE 5-11 Sketched areas for floor plan image map.

Mapping Image Coordinates

After you have determined how to divide the image into areas, you must determine the x- and y-coordinates for those sections. The x- and y-coordinates are based on a position relative to the x- and y-axes. The **x-axis** runs horizontally along the base of the image, while the **y-axis** runs vertically along the left of the image. The top-left corner of an image thus is the coordinate pair (0,0), as shown in Figure 5-12. The first number of a **coordinate pair** is the x-coordinate, and the second number is the y-coordinate. Figure 5-12 shows some sample x- and y-coordinates in a Paint window that contains the image, floorplan.gif. The y-coordinate numbers increase as you move the mouse pointer down the image, and the x-coordinate numbers increase as you move the mouse pointer to the right on the image. As you move the mouse pointer, the coordinates of its position display on the status bar.

You can use a simple or a sophisticated image editing or paint program to determine the x- and y-coordinates of various image points. In this project, the Paint program is used to find the x- and y-coordinates used in the map definition that divides a single image into several areas.

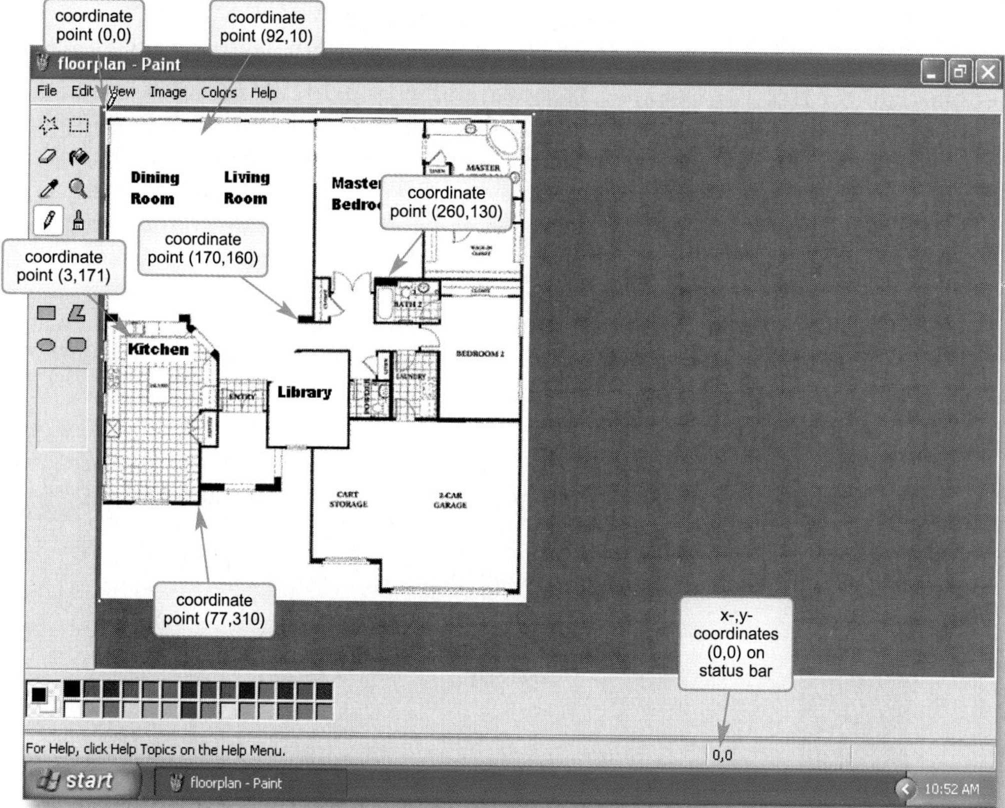

FIGURE 5-12 Floor plan image open in Paint.

Map areas can use one of three shapes: rectangle, circle, or polygon. These shapes are shown in Figure 5-13. To define a map area of an image, you must determine the x- and y-coordinates for that shape and then insert the coordinates for the various map shapes in the HTML code.

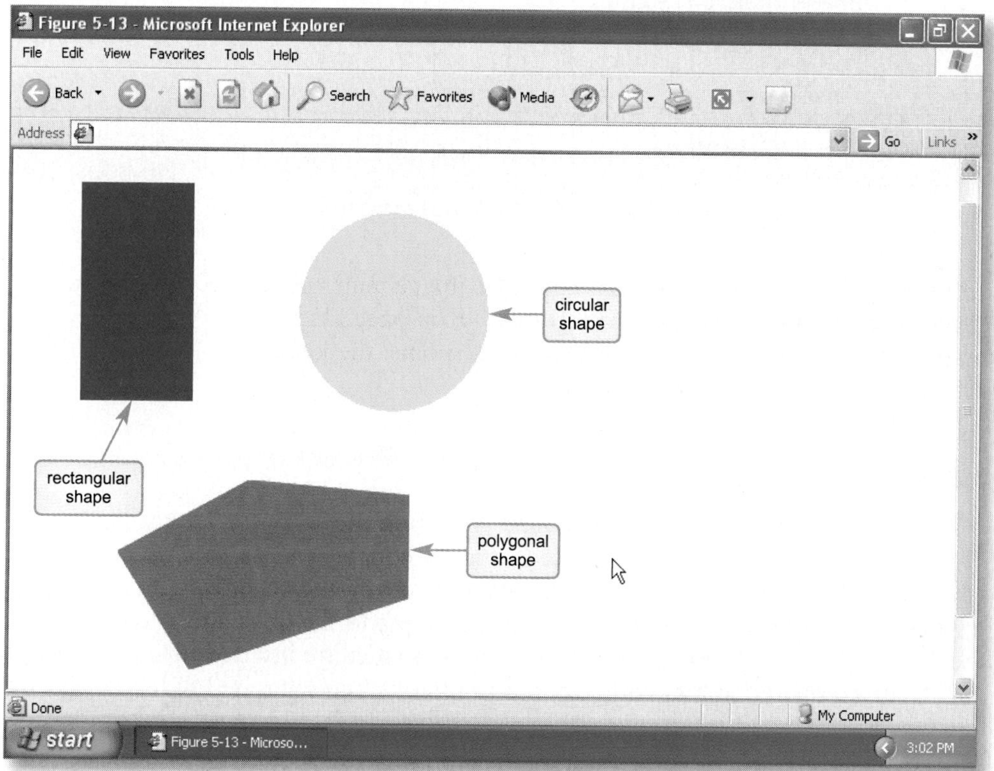

FIGURE 5-13 Shapes of map areas.

For a rectangular map area, you use the coordinates of the top-left and the bottom-right corners. For example, as shown in Figure 5-14, the rectangle's x- and y-coordinates are (46,35) for the top-left corner and (137,208) for the bottom-right corner. For a circular map area, you use the center point and the radius as the coordinates. The x- and y- coordinates of the center point of the circle in Figure 5-14 are (388,154). If the mouse pointer is moved along the y-axis (154) to the border of the circle, the x-axis is 459. The radius can be calculated by subtracting the x-axis value of the center point (388) from the x-axis value of the circle's right border (459), which gives a radius of 71 (459 – 388). For a polygonal map area, you must use the coordinates for each corner of the shape. For example, in Figure 5-14, the polygon has five corners with the coordinates (78,309), (183,251), (316,262), (317,344), and (136,402).

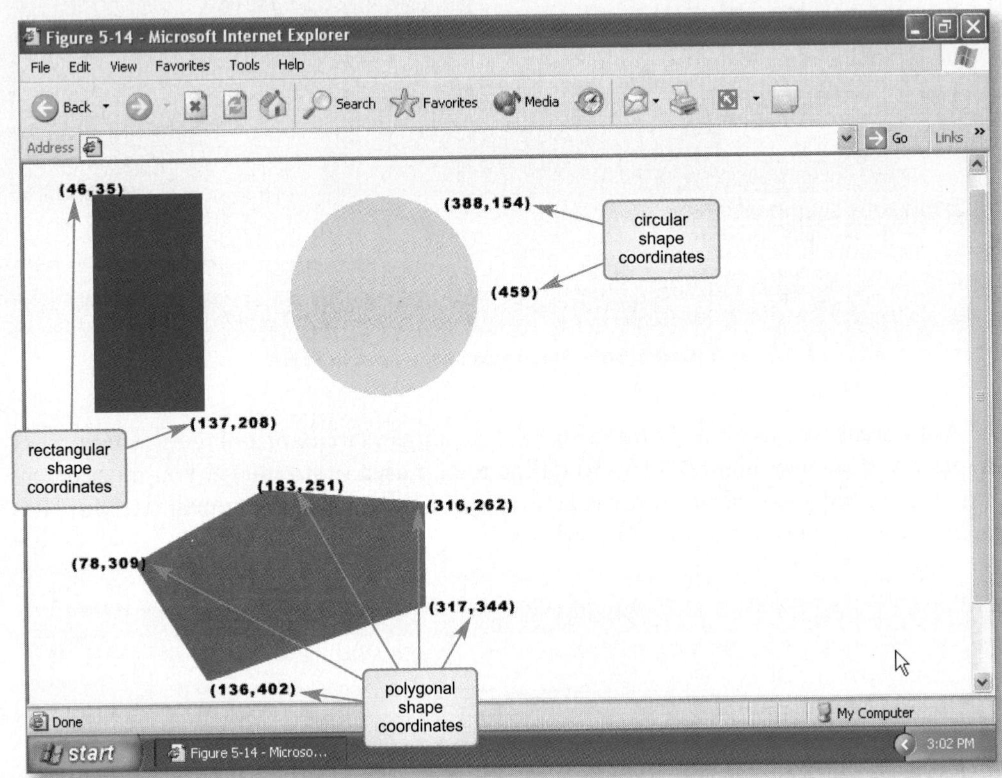

FIGURE 5-14 Coordinates of map areas.

In the floor plan image (floorplan.gif), the image map will use rectangular map areas for each room, as sketched in Figure 5-11 on page HTM 204. A clickable area is mapped in a rectangle around the following rooms: the kitchen, living room, dining room, library, and master bedroom.

Coding the Map

The final step in creating an image map is writing the HTML code for the map. To create a client-side image map, the tags <map> </map> and <area> are used. The map start tag (**<map>**) and map end tag (**</map>**) create the client-side image map. The **<area>** tag defines the specific areas of the map and the links and anchors for those areas. The x- and y-coordinates for each map area are inserted into the <area> tag with the **coords** attribute, within quotation marks and separated by commas.

Using Paint to Locate X- and Y-Coordinates

As you have learned, you can use a simple or a sophisticated image editing or paint program to determine the x- and y-coordinates of various points on an image. In this project, the Paint program is used to find the x- and y-coordinates used in the map definition that divides a single image into several areas. The following steps illustrate how to start Paint.

To Start Paint

1

- **Click the Start button on the taskbar.**

2

- **Point to All Programs on the Start menu, point to Accessories on the All Programs submenu, and then point to Paint on the Accessories submenu.**

The Paint command is highlighted on the Accessories submenu (Figure 5-15).

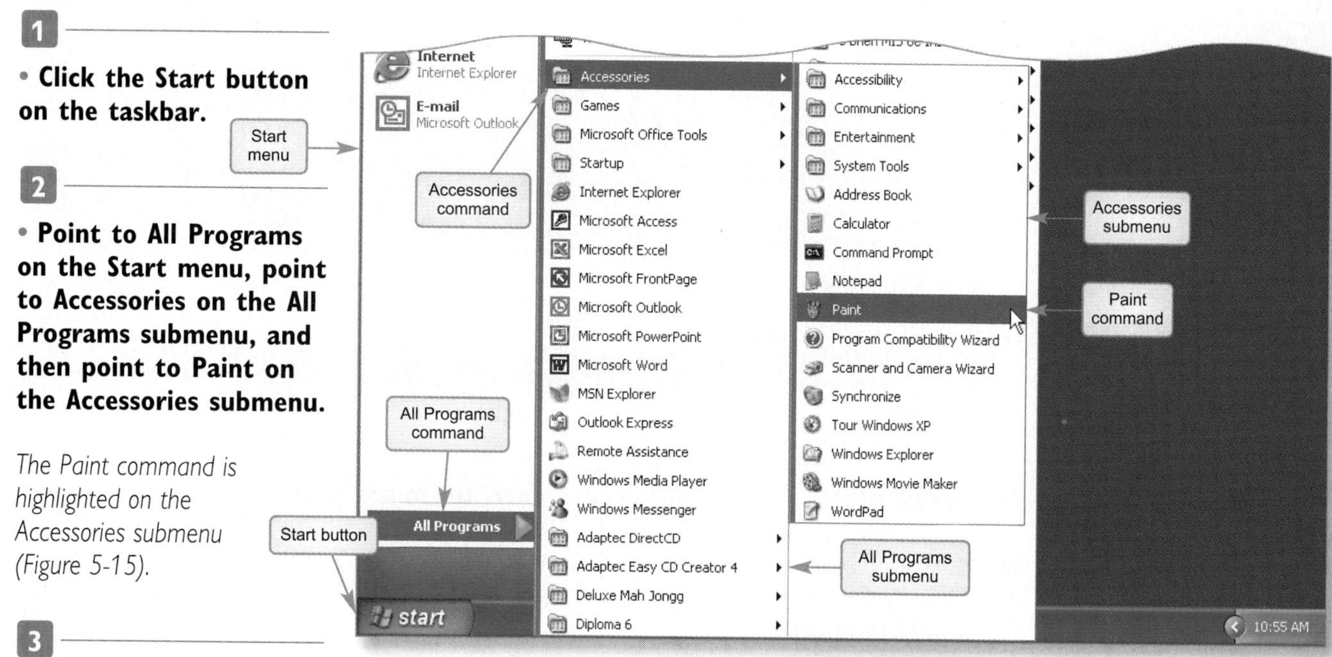

FIGURE 5-15

3

- **Click Paint.**
- **If necessary, click the Maximize button on the right side of the title bar to maximize the window.**

The Paint window appears (Figure 5-16 on the next page).

The Paint Window

The Paint window contains several elements similar to the document windows in other applications. The main elements of the Paint window are the drawing area, the toolbox, the color box, the menu bar, and the status bar (Figure 5-16).

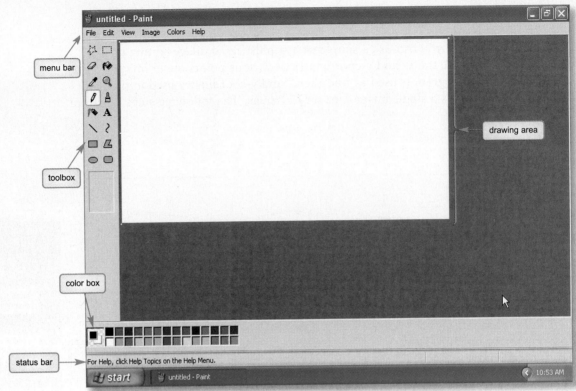

FIGURE 5-16

DRAWING AREA The **drawing area** is where the image is displayed.

TOOLBOX The **toolbox** displays tools that are used to edit or draw an image. In this project, the Select tool in the toolbox is used to find the x- and y-coordinates of the floor plan image.

COLOR BOX The **color box** displays a palette of colors that can be used to set the colors of the foreground, the background, or other elements in a drawing.

MENU BAR The **menu bar** displays at the top of the window just below the title bar and shows the Paint menu names. Each menu name contains a list of commands that can be used to open, save, and print the image in a file; edit the image; change the view of the Paint window; and perform other tasks.

STATUS BAR The **status bar** displays the coordinates of the center of the mouse pointer at its current position on the image.

> **Q&A**
>
> **Q:** Why would I use Paint for image mapping?
>
> **A:** The main reason to use Paint is that it is available on most computers. Many other graphic software tools are available that you can use to find the x- and y-coordinates. Paint, however, is easy to use and generally is available.

Opening an Image File in Paint

The floor plan image file used for the image map is stored on the HTML Data Disk. See the inside back cover for instructions for downloading the HTML Data Disk or see your instructor for information about accessing the files required for this book. The following steps illustrate how to open an image file in Paint.

To Open an Image File in Paint

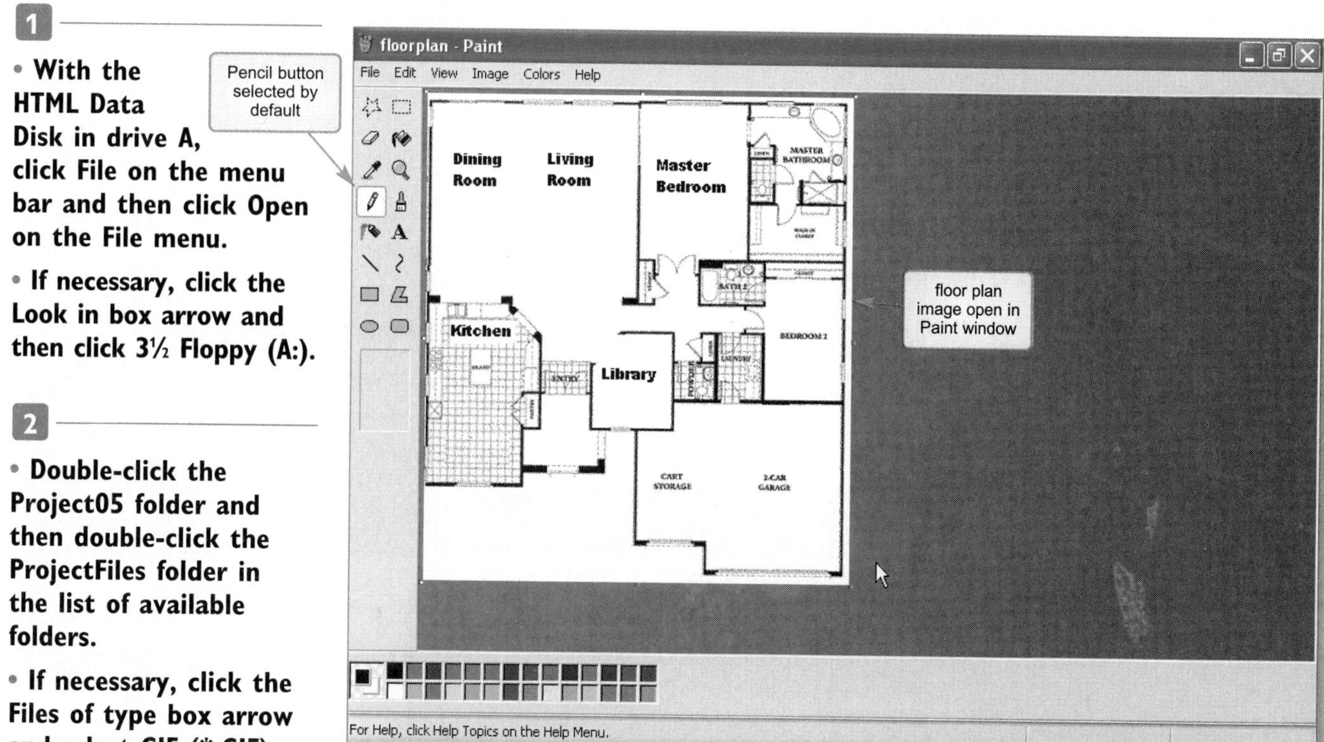

FIGURE 5-17

1

- **With the HTML Data Disk in drive A, click File on the menu bar and then click Open on the File menu.**
- **If necessary, click the Look in box arrow and then click 3½ Floppy (A:).**

2

- **Double-click the Project05 folder and then double-click the ProjectFiles folder in the list of available folders.**
- **If necessary, click the Files of type box arrow and select GIF (*.GIF).**
- **Click floorplan.gif in the list of files.**

3

- **Click the Open button in the Open dialog box.**

The image, floorplan.gif, is displayed in the Paint window (Figure 5-17).

Locating X- and Y-Coordinates of an Image

The next step is to locate the x- and y-coordinates of the areas that should be mapped on the image. As shown in Figure 5-18 on the next page, the image map should include five clickable rectangular areas that will link to other Web pages. For each of the five rectangular map areas, the x- and y-coordinate pairs of the top-left and the bottom-right corners must be determined.

As you have learned, the x- and y-coordinates begin with (0,0) in the top-left corner of the image, as shown in Figure 5-18. Moving the mouse pointer to the right (horizontally) increases the x-coordinate, and moving the mouse pointer down (vertically) increases the y-coordinate. Because all five clickable areas sketched on the floorplan.gif image are rectangular, the map definition must include the x- and y-coordinates of the top-left and bottom-right corner of each rectangular area (Figure 5-18).

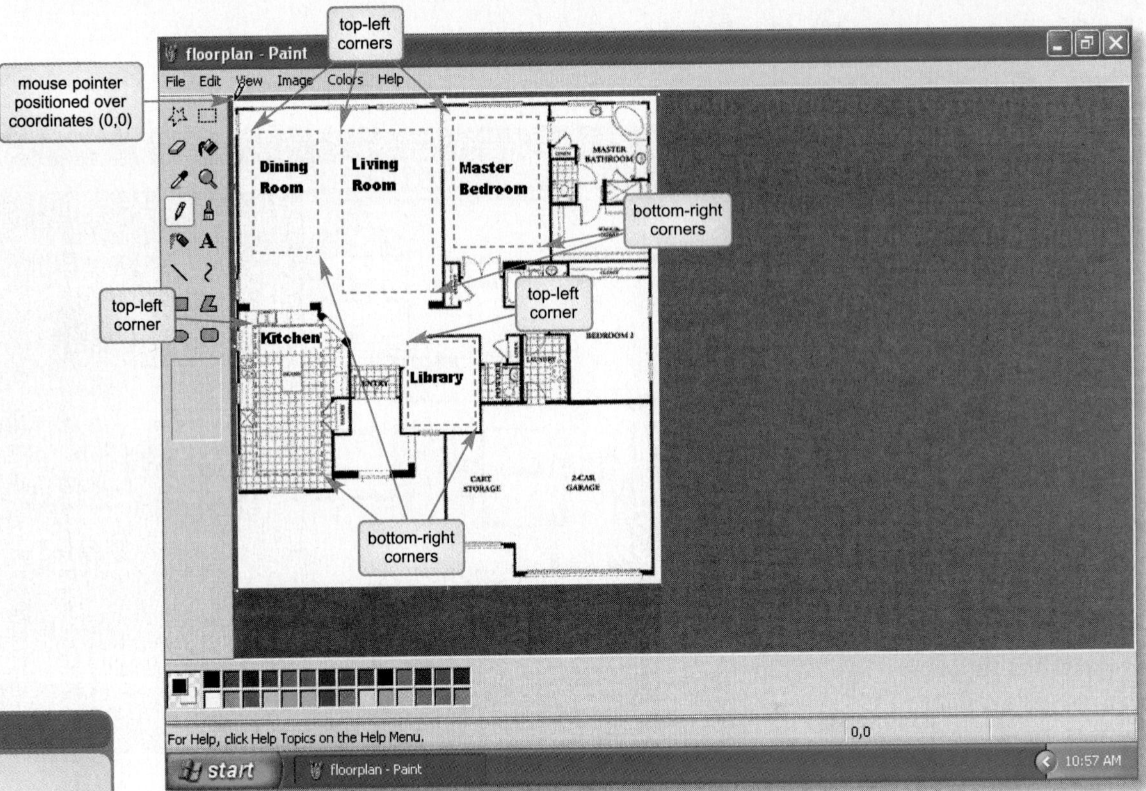

FIGURE 5-18

More About

Paint

The Help feature of Paint can answer your questions about the use of this popular tool. Paint can be used to identify the x- and y-coordinates in an image used as an image map. It also can be used to create images that are used as image maps.

Table 5-1 shows the x- and y-coordinates for the top-left and bottom-right corners of all five rectangular map areas. The first number is the x-coordinate, and the second number is the y-coordinate. For example, in the kitchen rectangle in Table 5-1, the top-left x-coordinate is 3 and the top-left y-coordinate is 171. The kitchen bottom-right x-coordinate is 77 and the bottom-right y-coordinate is 310. These x- and y-coordinates are used in the <area> tag to create the map definition for an image map.

Table 5-1 X- and Y-Coordinates

ROOM	TOP-LEFT X- AND Y-COORDINATES	BOTTOM-RIGHT X- AND Y-COORDINATES
Kitchen (points A and B)	(3,171)	(77,310)
Living Room (points C and D)	(92,10)	(170,160)
Dining Room (points E and F)	(4,10)	(78,160)
Library (points G and H)	(140,198)	(200,266)
Master Bedroom (points I and J)	(177,10)	(260,130)

The following steps illustrate how to locate the x- and y-coordinates of each clickable rectangular area by moving the mouse pointer to the top-left and bottom-right corners of each area. You will compare the coordinates with those shown in Table 5-1, which lists the exact coordinates used in the <area> tags for this project.

To Locate X- and Y-Coordinates of an Image

1

- **If necessary, click the Select button in the toolbox.**

The Select button is selected as shown in Figure 5-19.

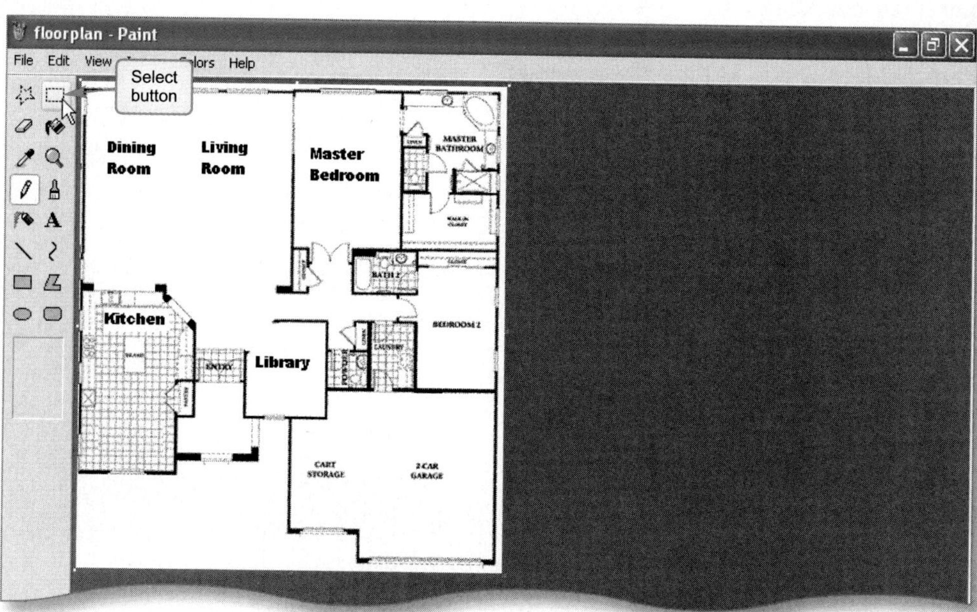

FIGURE 5-19

2

- **Move the mouse pointer to coordinates (3,171) as indicated in Figure 5-20.**

The x- and y-coordinates at the center of the mouse pointer display on the status bar and change as the mouse pointer is moved within the drawing area.

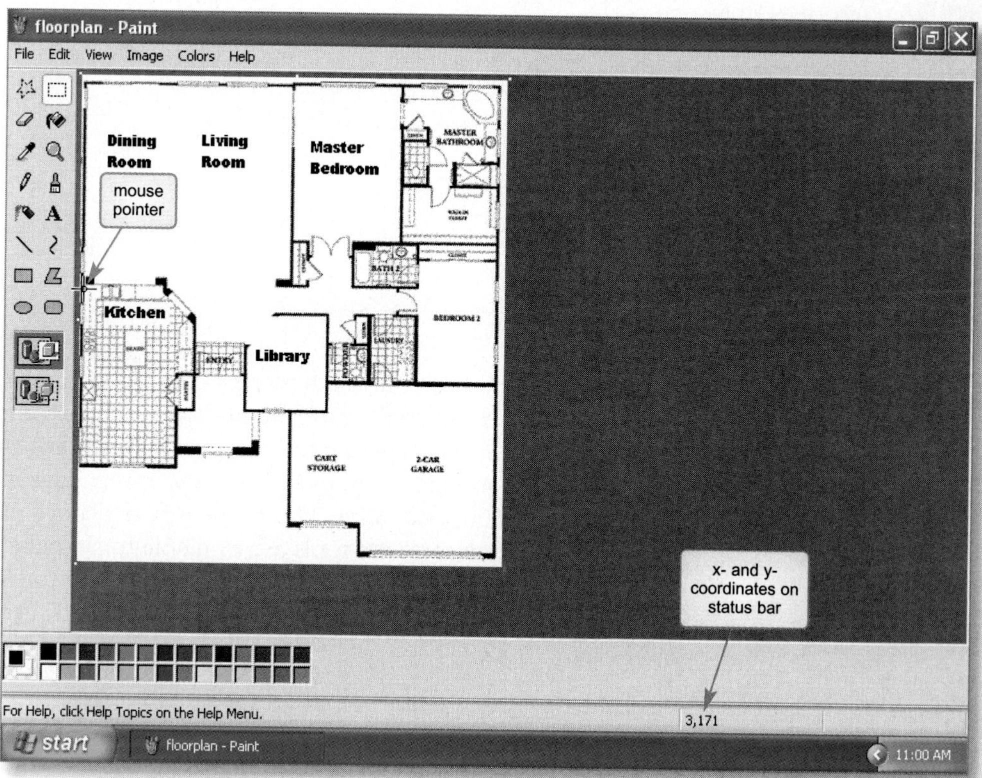

FIGURE 5-20

3

• Move the mouse pointer to coordinates (77,310) as indicated in Figure 5-21.

Point A indicates the top-left x- and y-coordinates of the rectangular map area for the kitchen, while point B indicates the bottom-right x- and y-coordinates (Figure 5-21).

4

• Move the mouse pointer to points C through J as shown in Figure 5-21 to verify the x- and y-coordinates listed in Table 5-1 on page HTM 210.

5

• After you have finished, click the Close button on the right side of the title bar.

The Paint window closes.

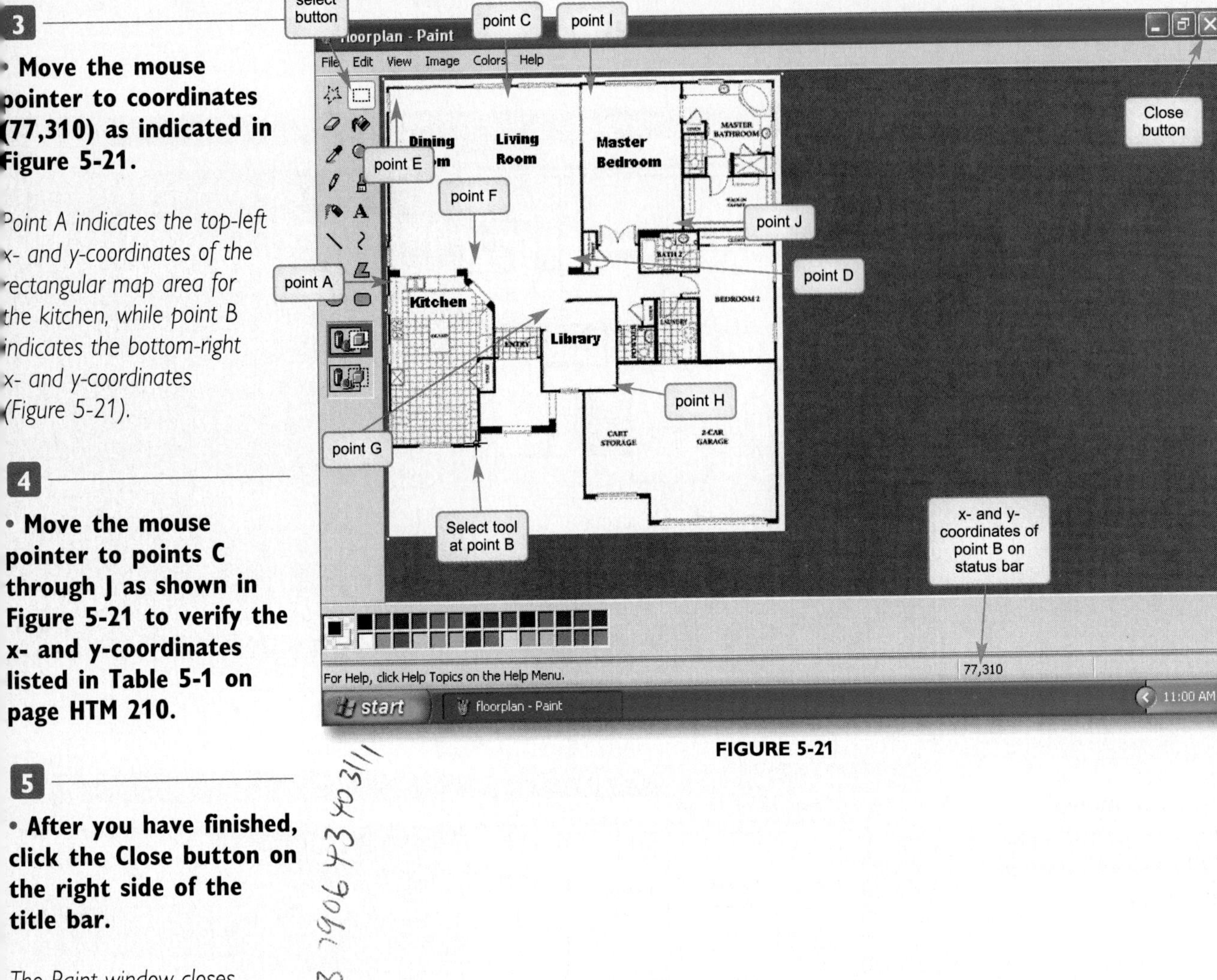

FIGURE 5-21

The previous steps showed how to locate the x- and y-coordinates listed in Table 5-1 by moving the mouse to the top-left and bottom-right corners of the five rectangular map areas and then comparing the coordinates with those in the table. Later in the project, those coordinates are included in the <area> tags in the HTML code.

Although Paint does allow you to identify the coordinates for a map area manually, several image map software tools are available to simplify this process. Table 5-2 lists several of these software tools. These tools allow you to click the image to define the clickable areas of the image map and then automatically generate the x- and y-coordinates and HTML code needed for the image map.

Table 5-2 Image Map Software Tools

TOOL	PLATFORM
Mapedit	Windows, UNIX, Mac OS
Cute MAP	Windows
CoffeeCup Image Mapper	Windows
Imaptool	Linux/X-Window

Creating the Home Page

Before the image map can be added to the home page of the Ibrahim Real Estate Web site, the home page must be created. The home page includes a borderless table, a logo image, and paragraphs of text, along with text links to other pages in the Web site (kitchen.htm, dining.htm, living.htm, library.htm, and master.htm). The first steps in creating the home page are to start Notepad and then enter an initial set of HTML tags to define the overall structure of the Web page, as shown in Table 5-3.

Table 5-3 HTML Code to Define Web Page Structure

LINE	HTML TAG AND TEXT
1	<!DOCTYPE html
2	PUBLIC "-//W3C//DTD XHTML 1.0 Transitional//EN"
3	"http://www.w3.org/TR/xhtml1/DTD/xhtml1-transitional.dtd">
4	
5	<html>
6	<head>
7	<title>Home Tour Home Page</title>
8	</head>
9	<body>
10	
11	</body>
12	</html>

More About

Server-Side Image Maps

When a hotspot on an image map is clicked, a special image map program that is stored on the Web server is run. In addition, the browser also sends the x- and y-coordinates to the Web server for the position of the link on the image map. Most, if not all, browsers support server-side image maps.

Starting Notepad and Entering Initial HTML Tags

The following steps illustrate how to start Notepad and enter HTML tags to define the Web page structure.

To Start Notepad and Enter Initial HTML Tags

1. **Click the Start button on the taskbar and then point to All Programs on the Start menu.**
2. **Point to Accessories on the All Programs submenu and then click Notepad on the Accessories submenu.**
3. **If necessary, click the Maximize button.**
4. **If necessary, click Format on the menu bar and click Word Wrap to turn on word wrap.**
5. **Enter the HTML code as shown in Table 5-3.**
6. **Position the insertion point on the blank line (line 10) between the `<body>` and `</body>` tags.**

The HTML code is displayed in Notepad (Figure 5-22 on the next page) and the insertion point is on line 10.

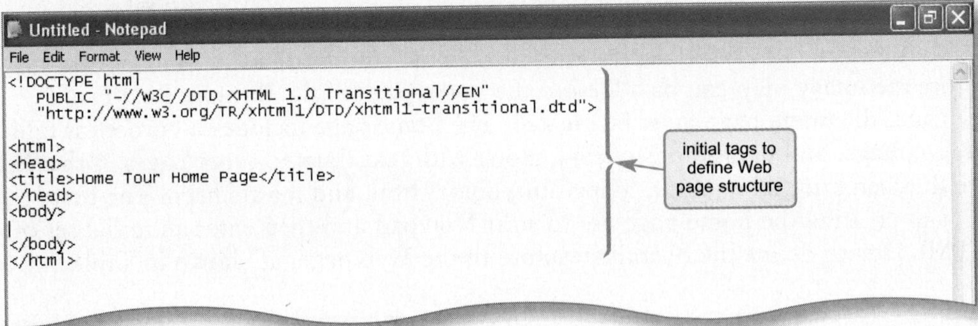

FIGURE 5-22

Creating a Table

The next task in developing the home page is to create a left-aligned, borderless table with two rows and two columns, as shown in Figure 5-23. The first row contains the logo and paragraphs of information about Ibrahim Real Estate, along with the image, floorplan.gif, which will be used for the image map. The second row contains the text links on the bottom of the Web page.

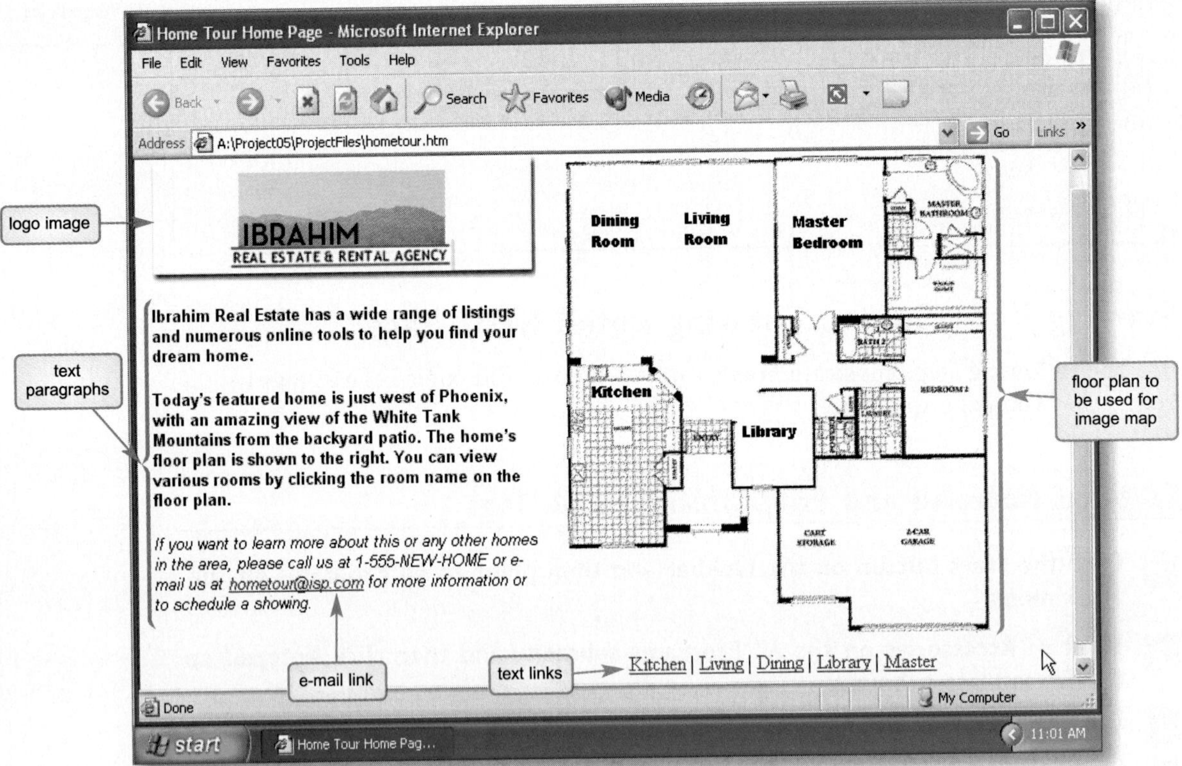

FIGURE 5-23

The <table> tag used on the home page uses the form

```
<table align="left" border="0" cols="2" rows="2" width="75%">
```

where the align="left" attribute aligns the table on the left of the Web page and border="0" creates a borderless table. The cols="2" attribute creates two columns in the table, while the rows="2" attribute creates two rows in the table. The width attribute used sets the table to use a width that is 75 percent of the total width of the Web page.

The two cells of the table are created using <td> tags that create table data cells. As you learned in Project 4, the <td> tag aligns the contents of a cell in the center of the cell vertically and to the left horizontally, by default. As shown in Figure 5-23, the table should use a vertical alignment so the contents of all cells are aligned with the top of the cell. The HTML code thus should use a <tr> tag with the valign="top" attribute to create a table row that uses vertical alignment. Using this tag eliminates the need to set each table data cell to use vertical alignment.

The following steps create a two-row, two-column borderless table, with a first table row that uses vertical alignment. This row will be used to position the logo, paragraph text, and floor plan image.

To Create a Table

1

- **With the insertion point on line 10, type** `<table align="left" border="0" cols="2" rows="2" width="75%">` **and then press the ENTER key.**

2

- **Type** `<tr valign="top">` **and then press the ENTER key.**

The HTML code is displayed (Figure 5-24).

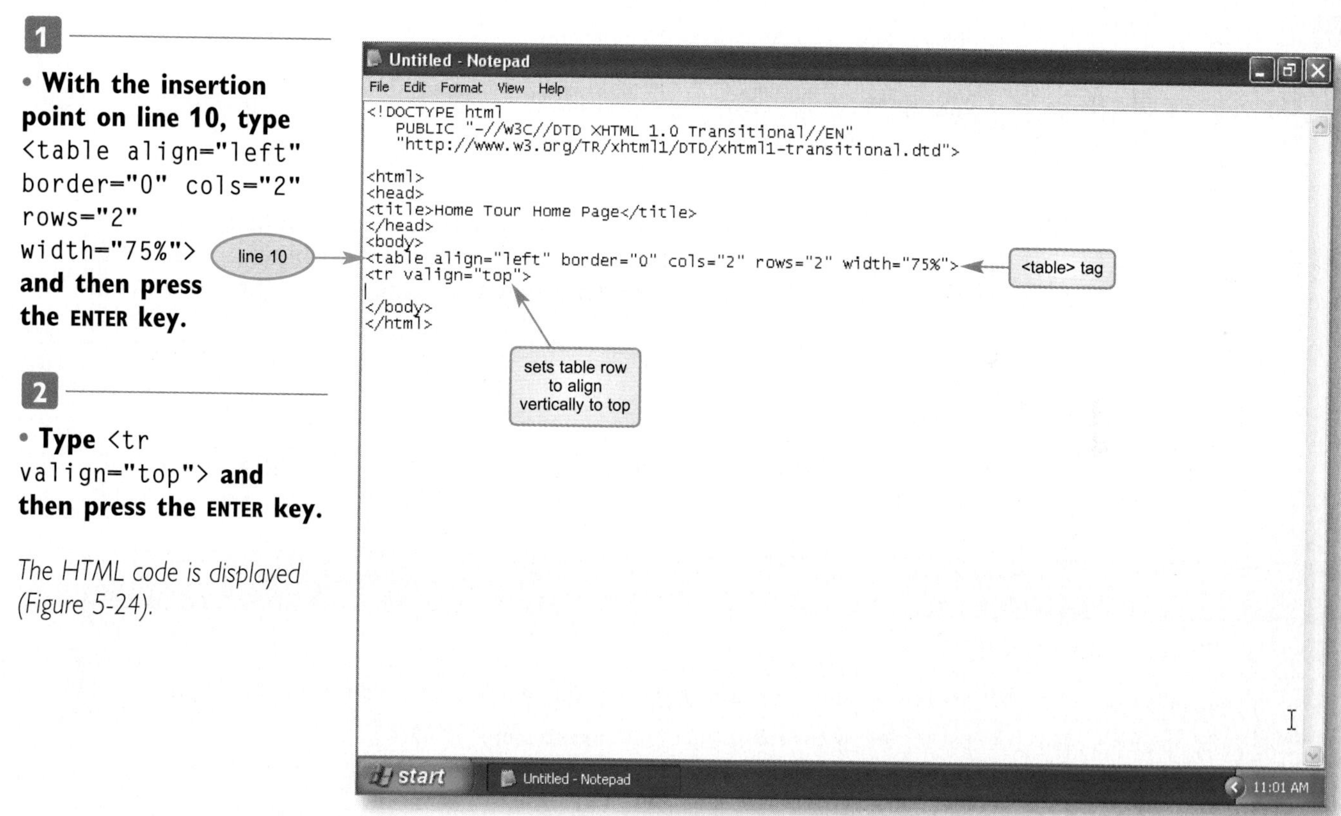

FIGURE 5-24

Inserting an Image in a Table

The next step in creating the home page is to add the logo image in the first row of the table. The corporate logo clearly identifies the company name and balances the larger floor plan image to the right. Because the floor plan image is a simple black and white image, the colorful logo image adds color and pizzazz to the Web page. The logo image, ibrahimlogo.gif, is stored on the HTML Data Disk.

The steps on the next page show how to insert an image in the first row of the table.

> **More About**
>
> **Image Map Tutorials**
>
> Many great resources are available on the Web that discuss image maps. The HTML Goodies Web site has an Image Map Tutorial that can be helpful for Web developers. For more information about these tutorials, visit the HTML More About Web page (scsite.com/html3e/more.htm) and then click image map tutorials.

To Insert an Image in a Table

1. **If necessary, click line 12.**
2. **Type** `<td><p><img src="ibrahimlogo.gif" width="320" height="97" /></p>` **and then press the ENTER key.**

The HTML code is displayed (Figure 5-25) and the insertion point is on line 13.

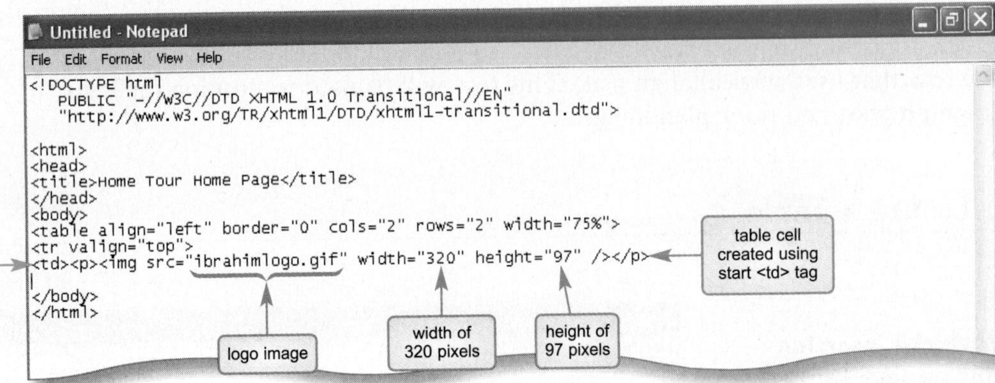

FIGURE 5-25

As you have learned in earlier projects, specifying the width and height attributes helps to improve page loading time. By identifying these attributes in the HTML code, the browser does not have to determine the width and height of the image.

Adding Text to a Table Cell

The home page also contains three paragraphs of text in the right column of the first row. The HTML code for this text is shown in Table 5-4.

Table 5-4 HTML Code for Inserting Paragraphs

LINE	HTML TAGS AND TEXT
13	`<b><p><font size="2" face="arial">Ibrahim Real Estate has a wide range of listings`
14	`and numerous online tools to help you find your dream home.</p>`
15	
16	`<p>Today's featured home is just west of Phoenix, with an amazing view of the`
17	`White Tank Mountains from the backyard patio. The home's floor plan is shown to`
18	`the right. You can view various rooms by clicking the room name on the floor`
19	`plan.</p></b>`
20	
21	`<p><em><font size="-1">If you want to learn more about this or any other homes`
22	`in the area, please call us at 1-555-NEW-HOME or e-mail us at`
23	`<a href="mailto:housetour@isp.com">hometour@isp.com</a> for more information or to`
24	`schedule a showing.</font></em></p>`
25	`</td>`

Entering the HTML code shown in Table 5-4 adds three paragraphs of text describing the company and an e-mail link. As you have learned, a Web page always should include an e-mail address on the home page for visitor contact. The following steps show how to enter the tags for the paragraphs of text.

To Add Text to a Table Cell

1. **If necessary, click line 13.**
2. **Enter the HTML code shown in Table 5-4 and then press the ENTER key twice.**

The HTML code is displayed (Figure 5-26) and the insertion point is on line 27.

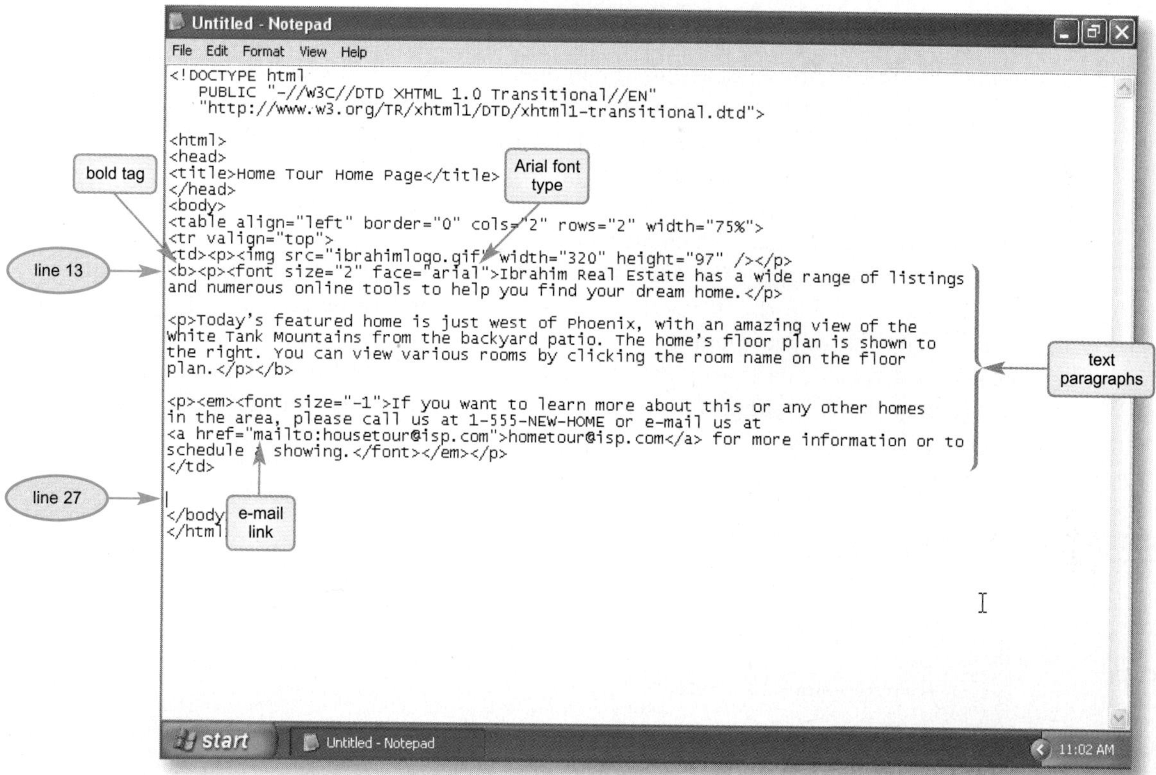


```
<!DOCTYPE html
   PUBLIC "-//W3C//DTD XHTML 1.0 Transitional//EN"
   "http://www.w3.org/TR/xhtml1/DTD/xhtml1-transitional.dtd">

<html>
<head>
<title>Home Tour Home Page</title>
</head>
<body>
<table align="left" border="0" cols="2" rows="2" width="75%">
<tr valign="top">
<td><p><img src="ibrahimlogo.gif" width="320" height="97" /></p>
<b><p><font size="2" face="arial">Ibrahim Real Estate has a wide range of listings
and numerous online tools to help you find your dream home.</p>

<p>Today's featured home is just west of Phoenix, with an amazing view of the
White Tank Mountains from the backyard patio. The home's floor plan is shown to
the right. You can view various rooms by clicking the room name on the floor
plan.</p></b>

<p><em><font size="-1">If you want to learn more about this or any other homes
in the area, please call us at 1-555-NEW-HOME or e-mail us at
<a href="mailto:housetour@isp.com">hometour@isp.com</a> for more information or to
schedule a showing.</font></em></p>
</td>

</body>
</html>
```

FIGURE 5-26

The home page now includes a borderless table. The first cell of the table includes the logo image, ibrahimlogo.gif, and three paragraphs of text, including an e-mail link. This completes the first cell of the table on the home page.

Adding an Image to Use as an Image Map

The floor plan image, floorplan.gif, will be used as an image map on the home page. Table 5-5 on the next page lists two <img> tag attributes that are used when adding an image to use as an image map.

Table 5-5 Tag Attributes Used to Create Image Maps		
TAG	ATTRIBUTE	FUNCTION
<img>	usemap	• Indicates the URL of a client-side image map
	ismap	• Indicates a server-side image map

The Ibrahim Real Estate home page will use a client-side image map. The HTML code to add the image thus will use four attributes of the <img> tag — src, hspace, usemap, and border — as follows:

```
<p><img src="floorplan.gif" width="350" height="389" border="0" hspace="20"
usemap="#tour" /></p>
```

where the src attribute identifies the image, the width and height attributes define the image size, and the border attribute makes the image borderless. The hspace attribute adds 20 pixels of horizontal space between the image and the text, so the text does not run right up against the image.

The usemap attribute indicates to the browser which client-side image map will be used for that image. The client-side image map is placed within the <map> tag and defines the x- and y-coordinates of the areas on the image being used for the image map. Later in this project, a map named tour will be created using the <map> tag. When adding the image to use as an image map, the value of the usemap attribute — in this case, usemap="#tour" — indicates that the browser should use the image map named tour as its image map source. The following steps show how to add an image to use as an image map.

To Add an Image to Use as an Image Map

1

• **If necessary, click line 27.**

2

• **Type** `<td>` **and then press the ENTER key.**

3

• **Type** `<p> <imgsrc= "floorplan.gif" width="350" height="389" border="0" hspace="20"` **and then press the ENTER key.**

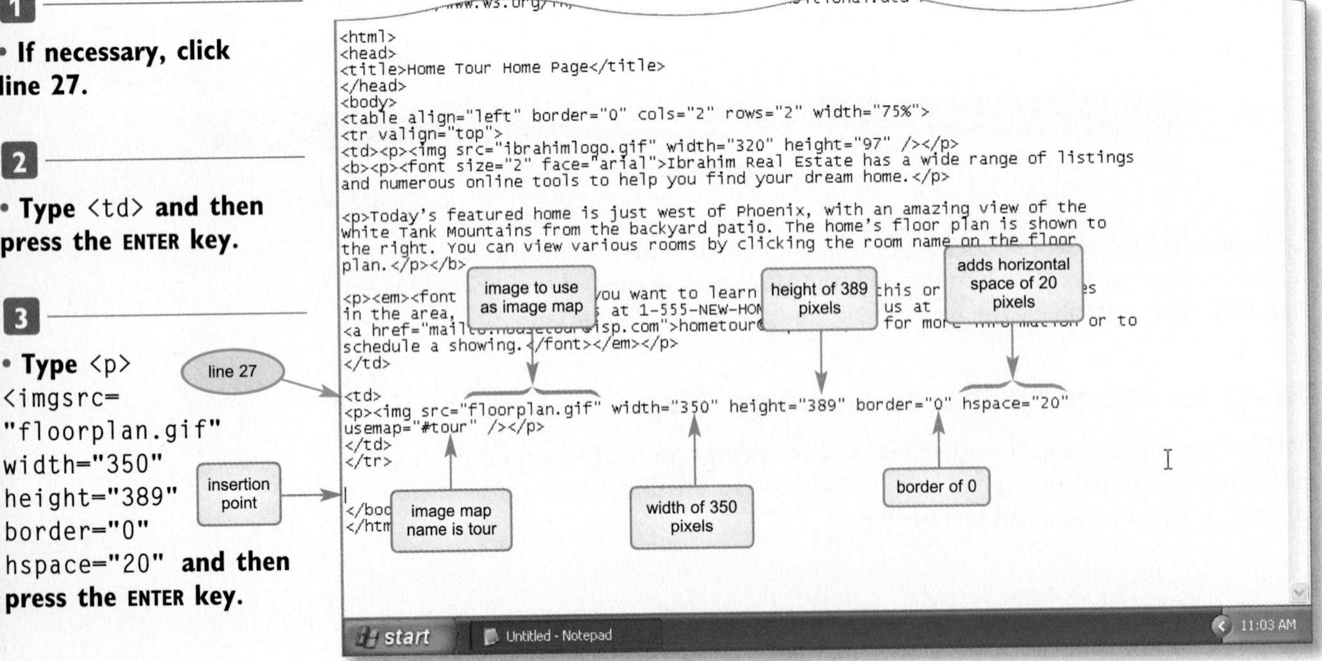

FIGURE 5-27

4

- **Type** usemap="#tour" /></p> **and then press the ENTER key.**

5

- **Type** </td> **and then press the ENTER key.**

6

- **Type** </tr> **and then press the ENTER key twice.**

The HTML code is displayed (Figure 5-27) and the insertion point is on line 33.

The floor plan image is added and the usemap target of tour is specified. Later in the project, the steps to create an image map named tour are discussed.

Creating a Horizontal Menu Bar with Text Links

The next step in creating the Ibrahim Real Estate home page is to create a horizontal menu bar of text links at the bottom of the page that mirror the image map links. As previously discussed, it is important that a Web page include text links to all URLs in the image map, in the event the image does not download or a user's browser is set to not display images.

Table 5-6 shows the HTML code used to create the horizontal menu bar. As shown in lines 34 and 35, the HTML code adds two data cells to the second row of the table. The first data cell uses the <br /> tag (line 34) to give the cell space without any text or image. This is necessary so the text links are aligned beneath the image map. Without this empty data cell, the text links would align under the paragraphs of text.

Q&A

Q: Why do I need to include text links?

A: Text links are very important to provide on all Web pages in addition to an image map. Some people turn graphics off while browsing the Web. If you did not have text links, they could not access your other Web pages with graphics turned off. Additionally, you want to give your Web site visitors access to all Web pages in the Web site. Text links should provide that access.

Table 5-6 HTML Code for Creating a Horizontal Menu Bar

LINE — HTML TAGS AND TEXT

```
33 <tr>
34 <td><br /></td>
35 <td align="center"><a href="kitchen.htm">Kitchen</a> |
36 <a href="living.htm">Living</a> |
37 <a href="dining.htm">Dining</a> |
38 <a href="library.htm">Library</a> |
39 <a href="master.htm">Master</a>
40 </td>
41 </tr>
42 </table>
```

Lines 35 through 39 create five links to the other Web pages in the Ibrahim Real Estate Web site, to mirror the five links that will be included in the image map. The links are separated visually using a | symbol. Line 42 ends the table with an end </table> tag.

The following steps show how to create the text links at the bottom of the home page.

To Create a Horizontal Menu Bar with Text Links

1. **If necessary, click line 33.**
2. **Enter the HTML code shown in Table 5-6 on the previous page and then press the ENTER key twice.**

The HTML code is displayed (Figure 5-28) and the insertion point is on line 44.

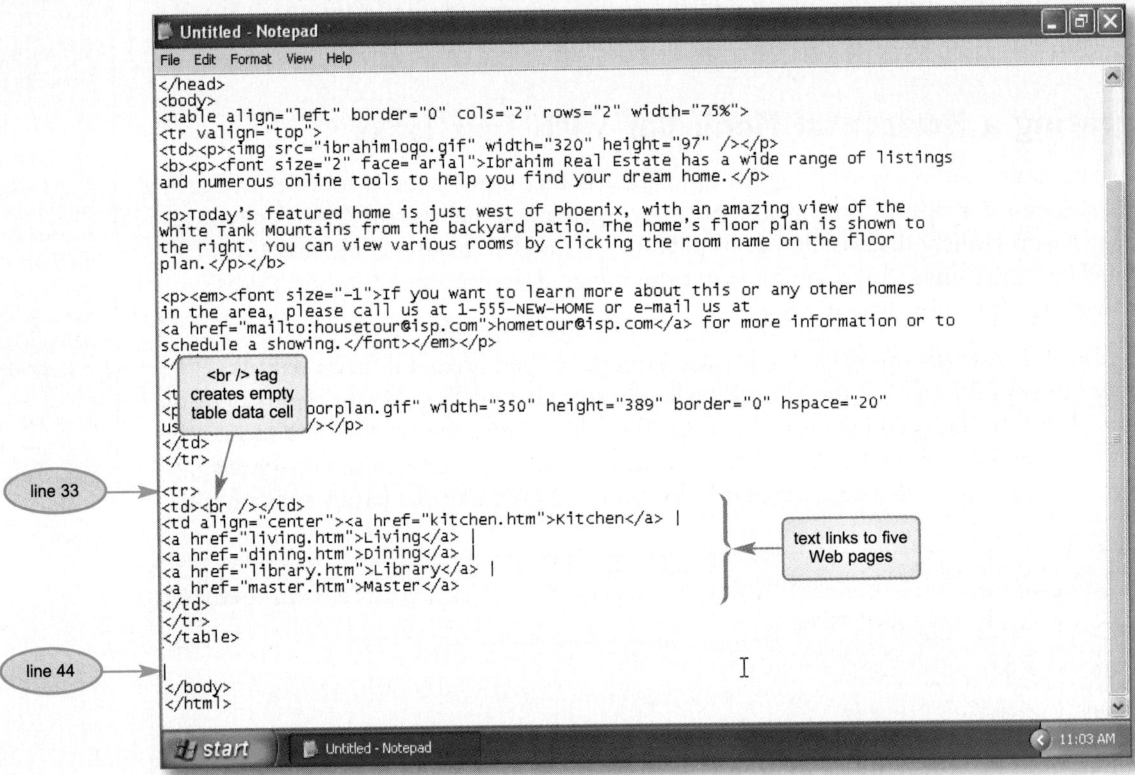

FIGURE 5-28

The borderless table on the Ibrahim Real Estate home page is complete. The image used as the image map, floorplan.gif, already is specified in the <img> tag on line 28. The next set of steps creates the image map used to map the coordinates of the floor plan image and create five clickable areas.

Coding the Image Map Using HTML Tags and Attributes

Thus far, the project has addressed three of the four steps in creating an image map: the floor plan image to use as an image map has been selected and added to the home page, the hotspots have been sketched on the floor plan image, and Paint was used to locate the x- and y-coordinates for each rectangular map area on the image. With these steps completed, the final step is to code the image map using HTML. Table 5-7 shows the two HTML tags used to create an image map, along with several key attributes of each.

Table 5-7 Tags and Tag Attributes Used to Create Image Maps

TAG	ATTRIBUTE	FUNCTION
<map> </map>		• Creates a client-side image map
	name	• Defines the map's name
<area>		• Defines clickable areas within a <map> element, as well as links and anchors
	shape coords href alt	• Indicates the shape of the map area; possible values are rect, poly, and circle • Indicates the x- and y-coordinates of the points bounding the map area • Indicates the link (URL) used for a map area • Indicates the alternate text for the image

The start <map> tag and end </map> tag define the section of code that includes the client-side image map. The <area> tag is used to define the clickable areas on the image map. The general form of the <area> tag is

```
<area shape="rect" alt="floor plan" coords="3,171,77,310" href="kitchen.htm">
```

where the **shape** attribute with the **rect** value defines the clickable map area as a rectangle. Other possible values for the shape attribute are circle and poly (polygon). The alt attribute defines alternate text for the image. The **coords** attribute indicates the x- and y-coordinates of the top-left and bottom-right of the rectangle. In a rectangle, the first two numbers indicate the x- and y-coordinates of the top-left corner of the rectangle (3,171). The next two numbers (77,310) denote the x- and y-coordinates of the bottom-right corner of the rectangle. Finally, the href attribute designates the URL of the link. In this example, a Web page visitor clicking anywhere within the rectangle bordered by x,y (3, 171) and x,y (77,310) will link to the Web page kitchen.htm.

To insert the <area> tag for the circle and polygon shapes, such as those shown in Figure 5-14 on page HTM 206, the HTML code would be as follows:

```
<area shape="circle" coords="388,154,71" href="kitchen.htm">
<area shape="poly" coords="78,309,183,251,316,262,317,344,136,402" href="kitchen.htm">
```

Creating an Image Map

For the image map on the Ibrahim Real Estate home page, five clickable areas are created, one for each room with a detailed Web page: Kitchen, Dining, Living, Library, and Master Bedroom. All five clickable areas are rectangular in shape. Table 5-8 on the next page shows the HTML code used to create the image map for the floor plan image on the home page. Line 44 defines the name of the image map as tour, which is the name referenced in the usemap attribute of the <img> tag that added the floor plan image. Lines 45 through 49 define the five rectangular map areas for the image map, based on the x- and y-coordinates listed in Table 5-1 on page HTM 210. Each rectangular map area links to one of the five other Web pages in the Web site.

Table 5-8 HTML Code for Creating an Image Map

LINE	HTML TAGS AND TEXT
44	`<map name="tour">`
45	`<area shape="rect" coords="3,171,77,310" href="kitchen.htm">`
46	`<area shape="rect" coords="92,10,170,160" href="living.htm">`
47	`<area shape="rect" coords="4,10,78,160" href="dining.htm">`
48	`<area shape="rect" coords="140,198,200,266" href="library.htm">`
49	`<area shape="rect" coords="177,10,260,130" href="master.htm">`
50	`</map>`

The following steps illustrate how to enter the HTML code to create the image map for the floor plan image.

To Create an Image Map

1

• **If necessary, click line 44.**

2

• **Enter the HTML code shown in Table 5-8.**

The HTML code is displayed (Figure 5-29).

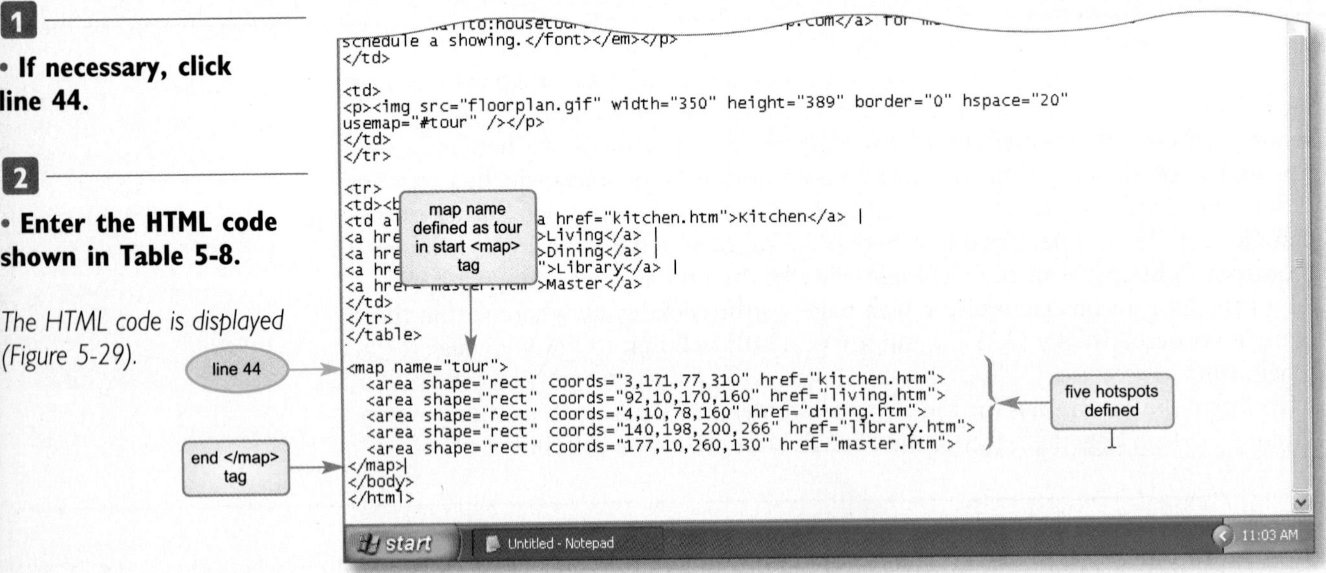

FIGURE 5-29

The image map is complete. Line 44 of the HTML code names the image map tour, which is the name referenced by the usemap attribute in the <img> tag in line 29. Lines 45 through 49 set five separate areas as hotspots by naming the top-left and the bottom-right x- and y-coordinates. A Web page visitor who clicks any of these hotspots will link to the appropriate URL as indicated by the href attribute. The end </map> tag on line 50 ends the image map.

Changing Link Colors

The next task is to change the color of the links to maintain consistency throughout the Web page. As you learned in Project 3, text link colors vary as the status of the link changes. The standard color of a normal (unvisited) link is blue in most browsers. A clicked (visited) link generally is green or purple. An active link varies in color depending on the browser. For the Ibrahim Real Estate home page, all links should be set to navy, to maintain color consistency on the Web page, regardless of the link status. To do this, the normal link (link), active link (alink), and visited link (vlink) attributes in the <body> tag must be set to navy. The following steps illustrate how to change link colors to override the browser defaults.

To Change Link Colors

1

- **Click immediately to the right of the y in the <body> tag on line 9 and then press the SPACEBAR.**

2

- **Type** `link="navy" alink="navy" vlink="navy"` **for the link colors.**

The HTML code is displayed (Figure 5-30).

Untitled - Notepad

File Edit Format View Help

navy color for normal link

navy color for visited active link

navy color for active link

```
<!DOCTYPE html
    PUBLI        D XHTML 1.0 T          /EN"
    "http        g/TR/xhtml1/DT         nsitional.dtd">
<html>
<head>
<title>Home Tour Home Page</title>
</head>
<body link="navy" alink="navy" vlink="navy">
<table align="left" border="0" cols="2" rows="2" width="75%">
<tr valign="top">
<td><p><img src="ibrahimlogo.gif" width="320" height="97" /></p>
<b><p><font size="2" face="arial">Ibrahim Real Estate has a wide range of listings
and numerous online t              you find your dream home.</p>

<p>Today's featured h              west of Phoenix, with an amazing view of the
White Tank Mountains              yard patio. The home's floor plan is shown to
the right. You can view various rooms by clicking the room name on the floor
plan.</p></b>

<p><em><font size="-1">If you want to learn more about this or any other homes
in the area, please call us at 1-555-NEW-HOME or e-mail us at
<a href="mailto:housetour@isp.com">hometour@isp.com</a> for more information or to
schedule a showing.</font></em></p>
</td>

<td>
<p><img src="floorplan.gif" width="350" height="389" border="0" hspace="20"
usemap="#tour" /></p>
</td>
</tr>

<tr>
<td><br /></td>
<td align="center"><a href="kitchen.htm">Kitchen</a> |
<a href="living.htm">Living</a> |
<a href="dining.htm">Dining</a> |
<a href="library.htm">Library</a> |
<a href="master.htm">Master</a>
```

start | Untitled - Notepad | 11:04 AM

FIGURE 5-30

The colors of text links are set to appear in the color, navy, regardless of whether the link is normal, visited, or active. The HTML code for the Ibrahim Real Estate home page is complete. The home page includes a two-row, two-column borderless table. The first cell in the first row positions a logo image and three paragraphs of text, including an e-mail link. The second cell in the first row positions the floor plan image that is defined as the image map with five hotspots that link to other Web pages in the Web site. The second row contains a series of six text links that mirror the links in the image map.

With the HTML code for the Ibrahim Real Estate home page complete, the file should be saved and a copy should be printed as a reference. The steps on the next page illustrate how to save and print the HTML file.

To Save and Print the HTML File

1. **With a floppy disk in drive A, click File on the menu bar and then click Save As. Type** hometour.htm **in the File name text box.**
2. **If necessary, click 3½ Floppy (A:) in the Save in list. Click the Project05 folder and then double-click the ProjectFiles folder in the list of available folders. Click the Save button in the Save As dialog box.**
3. **Click File on the menu bar and then click Print on the File menu.**

Notepad prints the HTML file (Figure 5-31). Notepad saves the HTML file in the Project05\ProjectFiles folder on the floppy disk in drive A using the file name, hometour.htm.

```
<!DOCTYPE html
   PUBLIC "-//W3C//DTD XHTML 1.0 Transitional//EN"
   "http://www.w3.org/TR/xhtml1/DTD/xhtml1-transitional.dtd">

<html>
<head>
<title>Home Tour Home Page</title>
</head>
<body link="navy" alink="navy" vlink="navy">
<table align="left" border="0" cols="2" rows="2" width="75%">
<tr valign="top">
<td><img src="ibrahimlogo.gif" width="320" height="97" />
<b><p><font size="2" face="arial">Ibrahim Real Estate has a wide range of listings
and numerous online tools to help you find your dream home.</p>

<p>Today's featured home is just west of Phoenix, with an amazing view of the
White Tank Mountains from the backyard patio. The home's floor plan is shown to
the right. You can view various rooms by clicking the room name on the floor
plan.</p></b>

<p><em><font size="-1">If you want to learn more about this or any other homes
in the area, please call us at 1-555-NEW-HOME or e-mail us at
<a href="mailto:housetour@isp.com">hometour@isp.com</a> for more information or to
schedule a showing.</font></em></p>
</td>

<td>
<p><img src="floorplan.gif" width="350" height="389" border="0" hspace="20"
usemap="#tour" /></p>
</td>
</tr>

<tr>
<td><br /></td>
<td align="center"><a href="kitchen.htm">Kitchen</a> |
<a href="living.htm">Living</a> |
<a href="dining.htm">Dining</a> |
<a href="library.htm">Library</a> |
<a href="master.htm">Master</a>
</td>
</tr>
</table>

<map name="tour">
   <area shape="rect" coords="3,171,77,310" href="kitchen.htm">
   <area shape="rect" coords="92,10,170,160" href="living.htm">
   <area shape="rect" coords="4,10,78,160" href="dining.htm">
   <area shape="rect" coords="140,198,200,266" href="library.htm">
   <area shape="rect" coords="177,10,260,130" href="master.htm">
</map>
</body>
</html>
```

FIGURE 5-31

Viewing and Printing the Web Page Using a Browser

After the HTML file for the Ibrahim Real Estate home page is saved, it should be viewed in a browser to confirm that the Web page appears as desired and that the links function as expected. To test the Ibrahim Real Estate home page, click the e-mail link to verify that it works correctly. Next, test the links to the Living Room, Dining Room, Library, and Master Bedroom pages by clicking the corresponding mapped areas of the image and the text links at the bottom of the page. These links work at this time because the files dining.htm, living.htm, library.htm, and master.htm are stored on the HTML Data Disk. The Kitchen hotspot and text link cannot be tested yet, because the Kitchen Web page has not been created yet.

The following steps show how to view and print the Web page.

To View and Print the Web Page Using a Browser

1

- **Start the browser.**
- **If necessary, click the Maximize button to maximize the browser window.**

2

- **Type** `a:\Project05\ProjectFiles\hometour.htm` **in the Address box and then press the ENTER key.**

The browser displays the Ibrahim Real Estate home page (Figure 5-32).

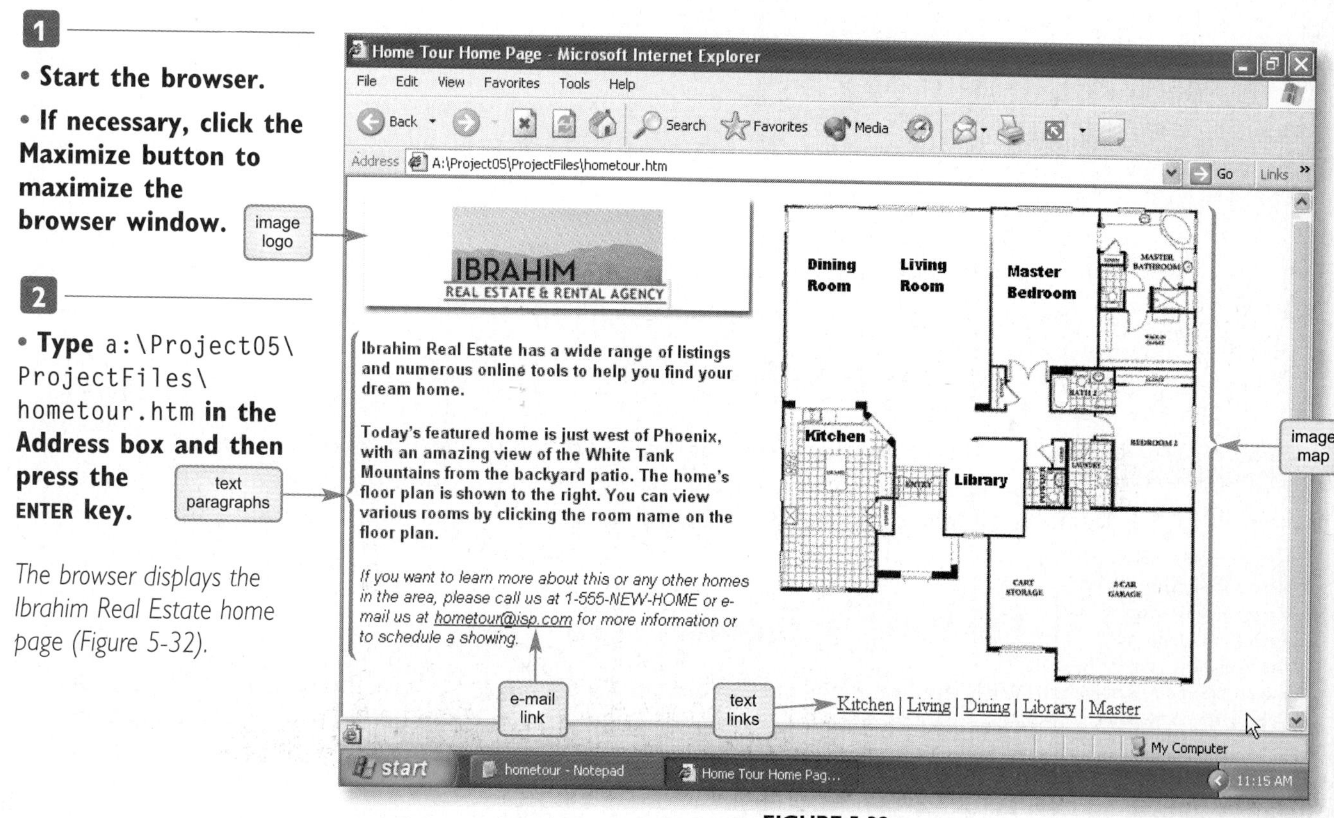

FIGURE 5-32

3 **Click the Print button on the Standard Buttons toolbar.**

The home page prints (Figure 5-33).

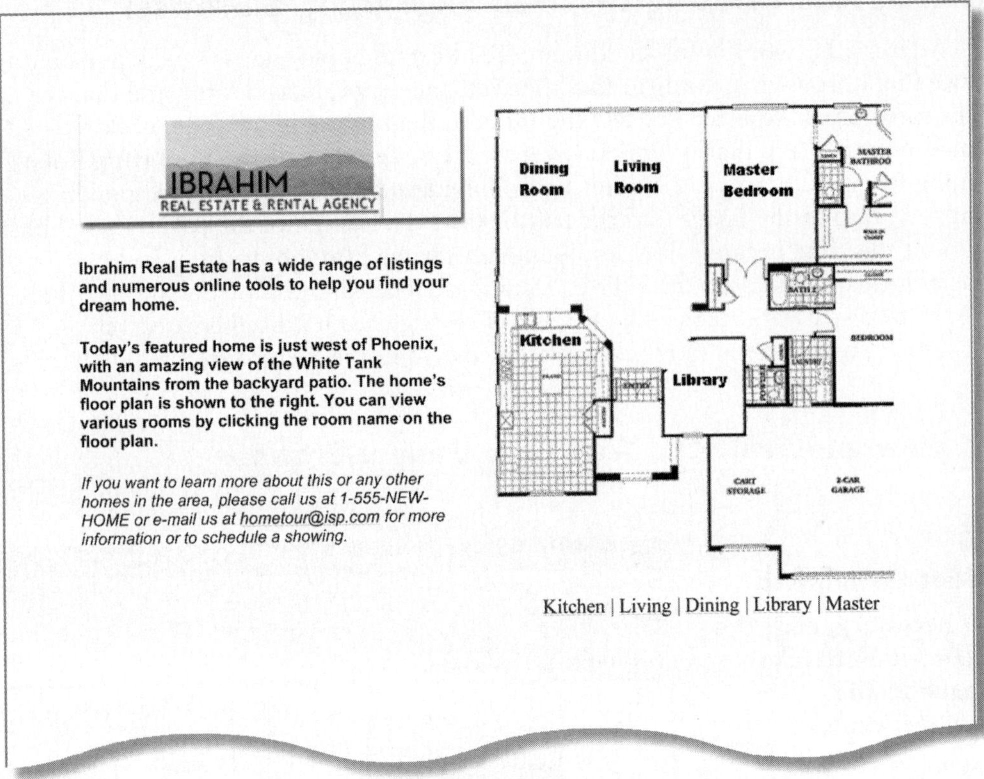

FIGURE 5-33

> *More About*
>
> **Accessibility**
>
> Developers should utilize suggestions from accessibility guidelines when developing Web pages. It is important that the Web page content is understandable and navigable. The W3C gives some good suggestions for Web site accessibility issues that should be reviewed. For more information about accessibility, visit the HTML More About Web page (scsite.com/html3e/more.htm) and then click Accessibility.

If you find any errors, double-check the spelling, symbols, and quotation marks in the HTML code. After the changes are made, you then can save the HTML file again and redisplay the Web page using the Refresh button in your browser.

Creating a Second Web Page

With the home page complete, the next step is to create the Kitchen Web page. As shown in Figure 5-1 on page HTM 195, each room represented in the image map (Kitchen, Living, Dining, Library, and Master) has a separate Web page that contains text that describes the room, together with a picture of the room. The individual room Web pages also have text links to the home page, as well as to all other Web pages in the Web site. This section discusses how to create the Kitchen Web page (kitchen.htm), as shown in Figure 5-34. The other pages in the Web site (living.htm, dining.htm, library.htm, and master.htm) are completed and stored on the HTML Data Disk.

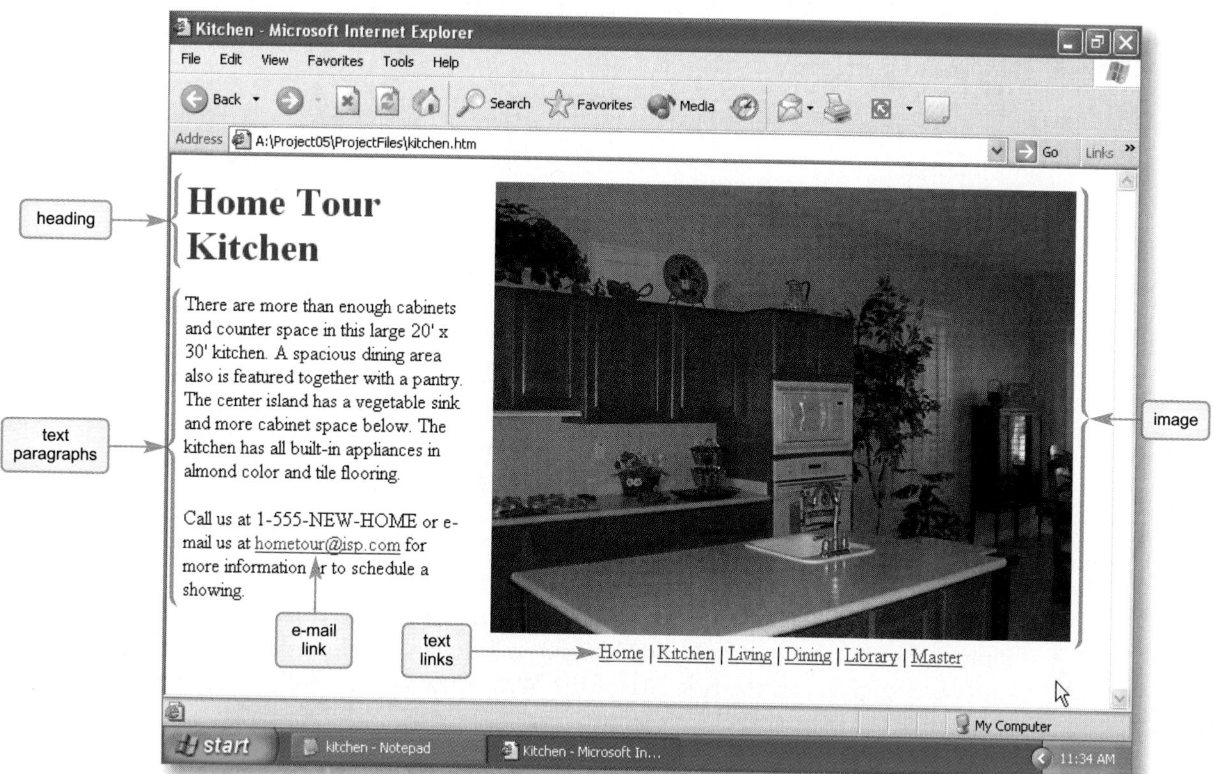

FIGURE 5-34

The easiest way to start creating the Kitchen Web page is to reuse code from the home page, wherever possible. For example, the first nine lines of HTML code in the home page, which are used to describe the Web page structure, can be used in the Kitchen Web page. The following steps illustrate how to copy the first nine lines of HTML code from the HTML file for the home page and then paste the lines in the HTML file for the Kitchen Web page.

To Copy and Paste HTML Code to a New File

1. **Click the Notepad button on the taskbar.**
2. **When the hometour.htm file is displayed in the Notepad window, click immediately to the left of the < in the <!DOCTYPE html tag on line 1. Drag through the <body link="navy" alink="navy" vlink="navy"> tag on line 9 to highlight lines 1 through 9.**
3. **Press CTRL+C to copy the selected lines to the Clipboard.**
4. **Click File on the menu bar and then click New.**
5. **Press CTRL+V to paste the contents of the Clipboard into a new file.**

The HTML code is displayed in the new file (Figure 5-35 on the next page).

Untitled - Notepad

File Edit Format View Help

```
<!DOCTYPE html
   PUBLIC "-//W3C//DTD XHTML 1.0 Transitional//EN"
   "http://www.w3.org/TR/xhtml1/DTD/xhtml1-transitional.dtd">

<html>
<head>
<title>Home Tour Home Page</title>
</head>
<body link="navy" alink="navy" vlink="navy">
```

copied lines of HTML code

link colors changed from default

FIGURE 5-35

Changing the Title

The next step is to edit the pasted code to change the title of the Web page. The title of the Web page should be changed to Kitchen, so the title of the current Web page is displayed on the title bar of the Web browser. The following steps show how to change the title of the Web page.

To Change the Title

1. **Highlight the words, Home Tour Home Page, between the <title> and </title> tags on line 7. Type** `Kitchen` **as the title to delete the words, Home Tour Home Page, and replace them with the word Kitchen.**
2. **Click immediately to the right of the vlink="navy"> tag on line 9 and then press the ENTER key twice.**
3. **Type** `</body>` **and then press the ENTER key.**
4. **Type** `</html>` **and then click line 11.**

The HTML code is displayed (Figure 5-36) and the insertion point is on line 11.

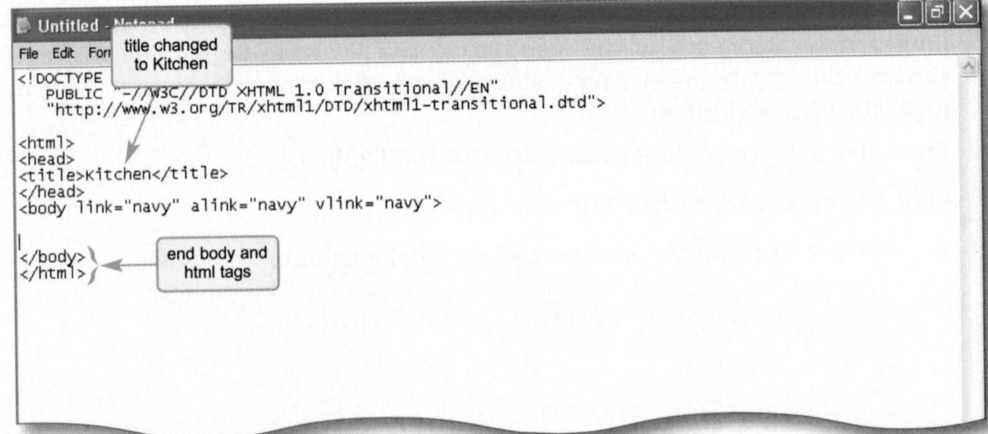

FIGURE 5-36

Adding a Heading and Paragraphs of Text

The next step is to add a table with two rows and two columns to the Kitchen Web page. As shown in Figure 5-34 on page HTM 227, the first cell of the first row contains a heading and paragraphs of text that describe the room. The second cell of the first row contains an image (kitchen.jpg). In the second row, the first cell is blank, while the second cell contains a horizontal menu bar with text links to all other room Web pages and the home page.

Table 5-9 lists the HTML code used to create the first row of the table and enter the heading to identify the Web page.

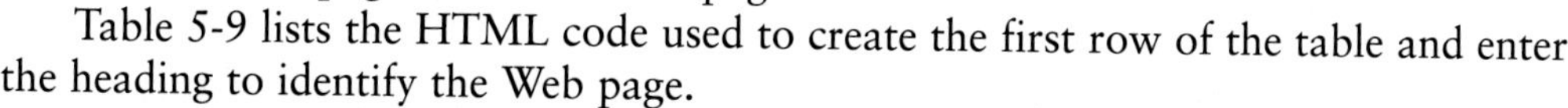

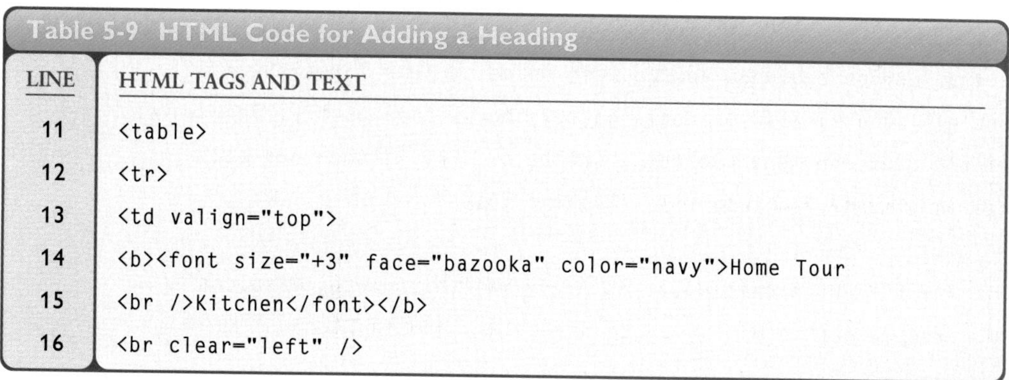

Table 5-9 HTML Code for Adding a Heading

LINE	HTML TAGS AND TEXT
11	`<table>`
12	`<tr>`
13	`<td valign="top">`
14	`<b><font size="+3" face="bazooka" color="navy">Home Tour`
15	` Kitchen</font></b>`
16	`<br clear="left" />`

The following steps illustrate how to enter HTML code to create a table and then add a heading in the first cell of the first row.

To Add a Heading

1. **If necessary, click line 11.**
2. **Enter the HTML code shown in Table 5-9 and then press the ENTER key.**

The HTML code is displayed (Figure 5-37) and the insertion point is on line 17.

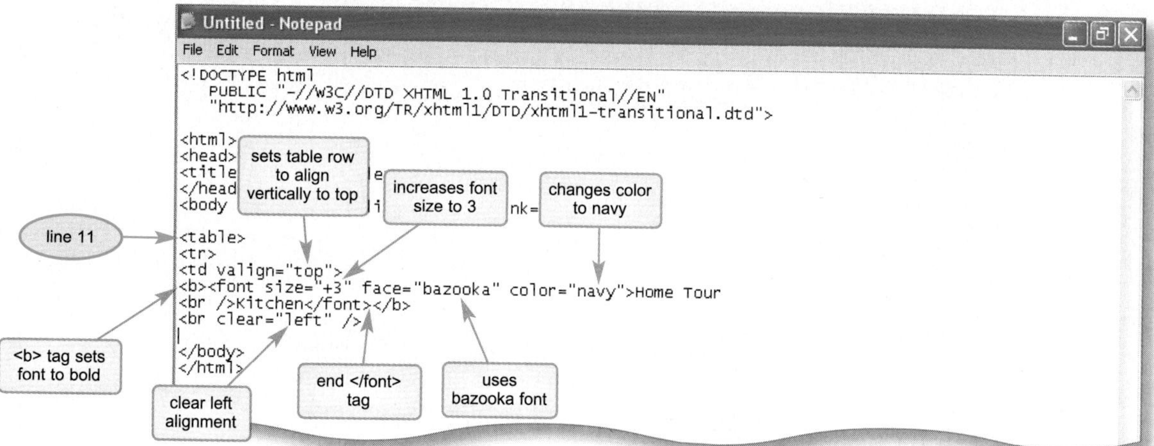

FIGURE 5-37

On line 13, the valign="top" attribute sets the vertical alignment of the text to the top of the data cell. Without this setting, the text would be vertically aligned in the center of the cell, which is the default. Lines 14 and 15 create a heading that has the same font face and color as headings on all other Web pages in the Ibrahim Real Estate Web site. Line 16 clears the image alignment on the left.

Next, two paragraphs of text must be added below the heading in the first row of the table. Table 5-10 shows the HTML code used to add paragraphs of text to the Kitchen Web page.

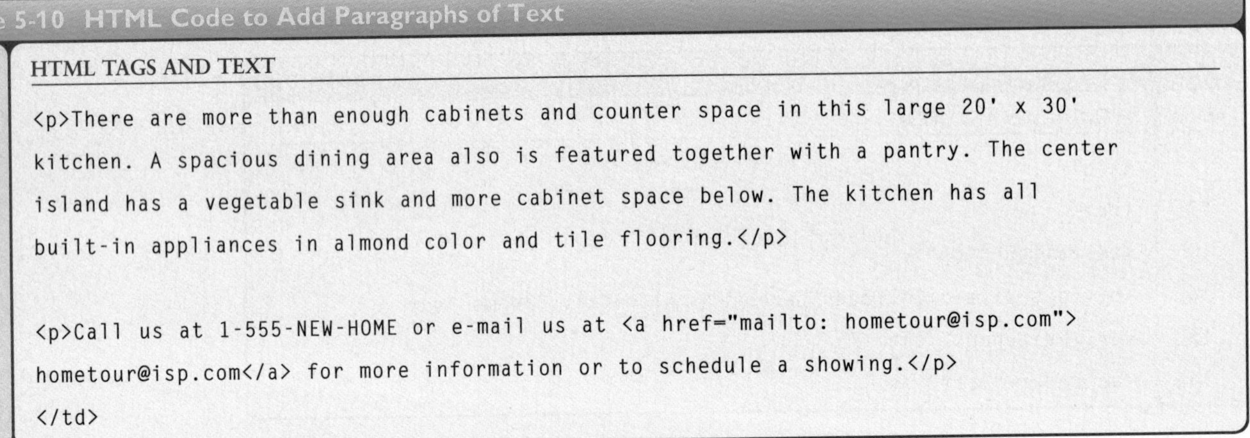

Table 5-10 HTML Code to Add Paragraphs of Text

LINE	HTML TAGS AND TEXT
17	`<p>There are more than enough cabinets and counter space in this large 20' x 30'`
18	`kitchen. A spacious dining area also is featured together with a pantry. The center`
19	`island has a vegetable sink and more cabinet space below. The kitchen has all`
20	`built-in appliances in almond color and tile flooring.</p>`
21	
22	`<p>Call us at 1-555-NEW-HOME or e-mail us at <a href="mailto: hometour@isp.com">`
23	`hometour@isp.com</a> for more information or to schedule a showing.</p>`
24	`</td>`

The following steps show how to add paragraphs of text.

To Add Paragraphs of Text

1 **If necessary, click line 17.**

2 **Enter the HTML code shown in Table 5-10 and then press the ENTER key twice.**

The HTML code is displayed (Figure 5-38) and the insertion point is on line 26.

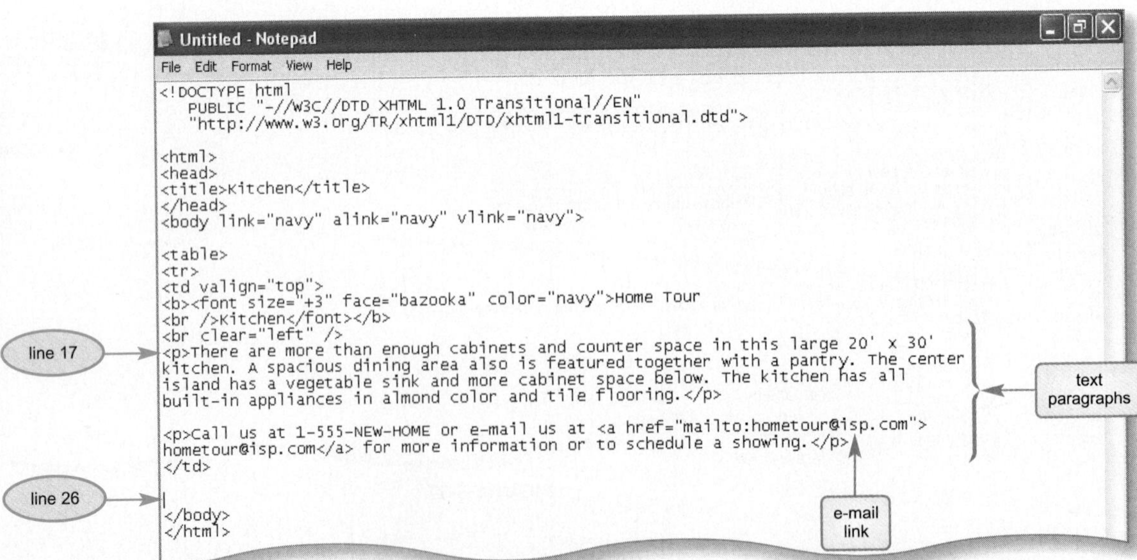

FIGURE 5-38

Adding an Image

The next step in creating the Kitchen Web page is to create a second table data cell in the first row and then add the photo image of the kitchen, as shown in Figure 5-34 on page HTM 227. The image file, kitchen.jpg, is stored on the HTML Data Disk. Table 5-11 shows the HTML code to add the photo image of the kitchen to the Kitchen Web page.

Table 5-11 HTML Code for Adding an Image

LINE	HTML TAGS AND TEXT
26	`<td>`
27	`<img src="kitchen.jpg" hspace="20" border="0" align="left" alt="Kitchen" width="480"`
28	`height="360" />`
29	`</td>`
30	`</tr>`

Line 26 creates the second table data cell in the first row of the table, to which the image is added in line 27. The src attribute specifies that the page should display the image, kitchen.jpg, while the hspace="20" attribute inserts a horizontal space of 20 pixels to provide space between the image and the text. The border="0" attribute makes the image borderless and the align="left" attribute aligns the image to the left of the table data cell. The alt attribute displays alternate text that gives the Web page visitor information about the image as the image is being loaded. The following steps show how to enter the tags and text given in Table 5-11 to add an image to the Kitchen Web page.

To Add an Image

1

• **If necessary, click line 26.**

2

• **Enter the HTML code shown in Table 5-11 and then press the ENTER key twice.**

The HTML code is displayed (Figure 5-39) and the insertion point is on line 32.

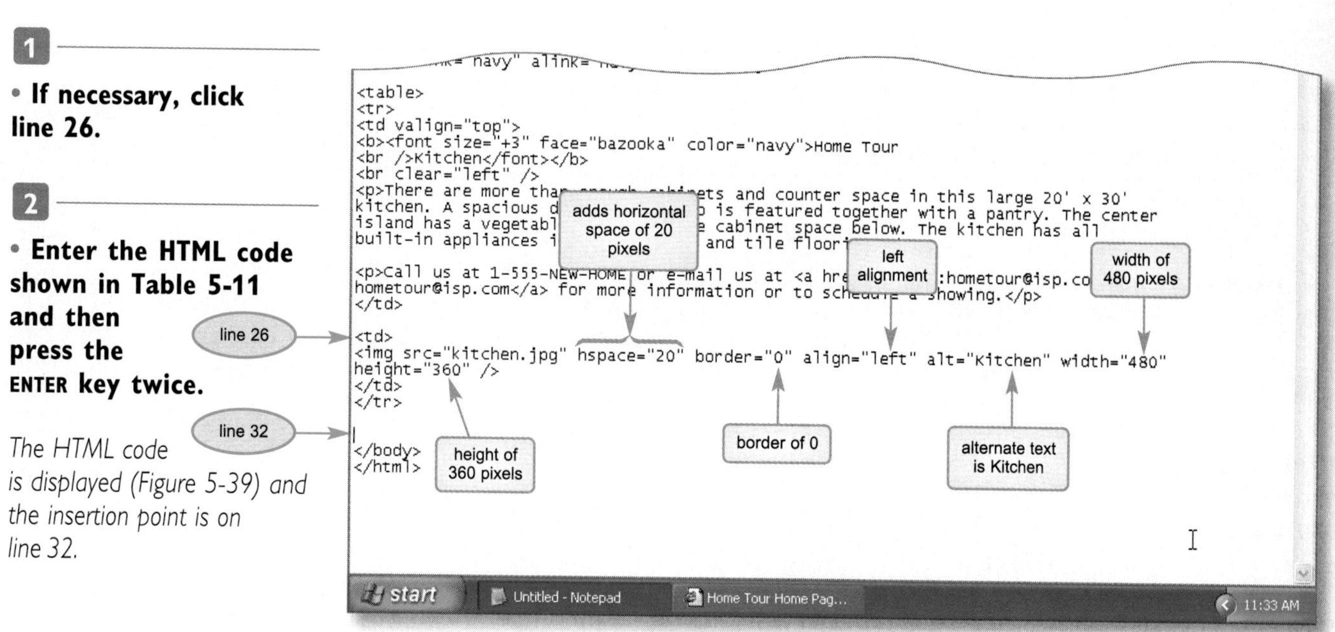

FIGURE 5-39

The HTML code for the first row of the Kitchen Web page is complete. The Kitchen Web page includes a table with text in the first cell of the first row and the photo image of the kitchen in the second cell of the first row. The image is left-aligned and adequate spacing is included between the text and the image by using the hspace="20" attribute. As the Web page loads, the alternate text, Kitchen, is displayed.

Creating a Horizontal Menu Bar

As shown in Figure 5-34 on page HTM 227, the Kitchen Web page includes a horizontal menu bar of text links, which allow a user to navigate to all of the other pages in the Web site. The horizontal menu bar is aligned below the image of the kitchen. Table 5-12 shows the HTML code used to create a horizontal menu bar on the Kitchen Web page.

Table 5-12 HTML Code for Creating a Horizontal Menu Bar

LINE	HTML TAGS AND TEXT
32	`<tr>`
33	`<td> </td>`
34	`<td align="center"><a href="hometour.htm">Home</a> |`
35	`<a href="kitchen.htm">Kitchen</a> |`
36	`<a href="living.htm">Living</a> |`
37	`<a href="dining.htm">Dining</a> |`
38	`<a href="library.htm">Library</a> |`
39	`<a href="master.htm">Master</a>`
40	`</td>`
41	`</tr>`
42	`</table>`

The following steps show how to enter the code to create the horizontal menu bar.

To Create a Horizontal Menu Bar

1

• **If necessary, click line 32.**

2

• **Enter the HTML code shown in Table 5-12 as the tags.**

The HTML code is displayed (Figure 5-40) and the insertion point is on line 42.

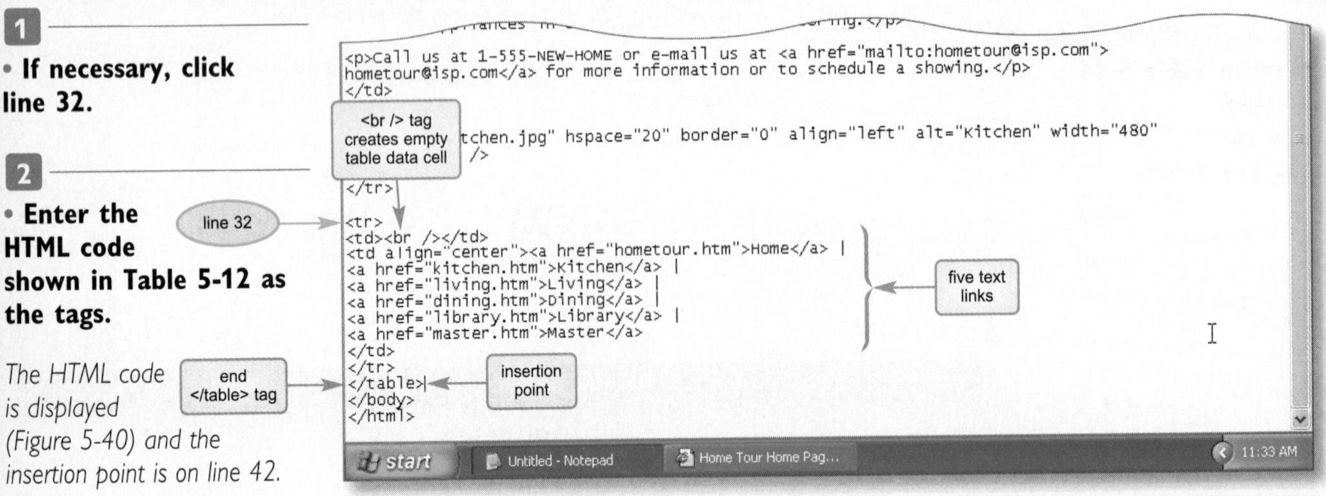

FIGURE 5-40

Line 32 starts the second row of the table on the Kitchen Web page. On line 34, the align="center" attribute center-aligns the horizontal menu bar within the table data cell. Lines 34 through 39 establish six text links. The first link links to the home page. The second and subsequent links take the Web site visitor to the Web pages, kitchen.htm, living.htm, dining.htm, library.htm, and master.htm, which are stored on the HTML Data Disk.

The HTML code for the Kitchen Web page is complete. With the HTML code for the Kitchen Web page complete, the file should be saved and a copy should be printed as a reference. The following steps show how to save and print the HTML file.

More About

Graphics Software

Many graphics tools are available for advanced image creation and maintenance. One of the more popular tools is Adobe Photoshop. Photoshop allows you to create images that can be used as image maps or crop sections out of existing images. For more information about accessibility, visit the HTML More About Web page (scsite.com/html3e/more.htm) and then click Graphics Software.

To Save and Print the HTML File

1. **With a floppy disk in drive A, click File on the menu bar and then click Save As. Type** `kitchen.htm` **in the File name text box.**
2. **If necessary, click 3½ Floppy (A:) in the Save in list. Click the Project05 folder and then double-click the ProjectFiles folder in the list of available folders. Click the Save button in the Save As dialog box.**
3. **Click File on the menu bar and then click Print on the File menu.**

Notepad prints the HTML file (Figure 5-41). Notepad saves the HTML file in the Project05\ProjectFiles folder on the floppy disk in drive A using the file name, kitchen.htm.

```
<!DOCTYPE html
   PUBLIC "-//W3C//DTD XHTML 1.0 Transitional//EN"
   "http://www.w3.org/TR/xhtml1/DTD/xhtml1-transitional.dtd">

<html>
<head>
<title>Kitchen</title>
</head>
<body link="navy" alink="navy" vlink="navy">

<table>
<tr>
<td valign="top">
<b><font size="+3" face="bazooka" color="navy">Home Tour
<br />Kitchen</font></b>
<br clear="left" />
<p>There are more than enough cabinets and counter space in this large 20' x 30'
kitchen. A spacious dining area also is featured together with a pantry. The center
island has a vegetable sink and more cabinet space below. The kitchen has all
built-in appliances in almond color and tile flooring.</p>

<p>Call us at 1-555-NEW-HOME or e-mail us at <a href="mailto:hometour@isp.com">
hometour@isp.com</a> for more information or to schedule a showing.</p>
</td>

<td>
<img src="kitchen.jpg" hspace="20" border="0" align="left" alt="Kitchen" width="480" height="360"
/>
</td>
</tr>

<tr>
<td><br /></td>
<td align="center"><a href="hometour.htm">Home</a> |
<a href="kitchen.htm">Kitchen</a> |
<a href="living.htm">Living</a> |
<a href="dining.htm">Dining</a> |
<a href="library.htm">Library</a> |
<a href="master.htm">Master</a>
</td>
</tr>
</table>
</body>
</html>
```

FIGURE 5-41

Viewing and Printing the Web Page

After the HTML file for the Kitchen Web page is saved, it should be viewed in a browser to confirm that the Web page appears as desired and that the links function as expected. The following steps show how to view and print the Web page.

To View and Print the Web Page

1

- **Click the Internet Explorer button on the taskbar.**

2

- **Click the Kitchen area on the floor plan image map.**

The browser displays the Kitchen Web page (Figure 5-42).

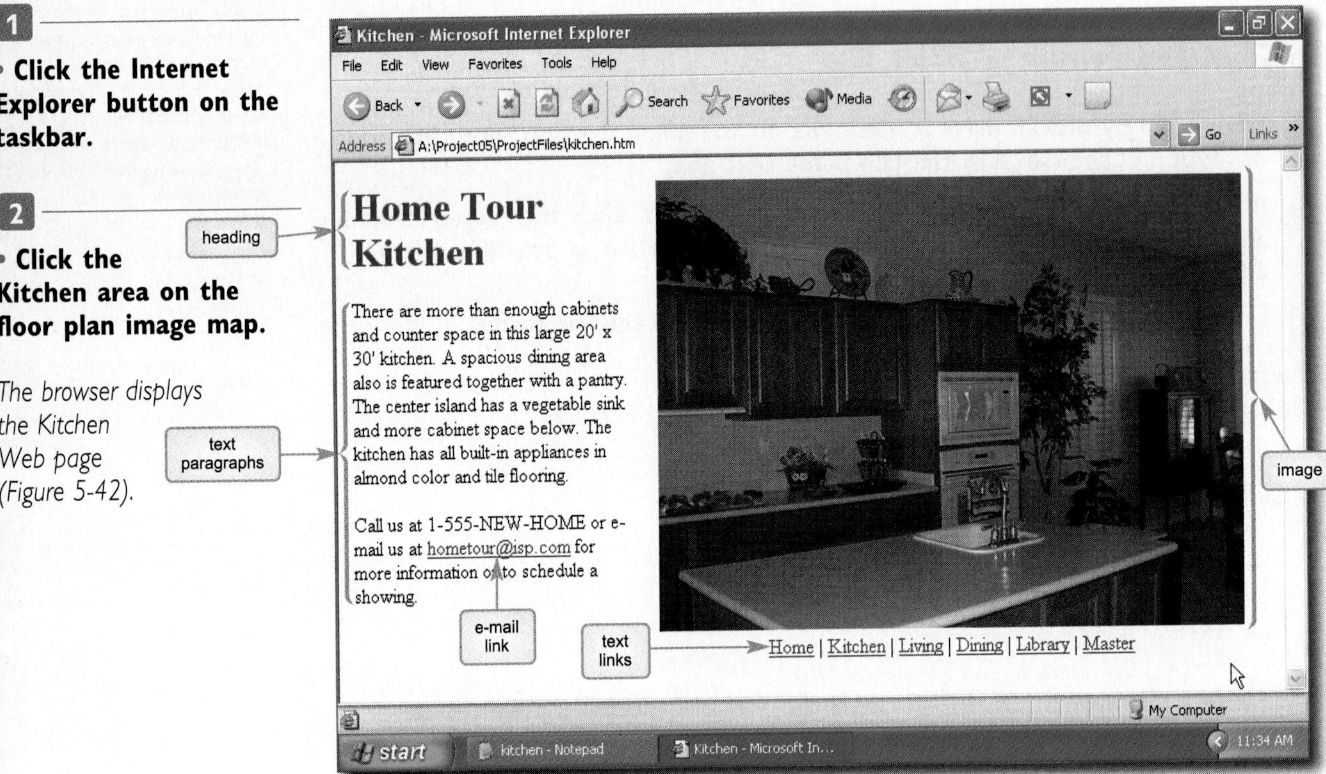

FIGURE 5-42

3

- **Click the Print button on the Standard Buttons toolbar.**

The Kitchen Web page prints (Figure 5-43).

Home Tour Kitchen

There are more than enough cabinets and counter space in this large 20' x 30' kitchen. A spacious dining area also is featured together with a pantry. The center island has a vegetable sink and more cabinet space below. The kitchen has all built-in appliances in almond color and tile flooring.

Call us at 1-555-NEW-HOME or e-mail us at hometour@isp.com for more information or to schedule a showing.

Home | Kitchen | Living | Dining | Library | Master

FIGURE 5-43

All six Web pages for the Ibrahim Real Estate Web site now are complete. In this project, two new Web pages (hometour.htm and kitchen.htm) were created and links were added to four existing Web pages (living.htm, dining.htm, library.htm, and master.htm).

More About

Testing

Especially with image maps, it is important to test the Web page thoroughly in the browser. If one incorrect number is typed as an x- or y-coordinate, the entire image map can be wrong as a result. Make sure that the clickable area is exactly where you want it to be by testing.

Testing the Links

The next step is to test the links on the various pages in the Web site to verify that each link connects to the appropriate Web page. If possible, view all of the Web pages in more than one browser type or version to ensure that the Web pages display correctly in different browsers. Links must be tested from the image map on the home page, as well as from the horizontal menu bar on each of the Web pages. The following steps show how to test the links.

To Test the Links

1. **Click the Home link on the Kitchen Web page.**
2. **Click the Master Bedroom area on the image map on the home page.**
3. **Click the Living link on the Master Bedroom Web page.**
4. **Click the Library link on the Living Room Web page.**
5. **Click the Dining link on the Library Web page.**

The Dining Room Web page displays (Figure 5-44).

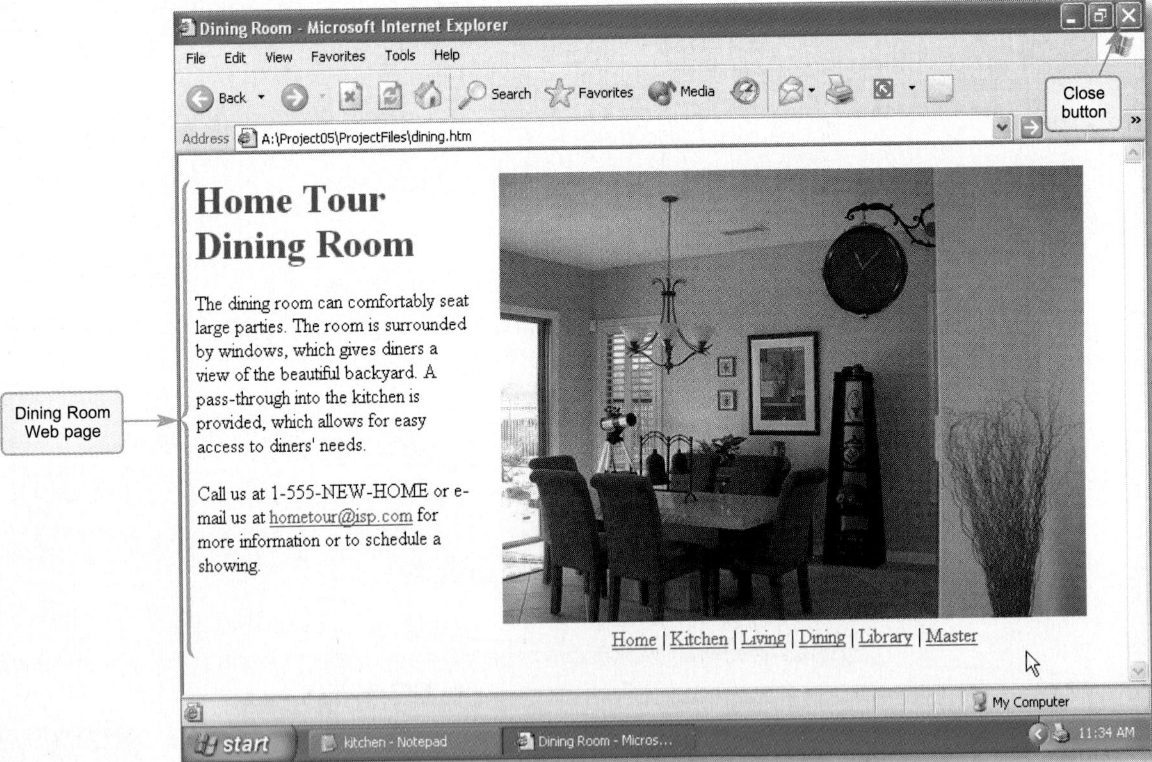

FIGURE 5-44

If any of the links do not work correctly, return to Notepad to modify the HTML code, save the changes, and then retest the links in the browser. After completing the project, quit Notepad and the browser. The following steps show how to quit Notepad and a browser.

To Quit Notepad and a Browser

1. **Click the Close button on the browser title bar.**
2. **Click the Close button on the Notepad window title bar.**

Both the browser and Notepad windows close, and the Windows desktop is displayed.

Project Summary

In this project, you used Notepad to create two HTML files, hometour.htm and kitchen.htm. You learned the four steps to implement an image map, including how to distinguish between appropriate and inappropriate images for image maps. After learning about the Paint program, you learned to use Paint to map the coordinates of an image. After explaining how to create a borderless table on the home page, the project covered how to insert an image with the usemap attribute for use as an image map. You then learned the HTML tags and attributes used to code an image map, including the <map> </map> tags to start and end a map and the <area> tag to indicate the shape, coordinates, and URL for a mapped area. You also learned to create a horizontal menu bar with links that correspond to the links in the image map and to change the link colors to appear always in navy. Finally, you tested the links and printed the HTML code and the Web pages.

What You Should Know

Having completed this project, you should be able to perform the tasks listed below. The tasks are listed in the same order they were presented in this project.

1. Start Paint (HTM 207)
2. Open an Image File in Paint (HTM 209)
3. Locate X- and Y-Coordinates of an Image (HTM 211)
4. Start Notepad and Enter Initial HTML Tags (HTM 213)
5. Create a Table (HTM 215)
6. Insert an Image in a Table (HTM 216)
7. Add Text to a Table Cell (HTM 217)
8. Add an Image to Use as an Image Map (HTM 218)
9. Create a Horizontal Menu Bar with Text Links (HTM 220)
10. Create an Image Map (HTM 222)
11. Change Link Colors (HTM 223)
12. Save and Print the HTML File (HTM 224, 233)
13. View and Print the Web Page Using a Browser (HTM 225)
14. Copy and Paste HTML Code to a New File (HTM 227)
15. Change the Title (HTM 228)
16. Add a Heading (HTM 229)
17. Add Paragraphs of Text (HTM 230)
18. Add an Image (HTM 231)
19. Create a Horizontal Menu Bar (HTM 232)
20. View and Print the Web Page (HTM 234)
21. Test the Links (HTM 236)
22. Quit Notepad and a Browser (HTM 237)

Learn It Online

Instructions: To complete the Learn It Online exercises, start your browser, click the Address bar, and then enter the Web address `scsite.com/html3e/learn`. When the HTML Learn It Online page is displayed, follow the instructions in the exercises below. Each exercise has instructions for printing your results, either for your own records or for submission to your instructor.

1 Project Reinforcement TF, MC, and SA

Below HTML Project 5, click the Project Reinforcement link. Print the quiz by clicking Print on the File menu for each page. Answer each question.

2 Flash Cards

Below HTML Project 5, click the Flash Cards link and read the instructions. Type 20 (or a number specified by your instructor) in the Number of playing cards text box, type your name in the Enter your Name text box, and then click the Flip Card button. When the flash card is displayed, read the question and then click the ANSWER box arrow to select an answer. Flip through Flash Cards. If your score is 15 (75%) correct or greater, click Print on the File menu to print your results. If your score is less than 15 (75%) correct, then redo this exercise by clicking the Replay button.

3 Practice Test

Below HTML Project 5, click the Practice Test link. Answer each question, enter your first and last name at the bottom of the page, and then click the Grade Test button. When the graded practice test is displayed on your screen, click Print on the File menu to print a hard copy. Continue to take practice tests until you score 80% or better.

4 Who Wants To Be a Computer Genius?

Below HTML Project 5, click the Computer Genius link. Read the instructions, enter your first and last name at the bottom of the page, and then click the PLAY button. When your score is displayed, click the PRINT RESULTS link to print a hard copy.

5 Wheel of Terms

Below HTML Project 5, click the Wheel of Terms link. Read the instructions, and then enter your first and last name and your school name. Click the PLAY button. When your score is displayed, right-click the score and then click Print on the shortcut menu to print a hard copy.

6 Crossword Puzzle Challenge

Below HTML Project 5, click the Crossword Puzzle Challenge link. Read the instructions, and then enter your first and last name. Click the submit button. Work the crossword puzzle. When you are finished, click the Submit button. When the crossword puzzle is redisplayed, click the Print Puzzle button to print a hard copy.

7 Tips and Tricks

Below HTML Project 5, click the Tips and Tricks link. Click a topic that pertains to Project 5. Right-click the information and then click Print on the shortcut menu. Construct a brief example of what the information relates to in HTML to confirm you understand how to use the tip or trick.

8 Newsgroups

Below HTML Project 5, click the Newsgroups link. Click a topic that pertains to Project 5. Print three comments.

9 Expanding Your Horizons

Below HTML Project 5, click the Expanding Your Horizons link. Click a topic that pertains to Project 5. Print the information. Construct a brief example of what the information relates to in HTML to confirm you understand the contents of the article.

10 Search Sleuth

Below HTML Project 5, click the Search Sleuth link. To search for a term that pertains to this project, select a term below the Project 5 title and then use the Google search engine at google.com (or any major search engine) to display and print two Web pages that present information on the term.

11 Online Help I

Below HTML Project 5, click the Online Help I link. Follow the instructions on the page to access Web pages that provide additional help on project topics. Hand in any printed information to your instructor.

12 Online Help II

Below HTML Project 5, click the Online Help II link. Follow the instructions on the page to access Web pages that provide additional help on project topics. Hand in any printed information to your instructor.

Apply Your Knowledge

1 Editing the Apply Your Knowledge Web Page

Instructions: Start Paint, Notepad, and a browser. Using Notepad, open the file, apply5-1.htm, from the Project05\AYK folder on the HTML Data Disk. See the inside back cover of this book for instructions for downloading the HTML Data Disk or see your instructor for information about accessing the files in this book. The apply5-1.htm file is a partially completed HTML file that contains errors. Figure 5-45 shows the Apply Your Knowledge Web page as it should appear in your browser after the errors are corrected. Perform the following steps using a computer:

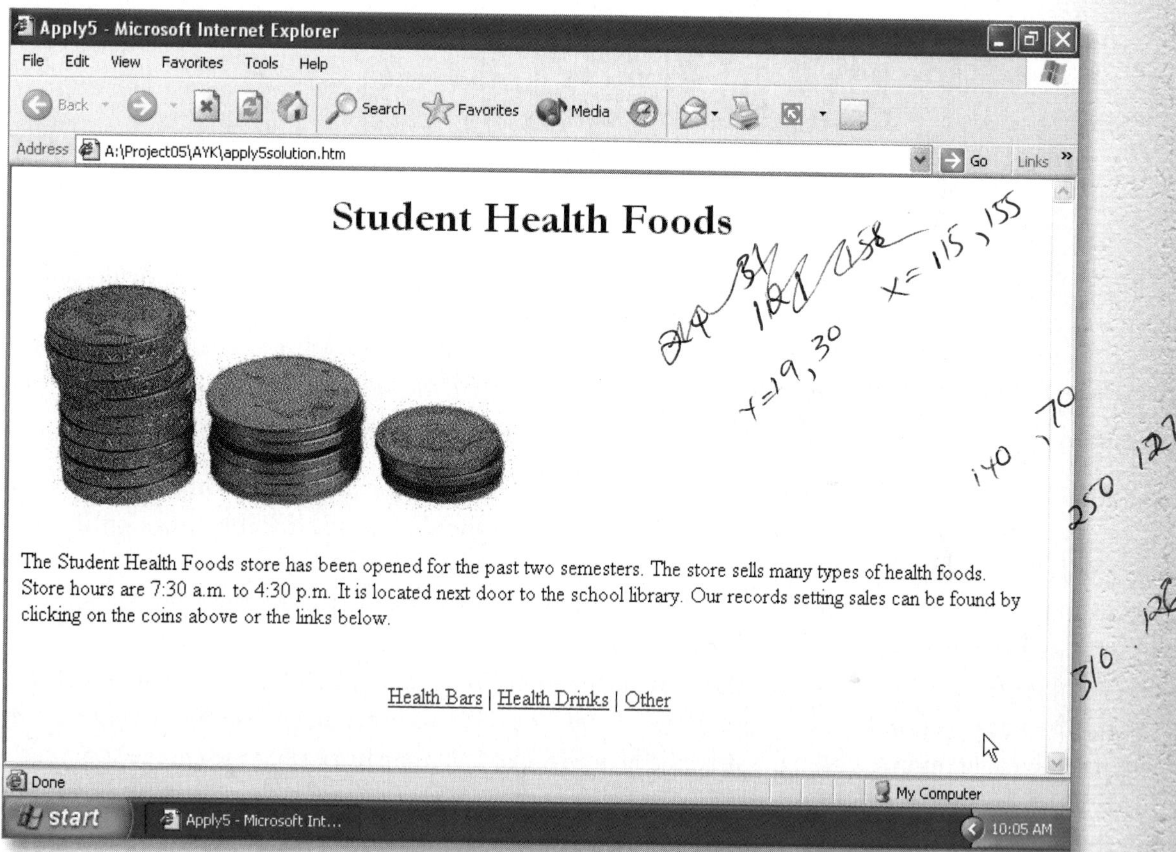

FIGURE 5-45

1. Enter the URL, `a:\Project05\AYK\apply5-1.htm`, to view the Web page in your browser.
2. Examine the HTML file and its appearance as a Web page in the browser.
3. Using Paint, open the file, coins.gif, from the Project05\AYK folder on the HTML Data Disk. Determine the x- and y-coordinates necessary to create three clickable areas on the coin image, one for each stack of coins. The first stack of coins should be a rectangular shape, the second stack should be a polygon, and the third stack of coins should be a circle.
4. Add HTML code to the apply5-1.htm file to create an image map that links each clickable area on the coin image to a different Web page of your choice. The rectangular shape should link to a Web page with information about health bars, the polygon shape should link to a Web page with information about health drinks, and the circle shape should link to a Web page with information about other health food products.

(continued)

Apply Your Knowledge

Editing the Apply Your Knowledge Web Page *(continued)*

5. Save the revised file in the Project05\AYK folder on the HTML Data Disk using the file name, apply5-1solution.htm.
6. Print the revised HTML file.
7. Enter the URL, `a:\Project05\AYK\apply5-1solution.htm`, to view the Web page in your browser.
8. Print the Web page.
9. Write your name on both printouts and hand them in to your instructor.

1 Creating a Money Map

Problem: Your Economics professor has asked each student to create a Web site that provides information on where tax dollars typically are spent. You decide to create a Web page similar to the Web page in Figure 5-46 on the next page, with the file, moneywheel.gif, as an image map that links to three government Web sites with information on taxes, housing, and education. The file, moneywheel.gif, is stored on the HTML Data Disk.

Instructions: Start Paint and Notepad. Perform the following steps using a computer:

1. Using Paint, open the file, moneywheel.gif, from the Project05\IntheLab folder on the HTML Data Disk.
2. Determine the x- and y-coordinates necessary to create three circular clickable areas on the coin image, one for each wheel. (Recall that for a circular map area, you use the center point and the radius as the coordinates. The radius can be calculated by subtracting the x-axis value of the center point from the x-axis value of the circle's right border.) Write down those coordinates for later use.
3. Using Notepad, create a new HTML file with the title, [Your name] Lab 5-1, in the main heading section.
4. Begin the body section by adding the Where Does Your $$$ Go? heading as shown in Figure 5-46.
5. Insert the image, moneywheel.gif, after the heading. Use the usemap attribute usemap="#money" in the <img> tag.
6. Enter the <map> </map> tags required to create the image map named money.
7. Enter the <area> tags required to define three circular clickable areas on the image, moneywheel.gif. Use the x- and y-coordinates determined in Step 2 and set the href attribute to use the URLs listed in Table 5-13.

FIGURE 5-46

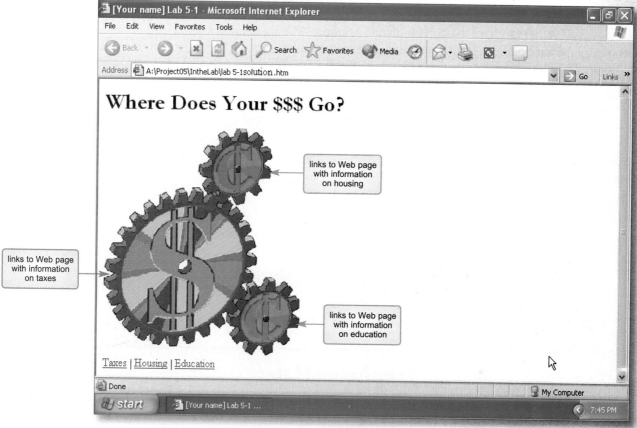

8. Add three text links at the bottom of the Web page as shown in Figure 5-46, using Table 5-13 for link names and URLs.
9. Save the HTML file in the Project05\IntheLab folder on the HTML Data Disk using the file name, lab5-1solution.htm. Print the HTML file.
10. Open the file, lab 5-1solution.htm, in your browser and test the image map and text links to verify they link to the correct Web pages.
11. Print the main Web page and the three linked Web pages.
12. Write your name on the printouts and hand them in to your instructor.

Table 5-13 Image Map Coordinates, URLs, and Text Links

TEXT LINK	IMAGE MAP COORDINATES	URLS
Taxes	123,199,81	http://ustreas.gov
Housing	199,60,45	http://hud.gov
Education	245,274,41	http://ed.gov

2 Mapping Hats

Problem: You decide to use your image mapping skills to create a Web page that describes the many hats you wear in life — for family, fun, and work. You plan to create a Web page similar to the one shown in Figure 5-47 on the next page, with the file, hats.gif, as an image map that links to three Web sites with information on family, fun, and work. The file, hats.gif, is stored on the HTML Data Disk.

Instructions: Start Paint and Notepad. Perform the following steps using a computer:

1. Using Paint, open the file, hats.gif, from the Project05\IntheLab folder on the HTML Data Disk.
2. Each hat has a distinct shape. Using Paint, determine the x- and y-coordinates necessary to create three clickable areas on the hat image, using a rectangle for the first hat, a polygon for the second hat, and a circle for the third hat. Write down those coordinates for later use.
3. Using Notepad, create a new HTML file with the title, [Your name] Lab 5-2, in the main heading section.
4. Begin the body section by adding the Your Many Hats heading as shown in Figure 5-47.
5. Insert the image, hats.gif, after the heading. Use the usemap attribute usemap="#hats" in the <img> tag.

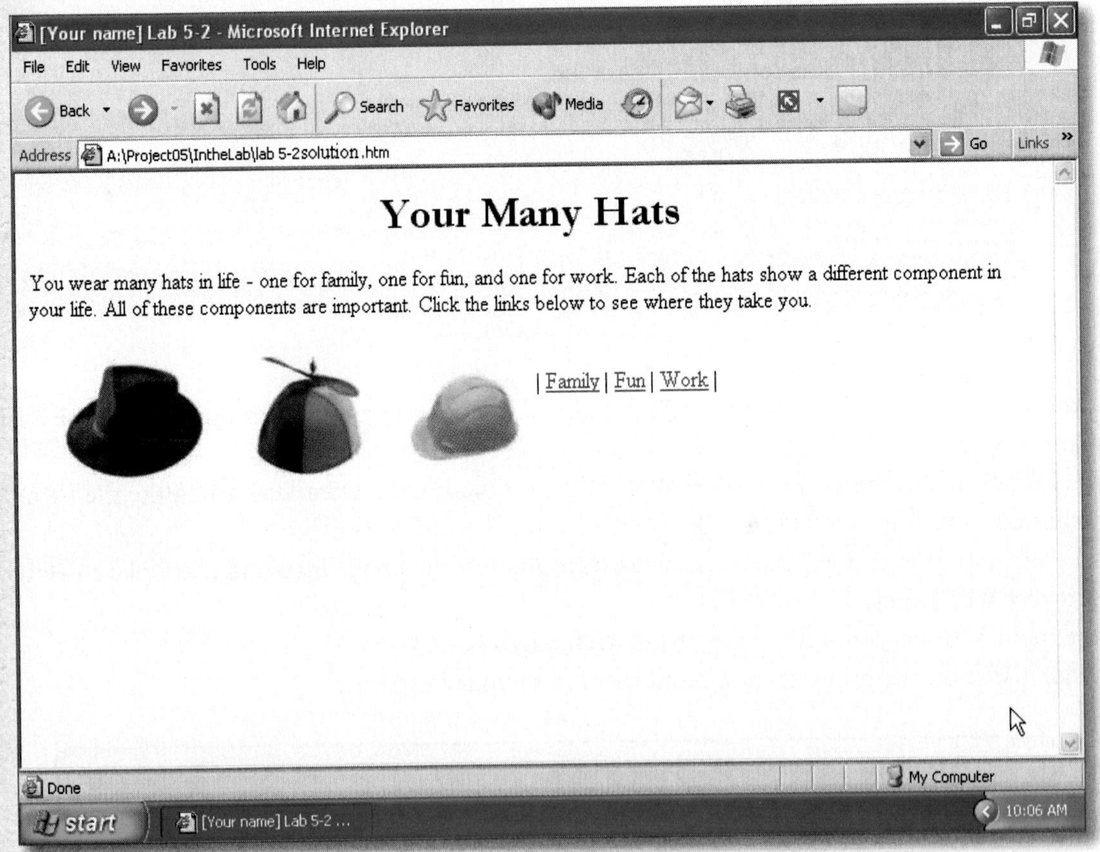

FIGURE 5-47

6. Enter the <map> </map> tags required to create the image map named hats.
7. Enter the <area> tags required to define three clickable areas on the image, hats.gif. Use the x- and y-coordinates determined in Step 2 and set the href attribute to use the URLs listed in Table 5-14.

Table 5-14 Image Map Coordinates, URLs, and Text Links

TEXT LINK	IMAGE MAP COORDINATES	URLS
Family	40,16,117,85	http://familyfun.go.com
Fun	175,6,247,33,250,74,206,97,168,75	http://disney.com
Work	335,53,30	http://www.dol.gov

8. Save the HTML file in the Project05\IntheLab folder using the file name, lab5-2solution.htm. Print the HTML file.
9. Open the file, lab 5-2solution.htm, in your browser and test the image map and text links to verify they link to the correct Web pages.
10. Print the main Web page and the three linked Web pages.
11. Write your name on the printouts and hand them in to your instructor.

3 Creating a Government Services Web Page

Problem: Your manager at the City Hall has asked you to create a Web page that provides easy access to important Web sites within your state and two other states of your choice. You plan to create a Web page similar to the one shown in Figure 5-48, with the file, states_good.gif, as an image map that links to three government Web sites. The file, states_good.gif, is stored on the HTML Data Disk. Browse the Web to find government Web sites that are common throughout three different states (e.g., Department of Education, tax information, and state departments) and then use these links in the image map.

Instructions: Start Paint and Notepad. Perform the following tasks using a computer:

1. Using Paint, open the file, states_good.gif, from the Project05\IntheLab folder on the HTML Data Disk.
2. Using Paint, determine the x- and y-coordinates necessary to create three clickable areas on the map image, using polygon shapes for each area. Write down those coordinates for later use.
3. Using Notepad, create a new HTML file with the title, [Your name] Lab 5-3, in the main heading section.
4. Begin the body section by adding the Important State Links heading as shown in Figure 5-48.
5. Insert the image, states_good.gif, after the heading. Use the usemap attribute usemap="#states" in the <img> tag.
6. Enter the <map> </map> tags required to create the image map named states.

(continued)

Creating a Government Services Web Page *(continued)*

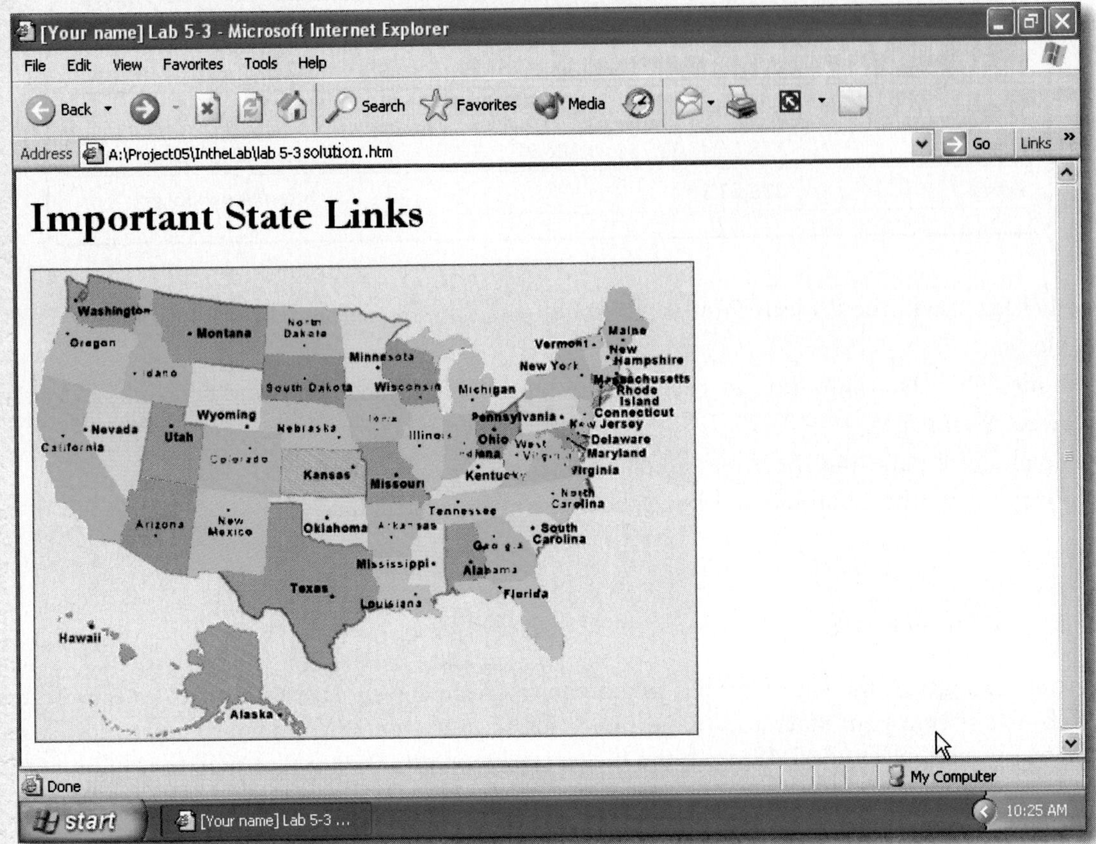

FIGURE 5-48

7. Enter the <area> tags required to define three clickable areas on the image, states_good.gif. Use the x- and y-coordinates determined in Step 2 and set the href attribute to use the URLs for the three government Web sites you have identified for three different states.
8. Save the HTML file in the Project05\IntheLab folder using the file name, lab5-3solution.htm. Print the HTML file.
9. Open the file, lab 5-3solution.htm, in your browser and test the image map and text links to verify they link to the correct Web pages.
10. Print the main Web page and the three linked Web pages.
11. Write your name on the printouts and hand them in to your instructor.

Cases and Places

The difficulty of these case studies varies:
■ are the least difficult and ■■ are the most difficult. The last exercise is a group exercise.

1 ■ Browse the Web to find two appropriate images for image mapping and two images that are not appropriate. Print the Web page with each image. On the appropriate printouts, list several reasons why an image is appropriate or inappropriate for use as an image map. For those that are appropriate for use as an image map, sketch borders around the sections of the images that can be utilized for hotspots. Be sure to sketch a specific map area shape (rectangular, circular, polygon) that you can use in creating the image map.

2 ■ The marketing director at Getaway Travel wants to create a bold, new graphical home page that highlights the unique travel packages the agency offers: ski & snow, surf & sun, golf & spa, and adventure. Using the image, getaway.gif, from the Project05\CasesandPlaces folder on the HTML Data Disk, create a simple home page for the Getaway Travel Web site. First, sketch the four areas on the image that are good for mapping and then use Paint to find the x- and y-coordinates for those hotspots. For each hotspot, create a link to a Web page with information on a destination you would recommend for each type of travel package. Be sure to include text links at the bottom of the page, to mirror the links in the image map.

3 ■■ As discussed in this project, some Web site visitors turn graphics off while browsing. Determine in your Web development (or any other) class how many students do turn graphics off. With this information in hand, search the Web to find three Web sites that utilize image maps. Track the time that it takes to load the three Web pages with image maps. Turn graphics off in your browser (in Internet Explorer, click Internet Options on the Tools menu and then click the Advanced tab; scroll down and click Show Pictures under Multimedia to deselect it). Next, clear the browser's history (in Internet Explorer, click Internet Options on the Tools menu and then click the Clear History button). Reload each of the three Web pages and again track the time it takes for the pages to load, this time without images. Determine if the Web pages load more quickly with images off. Review each Web page and determine if you can use all of the links despite having graphics turned off.

Cases and Places

4 ■■ The Graphics Design Director at Axcelent has asked you to search the Web to learn more about the image mapping software tools listed in Table 5-2 on page HTM 212, as well as additional software tools not listed in Project 5. Read the information about each tool, including its costs, free trial version availability, platform(s) supported, and ease of use. If a free trial version is offered at any of the Web sites and you are using your own computer (or your instructor or lab coordinator allows it), download the software and use it to create an image map. Compare the technique of using these tools to the technique used in this project using Paint. Write a synopsis of the available products, including cost, free trial version availability, platform(s) supported, and ease of use.

5 ■■ **Working Together** The local university is hoping to revamp its Web site to celebrate the school's fiftieth anniversary. The Anniversary Committee Chairman has asked LightWorks Design to create a prototype Web site that the committee can review. The prototype should include six pages: a home page, Academics, Admissions, Libraries & Museums, News & Events, and About. Two images that can be used in the Web site, schoolmontagebar.gif and schoolheaderbar.gif, are included in the Project05\ CasesandPlaces folder on the HTML Data Disk. Sketch out the overall plan for the Web site and then have each team member create one or more Web pages. On each Web page, include at least one image map, one or more text paragraphs, and a corresponding set of text links.

HTML

Using Frames in a Web Site

PROJECT

CASE PERSPECTIVE

For the final project in your Advertising class, you must determine a cost-effective advertising plan for a fictional or real company. Your first idea is to create a Web site to showcase your Uncle Bill's illustrations. This not only will be a great final project for your Advertising class, but also will help his business by making his illustrations available to anyone in the world. Your uncle is very enthusiastic about the idea and quickly agrees to allow you to scan his illustrations and use them in the Web site.

One of the first challenges you face in designing the Web site is how to display the illustrations effectively, while making the Web site easy to navigate. After considering several design techniques, you settle on a Web site using frames to display the illustrations in a user-friendly manner.

As you complete this project, you will learn how to use frames in a Web site. You will develop three frame Web pages to display in the frames: a header Web page, a menu Web page, and a home (or target) Web page to display the main Web site content.

Using Frames in a Web Site

Objectives

You will have mastered the material in this project when you can:

- Define terms related to frames
- Describe the steps used to design a frame structure
- Plan and lay out a frameset
- Create a frame definition file that defines three frames
- Use the <frameset> tag
- Use the <frame> tag
- Change frame scrolling options
- Name a frame content target
- Identify Web pages to display at startup
- Set frame rows
- Set frame columns
- Create a header page with text
- Create a navigation menu page with text links
- Create a home page

Introduction

Project 6 introduces frames and their use in Web page development. A **frame** is a rectangular area of a Web page — basically, a window — in which a Web page can be displayed. Web pages that include frames look and act differently than the Web pages created in previous projects. Frames allow a user to display several Web pages at one time in a single browser window. Each frame displays a different, individual Web page, each of which is capable of interacting with other Web pages.

When designed and implemented properly, frames provide Web pages with a cleaner look and make the pages easier to navigate. For example, frames can be used in place of tables and menu bars to organize content on a Web page and provide navigation options. Frames also can be used to organize Web pages by displaying more than one page in the browser window at the same time.

In this project, you will learn how to create Web pages that use frames. You will learn how to plan and design a frameset, create a frame definition file, define scrolling options for frames, and identify which Web pages should display in each frame when a user first visits the Web page address. Finally, you will learn to set frame rows and columns and create a header page, a navigation page, and a home page in each frame.

Project Six — Bill Thomas Illustrations

As shown in Figure 6-1a, the Bill Thomas Illustrations Web site uses three frames, each of which displays a different Web page. Frame 1 contains a header with the Bill Thomas Illustrations name. Frame 2, located below the header in the left column, contains a navigation menu with a list of text links to other Web pages and image files in the Web site. Frame 3, located in the right column, is the only frame in which content changes. The Web page, home.htm, displays in frame 3 at startup — that is, when the site first is accessed by a visitor (Figure 6-1a). When a link in frame 2 is clicked, frame 3 displays the content of the linked Web page, thus replacing the previous content of the frame. The Web page to define the frames and the three Web pages that are displayed in the frames at startup — header.htm, menu.htm, and home.htm — are created in the project.

The Bill Thomas Illustrations Web site also uses three image files (thomascross.jpg, thomasfull.jpg, and thomasink.jpg) and one Web page file (orderform.htm), which are stored on the HTML Data Disk. As shown in Figures 6-1b through 6-1e, the navigation menu Web page (frame 2 in Figure 6-1a) includes links to each of these files. Clicking a text link on the navigation menu Web page causes the corresponding linked Web page or image file to display in frame 3, replacing that frame's previous content.

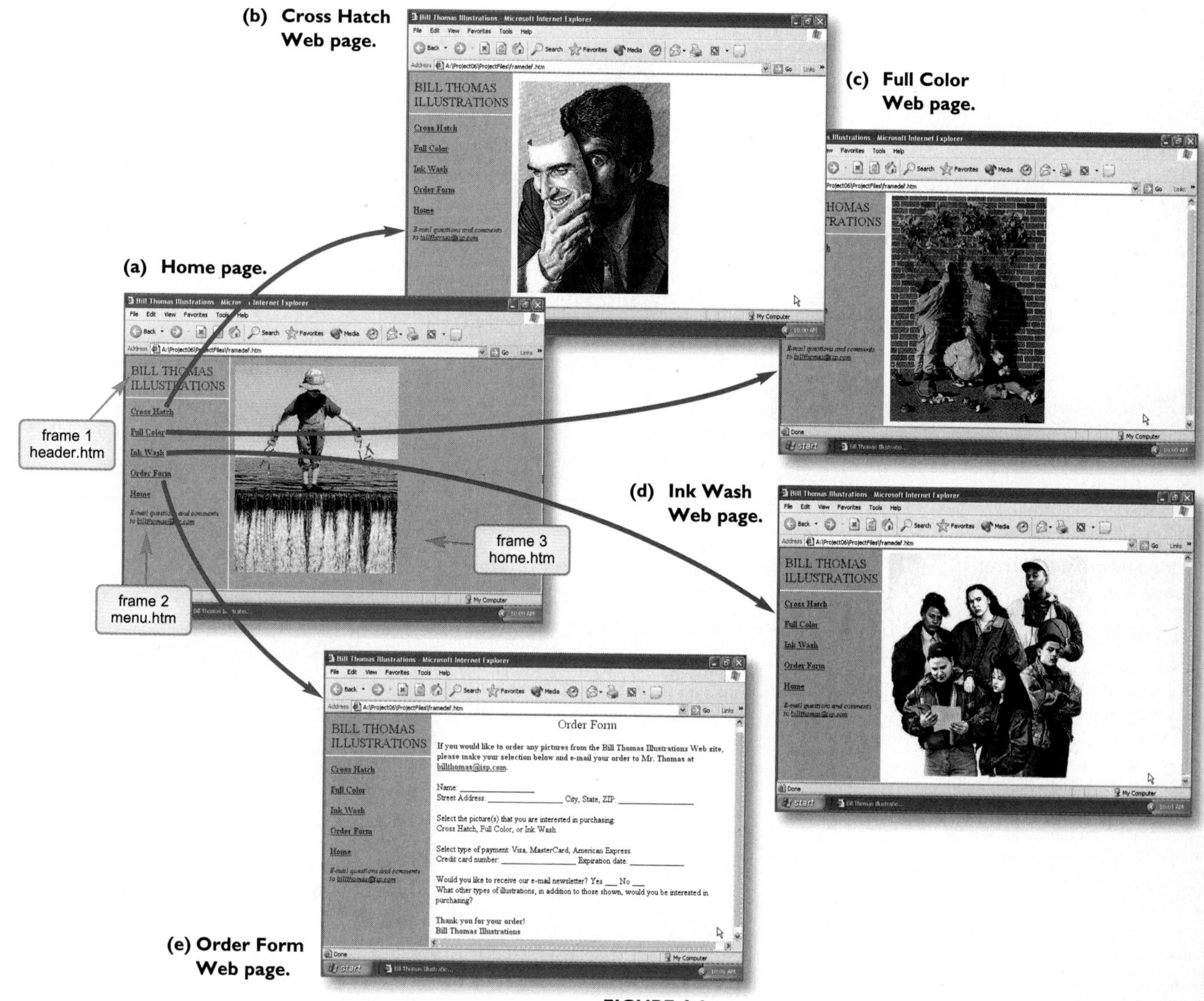

FIGURE 6-1

Creating Frames

When frames are used, the browser window contains multiple Web page or image files. Frames can be used for the following:

- To allow a Web site visitor to view more than one Web page at a time
- To create a navigation menu, as a replacement for such objects as menu lists and menu bars
- To display headers, navigation menus, or other information that needs to remain on the screen as other parts of the Web page change

Creating a Frame Definition File

The first step in creating frames for a Web site is to create a frame definition file. A **frame definition file** defines the layout of the frames in a Web site and specifies the Web page contents of each frame. The frame definition file is the Web page that opens when the visitor enters the URL of the Web site in the Address box. The information in the frame definition file defines which Web pages appear in each frame when the page first is loaded and when a user clicks a link.

For the Bill Thomas Illustrations Web site created in this project, the frame definition file is named framedef.htm. The frame definition file specifies that the Web site will use three frames — one to display a header, one to provide a navigation menu, and one to display the main Web page with the illustrations.

Creating a frame definition file uses a combination of three HTML tags and attributes, as shown in Table 6-1.

Table 6-1 Frame Tags

TAG	FUNCTION
<frameset> </frameset>	• Defines the structure of the frames within a window • Required end tag when creating frames
<frame>	• Defines a given frame; required for each frame • No end tag required
<noframes> </noframes>	• Defines alternate content that appears if the browser does not support frames • Supported by multiple types and versions of browsers

More About

Framesets

A frameset can be thought of as a window with various windowpanes. Within each windowpane is a separate Web page. The frame definition file is the HTML file that defines the Web pages that display in the individual windowpanes. Every Web page used in a frameset can be viewed independently in the browser as well as within the frameset.

A **frameset** is used to define the layout of the frames that are displayed. A start <frameset> tag and end </frameset> tag are used to enclose the content and structure of the frame definition file. Within these tags, a <frame> tag is used to define each frame. No end </frame> tag is used. The start <noframes> and end </noframes> tags are used to specify alternate text that displays on a visitor's screen if the visitor's browser does not support frames.

A frame definition file also contains additional information, specified in attributes and values. Table 6-2 summarizes the attributes for each frame-related tag.

Figure 6-2a shows the HTML code for the frame definition file, framedef.htm, which is used in the Bill Thomas Illustrations Web site. The HTML code uses the <frame> tag to define three frames within the start <frameset> and end </frameset> tags. For each frame, the src attribute is used to define which Web page should be displayed in the frame at startup. These three Web pages (header.htm, menu.htm, and home.htm) are shown in Figures 6-2b, 6-2c, and 6-2d. When the frame definition file, framedef.htm, is displayed in the browser window, it will display as shown in Figure 6-1a on the previous page.

Table 6-2 Frame Tag Attributes

TAG	ATTRIBUTE	FUNCTION
<frameset>	cols rows	• Indicates the number of columns • Indicates the number of rows
<frame>	frameborder bordercolor marginwidth marginheight noresize name scrolling src	• Turns frame borders on or off • Changes the border color • Adjusts the margin on the left and right of a frame • Adjusts the margin above and below a document within a frame • Locks the borders of a frame to prohibit resizing • Defines the name of a frame that is used as a target • Indicates whether a scroll bar is present • Indicates the Web page or other file to be displayed in the frame

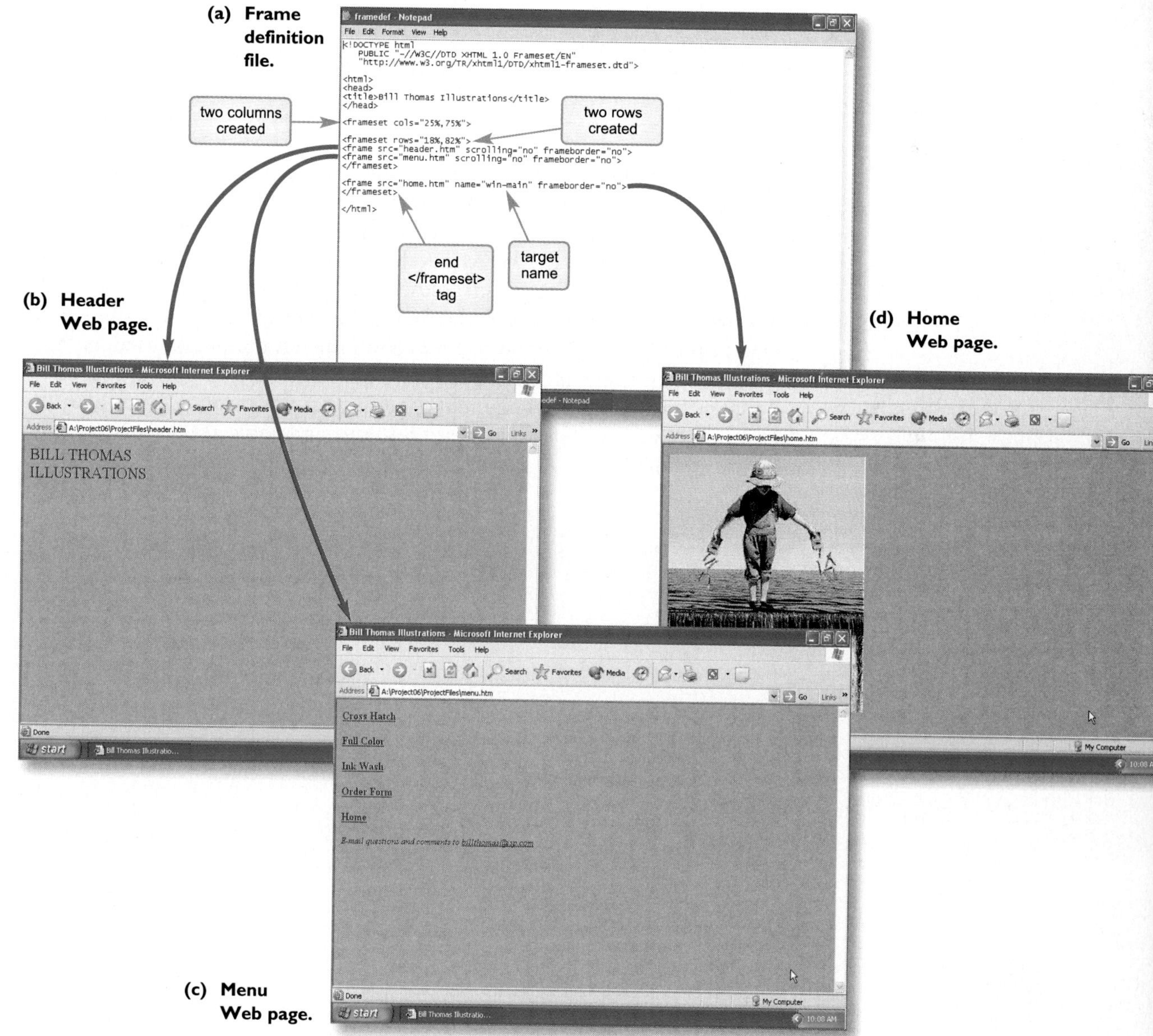

FIGURE 6-2

Defining Columns and Rows in a Frameset

The cols and rows attributes of the <frameset> tag set the number of columns and rows of the display area. Figure 6-3a shows a frameset with two rows and Figure 6-3b shows a frameset with two columns. The HTML code used to create the Web page shown in Figure 6-3a is:

```
<frameset rows="30%,70%">
<frame src="menu2.htm">
<frame src="home2.htm" name="win-main">
</frameset>
```

The HTML code used to create the Web page shown in Figure 6-3b is:

```
<frameset cols="30%,70%">
<frame src="menu1.htm">
<frame src="home1.htm" name="win-main">
</frameset>
```

As shown in Figure 6-2a on the previous page, <frameset> tags also can be nested to create three frames in a window, as used in the Bill Thomas Illustration Web site and shown in Figure 6-1a on page HTM 249. The first set of <frameset></frameset> tags in the HTML code in Figure 6-2a divides the window into two columns. The second set of <frameset></frameset> tags then divides the first column into two rows. In this project, the first cell in the left column is used as the frame for the header page, while the second cell in the left column is used as the frame for the navigation menu page. The right column is used to display the main Web page content, including the home page, additional illustrations, and the order form. The steps required to define frameset columns and rows are discussed in more detail later in the project.

More About

Frames

The World Wide Consortium Web site is an example of a Web site where you can find a thorough discussion of frames. The document contains an introduction to frames as well as frame layouts. All possible frame tags and attributes are discussed. For more information about frames, visit the HTML More About Web page (scsite.com/html3e/more.htm) and then click Frames.

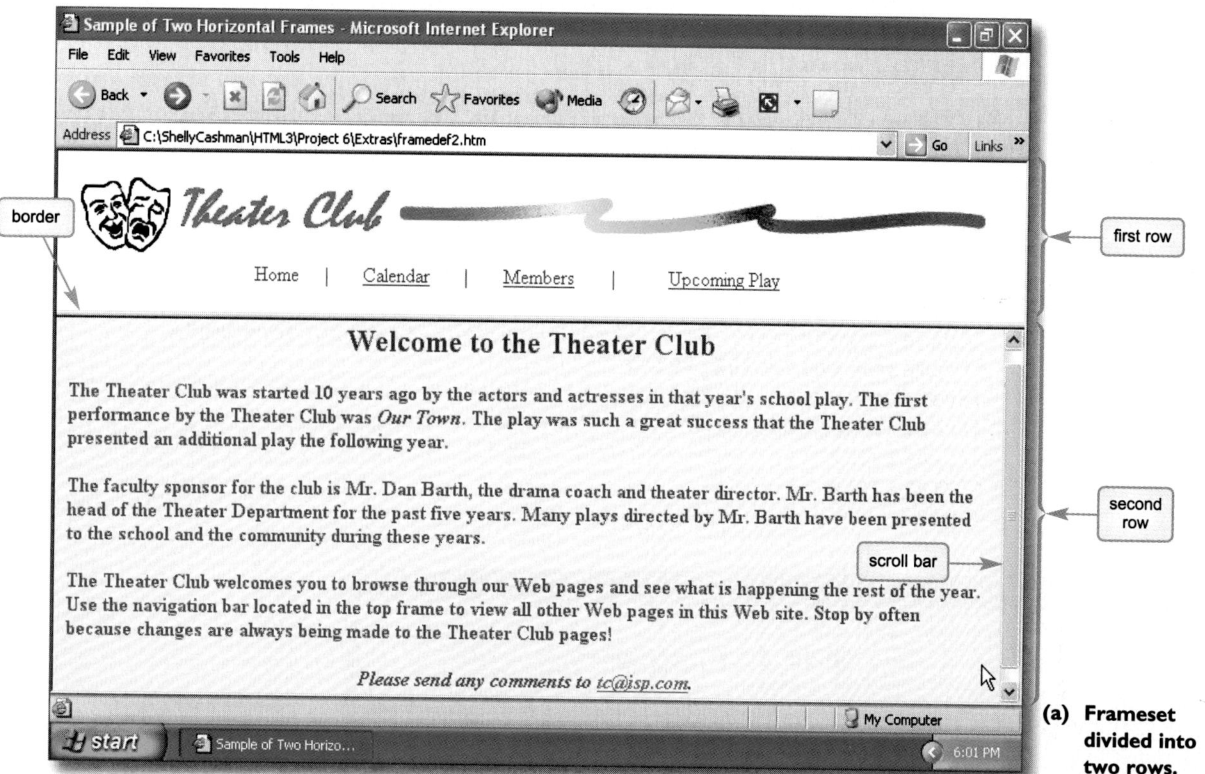

(a) Frameset divided into two rows.

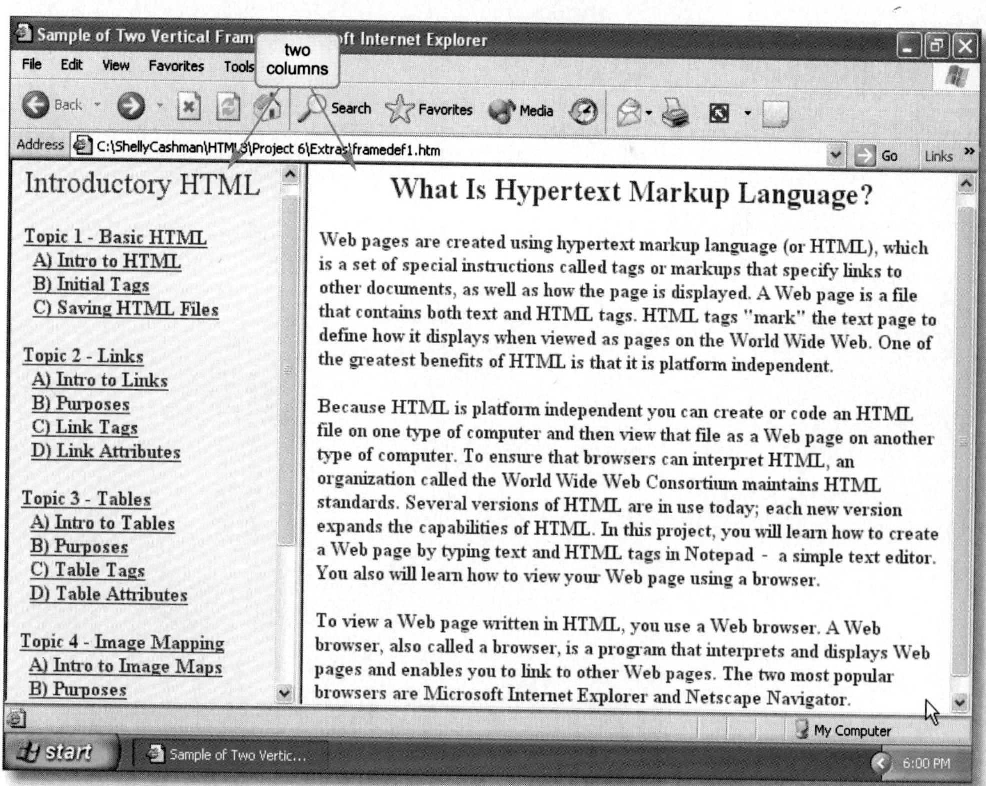

(b) Frameset divided into two columns.

FIGURE 6-3

Defining Frame Attributes

As shown in Table 6-2 on page HTM 251, the <frame> tag has several attributes that can be used to define how the frame appears. In the <frame> tag, the **frame border** attribute defines the border that separates frames. This attribute may be turned on, as shown in Figure 6-4a, or off, as shown in Figure 6-4b. The HTML code used to turn frameborders off in Figure 6-4b is:

```
<frameset rows="30%,70%">
<frame src="header.htm" scrolling="no" frameborder="no">
<frameset cols="25%,75%">
<frame src="menu.htm" scrolling="no" frameborder="no">
<frame src="home.htm" name="win-main" frameborder="no">
</frameset>
</frameset>
```

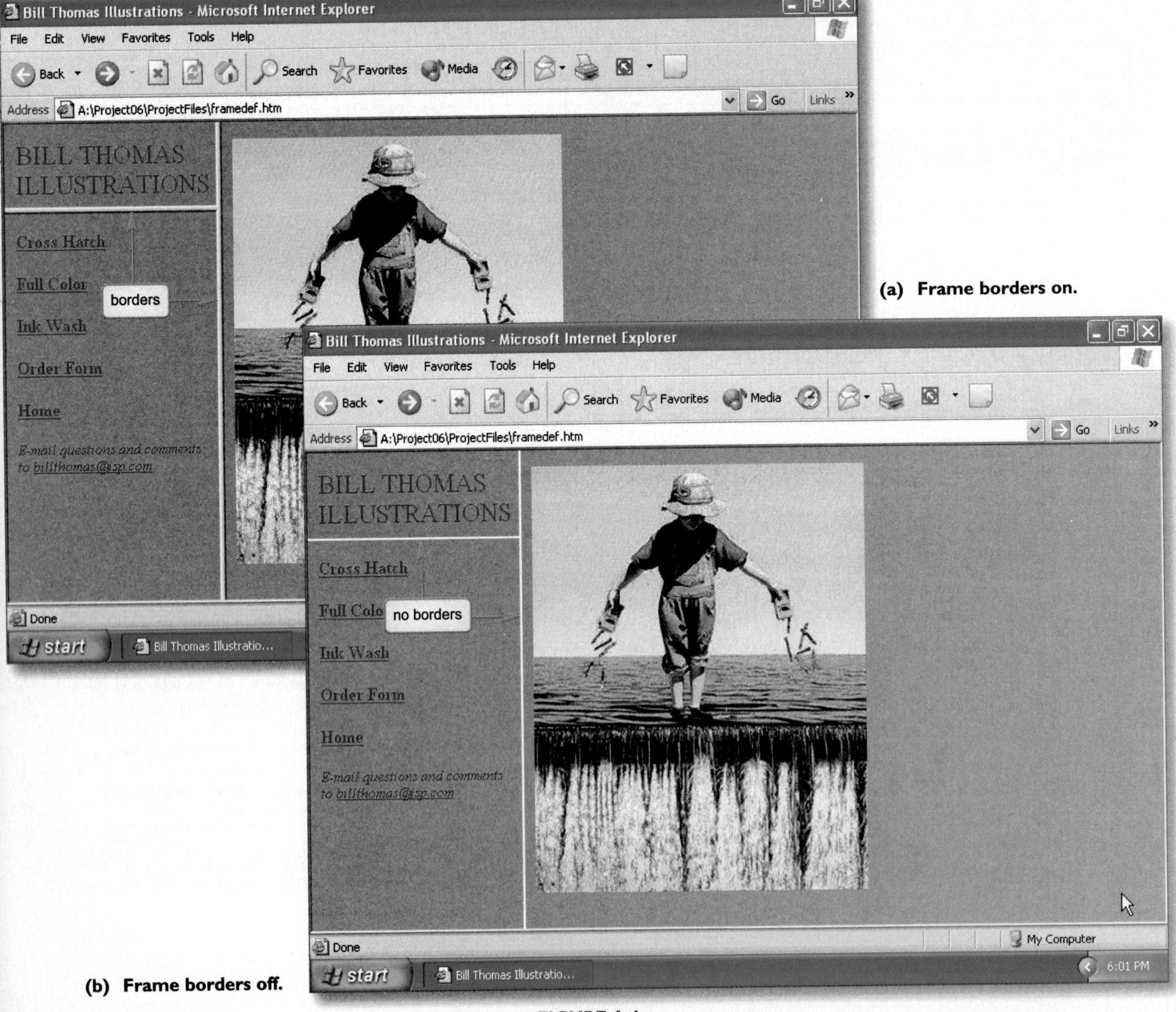

(a) Frame borders on.

(b) Frame borders off.

FIGURE 6-4

If the border is turned off, the browser automatically inserts five pixels of space to separate the frames. The amount of space, in pixels, can be increased or decreased.

By default, a border is gray (see Figure 6-4a). The **bordercolor** attribute of the <frame> tag can be used to change the border to any other color. Figure 6-5 shows the same set of frames as shown in Figure 6-4a, but with a bordercolor="navy" attribute and value that changes the border color to navy.

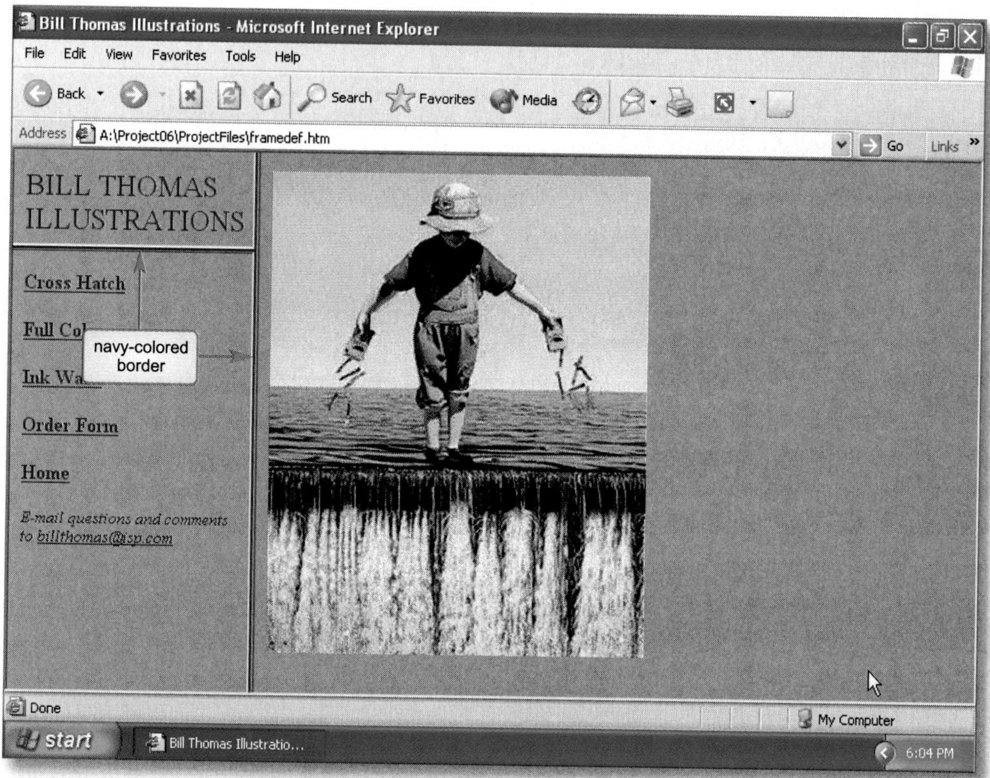

FIGURE 6-5 Frame borders with color specified.

The **marginwidth** attribute lets you change the margin on the left and/or right of a frame. The **marginheight** attribute lets you change the margin above and below a document within a frame. In both cases, you specify the size of the margin in number of pixels.

As you have learned in previous projects, scroll bars allow a Web page visitor to scroll vertically or horizontally through a Web page when the page is longer or wider than the screen. By default, the browser window displays a horizontal or vertical scroll bar, or both, to be added automatically whenever the content of a Web page exceeds the length or width of the frame area. The **scrolling** attribute of the <frame> tag instructs the browser that scroll bars should not be displayed and thus turns off scrolling in a frame. For example, as shown in Figure 6-6a on the next page, scrolling in frames 1 and 2 is not necessary because all the information appears in the frames without the need to scroll. Frame 3, however, may need a scroll bar. In Figure 6-6a, no scroll bar is needed for that frame, but in Figure 6-6b, a scroll bar is needed because the Web page content exceeds the length of the frame area. If scroll bars should appear in a frame, no HTML code is required; by default, scroll bars will appear in the frame as needed. To turn off scroll bars, the <frame> tag must include the **scrolling="no"** attribute and value. In the Bill Thomas Illustrations Web site, scrolling is turned off for frames 1 and 2, as shown in the HTML code in Figure 6-2a on page HTM 251.

More About

Margin Width and Height

By default, the primary browsers display a frame's contents with margins of eight pixels on each side of the frame. You use the marginwidth and marginheight attributes to adjust those margins. These attributes are used within the <frame> tag.

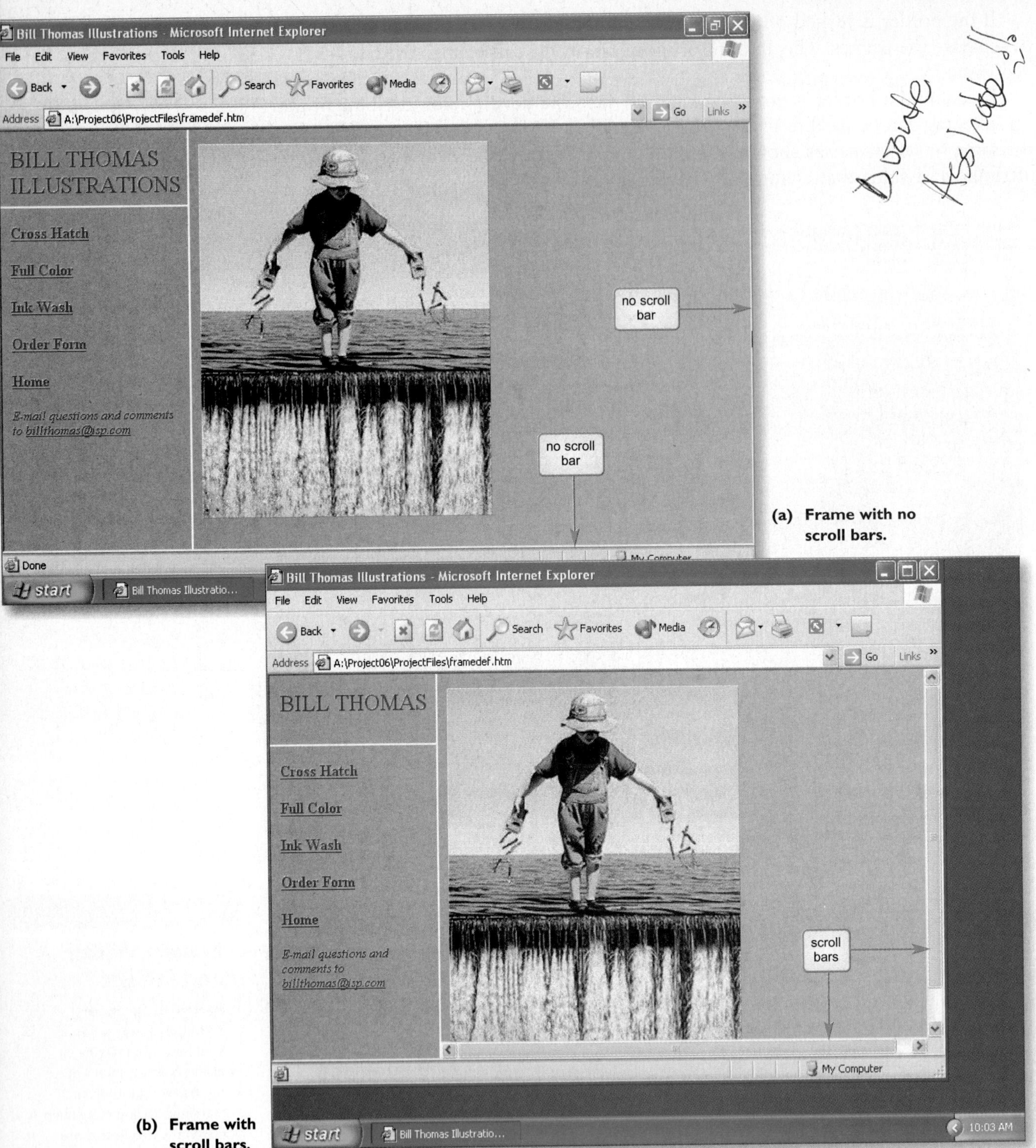

(a) **Frame with no scroll bars.**

(b) **Frame with scroll bars.**

FIGURE 6-6

One important frame attribute not used in this project is noresize. By default, Web page visitors can resize any frame on the screen by moving the mouse pointer to the frame's border and dragging the border (Figure 6-7). In many cases, however, a Web developer may want to restrict a user's ability to resize frames.

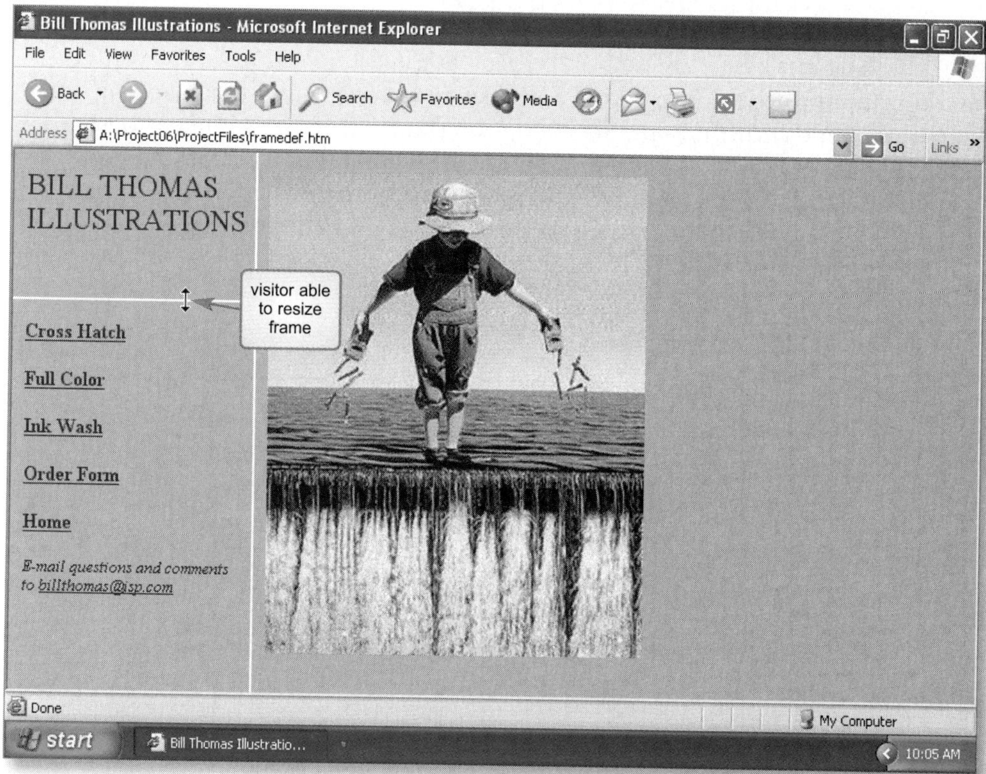

FIGURE 6-7 Sample layout for three-frame structure.

Including the **noresize** attribute in the <frame> tag locks the borders of a frame to prohibit resizing. For example, to eliminate resizing for the frames in this project, the noresize attribute would be added to the <frame> tags in the frame definition file, as follows:

```
<frame src="header.htm" scrolling="no" noresize>
<frame src="menu.htm" noresize>
<frame src="home.htm" name="win-main" noresize>
```

If the noresize attribute is not specified, visitors are able to resize a frame. The frame returns to its original size when the Web page is refreshed in the browser.

Additional frame attributes, such as name and src, are discussed in detail later in the project, as they are used.

Planning and Laying Out Frames

The most important step in creating an effective frame structure is planning and laying out a good frame design. Sketching the frame structure on paper before writing the HTML code, as shown in Figure 6-8, can help save time when determining which HTML <frameset> and <frame> tags and attributes to use. Once the structure is on paper, the number of rows and columns required, as well as whether scrolling is needed, is more apparent.

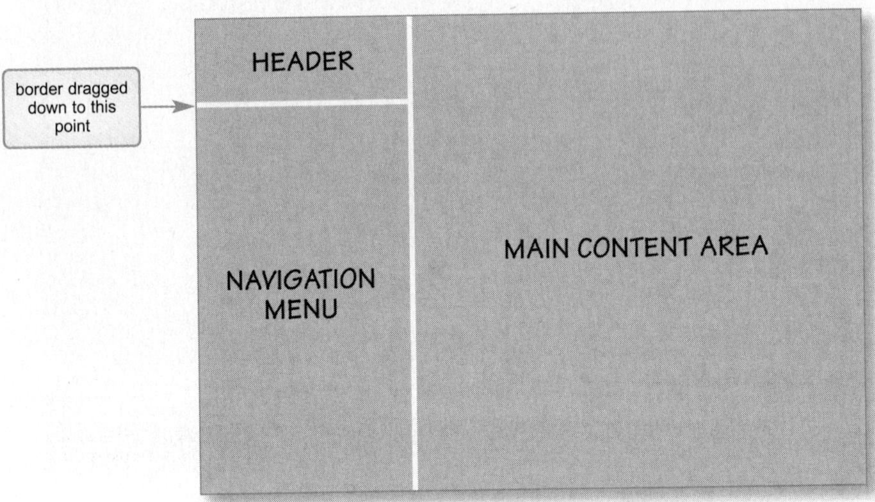

FIGURE 6-8 Resizable frames.

> *More About*
>
> **Frame Design**
>
> Whether you are using frames or any other navigation technique, design is very important. Many Web sites are available that provide information about the use of frames and link to example Web sites that talk about advanced Web design issues and topics. Many design tips also are available that can help you create a Web site that is informative as well as attractive. For more information about frame design, visit the HTML More About Web page (scsite.com/html3e/more.htm) and then click Frame Design.

Frame layouts can be designed in a variety of ways. The goal and purpose of the Web site determine which layout is appropriate. For example, as shown in Figure 6-1a on page HTM 249, the Bill Thomas Illustrations Web site uses a basic three-frame structure. This frame layout is appropriate for a Web site that needs to display a company, school, or personal logo or banner on the Web page and needs to provide a form of available navigation. In addition, the content frame is the only frame whose content changes. An example of the HTML code to define a three-frame structure is as follows:

```
<html>
<head>
<title>Sample of Three-Frame Structure</title>
</head>
<frameset cols="30%,70%">
<frameset rows="25%,75%">
<frame src="header.htm" scrolling="no">
<frame src="menu.htm" scrolling="no">
</frameset>
<frame src="home.htm" name="win-main">
</frameset>
</html>
```

A four-frame structure, as shown in Figure 6-9, can be used to split a header image from the header text.

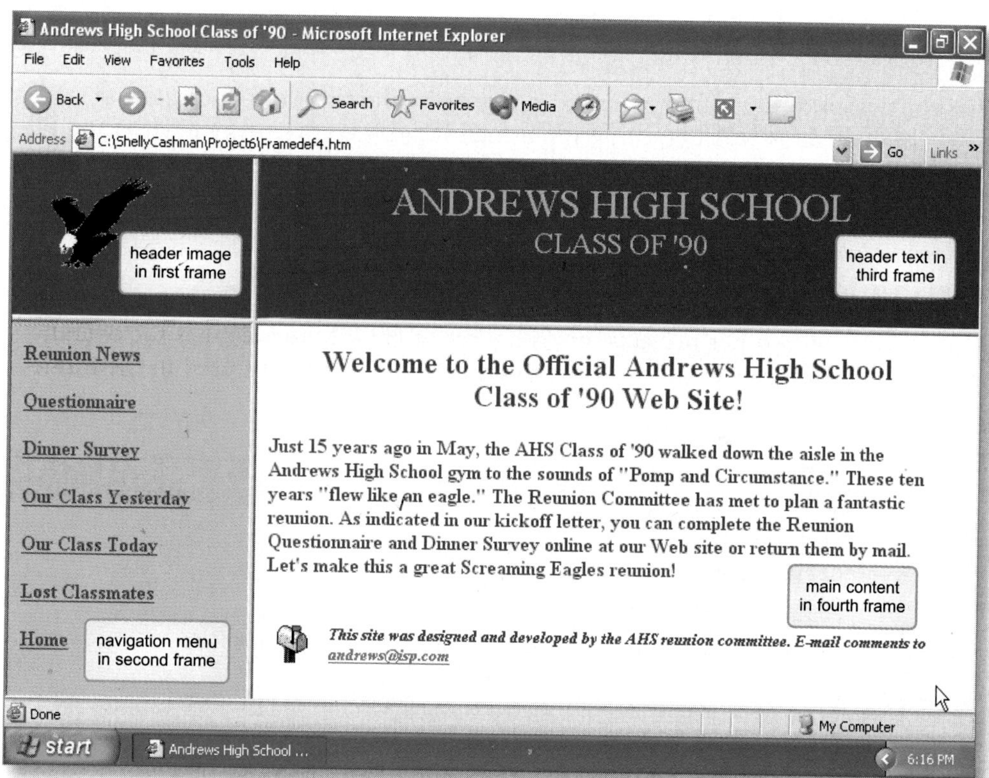

FIGURE 6-9 **Sample layout for four-frame structure.**

An example of the HTML code to define a four-frame structure is as follows:

```
<html>
<head>
<title>Sample of Four-Frame Structure</title>
</head>
<frameset rows="30%,70%">
<frameset cols="25%,75%">
<frame src="logo.htm" scrolling="no">
<frame src="header.htm" scrolling="no">
</frameset>
<frameset cols="25%,75%">
<frame src="menu.htm" scrolling="no">
<frame src="home.htm" name="win-main">
</frameset>
</frameset>
</html>
```

Notice that the four-frame structure includes an additional set of <frameset> tags to increase the number of frames from three to four. The most important task to manipulate multiple rows and columns is the placement of the </frameset> tags, as shown in this example.

Although the widths of the columns do not have to be the same (25% and 75% in this example), defining them the same maintains a border that is straight down the page. Using this basic structure, you can define any number of rows and columns in a frame structure.

More About

Noframes

The two main browsers have supported frames for a number of versions. A small number of browsers, however, do not support frames. To notify those visitors that the Web page is utilizing frames, you use a <noframes> tag after the last </frameset> tag to create the alternate text that displays in lieu of the frames. You must end this section of HTML code with the </noframes> tag.

Creating a Frame Definition File

After the design of the frame structure is complete, the first step in creating the Web page is to code the frame definition file using HTML tags. The frame definition file created in this project (framedef.htm) is used to define a three-frame structure and to indicate the names of the HTML files that will be displayed in the frames.

Starting Notepad and Entering Initial HTML Tags

As described in other projects, an initial set of HTML tags defines the overall structure of a Web page. Table 6-3 shows the initial HTML tags used in the frame definition file.

Table 6-3 Code for Initial HTML Tags in a Frame Definition File

LINE	HTML TAG AND TEXT
1	<!DOCTYPE html
2	PUBLIC "-//W3C//DTD XHTML 1.0 Frameset//EN"
3	"http://www.w3.org/TR/xhtml1/DTD/xhtml1-frameset.dtd">
4	
5	<html>
6	<head>
7	<title>Bill Thomas Illustrations</title>
8	</head>
9	
10	
11	</html>

Q: What is positive about using noframes?

A: Because Web page visitors use so many different browsers, it is difficult to plan for all browser types and versions. The noframes tag allows you to accommodate those visitors who cannot otherwise see your Web page in frames.

Notice that the DOCTYPE statement in lines 1 through 3 is different than the one used in previous projects. As discussed in Project 2, the <!DOCTYPE> tag is used to tell the browser which HTML or XHTML version and type the document uses. Recall that HTML and XHTML support three document types: strict, transitional, and frameset. In all previous projects, the transitional document type was used. Because this project utilizes frames, the frameset document type is used. The frameset document type, which is used to support frames on a Web page, allows the use of deprecated tags.

The initial HTML tags in Table 6-3 and those used in other projects have one important difference: the initial HTML tags used in this project do not include the <body> and </body> tags. These tags are not needed in a frame definition file. If you have a <frameset> tag in an HTML file, you cannot have a <body> tag. The two tags are mutually exclusive.

The first step in creating a frame definition file is to start Notepad and then enter the initial HTML tags to define the overall structure of a Web page. The following steps illustrate how to start Notepad and enter HTML tags to define the Web page structure for a frame definition file.

To Start Notepad and Enter Initial HTML Tags

1. **Click the Start button on the taskbar and then point to All Programs on the Start menu.**
2. **Point to Accessories on the All Programs submenu and then click Notepad on the Accessories submenu.**
3. **If necessary, click the Maximize button.**
4. **If necessary, click Format on the menu bar and click Word Wrap to turn on the Word Wrap feature.**
5. **Enter the HTML code as shown in Table 6-3.**
6. **Position the insertion point on the blank line (line 10).**

The HTML code is displayed in Notepad (Figure 6-10) and the insertion point is on line 10.

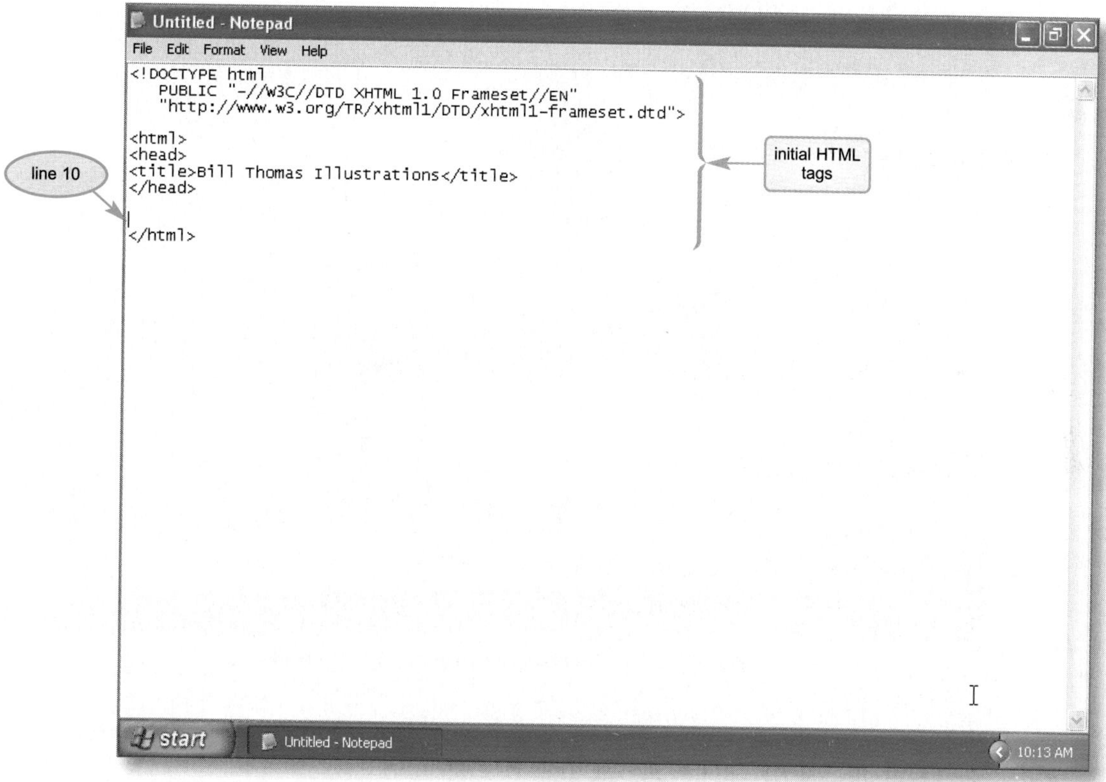

FIGURE 6-10

Defining the Frameset Columns and Rows

After the document type is declared for the Bill Thomas Illustrations Web site, the next step in creating the frame definition file is to enter <frameset> tags to define the frame structure, that is, the number of columns and rows of the display area. As shown in Figure 6-11, the frame definition file (framedef.htm) used in the Bill Thomas Illustrations Web site includes two columns that divide the screen vertically. The first column is divided horizontally into two rows. When the framedef.htm file is opened in a browser, the header displays in the top-left frame and the navigation menu displays in the bottom-left frame. While the contents of these two frames remain constant, the Web page displayed in the right column frame changes. At startup, it contains the Web page, home.htm.

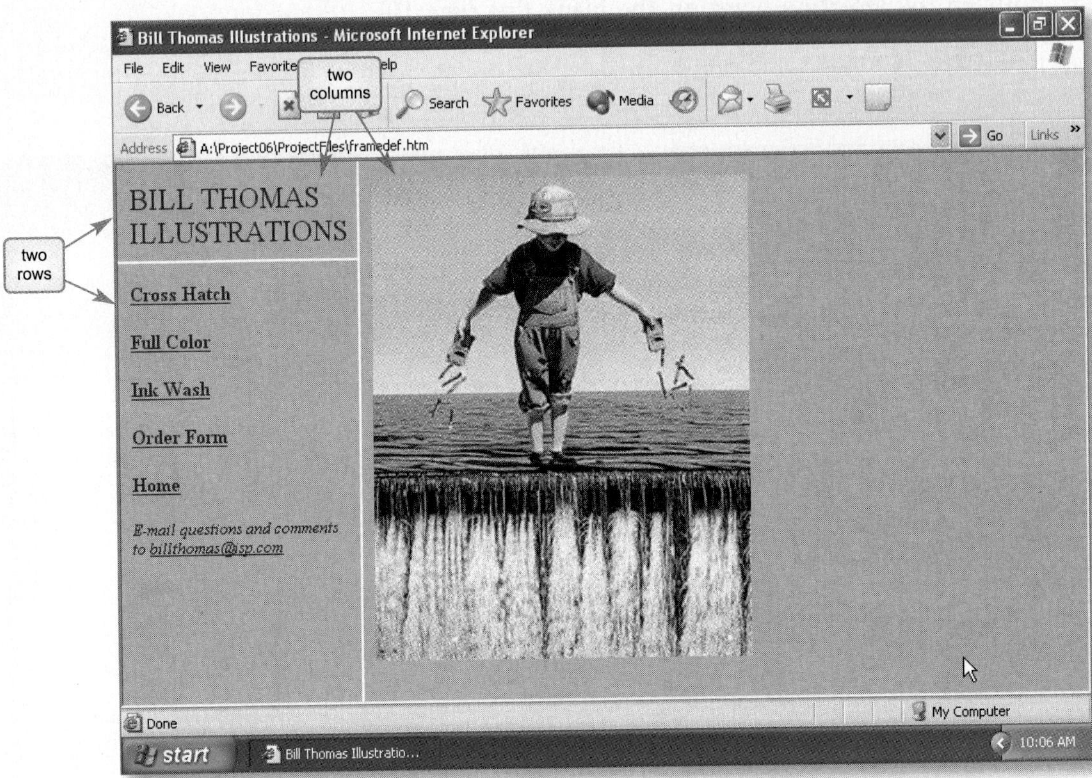

FIGURE 6-11 Three-frame structure for Web site.

> *More About*
>
> **Frame Sizes**
>
> The size of a frame should be determined by the content that it displays. If a frame is too small, the visitor has to scroll vertically or horizontally to read the content. If the frame is too large for the material, the space around the text makes the page look unattractive. When you create your frame size, think in terms of effectively using the space.

The cols attribute of the <frameset> tag is used to set the number and sizes of columns. For example, entering the HTML code:

```
<frameset cols="25%,75%">
```

creates two columns in the frameset. The cols="25%,75%" attribute indicates that the page consists of two columns, which will display in 25 percent and 75 percent of the screen, respectively. As shown in Figure 6-11, the Bill Thomas Illustrations Web site has two columns in the frame structure. The left column uses 25 percent of the total screen size, while the right column uses the remaining 75 percent of the total screen size.

If a frame structure needs more than two frame columns, additional column widths can be specified in the cols attribute of the <frameset> tag. For example, the HTML code:

```
<frameset cols="20%,65%,15%">
```

is used to create three columns, with widths of 20 percent, 65 percent, and 15 percent, respectively.

The rows attribute of the <frameset> tag is used to set the number and sizes of rows. Rows divide the screen horizontally. The rows attribute works in the same way as the cols attribute. For example, entering the HTML code:

```
<frameset rows="18%,82%">
```

creates two rows in a frameset. As shown in Figure 6-11, the Bill Thomas Illustrations Web site has two rows in the left column of the frame structure. The top row uses 18 percent of the total screen size, while the bottom row uses the remaining 82 percent of the total screen size. As with the cols attribute, if a frame structure needs more than two frame rows, additional row heights can be specified in the rows attribute of the <frameset> tag.

The size of a frame column or row may be specified as a percentage of the total screen size, as a number of pixels, or with an asterisk (*). Using a percentage has an advantage in that the width and height of the column or row will change as the browser window is resized. This maintains the set proportion of the frames. By contrast, if the frame column width or row height is defined in pixels, the size of the frame is fixed and does not resize when the browser window is resized. If you use an asterisk, the browser determines how much space is necessary for the frame based on information you include in the attribute. For example, an asterisk can be used to split a screen into three equal-sized column frames by indicating cols="*,*,*". In this case, each column will be 33.3 percent of the total screen size. An asterisk also can be used to set a row to split equally whatever space is left for the unspecified frames, as in rows="*,25,*". Here, the first and third rows each would be 37.5 percent of the total screen size.

The steps on the next page show how to enter HTML code to define the columns and rows in the frameset.

Q&A

Q: What is negative about eliminating scrolling from a menu frame?

A: The menu frame is generally used to provide links to all of the Web pages in the Web site. If you turn off scrolling in that frame, and a visitor has their screen resolution settings very low, you may not display all of the menu options. A visitor also may shrink the size of the browser window, which may not show all menu options.

To Define Columns and Rows in the Frameset

1

If necessary, click line 10 and then press the ENTER key twice.

2

• **Type** `<frameset cols="25%,75%">` **and then press the ENTER key.**

The <frameset> tag is displayed (Figure 6-12) and the insertion point is on line 12.

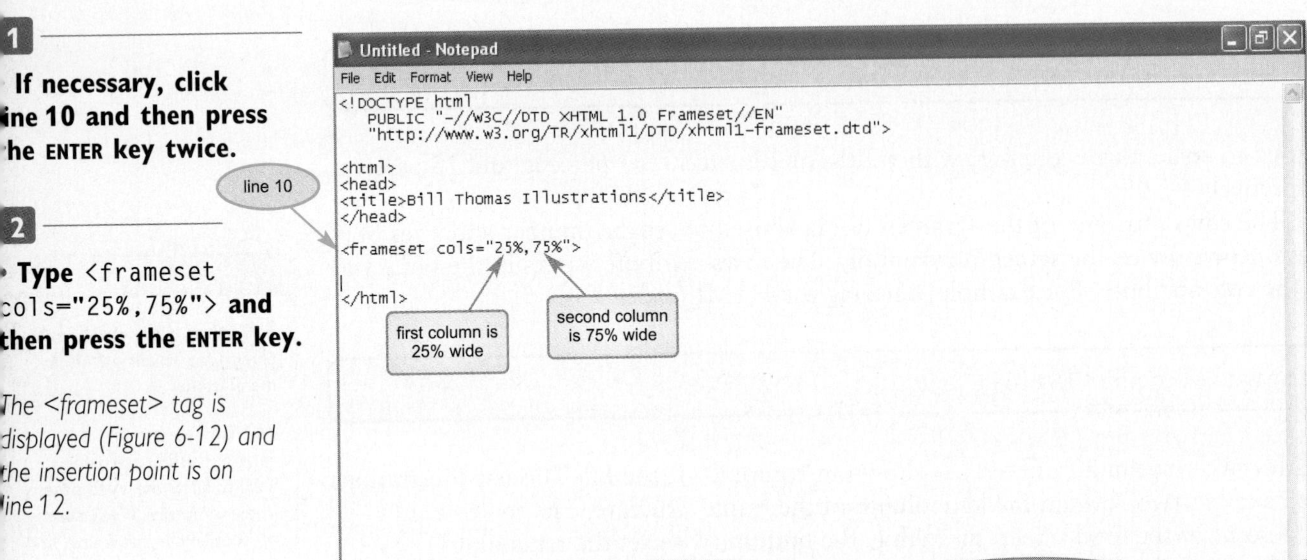

FIGURE 6-12

3

• **Type** `<frameset rows="18%,82%">` **and then press the ENTER key.**

The HTML code is displayed (Figure 6-13) and the insertion point is on line 13.

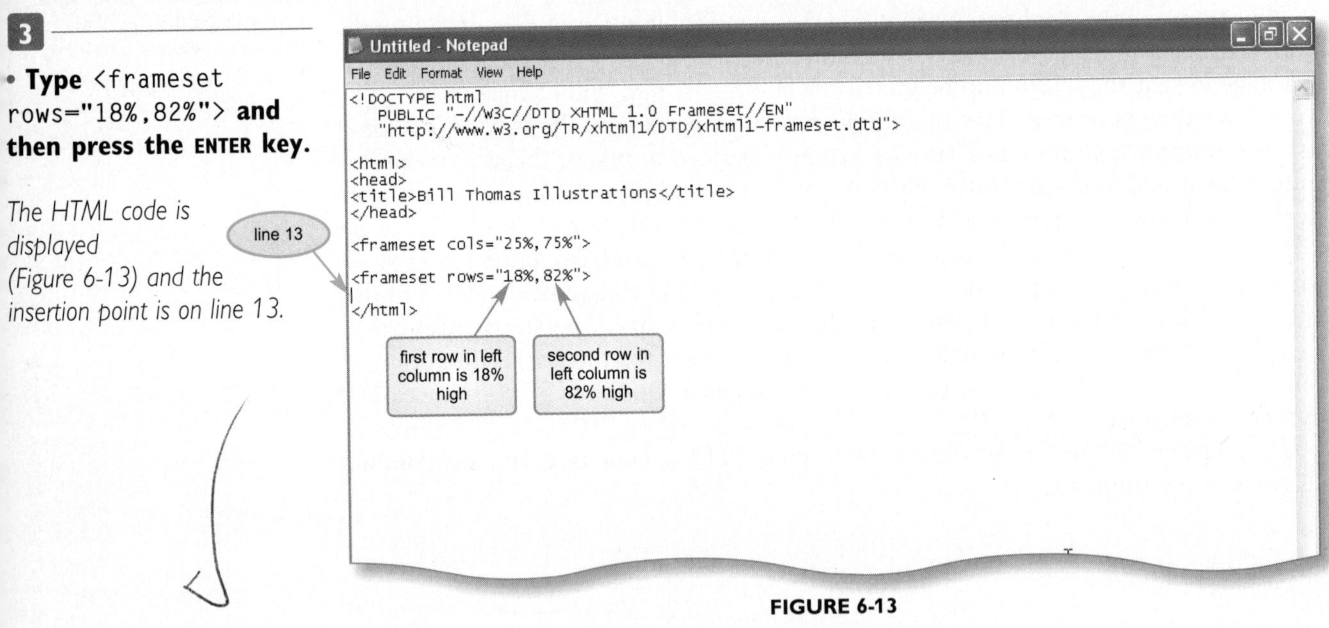

FIGURE 6-13

The HTML code creates a two-column frame structure with the left column divided into two rows. The header frame in the top row in the left column will display a header with the company name. The menu frame in the bottom row of the left column of the Web page will be used for the navigation menu. The main frame in the right column will display the home page at startup. All other Web pages in the Web site also will display in the main frame's right column, when the corresponding link is clicked in the navigation menu.

Identifying Attributes of the Header and Menu Frames

A <frame> tag is used to define each frame in a frame definition file. The src attribute of the <frame> tag is used to identify the Web page that will display in this frame.

For the Bill Thomas Illustrations Web site, three frames must be defined using <frame> tags. The frame in the top row of the first column displays the header Web page (header.htm) that contains the Bill Thomas Illustrations company name. (The file, header.htm, is created later in this project.) The header.htm Web page will remain constant as users browse through the Web site; no other Web page displays in that frame. In this <frame> tag, scrolling should be turned off, because the content of the header.htm Web page displays completely without having to scroll. Frame borders also should be turned off to give the Web page a polished look.

The second <frame> tag identifies the frame in the bottom row of the first column. This frame displays the navigation menu page, menu.htm, which is used for navigation of the Web site. (The file, menu.htm, is created later in this project.) The menu.htm Web page will remain constant as users browse through the Web site; no other Web page displays in that frame. Scrolling and borders should be turned off for this frame as well.

The following steps show how to enter HTML code to identify attributes of the header and menu frames.

To Identify Attributes of the Header and Menu Frames

1

- **If necessary, click line 13.**

2

- **Type** `<frame src="header.htm" scrolling="no" frameborder="no">` **and then press the ENTER key.**

3

- **Type** `<frame src="menu.htm" scrolling="no" frameborder="no">` **and then press the ENTER key twice.**

The HTML code is displayed (Figure 6-14) and the insertion point is on line 16.

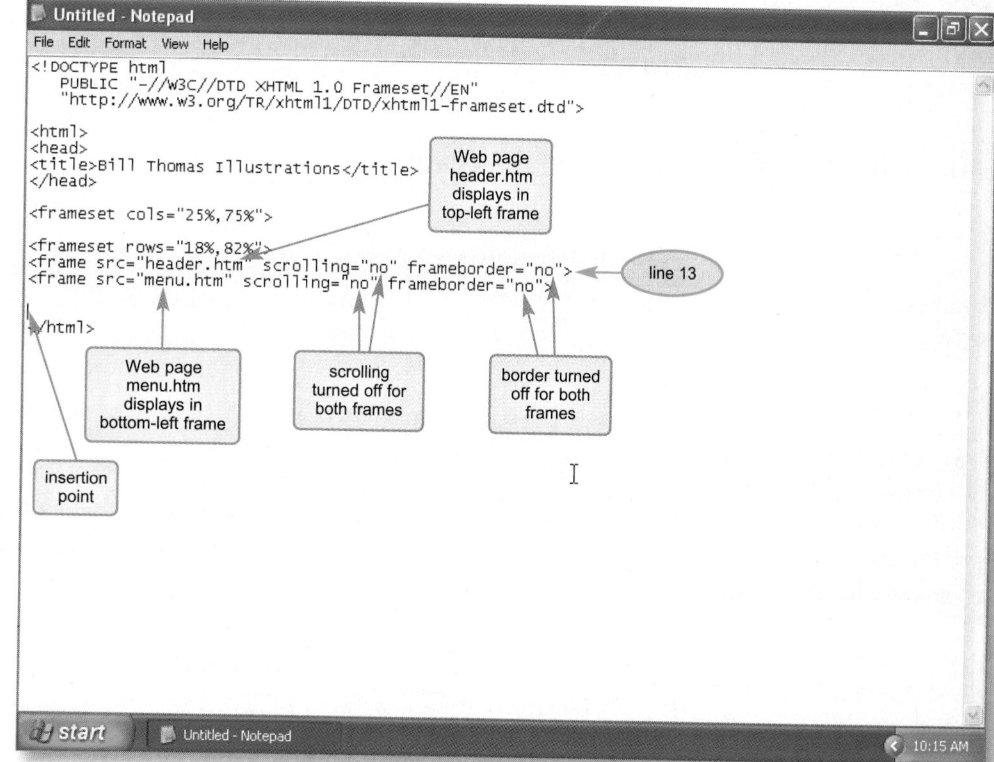

FIGURE 6-14

The attributes for the header frame and the menu frame in the left column are set. Next, the attributes for the main frame in the right column must be defined.

Identifying Attributes of the Main Frame

To identify the attributes of the frame in the right column, a <frame> tag is used along with the src attribute to specify that the Web page, home.htm, will display in the frame at startup.

In this project, the contents of the header and menu frames will remain constant — that is, the pages header.htm and menu.htm, respectively, always will be displayed in those frames. The main frame in the right column will display variable content. At startup, the main frame displays the Web page, home.htm. When a user clicks a link in the navigation menu, the Web page in the main frame changes to display the linked content. For example, if a user clicks the Order Form link in the menu frame, the Web page, orderform.htm, will be displayed in the main frame.

The name attribute, name="win-main", is used to assign the target name, win-main, to the main frame. The links in the navigation menu will use the target name, win-main, to indicate that all linked Web pages should be displayed in the main frame. Note that any frame may be named using the name attribute of the <frame> tag. For example, if you needed to display additional Web pages in the header or menu frames, you could specify target names for those frames. In the Bill Thomas Illustrations Web site, no additional target names are necessary, because the main frame is the only frame that displays the variable content.

Finally, borders will be turned off for the main frame, to match the other frames. Scrolling will not be turned off for this frame, because the content in this frame may require scroll bars to view all of the content.

The following steps show how to enter HTML code to identify attributes of the main frame.

More About

Files

In the projects in this book, you save your HTML file after inserting all of the HMTL tags and text. When developing Web pages, it is a good idea to save your file periodically so that you do not accidentally lose anything that you have entered. In case of a power outage or other unforeseen interruption before your file is saved, the file is not lost. Give the file a name that makes sense and identifies the purpose of the Web page.

To Identify Attributes of the Main Frame

1

• **If necessary, click line 16.**

2

• **Type** `<frame src="home.htm" name="win-main" frameborder="no">` **and then press the ENTER key.**

The HTML code is displayed (Figure 6-15) and the insertion point is on line 17.

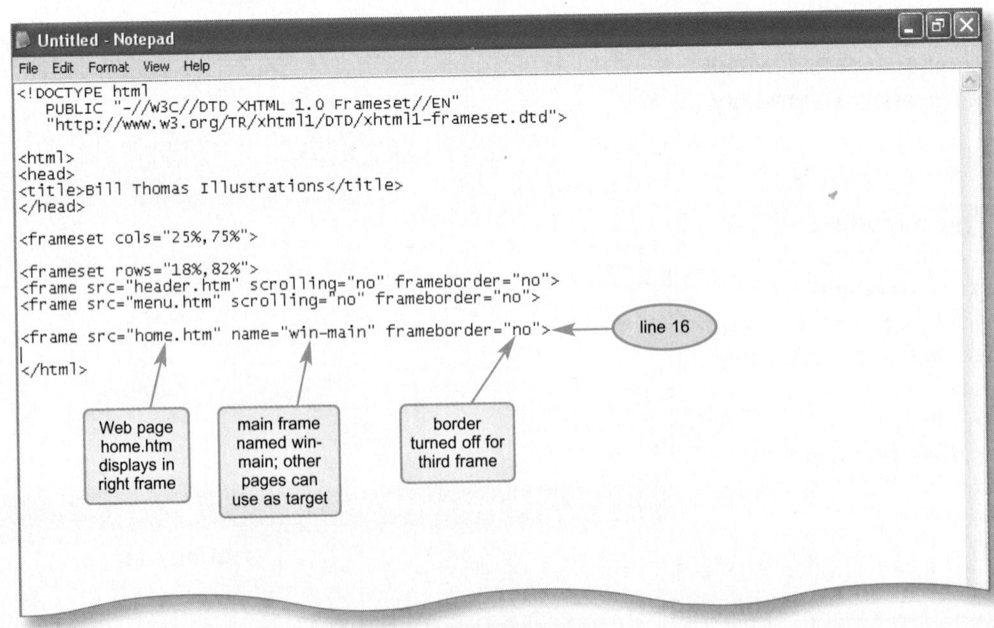

FIGURE 6-15

The attributes for the main frame in the right column are set. The next step is to end the framesets. An end </frameset> tag is needed to close every start <frameset> tag. The following steps show how to add the end </frameset> tags to end the framesets.

To End the Framesets

1

- **If necessary, click line 17.**

2

- **Type** `</frameset>` **as the tag.**

3

- **Click line 15 to position the insertion point.**

4

- **Type** `</frameset>` **and then press the ENTER key.**

The HTML code is displayed (Figure 6-16) and the insertion point is on line 16.

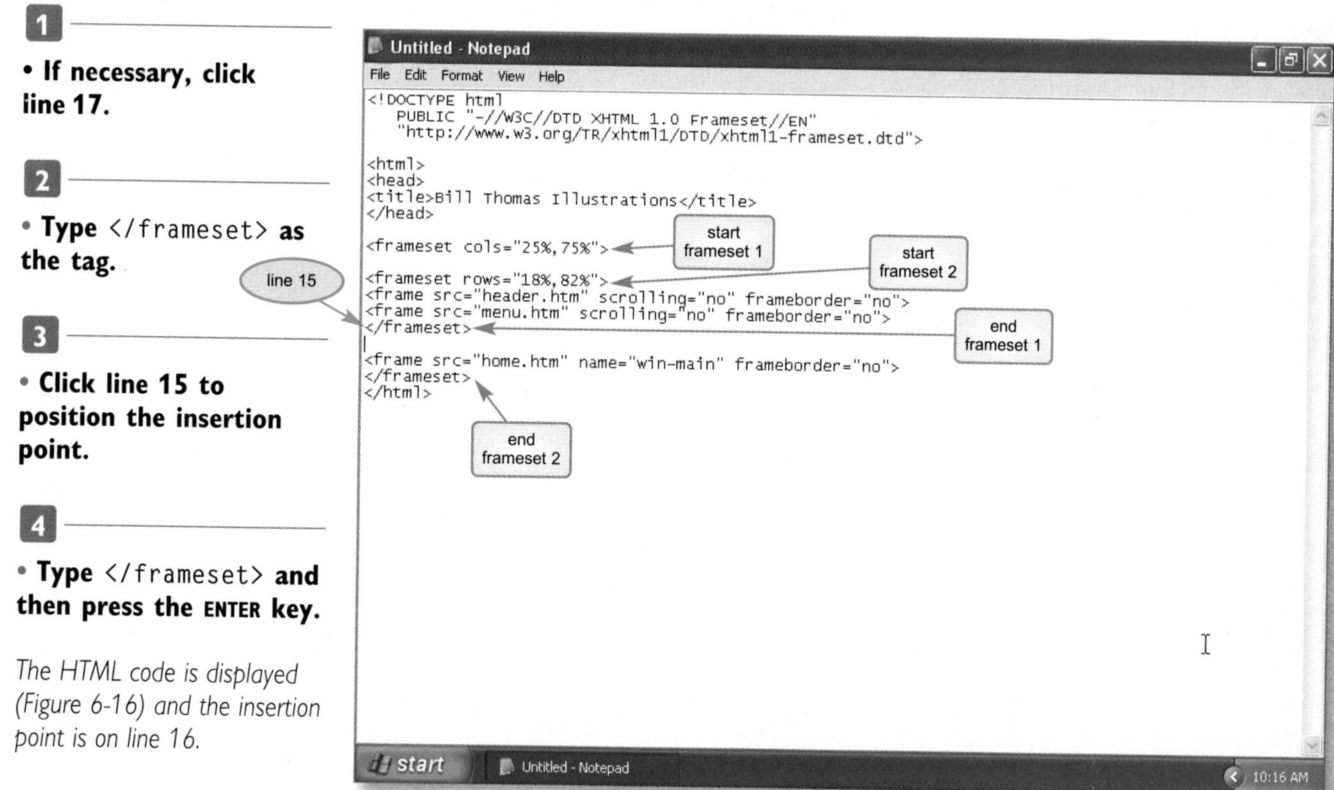

FIGURE 6-16

The frame definition file for the Bill Thomas Illustrations Web site is complete. The frameset divides the window into two columns and then further divides the left column into two rows. The header frame in the top row of the left column always displays the Web page, header.htm. The menu frame in the bottom row of the left column always displays the Web page, menu.htm, to provide a navigation menu. The main frame in the right column, named win-main, displays all other content in the Web site in the right column of the Web page. Note that no <body> </body> tags were used, as they are not needed when creating a frame definition file.

Saving the HTML File

With the HTML code for the frame definition file complete, the file should be saved. The steps on the next page illustrate how to save the frame definition file.

To Save the HTML File

1 **With a floppy disk in drive A, click File on the menu bar and then click Save As. Type** `framedef.htm` **in the File name text box.**

2 **If necessary, click 3½ Floppy (A:) in the Save in list. Click the Project06 folder and then click the ProjectFiles folder in the list of available folders. Click the Save button in the Save As dialog box.**

Notepad saves the HTML file in the Project06\ProjectFiles folder on the floppy disk in drive A using the file name, framedef.htm (Figure 6-17).

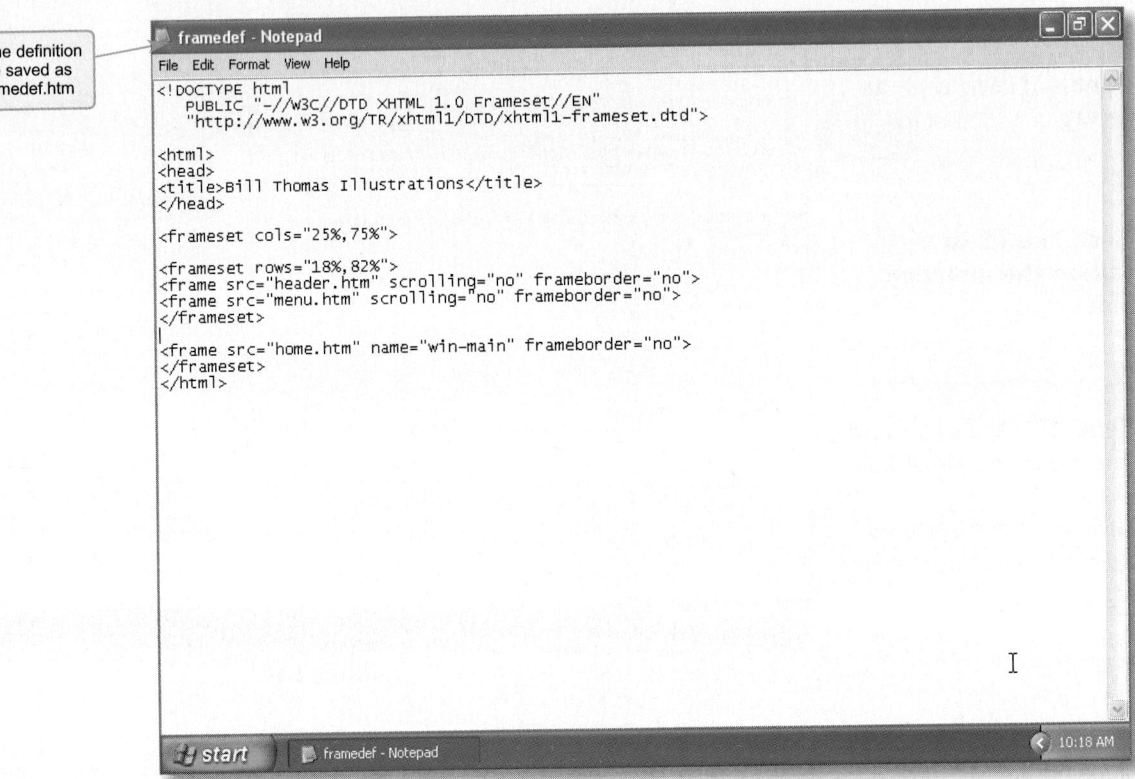

FIGURE 6-17

Creating the Header Page

As previously discussed, the header frame of the Bill Thomas Illustrations Web site always displays the header Web page, header.htm. The header page lists the name of the company, Bill Thomas Illustrations. For a fresh look, a silver-colored background is used in this project.

As with other Web pages, an initial set of HTML tags defines the overall structure of the Web page. Table 6-4 shows the initial HTML tags used in the header page. Note that the header page also uses the frameset document type.

Table 6-4 Code for Initial HTML Tags for Header Page

LINE	HTML TAG AND TEXT
1	<!DOCTYPE html
2	PUBLIC "-//W3C//DTD XHTML 1.0 Frameset//EN"
3	"http://www.w3.org/TR/xhtml1/DTD/xhtml1-frameset.dtd">
4	
5	<html>
6	<head>
7	<title>Bill Thomas Illustrations</title>
8	</head>
9	<body bgcolor="silver">
10	
11	
12	</body>
13	</html>

The following steps illustrate how to open a new document in Notepad and then enter HTML tags to define the Web page structure for the header page. Next, the steps show how to add the text, BILL THOMAS ILLUSTRATIONS, to the header page and change the font face, color, and size of the text. Finally, the steps show how save the HTML file.

To Create the Header Page

1

- **Click File on the menu bar and then click New on the File menu.**
- **Enter the HTML code as shown in Table 6-4.**
- **Position the insertion point on the second blank line (after the <body> tag) on line 11.**

The HTML code is displayed in Notepad (Figure 6-18) and the insertion point is on line 11.

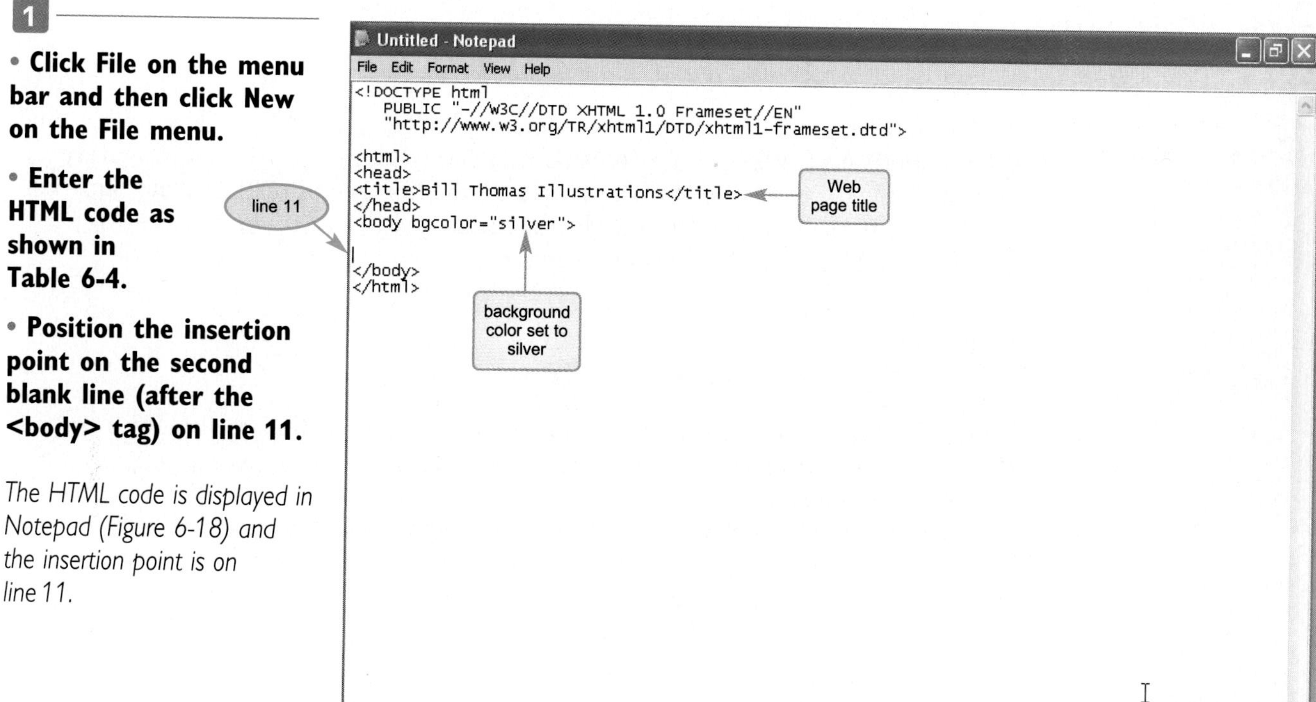

FIGURE 6-18

2

- **Type** `<font face="broadway" color="navy" size="+2">BILL THOMAS` **on line 11 and then press the ENTER key.**
- **Type** `<br />ILLUSTRATIONS </font>` **as the tag.**

3

- **With a floppy disk in drive A, click File on the menu bar and then click Save As. Type** `header.htm` **in the File name text box.**

4

- **If necessary, click 3½ Floppy (A:) in the Save in list. Click the Project06 folder and then click the ProjectFiles folder in the list of available folders. Click the Save button in the Save As dialog box.**

Notepad saves the header.htm file in the Project06\ProjectFiles folder on the floppy disk in drive A (Figure 6-19).

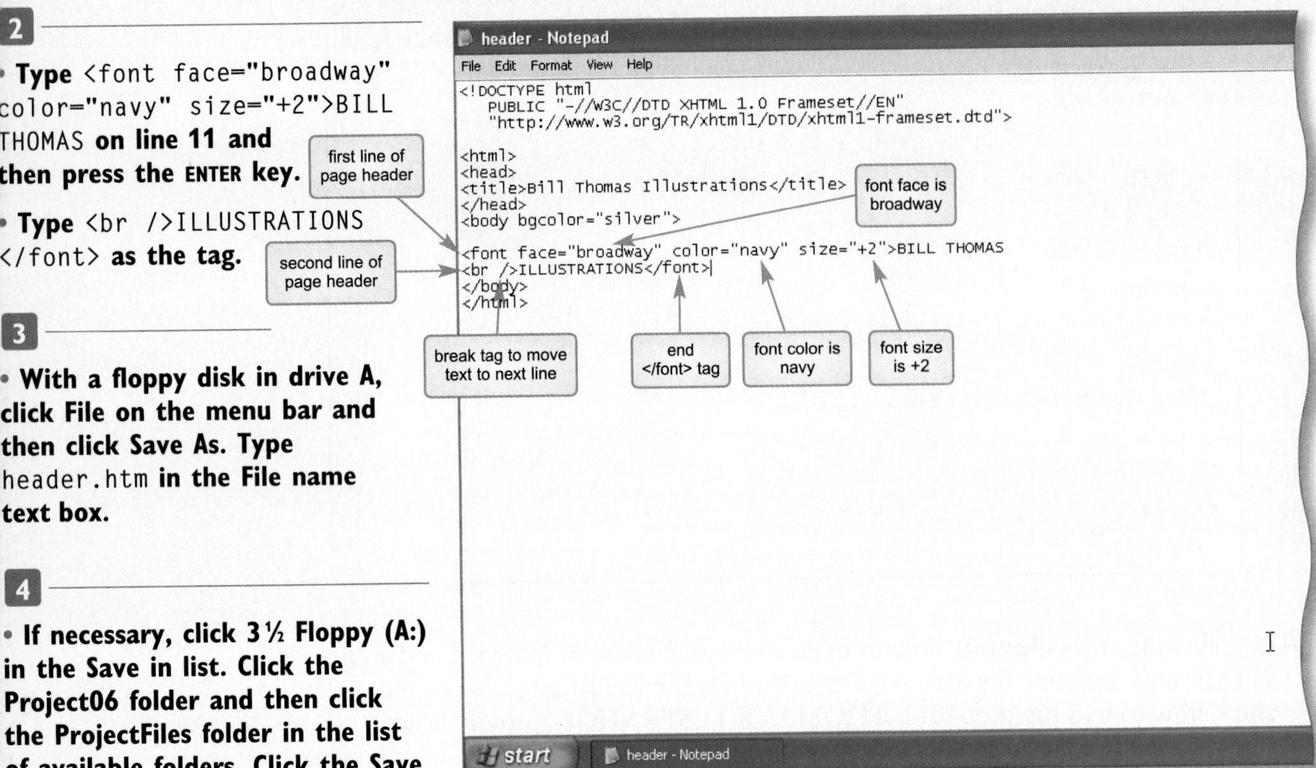

FIGURE 6-19

The header page (header.htm) is complete. The Web page uses a silver background color, with the title, BILL THOMAS ILLUSTRATIONS, in size +2 broadway navy font. A <br /> tag is used in line 12 to separate the first line of the title from the second line. In the frame definition file, the header page is set to appear in the top row of the left column of the frame structure.

Creating the Menu Page

As previously discussed, the menu frame of the Bill Thomas Illustrations Web site always displays the menu Web page, menu.htm. This Web page (menu.htm) contains the list of text links that is used as a navigation menu.

As with other Web pages, an initial set of HTML tags defines the overall structure of the Web page. Table 6-5 shows the initial HTML tags used in the menu page. Note that the menu page also uses the frameset document type.

Table 6-5 Code for Initial HTML Tags for Menu Page

LINE	HTML TAG AND TEXT
1	`<!DOCTYPE html`
2	`  PUBLIC "-//W3C//DTD XHTML 1.0 Frameset//EN"`
3	`  "http://www.w3.org/TR/xhtml1/DTD/xhtml1-frameset.dtd">`
4	
5	`<html>`
6	`<head>`
7	`<title>Bill Thomas Illustrations</title>`
8	`</head>`
9	`<body bgcolor="silver" text="navy" link="navy" vlink="navy" alink="navy">`
10	
11	
12	`</body>`
13	`</html>`

Line 9 sets the background color of the menu page to silver to match the header page and sets the text on the Web page to navy, as designated by the text="navy" attribute. Line 9 also includes HTML code to set the link colors to navy for normal, active, and visited links.

The following steps illustrate how to open a new document in Notepad and then enter HTML tags to define the Web page structure for the menu page.

To Start a New Document and Enter Initial HTML Tags

1. **Click File on the menu bar and then click New.**
2. **Enter the HTML code as shown in Table 6-5.**
3. **Position the insertion point on the second blank line (after the <body> tag) on line 11.**

The HTML code is displayed in Notepad (Figure 6-20) and the insertion point is on line 11.

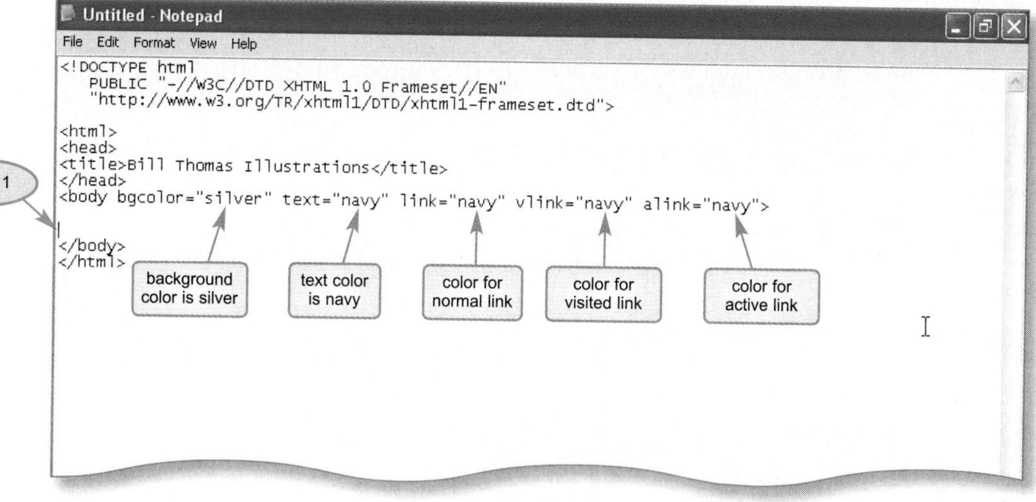

FIGURE 6-20

Adding Links with Targets to the Menu Page

The next step is to add the text links to the menu page. The menu page should contain five links that correspond to the five Web pages and images in the Bill Thomas Illustrations Web site: home.htm, thomascross.jpg, thomasfull.jpg, thomasink.jpg, and orderform.htm. Table 6-6 lists the HTML code used to create the links in the menu page.

Table 6-6 HTML Code for Creating Links

LINE	HTML TAG AND TEXT
11	<font face="broadway">
12	<b><p><a href="thomascross.jpg" target="win-main">Cross Hatch</a></p>
13	<p><a href="thomasfull.jpg" target="win-main">Full Color</a></p>
14	<p><a href="thomasink.jpg" target="win-main">Ink Wash</a></p>
15	<p><a href="orderform.htm" target="win-main">Order Form</a></p>
16	<p><a href="home.htm" target="win-main">Home</a></p></b>
17	</font>
18	
19	<p><em><font size="-1">E-mail questions and comments to
20	<a href="mailto:billthomas@isp.com">billthomas@isp.com</a></font></em></p>

In previous steps, the main frame was assigned the name, win-main, using the name attribute of the <frame> tag. As shown in lines 12 through 16, each link in the menu page has the target attribute, target="win-main", to indicate that all linked Web pages or images should be displayed in the main frame.

Line 11 sets the font face for the link text to broadway, so the link text matches the title text on the header page. Finally, lines 19 and 20 create an e-mail link so visitors can contact the owner of the Web site with questions or comments.

The following steps show how to add links with targets to the menu page and then save the HTML file using the file name, menu.htm.

To Add Links with Targets to the Menu Page and Save the HTML File

1

- **If necessary, click line 11.**

2

- **Enter the HTML code shown in Table 6-6.**

The HTML code is displayed in Notepad (Figure 6-21).

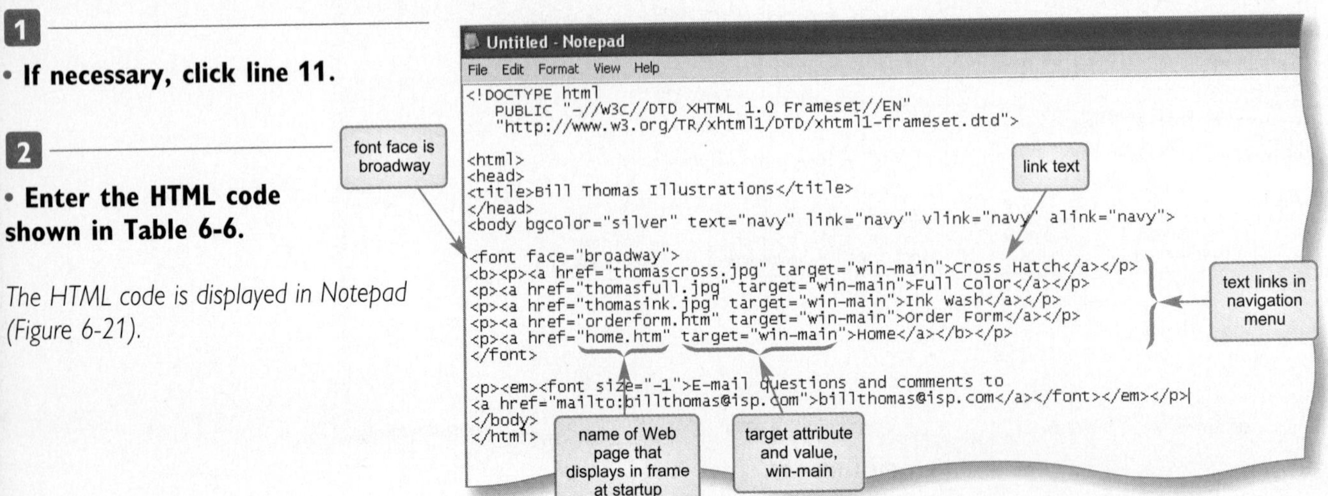

FIGURE 6-21

3

• **With a floppy disk in drive A, click File on the menu bar and then click Save As. Type** `menu.htm` **in the File name text box.**

4

• **If necessary, click 3½ Floppy (A:) in the Save in list. Click the Project06 folder and then click the ProjectFiles folder in the list of available folders. Click the Save button in the Save As dialog box.**

Notepad saves the menu.htm file in the Project06\ProjectFiles folder on the floppy disk in drive A.

Creating the Home Page

Three HTML files now are complete: the frame definition file, the header page that will be used as a header (header.htm), and the menu page that will be used for navigation (menu.htm). The next step is to create the home page (home.htm) that will display in the main frame of the frame structure at startup.

Table 6-7 shows the initial HTML tags used in the home page.

> *More About*
>
> **Noresize**
>
> If the noresize attribute is not used, Netscape displays a small hash mark in the middle of the border. This indicates that the frame can be resized. If noresize is used, the hash mark does not appear in Netscape. Internet Explorer does not display a hash mark for frames that allow resizing. You would use the noresize attribute when you do not want the Web page visitor to resize the frame. You can allow them to resize some of the frames and not others by using noresize in the various <frame> tags.

Table 6-7 Code for Initial HTML Tags for Home Page

LINE	HTML TAG AND TEXT
1	`<!DOCTYPE html`
2	`  PUBLIC "-//W3C//DTD XHTML 1.0 Frameset//EN"`
3	`  "http://www.w3.org/TR/xhtml1/DTD/xhtml1-frameset.dtd">`
4	
5	`<html>`
6	`<head>`
7	`<title>Bill Thomas Illustrations</title>`
8	`</head>`
9	`<body bgcolor="silver">`
10	
11	
12	`</body>`
13	`</html>`

Lines 1 through 3 set the home page to use the frameset document type, as did the other Web pages in the Web site. Line 9 sets the background color of the home page to silver to match the header and menu pages.

In addition to the initial HTML tags, the home page must include HTML code to add an image. As shown in Figure 6-1 on page HTM 249, the home page for the Bill Thomas Illustrations Web site includes one image file, thomaswaterfall.jpg. When a user first views the frame definition file (framedef.htm), the home page with the thomaswaterfall.jpg image appears in the main frame.

The following steps illustrate how to open a new document in Notepad and then enter HTML tags to define the Web page structure for the home page. Next, the steps show how to add the image, thomaswaterfall.jpg, to the home page. Finally, the steps show how to save the HTML file.

To Create the Home Page

1

- **Click File on the menu bar and then click New on the File menu.**
- **Enter the HTML code as shown in Table 6-7 on the previous page.**
- **Position the insertion point on the second blank line (line 11).**

The HTML code is displayed in Notepad (Figure 6-22) and the insertion point is on line 11.

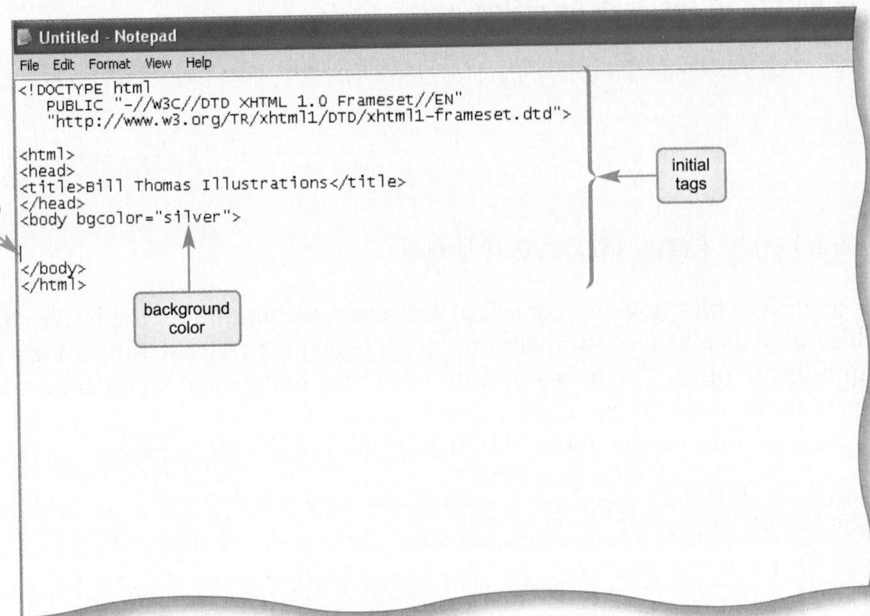

FIGURE 6-22

2

- **Type** `<img src="thomaswaterfall.jpg">` **as the tag.**

3

- **With a floppy disk in drive A, click File on the menu bar and then click Save As. Type** `home.htm` **in the File name text box.**

4

- **If necessary, click 3½ Floppy (A:) in the Save in list. Click the Project06 folder and then click the ProjectFiles folder in the list of available folders. Click the Save button in the Save As dialog box.**

Notepad saves the home.htm file in the Project06\ProjectFiles folder on the floppy disk in drive A (Figure 6-23).

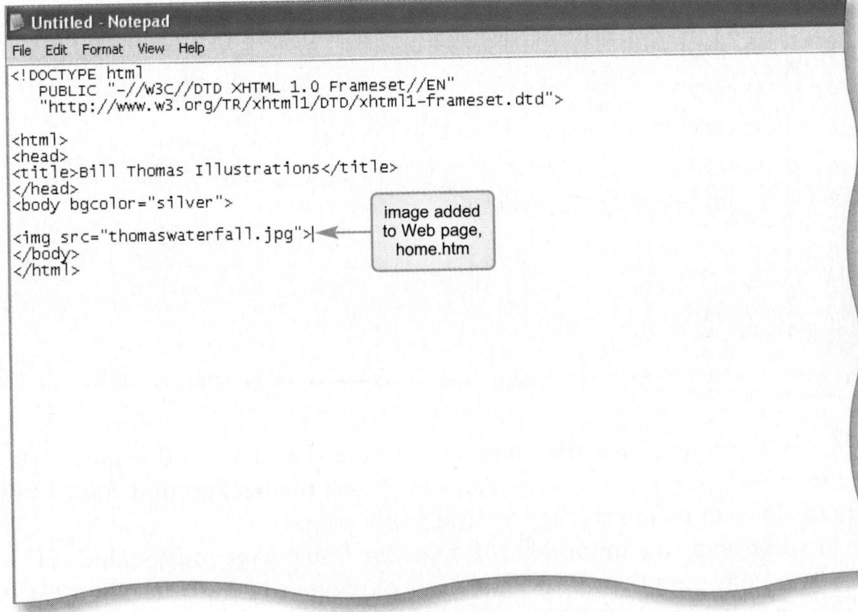

FIGURE 6-23

With the HTML code for the home page complete, all the Web pages to be created for the Bill Thomas Illustrations Web site — framedef.htm, header.htm, menu.htm, and home.htm — are complete. The additional Web pages and images used in the Web site (orderform.htm, thomascross.jpg, thomasfull.jpg, and thomasink.jpg) are stored on the HTML Data Disk.

The Web site includes a frame definition file (framedef.htm) that defines the layout of the frames as displayed in the window. The frame definition file divides the window into three frames: a top-left frame, a bottom-left frame, and a right frame.

When the frame definition file (framedef.htm) initially appears in the browser window, the Web page, header.htm, appears in the top-left frame, menu.htm appears in the bottom-left frame, and home.htm appears in the right frame. As a user clicks links in the menu bar in the bottom-left frame, the contents of the right frame, named win-main, change to reflect the contents of the linked Web page or image. The contents of the top-left frame and the bottom-left frame do not change.

Viewing, Testing, and Printing Web Pages and HTML Code

With the Bill Thomas Illustrations Web site complete, each of the Web pages in the Web site should be viewed in a browser to confirm that the Web page appears as desired and that the links function as expected. After testing the links, the Web pages and HTML code for each Web page should be printed for future reference.

Viewing and Printing the Frame Definition File Using a Browser

To test the Web pages in the Bill Thomas Illustrations Web site, the framedef.htm page first should be opened in the browser to verify that the correct pages display in the frame structure at startup. After verifying that the correct pages are displayed, the Web page should be printed for future reference. Because the Web site home page is divided into frames, three printing options are available. You can print the Web page as it displays on the screen or print each individual framed Web page separately. The Options tab of the browser's Print dialog box includes these three options:

- As laid out on screen
- Only the selected frame
- All frames individually

The default is to print only the selected frame. To print all three frames of the frame definition file in one printout, the As laid out on screen option should be used.

The steps on the next page show how to view and print the frame definition file using a browser.

More About

Frame Printing

The three ways to print a Web page with frames are (1) as laid out on the page, (2) only the selected frame, and (3) all frames individually. Your purpose for printing the page determines which option you should select. If the Web page does not contain frames, these options are not available in the Print dialog Options window.

To View and Print the Frame Definition File Using a Browser

1

- **Start your browser.**

2

- **Type** `a:\Project06\ProjectFiles\framedef.htm` **in the Address box and then press the ENTER key.**

The frame definition file, framedef.htm, is displayed (Figure 6-24).

FIGURE 6-24

3

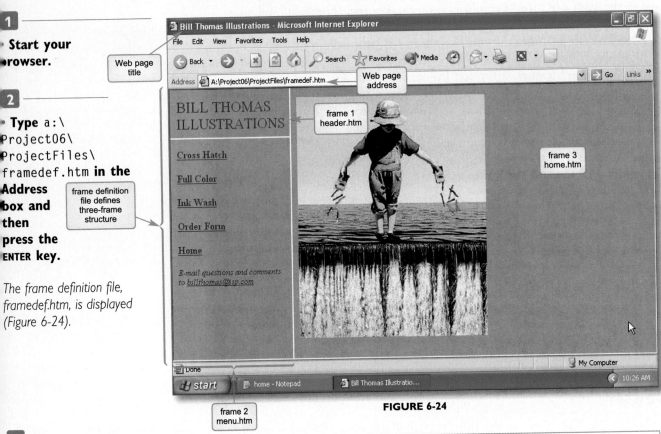

- **Click File on the menu bar and then click Print on the File menu.**
- **Click the Options tab in the Print dialog box.**
- **Click As laid out on screen to select it and then click the Print button.**

The Web page prints with the frames laid out as shown in the browser window (Figure 6-25).

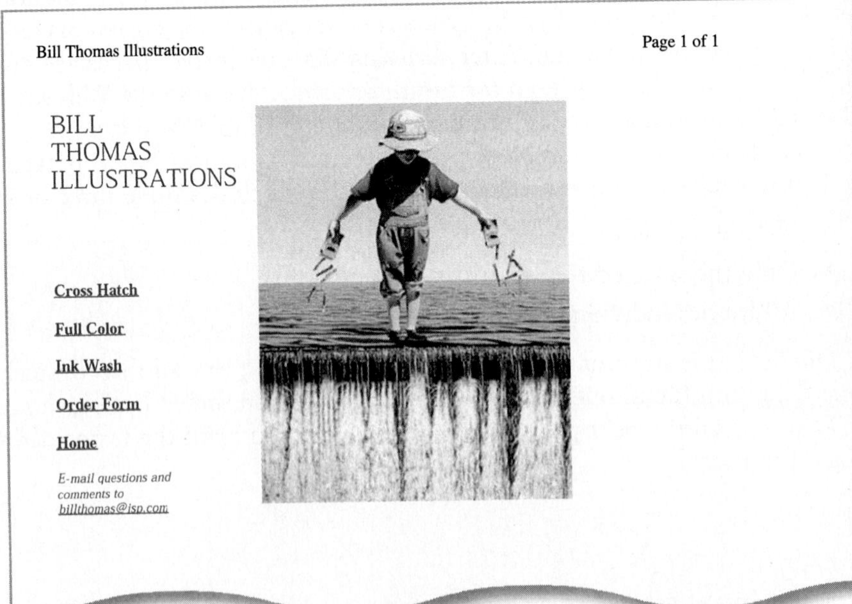

Bill Thomas Illustrations

Page 1 of 1

BILL THOMAS ILLUSTRATIONS

Cross Hatch

Full Color

Ink Wash

Order Form

Home

E-mail questions and comments to billthomas@isp.com

FIGURE 6-25

As shown in Figure 6-24, when the frame definition file is opened, the three Web pages created in this project display in the three frames shown in the browser window. The Web page, header.htm, is shown in the top-left frame. The Web page, menu.htm, appears in the bottom-left frame and includes text links to all the other Web pages in the site. The Web page, home.htm, appears in the right frame. The Web page, home.htm, is set to appear at startup in the main frame, named win-main. All other Web pages display in the main frame when their corresponding link is clicked.

More About

Frameset Tags

Be sure to use the </frameset> tag when developing Web pages with frames. If you do not add that tag, some older browsers will display a blank page. The Web server log collects statistics about your Web site visitors' browser types and versions. These statistics are an excellent source of information about who is visiting your Web site.

Testing the Links

The next step is to test the links by clicking each link in the menu bar to ensure the correct Web page displays in the main frame. Finally, test the e-mail address link to ensure it works correctly.

To Test the Links

1. **Click the Cross Hatch link on the navigation menu.**
2. **Click the Full Color link on the navigation menu.**
3. **Click the Ink Wash link on the navigation menu.**
4. **Click the Order Form link on the navigation menu.**
5. **Click the Home link on the navigation menu.**
6. **Click the e-mail link and verify that the New Message window shows billthomas@isp.com as the address. Click the Close button to close the New Message window and quit the e-mail program.**

The Web page, home.htm, displays in the browser's main frame.

If any of the links do not work correctly, return to Notepad to modify the HTML code, save the changes, and then retest the links in the browser.

Printing the HTML Files

After you have tested the Web page links, the HTML files created in this project should be printed for future reference.

To Print All HTML Files

1. **Click the Notepad button on the taskbar.**
2. **Click File on the menu bar and then click Print. Click Print in the Print dialog box to print the home.htm file.**
3. **Using Notepad, open the file, framedef.htm, from the Project06\ProjectFiles folder on the HTML Data Disk.**
4. **Click File on the menu bar and then click Print. Click Print in the Print dialog box to print the file, framedef.htm.**
5. **Repeat Steps 3 and 4 to open and print the header.htm and menu.htm files.**

The HTML files print (Figure 6-26 on the next page).

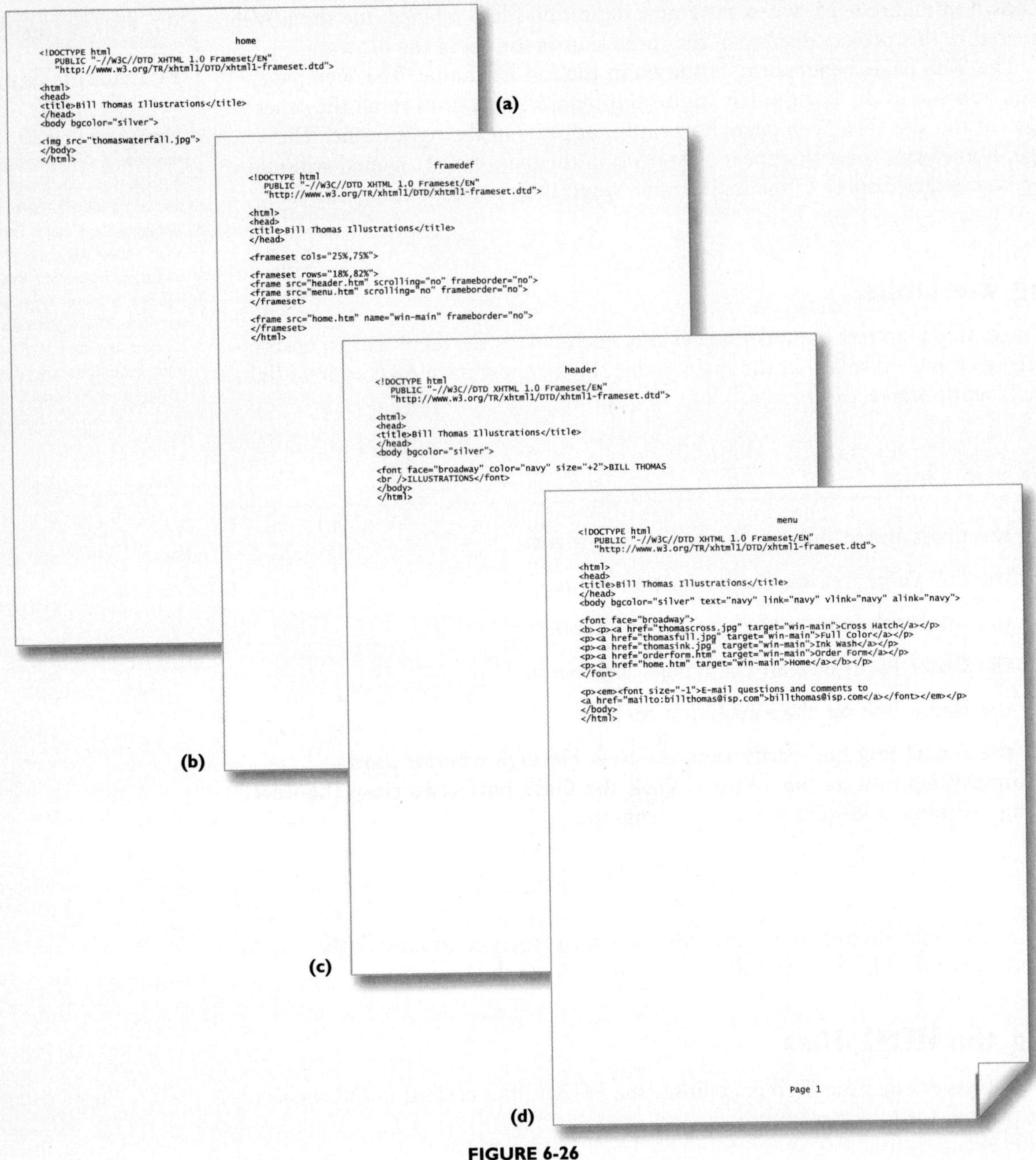

(a)

```
home
<!DOCTYPE html
   PUBLIC "-//W3C//DTD XHTML 1.0 Frameset/EN"
   "http://www.w3.org/TR/xhtml1/DTD/xhtml1-frameset.dtd">

<html>
<head>
<title>Bill Thomas Illustrations</title>
</head>
<body bgcolor="silver">

<img src="thomaswaterfall.jpg">
</body>
</html>
```

(b)

```
framedef
<!DOCTYPE html
   PUBLIC "-//W3C//DTD XHTML 1.0 Frameset/EN"
   "http://www.w3.org/TR/xhtml1/DTD/xhtml1-frameset.dtd">

<html>
<head>
<title>Bill Thomas Illustrations</title>
</head>

<frameset cols="25%,75%">

<frameset rows="18%,82%">
<frame src="header.htm" scrolling="no" frameborder="no">
<frame src="menu.htm" scrolling="no" frameborder="no">
</frameset>

<frame src="home.htm" name="win-main" frameborder="no">
</frameset>
</html>
```

(c)

```
header
<!DOCTYPE html
   PUBLIC "-//W3C//DTD XHTML 1.0 Frameset/EN"
   "http://www.w3.org/TR/xhtml1/DTD/xhtml1-frameset.dtd">

<html>
<head>
<title>Bill Thomas Illustrations</title>
</head>
<body bgcolor="silver">

<font face="broadway" color="navy" size="+2">BILL THOMAS
<br />ILLUSTRATIONS</font>
</body>
</html>
```

(d)

```
menu
<!DOCTYPE html
   PUBLIC "-//W3C//DTD XHTML 1.0 Frameset/EN"
   "http://www.w3.org/TR/xhtml1/DTD/xhtml1-frameset.dtd">

<html>
<head>
<title>Bill Thomas Illustrations</title>
</head>
<body bgcolor="silver" text="navy" link="navy" vlink="navy" alink="navy">

<font face="broadway">
<b><p><a href="thomascross.jpg" target="win-main">Cross Hatch</a></p>
<p><a href="thomasfull.jpg" target="win-main">Full Color</a></p>
<p><a href="thomasink.jpg" target="win-main">Ink Wash</a></p>
<p><a href="orderform.htm" target="win-main">Order Form</a></p>
<p><a href="home.htm" target="win-main">Home</a></b></p>
</font>

<p><em><font size="-1">E-mail questions and comments to
<a href="mailto:billthomas@isp.com">billthomas@isp.com</a></font></em></p>
</body>
</html>

Page 1
```

FIGURE 6-26

After completing the project, quit Notepad and the browser. The following steps show how to quit Notepad and a browser.

To Quit Notepad and a Browser

1. **Click the Close button on the browser title bar.**
2. **Click the Close button on the Notepad window title bar.**

Both the browser and Notepad windows close, and the Windows desktop is displayed.

Project Summary

In Project 6, you learned how to plan and lay out a frame structure before entering HTML code. You also learned how to create a frame definition file that defines the structure of the frames, specifies which Web page should appear in each frame at startup, and assigns a name to a frame to be used as a target. You then learned how to enter HTML code for a header page that contains a text heading. You also learned how to enter HTML code to create a navigation menu page with text links that link to the other Web pages and specify a target frame. Finally, after completing the Web site by creating a home page with one image, you learned how to use a browser to view and print the frame definition file using the As laid out on screen option.

What You Should Know

Having completed this project, you should be able to perform the tasks listed below. The tasks are listed in the same order they were presented in this project.

1. Start Notepad and Enter Initial HTML Tags (HTM 261)
2. Define Columns and Rows in the Frameset (HTM 264)
3. Identify Attributes of the Header and Menu Frames (HTM 265)
4. Identify Attributes of the Main Frame (HTM 266)
5. End the Framesets (HTM 267)
6. Save the HTML File (HTM 268)
7. Create the Header Page (HTM 269)
8. Start a New Document and Enter Initial HTML Tags (HTM 271)
9. Add Links with Targets to the Menu Page and Save the HTML File (HTM 272)
10. Create the Home Page (HTM 274)
11. View and Print the Frame Definition File Using a Browser (HTM 276)
12. Test the Links (HTM 277)
13. Print All HTML Files (HTM 277)
14. Quit Notepad and a Browser (HTM 278)

Learn It Online

Instructions: To complete the Learn It Online exercises, start your browser, click the Address bar, and then enter the Web address `scsite.com/html3e/learn`. When the HTML Learn It Online page is displayed, follow the instructions in the exercises below. Each exercise has instructions for printing your results, either for your own records or for submission to your instructor.

1 Project Reinforcement TF, MC, and SA

Below HTML Project 6, click the Project Reinforcement link. Print the quiz by clicking Print on the File menu for each page. Answer each question.

2 Flash Cards

Below HTML Project 6, click the Flash Cards link and read the instructions. Type 20 (or a number specified by your instructor) in the Number of playing cards text box, type your name in the Enter your Name text box, and then click the Flip Card button. When the flash card is displayed, read the question and then click the ANSWER box arrow to select an answer. Flip through Flash Cards. If your score is 15 (75%) correct or greater, click Print on the File menu to print your results. If your score is less than 15 (75%) correct, then redo this exercise by clicking the Replay button.

3 Practice Test

Below HTML Project 6, click the Practice Test link. Answer each question, enter your first and last name at the bottom of the page, and then click the Grade Test button. When the graded practice test is displayed on your screen, click Print on the File menu to print a hard copy. Continue to take practice tests until you score 80% or better.

4 Who Wants To Be a Computer Genius?

Below HTML Project 6, click the Computer Genius link. Read the instructions, enter your first and last name at the bottom of the page, and then click the PLAY button. When your score is displayed, click the PRINT RESULTS link to print a hard copy.

5 Wheel of Terms

Below HTML Project 6, click the Wheel of Terms link. Read the instructions, and then enter your first and last name and your school name. Click the PLAY button. When your score is displayed, right-click the score and then click Print on the shortcut menu to print a hard copy.

6 Crossword Puzzle Challenge

Below HTML Project 6, click the Crossword Puzzle Challenge link. Read the instructions, and then enter your first and last name. Click the SUBMIT button. Work the crossword puzzle. When you are finished, click the Submit button. When the crossword puzzle is redisplayed, click the Print Puzzle button to print a hard copy.

7 Tips and Tricks

Below HTML Project 6, click the Tips and Tricks link. Click a topic that pertains to Project 6. Right-click the information and then click Print on the shortcut menu. Construct a brief example of what the information relates to in HTML to confirm you understand how to use the tip or trick.

8 Newsgroups

Below HTML Project 6, click the Newsgroups link. Click a topic that pertains to Project 6. Print three comments.

9 Expanding Your Horizons

Below HTML Project 6, click the Expanding Your Horizons link. Click a topic that pertains to Project 6. Print the information. Construct a brief example of what the information relates to in HTML to confirm you understand the contents of the article.

10 Search Sleuth

Below HTML Project 6, click the Search Sleuth link. To search for a term that pertains to this project, select a term below the Project 6 title and then use the Google search engine at google.com (or any major search engine) to display and print two Web pages that present information on the term.

11 Online Help I

Below HTML Project 6, click the Online Help I link. Follow the instructions on the page to access Web pages that provide additional help on project topics. Hand in any printed information to your instructor.

12 Online Help II

Below HTML Project 6, click the Online Help II link. Follow the instructions on the page to access Web pages that provide additional help on project topics. Hand in any printed information to your instructor.

Apply Your Knowledge

1 Editing the Apply Your Knowledge Web Page

Instructions: Start Notepad and a browser. Open the file, apply6-1.htm, from the Project06\AYK folder on the HTML Data Disk. See the inside back cover of this book for instructions for downloading the HTML Data Disk or see your instructor for information about accessing the files in this book. The apply6-1.htm file is a partially completed HTML file that contains errors. Figure 6-27 shows the Apply Your Knowledge Web page as it should appear in your browser after the errors are corrected. With the Web page corrected, a user should be able to click a link in the top frame to display the corresponding linked page in the bottom frame. Perform the following steps using a computer:

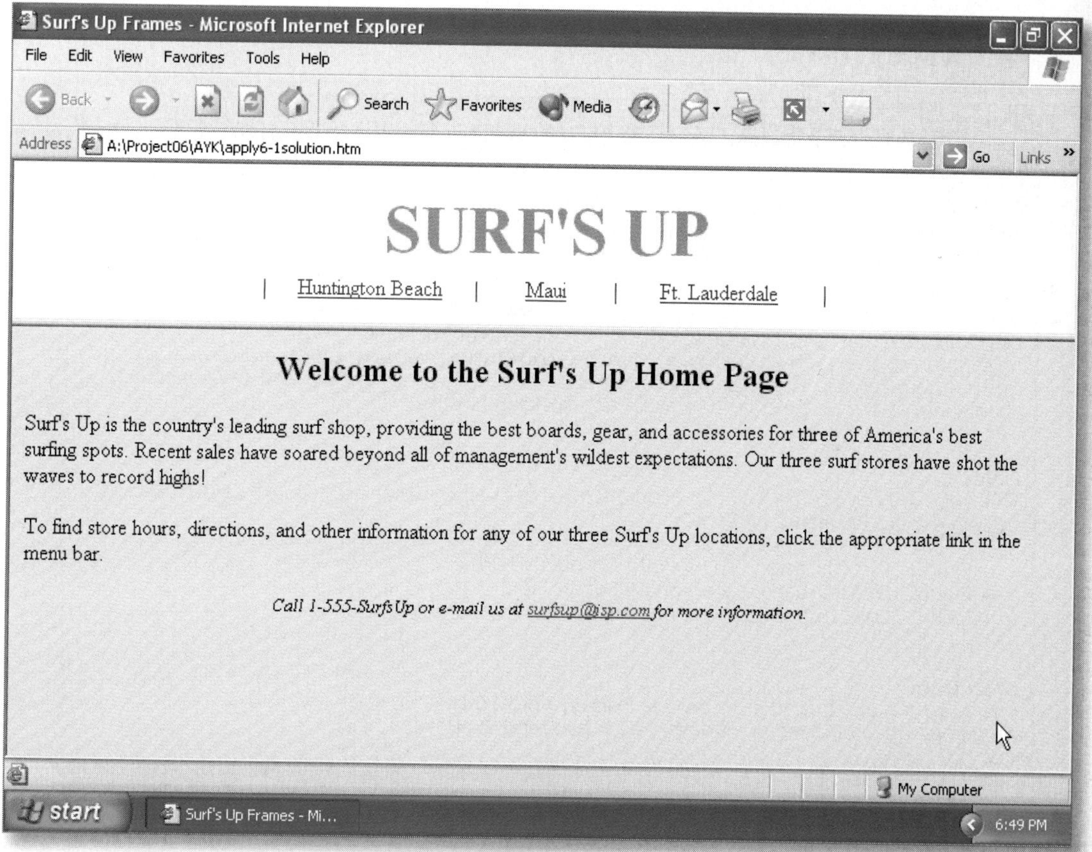

FIGURE 6-27

1. Open the file, apply6-1.htm, in Notepad.
2. Enter the URL, `a:\Project06\AYK\apply6-1.htm`, to view the Web page in your browser.
3. Examine the HTML file and its appearance as a Web page in the browser.
4. Using Notepad, correct the HTML errors to make the Web page look similar to the one shown in Figure 6-27.
5. Add any HTML code necessary to create additional features shown in the Web page.
6. Save the revised file in the Project06\AYK folder on the HTML Data Disk using the file name, apply6-1solution.htm.
7. Print the revised HTML file.
8. Enter the URL, `a:\Project06\AYK\apply6-1solution.htm`, to view the Web page in your browser.
9. Print the Web page.
10. Write your name on the printouts and hand them in to your instructor.

1 Creating a Two-Frame Structure for a Softball Web Site

Problem: The Director of Recreational Sports at your school has asked you to create a new Web site with information on the upcoming softball season. After reviewing the content with the Director, you suggest using a two-frame structure with two horizontal frames, as shown in Figure 6-28. The top frame will display a header and menu bar for navigation, while the bottom frame will display schedules, standings, rules, and other information.

FIGURE 6-28

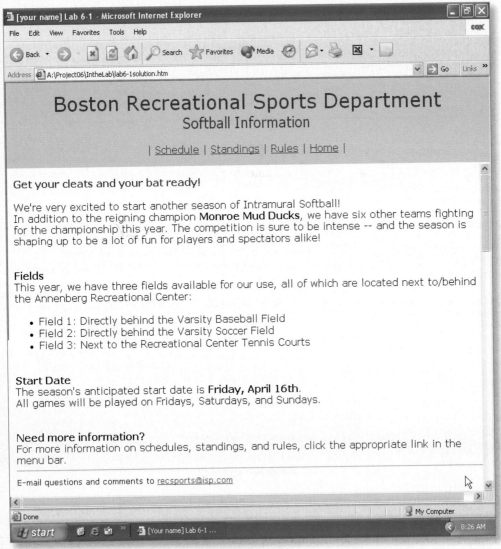

Instructions: Start Notepad. Perform the following steps using a computer:

1. Using Notepad, create a new HTML file with the title, [your name] lab6-1, in the main heading section.
2. Begin the frame definition file by specifying two rows. The first row should be 25 percent of the total screen width and the second row should be 75 percent of the screen width.
3. For the top frame, set the frame to display the Web page, lab6-1menu.htm, at startup. Turn off scrolling and borders.

4. For the bottom frame, set the frame to display the Web page, lab6-1home.htm, at startup. Turn off borders. Assign the frame the name, win-main.
5. Save the HTML file in the Project06\IntheLab folder on the HTML Data Disk using the file name, lab6-1solution.htm. Print the HTML file.
6. Open the HTML file, lab6-1solution.htm, in your browser and test the menu bar links to verify they link to the correct Web pages.
7. Click the Home link on the menu bar and then print the file, lab6-1solution.htm, using the As laid out on screen option.
8. Write your name on the printouts and hand them in to your instructor.

2 Greyhound Adoption Web Site

Problem: The Greyhound Adoption Center has decided to advertise on the Internet. You have been asked to create a Web site with a two-frame structure, as shown in Figure 6-29. First, you need to create a frame definition file that specifies a two-column structure, with columns set to 30 percent and 70 percent. At startup, the left frame displays the Web page, lab6-2menu.htm, which includes links to additional Web pages about the Greyhound Adoption Center. At startup, the right frame displays the Web page, lab6-2home.htm, which serves as a home page.

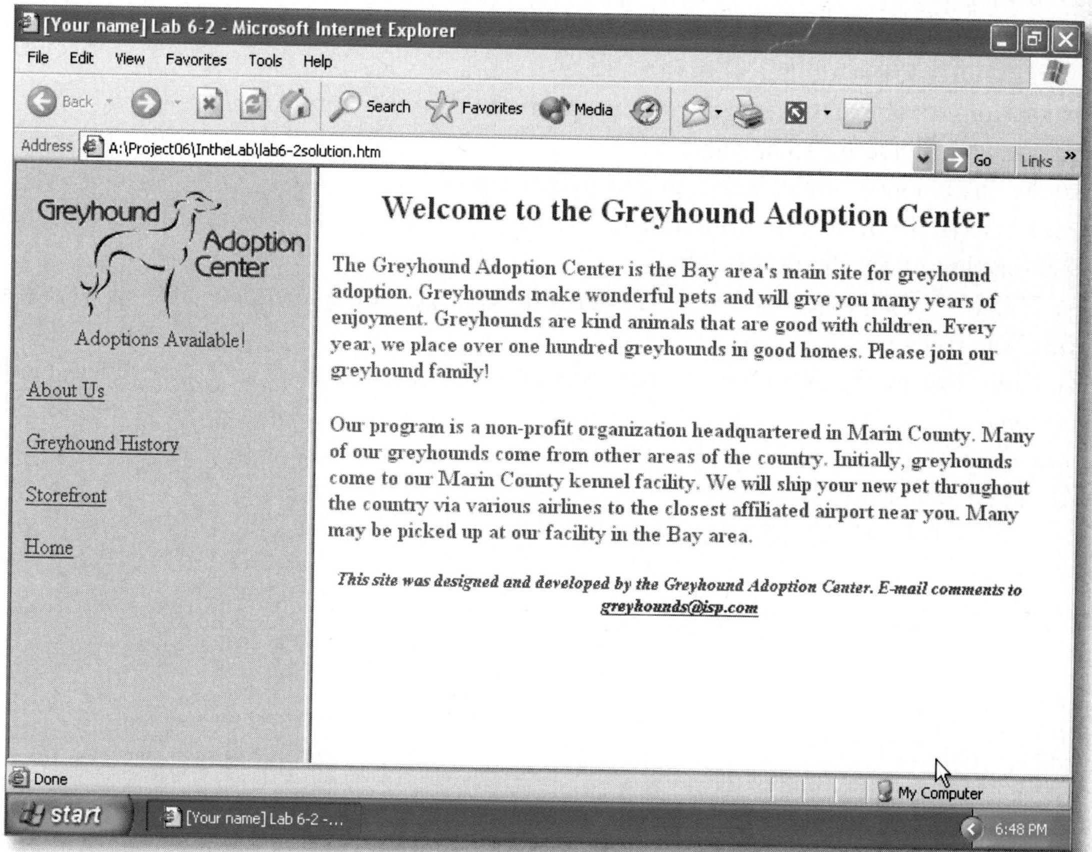

FIGURE 6-29

(continued)

Greyhound Adoption Web Site *(continued)*

Instructions: Start Notepad. Perform the following steps using a computer:

1. Using Notepad, create a new HTML file with the title, [Your name] lab6-2, in the main heading section.
2. Create a frame definition file that specifies a two-frame structure with two columns set to 30 percent and 70 percent, respectively. Save the HTML file in the Project06\IntheLab folder on the HTML Data Disk using the file name, lab6-2solution.htm. Print the HTML file.
3. Create a menu page to appear in the left frame by completing the following steps:
   a. Create a new file in Notepad.
   b. Set a background color of #e0e0e0. Set all links (normal, visited, active) to display in maroon text.
   c. Add the image, greyhound.gif, from the Project06\IntheLab folder on the HTML Data Disk.
   d. Add the text, Adoptions Available, below the image.
   e. Create four text links, as shown in Figure 6-29. Set the Home text link to link to the Web page, lab6-2home.htm. Set the other three links — About Us, Greyhound History, and Storefront — to link to any Web page on the HTML Data Disk.
   f. Save the HTML file in the Project06\IntheLab folder on the HTML Data Disk using the file name, lab6-2menu.htm. Print the HTML file.
4. Create a home page that contains the text shown in Figure 6-29 and appears in the right frame, by completing the following steps:
   a. Enter and format the heading to be center-aligned and bold, with a font size of +2 and a font color of maroon.
   b. Enter and format the remaining Web page text to be bold, with a font color of #808080.
   c. Format the e-mail address to be italic.
   d. Make the link colors (normal, active, and visited) maroon.
   e. Save the HTML file in the Project06\IntheLab folder on the HTML Data Disk using the file name, lab6-2home.htm. Print the HTML file.
5. Open the HTML file, lab6-2solution.htm, in your browser and test the menu bar links to verify they link to the correct Web pages.
6. Click the Home link on the menu bar and then print the file, lab6-2solution.htm, using the As laid out on screen option.
7. Write your name on the printouts and hand them in to your instructor.

3 Creating a Four-Frame Structure

Problem: You recently have started doing freelance Web development work for a few local companies. You want to create a Web site with a four-frame structure, as shown in Figure 6-30, to promote the Web development work you have done in previous projects. After creating the frame definition file, use any image stored on the HTML Data Disk as your logo. Use any of the Web pages previously created and stored on the HTML Data Disk to display in the bottom-right frame.

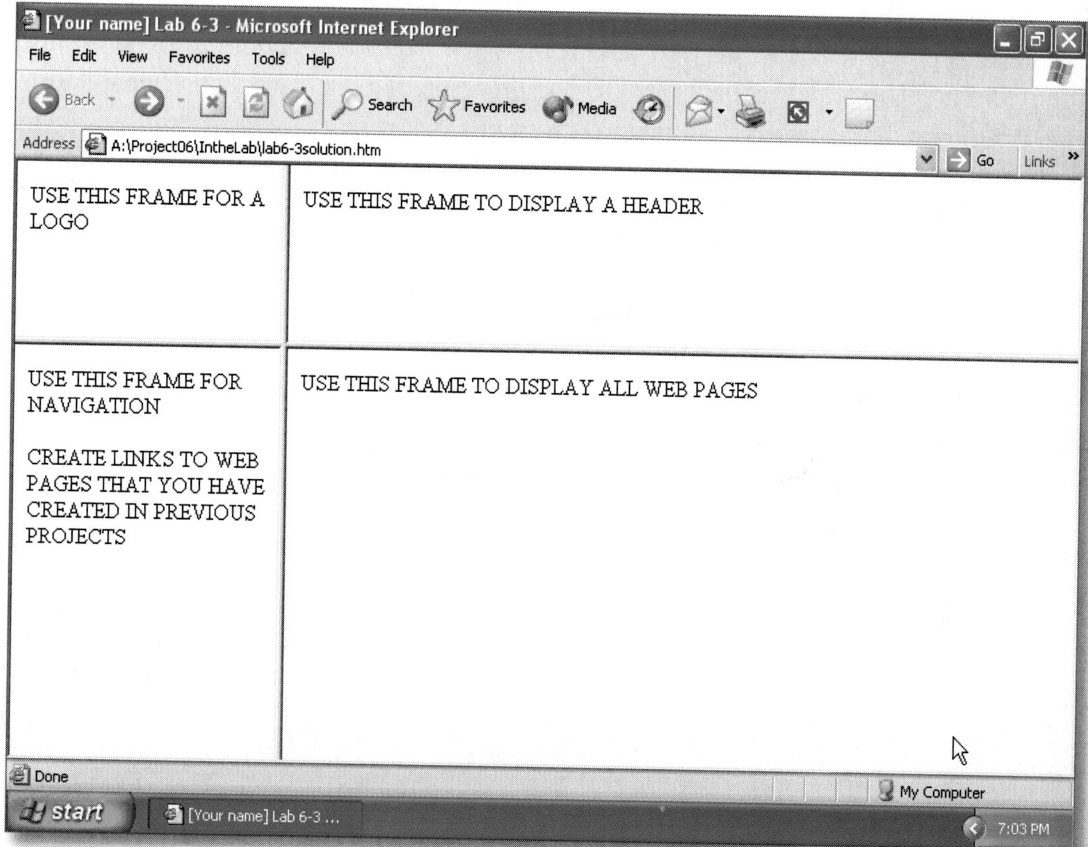

FIGURE 6-30

Instructions: Start Notepad. Perform the following steps using a computer:

1. Using Notepad, create a new HTML file with the title, [Your name] lab6-3, in the main heading section. Enter code to create a frame definition file that specifies a four-frame structure, similar to the one in Figure 6-30. For each frame, set the Web page to display at startup to lab6-3logo.htm for the logo frame, lab6-3header.htm for the header frame, lab6-3menu.htm for the navigation menu frame, and lab6-3home.htm for the main frame. Turn scrolling and borders for each frame on or off, as you think is appropriate.
2. Save the HTML file in the Project06\IntheLab folder on the HTML Data Disk using the file name, lab6-3solution.htm. Print the HTML file.

(continued)

Creating a Four-Frame Structure *(continued)*

3. Create a logo page to appear in the logo frame. Using any image stored on the HTML Data Disk, add a logo to the Web page. Save the HTML file in the Project06\IntheLab folder on the HTML Data Disk using the file name, lab6-3logo.htm. Print the HTML file.
4. Create a header page to appear in the header frame. Include a text heading that has a unique color and font face. Save the HTML file in the Project06\IntheLab folder on the HTML Data Disk using the file name, lab6-3header.htm. Print the HTML file.
5. Create a menu page to appear in the navigation menu frame. Include text links to several Web pages created in this or previous projects, as well as a text link to the home page (lab6-3home.htm). Save the HTML file in the Project06\IntheLab folder on the HTML Data Disk using the file name, lab6-3menu.htm. Print the HTML file.
6. Create a home page to appear in the navigation (or main) frame. Include text that describes your HTML and Web page development skills, along with contact information and an e-mail link. Save the HTML file in the Project06\IntheLab folder on the HTML Data Disk using the file name, lab6-3home.htm. Print the HTML file.
7. Open the HTML file, lab6-3solution.htm, in your browser and test the menu bar links to verify they link to the correct Web pages.
8. Click the Home link on the menu bar and then print the file, lab6-3solution.htm, using the As laid out on screen option.
9. Write your name on the printouts and hand them in to your instructor.

Cases and Places

The difficulty of these case studies varies:
■ are the least difficult and ■■ are the most difficult. The last exercise is a group exercise.

1 ■ In the In the Lab Question 1 on page HTM 282, you created a two-frame structure for an intramural softball Web site. Determine what changes you can make to the Web site to make it a more effective layout. How would you restructure this Web site so the e-mail link is always available? What other changes could you make to the Web site design or frame structure to make the Web site more effective or easier to navigate? Make these changes to the Web site, open the frame definition file in a browser, and then print the Web page using the As laid out on screen option. Turn that printout in to your instructor with a synopsis of why your design is a better solution than the previous two-frame structure used in the In the Lab Question 1.

2 ■ In preparation for a design planning session, the Manager of Web Development at Axcelent has asked you to locate two Web sites that use frames in their page structures, and view the HTML source code for the pages and see what frame options were used on the pages. Is the scrolling turned off, or is the default used? How many frames allow scrolling? Is the noresize attribute utilized? As part of this research, he has asked you to write a brief assessment of the intended purpose for using a frame structure, discussing whether the Web site is more or less effective because of the frames. Print each overall Web page (remember to use the As laid out on screen option in the Print dialog box) and then sketch a design for each Web page using a different frame structure or no frames. How does your structure compare with the originals? Which Web site layout is more effective?

3 ■■ The management at the Lower Keys Tourism Board was impressed by the Web site you developed for Bill Thomas Illustrations. They have asked you to design a prototype for a similar Web site they can use to sell souvenir photos. Because they have numerous pictures available, they want to utilize the thumbnail technique discussed in Project 3. Using the six images available in the Project06\CasesandPlaces folder on the HTML Data Disk, create a simple prototype Web site with frames for the Lower Keys Tourism Board. The Web site should use the smaller thumbnail images for the Web site visitors to review and then give users the option to click an image that they want to see enlarged. Be sure the thumbnail images and the selected large images are displayed in the same frame. Also, use the width and height attributes for all images.

Cases and Places

4 The Campus Tutoring Service has asked if you can create a reference Web site that can be used by students taking the Introductory HTML course. You suggest a Web site similar to the one shown in Figure 6-3b on page HTM 253, which is a Web site with a two-frame structure that provides an excellent reference Web site for information about HTML. Create a similar Web site using a two-frame structure, with the table of contents in the left frame and the content in the right frame. Include at least four topics in the table of contents and create Web pages that contain information about the topics shown in the table of contents.

5 **Working Together** LightWorks Design recently has contracted with several customers who want to use frames on their Web sites. Having read several articles suggesting that frames limit Web site usability, the Senior Web Developer has some concerns about using frames — and has asked everyone on the team to help research the pros and cons of using frames in a Web site. Find at least five Web sites (be sure to include the W3C Web site) that discuss the use of frames. Develop a matrix that describes when or if Web sites could be made more effective with the use of frames. Find some research that describes ways in which you can determine whether or not a browser supports frames. What do you need to do from a coding standpoint to display a Web site in browsers that do not support frames? From a Web site maintenance perspective, what would be the ramifications of this decision? Write a paper discussing the information that you find about using frames.

HTML

Creating a Form on a Web Page

PROJECT 7

CASE PERSPECTIVE

The Bill Thomas Illustrations Web site has been a great success. Many customers have viewed the illustrations on the Web site and followed the instructions on the Order Form Web page to send e-mails requesting to purchase illustrations. Although most of the e-mails are complete, your Uncle Bill has found that a number of e-mails are missing key information. Your uncle asks you if an easier, less error-prone way exists for customers to notify him of their selections.

Having recently learned how to develop forms using HTML, you suggest modifying the text-based order form to create a Web page with a form. Customers then will be able to fill in the online form and submit it to your uncle's e-mail address for collection, simply by clicking the Submit button.

As you read through this project, you will learn how to use HTML to create a Web page form with check boxes, a drop-down list, radio buttons, and text boxes. You also will add Submit and Reset buttons that customers can use to submit the completed form or clear the information previously entered into the form.

Creating a Form on a Web Page

PROJECT 7

Objectives

You will have mastered the material in this project when you can:

- Define terms related to forms
- Describe the different form controls and their uses
- Use the <form> tag
- Use the <input> tag
- Create a text box
- Create check boxes
- Create a selection menu with multiple options
- Use the <select> tag
- Use the <option> tag
- Create radio buttons
- Create a textarea box
- Create a Submit button
- Create a Reset button
- Use the <fieldset> tag to group form information

Introduction

The goal of projects completed thus far has been to present information to a Web page visitor. Getting information from the visitor is another important aspect of good Web page development and is vital to good communication between the Web site owner and Web page visitors.

In Project 6, the Order Form Web page for the Bill Thomas Illustrations Web site was created as a text-based Web page that listed the information needed to place an order. To place an order, customers had to type all of their order information into an e-mail and then send it to a specific e-mail address. While such an approach to information gathering does work, it is inefficient and prone to error. Users easily can forget to include required information or request options that are not available.

Using a Web page form reduces the potential for errors, because customers enter data or select options from the form included directly on the Web page. The form not only has input fields to remind users to enter information, but also provides only valid options to avoid incorrect data entry. Further, users can submit the data directly from the form by clicking the Submit button, rather than having to re-type and send the information via e-mail.

In this project, you will learn how to use HTML to create a form on a Web page. The form will include several controls, including check boxes, a drop-down list, radio buttons, and text boxes. You will also will learn to add Submit and Reset buttons that customers can use to submit the completed form or clear the information previously entered into the form. Finally, you will learn to use the <fieldset> tag to group information on a form in a user-friendly way.

Project Seven — Creating Forms on a Web Page

Web sites use forms to gather information from Web site visitors for a variety of purposes. A Web site can include a simple form such as a guest sign-in, a feedback form to collect visitor feedback about the Web site, a registration form to create an account on that Web site, or an order form to select and purchase products. All forms should be designed to allow visitors to submit information to the owners of the Web site easily and efficiently, by entering data or selecting options and then submitting the form.

In this project, you will learn to enter HTML tags to modify the text-based Order Form Web page on the Bill Thomas Illustrations Web site (Figure 7-1a) and to create an Order Form Web page with a form, as shown in Figure 7-1b. This page will request the same information as the text-based Web page, but will include a form that allows users to enter data, select options, and then submit the form to an e-mail address. The text-based Order Form Web page, orderform.htm, is stored on the HTML Data Disk.

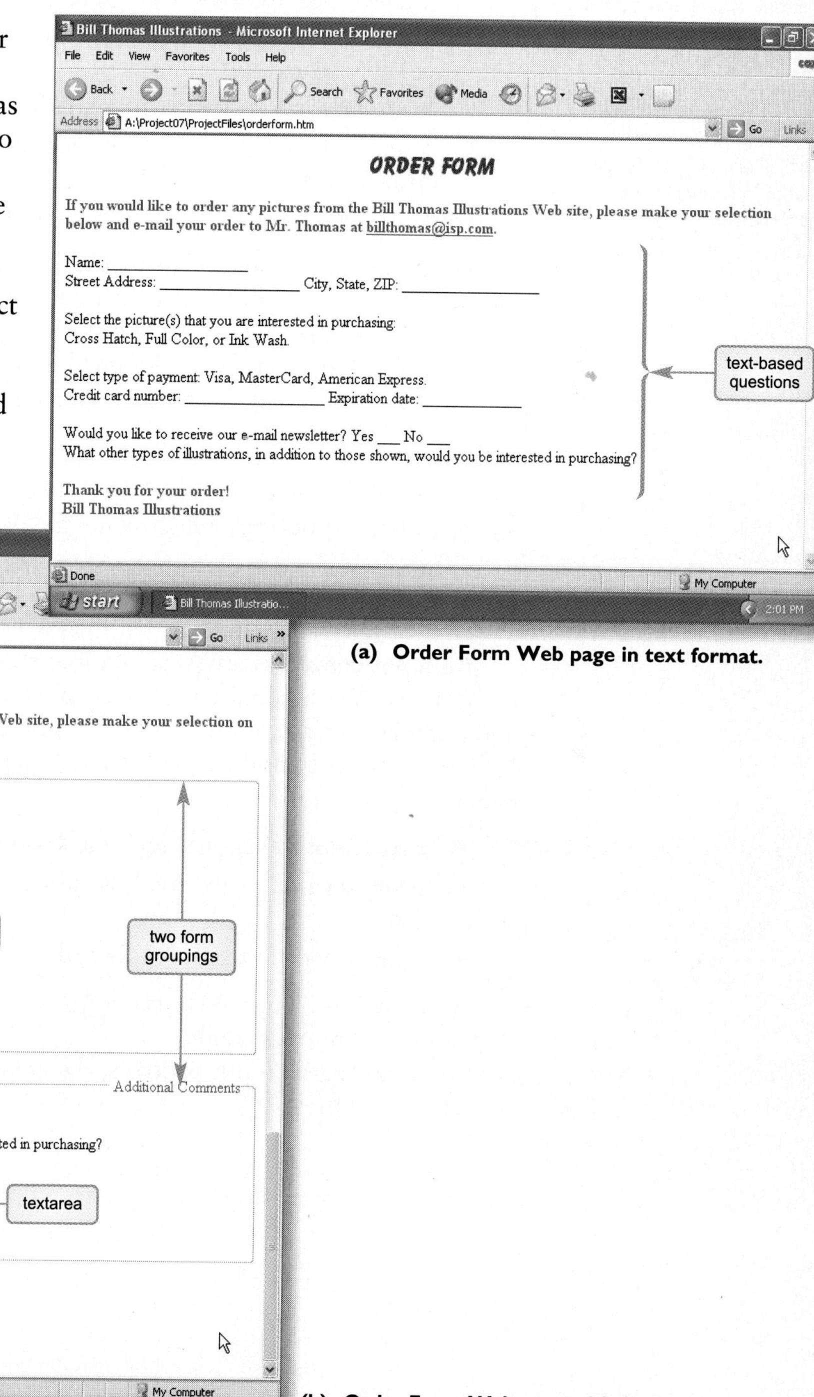

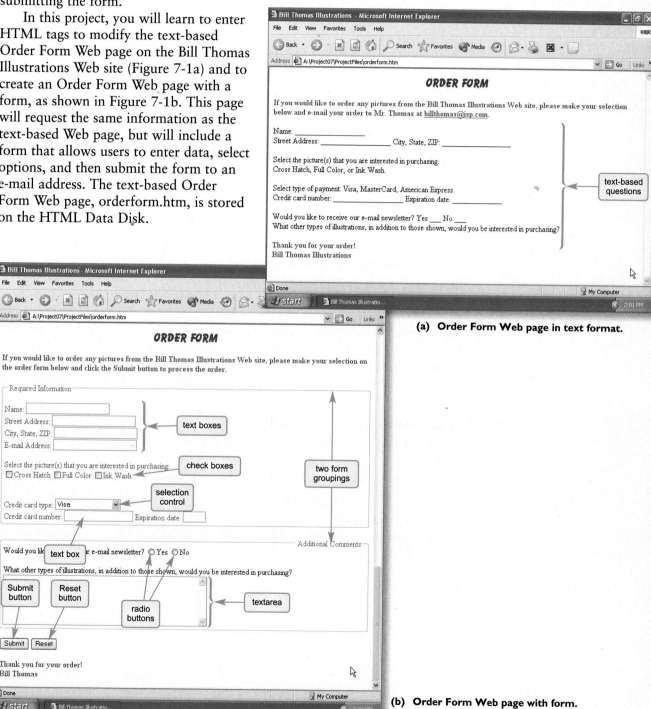

(a) Order Form Web page in text format.

(b) Order Form Web page with form.

FIGURE 7-1

Creating Web Page Forms

More About

Forms

A number of HTML guides on the Internet discuss the use of forms on Web pages. Many of these sites are created and maintained at universities. The guides give practical tips on the purpose and use of HTML tags and attributes. To view one HTML guide, visit the HTML More About Web page (scsite.com/html3e/more.htm) and then click Forms.

As previously discussed, many Web pages are designed to present information to a user. When a form is included on a Web page, the Web page can be used to gather information from Web site visitors for a number of purposes. Examples of forms commonly used on Web sites include:

- A feedback form to gather visitors' comments on the Web site
- A guestbook to allow users to sign in as visitors to the site
- A registration form for visitors to create an account, including a user name and password
- A survey form to gather information on any number of topics
- A search form for users to initiate a search for a word, a phrase, or other information
- An order form to select products and enter shipping and payment information

Whatever the purpose of the form, it should provide clear instructions to the users and allow users to fix any mistakes before submitting the form.

The Order Form Web page shown in Figure 7-1b on the previous page shows a example of a Web page form, designed to request specific information from the Web page visitor. A Web page form has three main components:

1. Input controls
2. A <form> tag, which contains the information necessary to process the form
3. A Submit button, which sends the data to be processed

Input Controls

An **input control** is any type of input mechanism on a form. A form may contain a number of different input controls classified as data or text input controls. A **data input control** is either a radio button (radio), a check box (checkbox), a Submit button (submit), a Reset button (reset), or a selection menu (select). A **text input control** is either

- a **text box** (text), in which the visitor may enter small amounts of text,
- a **textarea box** (textarea), in which the visitor may enter larger amounts of data, or
- a **password text box** (password), in which the visitor may enter a password.

As shown in Figure 7-1b, the form developed in this project uses several different data and text input controls.

Of the available input controls, the eight listed in Table 7-1 are used most often in form creation.

Table 7-1 Form Input Controls

CONTROL	FUNCTION	REMARKS
text	• Creates a single-line field for a relatively small amount of text	• Indicates both the size of the field and the total maximum length
password	• Identical to text boxes used for single-line data entry	• Echoes (or masks) back the entered text as asterisks or bullets
textarea	• Creates a multiple-line field for a relatively large amount of text	• Indicates the number of rows and columns for the area
select	• Creates a drop-down list or menu of choices from which a visitor can select an option or options	• Indicates the width of the list in number of rows
checkbox	• Creates a list item	• More than one item in a list can be chosen
radio	• Creates a list item	• Indicates only one item in a list can be chosen
submit	• Submits a form for processing	• Tells the browser to send the data on the form to the server
reset	• Resets the form	• Returns all input controls to the default status

Figures 7-2 through 7-5, on pages HTM 293 through HTM 295, show examples of the controls listed in Table 7-1.

A **text control** creates a text box that is used for a single line of input (Figure 7-2). The text control has two attributes:

1. **size**, which determines the number of characters that display on the form
2. **maxlength**, which specifies the maximum length of the input field

The maximum length of the field may exceed the size of the field that displays on the form. For example, consider a field size of three characters and a maximum length of nine characters. If a Web page visitor types in more characters than the size of the text box (three characters), the characters scroll to the left, to a maximum of nine characters entered.

A **password control** also creates a text box used for a single line of input (Figure 7-2), except that the characters entered into the field can display as asterisks or bullets. A password text box holds the password entered by a visitor. The password appears as a series of characters, asterisks, or bullets as determined by the Web developer, one per character in the password entered. This feature is designed to help protect the visitor's password from being observed by others as it is being entered.

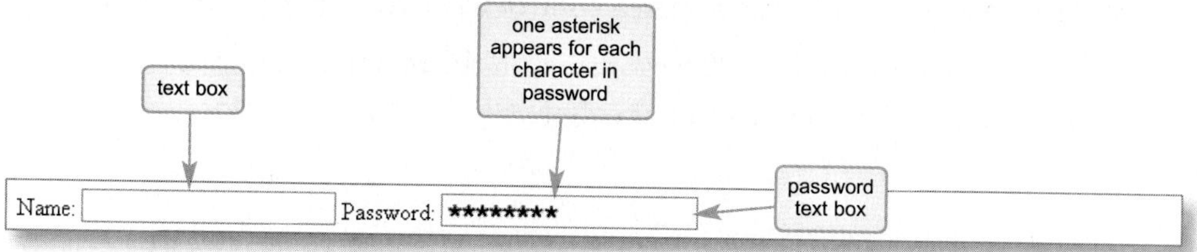

FIGURE 7-2 Text and password text controls.

A **radio control** limits the Web page visitor to only one choice from a list of choices (Figure 7-3). Each choice is preceded by a **radio button**, or option button, which typically appears as an open circle. When the visitor selects one of the radio buttons, all other radio buttons in the list automatically are deselected. By default, all radio buttons are deselected. The default can be changed so a particular button is pre-selected as the default, by using the checked value within the <input> tag.

FIGURE 7-3 Radio and checkbox controls.

A **checkbox control** allows a Web page visitor to select more than one choice from a list of choices (Figure 7-3). Each choice in a check box list can be either on or off. By default, all check boxes are deselected. The default can be changed so a particular check box is pre-selected as the default, by using the checked value within the <input> tag.

A **select control** creates a selection menu from which the visitor selects one or more choices (Figure 7-4). This eliminates the visitor's having to type information into a text or textarea field. A select control is suitable when a limited number of choices are available. The user clicks the list arrow to view all the choices in the menu. When clicked, the default appears first and is shown highlighted to indicate it is selected.

More About

Form Tutorial

What better way to learn more about the HTML form tag than using a tutorial on the Web? Lessons are grouped by topic, starting with initial HTML tags. An index is provided for ease of use. The tutorial uses illustrative examples to teach the important points of HTML to create Web pages. For more information about forms, visit the HTML More About Web page (scsite.com/html3e/more.htm) and then click Form Tutorial.

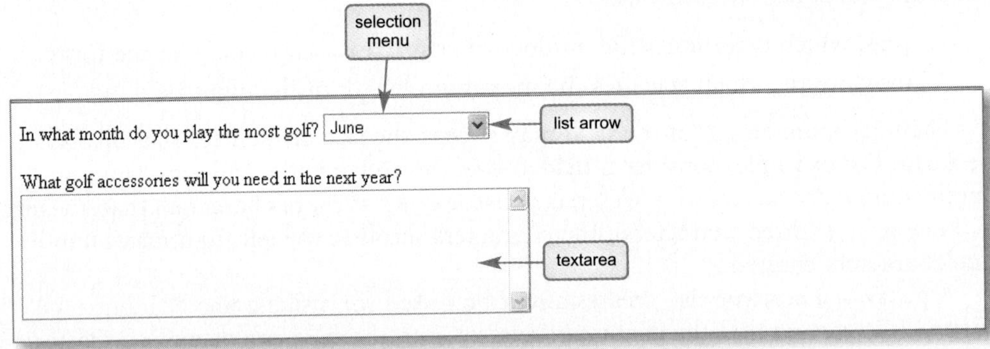

FIGURE 7-4 Select and textarea controls.

A **textarea control** creates a field that allows multiple lines of input (Figure 7-4). Textarea fields are useful when an extensive amount of input is required from, or desired of, a Web page visitor. The textarea control has two primary attributes:

1. **rows**, which specifies the number of rows in the textarea field
2. **cols** which specifies the number of columns in the textarea field

The **fieldset** control (Figure 7-5) helps to group related form elements together. This makes the form easier to read and complete. The form segment in Figure 7-5 shows two groupings: one for login information and one for information on golf playing habits. The Web page visitor immediately can see that two categories of information are included in the form. The easier that it is for a user to complete a form, the more likely it is that he or she will complete it.

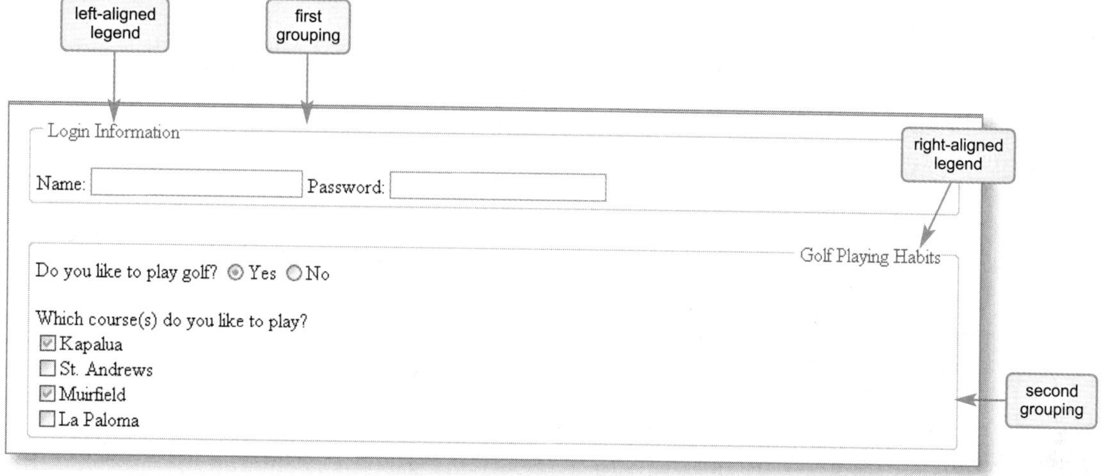

FIGURE 7-5 Fieldset control.

The **reset control** and the **submit control** create the Reset and Submit buttons, respectively (Figure 7-6). The **Reset button** clears any input that was entered in the form, resetting the input controls back to the defaults. The **Submit button** sends the information to the appropriate location for processing. A Web page form must include a Submit button, and most also include a Reset button.

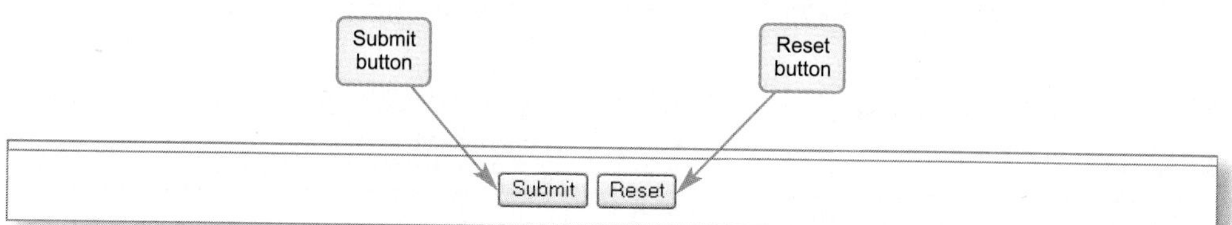

FIGURE 7-6 Submit and reset controls.

The type of information a form is intended to gather dictates what controls are used in the form. For example, to limit the number of choices a user can select, use radio buttons, check boxes, or selection menus. For less structured input or input that varies from user to user, such as user name, password, or comments, use a text or textarea field.

Regardless of the specific type, each input control has one or two attributes:

1. Name — the **name** attribute identifies the specific information that is being sent when the form is submitted for processing. All controls have a name.
2. Value — all controls except textarea also have a **value** attribute. The value attribute is the type of data that is contained in the named input control (that is, the data that the Web page visitor enters). For a textarea field, no value attribute is possible because of the variability of the input.

When a Web page visitor clicks the Submit button on the form, both the control name and the value of the data contained within that control are sent to be processed.

HTML Tags Used to Create Forms

Form statements start with the <form> tag and end with the </form> tag. The input controls in a form are created using either HTML tags or attributes of HTML tags. For example, the select and textarea controls are created using the HTML tags, <select> and <textarea>, respectively. Other input controls are created using attributes of HTML tags. For example, the text boxes, check boxes, radio buttons, and Submit and Reset buttons all are created using the type attribute of the <input> tag. The default type for the <input> tag is a text box. Therefore, if the type attribute is not used in the <input> tag, it creates a text box.

Table 7-2 lists the HTML tags used to create the order form in this project. Any combination of these elements can be used in a Web page form.

Table 7-2 HTML Tags Used to Create Forms

TAG	FUNCTION	REMARKS
<fieldset> </fieldset>	Groups related controls on a form	Optionally used for readability
<form> </form>	Creates a form that allows user input	Required when creating forms
<input>	Defines the controls used in the form, using a variety of type attribute values	Required for input controls
<legend> </legend>	Defines the text that displays in the grouping borders	Optionally used when using <fieldset> tags
<select> </select>	Creates a menu of choices from which a visitor selects	Required for selection choices
<option> </option>	Specifies a choice in a <select> tag	Required, one per choice
<textarea> </textarea>	Creates a multiple-line text input area	Required for longer text inputs that appear on several lines

More About

Margin CGI

Using CGI scripts to process forms is a much more efficient way to handle the data that is sent from a form. Many Web sites have free sample CGI scripts for Web developers to use. To view an interactive Web site with a multitude of information and free samples, visit the HTML More About Web page (scsite.com/html3e/more.htm) and then click CGI.

Attributes of HTML Tags Used to Create Forms

Many of the HTML tags used to create forms have several attributes. Table 7-3 lists several HTML tags used to create forms, along with their main attributes and their functions.

Table 7-3 Attributes of HTML Tags Used to Create Forms

TAG	ATTRIBUTE	FUNCTION
<form> </form>	action	• URL for action completed by the server
	method	• HTTP method (post)
	target	• Location at which the resource will display
<input>	type	• Type of input control (text, password, checkbox, radio, submit, reset, file, hidden, image, button)
	name	• Name of the control
	value	• Value submitted if a control is selected (required for radio and checkbox controls)
	checked	• Sets a radio button to a checked state (only one can be checked)
	disabled	• Disables a control
	readonly	• Used for text passwords
	size	• Number of characters that display on the form
	maxlength	• Maximum number of characters that can be entered
	src	• URL to the location of an image stored on the server
	alt	• Alternate text for an image control
	tabindex	• Sets tabbing order among control elements
<legend> </legend>	align	• Indicates how a legend should be aligned
<select> </select>	name	• Name of the element
	size	• Number of options visible when Web page is first opened
	multiple	• Allows for multiple selections in select list
	disabled	• Disables a control
	tabindex	• Sets the tabbing order among control elements
<option> </option>	selected	• Specifies whether an option is selected
	disabled	• Disables a control
	value	• Value submitted if a control is selected
<textarea> </textarea>	name	• Name of the control
	rows	• Width in number of rows
	cols	• Height in number of columns
	disabled	• Disables a control
	readonly	• Used for text passwords
	tabindex	• Sets the tabbing order among control elements

More About

Radio Buttons

Old-time car radios were operated by a row of large black plastic buttons. Push one button, and you get one preset radio station. You only could push one button at a time. Radio buttons on forms work the same way as the old-time radio buttons — one button at a time. With check boxes, more than one option can be selected at a time.

Creating a Form on a Web Page

In this project, you will learn to modify the text-based Order Form Web page (orderform.htm) used in the Bill Thomas Illustrations Web site. The file, orderform.htm, currently contains only text and does not utilize a form or form controls (Figure 7-1a on page HTM 291). Using this text-based order form is an inconvenient way for the user, who must re-type the required order information into an e-mail message and then e-mail that information to the address listed in the opening paragraph of text.

The file, orderform.htm, is stored on the HTML Data Disk. After opening this HTML file in Notepad, you will enter HTML code to convert this Web page into the Web page form shown in Figure 7-1b on page HTM 291. The following steps illustrate how to start Notepad and open the HTML file, orderform.htm.

To Start Notepad and Open an HTML File

1. **Start Notepad and, if necessary, maximize the window.**
2. **With the HTML Data Disk in drive A, click File on the menu bar and then click Open on the File menu. If necessary, click 3½ Floppy (A:) in the Look in list. Click the Project07 folder and then click the ProjectFiles folder in the list of available folders.**
3. **If necessary, click the Files of type box arrow and then click All Files.**
4. **Double-click orderform.htm in the list of files.**

Notepad displays the HTML code as shown in Figure 7-7.

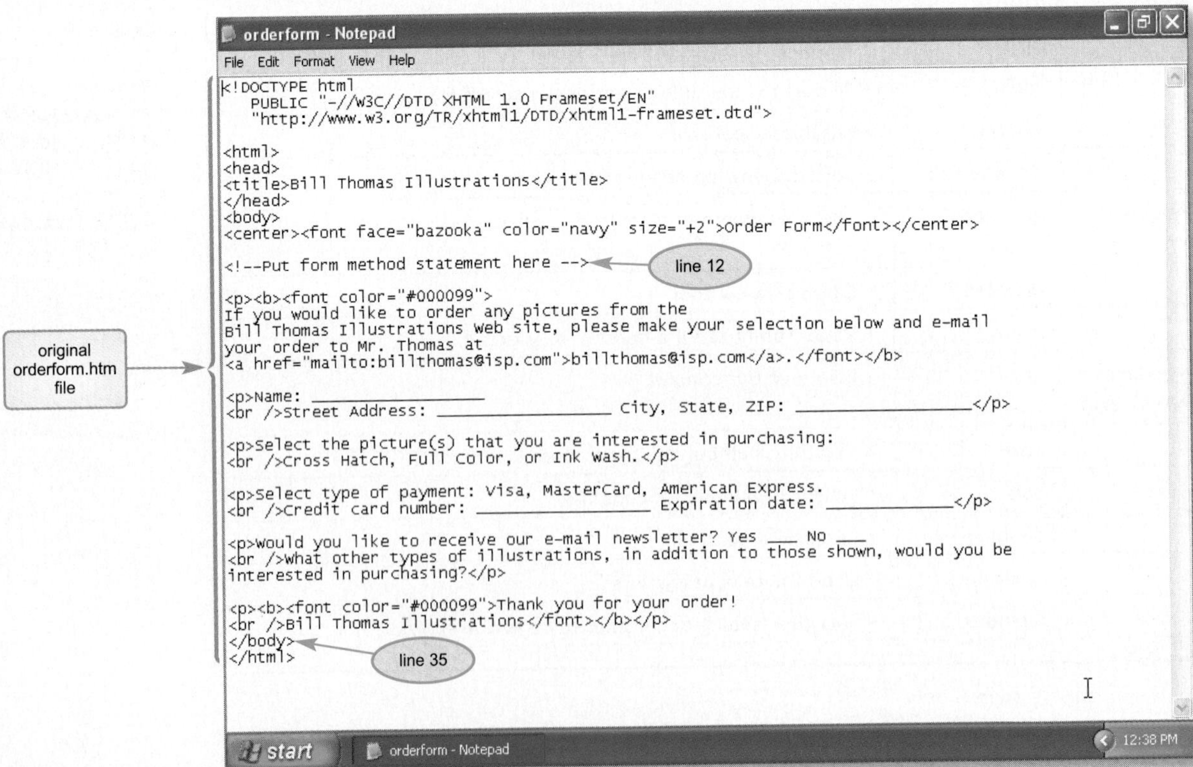


```
<!DOCTYPE html
   PUBLIC "-//W3C//DTD XHTML 1.0 Frameset/EN"
   "http://www.w3.org/TR/xhtml1/DTD/xhtml1-frameset.dtd">

<html>
<head>
<title>Bill Thomas Illustrations</title>
</head>
<body>
<center><font face="bazooka" color="navy" size="+2">Order Form</font></center>

<!--Put form method statement here -->

<p><b><font color="#000099">
If you would like to order any pictures from the
Bill Thomas Illustrations Web site, please make your selection below and e-mail
your order to Mr. Thomas at
<a href="mailto:billthomas@isp.com">billthomas@isp.com</a>.</font></b>

<p>Name: ____________________
<br />Street Address: ______________________ City, State, ZIP: ______________________</p>

<p>Select the picture(s) that you are interested in purchasing:
<br />Cross Hatch, Full Color, or Ink Wash.</p>

<p>Select type of payment: Visa, MasterCard, American Express.
<br />Credit card number: ______________________ Expiration date: _______________</p>

<p>Would you like to receive our e-mail newsletter? Yes ___ No ___
<br />What other types of illustrations, in addition to those shown, would you be
interested in purchasing?</p>

<p><b><font color="#000099">Thank you for your order!
<br />Bill Thomas Illustrations</font></b></p>
</body>
</html>
```

FIGURE 7-7

Creating a Form and Identifying the Form Process

When adding a form to a Web page, the first steps are creating the form and identifying how the form is sent and processed when it is submitted. The start <form> and end </form> tags designate an area of a Web page as a form. Between the <form> and </form> tags, form controls can be added to request different types of information and allow the appropriate input responses. A form can include any number of controls.

The **action attribute** of the <form> tag specifies the action that is taken when the form is submitted. Information entered in forms can be sent by e-mail to an e-mail address or can be used to update a database. Although the e-mail option is functional, many Web sites process information from forms using Common Gateway Interface (CGI) scripting. A **CGI script** is a program written in a programming language (such as Perl) that communicates with the Web server. The CGI script sends the information input on the Web page form to the server for processing. Because this type of processing involves programming tasks that are beyond the scope of this book, the information entered in the order form created in this project will be submitted in a file to an e-mail address. The e-mail address will be specified as the action attribute value in the <form> tag.

The **method attribute** of the <form> tag specifies the manner in which the data entered in the form is sent to the server to be processed. Two primary ways are used in HTML: the get method and the post method. The **get method** sends the name-value pairs to the end of the URL indicated in the action attribute. The **post method** sends a separate data file with the name-value pairs to the URL (or e-mail address) indicated in the action attribute. The post method is used for the forms in this project.

The HTML code shown below creates a form using the post method and an action attribute to indicate that the form information should be sent to an e-mail address in an attached data file:

```
<form method="post" action="mailto:billthomas@isp.com">
```

When the form is submitted, a file containing the input data is sent as an e-mail attachment to the e-mail address, billthomas@isp.com.

The following steps show how to enter HTML code to create a form and identify the form process.

To Create a Form and Identify the Form Process

1

• **Highlight the words <!--Put form method statement here --> on line 12 and then press the DELETE key.**

2

• **Type** `<form method="post" action="mailto:billthomas@isp.com">` **as the new tag.**

More About

Textareas

To create a textarea, the Web developer specifies the number of rows and columns in which the Web page visitor can enter information. The maximum number of characters for a textarea is 32,700. It is a good rule of thumb to keep the number of columns in a textarea to 50 or fewer. Using that as a limit, the textarea will fit on most screens.

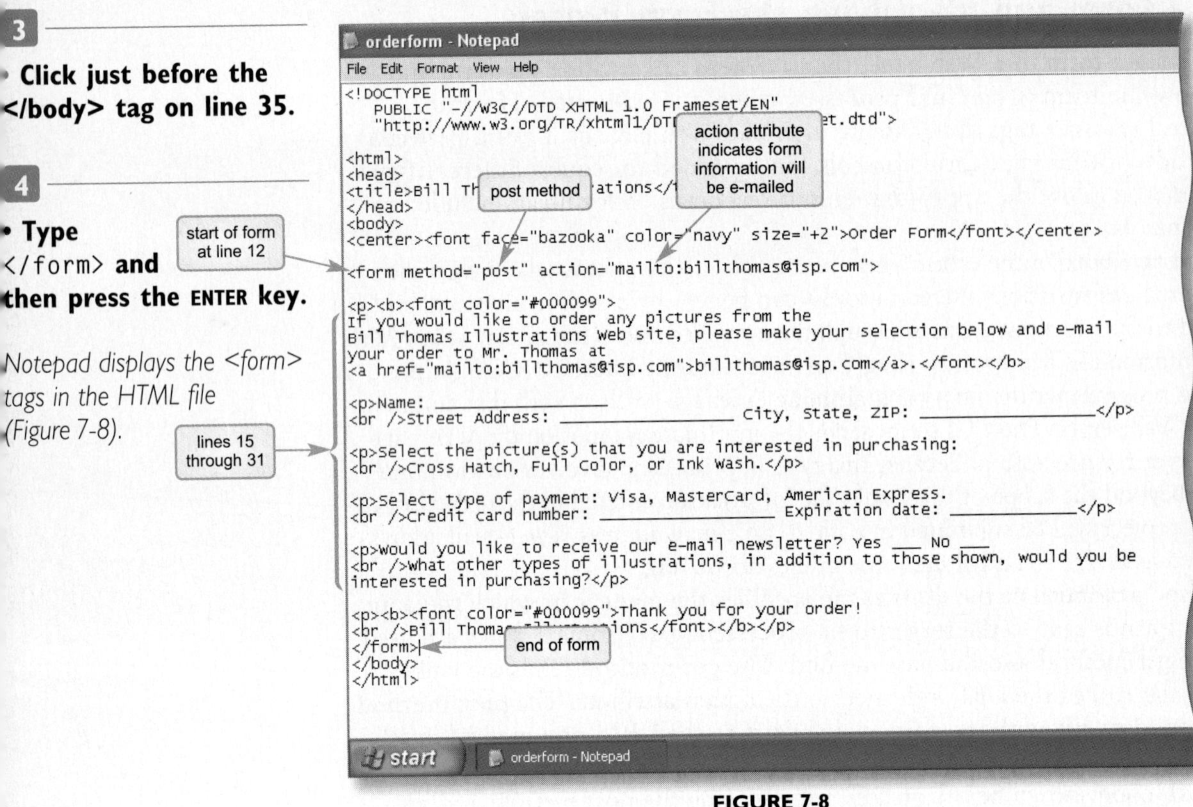

3

- **Click just before the </body> tag on line 35.**

4

- **Type** `</form>` **and then press the ENTER key.**

Notepad displays the <form> tags in the HTML file (Figure 7-8).

FIGURE 7-8

The HTML code, <form method="post" action="mailto:billthomas@isp.com">, creates a form and designates the form to use the post method to send the data. The information entered in the form thus will be sent in a file to the e-mail address, billthomas@isp.com. The </form> tag on line 35 just above the </body> tag ends the Web page form.

Changing the Text Message

The next step in updating the text-based Order Form Web page is to modify the text that tells the user to submit the questionnaire via e-mail. Table 7-4 shows the new HTML code used to provide instructions to users on how to submit the information on the order form.

Table 7-4 HTML Code to Change the Text Message

LINE	CODE
15	`If you would like to order any pictures from the Bill Thomas Illustrations`
16	`Web site, please make your selection on the order form below and click the`
17	`Submit button to process the order.</b></p>`

The following steps illustrate how to change the text message to provide instructions on how to use the order form.

To Change the Text Message

1

- **Select lines 15 through 31 and then press the DELETE key.**

2

- **With the insertion point on line 15, enter the HTML code shown in Table 7-4 and then press the ENTER key twice.**

Notepad displays the HTML code as shown in Figure 7-9.

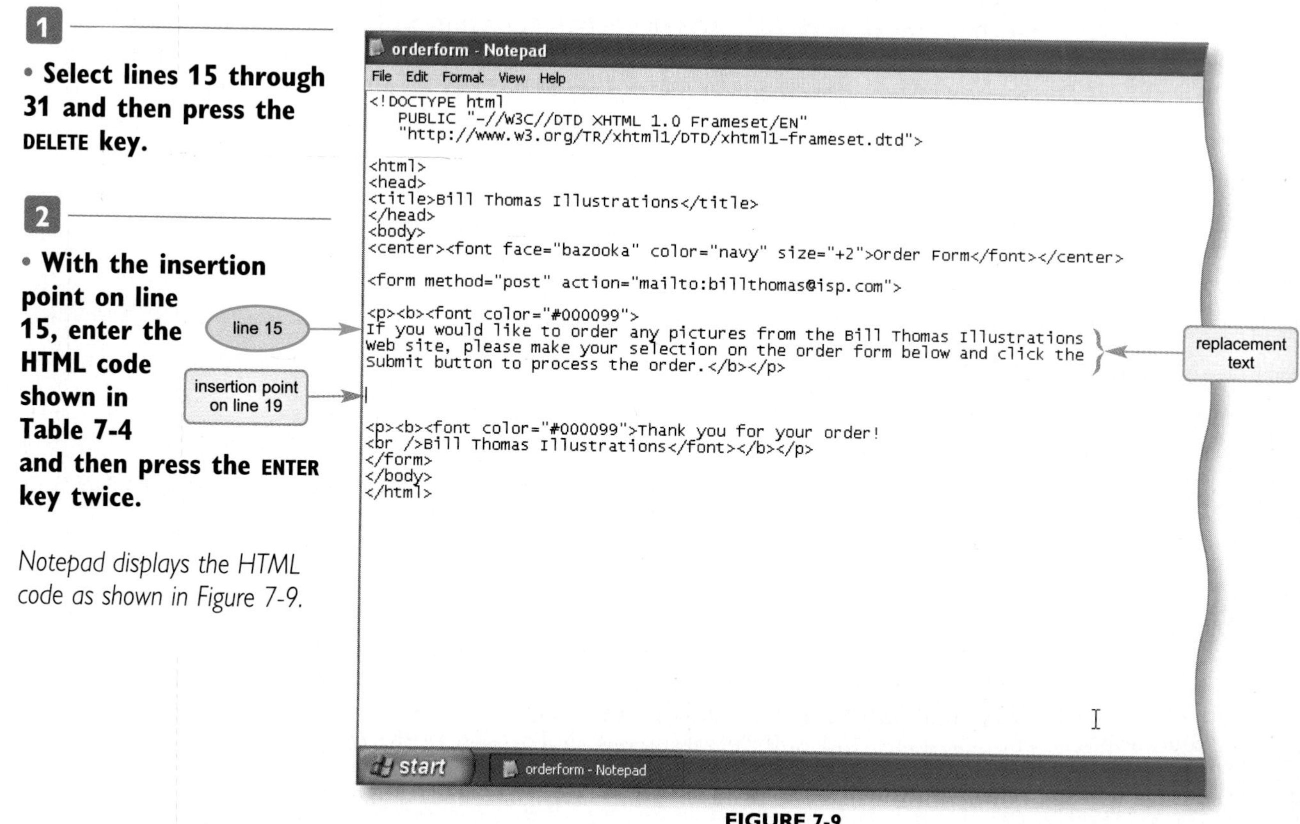

FIGURE 7-9

The updated text now directs users to submit the questionnaire via the Submit button that will be added at the bottom of the Web page form. The list of fields included in the text-based Order Form Web page is deleted; in the remainder of this project, various form controls will be added to replace them.

Adding Text Boxes

The next step in creating the order form is to add four text boxes to the form, for users to enter name; street address; city, state, ZIP; and e-mail address. As previously discussed, a text box allows for a single line of input. The HTML code below shows an example of the code used to add a text box to a form:

```
<input name="address" type="text" size="25" maxlength="25">
```

The <input> tag creates an input control, while the attribute and value, type="text", specifies that the input control is a text box. The name attribute of the input control is set to the value, address, to describe the information to be entered in this text box. When the form is submitted, the name is used to distinguish the value associated with that field from other fields.

The size attribute indicates the size of the text box that appears on the form. In the HTML code on the previous page, size="25" sets the text field to be 25 characters in length, which means only 25 characters will appear in the text box. The maxlength attribute, maxlength="25" sets the maximum number of characters that can be entered in the text box to 25 characters. The maxlength attribute specifies the same number of characters (25) as the size attribute (25), so all characters entered by a user will appear in the text box. If you specify a maximum number of characters that is greater than the number of characters specified in the size attribute, the additional characters scroll to the right in the text box as the user enters them.

Table 7-5 shows the HTML code to add four text boxes to the form.

Table 7-5 HTML Code to Add Text Boxes

LINE	CODE
19	 Name: <input name="name" type="text" size="25">
20	 Street Address: <input name="address" type="text" size="25">
21	 City, State, ZIP: <input name="citystatezip" type="text" size="25">
22	 E-mail Address: <input name="email" type="text" size="25">

Before the <input> tag for each text box, a descriptive text label, such as Name:, is added to tell the user what information to enter in the text box. The <input> tags on line 19 through 22 create four text boxes, each with a size of 25 characters. No maxlength attribute is specified, which means users can enter text items longer than 25 characters, but only 25 characters will appear in the text box.

The following steps illustrate how to add a text box to the form.

To Add Text Boxes

1

• **If necessary, click line 19.**

2

• **Enter the HTML code shown in Table 7-5 and then press the ENTER key twice.**

Notepad displays the HTML code to add four text boxes to the form (Figure 7-10). The insertion point is on line 24.

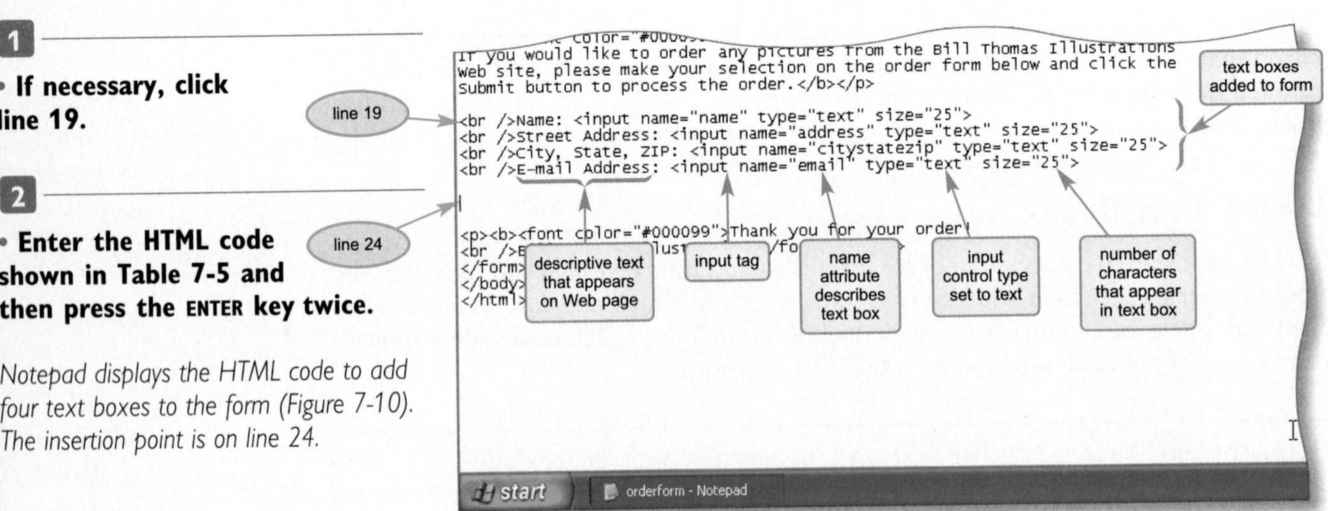

FIGURE 7-10

You now have created four text boxes for users to enter name; street address; city, state, ZIP; and e-mail address information in the order form.

Adding Check Boxes

The next step in creating the form is to add several check box options. Check boxes are similar to radio buttons, except they allow multiple options to be selected. Radio buttons should be used when only one option can be selected, while check boxes should be used when the user can select more than one option.

The HTML code below shows an example of the code used to add a check box to a form:

```
<input name="pictype" type="checkbox" value="cross">Cross Hatch
```

The <input> tag creates an input control, while the attribute and value, type="checkbox", specifies that the input control is a checkbox. The name attribute of the input control is set to the value, pictype. When the form is submitted, the name is used to distinguish the values associated with these checkbox fields from other fields. The value attribute, cross, indicates the value submitted in the file, if this check box is selected.

In the Order Form Web page, three check boxes are used to allow the user to select one or more types of pictures to purchase. Table 7-6 shows the HTML code to add three check boxes to the form.

Table 7-6 HTML Code to Add Check Boxes

```
LINE  CODE
24    <p>Select the picture(s) that you are interested in purchasing:
25    <br />
26    <input name="pictype" type="checkbox" value="cross">Cross Hatch
27    <input name="pictype" type="checkbox" value="fullcolor">Full Color
28    <input name="pictype" type="checkbox" value="ink">Ink Wash
29    </p>
```

Lines 26 through 28 add three check boxes to the form, one for each type of picture. For each check box, the value attribute is set to describe a specific type of picture — either cross hatch (cross), full color (fullcolor), or ink wash (ink). Finally, descriptive text is added to appear on the form next to the check box, so users know what each check box denotes.

The steps on the next page illustrate how to enter HTML code to add check boxes to the form.

Q&A

Q: Why use forms on a Web page?

A: In some Web applications, it is important to collect information from your Web site visitor. Forms provide an easy way to collect that needed information. Most Web surfers are used to completing online forms today, and this familiarity helps their comfort level when completing the form.

More About

Submit Buttons

A simplistic, default button is created when you use the type="submit" attribute and value within the <input> tag. The <button> tag also can be used to create a submit button. The <button> tag gives you the option of using an image for the button, rather than using the default button style. The appearance of the button text can be changed with the <style> tag. These tags give you more flexibility when creating submit or reset buttons.

To Add Check Boxes

1

- **If necessary, click line 24.**

2

- **Enter the HTML code shown in Table 7-6 on the previous page and then press the ENTER key twice.**

Notepad displays the HTML code as shown in Figure 7-11, and the insertion point is on line 31.

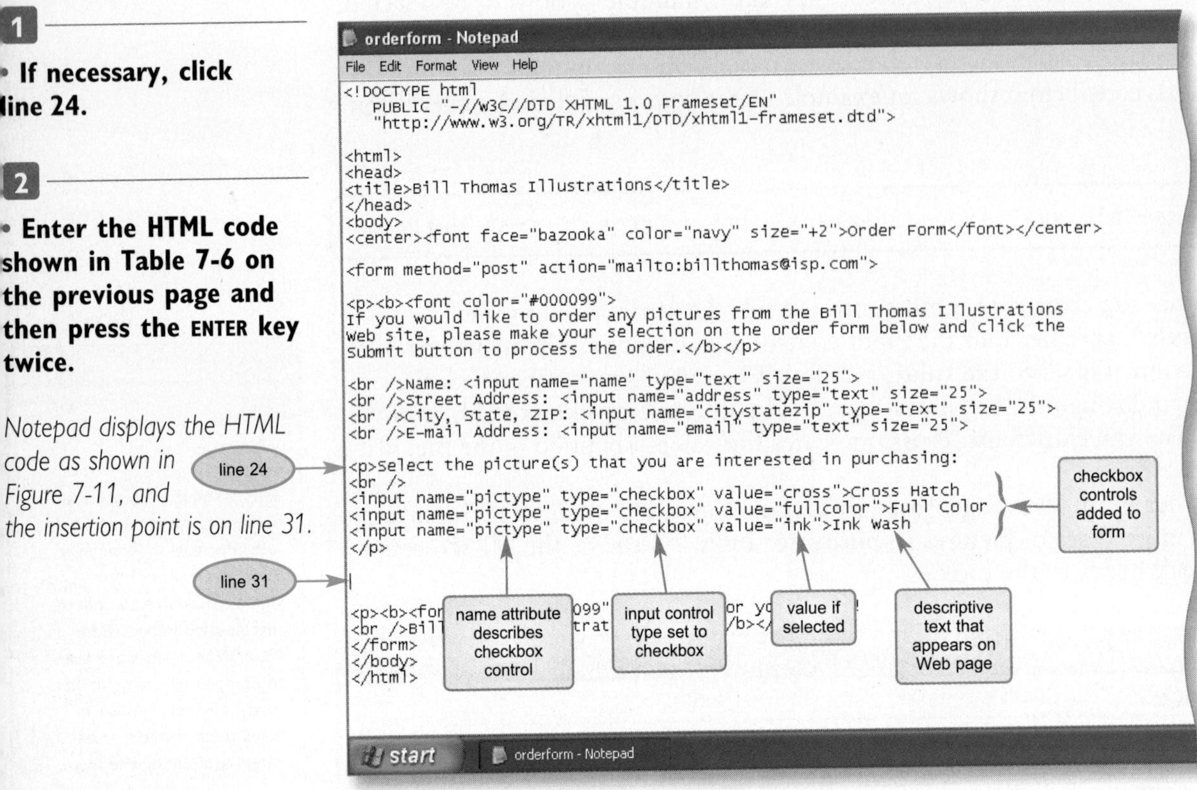

FIGURE 7-11

Adding a Selection Menu

As previously discussed, a select control is used to create a selection menu from which the visitor selects one or more choices. A select control is suitable when a limited number of choices are available. Figure 7-12 shows the basic selection menu used in the order form, with three credit card types (Visa, MasterCard, and American Express) as the choices in the list.

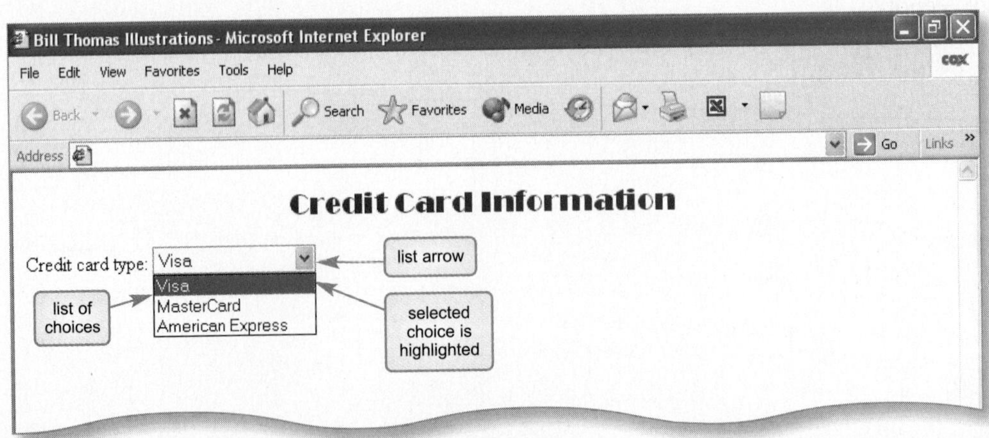

FIGURE 7-12

Table 7-7 shows the HTML code used to create the selection menu shown in Figure 7-12.

Table 7-7 HTML Code to Add Selection Menu

LINE	CODE
31	` Credit card type:`
32	`<select name="payment">`
33	`<option>Visa</option>`
34	`<option>MasterCard</option>`
35	`<option>American Express</option>`
36	`</select>`

The <select> tag on line 32 is used to start a selection menu and the end </select> tag indicates the end of the selection menu. The name attribute assigns the name, payment, to the selection menu. When the form is submitted to the e-mail address, the field is called payment, and the value associated with that field can be distinguished from other fields by that name.

All choices, or options, are contained within the <select> and </select> tags. The start <option> and end </option> tags define the text options that are available and appear in the list. Lines 33 through 35 create three options to appear in the selection menu: Visa, MasterCard, and American Express. The size attribute is not specified, so only one option displays, along with a list arrow, as shown in Figure 7-12. When the list arrow is clicked, the selection menu displays all selection options. When the user selects an option, such as Visa, in the list, it appears as highlighted. The following steps illustrate how to add a selection menu to the Web page form.

Q&A

Q: How can I better control placement of form elements?

A: You may use a table to place form elements more precisely. If you use a borderless table, the Web page visitor would never know that it is there.

To Add a Selection Menu

1 **If necessary, click line 31.**

2 **Enter the HTML code shown in Table 7-7 and then press the ENTER key twice.**

Notepad displays the HTML as shown in Figure 7-13, and the insertion point is on line 38.

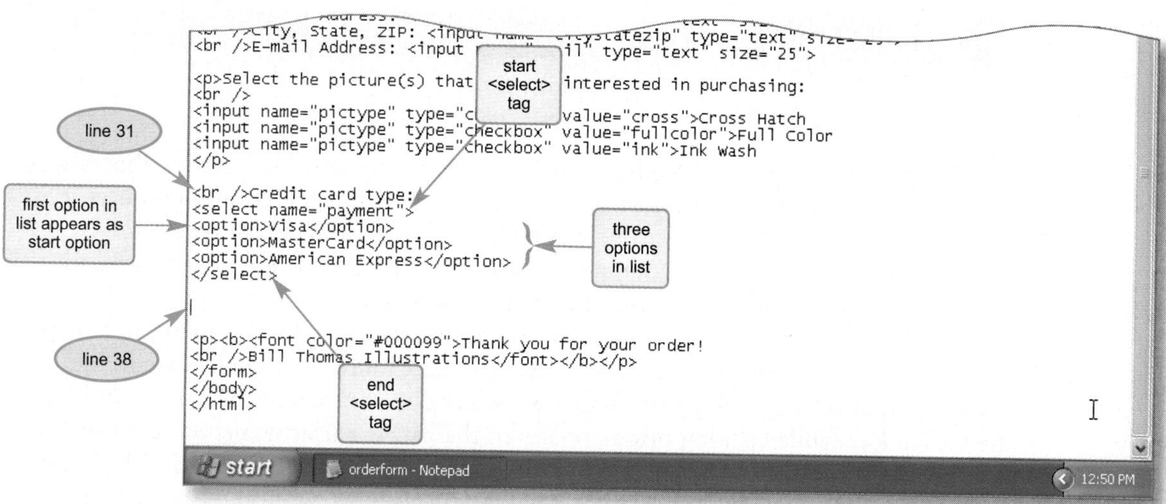

FIGURE 7-13

The Credit card type selection menu is added to the Web page form. The selection menu includes three options: Visa, MasterCard, and American Express. Because no size attribute value was specified, the selection menu initially displays only one option (in this case, Visa, the first option in the list), along with a list arrow to view other choices in the list. A user is allowed to select only one of the three choices in the list.

Adding More Advanced Selection Menus

Selection menus have many variations, beyond the simple selection menu used in the Order Form Web page. Table 7-3 on page HTM 297 lists several attributes for the <select> tag. Using these attributes, a selection menu can be set to display multiple choices or only one, with a drop-down list to allow a user to select another choice. Selection menus can be set to allow a user to select only one or multiple choices. A selection menu also can be defined to have one choice pre-selected as the default.

Figure 7-14 shows samples of selection menus. The HTML code used to create each selection menu is shown in Figure 7-15.

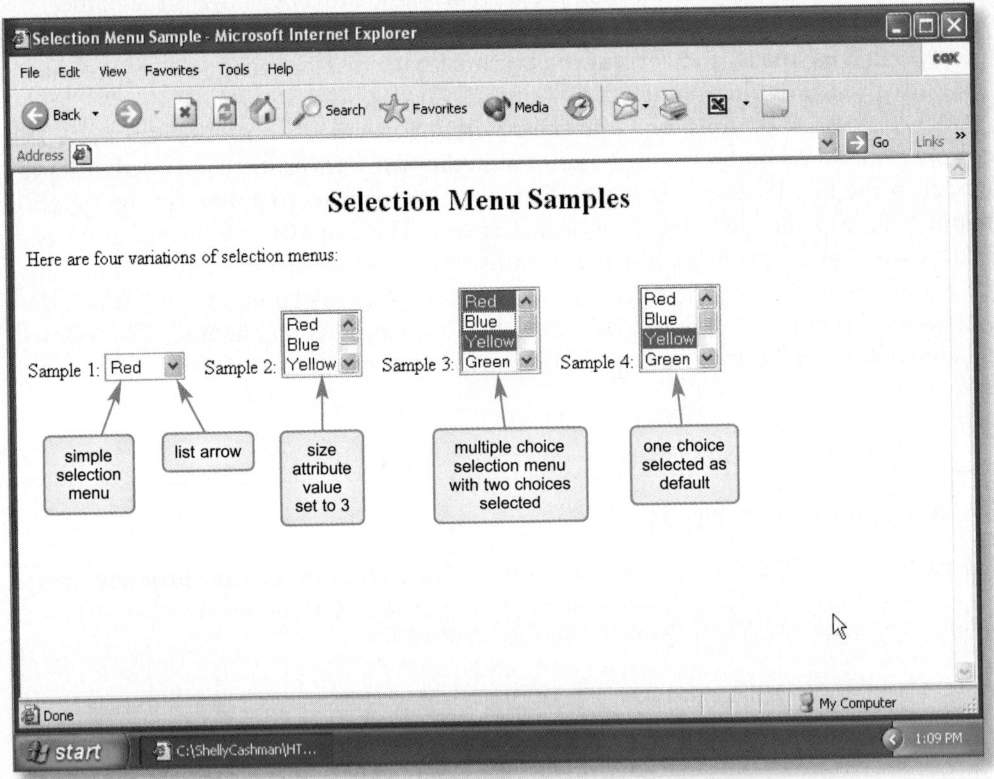

FIGURE 7-14

The selection menu in Sample 1 is a basic selection menu, with no attributes specified other than the name and the list options. This resulting selection menu uses a list menu that allows users to select one choice from the list. No choice is selected by default. The selection menu in Sample 2 uses a size attribute value of 3 to indicate that three choices should appear in the menu at startup. A user can use the UP and DOWN scroll arrows to view other choices in the list. The selection menu in Sample 3 uses the multiple attribute to allow a user to select more than one choice in the list. To select multiple choices, a user first must select one choice and then press and hold the CTRL key while clicking other choices in the list. If a user wants to select several consecutive choices, he or she can select the first choice and then press and hold the SHIFT key while selecting the last choice. All choices in between the first choice and last choice automatically will be selected. The selection menu in Sample 4 also contains the multiple attribute, so one or more choices can be selected. In addition, Sample 4 provides an example of one choice (in this case, Yellow) being selected at startup. As shown in the HTML code in Figure 7-15, the selected attribute is included in the <option> tag for Yellow, to indicate that Yellow should be selected at startup.

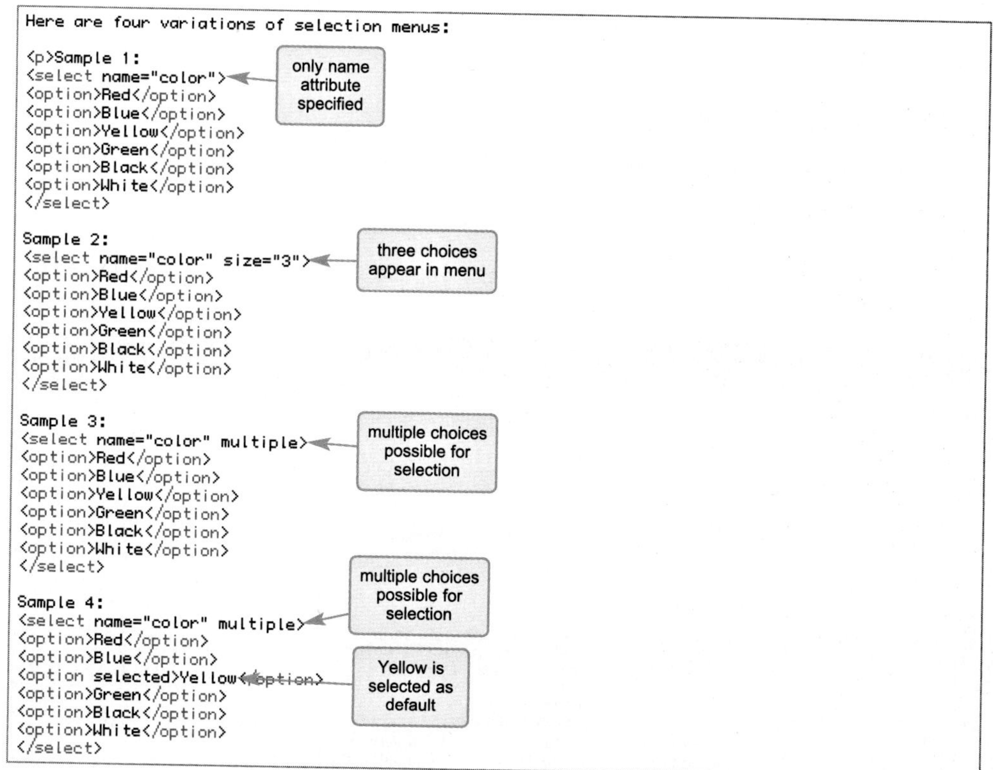

FIGURE 7-15 HTML code to create selection menus.

More About

Fonts

The Broadway font was selected for the titles in this project by using the <font face> tag and attribute. Not all Web page visitors have the Broadway font on their computers, however. If a visitor does not have the font used by the Web developer for a Web page, the text displays in the default font.

The purpose of the selection menu dictates the type of selection menu that should be used and the HTML code required to create that select control. Using the basic tags and attributes shown in Figure 7-15, you can create a wide variety of selection menus to suit almost any purpose.

Adding Additional Text Boxes

The next step in creating the Order Form Web page is to add two additional text boxes for credit card number and expiration date. Table 7-8 shows the HTML code used to add the additional text boxes.

Table 7-8 HTML Code to Add Additional Text Boxes

LINE	ATTRIBUTE
38	` Credit card number:`
39	`<input name="cardnum" type="text" size="20" maxlength="20">`
40	`Expiration date:`
41	`<input name="cardexp" type="text" size="4" maxlength="4">`

A text field is used rather than a textarea field because the user needs to enter only one row of characters. The Credit card number text box is set to have a size and maxlength value of 20, while the Expiration date text box is set to have a size and maxlength value of 4.

The following steps illustrate how to add two additional text boxes to the Web page form.

To Add Additional Text Boxes

1 **If necessary, click line 38.**

2 **Enter the HTML code shown in Table 7-8 on the previous page and then press the ENTER key twice.**

Notepad displays the HTML code as shown in Figure 7-16, and the insertion point is on line 43.

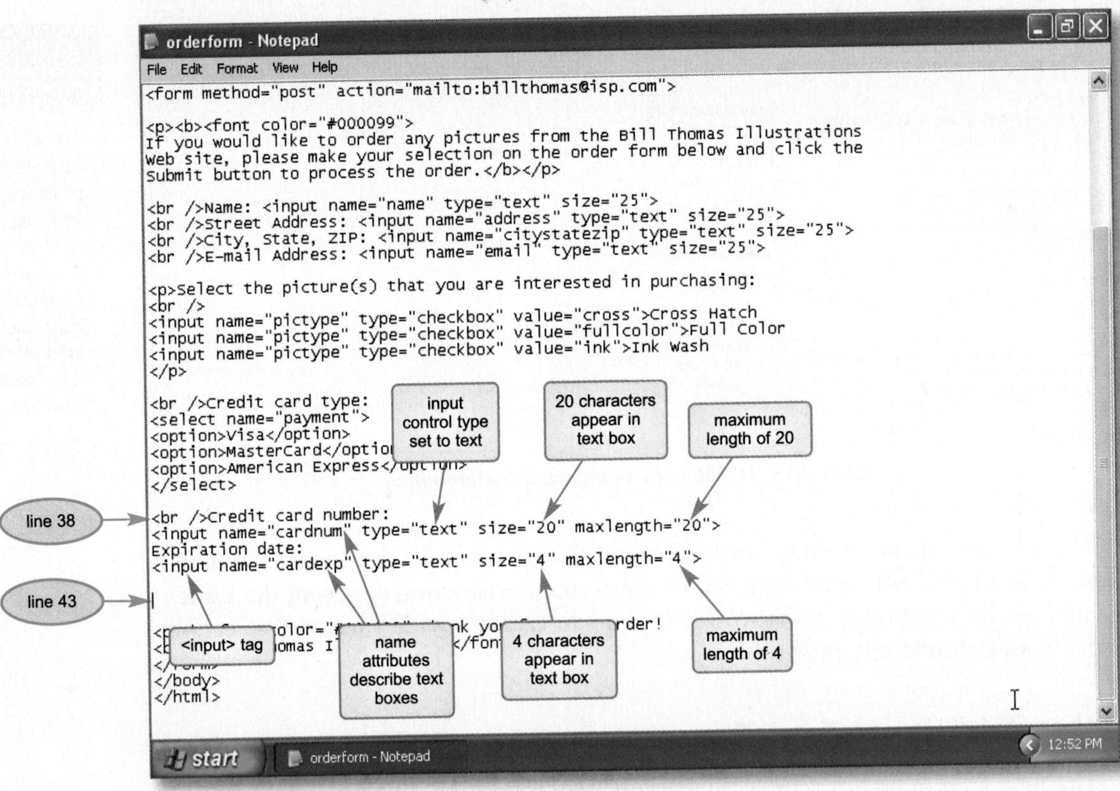

FIGURE 7-16

As previously noted, for both of these text boxes, the size and maxlength attributes (20 and 4) are the same. The credit card number has space for 20 characters, and the expiration date has space for only 4 characters — that is, the MM/YY characters that represent the expiration month and year. When determining the sizes of text boxes, consider how the field will be used and what possible responses could be entered for each type of text box. Set the size attribute of the text box to a size that will allow enough space to accommodate the need of the field.

Adding Radio Buttons and a Textarea

The next step is to add radio buttons and a textarea to the form. Remember that radio buttons are appropriate to use when a user can select only one choice from a set of two or more choices. Questions with a Yes or No answer are perfect for the use of radio buttons. On the Order Form Web page, radio buttons allow users to select a Yes or No answer to a question about receiving an e-mail newsletter.

The order form also includes a textarea that allows the user to add additional comments about other types of illustrations he or she might be interested in purchasing. Because the response can be longer than just one line, a textarea control is used.

Adding Radio Buttons

Table 7-9 contains the HTML code to add a set of radio buttons to the Order Form Web page.

Table 7-9 HTML Code to Add Radio Buttons

LINE	CODE
43	`Would you like to receive our e-mail newsletter?`
44	`<input name="newsletter" type="radio" value="yes">Yes`
45	`<input name="newsletter" type="radio" value="no">No`

The <input> tag creates an input control, while the attribute and value, type="radio", specifies that the input control is a radio button. Line 43 includes a yes or no question for which the user can select one of two answers: Yes or No. Using the same name attribute, "newsletter", for both radio buttons limits the users to selecting only one of the options. If the name attribute had been different for each radio button, the user could have selected both the Yes and No radio buttons.

The value attributes in lines 44 and 45 define the value for each radio button. The value (for example, yes or no) is associated with the field name and is the text that is sent to be processed when the visitor submits the form. For example, if a user clicks the Yes radio button named newsletter, the text string, newsletter=yes, is sent to be processed. The value attribute is required for the radio input control.

The following steps illustrate how to add a set of radio buttons to the form.

To Add Radio Buttons

1. **If necessary, click line 43.**
2. **Enter the HTML code shown in Table 7-9 and then press the ENTER key twice.**

Notepad displays the HTML code as shown in Figure 7-17 on the next page, and the insertion point is on line 47.

More About

Feedback

One good use of forms is to get feedback from your visitors. Suggestions from visitors not only can help improve the Web site, but can give your visitors the sense that you care about their opinions. Taking visitor feedback into account provides for better customer satisfaction. For more information about customer feedback, visit the HTML More About Web page (scsite.com/html3e/more.htm) and then click Feedback.

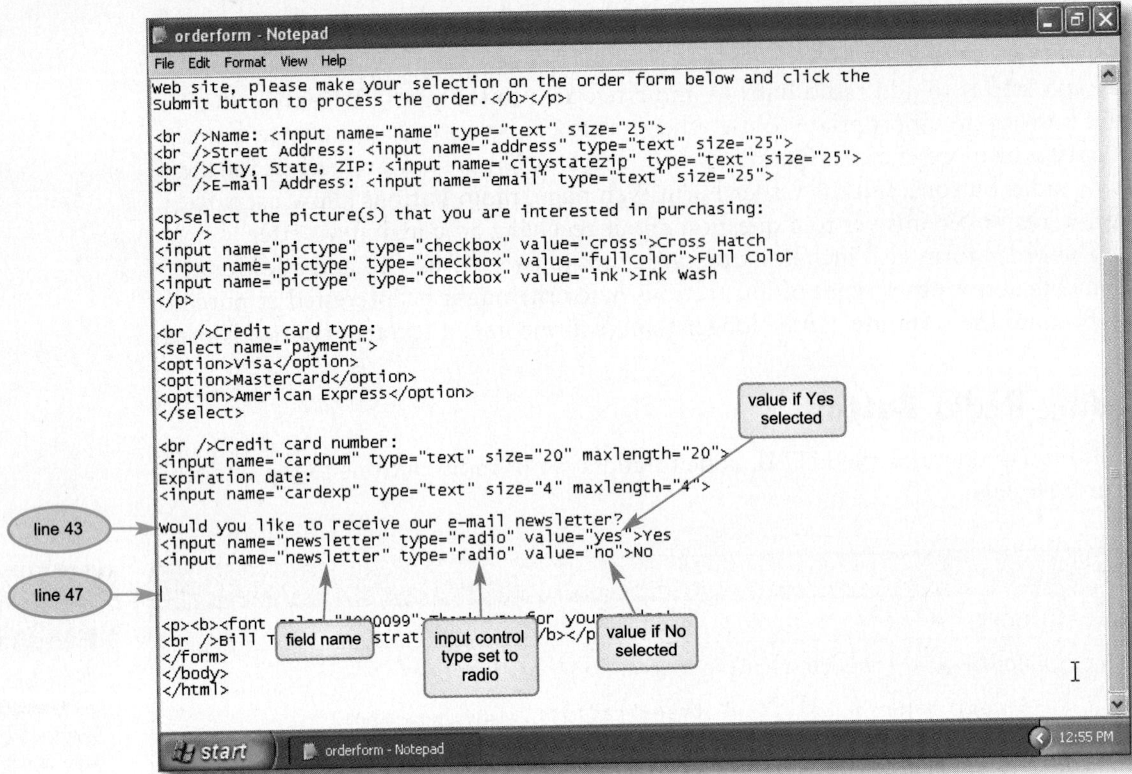

```
orderform - Notepad
File Edit Format View Help
Web site, please make your selection on the order form below and click the
Submit button to process the order.</b></p>

<br />Name: <input name="name" type="text" size="25">
<br />Street Address: <input name="address" type="text" size="25">
<br />City, State, ZIP: <input name="citystatezip" type="text" size="25">
<br />E-mail Address: <input name="email" type="text" size="25">

<p>Select the picture(s) that you are interested in purchasing:
<br />
<input name="pictype" type="checkbox" value="cross">Cross Hatch
<input name="pictype" type="checkbox" value="fullcolor">Full Color
<input name="pictype" type="checkbox" value="ink">Ink Wash
</p>

<br />Credit card type:
<select name="payment">
<option>Visa</option>
<option>MasterCard</option>
<option>American Express</option>
</select>

<br />Credit card number:
<input name="cardnum" type="text" size="20" maxlength="20">
Expiration date:
<input name="cardexp" type="text" size="4" maxlength="4">

Would you like to receive our e-mail newsletter?
<input name="newsletter" type="radio" value="yes">Yes
<input name="newsletter" type="radio" value="no">No


<p><b><font
<br />Bill T
</form>
</body>
</html>
start   orderform - Notepad   12:55 PM
```


FIGURE 7-17

A set of radio buttons are added to the Order Form Web page. By clicking one of the two radio buttons, a user can answer either yes or no to the question asked. Because no <br /> tags were included in the HTML, the buttons appear next to each other in the form. To have the radio buttons display on separate lines, include a <br /> tag before the <input> tags on lines 44 and 45.

Adding a Textarea

The next step is to add a textarea to the form. A single line of text is appropriate for some input, such as a street address or credit card number. In some cases, however, the input control requires more than one line to accommodate a larger amount of input. For example, the order form includes a question asking users for additional comments. Because the response can be longer than just one line, a textarea control is more appropriate than a text box.

Table 7-10 contains the tags and text to specify a textarea for multiple-line input.

Table 7-10 HTML Code to Add a Textarea

LINE	CODE
47	`<p>What other types of illustrations, in addition to those shown, would you be`
48	`interested in purchasing?`
49	` <textarea name="other" rows="6" cols="50"></textarea></p>`

The textarea is defined by start <textarea> and end </textarea> tags. The name attribute on line 49 gives the textarea input control a name to identify the information that is entered in the textarea. The rows and cols attributes are used to define the size of a textarea field on the form. In this example, the textarea is 6 rows high and 50 columns (or characters) wide. The following steps illustrate how to add a textarea to the order form.

To Add a Textarea

1 **If necessary, click line 47.**

2 **Enter the HTML code shown in Table 7-10 and then press the ENTER key twice.**

Notepad displays the HTML code as shown in Figure 7-18, and the insertion point is on line 51.

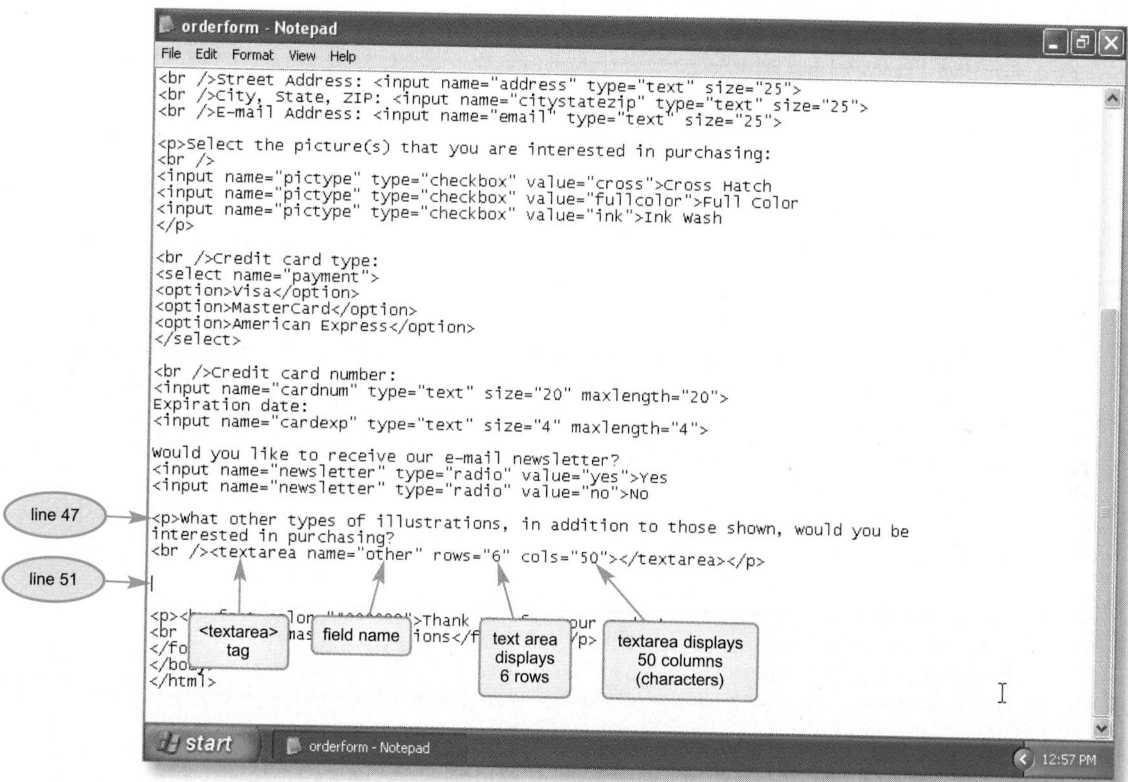

FIGURE 7-18

A textarea is added to the order form. The textarea displays on a new line directly below the question because the <br /> tag was used on line 49.

All of the controls have been added to the Web page form. First, text boxes were added to allow the user to enter name, address, city, state, ZIP, and e-mail address. Next, check boxes were added to allow the user to select more than one type of illustration. To gather credit card information, a selection menu with three possible credit card options and two text boxes for credit card number and expiration date were added. Finally, one set of radio buttons was added to allow the user to sign up for an e-mail newsletter and a textarea was added so users can provide multiple-line comments on other types of illustrations they might wish to purchase. The use of the various controls provides different types of input areas appropriate for various types of information.

Submit and Reset Buttons

The form controls are useless unless the information entered in the form can be submitted for processing. The next step in creating the order form is to add two buttons at the bottom of the Web page form. The first button, Submit, is for submitting the form. When the visitor clicks this button, the data entered into the form is sent to the appropriate location for processing. The second button, Reset, clears any data that was entered in the form.

Adding Submit and Reset Buttons

The HTML code below shows the <input> tags used to create the Submit and Reset buttons on a Web page form:

```
<p><input type="submit" value="Submit">
<input type="reset" value="Reset"></p>
```

More About

Options

The <select> and <option> tags are useful when you have a limited number of choices from which a Web page visitor can select. If the number of options becomes too large, however, the list is difficult to read. A better idea might be to group like options together into submenus. You can use the <optgroup> tag before the first <option> tag in the first group that you want to use in a submenu. After the last option in that group, use the </optgroup> tag.

The first line of HTML code creates a Submit button on the Web page form. A Submit button is created by using the attribute, type="submit", in an <input> tag. The value attribute is used to indicate the text that should appear on the button face — in this case, Submit.

When a user clicks the Submit button, all data currently entered in the form is sent to the appropriate location for processing. The action taken when a form is submitted is based on the method and action attributes specified in the <form> tag. In the <form> tag at the start of this form, the HTML code set the form attributes to method="post" and action="mailto:billthomas@isp.com". Thus, when a user clicks the Submit button, a data file that contains all the input data automatically is sent as an e-mail attachment to the e-mail address, billthomas@isp.com. By default, the data file is named Postdata.att.

The code below shows a sample of the data file that is sent to the e-mail address, when using the post method:

```
payment=American Express&newsletter=yes&other=I would be
interested in more abstract art work
```

The data entered in the form appears in the data file as name-value pairs — that is, the name of the control as specified in the name attribute, followed by the value entered or selected in the control. In the above example, the user selected American Express in the selection menu named payment and clicked the Yes radio button named newsletter. The user also entered a comment that he or she would be interested in more abstract art work in the textarea control named other. An ampersand (&) strings together all of the name-value pairs to make them easier to read.

The Reset button also is an important part of any form. Resetting the form clears any information previously typed into a text box or textarea and resets radio buttons, check boxes, selection menus, and other controls to their initial values. As shown in the second line of the HTML code above, a Reset button is created by using the attribute, type="reset", in an <input> tag. The value attribute is used to indicate the text that should appear on the button face — in this case, Reset.

The following steps illustrate how to add a Submit button and a Reset button to the form.

To Add Submit and Reset Buttons

1

- **If necessary, click line 51.**

2

- **Type** `<p><input type="submit" value="Submit">` **and then press the ENTER key.**

3

- **Type** `<input type="reset" value="Reset"></p>` **as the tag.**

Notepad displays the HTML code as shown in Figure 7-19, and the insertion point is on line 52.

orderforn - Notepad

File Edit Format View Help

```
<br />Street Address: <input name="address" type="text" size="25">
<br />City, State, ZIP: <input name="citystatezip" type="text" size="25">
<br />E-mail Address: <input name="email" type="text" size="25">

<p>Select the picture(s) that you are interested in purchasing:
<br />
<input name="pictype" type="checkbox" value="cross">Cross Hatch
<input name="pictype" type="checkbox" value="fullcolor">Full Color
<input name="pictype" type="checkbox" value="ink">Ink Wash
</p>

<br />Credit card type:
<select name="payment">
<option>Visa</option>
<option>MasterCard</option>
<option>American Express</option>
</select>

<br />Credit card number:
<input name="cardnum" type="text" size="20" maxlength="20">
Expiration date:
<input name="cardexp" type="text" size="4" maxlength="4">

Would you like      e our e-      tter?
<input name="ne     type="r       ="yes">Yes
<input name="ne     type="r       ="no">No

<p>What other t          llustrat        dition to those shown, would you be
interested in purchasing?
<br /><textarea name="other" rows="5" cols="50"></textarea></p>

<p><input type="submit" value="Submit">
<input type="reset" value="Reset"></p>

<p><b><font color="#000099">Thank you for your order!
<br />Bill Thomas Illustrations</font></b></p>
</form>
</body>
</html>
```

line 51

input control type set to submit

Submit appears on button face

input control type set to reset

Reset appears on button face

start Notepad

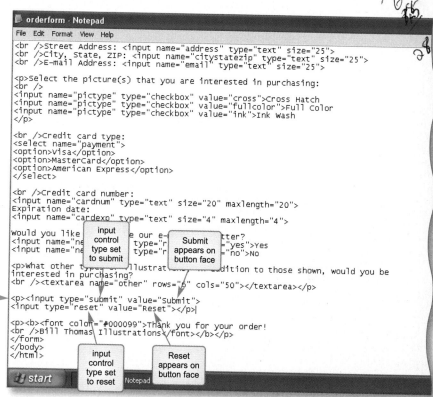

FIGURE 7-19

The Submit and Reset buttons have been added to the bottom of the form. The two buttons will appear on the same line, below the textarea field. As indicated by the value attributes, the button faces will read Submit and Reset, respectively.

Organizing a Form Using Form Groupings

An important aspect of creating a Web page form is making it easy for your audience to understand. Grouping similar information on a form, for example, makes it easier to read and understand — and, as a result, easier to complete. Using grouping is especially helpful in cases where some information is required and some is optional. In the order form, for example, all the personal information is required (e.g., name, address, and credit card number). The final questions on the form, however, are optional (e.g., newsletter and additional comments). The form thus should be modified to group required and optional information.

Using Fieldset Controls to Create Form Groupings

A fieldset control is used to group similar information on a form. The HTML code below shows the <fieldset> tag used to add a fieldset control to a Web page form:

```
<fieldset><legend align="left">Required Information</legend>
</fieldset>
```

The <legend> tag within the fieldset tag is optional. Using the <legend> tag creates a legend for the fieldset, which is the text that displays in the grouping borders, as shown in Figure 7-20. The align attribute is used to align the legend to the left or right of the fieldset control.

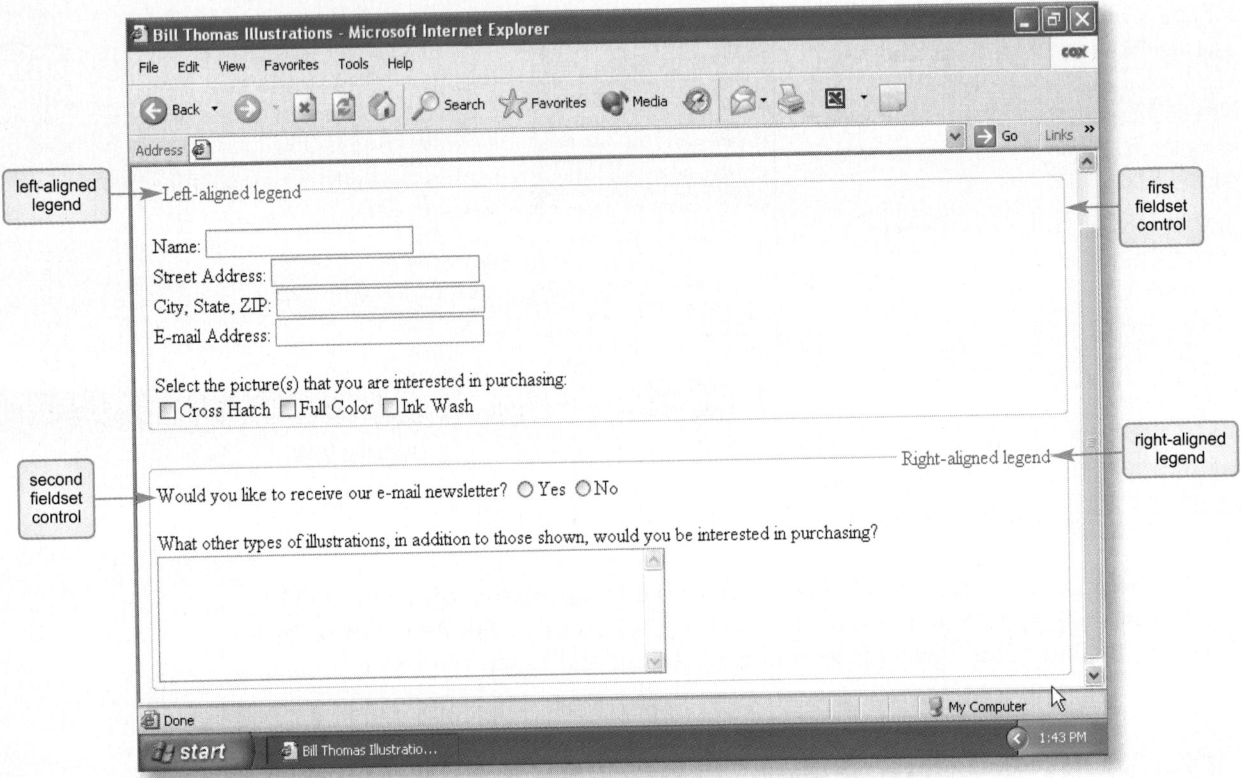

FIGURE 7-20

In the Order Form Web page, two fieldset controls are added to group similar information on the form. The first fieldset control is used to group required information on the form, as shown in Figure 7-21. The second fieldset control is used to group optional information. The first fieldset control has the legend, Required Information, aligned to the left. The second fieldset control has the legend, Additional Comments, aligned to the right. These groupings nicely divide the form so it is more readable and clearly defines what information is required and what is optional, or additional.

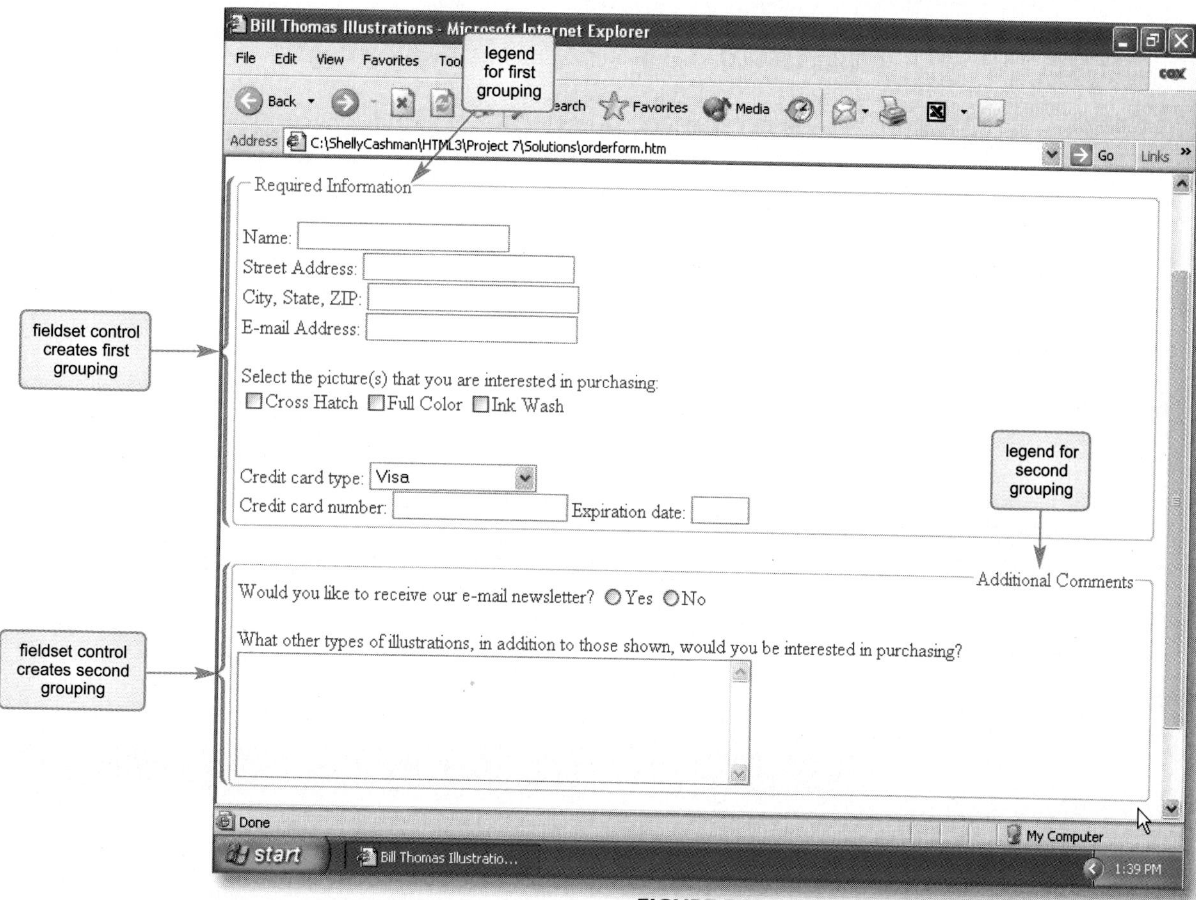

FIGURE 7-21

The following steps show how to add two sets of fieldset tags to create information groupings on the Web page form.

To Add Fieldset Controls to Create Form Groupings

1

- **Click just after the </p> on line 17 and then press the ENTER key.**

2

- **Type** `<fieldset><legend align="left">Required Information</legend>` **as the tag.**

3

- **Click to the right of maxlength="4"> on line 42 and then press the ENTER key.**

4

- **Type** `</fieldset>` **and then press the ENTER key twice.**

5

- **With the insertion point on line 45, type** `<br /><fieldset><legend align="right">Additional Comments</legend>` **as the tag.**

6

- **Click to the right of the </p> on line 53 and then press the ENTER key.**

7

- **Type `</fieldset>` as the tag.**

Notepad displays the HTML code as shown in Figure 7-22, and the insertion point is on line 54.

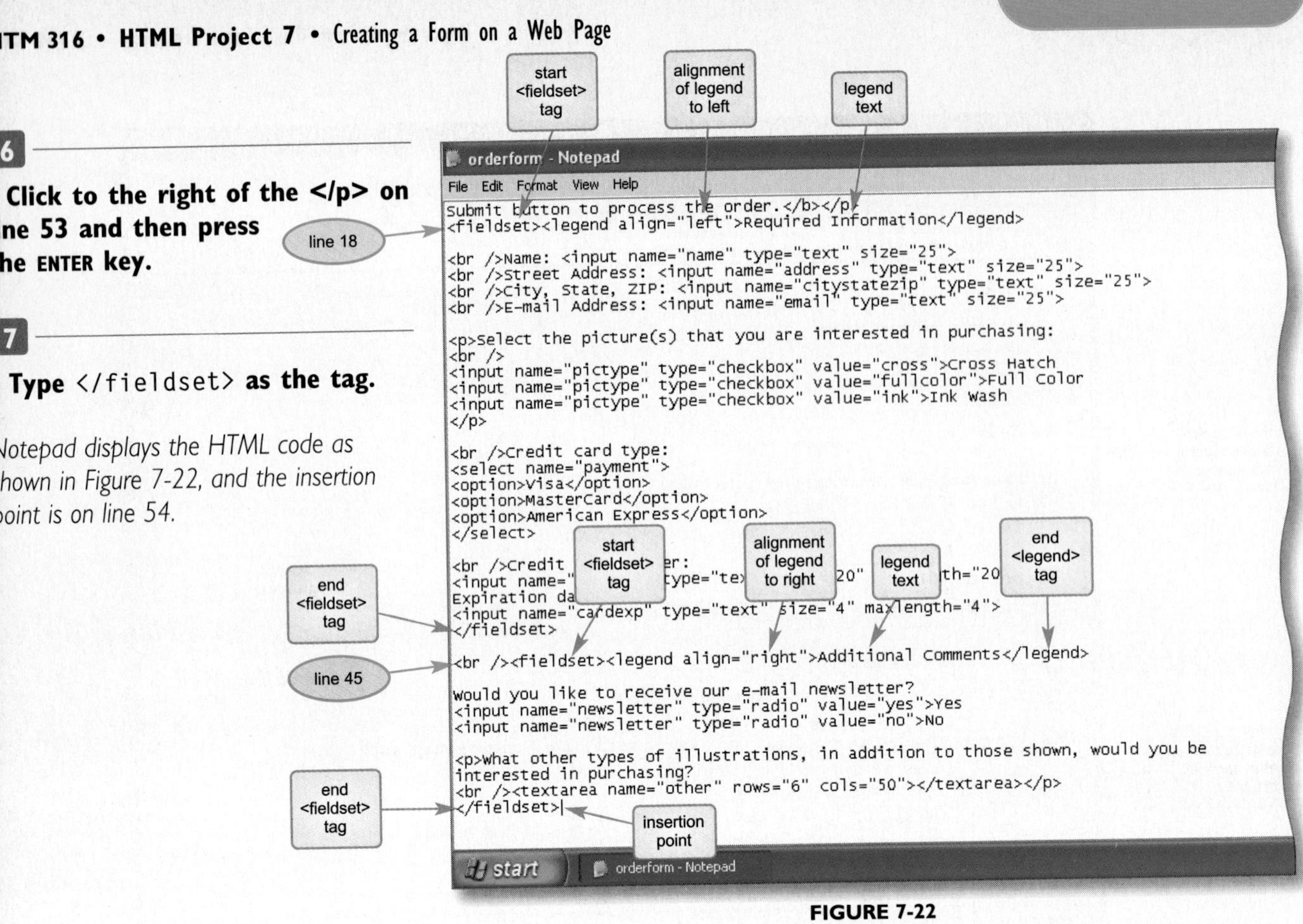

FIGURE 7-22

The form on the Web page, orderform.htm, is complete. The form contains six text fields, three check boxes, one selection menu, one question with radio button options, and one textarea field. It also contains two groupings around similar information, a Submit button that sends a file containing the form's input to the e-mail address, billthomas@isp.com, and a Reset button that clears any information that was entered in the form.

Saving the HTML File

With the Order Form Web page complete, the HTML file should be saved. The following steps illustrate how to save the orderform.htm file on the HTML Data Disk.

To Save the HTML File

1. **With the HTML Data Disk in drive A, click File on the menu bar and then click Save As. Type `orderform.htm` in the File name text box.**
2. **If necessary, click 3½ Floppy (A:) in the Save in list. Click the Project07 folder and then click the ProjectFiles folder in the list of available folders. Click the Save button in the Save As dialog box.**

Notepad saves the updated orderform.htm file in the Project07\ProjectFiles folder on the Data Disk in drive A.

Viewing, Testing, and Printing the Web Page and HTML Code

As shown in earlier projects, after completing the Order Form Web page, it should be viewed and tested in a browser to confirm that the Web page appears as desired and that the controls function as expected. After testing the controls, the Web page and HTML code for each Web page should be printed for future reference.

Review the form to make sure all spelling is correct and the controls are positioned appropriately. Next, test the Web page by completing the form. While entering information, verify the controls are operating correctly, using the following steps:

- Test all of the text boxes on the form. Try to type in more than the maximum number of allowable characters for each.
- Click the check boxes to test them. You should be able to choose one, two, or three of the boxes at the same time because check boxes are designed to select more than one option.
- Test the selection control by clicking the list arrow and selecting one of the three options.
- Click the radio buttons to test them. You should be able to choose only one choice (Yes or No).
- Test the textarea by entering in a paragraph of text. Verify that it allows more characters to be entered than are shown in the textarea.
- Click the Reset button again. It should clear and reset all controls to their original (default) state.

You cannot test the Submit button because it automatically generates an e-mail message to billthomas@isp.com, which is a nonexistent e-mail address. Alternatively, if you have an e-mail address you can use to test the submission process, you can modify the HTML code to use your e-mail address and then again save the HTML file. When you click the Submit button, the information entered in the form will be sent to your e-mail address in a data file that uses a format similar to the sample shown on page HTM 312.

The following steps illustrate how to view the HTML file in a browser, test the controls, and then print the Web page.

More About

Discussion Forums

Other HTML resources include a usenet newsgroup where HTML authoring issues are discussed. Among other things, visitors can ask "How To" questions here. Many issues related to forms and CGI are discussed. To find out more about this newsgroup, visit the HTML More About Web page (scsite.com/html3e/more.htm) and then click Newsgroup.

To View, Test, and Print the Web Page Using a Browser

1

- **Start your browser.**

2

- **Type** `a:\Project07\ProjectFiles\orderform.htm` **in the Address box and then press the ENTER key.**

3

- **Test all fields except the Reset button as described in the previous section.**

4

- **If you modified the HTML code to use your e-mail address as the action attribute value, click the Submit button.**

5

Click the Reset button.

The orderform.htm Web page appears, with all information cleared and controls reset to their original values (Figure 7-23).

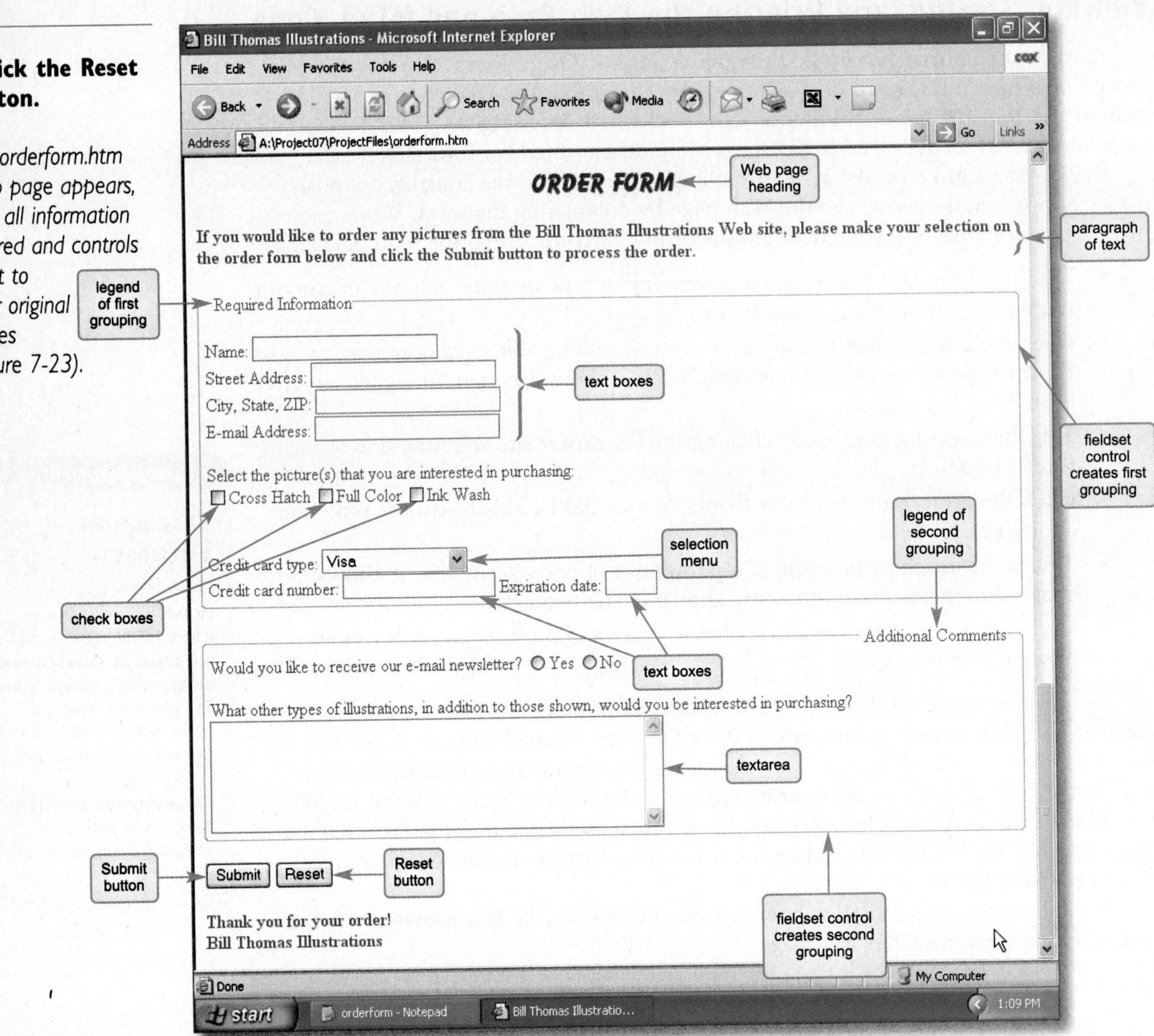

FIGURE 7-23

6

• **Click the Print button on the Standard Buttons toolbar.**

The Web page prints (Figure 7-24).

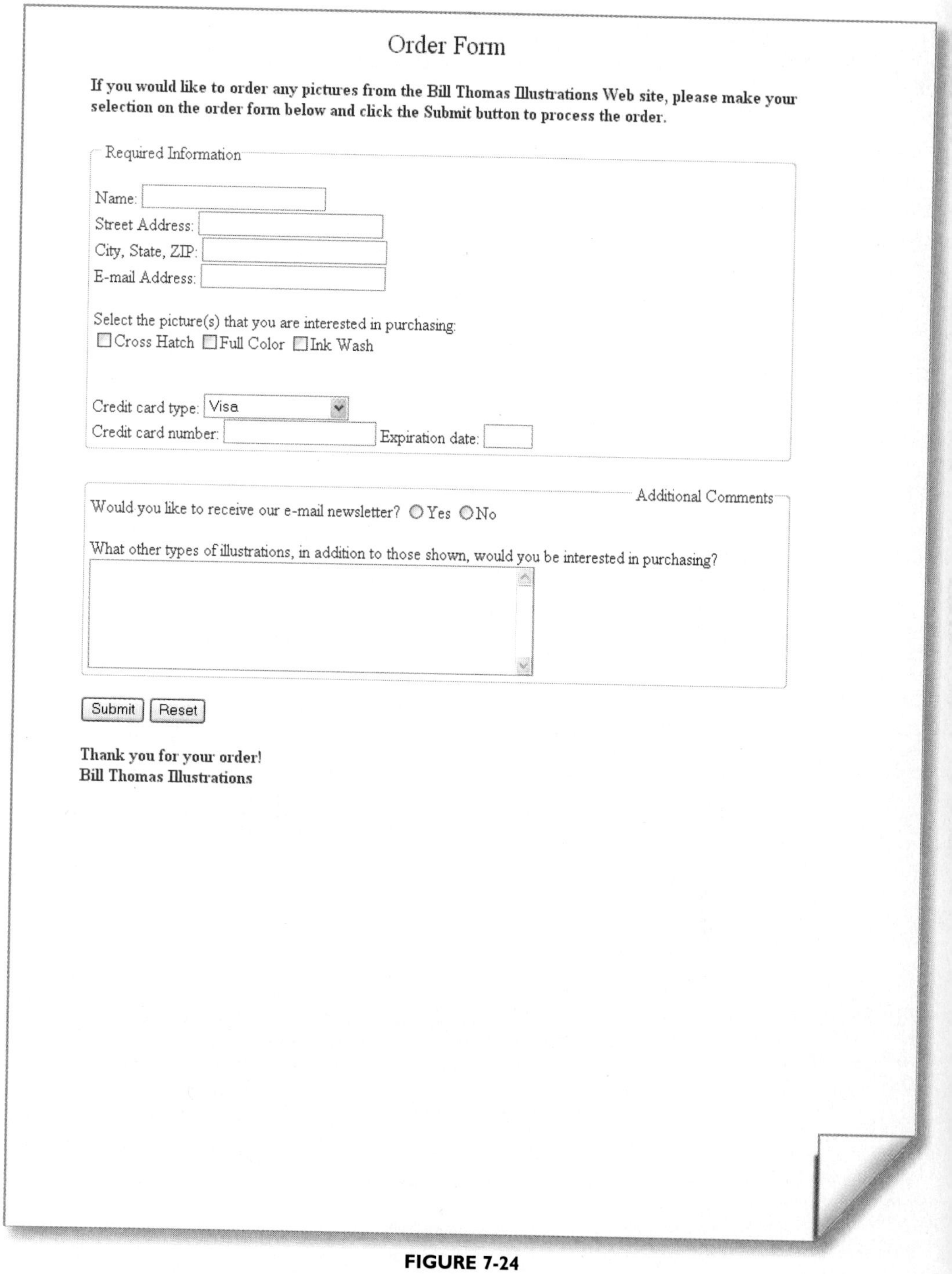

Order Form

If you would like to order any pictures from the Bill Thomas Illustrations Web site, please make your selection on the order form below and click the Submit button to process the order.

Required Information

Name:
Street Address:
City, State, ZIP:
E-mail Address:

Select the picture(s) that you are interested in purchasing:
☐Cross Hatch ☐Full Color ☐Ink Wash

Credit card type: Visa
Credit card number: Expiration date:

Additional Comments

Would you like to receive our e-mail newsletter? ○Yes ○No

What other types of illustrations, in addition to those shown, would you be interested in purchasing?

Submit Reset

Thank you for your order!
Bill Thomas Illustrations

FIGURE 7-24

As shown in Figure 7-24, when the Web page form is printed, all controls used on the form are printed, including the Submit and Reset buttons.

If a problem with the form is discovered during testing, return to Notepad and make the corrections to the HTML code before printing the Web page. If you submitted the form to your e-mail address, check your e-mail for the e-mail message and then open the attachment using Notepad. The name and value pairs from the form should be inserted into the file.

After you have verified that all controls on the Web page form work correctly, print the HTML file in Notepad. This printed file is a good source of reference for the HTML code used to create a form with different types of controls.

To Print the HTML File

1. **Click the Notepad button on the taskbar.**
2. **Click File on the menu bar and then click Print.**

The HTML file, orderform.htm, prints (Figure 7-25).

```
<!DOCTYPE html
  PUBLIC "-//W3C//DTD XHTML 1.0 Frameset/EN"
  "http://www.w3.org/TR/xhtml1/DTD/xhtml1-frameset.dtd">

<html>
<head>
<title>Bill Thomas Illustrations</title>
</head>
<body>
<center><font face="bazooka" color="navy" size="+2">Order Form</font></center>

<form method="post" action="mailto:billthomas@isp.com">

<p><b><font color="#000099">
If you would like to order any pictures from the Bill Thomas Illustrations
Web site, please make your selection on the order form below and click the
Submit button to process the order.</b></p>
<fieldset><legend align="left">Required Information</legend>

<br />Name: <input name="name" type="text" size="25">
<br />Street Address: <input name="address" type="text" size="25">
<br />City, State, ZIP: <input name="citystatezip" type="text" size="25">
<br />E-mail Address: <input name="email" type="text" size="25">

<p>Select the picture(s) that you are interested in purchasing:
<br />
<input name="pictype" type="checkbox" value="cross">Cross Hatch
<input name="pictype" type="checkbox" value="fullcolor">Full Color
<input name="pictype" type="checkbox" value="ink">Ink Wash
</p>

<br />Credit card type:
<select name="payment">
<option>Visa</option>
<option>MasterCard</option>
<option>American Express</option>
</select>

<br />Credit card number:
<input name="cardnum" type="text" size="20" maxlength="20">
Expiration date:
<input name="cardexp" type="text" size="4" maxlength="4">
</fieldset>

<br /><fieldset><legend align="right">Additional Comments</legend>

Would you like to receive our e-mail newsletter?
<input name="newsletter" type="radio" value="yes">Yes
<input name="newsletter" type="radio" value="no">No

<p>What other types of illustrations, in addition to those shown, would you be
interested in purchasing?
<br /><textarea name="other" rows="6" cols="50"></textarea></p>
</fieldset>

<p><input type="submit" value="Submit">
<input type="reset" value="Reset"></p>

<p><b><font color="#000099">Thank you for your order!
<br />Bill Thomas Illustrations</font></b></p>
</form>
</body>
</html>
```

FIGURE 7-25

After completing the project, quit Notepad and the browser. The following steps show how to quit Notepad and a browser.

To Quit Notepad and a Browser

1. **Click the Close button on the browser title bar.**
2. **Click the Close button on the Notepad window title bar.**

Both the browser and Notepad windows close, and the Windows desktop is displayed.

Project Summary

In Project 7, you used Notepad to convert a text-based Web page to a Web page form with a number of different controls. You learned the terms and definitions relating to forms and used numerous form tags and attributes. In the form, you created several sets of text boxes for single-line input, one set of check boxes, and a selection menu with three options. You also created a set of radio buttons and a textarea for multiple-line input. Finally, you created a Submit button to send the form data to the server to be processed and a Reset button to clear all input from the form.

What You Should Know

Having completed this project, you now should be able to perform the tasks listed below. The tasks are listed in the same order they were presented in this project.

1. Start Notepad and Open an HTML File (HTM 298)
2. Create a Form and Identify the Form Process (HTM 299)
3. Change the Text Message (HTM 301)
4. Add Text Boxes (HTM 302)
5. Add Check Boxes (HTM 304)
6. Add a Selection Menu (HTM 305)
7. Add Additional Text Boxes (HTM 308)
8. Add Radio Buttons (HTM 309)
9. Add a Textarea (HTM 311)
10. Add Submit and Reset Buttons (HTM 313)
11. Add Fieldset Controls to Create Form Groupings (HTM 315)
12. Save the HTML File (HTM 316)
13. View, Test, and Print the Web Page Using a Browser (HTM 317)
14. Print the HTML File (HTM 320)
15. Quit Notepad and a Browser (HTM 321)

Learn It Online

Instructions: To complete the Learn It Online exercises, start your browser, click the Address bar, and then enter the Web address `scsite.com/html3e/learn`. When the HTML Learn It Online page is displayed, follow the instructions in the exercises below. Each exercise has instructions for printing your results, either for your own records or for submission to your instructor.

1 Project Reinforcement TF, MC, and SA

Below HTML Project 7, click the Project Reinforcement link. Print the quiz by clicking Print on the File menu for each page. Answer each question.

2 Flash Cards

Below HTML Project 7, click the Flash Cards link and read the instructions. Type `20` (or a number specified by your instructor) in the Number of playing cards text box, type your name in the Enter your Name text box, and then click the Flip Card button. When the flash card is displayed, read the question and then click the ANSWER box arrow to select an answer. Flip through Flash Cards. If your score is 15 (75%) correct or greater, click Print on the File menu to print your results. If your score is less than 15 (75%) correct, then redo this exercise by clicking the Replay button.

3 Practice Test

Below HTML Project 7, click the Practice Test link. Answer each question, enter your first and last name at the bottom of the page, and then click the Grade Test button. When the graded practice test is displayed on your screen, click Print on the File menu to print a hard copy. Continue to take practice tests until you score 80% or better.

4 Who Wants To Be a Computer Genius?

Below HTML Project 7, click the Computer Genius link. Read the instructions, enter your first and last name at the bottom of the page, and then click the PLAY button. When your score is displayed, click the PRINT RESULTS link to print a hard copy.

5 Wheel of Terms

Below HTML Project 7, click the Wheel of Terms link. Read the instructions, and then enter your first and last name and your school name. Click the PLAY button. When your score is displayed, right-click the score and then click Print on the shortcut menu to print a hard copy.

6 Crossword Puzzle Challenge

Below HTML Project 7, click the Crossword Puzzle Challenge link. Read the instructions, and then enter your first and last name. Click the SUBMIT button. Work the crossword puzzle. When you are finished, click the Submit button. When the crossword puzzle is redisplayed, click the Print Puzzle button to print a hard copy.

7 Tips and Tricks

Below HTML Project 7, click the Tips and Tricks link. Click a topic that pertains to Project 7. Right-click the information and then click Print on the shortcut menu. Construct a brief example of what the information relates to in HTML to confirm you understand how to use the tip or trick.

8 Newsgroups

Below HTML Project 7, click the Newsgroups link. Click a topic that pertains to Project 7. Print three comments.

9 Expanding Your Horizons

Below HTML Project 7, click the Expanding Your Horizons link. Click a topic that pertains to Project 7. Print the information. Construct a brief example of what the information relates to in HTML to confirm you understand the contents of the article.

10 Search Sleuth

Below HTML Project 7, click the Search Sleuth link. To search for a term that pertains to this project, select a term below the Project 7 title and then use the Google search engine at google.com (or any major search engine) to display and print two Web pages that present information on the term.

11 Online Help I

Below HTML Project 7, click the Online Help I link. Follow the instructions on the page to access Web pages that provide additional help on project topics. Hand in any printed information to your instructor.

12 Online Help II

Below HTML Project 7, click the Online Help II link. Follow the instructions on the page to access Web pages that provide additional help on project topics. Hand in any printed information to your instructor.

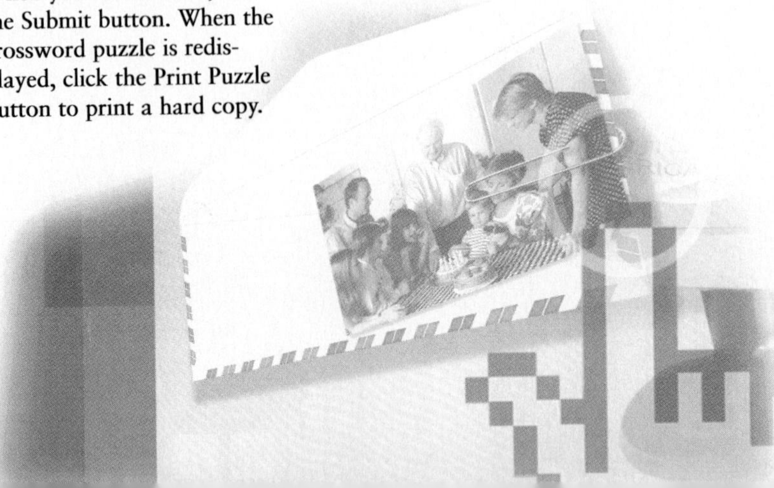

Apply Your Knowledge

1 Editing the Apply Your Knowledge Web Page

Instructions: Start Notepad. Open the file, apply7-1.htm, from the Project07\AYK folder on the HTML Data Disk. See the inside back cover of this book for instructions for downloading the HTML Data Disk or see your instructor for information about accessing the files in this book. The apply7-1.htm file is a partially completed HTML file that contains some errors. Figure 7-26 shows the Apply Your Knowledge Web page as it should appear in your browser after the errors are corrected.

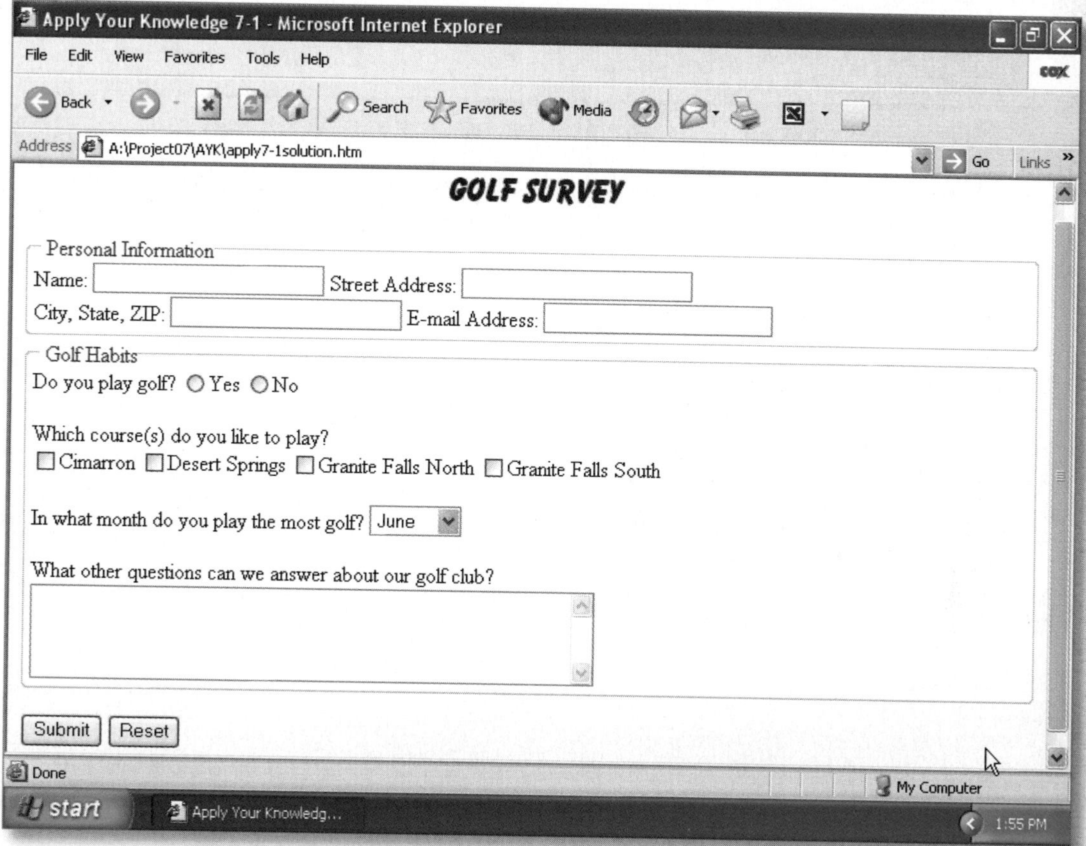

FIGURE 7-26

Perform the following steps using a computer:

1. Using Notepad, open the file, apply7-1.htm, from the Project 07\AYK folder on the HTML Data Disk.
2. Open your browser and then enter the URL, `a:\Project07\AYK\apply7-1.htm`, to view the Web page.
3. Examine the HTML file and its appearance in the browser.
4. Using Notepad, correct the HTML errors, making the Web page look similar to the one shown in Figure 7-26.
5. Add any HTML code necessary to include any additional features shown on the Web page.
6. Save the revised file on the HTML Data Disk using the file name, apply7-1solution.htm.
7. Print the revised HTML file.
8. Enter the URL, `a:\Project07\AYK\apply7-1solution.htm`, to view the Web page in your browser.
9. Print the Web page.
10. Write your name on both printouts and hand them in to your instructor.

1 Creating a School Cafeteria Survey

Problem: The staff of the school cafeteria are considering changing the lunch menus. They first want to survey the students at the school to find out how frequently they eat in the cafeteria and what types of food they like. The staff have asked you to create a Web page form that contains the questions as shown in Figure 7-27.

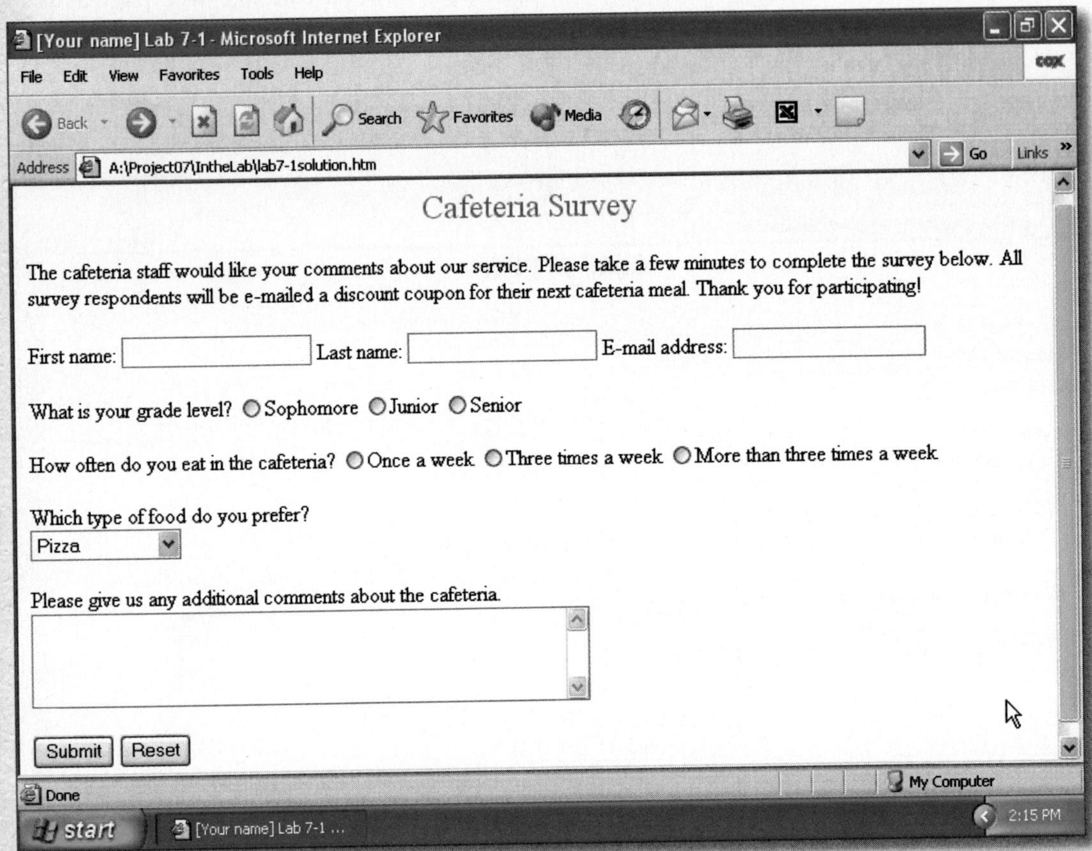

FIGURE 7-27

Instructions: Start Notepad. Perform the following steps using a computer:

1. Using Notepad, create a new HTML file with the title, [Your name] lab7-1, in the main heading section. Add the Web page heading, Cafeteria Survey, and the instructional text message at the top of the page.
2. Create a form and identify the form process using the post method with the action attribute set to email@isp.com.
3. Add three text boxes for first name, last name, and e-mail address.
4. Add three radio buttons for users to select grade level from the options Sophomore, Junior, and Senior.
5. Add three additional radio buttons for users to select how often they eat in the cafeteria from the options shown in Figure 7-27.
6. Create a selection menu as shown in Figure 7-27. Use four of your favorite foods for the options.
7. Create a textarea for additional comments and set it to 4 rows and 50 columns.
8. Add Submit and Reset buttons at the bottom of the Web page form.

9. Save the HTML file in the Project07\IntheLab folder on the HTML Data Disk using the file name, lab7-1solution.htm. Print the HTML file.
10. Open the lab7-1solution.htm file in your browser and test all controls (except the Submit button).
11. Print the Web page.
12. Write your name on the printouts and hand them in to your instructor.

2 School Fund-Raising Questionnaire

Problem: The school fund-raising committee is looking for new fund-raising ideas. They want to know the fund-raising activities in which students already have participated and what other activities they would like to see. They have asked you to create the survey as a Web page form, as shown in Figure 7-28.

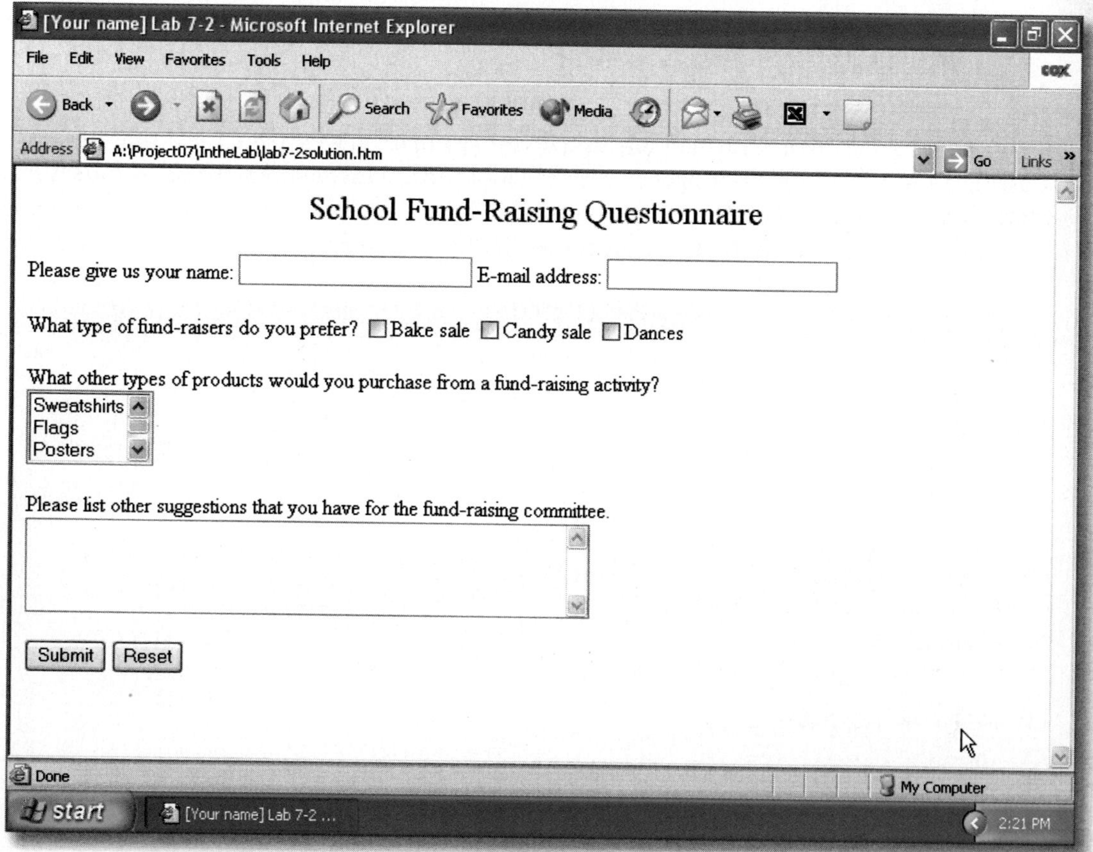

FIGURE 7-28

Instructions: Start Notepad. Perform the following steps using a computer:

1. Using Notepad, create a new HTML file with the title, [Your name] lab7-2, in the main heading section.
2. Create a form and identify the form process using the post method with the action attribute set to your e-mail address (if you do not have an e-mail address, use user@isp.com).
3. Add two text boxes for name and e-mail address, as shown in Figure 7-28.
4. Add three check boxes for users to select one or more types of fund-raisers.

(continued)

School Fund-Raising Questionnaire *(continued)*

5. Add a selection menu that initially displays 3 rows and allows multiple input. Use the following items as options in the selection menu: Sweatshirts, Flags, Posters, and Hats.
6. Insert a 5-row, 50-column textarea for users to provide additional suggestions.
7. Add a Submit button and a Reset button at the bottom of the Web page form.
8. Save the HTML file in the Project07\IntheLab folder on the HTML Data Disk using the file name, lab7-2solution.htm. Print the HTML file.
9. Open the lab7-2solution.htm file in your browser and test all controls. Test the Submit button only if you used your own e-mail address as the value for the form action attribute.
10. Print the Web page.
11. Write your name on the printouts and hand them in to your instructor.

3 Using Fieldset Controls to Group Controls in a Form

Problem: Your manager at Horizon Learning has asked you to create a Web page form that newer HTML developers can use as a model for a well-designed, user-friendly form. Having created forms for several different Web sites, you have learned that using fieldset controls to group form controls results in a well-organized, easily readable form. Create a Web page form that utilizes three fieldset controls, like the one shown in Figure 7-29.

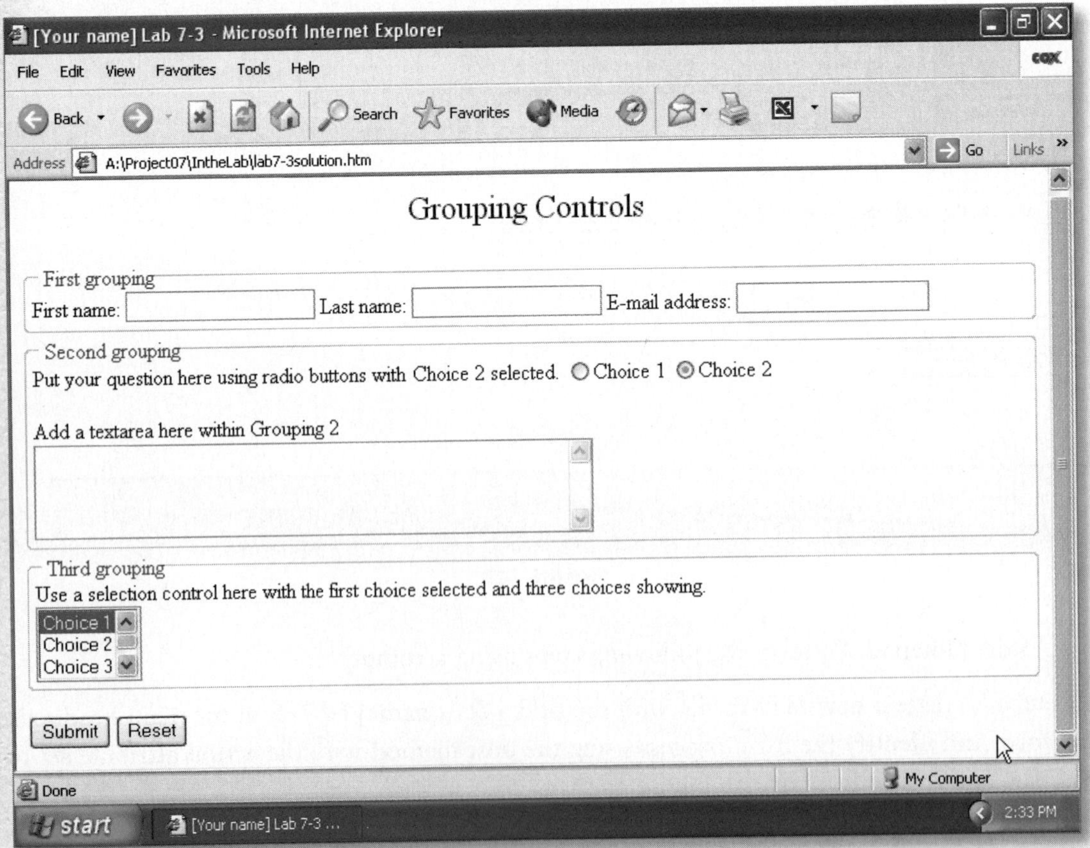

FIGURE 7-29

Instructions: Start Notepad. Perform the following steps using a computer:

1. Using Notepad, create a new HTML file with the title, [Your name] lab7-3, in the main heading section.
2. Add the Web page heading, Grouping Controls.
3. Create a form and identify the form process using the post method with the action attribute set to your e-mail address (if you do not have an e-mail address, use `user@isp.com`).
4. Add three text boxes for first name, last name, and e-mail address.
5. Add two radio buttons, with Choice 2 pre-selected, as shown in Figure 7-29.
6. Add a 4-row, 50-column textarea, as shown in Figure 7-29.
7. Insert a selection menu with options of Choice 1 through Choice 4. Set the selection menu to display 3 rows and have Choice 1 pre-selected as the default option.
8. Add a Submit button and a Reset button at the bottom of the Web page form.
9. Add three fieldset controls to group the other form controls, as shown in Figure 7-29.
10. Save the HTML file in the Project07\IntheLab folder on the HTML Data Disk using the file name, lab7-3solution.htm. Print the HTML file.
11. Open the lab7-3solution.htm file in your browser and test all controls. Test the Submit button only if you used your own e-mail address as the value for the form action attribute.
12. Print the Web page.
13. Write your name on the printouts and hand them in to your instructor.

Cases and Places

The difficulty of these case studies varies:
■ are the least difficult and ■■ are the most difficult. The last exercise is a group exercise.

1 ■ The marketing director at Getaway Travel asked you to create a Web page form to allow customers to request information on the four travel packages offered by the agency: ski & snow, surf & sun, golf & spa, and adventure. Using the techniques learned in this project, create a Web page form with input controls to allow customers to request information on one or more travel packages. By default, have all of the travel packages selected on the form. In addition, include input controls for customers to provide a mailing address, an e-mail address, and any suggestions for new travel packages. Include a Submit and Reset button and use your e-mail address in the action attribute for the form. After creating the Web page, enter information and submit the form. Print the data file with the information and indicate which name-value pairs are related to which controls on the form.

2 ■ As part of your Web development project, your instructor has asked you to find a text-based form that is currently in use by your school, a club, or another organization. Convert this text-based form to a Web page form. Start by designing the form on paper, taking into consideration the fields that are the most appropriate to use for each input area. Once your design is complete, use HTML to develop the Web page form. Test the form, and once testing is done, show the form to several people from the organization that controls the form. Explain to them why it is better to collect information using a Web page form, rather than a printed, text-based form.

3 ■■ You recently have started working for Miramar Web Group, L.L.C. The company has some great ideas about using Web pages to display information, but they are not as familiar with using the Web to collect information. You want to convince the head of Web development that Web page forms can be used to collect important information from the visitors to companies' Web sites. Search the Internet for two or three examples of Web page forms used in business. Print the forms as examples. If you were the Web developer for these Web sites, how would you update the forms to gather more information or make the forms easier to use? Sketch an updated form design for at least one of the Web sites on another sheet of paper, explaining why you chose the controls that you suggest. Develop the Web page form as an example to share with the head of Web development at Miramar.

4 ■■ Your manager at Hook Wholesale has asked you to update the order form on the Web site to make it easier to use. In Project 3, tables were used to lay out information in a more controlled manner. In this project, you used fieldset controls to group information so it was more readable and, thereby, easier to use. Forms also can be combined with tables to provide more control over the placement of the form controls. Create a Web page form that utilizes a table (either borderless or with borders) to structure the placement of controls and includes at least two fieldset controls that group other controls on a form.

5 ■■ **Working Together** Your team works in the Web development department for a small company in your community. You are interested in learning the latest programming techniques so you can stay current with the technology. In Project 7, data from a form was sent in a file to an e-mail address. The project mentioned CGI scripts and the Perl programming language as a better, more secure method to use for processing the information submitted in a form. While CGI scripts and Perl programming are beyond the scope of this book, they are important topics to study. Search the Web to find additional information about CGI scripts and Perl used in conjunction with forms. Try to find online tutorials that explain how to use these techniques. What other options are available for collecting information online? Develop a Web page that lists links to various Web sites that discuss these topics. Under each link, write a brief paragraph explaining the purpose of each Web site and why it is important to review.

HTML

Creating Style Sheets

PROJECT

8

CASE PERSPECTIVE

When the Stained Glass Club was started a few years ago, the head of advertising for the club, Tanya Wattigney, hired you to help the club members create the Web site. The original Stained Glass Club Web site was very basic, with a few simple pages of text information.

At Tanya's request, you recently have added several more Web pages to the Web site and updated it to use a frame structure. Recognizing that the Stained Glass Club Web site will continue to grow, you suggest to Tanya that you should modify the Web site to use Cascading Style Sheets (CSS). You then explain to her that Cascading Style Sheets are used to maintain a consistent look across a Web site — especially Web sites that contain many pages. Additionally, Cascading Style Sheets are the recommended technique to use that eliminates the use of deprecated HTML tags and attributes. Tanya is supportive of the plan and encourages you to start as soon as possible.

In this project, you will learn to use three different types of Cascading Style Sheets, including embedded style sheets, external style sheets, and inline style sheets. You also will learn the HTML tags used to define various styles in each style sheet type.

HTML

Creating Style Sheets

PROJECT

Objectives

You will have mastered the material in this project when you can:

- Describe the three different types of Cascading Style Sheets
- Add an embedded style sheet to a Web page
- Change the margin and link styles using an embedded style sheet
- Create an external style sheet
- Change the body margins and background using an external style sheet
- Change the link decoration and color using an external style sheet
- Change the font family and size for all paragraphs using an external style sheet
- Change table styles using an external style sheet
- Use the <link> tag to insert a link to an external style sheet
- Add an inline style sheet to a Web page
- Change the text style of a single paragraph using an inline style sheet
- Understand how to define style classes

Introduction

In previous projects, you learned how to use HTML tags to format text to use a heading style, italics, bold, colors, or other formatting to change the way the Web page appears in a Web browser. You also learned how to use HTML tags and attributes to change the look of an individual table on a Web page and to use the <bgcolor> tag to change the background color of an individual Web page.

While HTML allows Web page developers to make changes to the structure, design, and content of a Web page, HTML is limited in its ability to define the appearance, or style, of one or more Web pages. As a result, style sheets were created.

A **style** is a rule that defines the appearance of an element on a Web page. A **style sheet** is a series of rules that defines the style for a Web page or an entire Web site. With a style sheet, you can alter the appearance of a Web page, by changing characteristics such as font family, font size, margins, and link specifications. Style sheets allow you to change the style for a single element on a Web page, such as a paragraph, or to change the style of elements on all of the pages in a Web site.

Like HTML, style sheets adhere to a common language with set standards and rules. This language, called **Cascading Style Sheets**, or **CSS**, allows a Web developer to write code statements that control the style of elements on a Web page. CSS is not HTML; it is a separate language used to enhance the display capabilities of HTML. The World Wide Web Consortium (W3C), the same organization that defines HTML standards, defines the specifications for CSS.

CSS provides support for three types of style sheets: inline, embedded, and external (or linked). With an **inline style sheet**, you add a style to an individual HTML tag, such as a heading or paragraph. The style changes that specific tag, but does not affect other tags in the document. With an **embedded style sheet**, you add the style sheet within the <head> tags of the HTML document to define the style for an entire Web page. With a linked style sheet, or **external style sheet**, you create a text file that contains all of the styles you want to apply and then save the text file with the file extension, .css. You then add a link to this external style sheet into any Web page in the Web site. External style sheets give you the most flexibility and are ideal to apply the same formats to all of the Web pages in a Web site.

Project Eight — Using Style Sheets in the Stained Glass Club Web Site

In this project, you will use the three different types of style sheets to update and enhance the style of the Web pages in the Stained Glass Club Web site. The Web pages without style sheets are shown in Figure 8-1a. Notice the default elements in these pages. Figure 8-1b shows the Web pages with the style sheets applied. Adding the style sheets updates the pages so they display with new fonts, paragraph styles and spacing, and link placement and color.

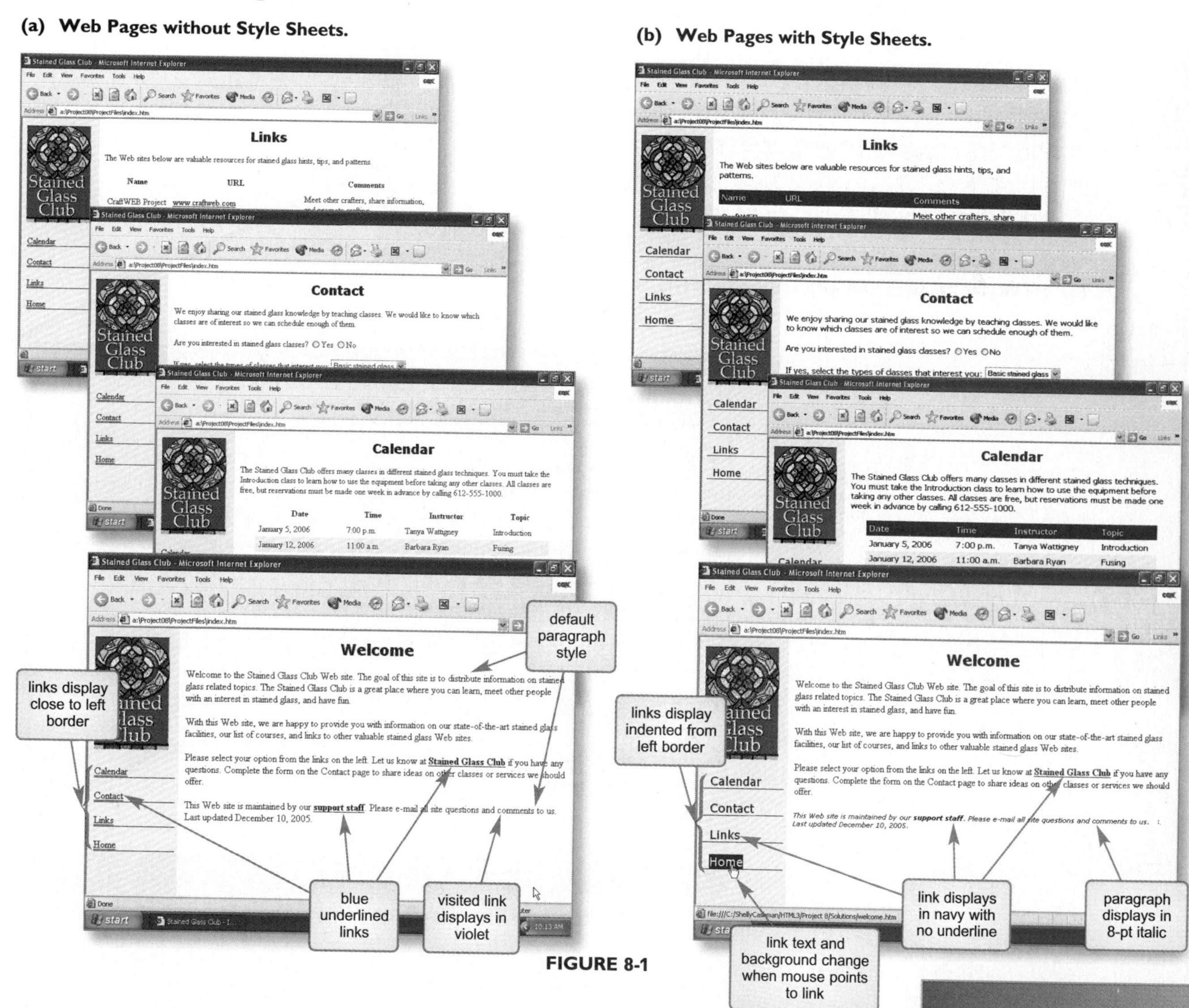

FIGURE 8-1

Without style sheets incorporated, the Web pages in the Stained Glass Club Web site use the default font, link, and margin styles (Figure 8-1a on the previous page). The navigation menu links therefore appear in a blue, underlined font and are positioned very close to the left border of the frame. When a link is clicked, or visited, the visited link's color changes to violet. By adding style sheets, you can update the Web page style to (1) set the link to 14-point Verdana with no underlines, (2) indent the navigation menu links away from the left margin, (3) set the text and background colors of a link to change when the mouse pointer points to, or **hovers**, over the link, (4) set the style of a single paragraph to 8-pt italic font, and (5) change the body, link, paragraph, and table styles of the Web pages that appear in the main frame (Figure 8-1b).

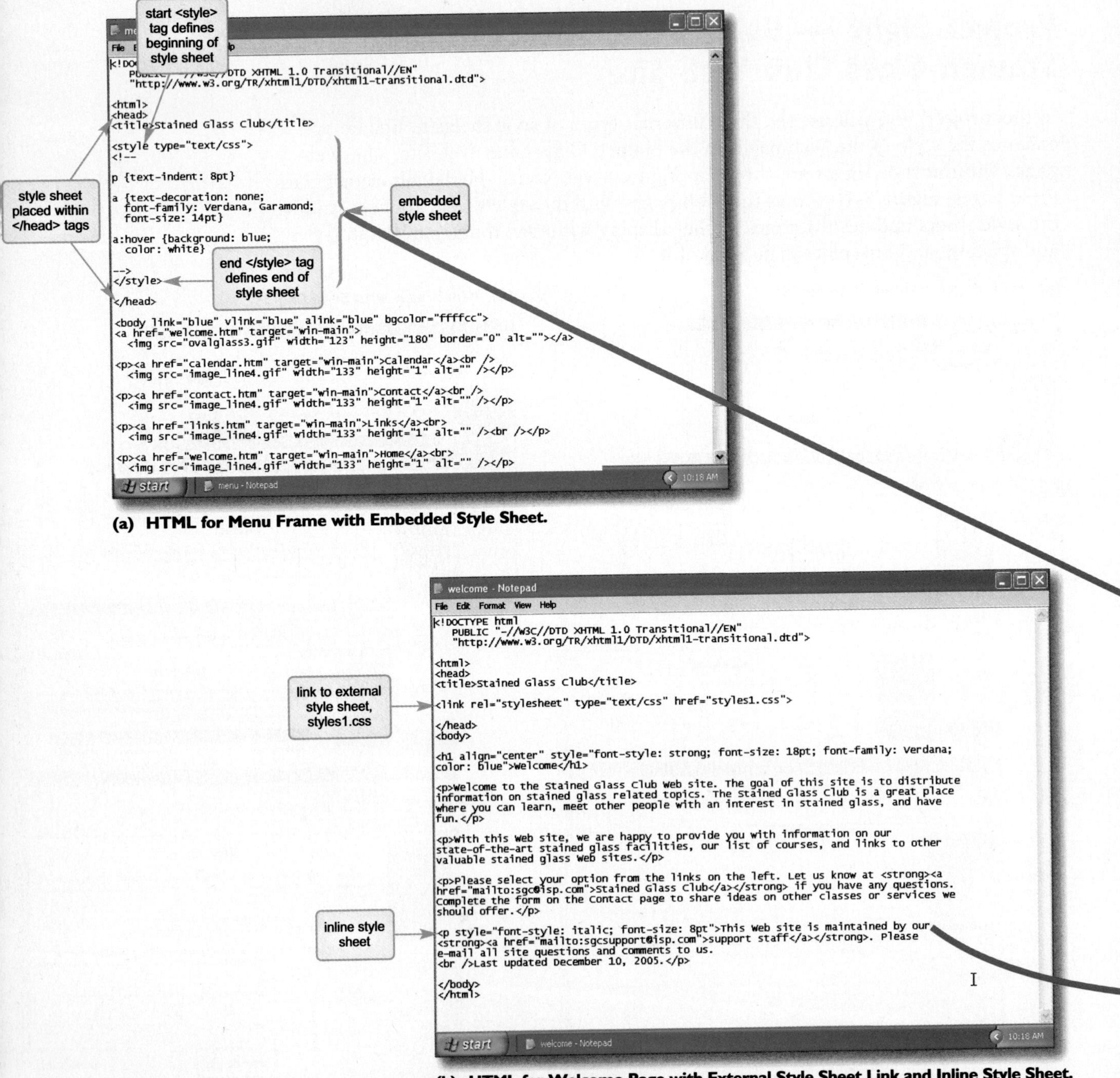

(a) HTML for Menu Frame with Embedded Style Sheet.

(b) HTML for Welcome Page with External Style Sheet Link and Inline Style Sheet.

In this project, you will learn to implement these design ideas using several different types of style sheets. First, an embedded style sheet is used to change the link styles in the menu in the left frame (Figure 8-2a). An inline style sheet is used to change the style for a single paragraph on the Welcome page (Figure 8-2b). An external style sheet is used to change the body, link, paragraph, and table styles in the main pages in the right frame (Figure 8-2c). After the three different style sheets are added to the Stained Glass Club Web site, the finished Web pages appear using styles that make them more attractive, polished, and professional-looking than the original Web pages (Figure 8-2d).

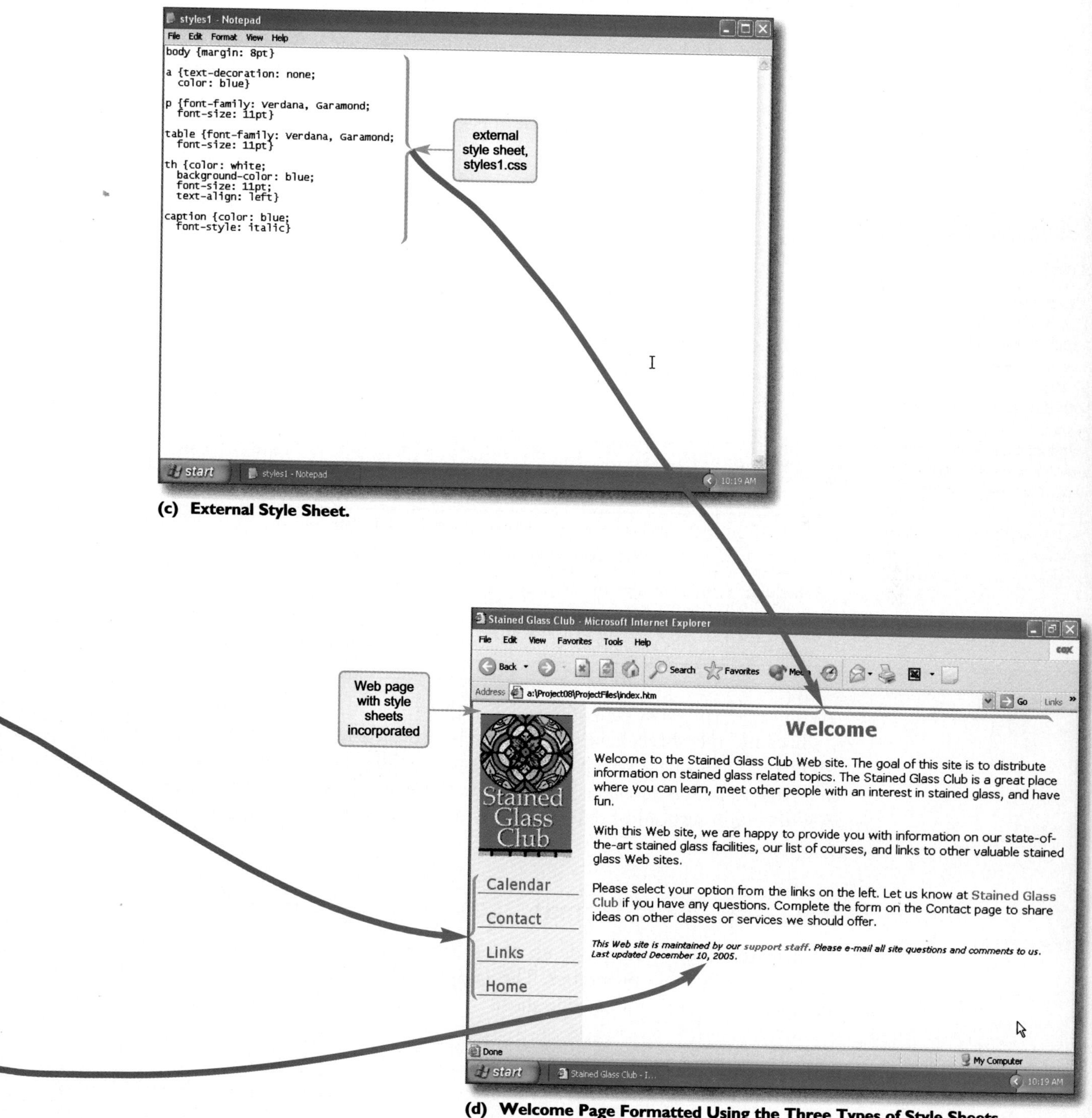

(c) External Style Sheet.

(d) Welcome Page Formatted Using the Three Types of Style Sheets.

FIGURE 8-2

Creating Style Sheets

Style sheets allow a Web developer to assign several properties at once to elements on a Web page. For instance, you can change all of the text in a paragraph to a particular font family and font size using a style sheet. While you could use HTML to specify the font family and font size within each individual paragraph tag, using style sheets allows you to change styles such as font family, font size, and others more easily and consistently. With an embedded style sheet, for example, you can control the style for an entire Web page. Alternatively, you can create an external style sheet to control the appearance of multiple pages in a Web site. If, however, you need to define a style for only a single HTML tag, you can use an inline style sheet to apply a style to just that tag. It is this flexibility that makes CSS such a useful tool for Web developers, giving them more control over Web page appearance and simplifying Web page maintenance.

Style Sheet Precedence

As shown in Table 8-1, the three style sheets supported by CSS control the appearance of a Web page at different levels. Each style sheet type also has a different level of precedence in relationship to the others. An external style sheet, for example, is used to define styles for multiple pages in a Web site. An embedded style sheet is used to change the style of one Web page, but overrides or takes precedence over any styles defined in an external style sheet. An inline style sheet is used to control the style within an individual HTML tag and takes precedence over the styles defined in both embedded and external style sheets.

More About

CSS

The World Wide Web Consortium (W3C) has a wealth of information about Cascading Style Sheets (CSS). You can find out what is new with CSS, access CSS testing suites, and find links to CSS authoring tools from this Web site. For more information about CSS, visit the HTML More About Web page (scsite.com/html3e/more.htm) and then click CSS.

Table 8-1 Three Types of Style Sheets

TYPE	LEVEL AND PRECEDENCE
Inline	• To change the style within an individual HTML tag • Overrides embedded and external style sheets
Embedded	• To change the style of one Web page • Overrides external style sheets
External	• To change the style of multiple pages in a Web site

Because style sheets have different levels of precedence, all three types of style sheets can be used in a single Web page. For example, while you may want some elements of a Web page to match the other Web pages in the Web site, you also may want to vary the look of certain sections of that Web page. You can do this by using the three types of style sheets.

Style Statement Format

A **style statement** is made up of a selector and a declaration that defines the style for one or more properties. The sample code below shows an example of a style statement used in an inline style sheet.

```
<h1 style ="font-family: Garamond; font-color: navy">
```

The part of the style statement that identifies the page elements is called the **selector**. The part of the style statement that identifies how the elements should display is called the **declaration**. A declaration includes at least one type of style, or

property, to apply to the selected element. Examples of properties include color, text-indent, border-width, and font-style. For each property, the declaration includes a related **value,** which specifies the display parameters for that specific property.

In the example above, the h1 (header size 1) element is the selector and the remainder of the code designates the declaration. The declaration includes two property-value statements, font-family: Garamond and font-color: navy, to specify that the header size 1 should display in navy Garamond font. Note that each property accepts specific values, based on the styles that property can define. The property, font-color, for example can accept the value, navy, but cannot accept the value, 10%, because that is not a valid color value.

The sample code below shows an example of style statements used in an embedded style sheet.

```
h1 {font-family: Garamond;
    font-size: 32pt}
```

In this style statement, the h1 (header size 1) element is the selector and the remainder of the code is the declaration. The declaration sets the values for two different properties. The first property-value statement sets the h1 font family to Garamond. The second property-value statement sets the font size to 32 point. This means that the browser will display all h1 headers in 32-point Garamond font.

As shown in these examples, style sheets allow you to control many different property values for various elements in a Web page. Table 8-2 lists six main properties and related options you can control with a value. A complete list of properties and property values that can be used in style sheets are included in Appendix C.

More About

CSS Tutorial

Information is available on the Web about CSS. A good CSS tutorial can be found at the Web site below. The site starts with CSS basics and then moves to more advanced topics. CSS examples and a quiz are available along with many CSS references. To view this tutorial, visit the HTML More About Web page (scsite.com/html3e/more.htm) and then click CSS tutorial.

Table 8-2 Properties and Values

PROPERTY NAME	OPTIONS THAT CAN BE CONTROLLED
background	• color • image • position
border	• color • style • width
font	• family • size • style • variant • weight
list	• image • position • type
margin	• length • percentage
text	• alignment • decoration • indentation • spacing • white space

Inline Style Sheets

As previously discussed, an *inline style sheet* is used to define the style of an individual HTML tag. An inline style sheet takes precedence over both embedded and external style sheets. Because an inline style sheet takes precedence, even if you set the font style and color of all paragraphs in a Web page using an embedded style sheet, you still can change the style of a single paragraph by inserting an inline style sheet. For example, to change the style of a single paragraph, you could add an inline style sheet with the <p> (paragraph) tag as the selector and a declaration that defines new font style and color values for that paragraph, as shown below.

```
<p style="font-style: italic; font-size: 8pt">
```

Because they take precedence over the other types of style sheets and affect the style for individual HTML tags, inline style sheets are helpful when one section of a Web page needs to have a different style than the rest of the Web page.

Embedded Style Sheets

An *embedded style sheet* is used to control the style of a single Web page. To add an embedded style sheet to a Web page, you insert a start <style> tag at the top of the Web page within the <head> tags that define the header section. After adding the desired style statements, you end the embedded style sheet by adding an end </style> tag. The code below shows an example of an embedded style sheet.

```
<style type="text/css">
<!--

p {text-indent: 8pt}

a {text-decoration: none;
   font-family: Verdana;
   font-size: 14pt;
   color: navy}

a:hover {background: navy;
   color: white}

-->
</style>
```

The embedded style sheet shown above defines the style for three elements on the page: paragraphs, links, and the link-hover property. The first style statement uses the **selector p** to specify that all text in a paragraph should be indented by 8 points. Adding space to indent the text ensures that the text does not run up against the left side of the Web page, thus giving the Web page a cleaner look.

The second style statement defines four properties of the link element. The **selector a** is used to indicate the link element. The property-value statement "text-decoration: none" changes the default, so that no line will appear under the links. The next two property-value statements change the font family and font size to 14-point Verdana. The final property-value statement changes the color of all link text to navy. Because the style statement uses a as the selector, it changes all link states (normal, visited, active) to these property values. You also can define a unique style for normal, visited, and active links by creating three separate style statements with **a:link**, **a:visited**, and **a:active** as the selectors.

The last style statement uses the **a:hover selector** to define the style of a link when the mouse pointer points to, or hovers over, a link. This statement tells the browser to display white link text on a navy background when the mouse hovers over the link (see the sample code above). Adding a link hover style significantly changes the look of the links and adds a dimension of interactivity to the Web page.

Recall that an embedded style sheet has the second highest level of precedence of the three types of style sheets. Although an inline style sheet overrides the properties of an embedded style sheet, the embedded style sheet takes precedence over an external style sheet.

External Style Sheets

External style sheets are the most comprehensive form of style sheet and can be used to control the consistency and look of many Web pages within a Web site. Adding an external style sheet to a Web page involves a two-step process of creating an external style sheet and then linking this style sheet into the desired Web pages.

An external style sheet is a text file that contains style statements for all of the styles you want to define. The sample code below shows an example of an external style sheet.

```
a {text-decoration: none;
  color: blue}

p {font-family: Verdana, Garamond;
  font-size: 11pt}

table {font-family: Verdana, Garamond;
  font-size: 11pt}

th {color: white;
  background-color: blue;
  font-size: 11pt;
  text-align: left}
```

The format of the external style sheet is very similar to the format of the embedded style sheet. An external style sheet, however, does not need <style> tags to start and end the style sheet; it includes just the style statements.

To create an external style sheet, enter all of the style statements in a text file using Notepad or another text editor and then save the text file with a **.css extension.** The code shown above, for example, can be saved with the file name, styles1.css, and then linked into multiple Web pages.

For each Web page to which you want to apply the styles in an external style sheet, a <link> tag similar to the sample code below must be inserted within the <head> tags of the Web page.

```
<link rel="stylesheet" type="text/css" href="styles1.css">
```

The <link> tag shown above indicates that the style sheet, styles1.css, should be applied to this Web page. The property-value statement rel="stylesheet" defines the relationship of the linked document (that is, that it is a style sheet). The property-value statement type="text/css" indicates the content and language used in the linked document. The property-value statement href="styles1.css" indicates the name and location of the linked style sheet, styles1.css. To apply this style sheet to other pages in the Web site, you would insert the same <link> tag within the <head> tag of each Web page.

Working with Classes in Style Sheets

More About

Classes

One very important advanced CSS topic is classes. With classes, you can create several different variations for any one tag. You might utilize three different classes of paragraphs, and each one can have a different style sheet declaration. You can name classes anything that you want, but make sure to use a period before the class name in the style sheets rule.

In some Web sites, you might need to have more control over the style in a Web page. For example, rather than having all paragraphs of text appear in the same style, you might want the style of the first paragraph on a page to be different than the other paragraphs of text. In order to gain more control for these purposes, you can define specific elements of an HTML file as a category, or **class**. You then can create a specific style for each class. Using classes in style sheets thus allows you to apply styles to HTML tags selectively. Using a class, for example, you could apply one style to a beginning paragraph and a different style to a closing paragraph in the same Web page.

Defining and using classes in a style sheet is a two-step process. First, any elements that belong to the class are marked by adding the tag

```
class="classname"
```

where classname is the identifier or name of the class. To define a class that includes any beginning paragraphs, for example, you would enter the code

```
<p class="beginning">
```

where beginning is the classname and the <p> tag indicates that the class is a specific type of paragraph style. Any word can be used as a classname, as long as it does not contain spaces. In general, however, you should use descriptive names that illustrate the purpose of a class (for example, beginning, legallanguage, or copyrighttext), rather than names that describe the appearance of the class (for example, bluetext, largereditalic, or boldsmallarial). Using names that describe the purpose makes the code easier to read and more flexible.

After you have named the classes, you can use the names in a selector and define a specific style for the class. For example, within the <style> tags in an embedded or external style sheet, you enter a style statement in the format

```
p.beginning {color: red;
   font: 20pt}
```

where the p indicates that the class applies to a specific category of the paragraph tag and beginning is the classname. The tag and the classname are separated by a period. Together, the tag and the classname make up the selector for the style statement. The declaration then lists the property-value statements that should be applied to elements in the class.

For instance, if you want to display the beginning paragraph text in a 20-point red font, you would add a style statement like the one shown in the sample code in

Figure 8-3a and then use the tag, <p class="beginning">, to apply the style defined by the declaration associated with the p.beginning selector. If the paragraph <p> tag is used without the classname, the paragraph displays in the default style or other style as defined by a style sheet.

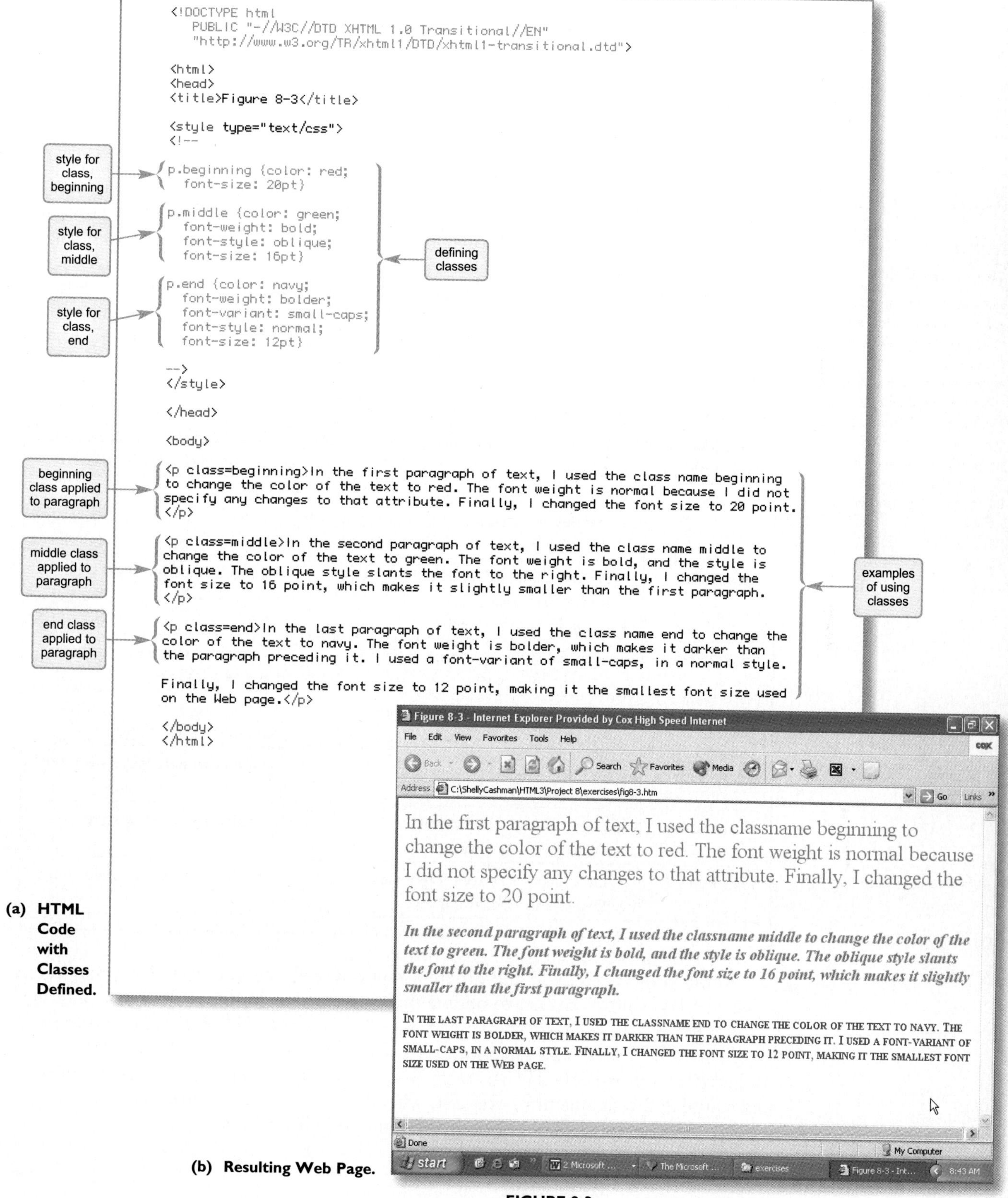

(a) HTML Code with Classes Defined.

(b) Resulting Web Page.

FIGURE 8-3

In addition to the style for the beginning paragraphs, Figure 8-3a on the previous page shows an example of HTML code with classes defined for and applied to the middle and end paragraphs. Figure 8-3b shows how the resulting Web page displays in the browser.

Classes allow you to have more control over the style used for different sections of a Web page. One drawback is that classes can be defined for use only in embedded or external style sheets. Because the purpose of using classes is to format a group of elements at once, not individual elements, classes do not work in inline style sheets.

Adding Style Sheets to the Stained Glass Club Web Site

More About

Inline Style Sheets

Inline style sheets give you a great amount of flexibility in Web page styling. Inline style sheets override both embedded and external style sheets. This means if you want all paragraph styles throughout the Web site except for one to be 10pt Garamond, for that one paragraph you can use an inline style sheet to alter its style.

The Stained Glass Club Web site in Project 8 consists of seven files, as shown in Table 8-3. The first Web page, index.htm, is the frame definition file, which contains the frame layout for the Web site. The frame definition file designates the Web page, menu.htm, to always display as the navigation menu in the left frame and sets the right frame to display various Web pages, depending on the link that the user chooses. When you first open the frame definition file, index.htm, the Web page, menu.htm, appears as the navigation menu in the left frame and the Web page, welcome.htm, appears in the right frame.

Table 8-3 Files Used in Project 8

FILE NAME	PURPOSE AND DISPLAY SPECIFICS	CHANGES MADE IN PROJECT 8
index.htm	• Frame definition file • Defines the layout of the frames on the Web page	• None
menu.htm	• Provides links to all other Web pages in the Web site • Displays in left frame	• Add an embedded style sheet
styles1.css	• External style sheet that is linked to next four pages	• Create as external style sheet • Save as a .css file
welcome.htm	• Provides welcome to Web site • Displays in right frame	• Add link to external style sheet • Add inline style sheet
calendar.htm	• Lists calendar of events • Displays in right frame	• Add link to external style sheet
contact.htm	• Lists contact information • Displays in right frame	• Add link to external style sheet
links.htm	• Lists links to related Web sites • Displays in right frame	• Add link to external style sheet

In this project, you will add different types of style sheets to the Web pages in the Stained Glass Club Web site, to update them from the style shown in Figure 8-1a on page HTM 331 to the style shown in Figure 8-1b on page HTM 331. To add the style sheets, you will make changes to five Web pages stored in the Project08/ProjectFiles folder on the HTML Data Disk: menu.htm, calendar.htm, contact.htm, links.htm, and welcome.htm. You also will create an external style sheet file, styles1.css. The list of files and changes are listed in Table 8-3.

Adding an Embedded Style Sheet

The first step in adding style sheets to the Stained Glass Club Web site is to add an embedded style sheet to the navigation menu, menu.htm. First, the HTML file, menu.htm, must be opened in Notepad. The following steps show how to start Notepad and open the HTML file, menu.htm.

To Start Notepad and Open an HTML File

1. **Start Notepad and, if necessary, maximize the window.**
2. **With the HTML Data Disk in drive A, click File on the menu bar and then click Open on the File menu. If necessary, click 3½ Floppy (A:) in the Look in list. Click the Project08 folder and then click the ProjectFiles folder in the list of available folders.**
3. **If necessary, click the Files of type box arrow and then click All Files.**
4. **Double-click menu.htm in the list of files.**

Notepad displays the HTML code as shown in Figure 8-4.

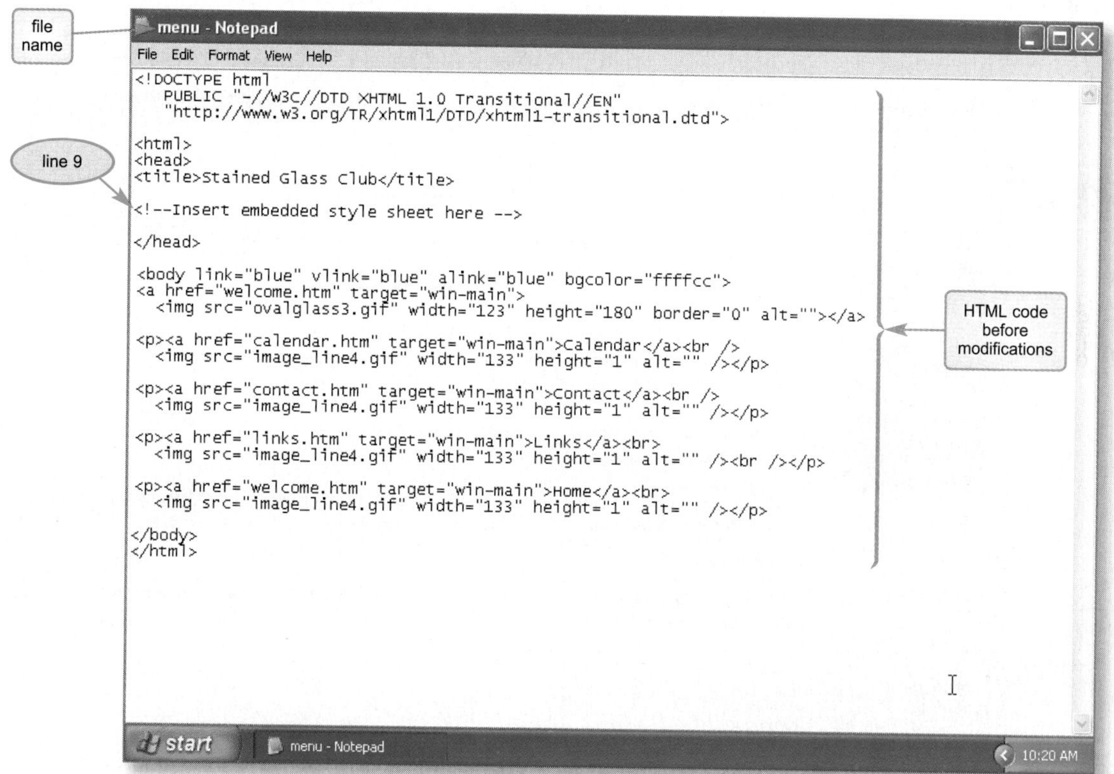

```
<!DOCTYPE html
   PUBLIC "-//W3C//DTD XHTML 1.0 Transitional//EN"
   "http://www.w3.org/TR/xhtml1/DTD/xhtml1-transitional.dtd">

<html>
<head>
<title>Stained Glass Club</title>

<!--Insert embedded style sheet here -->

</head>

<body link="blue" vlink="blue" alink="blue" bgcolor="ffffcc">
<a href="welcome.htm" target="win-main">
  <img src="ovalglass3.gif" width="123" height="180" border="0" alt=""></a>

<p><a href="calendar.htm" target="win-main">Calendar</a><br />
  <img src="image_line4.gif" width="133" height="1" alt="" /></p>

<p><a href="contact.htm" target="win-main">Contact</a><br />
  <img src="image_line4.gif" width="133" height="1" alt="" /></p>

<p><a href="links.htm" target="win-main">Links</a><br>
  <img src="image_line4.gif" width="133" height="1" alt="" /><br /></p>

<p><a href="welcome.htm" target="win-main">Home</a><br>
  <img src="image_line4.gif" width="133" height="1" alt="" /></p>

</body>
</html>
```


FIGURE 8-4

As shown in Figure 8-5a on the following page, the current style of the navigation menu uses the default settings for the paragraphs and all link states (normal, visited, active). After the embedded style sheet shown in Table 8-4 on page HTM 343 is added to menu.htm, the navigation menu appears as shown in Figure 8-5b. With the embedded style sheet added, the paragraph text appears indented 8 points from the left margin and all link states, except hover, display as 12-point Verdana (or Garamond if Verdana is not available) font with no underline. The link hover state is set so links appear as white text on a blue background when the mouse pointer hovers over the link (Figure 8-5b).

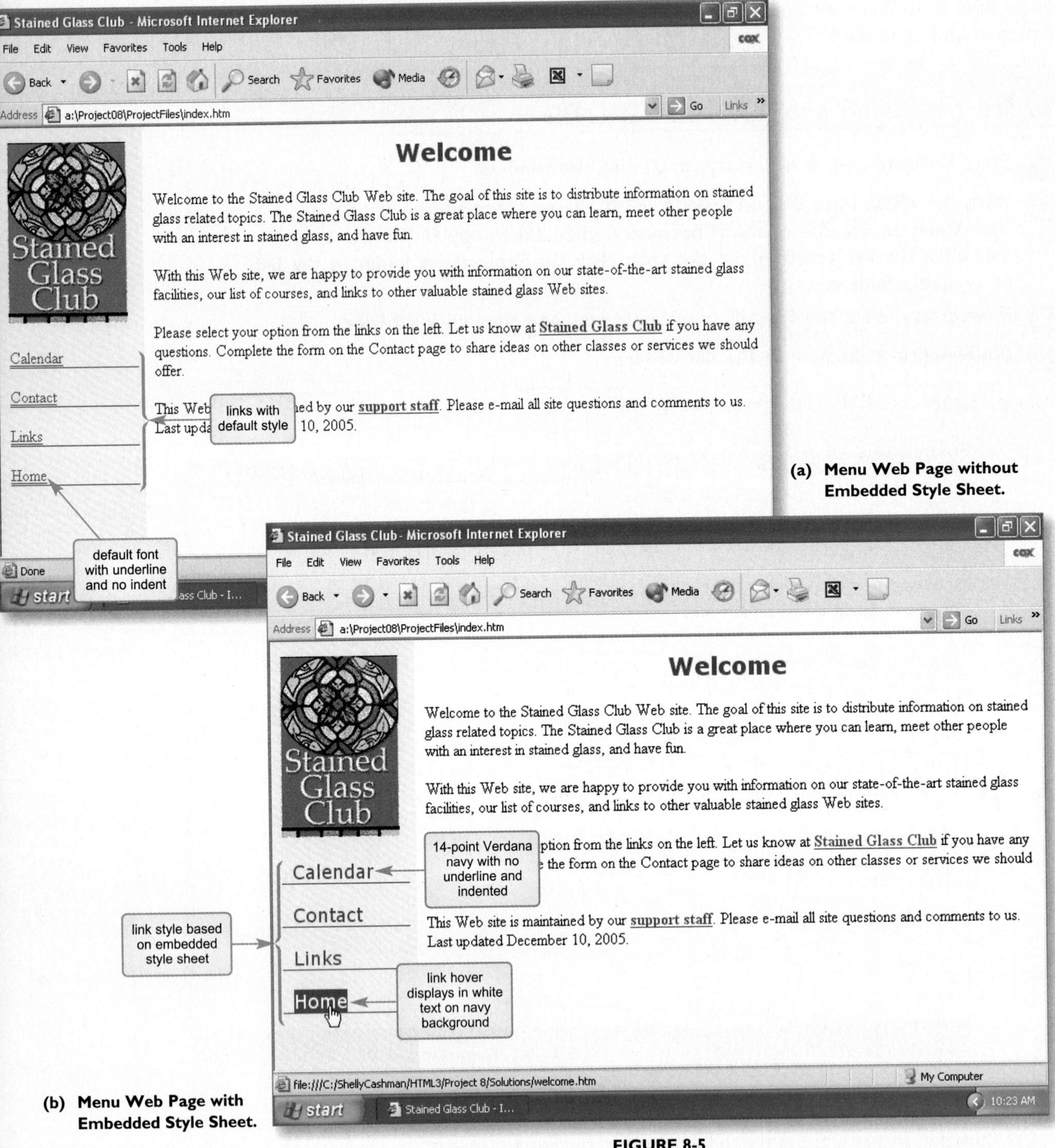

(a) Menu Web Page without Embedded Style Sheet.

(b) Menu Web Page with Embedded Style Sheet.

FIGURE 8-5

Table 8-4 Code for an Embedded Style Sheet

LINE	CSS CODE
9	`<style type="text/css">`
10	`<!--`
11	
12	`p {text-indent: 8pt}`
13	
14	`a {text-decoration: none;`
15	`font-family: Verdana, Garamond;`
16	`font-size: 14pt}`
17	
18	`a:hover {background: blue;`
19	`color: white}`
20	
21	`-->`
22	`</style>`

As shown in Table 8-4, the code for an embedded style sheet must be inserted within a start <style> tag (line 9) and an end </style> tag (line 22), which are positioned within the head element. Within the style tag container, Web developers generally follow the coding practice to add an HTML start comment code (line 10) and end comment code (line 21). The beginning and ending HTML comment lines hide any script language that a browser cannot interpret. Inserting these comment lines ensures that, if a browser does not support CSS, the comment lines take effect. The browser, therefore, will not try to interpret the code within the beginning and ending comment lines.

More About

Embedded Style Sheets

When you want to change the style of one Web page, you easily can do that with an embedded style sheet. The embedded style sheet needs to be put within the start <head> and end </head> tags. When you want to change the style of more than one Web page though, using an external style sheet (a .css file) and linking to that style sheet is a better, more efficient method.

Setting the Paragraph Style

The first style statement

```
p {text-indent: 8pt}
```

indents the first word of each paragraph 8 points from the left edge of the browser window to make the navigation menu page look less cramped and unattractive. In addition to the points value used here, the text-indent property allows you to specify a fixed value in inches, centimeters, or pixels. You also can specify a relative value for a text indent using a percentage as the value. For example, the style statement

```
p {text-indent: 10%}
```

indents the first line of each paragraph 10% of the total width of the screen. Because the percentage indent is based on the total width of the screen, the indent widens when the screen is widened.

In general, paragraphs stand out better when they are indented from the rest of the text. In standard text applications, paragraphs generally are indented five spaces. In a Web page, you can use the text-indent declaration to set that value for the indent.

Setting a Style for All Links

The next section of code in the embedded style sheet (lines 14 through 16) changes the style of the links in the menu page. The style statement uses the selector a and a series of property-value statements in the declaration to define the text decoration, font family, and font size for all links.

As you have learned, links have three states (normal, visited, and active). You can change the style of the three states individually by using the selectors, a:link, a:visited, or a:active, or use the selector a to set a style for all link states. In this project, the selector a is used to change all states of links to the same style.

Setting the text-decoration property to a value of none will remove the underline from all links. You also can set the text-decoration property to the following:

- **blink** – causes the text to blink on and off
- **line-through** – places a line through the middle of the text
- **overline** – places a line above the text
- **underline** – places a line below the text

If you wanted to apply two different text styles to a link, you can specify two text-decoration values by separating the choices with a space. For example, to give links a style with both an underline and an overline, you would add the property-value statement:

```
{text-decoration: underline overline}
```

to the embedded style sheet.

The font-family property allows you to define a font for use in a Web page. In this embedded style sheet, the font-family property is set to two different values: Verdana and Garamond. In general, it is good practice to specify more than one font-family value. If the first font is not available on the user's computer, the browser will display text in the second font. If neither of the fonts is available, the browser will display text in the default font.

To specify more than one value for a font-family property, you separate the font-family values with commas. Also, if you want to use a font family with a name that has spaces (such as Times New Roman or Courier New), you must put the font-family name in quotation marks. The resulting code would have

```
{font-family: "Times New Roman", Verdana)
```

as the style statement.

The font-family and font-size properties for the link are defined in lines 15 and 16 of the embedded style sheet. As shown in Table 8-4 on the previous page, line 15 sets the font family to Verdana or Garamond, if Verdana is not available. Line 16 sets the size of all links to a 14-point font.

Q&A

Q: Are there any negatives to using Cascading Style Sheets?

A: The bad news is, not all browsers support CSS, so not all users will be viewing the same style on your Web pages. The good news is, over 75 percent of users use a browser that does support CSS. For specific details, you need to test your Web pages with multiple browsers.

Setting the Link Hover Style

The final section of the embedded style sheet (lines 18 and 19) defines the style of the link:hover property. As you have learned, the link:hover property defines the way a link displays when a mouse pointer points to, or hovers over, the link. In this project, the selector a:hover is used to change the hover state of all links. The code in lines 18 and 19 of Table 8-4 sets the link background to display in blue and the text to display in white when the mouse hovers over the link. Using a link:hover style gives the menu page an aspect of interactivity.

To add the embedded style sheet shown in Table 8-4 to the Web page, menu.htm, the CSS code for the style sheet is entered directly in the header section of the HTML code for the Web page. The following steps illustrate how to add an embedded style sheet to the Web page, menu.htm.

To Add an Embedded Style Sheet

1

- **Highlight the comment, <!--Insert embedded style sheet here -->, on line 9 and then press the DELETE key.**

2

- **Enter the CSS code as shown in Table 8-4.**

Notepad displays the CSS and HTML code as shown in Figure 8-6.

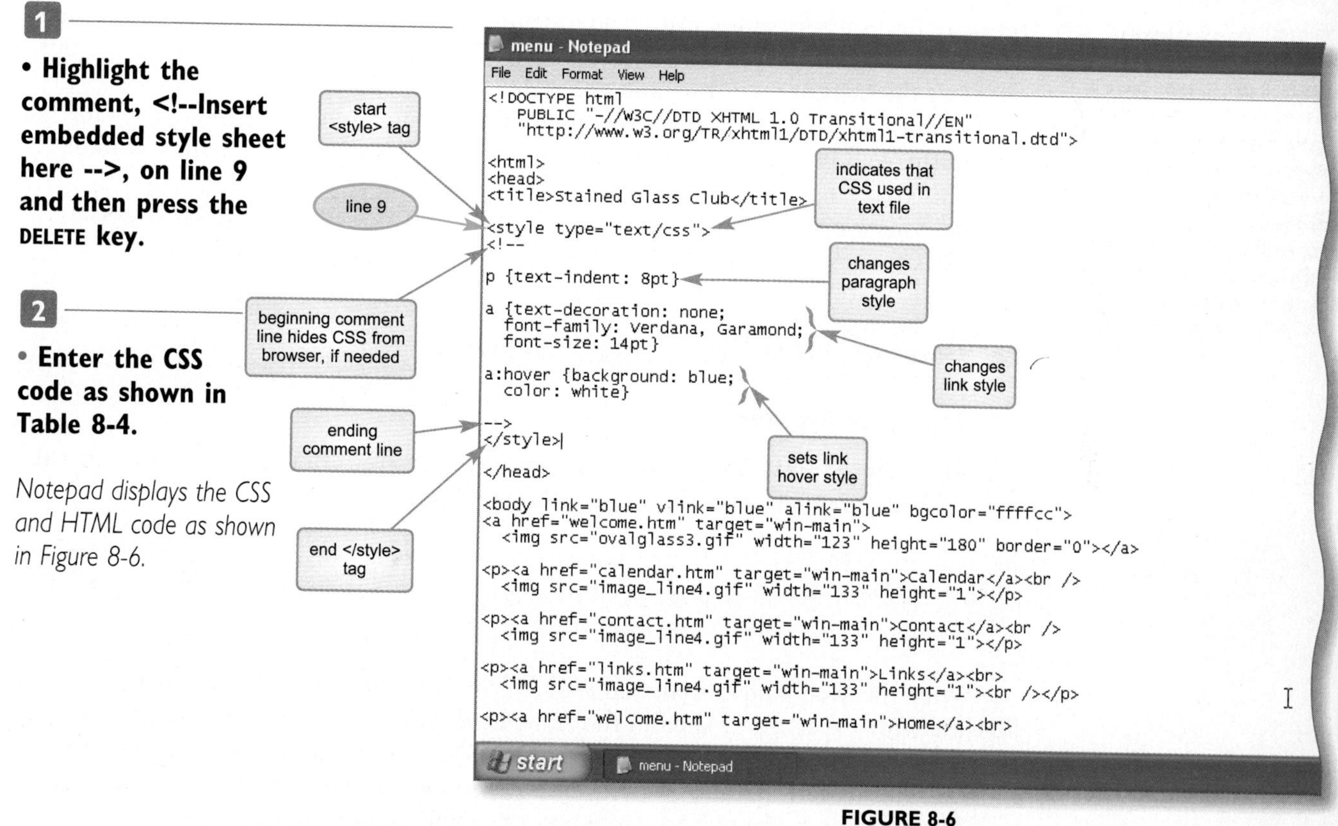

FIGURE 8-6

After the embedded style sheet has been added, the next step is to save the menu Web page, view it in the browser, and then print the HTML file.

Saving, Viewing, and Printing the HTML File

After you have added the embedded style sheet to the menu.htm Web page, you should save the HTML file, view the Web page to review the style changes, and then print the HTML code. Before you can view the Web page to review the style changes, you must save the HTML file with the embedded style sheet. The following steps illustrate how to save the HTML file.

To Save an HTML File

1. **With the HTML Data Disk in drive A, click File on the menu bar and then click Save As. If necessary, type** `menu.htm` **in the File name text box.**
2. **If necessary, click 3½ Floppy (A:) in the Save in list. Click the Project08 folder, and then click the ProjectFiles folder in the list of available folders.**
3. **Click the Save button in the Save As dialog box. If a Save As dialog box displays, click Yes to continue saving.**

More About

CSS Precedence

Although the three types of CSS (inline, embedded, and external) can co-exist, there is precedence to their order of importance. Any embedded style sheet overrides the external style sheet. So if you specify the style for your paragraphs in both embedded and inline style sheets, the style of the inline style sheet would override the embedded style.

Having added the embedded style sheet, you should view the HTML file in your browser to confirm that the styles defined in the style sheet appear correctly in the Web page. To view the style changes in the menu.htm Web page, open the frame definition file, index.htm. The index.htm file is the frame definition file that defines the Web page as two vertical frames. The menu.htm file appears in the left frame of the browser window and the welcome.htm file displays in the right frame. By opening the frame definition file, index.htm, you can view the new styles for the menu.htm Web page within its frame structure, just as a Web site visitor would view the Web page.

The following steps show how to view an HTML file in the browser to review the style changes added by the embedded style sheet.

To View an HTML File Using a Browser

1. **Start your browser.**
2. **Click the Address bar. Type** `a:\Project08\ProjectFiles\index.htm` **in the Address text box and then press the ENTER key.**

The index.htm frame definition file opens and displays menu.htm in the left frame and welcome.htm in the right frame (Figure 8-7). If your computer does not have the Verdana or Garamond font, the links display with the default font for your system.

When the Web page initially appears, verify that the menu.htm Web page appears with the styles defined in the embedded style sheet. The menu links should be indented 8 points to add space on the left side and display in 14-point Verdana font with no underline. As you move the mouse over any of the links, the link:hover style should change the text to white text on a blue background.

After you have confirmed that the Web page displays the desired styles, you should print the HTML file using Notepad so you can use it as a reference for other style sheets. If you discover a problem with the Web page when you view the page, return to Notepad to make any corrections before printing the HTML file. The following steps show how to print the HTML file.

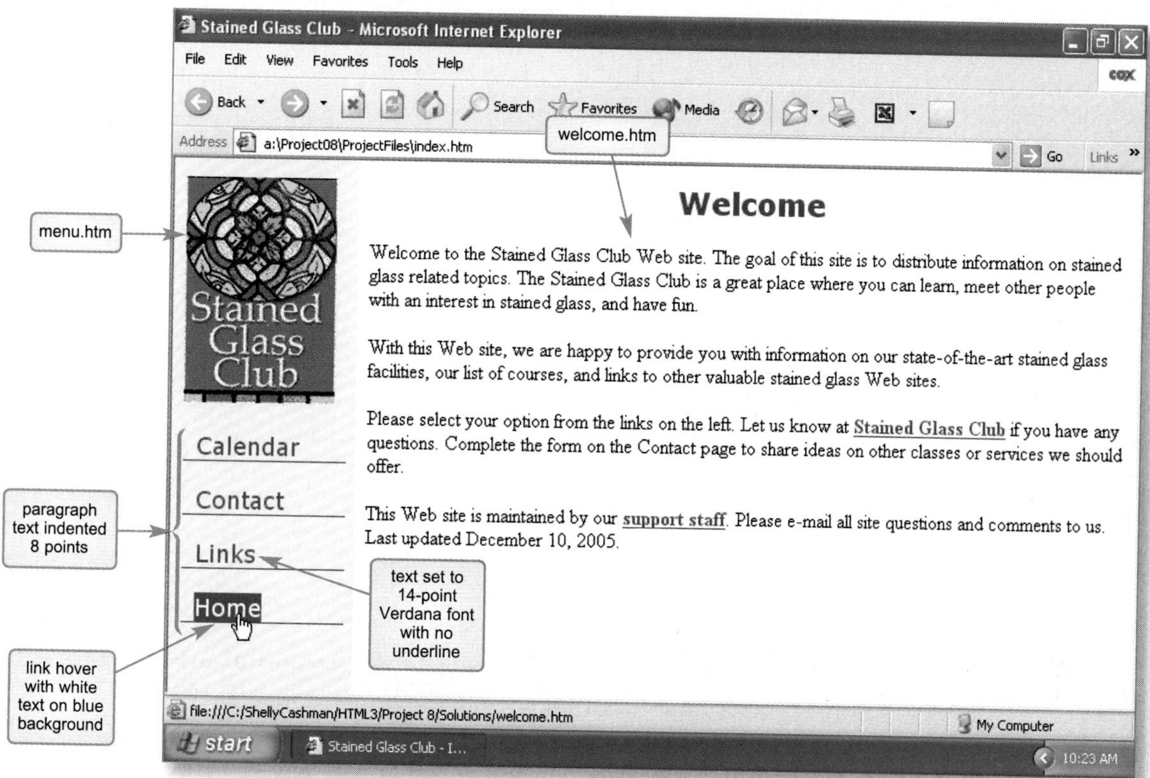

FIGURE 8-7

To Print an HTML File

1. **Click the Notepad button on the taskbar.**
2. **Click File on the menu bar and then click Print on the File menu.**
3. **Click the Print button in the Print dialog box.**

The HTML file prints (Figure 8-8 on the next page).

The embedded style sheet now is added to the menu.htm file. Recall that an embedded style sheet is added within the <head> tags of the page to which you want to apply the styles and defines the style for only that one Web page. If you want to apply the styles to more than one page in a Web site, you should use an external style sheet.

```
<!DOCTYPE html
   PUBLIC "-//W3C//DTD XHTML 1.0 Transitional//EN"
   "http://www.w3.org/TR/xhtml1/DTD/xhtml1-transitional.dtd">

<html>
<head>
<title>Stained Glass Club</title>

<style type="text/css">
<!--

p {text-indent: 8pt}

a {text-decoration: none;
  font-family: Verdana, Garamond;
  font-size: 14pt}

a:hover {background: blue;
  color: white}

-->
</style>

</head>

<body link="blue" vlink="blue" alink="blue" bgcolor="ffffcc">
<a href="welcome.htm" target="win-main">
  <img src="ovalglass3.gif" width="123" height="180" border="0" alt="" /></a>

<p><a href="calendar.htm" target="win-main">Calendar</a><br />
  <img src="image_line4.gif" width="133" height="1" alt="" /></p>

<p><a href="contact.htm" target="win-main">Contact</a><br />
  <img src="image_line4.gif" width="133" height="1" alt="" /></p>

<p><a href="links.htm" target="win-main">Links</a><br />
  <img src="image_line4.gif" width="133" height="1" alt="" /><br /></p>

<p><a href="welcome.htm" target="win-main">Home</a><br />
  <img src="image_line4.gif" width="133" height="1" alt="" /></p>

</body>
</html>
```

FIGURE 8-8

Adding an External Style Sheet

External style sheets are ideal for giving multiple pages in a Web site a common look or style. Instead of displaying styles based on an embedded style sheet added to each Web page, each Web page in the Web site references the same external style sheet for style information, thus ensuring each Web page uses a consistent style. In the Stained Glass Club Web site, for example, each of the four main pages (welcome.htm, calendar.htm, contact.htm, and links.htm) can be linked to the same external style sheet that defines a common style.

As you have learned, adding an external style sheet to a Web page is a two-part process that involves: (1) creating an external style sheet and (2) adding a link to the external style sheet into the Web pages. An external style sheet is a separate text file that contains the style statements that define how the Web page elements will display. Table 8-5 shows an example of the style statements used in an external style sheet. After you have created the text file with all of the desired style statements, you save the file with the file extension, .css, to identify it as a CSS file. You then can use a <link> tag to link the external style sheet to any Web pages to which you want to apply the style.

Table 8-5 Code for an External Style Sheet

LINE	CSS CODE
1	`body {margin: 8pt}`
2	
3	`a {text-decoration: none;`
4	`color: blue}`
5	
6	`p {font-family: Verdana, Garamond;`
7	`font-size: 11pt}`
8	
9	`table {font-family: Verdana, Garamond;`
10	`font-size: 11pt}`
11	
12	`th {color: white;`
13	`background-color: blue;`
14	`font-size: 11pt;`
15	`text-align: left}`
16	
17	`caption {color: blue;`
18	`font-style: italic}`

Q&A

Q: What is an easy way to find out the fonts supported on your computer system?

A: One easy way to find out the fonts supported on your system is to review the font names as they appear in the font menu of an application, such as Microsoft Word.

Setting a Body Style

The CSS code for the external style sheet shown in Table 8-5 defines a new style for four main elements in a Web page: body, links, paragraphs, and tables. For example, the first style statement on line 1 is entered as

```
body {margin: 8pt}
```

to change the margin of the Web page body to 8 points. The margin is the amount of transparent space between elements on the page. Because it uses the margin property, the style statement sets the margin for all sides of the Web page. If desired, you also can set the margin for the top, bottom, left, or right of a page by using the properties margin-top, margin-bottom, margin-left, or margin-right, respectively. Like the text-indent property, the margin property can be set as a fixed length in points, pixels, inches, or centimeters, or as a relative length based on a percentage.

Setting Link and Paragraph Styles

Lines 3 and 4 set the style for all link states to have no text decoration (that is, no underline) and display in the color blue. The style statement in line 6 changes the style of all paragraph text to the font family Verdana or Garamond, depending on the fonts available on the user's computer. Line 7 sets the font size to 11 point, which is slightly smaller than the font selected for the link text in the navigation menu.

Q&A

Q: What is the real benefit of using CSS?

A: With CSS, you can establish a standard look for all Web pages in a Web site. Using CSS, you avoid the tedious steps of putting repetitive codes to format the same types of information. Instead of making all paragraphs of text 10pt Verdana in individual <p> tags, you can define that in a .css file and link that external file to all Web pages.

Setting Table and Caption Styles

The next section of CSS code, lines 9 through 18, define the styles to be applied to tables. The style statement in lines 9 and 10 is entered as

```
table {font-family: Verdana, Garamond;
  font-size: 11pt}
```

to set the style for table text to match the style used for paragraph text (11-point Verdana or Garamond). The style statement in lines 12 through 15 sets the table header styles. Recall that table headers are bold and centered by default. In this code, all table headers display in 11-point white font with a blue background. The text will also be left-aligned, rather than the default header alignment of centered.

Finally, lines 17 and 18 set the style of all table captions to display in blue italic font. Setting the caption to italic makes the table caption text distinctly different from the text in the table itself. The font-style property also can be set to values of normal (the default style) or oblique. An oblique font — one that is slanted to the right by the browser — can be used when the font itself does not provide an italic version. If you want to change italic or oblique text back to display in the default or normal style, you insert a property-value statement font-style: normal in the style sheet.

Creating an External Style Sheet

After you have defined the styles you want to use for various page elements, you can create the external style sheet. To create an external style sheet, you open a new text file and enter CSS code for the style statements that define the Web page style. After coding the style statements, you save the file with the file extension, .css, to identify it as a CSS file.

The following steps illustrate how to create an external style sheet.

To Create an External Style Sheet

1

• **If necessary, click the Notepad button on the taskbar. Click File on the menu bar and then click New.**

Notepad displays a blank text file.

2

• **Enter the CSS code as shown in Table 8-5 on page HTM 349.**

3

• **With the HTML Data Disk in drive A, click File on the menu bar and then click Save As. Type** `styles1.css` **in the File name text box. If necessary, click 3½ Floppy (A:) in the Save in list. Click the Project08 folder and then click the ProjectFiles folder in the list of available folders. Click the Save button in the Save As dialog box.**

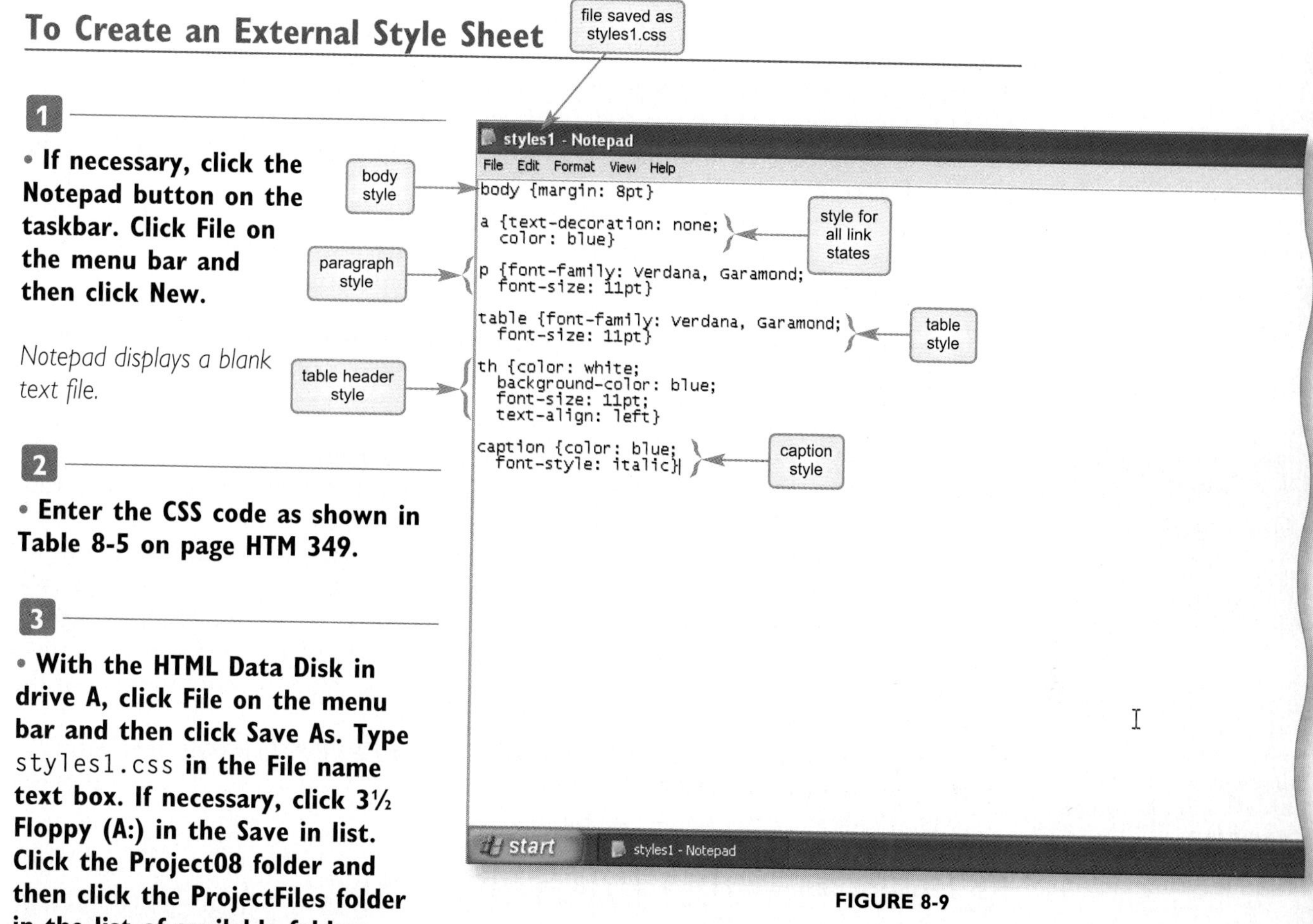

FIGURE 8-9

The external style sheet, styles1.css, displays in the Notepad window as shown in Figure 8-9.

4

• **Click the File menu and then click Print on the File menu.**

After you have added the style statements in Notepad, you save the text file with a file name and the file extension, .css, to identify the file as a Cascading Style Sheet file. In most cases, the external style sheet is saved in the main or root directory of the Web site. Printing the style sheet will allow you to reference it when creating style sheets for other Web sites or making changes to the style sheet for this Web site.

To apply the styles defined in the styles1.css style sheet to one or more Web pages, you must add a link statement to each Web page.

Linking to an External Style Sheet

As previously discussed, four Web pages in the Stained Glass Club Web site require the same style: welcome.htm, calendar.htm, contact.htm, and links.htm. Linking the external style sheet to each of these Web pages gives them the same styles for margin, paragraph text, links, and tables.

To link to the external style sheet, a <link> tag must be inserted into each of these four Web pages. The <link> tag used to link an external style sheet is added within the <head> tag of the Web page HTML. The general format of the <link> tag is

```
<link rel="stylesheet" type="text/css" href="styles1.css">
```

where rel="stylesheet" establishes that the linked document is a style sheet, type="text/css" indicates that the CSS language is used in the text file containing the style sheet, and href="styles1.css" provides the name and location (URL) of the linked style sheet. In order to link a style sheet to a Web page, the <link> tag must use "stylesheet" as the value for the rel property and text/css as the value for the type property. The URL used as the value for the href property varies, based on the name and location of the file used as the external style sheet. The URL used here indicates that the external style sheet, styles1.css, is located in the main or root directory of the Web site.

The following steps illustrate how to add a link to an external style sheet using a <link> tag and then save the HTML file.

More About

Font Families

You also can specify font-weight using numerical values from 100 to 900. Normal text that is not bold has a value of 400. Each larger number is at least as bold as the one above it, and 900 is the boldest option of the font. The browser determines how bold each value is as it is displaying the Web page.

To Link to an External Style Sheet

1. **If necessary, click the Notepad button on the taskbar.**
2. **With the HTML Data Disk in drive A, click File on the menu bar and then click Open on the File menu.**
3. **Type** `calendar.htm` **in the File name text box. If necessary, click 3½ Floppy (A:) in the Look in list, click the Project08 folder, and then click the ProjectFiles folder in the list of available folders.**
4. **Click the Open button in the Open dialog box.**
5. **Highlight the text, <!--Insert link statement here -->, in line 9 and then press the DELETE key.**
6. **Type** `<link rel="stylesheet" type="text/css" href="styles1.css" />` **as the tag.**
7. **Click File on the menu bar and then click Save on the File menu.**

Notepad displays the calendar.htm HTML file as shown in Figure 8-10.

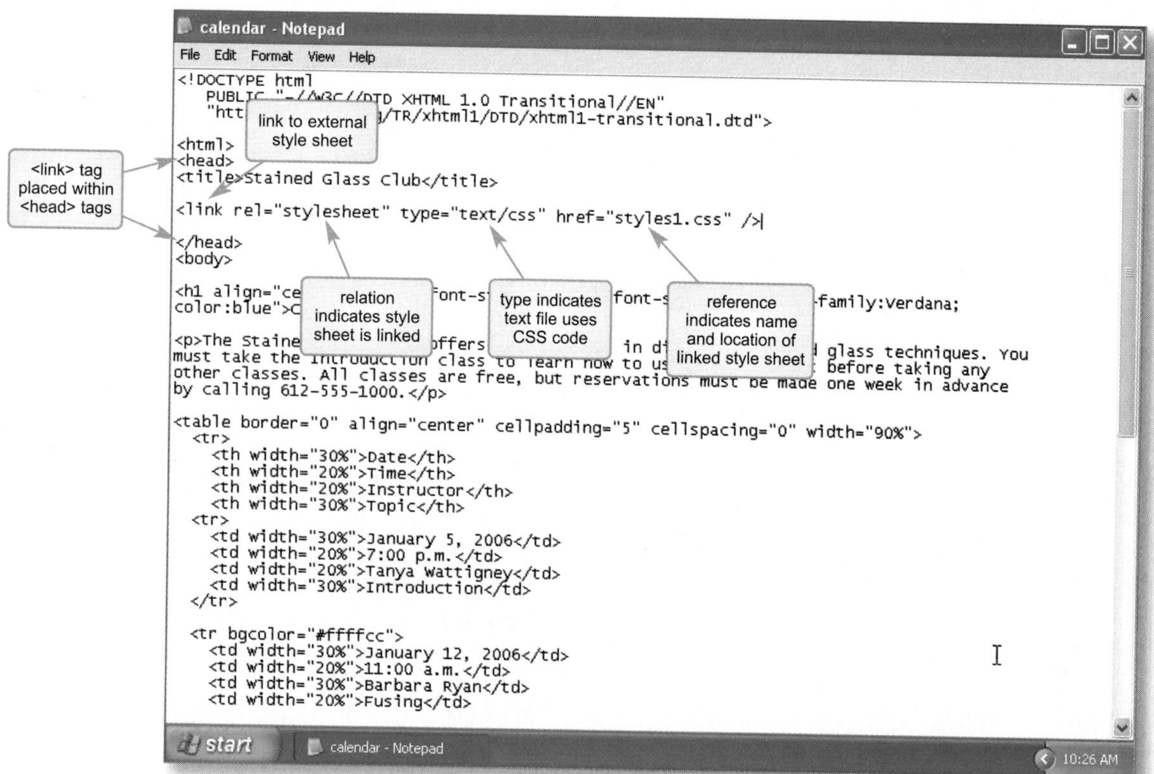

FIGURE 8-10

After the <link> tag is inserted in the calendar.htm Web page and the file is saved, the calendar.htm Web page will appear in the browser using the styles indicated in the external style sheet, styles1.css. As a result, the Web page style changes from the style shown in Figure 8-11a on the next page to the style shown in Figure 8-11b. Based on the style statements in the external style sheet, the calendar.htm page displays with an 8-point margin around all sides. The text for all paragraphs and tables uses 11-point Verdana as the first font choice and 11-point Garamond as the second font choice, if Verdana is not available on the user's computer. The table header appears with white text on a blue background, with the header text left-aligned. Links appear in blue font with no underline, while captions appear in blue italic font.

Linking the Remaining HTML Files to an External Style Sheet

A link to the external style sheet, styles1.css, has been added to the Web page, calendar.htm. As you have learned, the Stained Glass Club Web site includes three other Web pages that display in the right frame of the browser when the corresponding menu link is clicked: contact.htm, links.htm, and welcome.htm. To ensure that all of the Web pages in the Stained Glass Club Web site have a consistent look, a link to the styles1.css external style sheet should be added to the other Web pages.

The steps on the next page show how to add a <link> tag to the remaining three Web pages and then save the files.

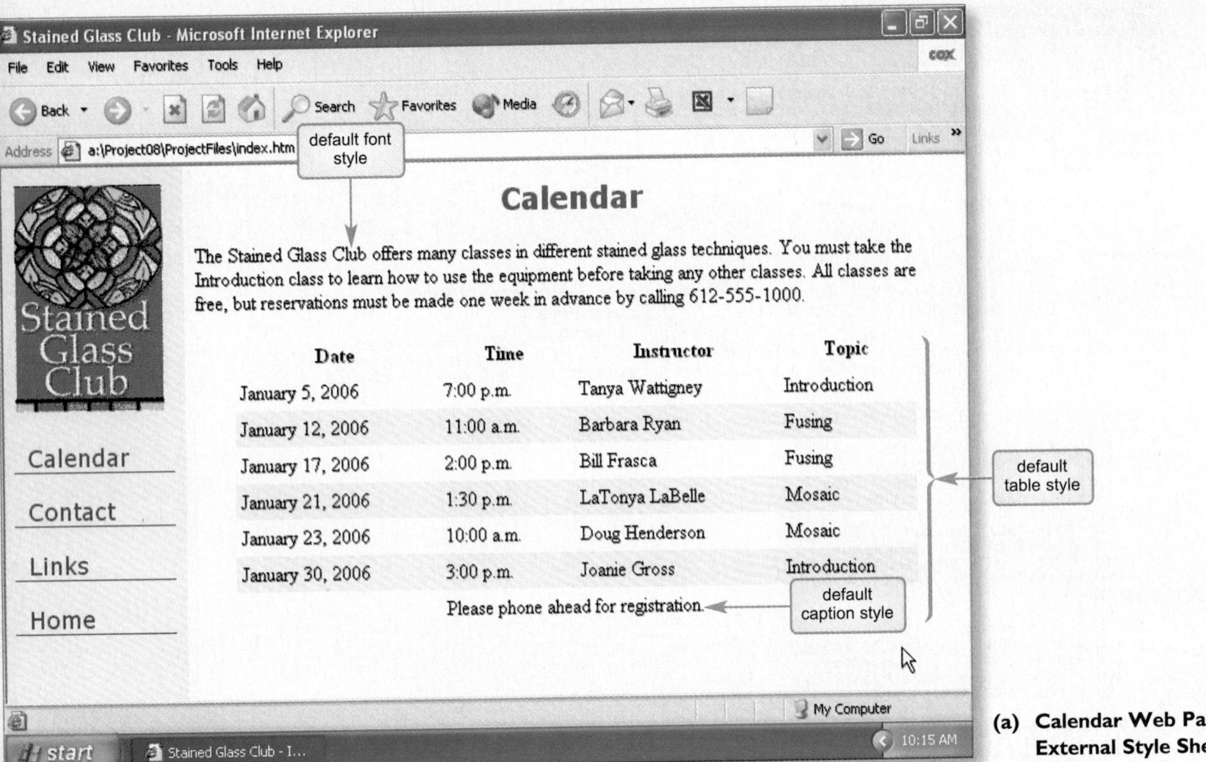

(a) **Calendar Web Page without External Style Sheet.**

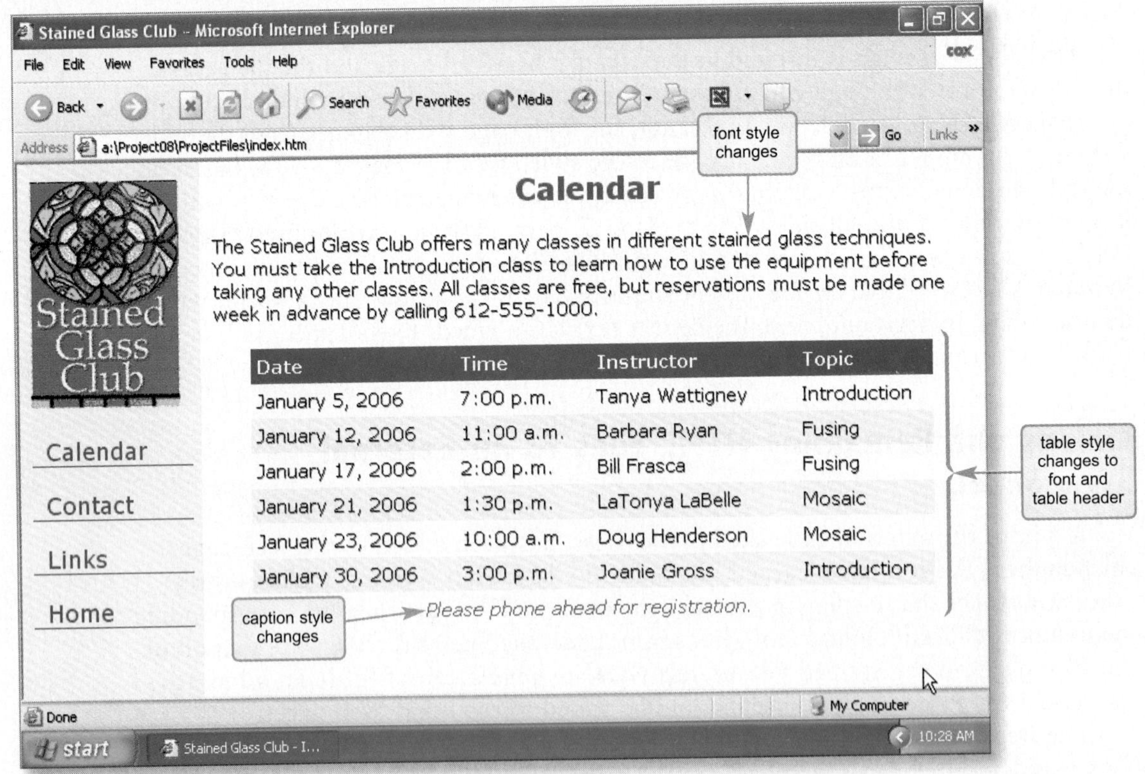

(b) **Calendar Web Page with External Style Sheet.**

FIGURE 8-11

To Link the Remaining HTML Files to an External Style Sheet

1. **With the HTML Data Disk in drive A, click File on the menu bar and then click Open on the File menu.**
2. **Type** `contact.htm` **in the File name text box. If necessary, click 3½ Floppy (A:) in the Look in list, click the Project08 folder, and then click the ProjectFiles folder in the list of available folders.**
3. **Click the Open button in the Open dialog box.**
4. **Highlight the text, <!--Insert link statement here -->, and press the DELETE key.**
5. **Type** `<link rel="stylesheet" type="text/css" href="styles1.css" />` **as the tag.**
6. **Click File on the menu bar and then click Save on the File menu.**
7. **One at a time, open the remaining HTML files, links.htm and welcome.htm, and repeat Steps 4 through 6.**

The Web pages, contact.htm, links.htm, and welcome.htm, now have a <link> tag that links to the external style sheet, styles1.css. The file, welcome.htm, is open in the Notepad window.

With the <link> tag inserted, each of the four main Web pages (calendar.htm, contact.htm, links.htm, and welcome.htm) is linked to the external style sheet, styles1.css. Because they are linked to the same external style sheet, all of the main Web pages in the Web site will share a common look or style.

Another way to define a common style for multiple pages in a Web site is to insert an embedded style sheet in each Web page. Using this approach, you could copy and paste the embedded style sheet into all of the Web pages for which you want the same style. While this would not be very difficult or time-consuming if the Web site consisted of only a few Web pages, making a change to any style requires you to update the embedded style sheet in every page.

Using external style sheets is a more efficient way of defining and maintaining a common style across multiple pages in a Web site. With an external style sheet, style changes are made once, in the style statements in the external style sheet. The <link> tag in each Web page automatically references the updated style sheet when it displays the Web page, thus displaying it with the new styles. For Web sites with a significant number of Web pages, using external style sheets makes it much easier for Web developers to keep all of the pages in the Web site consistent and maintainable.

More About

Word Spacing

The word-spacing property is a good way to add additional space between words. You can use any of the length units including: inches, centimeters, millimeters, points, picas, ems, x-height, and pixels.

Adding an Inline Style Sheet

The Stained Glass Club Web site now includes two of the three types of style sheets: an embedded style sheet and an external style sheet. The embedded style sheet defines the style for the menu Web page, menu.htm, which displays in the left frame. The external style sheet is linked to and defines the style of the main Web pages that display in the right frame. To complete the new design for the Stained Glass Club Web site, one additional type of style sheet — an inline style sheet — is needed to define a paragraph style for the Welcome page that users see when they first visit the site.

The last paragraph on the welcome.htm Web page provides basic information about Web site development and support. The paragraph style for this paragraph should be set to display in a smaller font size with an italic style, so that it does not distract users from the more important information on the Welcome page.

As you have learned, an inline style sheet allows you to add a style to an individual HTML tag, such as a heading or paragraph. The style changes only that specific tag and does not affect other tags in the document. Because an inline style sheet also overrides the styles defined in embedded and external style sheets, it is ideal to make style changes to a single paragraph of text. For example, based on the external style sheet linked to the page, all text displays in 11-point normal font (Figure 8-12a). Using an inline style sheet, the external style sheet can be overridden to set the style of that one paragraph to display with a font style of italic and a font size of 8 points, as shown in Figure 8-12b.

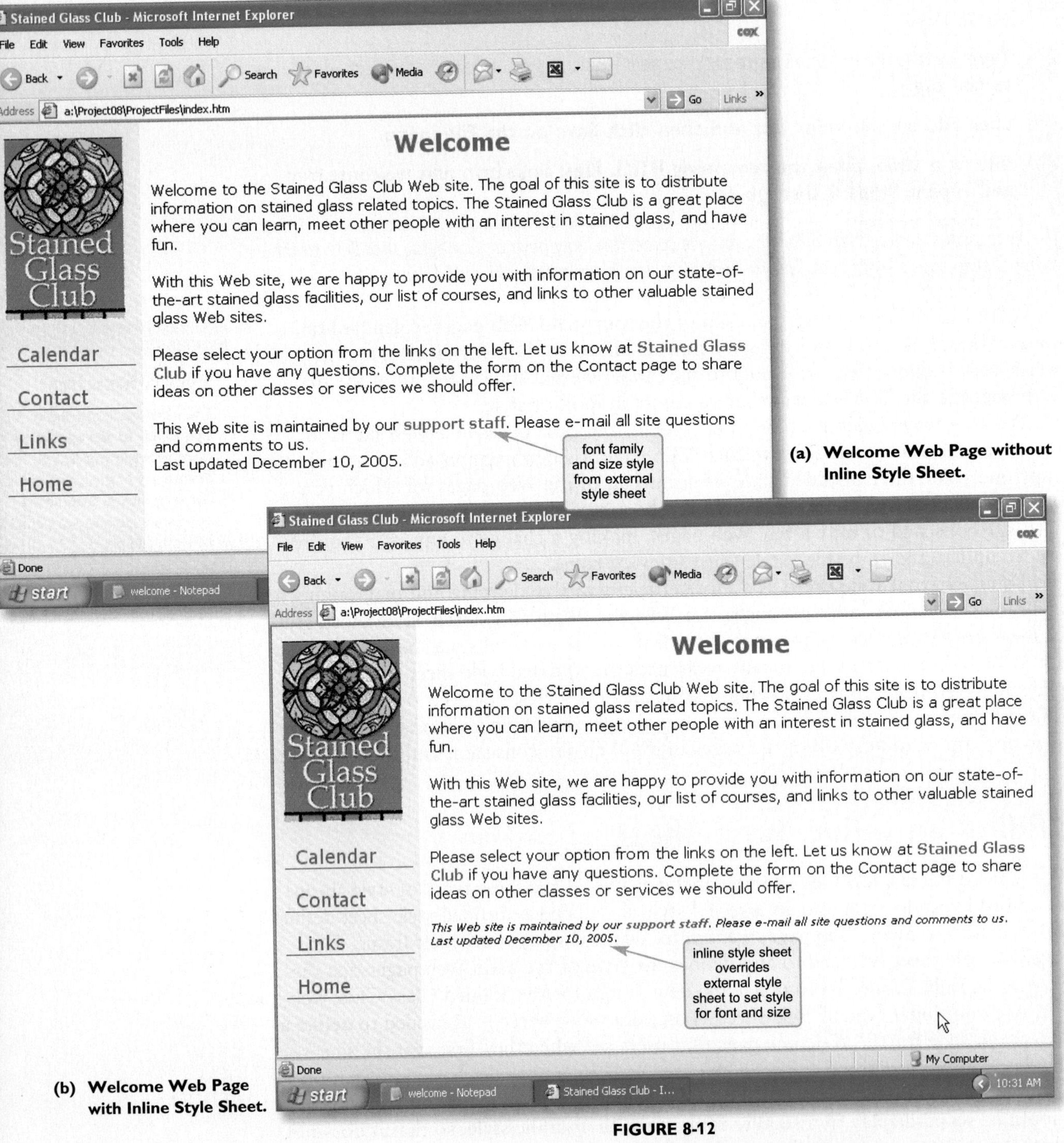

(a) **Welcome Web Page without Inline Style Sheet.**

(b) **Welcome Web Page with Inline Style Sheet.**

FIGURE 8-12

To add an inline style sheet, you enter the declaration within the HTML tag to which you want to apply the style. For example, for the Welcome Web page, the format of the inline style sheet is

```
<p style="font-style: italic; font-size: 8pt">
```

with the HTML tag <p> functioning as the selector and the remainder of the style sheet functioning as the declaration.

The following steps show how to add an inline style sheet to the Welcome Web page.

To Add an Inline Style Sheet

1

- **If necessary, click the Notepad button on the taskbar to display the file, welcome.htm.**

The file, welcome.htm, displays in the Notepad window.

2

- **Click immediately to the right of the p in the <p> tag on line 31. Press the SPACEBAR and then type** `style="font-style: italic; font-size: 8pt"` **as the code.**

3

- **Click File on the menu bar and then click Save.**

Notepad displays the HTML file as shown in Figure 8-13. The style statement is entered within the <p> tag, so that the style applies to only that paragraph.

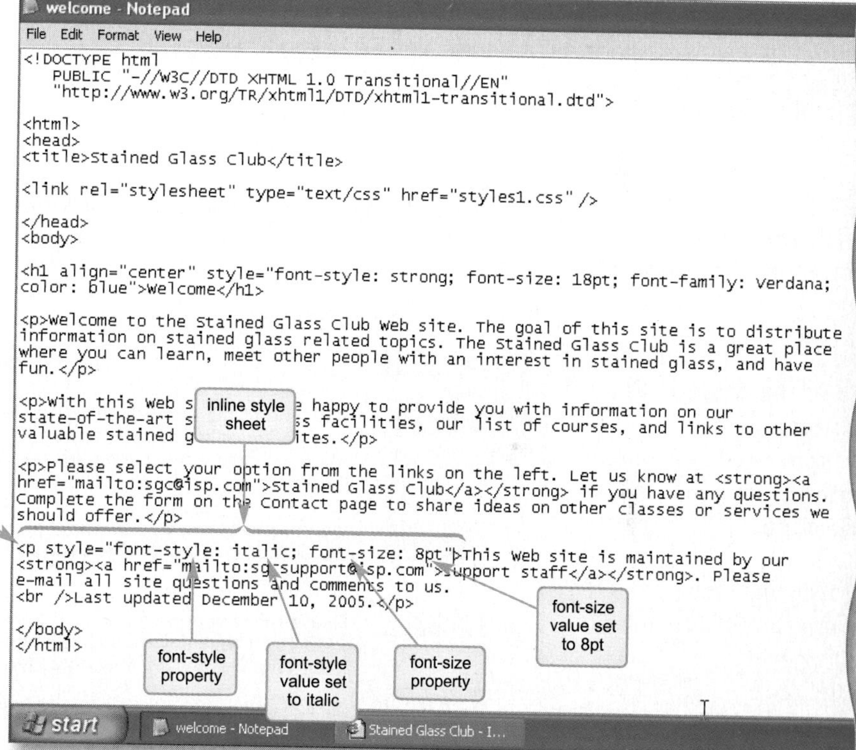

FIGURE 8-13

The inline style sheet is added to the Welcome Web page. Because an inline style sheet takes precedence over the other style sheets and can apply to an individual HTML tag, it provides the most flexibility and control over Web page style.

Viewing and Printing Framed Web Pages

Having added links to the external style sheet to all of the Web pages and an inline style sheet to the Welcome Web page, you should view the HTML files in your browser to confirm that the styles defined in the style sheets appear correctly in the

Web page. To view the style changes in the menu.htm Web page, you must open the frame definition file, index.htm.

After viewing the Web page in the browser, you should print a copy of each Web page for reference. Because the Web pages display in frames defined by the frame definition file, index.htm, several printing options are available. As you learned in Project 5, you can print all of the Web pages as they display on the screen or print each framed Web page separately. The Print dialog box of the browser includes three options in the Print frames area:

- As laid out on screen
- Only the selected frame
- All frames individually

The Print dialog box default is to print all frames individually. To print the Web pages as they are displayed in the browser, select the As laid out on screen option.

Perform the following steps to view and print all of the framed Web pages in the Web site as laid out on screen.

To View and Print Framed Web Pages

1

• **Click the browser button on the taskbar.**

2

• **Click the Stained Glass Club logo in the upper-left corner of the Web page.**

The Welcome Web page is displayed in the main frame of the Stained Glass Club Web site (Figure 8-14). The last paragraph displays in 8-point Verdana italic font, as defined by the inline style sheet.

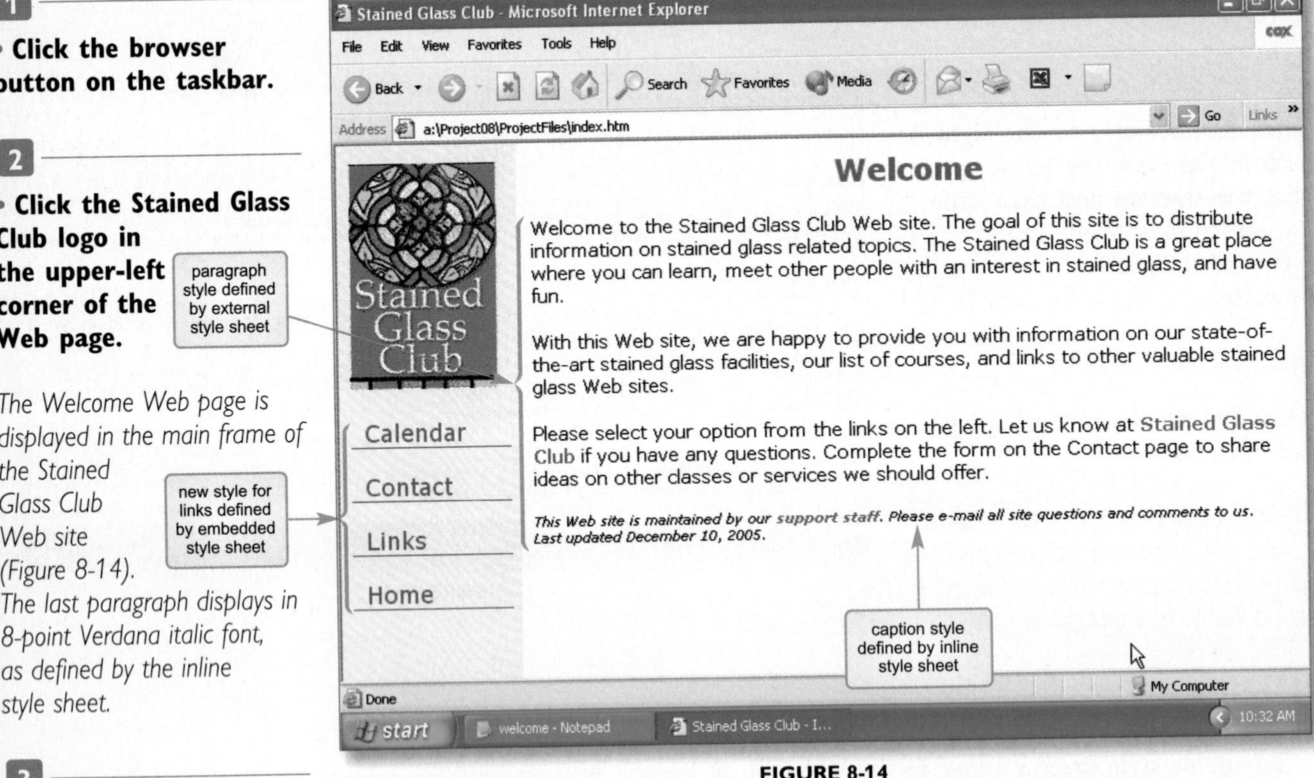

FIGURE 8-14

3

• **Click File on the menu bar and then click Print on the File menu.**

4

• **When the Print dialog box is displayed, click the Options tab.**

5

- **Click As laid out on screen and then click the Print button.**

6

- **One at a time, click the remaining links, Calendar, Contact, and Links, and repeat Steps 3 through 5.**

Each of the four main Web pages — Welcome, Calendar, Contact, and Links — appears in the browser with styles defined by the external style sheet. Each Web page then is printed as laid out on screen.

By clicking the links to display the four Web pages in the main frame on the right, you can verify that the styles defined by the external style sheet, styles1.css, appear correctly in each of the five Web pages with the <link> tag. You also can confirm that the paragraph style defined by the inline style sheet displays correctly on the Web page, welcome.htm.

More About

Line Height

Another useful CSS property gives you the ability to control line height. With the line-height property, you can control the vertical spacing between lines of text. There are three different ways to add the line-height value: by number, by length unit, and by percentage. If you specify by number, the browser uses the font-size property to determine the space. You also can use em and pt to set the height by unit. Finally, you can determine the line spacing by a percentage.

Viewing and Printing HTML Files

After verifying that each Web page is displayed correctly in the browser window, you should print the HTML file for each Web page for reference. Because these Web pages are in a frame structure, printing the HTML source code requires you to right-click the Web page that you want to print in the frame and then click View Source on the shortcut menu to open the Web page file in Notepad. After the file is open in Notepad, you then can print the HTML file using Notepad.

To print the HTML files for all the Web pages that display in the right frame — Calendar, Contact, Links, and Home (Welcome) — you must click each of the four menu links to display the page in the browser and then follow the steps outlined below. If you discover a problem with the Web page when you view it in the browser or when you view the HTML source code in Notepad, use Notepad to make the necessary changes in the HTML file and then save it before you print the HTML code. After the HTML files are printed, you can use the printed HTML files as a good source of reference for style sheet formatting, selectors, and declarations.

The following steps show how to view and print the HTML files.

To View and Print HTML Files

1. **If necessary, click the browser button on the taskbar. If necessary, click the Home link in the menu frame to display the Welcome Web page (welcome.htm) in the right frame.**
2. **Right-click anywhere on the Welcome page except on a link.**
3. **Click View Source on the shortcut menu.**
4. **After the file, welcome.htm, is opened in Notepad, click File on the menu bar and then click Print on the File menu. Click the Print button on the Print dialog box.**
5. **Click the browser button on the taskbar, click the Calendar link, and then repeat Steps 2 through 4.**

6 **Click the browser button on the taskbar, click the Contacts link, and then repeat Steps 2 through 4.**

7 **Click the browser button on the taskbar, click the Links link, and then repeat Steps 2 through 4.**

The HTML files print (Figure 8-15). The <link> tag to the external style sheet displays within the <head> tag of the HTML for each Web page.

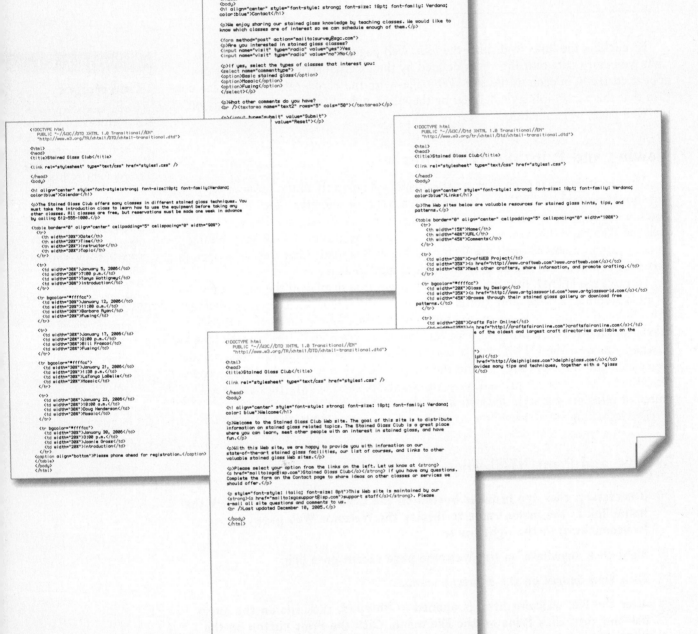

```
<!DOCTYPE html
   PUBLIC "-//W3C//DTD XHTML 1.0 Transitional//EN"
   "http://www.w3.org/TR/xhtml1/DTD/xhtml1-transitional.dtd">

<html>
<head>
<title>Stained Glass Club</title>

<link rel="stylesheet" type="text/css" href="styles1.css" />

</head>
<body>
<h1 align="center" style="font-style: strong; font-size: 18pt; font-family: Verdana;
color:blue">Contact</h1>

<p>We enjoy sharing our stained glass knowledge by teaching classes. We would like to
know which classes are of interest so we can schedule enough of them.</p>

<form method="post" action="mailto:survey@sgc.com">
<p>Are you interested in stained glass classes?
<input name="visit" type="radio" value="yes">Yes
<input name="visit" type="radio" value="no">No</p>

<p>If yes, select the types of classes that interest you:
<select name="commenttype">
<option>Basic stained glass</option>
<option>Mosaic</option>
<option>Fusing</option>
</select></p>

<p>What other comments do you have?
<br /><textarea name="text2" rows="5" cols="50"></textarea></p>

<p><input type="submit" value="Submit">
                 value="Reset"></p>
```

```
<!DOCTYPE html
   PUBLIC "-//W3C//DTD XHTML 1.0 Transitional//EN"
   "http://www.w3.org/TR/xhtml1/DTD/xhtml1-transitional.dtd">

<html>
<head>
<title>Stained Glass Club</title>

<link rel="stylesheet" type="text/css" href="styles1.css" />

</head>
<body>

<h1 align="center" style="font-style:strong; font-size:18pt; font-family:Verdana;
color:blue">Calendar</h1>

<p>The Stained Glass Club offers many classes in different stained glass techniques. You
must take the Introduction class to learn how to use the equipment before taking any
other classes. All classes are free, but reservations must be made one week in advance
by calling 612-555-1000.</p>

<table border="0" align="center" cellpadding="5" cellspacing="0" width="90%">
  <tr>
    <th width="30%">Date</th>
    <th width="20%">Time</th>
    <th width="20%">Instructor</th>
    <th width="30%">Topic</th>
  </tr>

  <tr>
    <td width="30%">January 5, 2006</td>
    <td width="20%">7:00 p.m.</td>
    <td width="20%">Tanya Wattigney</td>
    <td width="30%">Introduction</td>
  </tr>

  <tr bgcolor="#ffffcc">
    <td width="30%">January 12, 2006</td>
    <td width="20%">11:00 a.m.</td>
    <td width="30%">Barbara Ryan</td>
    <td width="20%">Fusing</td>
  </tr>

  <tr>
    <td width="30%">January 17, 2006</td>
    <td width="20%">2:00 p.m.</td>
    <td width="30%">Bill Frasca</td>
    <td width="20%">Fusing</td>
  </tr>

  <tr bgcolor="#ffffcc">
    <td width="30%">January 21, 2006</td>
    <td width="20%">1:30 p.m.</td>
    <td width="30%">LaTonya LaBelle</td>
    <td width="20%">Mosaic</td>
  </tr>

  <tr>
    <td width="30%">January 23, 2006</td>
    <td width="20%">10:00 a.m.</td>
    <td width="30%">Doug Henderson</td>
    <td width="20%">Mosaic</td>
  </tr>

  <tr bgcolor="#ffffcc">
    <td width="30%">January 30, 2006</td>
    <td width="20%">3:00 p.m.</td>
    <td width="30%">Joanie Gross</td>
    <td width="20%">Introduction</td>
  </tr>
<caption align="bottom">Please phone ahead for registration.</caption>
</table>
</body>
</html>
```

```
<!DOCTYPE html
   PUBLIC "-//W3C//Dtd XHTML 1.0 Transitional//EN"
   "http://www.w3.org/tr/xhtml1/Dtd/xhtml1-transitional.dtd">

<html>
<head>
<title>Stained Glass Club</title>

<link rel="stylesheet" type="text/css" href="styles1.css">

</head>
<body>

<h1 align="center" style="font-style: strong; font-size: 18pt; font-family: Verdana;
color:blue">Links</h1>

<p>The Web sites below are valuable resources for stained glass hints, tips, and
patterns.</p>

<table border="0" align="center" cellpadding="5" cellspacing="0" width="100%">
  <tr>
    <th width="15%">Name</th>
    <th width="40%">URL</th>
    <th width="45%">Comments</th>
  </tr>

  <tr>
    <td width="20%">CraftWEB Project</td>
    <td width="35%"><a href="http://www.craftweb.com">www.craftweb.com</a></td>
    <td width="45%">Meet other crafters, share information, and promote crafting.</td>
  </tr>

  <tr bgcolor="#ffffcc">
    <td width="20%">Glass by Design</td>
    <td width="35%"><a href="http://www.artglassworld.com">www.artglassworld.com</a></td>
    <td width="45%">Browse through their stained glass gallery or download free
patterns.</td>
  </tr>

  <tr>
    <td width="20%">Crafts Fair Online</td>
    <td width="35%"><a href="http://craftsfaironline.com">craftsfaironline.com</a></td>
                   e of the oldest and largest craft directories available on the

                   ">
                   lphi</td>
                    href="http://delphiglass.com">delphiglass.com</a></td>
                   ovides many tips and techniques, together with a "glass
                   </td>
```

```
<!DOCTYPE html
   PUBLIC "-//W3C//DTD XHTML 1.0 Transitional//EN"
   "http://www.w3.org/TR/xhtml1/DTD/xhtml1-transitional.dtd">

<html>
<head>
<title>Stained Glass Club</title>

<link rel="stylesheet" type="text/css" href="styles1.css" />

</head>
<body>

<h1 align="center" style="font-style: strong; font-size: 18pt; font-family: Verdana;
color: blue">Welcome</h1>

<p>Welcome to the Stained Glass Club Web site. The goal of this site is to distribute
information on stained glass related topics. The Stained Glass Club is a great place
where you can learn, meet other people with an interest in stained glass, and have
fun.</p>

<p>With this Web site, we are happy to provide you with information on our
state-of-the-art stained glass facilities, our list of courses, and links to other
valuable stained glass Web sites.</p>

<p>Please select your option from the links on the left. Let us know at <strong>
<a href="mailto:sgc@isp.com">Stained Glass Club</a></strong> if you have any questions.
Complete the form on the Contact page to share ideas on other classes or services we
should offer.</p>

<p style="font-style: italic; font-size: 8pt">This Web site is maintained by our
<strong><a href="mailto:sgcsupport@isp.com">support staff</a></strong>. Please
e-mail all site questions and comments to us.
<br />Last updated December 10, 2005.</p>

</body>
</html>
```

FIGURE 8-15

Quitting Notepad and a Browser

After you have viewed and printed the HTML files, the project is complete. After completing the project, quit Notepad and the browser. The following steps show how to quit Notepad and a browser.

To Quit Notepad and a Browser

1. **Click the Close button on the browser title bar.**
2. **Click the Close button on the Notepad window title bar.**

Both the browser and Notepad windows close, and the Windows desktop is displayed.

Project Summary

In Project 8, you learned how to add embedded, external, and inline style sheets to define new styles for the Web pages in the Stained Glass Club Web site. You also learned how to use classes in style sheets to allow for greater flexibility with style sheets. You then learned how to add an embedded style sheet to the menu Web page to define new styles for the paragraphs, links, and link hover state. You learned how to create an external style sheet and link it to the four Web pages that display in the main right frame, as well how to add an inline style sheet to the Welcome Web page to change the appearance of one paragraph of text. You then learned how to print Web pages as laid out in the browser, as well as how to print HTML source code from Web pages in frame structure.

What You Should Know

Having completed this project, you should be able to perform the tasks listed below. The tasks are listed in the same order they were presented in this project.

1. Start Notepad and Open an HTML File (HTM 341)
2. Add an Embedded Style Sheet (HTM 345)
3. Save an HTML File (HTM 346)
4. View an HTML File Using a Browser (HTM 346)
5. Print an HTML File (HTM 347)
6. Create an External Style Sheet (HTM 351)
7. Link to an External Style Sheet (HTM 352)
8. Link the Remaining HTML Files to an External Style Sheet (HTM 355)
9. Add an Inline Style Sheet (HTM 357)
10. View and Print Framed Web Pages (HTM 358)
11. View and Print HTML Files (HTM 359)
12. Quit Notepad and a Browser (HTM 361)

Learn It Online

nstructions: To complete the Learn It Online exercises, start your browser, click the Address bar, and then enter the Web address `scsite.com/html3e/learn`. When the HTML Learn It Online page is displayed, follow the instructions in the exercises below. Each exercise has instructions for printing your results, either for your own records or for submission to your instructor.

1 Project Reinforcement TF, MC, and SA

Below HTML Project 8, click the Project Reinforcement link. Print the quiz by clicking Print on the File menu for each page. Answer each question.

2 Flash Cards

Below HTML Project 8, click the Flash Cards link and read the instructions. Type 20 (or a number specified by your instructor) in the Number of playing cards text box, type your name in the Enter your Name text box, and then click the Flip Card button. When the flash card is displayed, read the question and then click the ANSWER box arrow to select an answer. Flip through Flash Cards. If your score is 15 (75%) correct or greater, click Print on the File menu to print your results. If your score is less than 15 (75%) correct, then redo this exercise by clicking the Replay button.

3 Practice Test

Below HTML Project 8, click the Practice Test link. Answer each question, enter your first and last name at the bottom of the page, and then click the Grade Test button. When the graded practice test is displayed on your screen, click Print on the File menu to print a hard copy. Continue to take practice tests until you score 80% or better.

4 Who Wants To Be a Computer Genius?

Below HTML Project 8, click the Computer Genius link. Read the instructions, enter your first and last name at the bottom of the page, and then click the PLAY button. When your score is displayed, click the PRINT RESULTS link to print a hard copy.

5 Wheel of Terms

Below HTML Project 8, click the Wheel of Terms link. Read the instructions, and then enter your first and last name and your school name. Click the PLAY button. When your score is displayed, right-click the score and then click Print on the shortcut menu to print a hard copy.

6 Crossword Puzzle Challenge

Below HTML Project 8, click the Crossword Puzzle Challenge link. Read the instructions, and then enter your first and last name. Click the SUBMIT button. Work the crossword puzzle. When you are finished, click the Submit button. When the crossword puzzle is redisplayed, click the Print Puzzle button to print a hard copy.

7 Tips and Tricks

Below HTML Project 8, click the Tips and Tricks link. Click a topic that pertains to Project 8. Right-click the information and then click Print on the shortcut menu. Construct a brief example of what the information relates to in HTML to confirm you understand how to use the tip or trick.

8 Newsgroups

Below HTML Project 8, click the Newsgroups link. Click a topic that pertains to Project 8. Print three comments.

9 Expanding Your Horizons

Below HTML Project 8, click the Expanding Your Horizons link. Click a topic that pertains to Project 8. Print the information. Construct a brief example of what the information relates to in HTML to confirm you understand the contents of the article.

10 Search Sleuth

Below HTML Project 8, click the Search Sleuth link. To search for a term that pertains to this project, select a term below the Project 8 title and then use the Google search engine at google.com (or any major search engine) to display and print two Web pages that present information on the term.

11 Online Help I

Below HTML Project 8, click the Online Help I link. Follow the instructions on the page to access Web pages that provide additional help on project topics. Hand in any printed information to your instructor.

12 Online Help II

Below HTML Project 8, click the Online Help II link. Follow the instructions on the page to access Web pages that provide additional help on project topics. Hand in any printed information to your instructor.

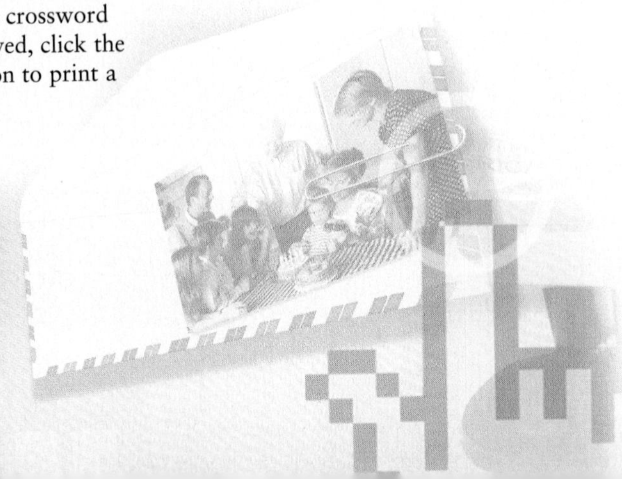

Apply Your Knowledge

1 Editing a Web Page

Instructions: Start Notepad and a browser. Using your browser, open the apply8-1.htm file from the Project08\AYK folder on the HTML Data Disk. If you do not have the HTML Data Disk, see the inside back cover for instructions or see your instructor. The apply8-1.htm file is the frame definition file that displays the apply8menu.htm file in the left frame and the apply8home.htm file in the right frame. The apply8menu.htm and apply8home.htm files are partially completed HTML files that contain some errors. Figure 8-16 shows the Apply Your Knowledge Web page as it should display in the browser after the errors are corrected.

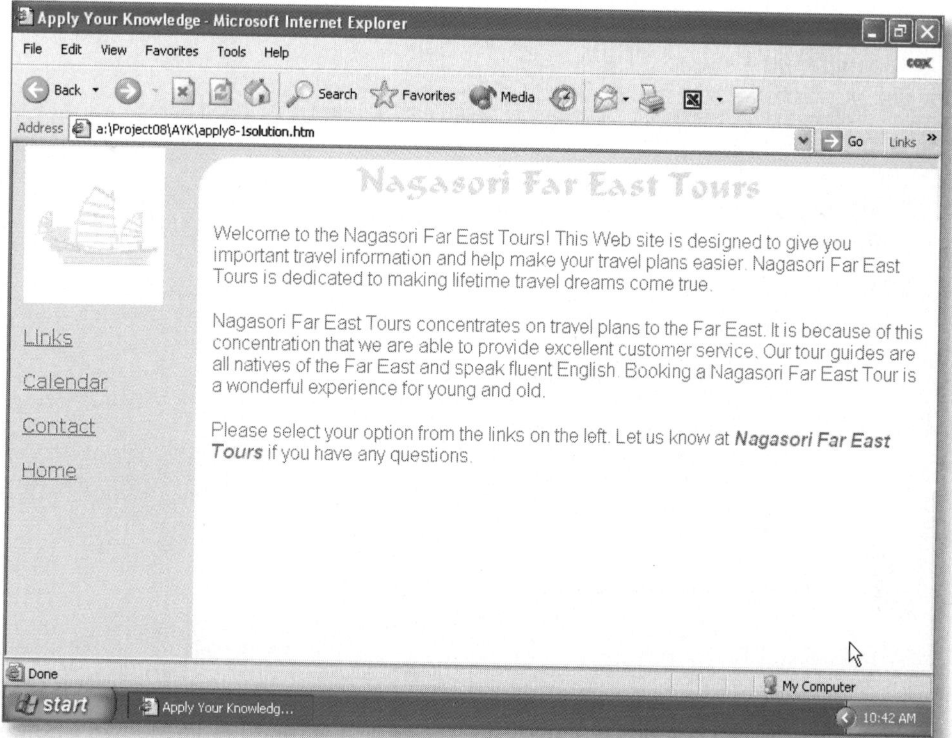

FIGURE 8-16

Perform the following steps using a computer.

1. Enter the URL, `a:\Project08\AYK\apply8-1.htm`, to view the Web page in your browser. Examine the HTML files within the frames and their appearance in the browser.
2. As needed, right-click the pages to view the HTML code in Notepad and then correct style sheet errors, so that the Web pages appear as shown in Figure 8-16.
3. As needed, open the external style sheet, styles5.css, in Notepad to add CSS code required to include any additional features shown on the Web page.
4. Save the revised file on the HTML Data Disk using the file name, apply8-1solution.htm.
5. Print the revised HTML file.
6. Enter the URL, `a:\Project08\AYK\apply8-1solution.htm`, to view the Web page in your browser.
7. Print the Web page as laid out on screen.
8. Write your name on both printouts and hand them in to your instructor.

1 Using External and Internal Styles

Problem: Your school is having its annual Halloween Dinner & Dance on October 3 and wants to create a Web page to notify students and provide information about the event. The event coordinator asks you to create a Web page that contains information about the dance and an e-mail address link, as shown in Figure 8-17. The Web page should have a link to the external style sheet, styles2.css, which is in the Project08\IntheLab folder on the HTML Data Disk. The external style sheet is not complete, so you must add some selectors and declarations to complete it.

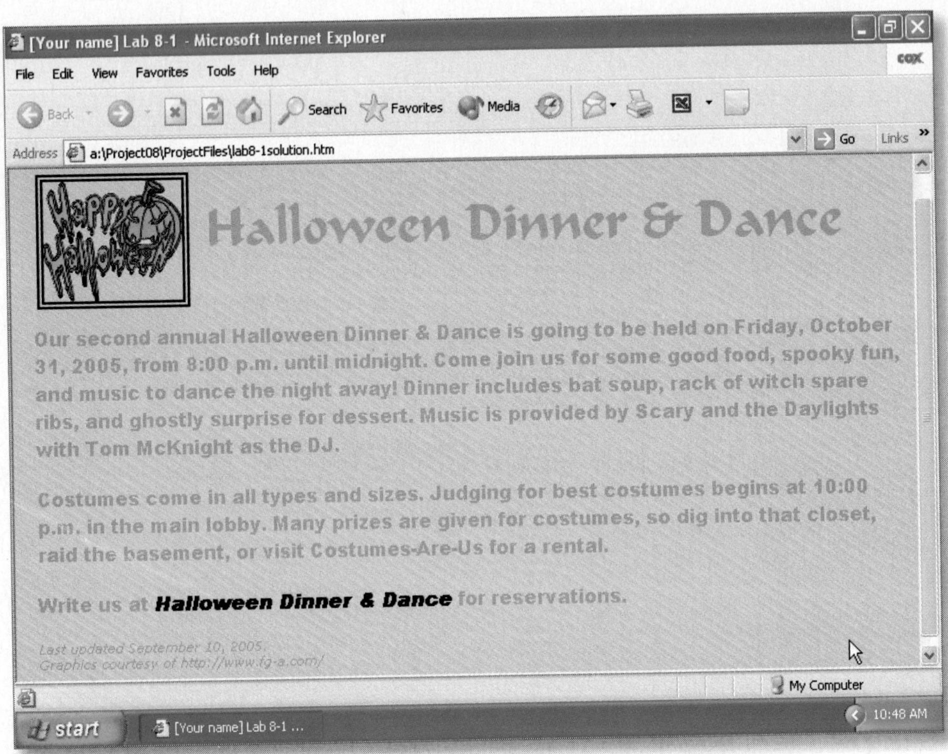

FIGURE 8-17

Instructions: Start Notepad. Perform the following steps using a computer.

1. Using Notepad, open the HTML file, lab8-1.htm, on the HTML Data Disk.
2. Add the title, [Your name] Lab 8-1, as the Web page title.
3. Add a link to the external style sheet, styles2.css.
4. Insert the image, happyh1.gif, as the pumpkin image in the first table data cell.
5. Add an inline style sheet to the last paragraph with the declarations:

```
style="font-style:italic; font-family:Verdana; font-size=8pt"
```

6. Save the HTML file in the Project08\IntheLab folder as lab8-1solution.htm.
7. Open the file, styles2.css, in Notepad. This is a partially completed external style sheet.
8. Insert a style to set the body background-color property to the value, #ffcc99.

9. Enter the following code to define paragraph styles:

```
p {font-family: "Arial Black", Boulder;
   color: #ff8429;
   margin-left: 10}
```

10. Enter the following code to define all link states:

```
a {text-decoration: none;
   color: black;
   font-style: italic}
```

11. Enter the following code to define the style for image borders and margins:

```
img {border-style: double;
   border-width: thick;
   margin: 10}
```

12. Save the CSS file as styles2.css.
13. Print the lab8-1solution.htm file.
14. Print the styles2.css file.
15. Open the lab8-1solution.htm file in your browser and test all styles to ensure they display as shown in Figure 8-17.
16. Print the Web page.
17. Write your name on the printouts and hand them in to your instructor.

2 Creating Embedded Style Sheets

Problem: Signs Etc., a small company that provides signs for both office and party use, is planning to advertise its business on the Internet. You will use inline, embedded, and external style sheets to create the framed Web pages shown in Figure 8-18 on the next page. The lab8-2solution.htm file included in the Project08\IntheLab folder on the HTML Data Disk is the frame definition file that displays the lab8-2menu.htm in the top frame and lab8-2home.htm in the bottom frame. You will change those two files by adding inline, embedded, and external style sheets to define the styles in the pages.

Instructions: Start Notepad. Perform the following steps using a computer.

1. Using Notepad, open the HTML file, lab8-2menu.htm, on the HTML Data Disk.
2. Add an embedded style sheet that defines the following styles:
   a. links: color red, font weight of bolder, and no text decoration
   b. tables: left margin of 140, color red, and a font size of 14 point
   c. link:hover: red background, yellow text
3. Add the image, sign.gif, in the top frame of the Web page. Insert a <br /> tag below the image.

(continued)

Creating Embedded Style Sheets *(continued)*

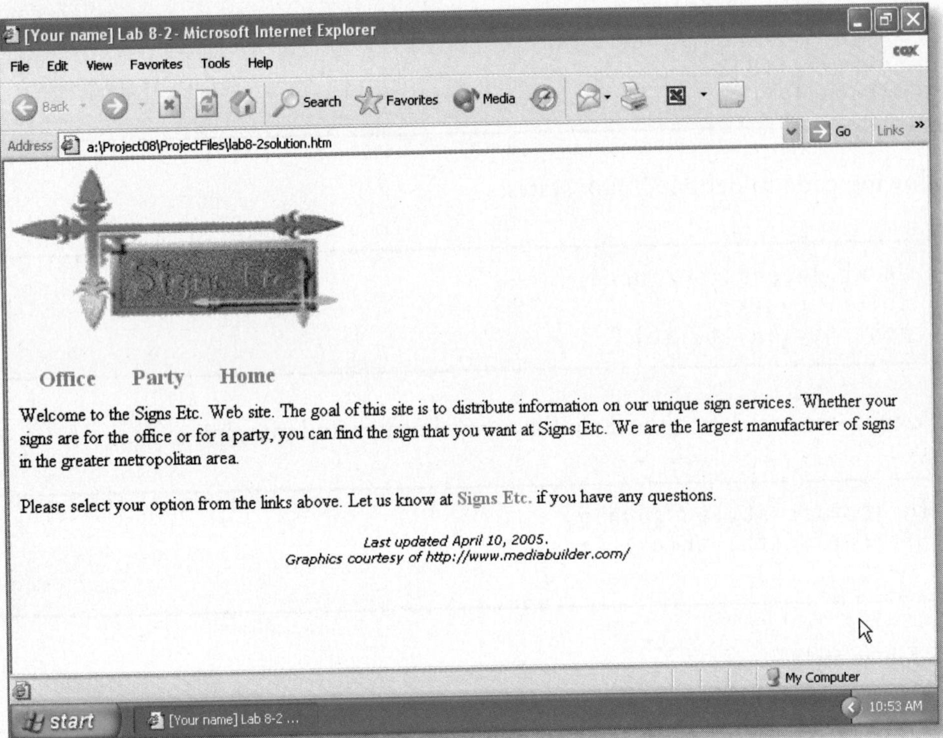

FIGURE 8-18

4. Insert a table with one row. In the table row, enter three links using bold font style:
   a. Office: links to file, lab8-2office.htm
   b. Party: links to the file, lab8-2party.htm
   c. Home: links to the file, lab8-2home.htm
5. Save the file as lab8-2menu.htm.
6. Using Notepad, open the HTML file, Project08\IntheLab\lab8-2home.htm, on the HTML Data Disk.
7. Copy and paste the embedded style sheet from Project08\IntheLab\lab8-2menu.htm into this file.
8. Add an inline style sheet to set the style of the last paragraph to display in 8-point Verdana italic font, with center alignment.
9. Save the file in the Project08\IntheLab folder as lab8-2home.htm.
10. Open the Project08\IntheLab\lab8-2solution.htm file in your browser.
11. Print the Web page using the option to print frames as laid out on screen.
12. Right-click each frame individually to view the HTML source code for lab8-2menu.htm and lab8-2home.htm. Print the HTML files from Notepad.
13. Write your name on all printouts and hand them in to your instructor.

3 Developing External and Inline Style Sheets

Problem: You want to create a Web site that uses all three types of style sheets to give the look shown in Figure 8-19. The file, lab8-3solution.htm, is a frame definition file that defines a menu frame on the left and a

main page frame on the right. The file, lab8-3solution.htm, is included in the Project08\IntheLab folder on the HTML Data Disk. In this exercise, you will create a menu Web page for the left menu frame and a main Web page for the right main frame, both of which use style sheets to give them a specific look.

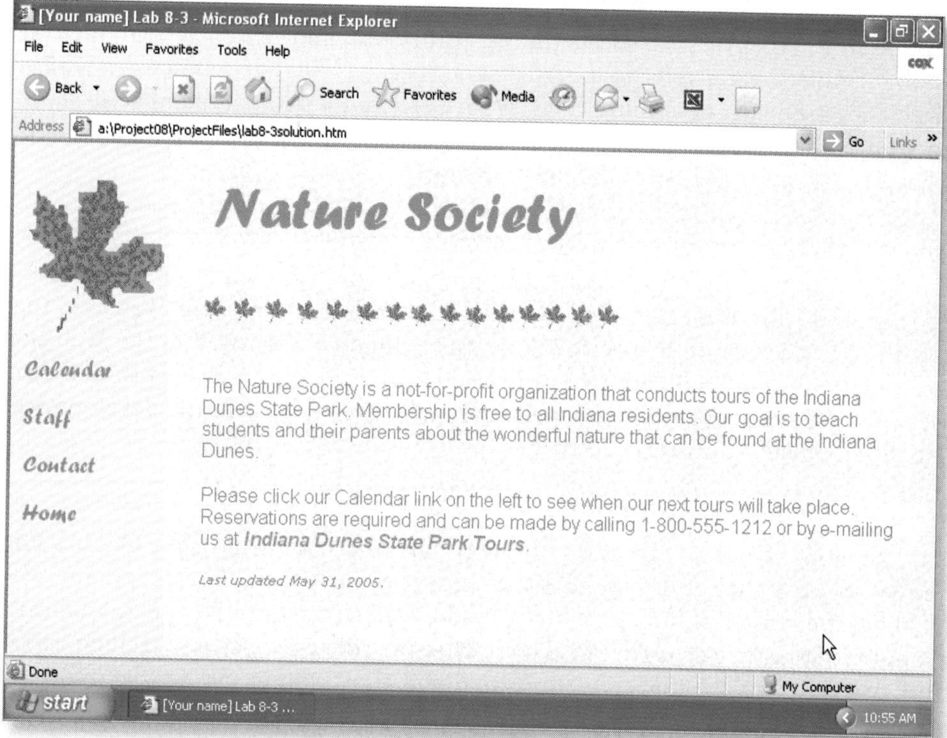

FIGURE 8-19

Instructions: Start Notepad. Perform the following steps using a computer.

1. Open a new file in Notepad and create a menu Web page similar to the one shown in Figure 8-19.
2. Insert four links, using the font family Verdana. Use a style sheet to set a link hover style for the links.
3. Add the image, leaf2.gif, at the top of the menu Web page.
4. Save the menu Web page using the file name, lab8-3menu.htm.
5. Open a new file in Notepad and create an external style sheet that controls the h1, paragraph, link, and image styles. Set paragraph styles to display in green Arial or Boulder font (or a similar font), with 20-point margins. Set the image style to add 15 points of space around all images.
6. Save the external style sheet as styles4.css.
7. Open a new file in Notepad and create a main Web page similar to the one shown in Figure 8-19.
8. Add the image, yellowbkgrnd.jpg, as the background and the image, leafline2.gif, as the horizontal rule.
9. Use an inline style sheet to change the last paragraph of text to display as shown in Figure 8-19.
10. Save the Web page using the file name, lab8-3home.htm.
11. Print the Web page using the option to print frames as laid out on screen.
12. Right-click each frame individually to view the HTML source code for lab8-3menu.htm and lab8-3home.htm. Print the HTML files from Notepad.
13. Write your name on the printouts and hand them in to your instructor.

Cases and Places

The difficulty of these case studies varies:
■ are the least difficult and ■■ are the most difficult. The last exercise is a group exercise.

1 ■ Browse the Internet to find two Web sites that discuss Cascading Style Sheets (CSS). How do these sites describe the three types of style sheets (inline, embedded, and external)? Are their definitions different or similar? Some sources refer to external style sheets as linked style sheets. What terminology do these two Web sites use when describing CSS? What determines which type of style sheet should be used? When would an embedded (or linked) style sheet be more appropriate than an external style sheet? In what cases would you use an inline style sheet?

2 ■ Your manager at WebSource has asked you to prepare a brief presentation on the use of classes in style sheets, as described in Project 8. He has asked to you find at least two Web sites that describe the use of classes in style sheets and then review how the techniques discussed in the Web sites compare to the style sheet methods described and used in Project 8. The presentation also should discuss how the use of classes can help make Web development more effective — both in the development of one Web page and the development of an entire Web site.

3 ■■ You are planning to use an external style sheet in the development of the Ocean's Edge Spa Web site, so that you can change the site's look according to the season. Create a home Web page with information about the resort, including an <h1> header style, a paragraph of text, a table of special events, and an e-mail link to oceansedge@isp.com. Based on the concepts and techniques discussed in the project, create two different external style sheets that will allow you to modify the resort Web page to reflect a summer look and a fall look. Link the first style sheet to the home Web page and then view how it appears in the browser. Modify the home Web page to link to the second style sheet and then view how it appears in the browser. Print the HTML source code for both style sheets and the home page.

4 ■■ Tanya Wattigney is very impressed by the use of style sheets in the Stained Glass Club Web site and would like to explore additional styles that can be applied to the Web pages. Using Appendix C, find three CSS properties that were not used in Project 8, modify the styles1.css style sheet to include these properties and values, and then save the style sheet as styles1new.css. Update the link in the Web page, welcome.htm, and then view the Web page in the browser using the new style sheet. How did the use of these new properties improve the appearance of the Web page?

5 ■■ **Working Together** Your design team at SolidWorks Design has been asked to create a proposal for an existing customer, to explain the value of using Cascading Style Sheets. Select a Web site with which you are familiar. Verify that the Web site does not utilize any of the three types of style sheets. Develop a graphic of the Web site hierarchy. Determine how the three types of style sheets could be utilized in this Web site and develop an outline explaining how they would help enhance pages or sections of the site, add style consistency, or make the site easier to maintain. Write a proposal to the owners of the Web site that describes the features you could add with style sheets and the benefits of doing so, relative to the formatting techniques currently used in the Web site. As an example, you might want to address the number of times that a particular <font> tag is used in the site and contrast that with the ease of using one external style sheet and a link statement per page. Use other ideas as discussed in the project to stress the other benefits of style sheets. Write the proposal in the form of a bid, giving time estimates and costs associated with the development effort. Include your hierarchy chart and style sheet outline as appendices to the proposal.

Appendix A

HTML Quick Reference

HTML Tags and Attributes

HTML is the original language used for publishing hypertext on the World Wide Web. It is a non-proprietary format based on Standard Generalized Markup Language (SGML). HTML documents can be created with a wide variety of tools, from simple plain text editors, such as Notepad, to sophisticated WYSIWYG authoring tools, such as FrontPage. HTML uses tags such as <h1> and <p> to structure text into headings, paragraphs, lists, hypertext links, and so on.

Many HTML tags have attributes that can be defined in different ways to alter the look of the Web page even more. Table A-1 lists HTML tags and their associated attributes. The list provides a brief description of each tag and its attributes. The default value for each attribute is indicated by bold text. For a comprehensive list, more thorough descriptions, and examples of all HTML tags, visit the World Wide Web Consortium Web site at www.w3.org.

As the World Wide Web Consortium updates the current HTML specifications, HTML tags constantly are being added to, deleted, and replaced by newer tags. In this list, deprecated elements — that is, tags that can be replaced with newer elements — are indicated with an asterisk. Deprecated elements still are available for use, and most browsers still support them. Obsolete elements are elements that no longer are in use or supported by common browsers. This appendix does not list obsolete elements.

Table A-1 HTML Tags and Attributes

HTML TAG AND ATTRIBUTES	DESCRIPTION
<a>....</a>	Anchor; creates a hyperlink or fragment identifier
charset=*character set*	Specifies the character encoding of the linked resource
href=*url*	Hyperlink reference that specifies the target URL
name=*text*	Specifies a name for enclosed text, allowing it to be the target of a hyperlink
rel=*relationship*	Indicates the relationship going from the current page to the target
rev=*relationship*	Indicates the relationship going from the target to the current page
target=*name*	Defines the name of the window or frame in which the linked resource will display
<address>....</address>	Used for information such as authorship, e-mail addresses, or addresses; enclosed text displays italicized and indented in some browsers
No attributes	
<area>....</area>	Creates a clickable area, or hotspot, on a client-side imagemap
coords=*value1, value2*	Specifies the coordinates that define the edges of the hotspot; a comma-delimited list of values
href=*url*	Hyperlink reference that specifies the target URL
nohref	Indicates that no link is associated with the area
shape=*shape*	Identifies the shape of the area (poly, rect)
target=*name*	Defines the name of the window or frame in which the linked resource will display
<b>....</b>	Specifies text to display in bold
No attributes	
<base />	Identifies the base in all relative URLs in the document
href=*url*	Specifies the absolute URL used to resolve all relative URLs in the document
target=*name*	Defines the name for the default window or frame in which the hyperlinked pages display
<big>....</big>	Increases the size of the enclosed text to a type size bigger than the surrounding text; exact display size depends on the browser and default font
No attributes	
<blockquote>....</blockquote>	Sets enclosed text to display as a quotation, indented on the right and left
No attributes	
<body>....</body>	Defines the start and end of a Web page
alink=*color*	Defines the color of an active link
background=*url*	Identifies the image to be used as a background
bgcolor=*color*	Sets the document's background color
link=*color*	Defines the color of links not yet visited
vlink=*color*	Defines the color of visited links
<bold>....</bold>	Sets enclosed text to display in bold
No attributes	

Table A-1 HTML Tags and Attributes

HTML TAG AND ATTRIBUTES	DESCRIPTION
** **	Inserts a line break
clear=*margin*	Sets the next line to start in a spot where the requested margin is clear (left, right, all, none); used to stop text wrap
<caption>....</caption>	Creates a caption for a table
align=*position*	Sets caption position (top, bottom, left, right)
<center>....</center> *	Centers the enclosed text horizontally on the page
No attributes	
<cite>....</cite>	Indicates that the enclosed text is a citation; text usually displays in italics
No attributes	
<code>....</code>	Indicates that the enclosed text is a code sample from a program; text usually displays in fixed width font such as Courier
No attributes	
<col>....</col>	Organizes columns in a table into column groups to share attribute values
align=*position*	Sets horizontal alignment of text within the column (char, center, top, bottom, left, right)
span=*value*	Sets the number of columns that span the <col> element
valign=*position*	Specifies vertical alignment of text within the column (top, middle, bottom)
width=*value*	Sets the width of each column in the column group
<colgroup>....</colgroup>	Encloses a group of <col> tags and groups the columns to set properties
align=*position*	Specifies horizontal alignment of text within the column (char, center, top, bottom, left, right)
char=*character*	Specifies a character on which to align column values (e.g., a period is used to align monetary values)
charoff=*value*	Specifies a number of characters to offset data aligned with the character specified in the char property
span=*number*	Sets the number of columns the <col> element spans
valign=*position*	Specifies vertical alignment of text within the column (top, middle, bottom)
width=*value*	Sets the width of each column spanned by the colgroup statement
<dd>....</dd>	Indicates that the enclosed text is a definition in the definition list
No attributes	
<div>....</div>	Defines block-level structure or division in the HTML document
align=*position*	Specifies alignment of the content block (center, left, right)
class=*name*	Assigns the class name to each class of divisions
id=*name*	Assigns a unique name to a specific content block
<dl>....</dl>	Creates a definition list
No attributes	
<dt>....</dt>	Indicates that the enclosed text is a term in definition list
No attributes	

(continued)

Table A-1 HTML Tags and Attributes *(continued)*

HTML TAG AND ATTRIBUTES	DESCRIPTION
<em>....</em>	Indicates that the enclosed text should be emphasized; usually displays in italics
No attributes	
<fieldset>....</fieldset>	Groups related form controls and labels
align=*position*	Specifies alignment of a legend as related to the fieldset (top, bottom, middle, left, right)
<font>....</font> *	Defines the appearance of enclosed text
size=*value*	Sets the font size in absolute terms (1 through 7) or as a relative value (e.g., +2)
color=*color*	Sets the font color; can be a hexadecimal value (#rrggbb) or a word for a predefined color value (e.g., navy)
face=*list*	Identifies the font face; multiple entries should be separated by commas
point-size=*value*	Sets the point size of text for downloaded fonts
weight=*value*	Sets the weight of the font, ranging from 100 (lightest) to 900 (heaviest)
<form>....</form>	Marks the start and end of a Web page form
action=*url*	Specifies the URL of the application that will process the form; required attribute
enctype=*encoding*	Specifies how the form element values will be encoded
method=*method*	Specifies the method used to pass form parameters (data) to the server
target=*text*	Specifies the frame or window that displays the form's results
<frame>....</frame>	Delimits a frame within a frameset
frameborder=*option*	Specifies whether the frame border displays (yes, no)
marginheight=*value*	Adds *n* pixels of space above and below the frame contents
marginwidth=*value*	Adds *n* pixels of space to the left and the right of the frame contents
name=*text*	Specifies the name of the frame
noresize	Prevents the user from resizing the frame
scrolling=*option*	Defines the URL of the source document that is displayed in the frame
src=*url*	Adds scroll bars or not – always (yes), never (no), or add when needed (**auto**)
<frameset>....</frameset>	Defines a collection of frames in a frameset
cols=*value1, value2,...*	Defines the number and width of frames within a frameset
rows= *value1, value2,...*	Defines the number and height of frames within a frameset
frameborder=*option*	Specifies whether the frame border displays (yes, no)
<h*n*>....</h*n*>	Defines a header level *n*, ranging from the largest (h1) to the smallest (h6)
align=*position*	Specifies the header alignment (**left**, center, right)
<head>....</head>	Delimits the start and end of the HTML document's head
No attributes	
<hr />	Inserts a horizontal rule
align=*type*	Specifies the alignment of the horizontal rule (left, **center**, right)
noshade	Specifies to not use 3D shading and to round the ends of the rule
size=*value*	Sets the thickness of the rule to a value in pixels
width=*value or %*	Sets the width of the rule to a value in pixels or a percentage of the page width; percentage is preferred

Table A-1 HTML Tags and Attributes

HTML TAG AND ATTRIBUTES	DESCRIPTION
<html>....</html>	Indicates the start and the end of the HTML document
version=*data*	Indicates the HTML version used; not usually used
<i>....</i>	Sets enclosed text to display in italics
No attributes	
<iframe>....</iframe>	Creates an inline frame, also called a floating frame or subwindow, within an HTML document
align=*position*	Aligns the frame with respect to context (top, middle, **bottom**, left, right)
frameborder=*option*	Specifies whether a frame border displays (1=yes; 0=no)
height=*value*	Sets the frame height to a value in pixels
marginheight=*value*	Sets the margin between the contents of the frame and its top and bottom borders to a value in pixels
marginwidth=*value*	Sets the margin between the contents of the frame and its left and right borders to value in pixels
name=*text*	Assigns a name to the current frame
noresize	Prevents the user from resizing the frame
src=*url*	Defines the URL of the source document that is displayed in the frame
width=*value*	Sets the frame width to a value in pixels
scrolling=*option*	Adds scroll bars or not – always (yes), never (no), or add when needed (**auto**)
<img>....</img>	Inserts an image into the current Web page
align=*type*	Defines image alignment in relation to the text or the page margin (top, middle, bottom, right, left)
alt=*text*	Provides a text description of an image if the browser cannot display the image; always should be used
border=*value*	Sets the thickness of the border around the image to a value in pixels; default size is 3
height=*value*	Sets the height of the image to a value in pixels; always should be used
src=*url*	Specifies the URL of the image to be displayed; required
usemap=*url*	Specifies the map of coordinates and links that defines the href within this image
width=*value*	Sets the width of the image to a value in pixels; always should be used
<input>....</input>	Defines controls used in forms
alt=*text*	Provides a short description of the control or image button; for browsers that do not support inline images
checked	Sets radio buttons and check boxes to the checked state
disabled	Disables the control
maxlength=*value*	Sets a value for the maximum number of characters allowed as input for a text or password control
name=*text*	Assigns a name to the control
readonly	Prevents changes to the control
size=*value*	Sets the initial size of the control to a value in characters
src=*url*	Identifies the location of the image if the control is set to an image

(continued)

Table A-1 HTML Tags and Attributes *(continued)*

HTML TAG AND ATTRIBUTES	DESCRIPTION
<input>....</input> *(continued)*	
tabindex=*value*	Specifies the tab order between elements in the form, with 1 as the first element
type=*type*	Defines the type of control (**text**, password, checkbox, radio, submit, reset, file, hidden, image, button)
usemap=*url*	Associates an imagemap as defined by the <map> element
value=*data*	Sets the initial value of the control
<ins>....</ins>	Identifies and displays text as having been inserted in the document in relation to a previous version
cite=*url*	Specifies the URL of a document that has more information on the inserted text
datetime=*datetime*	Date and time of a change
<kbd>....</kbd>	Sets enclosed text to display as keyboard-like input
No attributes	
<label>....</label>	Creates a label for a form control
for=*data*	Indicates the name or ID of the element to which the label is applied
<legend>....</legend>	Assigns a caption to a fieldset element, as defined by the <fieldset> tags
No attributes	
<li>....</li>	Defines the enclosed text as a list item in a list
value=*value1*	Inserts or restarts counting with value1
<link>....</link>	Establishes a link between the HTML document and another document, such as an external style sheet
charset=*character set*	Specifies the character encoding of the linked resource
href=*url*	Defines the URL of the linked document
name=*text*	Names the current anchor so that it can be the destination to other links
rel=*relationship*	Indicates the relationship going from the current page to the target
rev=*relationship*	Indicates the relationship going from the target to the current page
target=*name*	Defines the name of the frame into which the linked resource will display
type=*mime-type*	Indicates the data or media type of the linked document (e.g., text/css for linked style sheets)
<map>....</map>	Specifies a client-side imagemap; must enclose <area> tags
name=*text*	Assigns a name to the imagemap
<meta />	Provides additional data (metadata) about an HTML document
content=*text*	Specifies the value for the <meta> information; required
http-equiv=*text*	Specifies the HTTP-equivalent name for metadata; tells the server to include that name and content in the HTTP header when the HTML document is sent to the client
name=*text*	Assigns a name to metadata
scheme=*text*	Provides additional context for interpreting the information in the content attribute

Table A-1 HTML Tags and Attributes

HTML TAG AND ATTRIBUTES	DESCRIPTION
<noframes>....</noframes>	Defines content to be displayed in browsers that do not support frames; very important to include
No attributes	
<object>....</object>	Includes an external object in the HTML document such as an image, a Java applet, or other external object, not well-supported by most browsers
archive=*url*	Specifies the URL of the archive containing classes and other resources that will be preloaded for use by the object
classid=*url*	Specifies the URL of the embedded object
codebase=*url*	Sets the base URL for the object; helps resolve relative references
codetype=*type*	Identifies the content type of the data in the object
data=*url*	Identifies the location of the object's data
declare	Indicates the object will be declared only, not installed in the page
height=*value*	Sets the height of the object to a value in pixels
name=*text*	Assigns a control name to the object for use in forms
standby=*text*	Defines the message to display while the object loads
tabindex=*value*	Specifies the tab order between elements, with 1 as the first element
type=*type*	Specifies the content or media type of the object
usemap=*url*	Associates an imagemap as defined by the <map> element
width=*value*	Sets the width of the object to a value in pixels
<ol>....</ol>	Defines an ordered list that contains numbered list item elements (<li>)
type=*option*	Sets or resets the numbering format for the list; options include: A=capital letters, a=lowercase letters, I=capital Roman numerals, i=lowercase Roman numerals, or **1**=Arabic numerals
<option>....</option>	Defines individual options in a selection list, as defined by <select> element
label=*text*	Provides a shorter label for the option than that specified in its content
selected	Sets the option to be the default or the selected option in a list
value=*value*	Sets a value returned to the server when the user selects the option
disabled	Disables the option items
<p>....</p>	Delimits a paragraph; automatically inserts a blank line between text
align=*position*	Aligns text within the paragraph (left, center, right)
<param>....</param>	Passes a parameter to an object or applet, as defined by <object> or <applet> element
id=*text*	Assigns an identifier to the element
name=*text*	Defines the name of the parameter required by an object
type=*type*	Specifies the content or media type of the object
value=*data*	Sets the value of the parameter
valuetype=*data*	Identifies the type of parameter used in the value attribute (data, ref, object)
<pre>....</pre>	Preserves the original format of the enclosed text; keeps line breaks and spacing the same as the original
No attributes	

(continued)

Table A-1 HTML Tags and Attributes *(continued)*

HTML TAG AND ATTRIBUTES	DESCRIPTION
<q>....</q>	Sets enclosed text as a short quotation
lang=*option*	Defines the language in which the quotation will display
<samp>....</samp>	Sets enclosed text to display as sample output from a computer program or script; usually displays in a monospace font
No attributes	
<script>....</script>	Inserts a client-side script into an HTML document
defer	Indicates that the browser should defer executing the script
src=*url*	Identifies the location of an external script
type=*mime-type*	Indicates the data or media type of the script language (e.g., text/javascript for JavaScript commands)
<select>....</select>	Defines a form control to create a multiple-choice menu or scrolling list; encloses a set of <option> tags to define one or more options
name=*text*	Assigns a name to the selection list
multiple	Sets the list to allow multiple selections
size=*value*	Sets the number of visible options in the list
disabled	Disables the selection list
tabindex=*value*	Specifies the tab order between list items, with 1 as the first element
<small>....</small>	Sets enclosed text to display in a smaller typeface
No attributes	
<span>....</span>	Creates a user-defined container to add inline structure to the HTML document
No attributes	
<strong>....</strong>	Sets enclosed text to display with strong emphasis; usually displayed as bold text
No attributes	
<style>....</style>	Encloses embedded style sheet rules for use in the HTML document
media=*data*	Identifies the intended medium of the style (**screen**, tty, tv, projection, handheld, print, braille, aural, all)
title=*data*	Indicates the title of the style sheet
type=*data*	Specifies the content or media type of the style language (e.g., text/css for linked style sheets)
_{....}	Sets enclosed text to display in subscript
No attributes	
^{....}	Sets enclosed text to display in superscript
No attributes	
<table>....</table>	Marks the start and end of a table
align=*position*	Aligns the table text (left, right, center, justify, char)
border=*value*	Sets the border around a table to a value in pixels
cellpadding=*value*	Sets padding around each cell's contents to a value in pixels
cellspacing=*value*	Sets spacing between cells to a value in pixels
summary=*text*	Provides a summary of the table's purpose and structure
width=*value or %*	Sets table width in pixels or a percentage of the window

Table A-1 HTML Tags and Attributes

HTML TAG AND ATTRIBUTES	DESCRIPTION
<table>....</table> *(continued)*	
frame=*option*	Defines which parts of the outer border (frame) to display (void, above, below, hsides, lhs, rhs, vsides, box, border)
rules=*option*	Specifies which inner borders are to display between the table cells (none, groups, rows, cols, all)
<tbody>....</tbody>	Defines a groups of rows in a table body
align=*option*	Aligns text (left, center, right, justify, char)
char=*character*	Specifies a character on which to align column values (e.g., a period is used to align monetary values)
charoff=*value*	Specifies a number of characters to offset data aligned with the character specified in the char property
valign=*position*	Sets vertical alignment of cells in a group (top, middle, bottom, baseline)
<td>....</td>	Defines a data cell in a table; contents are left-aligned and normal text by default
bgcolor=*color*	Defines the background color for the cell
colspan=*value*	Defines the number of adjacent columns spanned by the cell
rowspan=*value*	Defines the number of adjacent rows spanned by the cell
width=*n* or *%*	Sets the width of the table in either pixels or a percentage of the whole table width
headers=*idrefs*	Defines the list of header cells for the current cell
abbr=*text*	Provides an abbreviated version of the cell's contents that browsers can use if space is limited
scope=*option*	Specifies cells for which the element defines header cells (row, col, rowgroup, colgroup)
align=*position*	Specifies horizontal alignment (left, center, right, justify, char)
char=*character*	Specifies a character on which to align column values (e.g., a period is used to align monetary values)
charoff=*value*	Specifies a number of characters to offset data aligned with the character specified in the char property
valign=*position*	Sets vertical alignment of cells in the group (top, middle, bottom, baseline)
<textarea>....</textarea>	Creates a multiline text input area within a form
cols=*value*	Defines the number of columns in the text input area
name=*data*	Assigns a name to the text area
rows=*value*	Defines the number of rows in the text input area
disabled	Disables the element
readonly	Prevents the user from editing content in the text area
tabindex=*value*	Specifies the tab order between elements, with 1 as the first element
<tfoot>....</tfoot>	Identifies and groups rows into a table footer
align=*position*	Specifies horizontal alignment (left, center, right, justify, char)
char=*character*	Specifies a character on which to align column values (e.g., a period is used to align monetary values)
charoff=*value*	Specifies a number of characters to offset data aligned with the character specified in the char property
valign=*position*	Sets vertical alignment of cells in a group (top, middle, bottom, baseline)

(continued)

Table A-1 HTML Tags and Attributes *(continued)*

HTML TAG AND ATTRIBUTES	DESCRIPTION
<th>....</th>	Defines a table header cell; contents are bold and center-aligned by default
bgcolor=*color*	Defines the background color for the cell
colspan=*value*	Defines the number of adjacent columns spanned by the cell
rowspan=*value*	Defines the number of adjacent rows spanned by the cell
width=*n* or *%*	Sets the width of the table in either pixels or a percentage of the whole table width
<thead>....</thead>	Identifies and groups rows into a table header
align=*position*	Specifies horizontal alignment (left, center, right, justify, char)
char=*character*	Specifies a character on which to align column values (e.g., a period is used to align monetary values)
charoff=*value*	Specifies a number of characters to offset data aligned with the character specified in the char property
valign=*position*	Sets vertical alignment of cells in a group (top, middle, bottom, baseline)
<title>....</title>	Defines the title for the HTML document; always should be used
No attributes	
<tr>....</tr>	Defines a row of cells within a table
bgcolor=*color*	Defines the background color for the cell
align=*position*	Specifies horizontal alignment (left, center, right, justify, char)
char=*character*	Specifies a character on which to align column values (e.g., a period is used to align monetary values)
charoff=*value*	Specifies a number of characters to offset data aligned with the character specified in the char property
valign=*position*	Sets vertical alignment of cells in a group (top, middle, bottom, baseline)
<tt>....</tt>	Formats the enclosed text in teletype- or computer-style monospace font
No attributes	
<u>....</u> *	Sets enclosed text to display with an underline
No attributes	
<ul>....</ul>	Defines an unnumbered list that contains bulleted list item elements (<li>)
type=*option*	Sets or resets the bullet format for the list; options include: circle, **disc**, square
<var>....</var>	Indicates the enclosed text is a variable's name; used to mark up variables or program arguments
No attributes	

Appendix B

Browser-Safe Color Palette

Browser-Safe Colors

Three hardware components help to deliver color to a computer user: the processor, the video card, and the monitor. Because of the wide variety of components that exist, the color quality that users see varies greatly. The software on a user's computer, specifically the Web browser, also affects the way that color is displayed on a monitor. For Web developers, it is the browser that limits color significantly. It is very difficult, if not impossible, to plan for all possible color variations created by a Web browser. Using browser-safe colors allows for the browser variations, but limits the number of colors used on the Web page.

A total of 216 browser-safe colors display well on different monitors, operating systems, and browsers — including both Windows and Mac OS operating systems and Internet Explorer and Netscape Navigator browsers. When using color on your Web site, keep in mind that using only the 216 browser-safe colors can be very restrictive, especially for the approximately ten percent of Web visitors who have 256-color monitors. On those monitors, only the browser-safe colors will display. If you decide to use a non-browser-safe color, the visitor's browser will try to create the color by combining (a process called dithering) any number of the 216 acceptable colors. The resulting color could be slightly different from the color you had intended.

For a complete list of the 216 browser-safe colors, see Table B-1 on the next page or visit the Shelly Cashman Series HTML Web page (scsite.com/html3e) and click Color Chart. Links to other Web sites with information about browser-safe colors also are available.

Table B-1 Browser-Safe Colors

#ffffff	#ffffcc	#ffff99	#ffff66	#ffff33	#ffff00
#ffccff	#ffcccc	#ffcc99	#ffcc66	#ffcc33	#ffcc00
#ff99ff	#ff99cc	#ff9999	#ff9966	#ff9933	#ff9900
#ff66ff	#ff66cc	#ff6699	#ff6666	#ff6633	#ff6600
#ff33ff	#ff33cc	#ff3399	#ff3366	#ff3333	#ff3300
#ff00ff	#ff00cc	#ff0099	#ff0066	#ff0033	#ff0000
#ccffff	#ccffcc	#ccff99	#ccff66	#ccff33	#ccff00
#ccccff	#cccccc	#cccc99	#cccc66	#cccc33	#cccc00
#cc99ff	#cc99cc	#cc9999	#cc9966	#cc9933	#cc9900
#cc66ff	#cc66cc	#cc6699	#cc6666	#cc6633	#cc6600
#cc33ff	#cc33cc	#cc3399	#cc3366	#cc3333	#cc3300
#cc00ff	#cc00cc	#cc0099	#cc0066	#cc0033	#cc0000
#99ffff	#99ffcc	#99ff99	#99ff66	#99ff33	#99ff00
#99ccff	#99cccc	#99cc99	#99cc66	#99cc33	#99cc00
#9999ff	#9999cc	#999999	#999966	#999933	#999900
#9966ff	#9966cc	#996699	#996666	#996633	#996600
#9933ff	#9933cc	#993399	#993366	#993333	#993300
#9900ff	#9900cc	#990099	#990066	#990033	#990000
#66ffff	#66ffcc	#66ff99	#66ff66	#66ff33	#66ff00
#66ccff	#66cccc	#66cc99	#66cc66	#66cc33	#66cc00
#6699ff	#6699cc	#669999	#669966	#669933	#669900
#6666ff	#6666cc	#666699	#666666	#666633	#666600
#6633ff	#6633cc	#663399	#663366	#663333	#663300
#6600ff	#6600cc	#660099	#660066	#660033	#660000
#33ffff	#33ffcc	#33ff99	#33ff66	#33ff33	#33ff00
#33ccff	#33cccc	#33cc99	#33cc66	#33cc33	#33cc00
#3399ff	#3399cc	#339999	#339966	#339933	#339900
#3366ff	#3366cc	#336699	#336666	#336633	#336600
#3333ff	#3333cc	#333399	#333366	#333333	#333300
#3300ff	#3300cc	#330099	#330066	#330033	#330000
#00ffff	#00ffcc	#00ff99	#00ff66	#00ff33	#00ff00
#00ccff	#00cccc	#00cc99	#00cc66	#00cc33	#00cc00
#0099ff	#0099cc	#009999	#009966	#009933	#009900
#0066ff	#0066cc	#006699	#006666	#006633	#006600
#0033ff	#0033cc	#003399	#003366	#003333	#003300
#0000ff	#0000cc	#000099	#000066	#000033	#000000

Appendix C

Style Sheet Browser Compatibility Tables

Style Sheet Properties and Values

This appendix provides a listing of the CSS (cascading style sheet) properties and values supported by the following fully released browsers:

- Internet Explorer 4.x, 5.x, and 6.x for Windows (IE 4.x, IE5.x, IE6.x)
- Netscape 4.x, 6.x, and 7.x for Windows (N4.x, N6.x, N7.x)

The table lists the property name and description for each property, along with valid values. Values listed in bold are the default. For each browser version listed above, the table then indicates whether or not the browser type and version supports that specific property.

Because of the rapid changes in browser versions, you may find that a newly released browser version is not reflected in the list. To view an updated version of the appendix, visit the Shelly Cashman Series HTML Web site (scsite.com/html3e) and then click Style Sheet.

Background and Color Styles

Colors and subtle backgrounds can enhance the style of a Web page significantly. You can set the background or color of an element using these style sheet properties. Not all browser versions support these style attributes, however, so be aware that not all users will be able to see the background and color styles set by these properties. Table C-1 provides a list of background and color properties.

Table C-1 Background and Color Properties

PROPERTY NAME	DESCRIPTION	VALUES	IE4.X	IE5.X	IE6.X	N4.X	N6.X	N7.X
background-attachment	Sets the background image to fixed or scrolls with the page	**scroll** fixed	Yes Yes	Yes Yes	Yes Yes	No No	Yes Yes	Yes Yes
background-color	Sets the background color of an element	**transparent** <color>	Yes Yes	Yes Yes	Yes Yes	Yes Yes	Yes Yes	Yes Yes
background-image	Sets an image as the background	**none** <url>	Yes Yes	Yes Yes	Yes Yes	Yes Yes	Yes Yes	Yes Yes
background-position	Sets the starting position of a background image	<percentage> <length> bottom center left right top	Yes Yes Yes Yes Yes Yes Yes	Yes Yes Yes Yes Yes Yes Yes	Yes Yes Yes Yes Yes Yes Yes	No No No No No No No	Yes Yes Yes Yes Yes Yes Yes	Yes Yes Yes Yes Yes Yes Yes

(continued)

Table C-1 Background and Color Properties *(continued)*

PROPERTY NAME	DESCRIPTION	VALUES	IE4.X	IE5.X	IE6.X	N4.X	N6.X	N7.X
background-repeat	Sets if/how a background image will be repeated	**repeat**	Yes	Yes	Yes	Yes	Yes	Yes
		repeat-x	Yes	Yes	Yes	Yes	Yes	Yes
		repeat-y	Yes	Yes	Yes	Yes	Yes	Yes
		no-repeat	Yes	Yes	Yes	Yes	Yes	Yes
color	Sets the background color of an element	<color>	Yes	Yes	Yes	Yes	Yes	Yes
		transparent	Yes	Yes	Yes	Yes	Yes	Yes

Border Styles

Many changes can be made to the style, color, and width of any or all sides of a border using the border properties listed in Table C-2. Using the border-color, border-width, or border-style border properties allows you to set the style for all sides of a border. Using style properties such as border-top-width, border-right-color, or border-bottom-style gives you the option to set the width, color, or style for only the top, right, bottom, or left border of a table cell. If you do not make changes to the border style using style sheet properties, the default border will display.

Table C-2 Border Properties

PROPERTY NAME	DESCRIPTION	VALUES	IE4.X	IE5.X	IE6.X	N4.X	N6.X	N7.X
border-color	Sets the color of the four borders; can have from one to four colors	<color>	Yes	Yes	Yes	Yes	Yes	Yes
border-top-color border-right-color border-bottom-color border-left-color	Sets the respective color of the top, right, bottom, and left borders individually	<color>	Yes	Yes	Yes	Yes	Yes	Yes
border-style	Sets the style of the four borders; can have from one to four styles	**none**	Yes	Yes	Yes	Yes	Yes	Yes
		dashed	No	Yes	Yes	No	Yes	Yes
		dotted	No	Yes	Yes	No	Yes	Yes
		double	Yes	Yes	Yes	Yes	Yes	Yes
		groove	Yes	Yes	Yes	Yes	Yes	Yes
		inset	Yes	Yes	Yes	Yes	Yes	Yes
		outset	Yes	Yes	Yes	Yes	Yes	Yes
		ridge	Yes	Yes	Yes	Yes	Yes	Yes
		solid	Yes	Yes	Yes	Yes	Yes	Yes
border-top-style border-right-style border-bottom-style border-left-style	Sets the respective style of the top, right, bottom, and left borders individually	**none**	Yes	Yes	Yes	Yes	Yes	Yes
		dashed	No	Yes	Yes	No	Yes	Yes
		dotted	No	Yes	Yes	No	Yes	Yes
		double	Yes	Yes	Yes	Yes	Yes	Yes
		groove	Yes	Yes	Yes	Yes	Yes	Yes
		inset	Yes	Yes	Yes	Yes	Yes	Yes
		outset	Yes	Yes	Yes	Yes	Yes	Yes
		ridge	Yes	Yes	Yes	Yes	Yes	Yes
		solid	Yes	Yes	Yes	Yes	Yes	Yes

Table C-2 Border Properties *(continued)*

PROPERTY NAME	DESCRIPTION	VALUES	IE4.X	IE5.X	IE6.X	N4.X	N6.X	N7.X
border-width	Shorthand property for setting the width of the four borders in one declaration; can have from one to four values	**medium**	Yes	Yes	Yes	Yes	Yes	Yes
		<length>	Yes	Yes	Yes	Yes	Yes	Yes
		thick	Yes	Yes	Yes	Yes	Yes	Yes
		thin	Yes	Yes	Yes	Yes	Yes	Yes
border-top-width border-right-width border-bottom-width border-left-width	Sets the respective width of the top,right, bottom, and left borders individually	**medium**	Yes	Yes	Yes	Yes	Yes	Yes
		<length>	Yes	Yes	Yes	Yes	Yes	Yes
		thick	Yes	Yes	Yes	Yes	Yes	Yes
		thin	Yes	Yes	Yes	Yes	Yes	Yes

Font Styles

An element's font can be changed using the font attribute and various font properties. When you set the font family for an element, you can set one or more fonts or font families by using a comma-delimited list. Each font family generally includes several font definitions. For example, the Arial font family includes Arial Black and Arial Narrow. If you specify more than one font, the browser assesses the user's system and finds the first font family installed on the system. If the system has none of the font families specified in the style sheet, the browser uses the default system font. Table C-3 lists common font properties.

Table C-3 Font Properties

PROPERTY NAME	DESCRIPTION	VALUES	IE4.X	IE5.X	IE6.X	N4.X	N6.X	N7.X
font-family	A prioritized list of font-family names and/or generic family names for an element	<family-name>	Yes	Yes	Yes	Yes	Yes	Yes
		cursive	Yes	Yes	Yes	No	Yes	Yes
		fantasy	Yes	Yes	Yes	No	Yes	Yes
		monospace	Yes	Yes	Yes	Yes	Yes	Yes
		sans-serif serif	Yes	Yes	Yes	Yes	Yes	Yes
font-size	Sets the size of a font	<length>	Yes	Yes	Yes	Yes	Yes	Yes
		<percentage>	Yes	Yes	Yes	Yes	Yes	Yes
		large	Yes	Yes	Yes	Yes	Yes	Yes
		medium	Yes	Yes	Yes	Yes	Yes	Yes
		small	Yes	Yes	Yes	Yes	Yes	Yes
		x-large	Yes	Yes	Yes	Yes	Yes	Yes
		x-small	No	Yes	Yes	Yes	Yes	Yes
		xx-large	No	Yes	Yes	Yes	Yes	Yes
		xx-small	No	Yes	Yes	Yes	Yes	Yes
font-style	Sets the style of a font	**normal**	Yes	Yes	Yes	Yes	Yes	Yes
		italic	Yes	Yes	Yes	Yes	Yes	Yes
		oblique	Yes	Yes	Yes	No	Yes	Yes
font-variant	Displays text in a small-caps font or a normal font	**normal**	Yes	Yes	Yes	No	Yes	Yes
		small-caps	Yes	Yes	Yes	No	Yes	Yes
font-weight	Sets the weight of a font	**normal**	Yes	Yes	Yes	Yes	Yes	Yes
		bold	Yes	Yes	Yes	Yes	Yes	Yes
		bolder	Yes	Yes	Yes	Yes	Yes	Yes
		lighter	Yes	Yes	Yes	Yes	Yes	Yes

List Styles

Using the properties associated with list styles allows you to set the kind of marker that identifies a list item. An unnumbered list marker, for example, can be a filled disc, an empty circle, or a square. A numbered list marker can be decimal, lower-alpha, lower-roman, upper-alpha, or upper-roman numeral. Table C-4 provides compatible browser list properties.

Table C-4 List Properties

PROPERTY NAME	DESCRIPTION	VALUES	IE4.X	IE5.X	IE6.X	N4.X	N6.X	N7.X
list-style-image	Sets an image as the list-item marker	**none**	Yes	Yes	Yes	No	Yes	Yes
		url	Yes	Yes	Yes	No	Yes	Yes
list-style-position	Indents or extends a list-item marker with respect to the item's content	**outside**	Yes	Yes	Yes	No	Yes	Yes
		inside	Yes	Yes	Yes	No	Yes	Yes
list-style-type	Sets the type of list-item marker	**disc**	Yes	Yes	Yes	Yes	Yes	Yes
		circle	Yes	Yes	Yes	Yes	Yes	Yes
		square	Yes	Yes	Yes	Yes	Yes	Yes
		decimal	Yes	Yes	Yes	Yes	Yes	Yes
		lower-alpha	Yes	Yes	Yes	Yes	Yes	Yes
		lower-roman	Yes	Yes	Yes	Yes	Yes	Yes
		upper-alpha	Yes	Yes	Yes	Yes	Yes	Yes
		upper-roman	Yes	Yes	Yes	Yes	Yes	Yes

Margin and Padding Styles

Many changes can be made to the width and spacing around an element using the margin and padding properties listed in Table C-5. Padding is the space that occurs between the edge of an element and the beginning of its border. If you increase padding around an element, you add space inside its border. The border, therefore, has a larger area to cover.

You can use the margin or padding property to set the widths of margins and padding amounts along all four sides of an element. Using margin and padding properties such as margin-top, margin-right, padding-left, or padding-bottom gives you the option to set the margin or padding for only the top, right, bottom, or left side of an element.

Table C-5 Margin and Padding Properties

PROPERTY NAME	DESCRIPTION	VALUES	IE4.X	IE5.X	IE6.X	N4.X	N6.X	N7.X
margin	Shorthand property for setting margin properties in one declaration	<length>	No	Yes	Yes	Yes	Yes	Yes
		<percentage>	No	Yes	Yes	Yes	Yes	Yes
		auto	No	Yes	Yes	No	Yes	Yes
margin-top margin-right margin-bottom margin-left	Sets the top, right, bottom, and left margin of an element individually	<length>	Yes	Yes	Yes	No	Yes	Yes
		<percentage>	Yes	Yes	Yes	No	Yes	Yes
		auto	No	Yes	Yes	No	No	Yes

Table C-5 Margin and Padding Properties *(continued)*

PROPERTY NAME	DESCRIPTION	VALUES	IE4.X	IE5.X	IE6.X	N4.X	N6.X	N7.X
padding	Shorthand property for setting padding properties in one declaration	<length> <percentage>	Yes Yes	Yes Yes	Yes Yes	Yes Yes	Yes Yes	Yes Yes
padding-top padding-right padding-bottom padding-left	Sets the top, right, bottom, and left padding of an element individually	<length> <percentage>	Yes Yes	Yes Yes	Yes Yes	Yes Yes	Yes Yes	Yes Yes

Text Styles

Text styles can be used to change the letter-spacing, alignment, line-height (not recommended), and text decoration, along with other text properties. The text-transform property can change text into all uppercase, all lowercase, or be used to change the first letter of each word to uppercase. With text-align, you can align text left, right, center, or justify the text.

Table C-6 Text Properties

PROPERTY NAME	DESCRIPTION	VALUES	IE4.X	IE5.X	IE6.X	N4.X	N6.X	N7.X
letter-spacing	Increases or decreases the space between characters	**normal** <length>	Yes Yes	Yes Yes	Yes Yes	No No	Yes Yes	Yes Yes
line-height	Sets the spacing between text baselines	**normal** <length> <number> <percentage>	Yes Yes Yes Yes	Yes Yes Yes Yes	Yes Yes Yes Yes	Yes Yes Yes Yes	Yes Yes Yes Yes	Yes Yes Yes Yes
text-align	Aligns the text in an element	left right center justify	Yes Yes Yes Yes	Yes Yes Yes Yes	Yes Yes Yes Yes	Yes Yes Yes Yes	Yes Yes Yes Yes	Yes Yes Yes Yes
text-decoration	Adds decoration to text	**none** blink line-through overline underline	Yes No Yes Yes Yes	Yes No Yes Yes Yes	Yes Yes Yes Yes Yes	Yes Yes Yes No Yes	Yes Yes Yes Yes Yes	Yes Yes Yes Yes Yes
text-indent	Indents the first line of text in an element	<length> <percentage>	Yes Yes	Yes Yes	Yes Yes	Yes Yes	Yes Yes	Yes Yes
text-transform	Controls text capitalization	**none** capitalize lowercase uppercase	Yes Yes Yes Yes	Yes Yes Yes Yes	Yes Yes Yes Yes	Yes Yes Yes Yes	Yes Yes Yes Yes	Yes Yes Yes Yes

(continued)

Table C-6 Text Properties *(continued)*

PROPERTY NAME	DESCRIPTION	VALUES	IE4.X	IE5.X	IE6.X	N4.X	N6.X	N7.X
vertical-align	Sets the vertical positioning of text	**baseline**	Yes	Yes	Yes	No	Yes	Yes
		<percentage>	No	No	Yes	No	Yes	Yes
		bottom	No	Yes	Yes	No	Yes	Yes
		middle	No	Yes	Yes	No	Yes	Yes
		sub	Yes	Yes	Yes	No	Yes	Yes
		super	Yes	Yes	Yes	No	Yes	Yes
		text-bottom	Yes	Yes	Yes	No	Yes	Yes
		text-top	No	Yes	Yes	No	Yes	Yes
		top	No	Yes	Yes	No	Yes	Yes
white-space	Sets how white space inside an element is handled	**normal**	No	Yes	Yes	Yes	Yes	Yes
		pre	No	Yes	Yes	Yes	Yes	Yes
		nowrap	No	Yes	Yes	No	Yes	Yes
word-spacing	Increases or decreases the space between words	**normal**	No	No	Yes	No	Yes	Yes
		<length>	No	No	Yes	No	Yes	Yes

Index

<a>tag, for target, HTM 94, HTM 110–111
a:active, **HTM 337,** HTM 344
Access document, converting into HTML file, HTM 14
Accessibility issues, HTM 16, HTM 19, HTM 226
Accessories submenu (All Programs submenu), Notepad command, HTM 34
action attribute, **HTM 299**
Active link
  color of, HTM 73, HTM 223
  style for, HTM 337
Actor Web page, HTM 168
Address bar, HTM 49
Address box, HTM 49
a:hover selector, **HTM 337**
align attribute, **HTM 56**
Alignment
  in cell, HTM 147
  data cells, HTM 149
  heading, HTM 56, HTM 80–82
  horizontal menu bar, HTM 233
  image, HTM 231
  table, HTM 214, HTM 215
  table caption, HTM 172
a:link, **HTM 337,** HTM 344
All Programs submenu (Start menu)
  Accessories, Notepad command, HTM 34
  Internet Explorer command, HTM 47–48
alt attribute, **HTM 51**
  Kitchen Web page, HTM 231
Alternative text, HTM 51
Anchor tag
  links, HTM 85–86
  moving within Web page, HTM 77
Animated, **HTM 33**
<area> tag, **HTM 206,** HTM 221
Attributes
  controls, HTM 293–295
  forms, HTM 293–295, HTM 296
  frame, HTM 254–257, HTM 265–266
  selection menu, HTM 305, HTM 306
a:visited, **HTM 337,** HTM 344

Background, **HTM 32**
  color. *see* Background color
  graphics, HTM 32
  image, HTM 32, HTM 85
Background color, HTM 32
  Campus Tutoring Service Web page, HTM 54–56
  cells, HTM 134, HTM 149
  font, HTM 350
  header page, HTM 270
  home page, HTM 273
  menu page, HTM 271
  style sheets, HTM 332
Bell Video home page, menu bar with text links for, HTM 148–150
Bell Video Web site, HTM 131–183
  borderless table, HTM 145–147
  cellpadding, HTM 169–172
  cellspacing, HTM 169–172
  home page, HTM 143–155
  secondary Web page, HTM 155–160
  table caption, HTM 137, HTM 172–173
  table with borders, HTM 160–168
Berners-Lee, Tim, HTM 11
bgcolor attribute, **HTM 54,** HTM 55, **HTM 149**
Bill Thomas Illustrations Web site, HTM 249–279
  form for, HTM 290–321
Blink property, **HTM 344**
blockquote tags, HTM 96
Body, **HTM 32**
Body style, HTM 349–350
<body> tag, **HTM 37,** HTM 38, HTM 50
  link color attributes, HTM 74
</body> tag, **HTM 37,** HTM 38, HTM 50
Bold format, HTM 12
  Desert Plants Web page, HTM 96–98
  heading, HTM 33
Bookmarks, **HTM 32**
Border
  around images, HTM 135
  color, HTM 74, HTM 255
  frame, HTM 254–257, HTM 259, HTM 265, HTM 266
  image map, HTM 196, HTM 203
  table, HTM 134, HTM 137, HTM 160–168
border attribute, image map and, HTM 218
bordercolor attribute, **HTM 255**
Borderless tables, HTM 145–147, HTM 214
  copying and pasting HTML code for, HTM 156

 tag, HTM 41
Breaking line of text, HTM 41
Broad Web site, **HTM 18**
Browser (Web browser), **HTM 9**
  bookmarks and, HTM 32
  client-side image map and, HTM 201
  favorites and, HTM 32
  frame definition file in, HTM 275–277
  frames in, HTM 250
  Internet Explorer, HTM 31
  noframes, HTM 250, HTM 259, HTM 260
  Print dialog box, HTM 358
  printing Web page from, HTM 60
  quitting, HTM 62
  refreshing view in, HTM 58
  starting, HTM 47–48
  testing Web page, HTM 20
  viewing HTML source code in, HTM 58–59
  viewing Web page in, HTM 44, HTM 47–50, HTM 225–226
Browser window, resized, HTM 263
Bulleted list. *See* Unordered (bulleted) list
Bullets
  default, HTM 42–43, HTM 83
  types of, HTM 41
Businesses
  extranet uses, HTM 8–9, HTM 15
  Web site uses, HTM 8, HTM 15
Button, radio, HTM 294

Calliau, Robert, HTM 11
Campus Tutoring Service Web page, HTM 30–62
Caption
  style for, HTM 350
  in table, HTM 137, HTM 172–173
Cascading Style Sheets, HTM 329, **HTM 330**–361
Cell, **HTM 136**
  background color, HTM 134, HTM 149
  creating, HTM 215
  data. *See* Data cell
  heading. *See* Heading cell
  headings spanning rows and columns, HTM 174–182
  image in, HTM 147
  spacing between, HTM 141, HTM 149, HTM 169–172
  spacing within, HTM 169–172
  text added to, HTM 151–152, HTM 216–217
  text in, HTM 162–164
  vertical alignment in, HTM 149
Cellpadding, **HTM 169**–172
Cellspacing, **HTM 149, HTM 169**–172
Centering heading, HTM 56
CGI script, HTM 296, **HTM 299**
Check box
  adding, HTM 303–304
  testing, HTM 317
Checkbox control, **HTM 294**
Circle bullet, HTM 41
Circular image map, HTM 206
Class, **HTM 338**–340
classname, HTM 338
Clearing text wrapping, HTM 104
Clickable element. *See* Hotspot
Client-side image map, **HTM 201–206,** HTM 218
Closing Notepad, HTM 59
Coding
  practices for HTML, HTM 12
  XHTML standards, HTM 82
  See also HTML code
Color
  background. *See* Background color
  border. *See* Border color
  browser-safe, HTM 9
  font. *See* Font color
  heading, HTM 33
  HTML, HTM 99
  links. *See* Link color
  list of, HTM 82
  Paint program, HTM 208
  style sheets, HTM 332
Color box (Paint window), **HTM 208**
cols attribute
  frameset, HTM 262–263
  textarea, HTM 311
  text area control, **HTM 294**
colspan attribute, HTM 134, **HTM 174–182**
Column, **HTM 136**
  frameset and, HTM 252–253, HTM 259, HTM 262–264
  newspaper-type, HTM 134
  number of, HTM 149
  spanning, HTM 174–182
  text in, HTM 151–152
  width, HTM 150, HTM 159, HTM 262–263
Comment, style sheet and, HTM 343
Company information, image maps for, HTM 200
Drawing image, using Paint, HTM 208
Content, HTM 12
  usability testing, HTM 20
Content type, of linked page, HTM 86
Control
  form, HTM 292–295, HTM 299, HTM 314
  input. *See* Input control
Coordinate pair, **HTM 204**
Coordinates, for image map, HTM 204–212, HTM 221
coords attribute, **HTM 206, HTM 221**
Copying
  embedded style sheet, HTM 355
  HTML code, HTM 115, HTM 156, HTM 227
CSS. *See* Cascading Style Sheets
.css extension, **HTM 337,** HTM 349, HTM 350, HTM 351

Data cell, **HTM 136**
  alignment, HTM 149
Data input control, **HTM 292**
<dd> tag, **HTM 43,** HTM 44
Declaration, **HTM 334**–335
  class and, HTM 338–339
  embedded style sheet, HTM 344
Deep Web site, **HTM 19**
Definition list, **HTM 43**
Deleting image, HTM 158
Deprecated tags, **HTM 36**
Desert Plants Web page
  editing, HTM 94–100
  image link within, HTM 115–117
  text link to, HTM 86–88
DHTML. *See* Dynamic HTML
Dining Room Web page, HTM 196

isabled users, Web site accessibility by, HTM 16,
HTM 51
sc bullet, HTM 41
il> tag, **HTM 43,** HTM 44
dl> tag, **HTM 43,** HTM 44
OCTYPE statement, frames and, HTM 260
DOCTYPE> tag, **HTM 36,** HTM 37, HTM 38,
HTM 260
ocument
HTML, HTM 14–15
types, HTM 36–37
on Web site, HTM 6
ocument Type Definition (DTD), **HTM 36–37**
dt> tag, **HTM 43,** HTM 44
rawing area (Paint window), **HTM 208**
TD. *See* Document Type Definition
ynamic HTML (DHTML), **HTM 13**
-commerce. *See* Electronic commerce
diting
Desert Plants Web page, HTM 94–100
image using Paint program, HTM 208
ditor
HTML, HTM 14, HTM 21
text, HTM 14, HTM 31
WYSIWYG, HTM 15, HTM 21, HTM 31
ducation, Web site uses in, HTM 8, HTM 15
lectronic commerce (e-commerce), **HTM 8**
image map for Web site, HTM 198
em> tag, HTM 98
E-mail, Submit button on form for, HTM 312,
HTM 317
E-mail access, HTM 5
E-mail link, **HTM 77**
Plant World home page, HTM 88–89
table, HTM 152
testing, HTM 91
Embedded style sheet, **HTM 331**
adding, HTM 336, HTM 341–348
inserting, HTM 355
precedence, HTM 334, HTM 337
use of, HTM 333, HTM 334
End tags, HTM 12, HTM 37
nesting tags, HTM 82
Error correction
HTML tags, HTM 39
URL, HTM 49
Excel document, converting into HTML file, HTM 14
Extensible Hypertext Markup Language (XHTML),
HTM 13–14
coding standards, HTM 82
Extensible Markup Language (XML), **HTM 13**
External style sheet, **HTM 331**
adding, HTM 348–351
creating, HTM 350–351
linking to, HTM 352–355
precedence, HTM 334, HTM 337
use of, HTM 333, HTM 334
Extranet, **HTM 8–9,** HTM 15
Favorites, **HTM 32**
Field, input. *See* Input field
Fieldset control, **HTM 295**
creating form groupings using, HTM 314–316
File
converting into HTML, HTM 14
copying and pasting HTML code to, HTM 227
frame definition. *See* Frame definition file
HTML, HTM 30
log, HTM 22
opening image, HTM 208–209
publishing, HTM 6
on Web site, HTM 6
File extension, HTM 45, HTM 51
File menu (Notepad)
Print command, HTM 61
Save As command, HTM 45
Save command, HTM 57
File names, HTM 45, HTM 46
Floor plan image file, opening, HTM 208–209
Font
alternative, HTM 114
background color, HTM 350
default, HTM 81
default styles, HTM 332
embedded style sheet, HTM 336, HTM 342,
HTM 344
inline style sheet, HTM 336, HTM 355, HTM 356
oblique, HTM 350
style sheets, HTM 332, HTM 334, HTM 336,
HTM 342, HTM 344, HTM 355, HTM 356
weight, HTM 352
Font attributes, heading, HTM 80–81
Font color, in Desert Plants Web page, HTM 99–100
Font size, HTM 82
headings, HTM 33
links, HTM 114
Form, HTM 289–291
controls, HTM 292–295, HTM 299, HTM 314
creating, HTM 299–300
HTML tags, HTM 296–300
organizing using form groupings, HTM 313–316
Reset button, HTM 312–313
selection menu, HTM 304–307
Submit button, HTM 312–313
testing, HTM 20
text message, HTM 300–301
textarea, HTM 310–311
Form groupings, HTM 313–316
Form process, identifying, HTM 299–300
<form> tag, HTM 299
</form> tag, HTM 299
Format menu (Notepad), Word Wrap command,
HTM 35–36
Formatting
headings, HTM 33, HTM 80–82
tables, HTM 134
text in Desert Plants Web page, HTM 96–100
Frame, HTM 135, **HTM 247–279**
attributes, HTM 254–257, HTM 265–266
creating, HTM 250–257
header. *See* Header frame
layout of, HTM 250, HTM 258–259
main. *See* Main frame
menu. *See* Menu frame
planning, HTM 258–259
sizes, HTM 257, HTM 262, HTM 273
style, HTM 332
Frame border, **HTM 254–**257, HTM 259,
HTM 265, HTM 266
Frame definition file, **HTM 250–251**
creating, HTM 260–267
saving, HTM 267–268
Stained Glass Club Web site, HTM 340
<frame> tag, HTM 250, HTM 251, HTM 265,
HTM 266
Frameset, **HTM 36,** HTM 37, **HTM 250,** HTM 260
columns in, HTM 252–253, HTM 259,
HTM 262–264
ending, HTM 267
header page, HTM 268
home page, HTM 273
menu page, HTM 270
rows in, HTM 252–253, HTM 259,
HTM 262–264
<frameset> tag, HTM 250, HTM 251, HTM 260,
HTM 262
</frameset> tag, HTM 250, HTM 277
FrontPage, used as WYSIWYG editor, HTM 15,
HTM 31
FTP site, link to, HTM 109
FTP software, publishing using, HTM 21
get method, **HTM 299**
GIF. *See* Graphics Interchange Format
Grammar, accuracy of, HTM 20
Graphical images, on menu bar, HTM 197
Graphics
background, HTM 32
for international audience, HTM 19
testing, HTM 20
Graphics Interchange Format (GIF), **HTM 51**
Graphics software, HTM 233
<h1> tag, HTM 39, HTM 40, HTM 50
</h1> tag, HTM 40
<h2> tag, HTM 50, HTM 83
Hard copy, **HTM 60–61**
<head> tag, **HTM 37,** HTM 38
style sheet within, HTM 331
</head> tag, **HTM 37,** HTM 38
Header
frames used to display, HTM 250
table, HTM 137
Header frame, HTM 264
attributes, HTM 265
Header page, frame for, HTM 252, HTM 268–270
Heading cell, **HTM 136,** HTM 137
code for, HTM 141
Headings, **HTM 33**
centering, HTM 56
entering, HTM 39–40
font, HTM 80–81
formatting, HTM 80–82
Kitchen Web page, HTM 229
left-aligned, HTM 80–82
levels, HTM 33
list, HTM 83
sizes of, HTM 39
spanning rows and columns, HTM 174–182
style, HTM 356
Height
image, HTM 216, HTM 218
margin, HTM 255
height attribute, of image map, HTM 218
Help feature, in Paint program, HTM 210
Hierarchical (Web site structure), **HTM 18**
Home page, **HTM 6, HTM 48**
Bell Video Web site, HTM 143–155
Ibrahim Real Estate Web site, HTM 196,
HTM 213–216
Internet Explorer, HTM 48
links to other Web pages within same Web site from,
HTM 75
main frame in, HTM 273–275
Plant World Web site, HTM 71, HTM 78–85
text links on, HTM 219–220
Web pages accessible through, HTM 18
Home Tour Web site, HTM 193–237
Horizontal menu bar, HTM 232–233
with text links, HTM 219–220
Horizontal rules, **HTM 33**
examples of, HTM 56–57
table with, HTM 137
Horizontal space, in Web page, HTM 231
Horizontal spacing, on Web page, HTM 106
Host. *See* Web server
Hotspot, **HTM 33**
dividing into geographical map, HTM 198
image map, HTM 194–237
Hovers, **HTM 332,** HTM 332, HTM 337,
HTM 342, HTM 345
<hr /> tag, HTM 57
href attribute, of image map, HTM 221

href attribute value
e-mail link, HTM 88
linked page, HTM 87
hspace attribute, HTM 106
of Kitchen Web page, HTM 231
.htm, **HTM 45**
HTML. *See* Hypertext Markup Language
.html, **HTM 45**
HTML code
copying and pasting, HTM 115, HTM 156, HTM 227
embedded style sheet, HTM 343, HTM 345
fieldset control, HTM 314
forms, HTM 296–300
frame definition file, HTM 250–251, HTM 260–261
frame structure, HTM 258–259
header page, HTM 268–270
horizontal menu bar, HTM 232–233
image map, HTM 206, HTM 220–223
understanding, HTM 50
viewing, HTM 58–60
HTML colors, HTM 99
HTML editor, **HTM 14,** HTM 21
HTML file
opening, HTM 95
printing, HTM 60–61
saving, HTM 44–47
saving documents as, HTM 14, HTM 30
viewing, HTM 47–50
HTML tag. *See* Tags
<html> tag, **HTM 37,** HTM 38
</html> tag, **HTM 37,** HTM 38
HTTP. *See* Hypertext Transfer Protocol
Hyperlink. *See* Link
Hypertext Markup Language (HTML), **HTM 9**
coding practices, HTM 12
dynamic, HTM 13
elements, HTM 12
Extensible, HTM 13–14
history of, HTM 11
introduction to, HTM 3–22
standards, HTM 11, HTM 12, HTM 20
tools, HTM 14–15
versions, HTM 12
Hypertext Transfer Protocol (HTTP), **HTM 6**

Ibrahim Real Estate Web site
home page, HTM 213–216
image map in, HTM 195–237
Kitchen Web page, HTM 226–236
Images
adding, HTM 53–54
adding to use as image map, HTM 217–219
alignment, HTM 231
animated, HTM 33
attributes, HTM 51–52, HTM 80
background, HTM 32, HTM 85
border around, HTM 135
coordinates of, HTM 204–212, HTM 221
deleting, HTM 158
frame around, HTM 135
home page, HTM 273
hotspot, HTM 33, HTM 194
inline, HTM 33
inserting in table, HTM 147–148, HTM 215–216
logo, HTM 215–216
obtaining, HTM 107
selecting for image map, HTM 201–202
size of, HTM 197
space around, HTM 106
tables used to position, HTM 135, HTM 145–147
thumbnail, HTM 106–107
tiled, HTM 32
types, HTM 51
wrapped text with, HTM 100–105
Image elements, in Web page, HTM 33
Image file, HTM 85
opening in Paint, HTM 208–209
Image link
border color, HTM 74
example of, HTM 72
Image logo, for Plant World Web site, HTM 79–80
Image map, **HTM 33,** HTM 193–237
adding image to use as, HTM 217–219
border for, HTM 196, HTM 203
borders of hotspots, HTM 203
clickable areas on, HTM 221
client-side. *See* Client-side image map
coding, HTM 206, HTM 220–223
company information, HTM 200
coordinates, HTM 204–206, HTM 221
creating, HTM 201–206, HTM 221–222
e-commerce site, HTM 198
image size and, HTM 197
introduction to, HTM 196–201
link colors, HTM 223
server-side. *See* Server-side image map
shapes, HTM 205
software tools, HTM 212
text links used with, HTM 197, HTM 219
uses, HTM 197–200
Image map button bar, **HTM 197**
<img> tag
for image map, HTM 218
for logo, HTM 54, HTM 80
Implementation, of Web site, HTM 21
Indentation
blocks of text, HTM 96
embedded style sheet and, HTM 336, HTM 343–344
Inline image, **HTM 33**
horizontal rule, HTM 56, HTM 57
image map as, HTM 194
Inline style sheet, **HTM 331**
adding, HTM 355–357
precedence, HTM 334, HTM 336, HTM 337, HTM 356, HTM 357
use of, HTM 333, HTM 334
Input control, **HTM 292–295**
check box, HTM 303
radio buttons, HTM 309
text box, HTM 301
textarea, HTM 311
Input field, length of, HTM 293
Inserting
embedded style sheet, HTM 355
images in table, HTM 147–148, HTM 215–216
text in cells, HTM 162–164
Internationalization, Web site design and, HTM 19
Internet, **HTM 4**
Internet backbone, **HTM 4–5**
Internet Explorer, HTM 31
Favorites, HTM 32
starting, HTM 47–48
Internet Explorer command (All Programs submenu), HTM 47–48
Internet service provider (ISP), **HTM 5**
Internet site, **HTM 7**
Intranet, **HTM 8**
ISP. *See* Internet service provider
Italic format
Desert Plants Web page, HTM 98–99
heading, HTM 33

Joint Photographic Experts Group (JPEG), **HTM 51,** HTM 80
JPEG. *See* Joint Photographic Experts Group

Kitchen Web page, HTM 196, HTM 226–236

Layout, of frames, HTM 250, HTM 258–259
Left-aligned heading, HTM 80–82
<li> tag, **HTM 41**
</li> tag, **HTM 41**
Library Web page, HTM 196
Linear (Web site structure), **HTM 17–18**
Lines
breaking, HTM 41, HTM 96
horizontal rules as, HTM 33
Line-through property, **HTM 344**
Link (hyperlink), **HTM 9, HTM 33,** HTM 70
active. *See* Active link
anchor tag, HTM 85–86
default styles, HTM 332
e-mail. *See* E-mail link
embedded style sheet, HTM 342, HTM 344
external style sheet, HTM 331, HTM 349, HTM 350, HTM 352–355
font size, HTM 114
frames and, HTM 249
FTP site, HTM 109
hovers over, HTM 332, HTM 337, HTM 342, HTM 345
image map. *See* Image map
internal, HTM 109–117
moving mouse pointer over, HTM 72, HTM 109, HTM 332, HTM 337, HTM 342, HTM 345
navigation menu. *See* Navigation menu
newsgroups, HTM 109
to other pages within Web site, HTM 85–88
Plant World Web site, HTM 70–120
to section within same Web page, HTM 77
style sheet, HTM 331, HTM 337–338, HTM 349, HTM 350, HTM 352–355
tag, HTM 85–86
target. *See* Target
testing, HTM 20, HTM 90–92, HTM 236
text. *See* Text links
text-decoration property, HTM 344
underlined, HTM 344
to Web page in another Web site, HTM 76, HTM 108
Web page sections, HTM 109–115
to Web page within same Web site, HTM 75, HTM 115
usability testing, HTM 20
visited. *See* Visited links
within Web page, HTM 109–117
Link color, HTM 33
active link, HTM 73, HTM 74, HTM 223
changing, HTM 73
embedded style sheet, HTM 336
text links, HTM 73, HTM 74
visited link, HTM 73, HTM 74, HTM 223
<link> tag, for external style sheet, HTM 352, HTM 353
Link-hover property, HTM 332, HTM 337, HTM 342, HTM 345
linktext, HTM 86
List, **HTM 33**
creating, HTM 41–44
definition, HTM 43
ordered. *See* Ordered (numbered) list
unordered. *See* Unordered (bulleted) list
List item, defining, HTM 41
Living Room Web page, HTM 196
Log, **HTM 22**
Logical style, HTM 96, HTM 118
Logo image, HTM 54, HTM 79–80, HTM 215–216

Macromedia Dreamweaver, HTM 31
Main frame, HTM 264
attributes, HTM 266
in home page, HTM 273–275
style, HTM 332
Maintenance, of Web site, HTM 21–22
<map> tag, **HTM 206,** HTM 218, HTM 221
</map> tag, **HTM 206,** HTM 221

Margin
default styles, HTM 332
external style sheet, HTM 349–350
height, HTM 255
style sheets, HTM 332, HTM 349–350
width, HTM 255
marginheight attribute, **HTM 255**
marginwidth attribute, **HTM 255**
Markup. *See* Tags
Master Bedroom Web page, HTM 196
Maximizing Notepad window, HTM 35
maxlength attribute, **HTM 293**
text box, HTM 302, HTM 308
Media type, of linked page, HTM 86
Menu, **HTM 35**
Notepad window, HTM 35
selection, HTM 304–307
Web page sections, HTM 109–115
Menu bar, **HTM 35**
graphical images on, HTM 197
horizontal, HTM 158–160, HTM 219–220, HTM 232–233
Notepad window, HTM 35
text links, HTM 148–150, HTM 158–160
text links on horizontal, HTM 219–220
vertical, HTM 148–150
Menu bar (Paint window), **HTM 208**
Menu frame, HTM 264
attributes, HTM 265
menu page and, HTM 270–273
scrolling in, HTM 263
Menu name (Notepad window), **HTM 35**
Menu page, creating, HTM 270–273
method attribute, **HTM 299**
MIME type, of linked page, HTM 86
Mouse pointer
hovers over link, HTM 332, HTM 337, HTM 342, HTM 345
image coordinates and, HTM 209, HTM 211–212
image map coordinates and, HTM 204
moving over link, HTM 72, HTM 109
Multimedia
Web site design and, HTM 19
World Wide Web and, HTM 6
multiple attribute, selection menu and, HTM 307–308
Multitasking, **HTM 47**

Name
anchor, HTM 86
class, HTM 338
file, HTM 45, HTM 46
menu, HTM 35
Name attribute
check box, HTM 303
frame, HTM 266
input control, **HTM 295**, HTM 301
link targets and, HTM 86, HTM 110–111
radio buttons, HTM 309
selection menu, HTM 305
textarea, HTM 311
Navigation
frames used in, HTM 248, HTM 264
image maps used for, HTM 196
issues, HTM 18–19
usability testing, HTM 20
Navigation menu
embedded style sheet, HTM 341–348
frames and, HTM 249, HTM 250, HTM 252, HTM 264, HTM 266, HTM 267
Navigation menu links
default styles, HTM 332
style sheets, HTM 332
Nesting tags, HTM 82
Netscape Navigator, Bookmarks in, HTM 32
Network, **HTM 4**
New Releases Web page
creating, HTM 155–160
table with borders, HTM 160–168
Newsgroups
access, HTM 5
links to, HTM 109
noframes, HTM 250, HTM 259, HTM 260
<noframes> tag, HTM 250, HTM 259
noresize attribute, HTM 256–**257**, HTM 273
Normal link, color of, HTM 73, HTM 74
Normal text, **HTM 32–33**
Notepad, HTM 14, HTM 30, **HTM 31**
activating, HTM 50
closing, HTM 59
opening HTML file using, HTM 95
quitting, HTM 62
starting, HTM 33–35
word wrap, HTM 35–36
Notepad button (Windows taskbar), HTM 50
Notepad command (Accessories submenu), HTM 34
Notepad window, HTM 35
Numbered list. *See* Ordered (numbered) list
Numbers, types of, HTM 41

Oblique font, HTM 350
<ol> tag, **HTM 41**
</ol> tag, **HTM 41**
Online form. *See* Forms
HTML code to new file, HTM 227
Opening
HTML file, HTM 95
image file in Paint, HTM 208–209
Order Form Web page, HTM 290–321
Ordered (numbered) list, HTM 33, **HTM 41**
Organizations, Web site uses by, HTM 8–9, HTM 15
Outline, of image map, HTM 196
Overline property, **HTM 344**

<p> tag, HTM 40, HTM 41
</p> tag, HTM 40, HTM 41
Paint program, HTM 194
Help feature, HTM 210
image map coordinates and, HTM 204, HTM 207–212
opening image file in, HTM 208–209
starting, HTM 207
Paint window, HTM 207–208
Paragraph
classes and, HTM 338–340
embedded style sheet, HTM 341–342, HTM 343
external style sheet, HTM 350
style, HTM 355, HTM 356
style sheets, HTM 332, HTM 341–342, HTM 343, HTM 350
Paragraphs of text
entering, HTM 40–41
Kitchen Web page, HTM 230
Password control, **HTM 293**
Password text box, **HTM 292**
Pasting
embedded style sheet, HTM 355
HTML code, HTM 115, HTM 156
Percentage, column width as, HTM 150, HTM 159
Photo elements, in logo image, HTM 80
Phrase, in text link, HTM 86
Physical style, HTM 96, HTM 118
Picture
as background, HTM 32
See also Images
Pixels
border, HTM 135
horizontal rule, HTM 56
image size, HTM 80
spacing between cells, HTM 141
Plant World Web site
editing Web page in, HTM 94–100
e-mail link, HTM 88–89
home page, HTM 71, HTM 78–85
image with wrapped text, HTM 100–105
links in, HTM 70–120
links within Web page, HTM 109–117
links to another Web site, HTM 108
text links, HTM 85–88, HTM 108
Platform independent, **HTM 10**
PNG. *See* Portable Network Graphics
Polygonal image map, HTM 206
Portable Network Graphics (PNG), **HTM 51**
post method, **HTM 299**
PowerPoint document, converting into HTML file, HTM 14
Precedence, style sheet, HTM 334, HTM 336, HTM 337, HTM 356, HTM 357
Presentation, usability testing, HTM 20
Print command (Notepad File menu), HTM 61
Print dialog box, of browser, HTM 358
Print frames area, HTM 358
Printing
Bell Video Web site, HTM 154, HTM 167, HTM 182
Desert Plants Web page, HTM 117
frame definition file, HTM 275–277
frame page, HTM 277, HTM 359
framed Web pages, HTM 357–359
Home Tour file, HTM 224
HTML file, HTM 60–61
Ibrahim Real Estate home page using browser, HTM 225–226
Kitchen Web page, HTM 233, HTM 234
order form file, HTM 320
Order Form Web page, HTM 317
Plant World home page, HTM 92–93
style sheet, HTM 351
testing, HTM 20
Web page, HTM 60–61
Printout, **HTM 60–61**
Proofreading Web site, HTM 20
Property, **HTM 335**
link element, HTM 336
See also Style
Property-value statements, HTM 335
class and, HTM 338
embedded style sheet, HTM 344
external style sheet, HTM 337–338
Publishing, **HTM 6**
using FTP software, HTM 21

Questionnaire, usability testing and, HTM 20–21
Quitting Notepad, HTM 62

Radio button, **HTM 294**
adding, HTM 309
testing, HTM 317
Radio control, **HTM 294**
rect value, **HTM 221**
Rectangular area. *See* Frame
Rectangular image map, HTM 206, HTM 221
rel (relationship) attribute, links and, HTM 86
Reset button, **HTM 295**, HTM 312–313
testing, HTM 317
Reset control, **HTM 295**
Resizing
browser window, HTM 263
frame, HTM 257, HTM 273
See also Size
rev (reverse) attribute, links and, HTM 86
Row, **HTM 136**
code for, HTM 141
creating data cells in, HTM 147
frameset, HTM 252–253, HTM 259, HTM 262–264
number of, HTM 215
spanning, HTM 174–182

row attribute, HTM 134
rows attribute
text area control, **HTM 294**
textarea, HTM 311
rowspan attribute, **HTM 174**–182
Rules, horizontal, HTM 33
Rules attribute, **HTM 137**

Save As command (Notepad File menu), HTM 45
Save command (Notepad File menu), HTM 57
Saving
Bell Video Web site, HTM 182
Desert Plants Web page, HTM 117
frame definition file, HTM 267–268
Home Tour file, HTM 224
HTML file, HTM 44–47
as HTML file, HTM 14, HTM 30
Kitchen Web page, HTM 233
Order Form file, HTM 316
Plant World home page file, HTM 89
Schools, Web site uses by, HTM 8
Screen reader, HTM 51
Scroll bar
Notepad window, **HTM 35**
Web page, HTM 255
Scroll box (Notepad window), **HTM 35**
scrolling attribute, **HTM 255**
Scrolling frames, HTM 255, HTM 263
scrolling="no" attribute, **HTM 255**
Searching, for images, HTM 107
Sections
table, HTM 176
Web page, HTM 56, HTM 77, HTM 109–115
Select button (Paint toolbox), HTM 211
Select control, **HTM 294**
Selecting images, for image map, HTM 201–202
Selection control, testing, HTM 317
Selection menu, HTM 304–307
Selector, **HTM 334,** HTM 335
class and, HTM 338
Selector a, **HTM 336**
embedded style sheet, HTM 344
Selector p, **HTM 336**
class and, HTM 338–339
embedded style sheet, HTM 343
Server, Web. *See* Web server
Server-side image map, **HTM 201,** HTM 203
SGML. *See* Standard Generalized Markup Language
Shading, for horizontal rule, HTM 56
Shape, of image map, HTM 205, HTM 221
shape attribute, **HTM 221**
Size
frame, HTM 262
of heading, HTM 39
image, HTM 197
See also Resizing
size attribute, **HTM 293**
selection menu, HTM 306
text box, HTM 302, HTM 308
Source code, **HTM 58–60**
Source command (Internet Explorer View menu), HTM 59
Space, horizontal. *See* Horizontal space
Spaces, between tags, HTM 12
Spacing
between cells, HTM 141, HTM 149, HTM 169–172
on Web page, HTM 106
within cells, HTM 169–172
word, HTM 355
Spanning rows and columns, HTM 174–182
Spelling, accuracy of, HTM 20
Square bullet, HTM 41
src attribute, **HTM 51**
frame, HTM 265
image map, HTM 218
Kitchen Web page, HTM 231
Stained Glass Club Web site, HTM 329–361
Standard Generalized Markup Language (SGML), HTM 12
Start menu (Windows taskbar)
All Programs, Accessories, Notepad command, HTM 34
All Programs, Internet Explorer command, HTM 47–48
Start page. *See* Home page
Start tags, HTM 12, HTM 37
nesting tags, HTM 82
Starting
browser, HTM 47–48
HTML, HTM 12, HTM 37
Notepad, HTM 33–35
Paint program, HTM 207
Status bar (Paint window), **HTM 208**
Strict (document type), **HTM 36**
Strong emphasis, HTM 96
Style, **HTM 330**
body, HTM 349–350
bullet, HTM 41
default, HTM 332
heading, HTM 33
logical, HTM 96, HTM 118
physical, HTM 96, HTM 118
Style sheet, HTM 329, **HTM 330–361**
adding, HTM 340–351
classes in, HTM 338–340
creating, HTM 334–338
embedded. *See* Embedded style sheet
external. *See* External style sheet
inline. *See* Inline style sheet
precedence, HTM 334, HTM 336, HTM 337, HTM 356, HTM 357
printing, HTM 351
Style statement, **HTM 334–335**
Style tag container, HTM 343
Submit button, **HTM 295,** HTM 303, HTM 312–313
Submit control, **HTM 295**
Survey, usability testing and, HTM 20

Table border, HTM 134, **HTM 137,** HTM 160–168
Table caption, **HTM 137,** HTM 172–173
Table header, **HTM 137**
Tables, HTM 131, **HTM 134–183**
alignment, HTM 214, HTM 215
borderless, HTM 145–147, HTM 214
borders, HTM 134, HTM 137, HTM 160–168
cellpadding, HTM 169–172
cellspacing, HTM 169–172
coding, HTM 141–412
design, HTM 176
elements, HTM 136
features, HTM 137
form elements and, HTM 305
formatting, HTM 134
header, HTM 137
Ibrahim Real Estate Web site, HTM 214–217
inserting images in, HTM 147–148, HTM 215–216
Kitchen Web page, HTM 229, HTM 231
need for, HTM 139
planning, HTM 139–140
positioning text and images using, HTM 135, HTM 145–147
rules attribute, HTM 137
sections, HTM 176
spanning rows and columns in, HTM 174–182
style, HTM 332, HTM 350
tag attributes, HTM 142
width, HTM 215
Tags, **HTM 9**
deprecated, HTM 36
end. *See* End tags
links, HTM 85–86
list, HTM 41
logical style, HTM 96
nesting, HTM 82
paragraph, HTM 40
physical style, HTM 96
Standard Generalized Markup Language, HTM 12
start. *See* Start tags
style for, HTM 331, HTM 334, HTM 356
table, HTM 141–142
text format, HTM 96
Web page structure and, HTM 36–38
Target, **HTM 94, HTM 109**
link to, HTM 109–115, HTM 272
menu page, HTM 272
Web page sections, HTM 109–115
targetname, HTM 110–111, HTM 112
<td> tag, **HTM 141,** HTM 147, HTM 152, HTM 164, HTM 215
</td> tag, **HTM 141,** HTM 147, HTM 152, HTM 164
Testing
Bell Video Web site, HTM 168
Desert Plants Web page, HTM 118
frame definition file, HTM 275
frame page, HTM 277
Ibrahim Real Estate home page, HTM 225, HTM 236
implemented Web site, HTM 21
links, HTM 20
Order Form Web page, HTM 317
Plant World home page, HTM 90–92
usability, HTM 20
Web site, HTM 20–21
Text
alternative, HTM 51
breaking line of, HTM 41
in cells, HTM 162–164, HTM 216–217
in column, HTM 151–152
entering paragraphs of, HTM 40–41
form, HTM 300–301
formatting. *See* Formatting
newspaper-type columns, HTM 134
normal, HTM 32–33
paragraphs of, HTM 82–83, HTM 230
table caption, HTM 172
tables used to position, HTM 135
text links, HTM 73
wrapped, HTM 35–36, HTM 100–105
Text area (Notepad window), **HTM 35**
Text box, **HTM 292**
adding, HTM 301–302, HTM 307–308
password control, HTM 293
testing, HTM 317
text control, HTM 293
Text color, style sheets for, HTM 332
Text control, **HTM 293**
Text editor, **HTM 14,** HTM 31. *See also* Notepad
Text elements, of Web page, HTM 32–33
Text file
external style sheet, HTM 337
external style sheet, HTM 349
style sheet, HTM 331, HTM 337, HTM 349
Text input control, **HTM 292**
Text links
color, HTM 33, HTM 73, HTM 74
descriptive text for, HTM 73
example of, HTM 72
horizontal menu bar with, HTM 158–160, HTM 219–220
image maps with, HTM 197
menu page, HTM 271
Plant World home page, HTM 85–88
vertical menu bar with, HTM 148–150
to Web page in another Web site, HTM 108
to Web page within same Web site, HTM 85, HTM 86–88
within Web page, HTM 109–115

xtarea
adding to form, HTM 310–311
testing, HTM 317
xtarea box, **HTM 292**
xtarea control, **HTM 294**
xt-decoration property, HTM 344
h> tag, **HTM 141**
th> tag, **HTM 141**
humbnail image, **HTM 106–107**
iled image, HTM 32
itle, Web page, **HTM 32,** HTM 37, HTM 157
changing, HTM 228
title> tag, **HTM 37,** HTM 38
/title> tag, **HTM 37**
itle bar (Notepad window), **HTM 35**
oolbox (Paint window), **HTM 208**
op alignment, of table, HTM 215
tr> tag, **HTM 141,** HTM 147, HTM 164
/tr> tag, **HTM 141,** HTM 147, HTM 164
ransitional (document type), **HTM 36,** HTM 37
ype attribute, **HTM 41**
links and, HTM 86
ype Web page, HTM 168
headings spanning rows and columns, HTM 174–182
ul> tag, **HTM 41**
/ul> tag, **HTM 41**
Jnderline property, **HTM 344**
Jnderlined, in text link, HTM 33, HTM 73
Jniform Resource Locator (URL), **HTM 9**
Address box, HTM 49
defining, HTM 51
Document Type Definition, HTM 36
external style sheet, HTM 352
image map, HTM 219, HTM 221
linked page, HTM 72, HTM 86, HTM 87
moving mouse pointer over link, HTM 72
text link, HTM 86
Universities, Web site uses by, HTM 8
Unordered (bulleted) list, HTM 33, **HTM 41**
creating, HTM 42–43
Plant World home page, HTM 83–84
table versus, HTM 139
Web page sections, HTM 109–115
URL. *See* Uniform Resource Locator
Usability, **HTM 20**
Usability testing, **HTM 20**
usemap attribute, HTM 218
User interface design, HTM 18, HTM 48
Users, usability testing and, HTM 20
valign attribute, **HTM 149**
valign="top" attribute, **HTM 149**
Value, for text decoration, HTM 344
value attribute
check box, HTM 303
input control, **HTM 295**
radio buttons, HTM 309
Vertical alignment
in data cells, HTM 149
of table, HTM 215
Vertical menu bar, with text links, HTM 148–150
Vertical rules, table with, HTM 137
Vertical spacing, on Web page, HTM 106
View menu (Internet Explorer), Source command, HTM 59
Viewing
Bell Video Web site, HTM 154, HTM 182
Desert Plants Web page, HTM 118
frame definition file, HTM 275–277
framed Web pages, HTM 357–359
frames pages, HTM 359
HTML file, HTM 47–50
HTML source code, HTM 58–60
Ibrahim Real Estate home page using browser, HTM 225–226
Kitchen Web page, HTM 234
Order Form Web page, HTM 317
Plant World home page, HTM 90
Web page in browser, HTM 44, HTM 47–50
Visited link
color of, HTM 73, HTM 223
style for, HTM 337
vspace attribute, HTM 106
Web. *See* World Wide Web
Web browser. *See* Browser
Web development life cycle, HTM 15–22
Web page structure
Bell Video Web site, HTM 143–144
Plant World Web site, HTM 78–79
tags and, HTM 36–38
Web pages, **HTM 6**
background, HTM 32, HTM 85
body of, HTM 32
Campus Tutoring Service, HTM 30–62
development, HTM 14–15, HTM 30–62, HTM 92
elements, HTM 32–33
form on, HTM 289–321
frame in. *See* Frame
Ibrahim Real Estate Web site, HTM 196
image elements, HTM 33, HTM 51–54
improving appearance of, HTM 52–58
Kitchen, HTM 226–236
link elements, HTM 33
linking to another, within same Web site, HTM 75, HTM 86–88, HTM 115
linking to in another Web site, HTM 76, HTM 108
links to other, HTM 148–150
links to section in same, HTM 77
links within, HTM 109–117
loading time, HTM 216
Order Form, HTM 290–321
printing, HTM 60–61
publishing, HTM 6
section, HTM 56, HTM 77, HTM 109–115
size, HTM 106
source code for, HTM 58–60
spacing on, HTM 106
style for, HTM 330
style sheets, HTM 329–361
testing, HTM 90–92
text elements, HTM 32–33
title of, HTM 32, HTM 37, HTM 157
viewing in browser, HTM 44, HTM 47–50, HTM 225–226
window elements, HTM 32
Web server, **HTM 6**
server-side image map and, HTM 201
Web site, **HTM 6**
accessibility, HTM 16, HTM 19
analysis, HTM 16–17
audience for, HTM 19
Bell Video, HTM 131–183
Bill Thomas Illustrations, HTM 249–279, HTM 290–321
broad, HTM 18
deep, HTM 19
design, HTM 17–20
development, HTM 17–20
form for, HTM 290–321
frame in. *See* Frame
home page. *See* Home page
Home Tour, HTM 193–237
Ibrahim Real Estate, HTM 195–237
implementation, HTM 21
linking to another Web page within same, HTM 75, HTM 115
linking to Web page in another, HTM 76, HTM 108
links to other pages within, HTM 85–88
maintenance, HTM 21–22
planning, HTM 15–16
Plant World, HTM 70–120
purposes of, HTM 7–9, HTM 15, HTM 30
Stained Glass Club, HTM 329–361
style sheets, HTM 329–361
tables in. *See* Tables
testing, HTM 20–21
types of, HTM 7–9
updates, HTM 21
usability, HTM 20
Web site structure
hierarchical, HTM 18
linear, HTM 17–18
webbed, HTM 18
Webbed (Web site structure), **HTM 18**
Width
border, HTM 135
column, HTM 150, HTM 159, HTM 262–263
image, HTM 216
margin, HTM 255
table, HTM 215
width attribute, **HTM 150**
for image map, HTM 218
Window, Paint, HTM 207–208
Windows, multitasking and, HTM 47
Word
spacing, HTM 355
in text link, HTM 86
Word document, converting into HTML file, HTM 14
Word wrap, **HTM 35–36**
WordPad, HTM 35
World Wide Web (WWW), **HTM 6**
access, HTM 5
history of, HTM 11
World Wide Web Consortium (W3C), HTM 6, **HTM 11,** HTM 12, HTM 20, HTM 36
Wrapped text, image with, HTM 100–105
WWW. *See* World Wide Web
WYSIWYG editor, **HTM 15,** HTM 21, HTM 31
X-axis, **HTM 204**
X-coordinate, HTM 204–212, HTM 221
XHTML. *See* Extensible Hypertext Markup Language
XML. *See* Extensible Markup Language
Y-axis, **HTM 204**
Y-coordinate, HTM 204–212, HTM 221